# THE RAGE OF
# INNOCENCE

# THE RAGE OF INNOCENCE

## How America Criminalizes
## Black Youth

## Kristin Henning

Pantheon Books, New York

Library of Congress Cataloging-in-Publication Data
Name: Henning, Kristin (law teacher), author.
Title: The rage of innocence : how America criminalizes Black youth /
Kristin Henning.
Description: First edition. New York : Pantheon Books, 2021.
Includes bibliographical references and index.
Identifiers: LCCN 2021002180 (print). LCCN 2021002181 (ebook).
ISBN 9781524748906 (hardcover). ISBN 9781524748913 (ebook).
Subjects: LCSH: Discrimination in juvenile justice administration—
United States. Discrimination in criminal justice administration—
United States. African American youth. Police–community
relations—United States. Racial profiling in law enforcement—
United States. Discrimination in law enforcement—United States.
Racism—United States.
Classification: LCC HV9104 .H46 2021 (print) |
LCC HV9104 (ebook) | DDC 364.36089/96073—dc23
LC record available at lccn.loc.gov/2021002180
LC ebook record available at https lccn.loc.gov/2021002181

www.pantheonbooks.com

Jacket design and illustration by Oliver Munday

Printed in the United States of America

First Edition

2 4 6 8 9 7 5 3 1

# Contents

*Introduction: Molotov Cocktail
  or Science Experiment?*                                        vii

1. American Adolescence in Black and White                        3

2. Toy Guns, Cell Phones, and Parties:
   Criminalizing Black Adolescent Play                           25

3. Hoodies, Headwraps, and Hip-Hop:
   Criminalizing Black Adolescent Culture                        48

4. Raising "Brutes" and "Jezebels":
   Criminalizing Black Adolescent Sexuality                      81

5. Policing Identity: The Politics of Adolescence and
   Black Identity Development                                   106

6. Cops in School                                               122

7. Contempt of Cop                                              147

8. Policing by Proxy                                            173

9. Policing as Trauma                                           204

10. The Dehumanization of Black Youth:
    When the Children Aren't Children Anymore                   236

11. Things Fall Apart: Black Families in an Era of
    Mass Incarceration                                          266

12. #BlackBoyJoy and #BlackGirlMagic:
   Adolescent Resilience and Systems Reform          298

   *Acknowledgments*          345

   *Notes*          349

   *Index*          465

# Introduction

*Molotov Cocktail or Science Experiment?*

I first heard about "Eric"* on the evening news when I saw the headline "Teen Arrested for Bringing Explosive Device to D.C. School." The story immediately caught my attention. It sounded serious, and as a defense attorney practicing in Washington, D.C.'s juvenile court, I knew I would likely see Eric in court the next day. Indeed, as fate would have it, just as I walked into the courthouse, a teenage girl approached me to ask if I could represent her brother—Eric. Coincidentally, I had met Eric's sister a few months earlier in a drama workshop at a local high school. As I checked in with the court staff, I learned that I had already been appointed to Eric's case.

Within minutes of talking to Eric in the juvenile lockup, I realized that what sounded so shocking on the news wasn't so serious after all. Eric was a typical thirteen-year-old boy who was watching a movie and saw someone with a Molotov cocktail. Eric thought it was "cool" and wanted to see if he could make something that "looked" like that. He grabbed an empty bottle from under the kitchen sink and started filling it with household products—bleach, Pine-Sol, stainless steel cleaner—whatever he could find. He didn't research it. He didn't look up "Molotov

---

*Throughout this book, I have changed the names of my clients and their family members to preserve their confidentiality.

cocktail" on the internet, and he didn't know if any of the products he grabbed were flammable. He was just being creative. He taped up the entire bottle with black tape and put a long piece of toilet paper underneath the cap so it hung out of the bottle like the wick of a cocktail. After admiring his design, Eric put the bottle in his book bag so it wouldn't spill on his mother's white carpet and moved on to his next source of entertainment for the day. This all happened on a Saturday night, and like most thirteen-year-olds, he had completely forgotten about it by Monday morning when his mother drove him to school.

As he did every school day, Eric walked through a metal detector and put his bag on an electronic conveyor belt. A police officer assigned to the school as a "school resource officer" saw the bottle and stopped Eric to ask about it. Eric responded without thinking, "Oh, that's nothing. You can throw it away." He walked on to class. Little did he know this was the beginning of a very long and painful ordeal for him and his family in juvenile court.

Eric was pulled out of class, questioned by the police, and arrested. No one believed him when he told them he forgot the bottle was there and was not planning to blow up the school. Eric spent the night in the local juvenile detention center and was brought to D.C. Superior Court the next day. The prosecutor charged him with possession of a Molotov cocktail, attempted arson, and carrying a dangerous weapon. When I heard the prosecutor read out the charges, I kept expecting there to be more to the story—maybe a letter or some cryptic online message by Eric threatening to hurt a teacher. Maybe Eric was sad, isolated, and bullied by his classmates. Maybe Eric had a history of depression and dressed in all black. None of that turned out to be true. There was nothing more to the story.

Quite to the contrary, Eric was a happy and creative Black boy living in Southeast D.C. with his mother and little brother. Although his father was in prison at the time, Eric was raised in a large close-knit family, including two older sisters in college and another in the U.S. Air Force. His mother worked in a hospital and catered food a bit on the side while studying for her nursing degree. His father was a college graduate who had worked for many years as an emergency medical technician before his incarceration. I visited Eric's home many times and met many of his family members over the next several months. I saw nothing other than a well-adjusted boy who loved to show me his kittens and play with his brother. He was active in youth theater, participated in the city's local youth orchestra, and tutored second- and third-grade students in reading four days a week. He also enjoyed youth activities at church. His teachers described him as calm and respectful, and he had never been in trouble at school or with the police.

The only thing that could really explain the school's extreme reaction to Eric's duct-taped bottle was our country's outsized fear of school shootings. And for a while, I accepted that as the reason. I let myself believe that our schools were just being extra careful in the era of mass violence. But then something happened that forever changed my view of this case. Several months after I met Eric, I shared his story at a conference in New Haven, Connecticut. When I finished, a White woman walked over and said, "My son did exactly what you described. He tried to make a Molotov cocktail and took it to school." When I asked what happened to her son, she said, "They rearranged his class schedule so he could take a chemistry course."

No, we are not just afraid of school shootings. And we are not just afraid of children with guns. We are afraid of Black children. There was nothing Eric could have done or said that day to convince the police or anyone else that he was not a threat to the school.

Eric was suspended and banned from all after-school activities. For the next nine months, he met weekly with a probation officer, was forced to attend anger management classes, and had to pee in a cup to prove he was not using drugs. At the city's expense, lawyers on both sides of the case spent hours investigating, preparing, and arguing about every legal question we could think of. Our defense team even hired an arson expert to prove that the liquids in the bottle would never catch on fire and the toilet paper hanging out of it would never work as a wick. Only after months of advocacy were we able to persuade the judge to dismiss Eric's case under a special law in D.C. that allows a judge to throw out a juvenile case when it is "in the interest of justice." Fortunately, our judge thought the school and the police had overreacted. Unfortunately, the dismissal could never undo the agony, embarrassment, and fear Eric and his family experienced that year.

That was ten years ago, when Eric was thirteen—one of the most important years in his, and any child's, life. He was in his early adolescence and beginning his teenage years. For most youth, adolescence offers a prolonged period of self-discovery from age ten to nineteen—and sometimes into the early twenties. It is the time when children complete their formal education and develop the mental, emotional, and social skills they need to succeed and thrive as adults. Although family remains important, adolescents seek independence and begin to forge new identities apart from their parents. Parents and teachers hope their children and students will grow into healthy young adults with a positive sense of who they are and a robust idea of what their futures might hold.

Adolescence is a time when young people enjoy the freedoms of childhood while starting to figure out how to be an adult. We hope they will be curious, creative, and at least a little adventurous. We anticipate that they will take risks, test boundaries, and challenge authority. We expect them to show off for their classmates and be fiercely loyal to their friends. We are not surprised when they are impulsive, make poor decisions, or even experiment with sex or drugs. And despite our nervousness about the seeming recklessness of adolescence, we tend to show teenagers a great deal of grace. We are confident that most youth will grow out of their mischief. "Boys will be boys," the adults say. Girls are "just going through a phase." The risk and adventure of adolescence is socially accepted as a rite of passage, and maybe even encouraged as a source of amusement. But those rules apply only if you are White.

Eric's adolescence looked quite different. While White youth have the freedom and privileges of adolescent irresponsibility, mischief, and play, Black youth like Eric are seen as a threat to White America. Two boys made a "Molotov cocktail," but only one was treated like a criminal. I was struck by everyone's refusal to believe Eric when he said the cocktail wasn't real. There was nothing intimidating about his appearance or suspicious about his behavior when he entered the building. Eric put his book bag through the conveyer belt without hesitation. He answered the resource officer's questions freely and handed over the bottle immediately when he was asked about it. He was searched thoroughly and clearly had nothing else in his possession by the time he went to class. With the bottle safely in their custody, the officers were able to remove any potential threat from the school and have the fire department examine the bottle's contents to confirm that it wasn't flammable. Yet nothing dispelled their fears. The officers and administrators treated Eric like a potential mass murderer—evacuating the school, disrupting learning for everyone in the building, and arresting him in front of his classmates and teachers.

By the next day, the whole school knew Eric was the reason for the evacuation. And everyone had their theories—teachers, students, and staff. Some, knowing that his father was incarcerated, speculated that "maybe his father put him up to it." Others thought he did it to get a day off from school. Still others were convinced he was a terrorist with a master plan to blow up the campus. Students started calling him "Osama bin Laden" and yelled out, "Ticktock boom!" whenever he walked by. Very few thought he was just being curious and creative. Although his teachers admitted that he was a quiet kid who had never been in trouble, they claimed not to know him well enough to say he wouldn't do anything violent. It was only those who knew him best—from drama, art, and the youth orchestra—who could see Eric for who he really was: an imaginative child who was just being a child.

Eric's arrest was a very public event that took on even greater importance in his thirteen-year-old mind. Every choice the adults made that day was critically important to Eric's development. The school resource officer created negative attention for Eric at a time when status and reputation matter a lot to young people. The police embarrassed him in front of his classmates when we want teenagers to develop a strong social network and feel good about themselves. Eric was still trying to make and keep friends, win approval from the adults in his life, and walk the thin line between fitting in with the crowd and standing out with a unique style and diverging interests. The public spectacle branded him a "troublemaker" when we want young people to resist the negative influence of students who are into mischief and gravitate toward those who are well behaved and excelling in their classes.

The arrest caused many to underestimate Eric's potential at a time when young people begin to internalize what others think of them. This was especially true for Eric, who was already thinking about what he wanted to do "when he grew up" and was keenly aware of what his teachers thought he could and could not achieve in the future. The school also suspended him when we most need to help adolescents think wisely about their actions and improve their decision-making skills. They excluded him from the drama program when we most want to encourage creativity and surround youth with mentors. And they removed him from class and structured activities when we most need young people to be supervised by adults who will keep them focused and help them regulate their emotions and control their behaviors.

This book grew out of my anger and indignation about what happened to Eric. But Eric is just one of the Black teenagers whose stories I share in this book. I have met many Black teens in the last twenty-five years whose adolescence was interrupted by police encounters like the one Eric experienced. And I have met many Black youth who were dehumanized in the court system instead of nurtured and supported in their community.

My first memory of juvenile court occurred when I was a college freshman in Durham, North Carolina, interning at the local district attorney's office. On my first day, I was instructed to meet the prosecutor at the courthouse at 9:00 a.m. As I turned down the hall leading to the youth division, I stopped dead in my tracks. Eight boys—mostly Black and Latino—were being escorted down the hall in a single file by a bailiff. They had metal handcuffs tight around their wrists. "Belly chains" locked their arms and hands close to their stomachs, and metal links connected the shackles on each of their ankles, clanking loudly as they walked slowly and clumsily from the awkwardness of the restriction. I had no idea we chained children in courts and detention facilities in America. As a Black woman born in the South, all I could think of was Alex Haley's 1970s television miniseries *Roots*. The imagery of slavery was unmistakable. But this was 1988 and slavery had ended more than a century before. That image has stuck with me. That was the day I knew I wanted to go to law school and fight for children.

My shock and outrage about the way we treat Black children in America continue today. In my first year of law school, I took a clinical course—much like an apprenticeship—that allowed me to represent children in special education, abuse and neglect, and delinquency cases. The children I met in New Haven looked like those I met in Durham. They were Black and Latinx in a city that had plenty of White children. And their judges, lawyers, and bailiffs, like those I saw in North Carolina, were almost all White.

After law school, I was drawn to Washington, D.C., to work at the Public Defender Service, an office known for its deep commitment to advocating for the rights of the accused and reforming the criminal legal system. This time, I went in expecting my clients to be Black based on the city's reputation. As James

Forman Jr. wrote in his book, *Locking Up Our Own,* D.C. is quite different from New Haven. It is a city where many—if not most—of the decision makers controlling the juvenile and criminal legal system are also Black: judges, bailiffs, probation officers, the city's attorney general, city council members, and the mayor. We have had a Black police chief and many police officers who are Black.

By the time I met Eric in 2011, I had already been representing teenagers in Washington, D.C., for fifteen years. I could—and still can—count on one hand the number of White children I have ever represented, or even seen, in D.C.'s juvenile court. By then it was easy to forget that White youth were committing the same kinds of "crimes" my clients were; they just weren't being arrested. My conversation with a White mother at the conference in New Haven was a jarring reminder that Eric's arrest wasn't a normal or necessary response to most adolescent behaviors. Eric's arrest was evidence of America's deep-seated fear, distrust, and intolerance of Black adolescence.

I have now been representing children in D.C. for twenty-five years, mostly as the director of the Juvenile Justice Clinic at Georgetown Law, where I supervise law students and new attorneys defending children charged with crimes in the city. I also spend a good deal of time traveling, training, and strategizing with juvenile defenders across the country in partnership with the National Juvenile Defender Center. From the East Coast to the West, from the Deep South to the North, Black children appear in juvenile and criminal courts in numbers that far exceed their presence in the population. Black children are accosted all over the nation for the most ordinary adolescent activities—shopping for prom clothes, playing in the park, listening to music, buying juice from the convenience store, wearing the latest fashion trend, and protesting for their social and political rights.

In D.C., our elected attorney general is more attentive now to the harms and disparities impacting people of color, so maybe the prosecutors wouldn't pursue Eric's case so zealously today. But even with these changes, I have still spent much of the last two decades fighting for Black children who have been arrested and prosecuted for "horseplay" on the Metro, breaking a school window, stealing a pass to a school football game, throwing snowballs (a.k.a. "missiles") at a passing police car, hurling pebbles across the street at another kid, playing "toss" with a teacher's hat, and snatching a cell phone from a boyfriend. I have seen Black children handcuffed at ages nine and ten; twelve- and thirteen-year-old Black boys stopped for riding their bicycles; and industrious sixteen- and seventeen-year-old Black boys detained for selling water on the National Mall. The list goes on.

We live in a society that is uniquely afraid of Black children. Americans become anxious—if not outright terrified—at the sight of a Black child ringing the doorbell, riding in a car with white women, or walking too close in a convenience store. Americans think of Black children as predatory, sexually deviant, and immoral. For many, that fear is subconscious, arising out of the historical and contemporary narratives that have been manufactured by politicians, business leaders, and others who have a stake in maintaining the social, economic, and political status quo. There is something particularly efficient about treating Black children like criminals in adolescence. Black youth are dehumanized, exploited, and even killed to establish the boundaries of Whiteness before they reach adulthood and assert their rights and independence.

It is no coincidence that Emmett Till was fourteen when he was lynched, Trayvon Martin was seventeen when he was shot by a volunteer neighborhood watchman, Tamir Rice was twelve when he was shot by the police at a park, Dajerria Becton was fifteen when she was slammed to the ground by police at a pool party, and four Black and Latina girls were twelve when they were strip-searched for being "hyper and giddy" in the hallway of their New York middle school. It is also no coincidence that George Stinney—the youngest person in modern America to be executed—was fourteen when he was sent to the electric chair. These early encounters with Whiteness teach Black children that there are limits on where they can go and what they can achieve in America. These encounters, and the self-serving claims of "Black threat" that follow, reinforce White fears about Black youth purportedly run amok in society.

Contrary to myth and legend, Black youth aren't as dangerous as people think they are. Very few youth arrests involve violent crimes like murder, rape, robbery, and aggravated assault. The same is true for Black youth. Violent crime makes up only a small portion, approximately 9 percent, of all arrests for Black youth.[1] Research on adolescent development offers additional evidence that Black children are no more dangerous or impulsive than their White peers.

Youth of every race, class, and ethnicity take risks, chase excitement, act impulsively, and are easily influenced by their friends. Yet, even as youth arrests and juvenile detention have gone down all across the country, disparities in the way we treat Black and White youth have held fast or continue to grow. Black youth were arrested at a rate 1.6 times that of White youth in 1980, 2.1 times that of White youth in 2008, and 2.6 times that of White youth in 2018.[2] Although Black youth made up 16 percent of the youth population aged ten to seventeen in 2018, they accounted for half (50 percent) of all youth arrests for violent crimes that year, and 42 percent of arrests for property crimes.[3]

After arrest, Black youth are more likely to be detained, prosecuted, and punished more harshly—even when they are charged with similar offenses and have similar prior histories.[4] Although the total number of youth whom juvenile court judges transferred to adult court decreased by almost half from 2005 to 2018, racial disparities grew.[5] The child was Black in 39 percent of the cases transferred to adult court in 2005. In 2018, Black youth made up more than 51 percent of these transfers despite accounting for only 35 percent of all cases in juvenile court that year. Meanwhile, White youth made up almost 44 percent of juvenile court cases, but accounted for only 32 percent of cases judges transferred to adult court. Even when White youth do exceptionally violent things, we still treat them like children.

Our nation's obsession with policing and incarcerating Black

America begins with Black children. The history of mass incarceration and police violence against Blacks has been well told in books like *The New Jim Crow* (Michelle Alexander), *Policing the Black Man* (edited by Angela Davis), *Chokehold* (Paul Butler), and *Locking Up Our Own* (James Forman Jr.), but the policing of Black adolescence requires a special telling. Although the recent flurry of highly visible police killings of Black Americans has drawn national and international attention, the day-to-day abuses of policing remain largely hidden from public view. These high-profile incidents don't tell us enough about the physical and psychological effects of policing in neighborhoods where law enforcement is a constant presence in the lives of Black youth.

There are now generations of Black youth who have grown up under the constant surveillance and persistent threat of abuse by the police. And the effects are traumatic—for the youth, their families, and the community. In many Black neighborhoods, police are parked on the corner, are stationed at the front door of the school, and drive through the community at all hours of the day and night asking young people to lift their shirts to prove they aren't carrying guns in their waistbands. Black youth are stopped and harassed by the police for doing what teenagers do all over the world—talking on the phone, laughing with friends, shooting hoops at the local recreation center, flirting with a classmate on social media, or posting political views online.

Tensions between Black youth and the police are at an all-time high, with bias and mistrust running in both directions. Police expect Black youth to be violent and aggressive; Black youth expect the police to be biased and antagonistic. Black children have learned to adapt their behaviors to survive under the relentless scrutiny of police officers who see and treat them as a perpetual threat. At its worst, the discriminatory and aggressive policing of Black adolescence has socialized a generation of Black teenagers to fear, resent, and resist the police.

This is a book about the criminalization of Black adolescence in America. It is a book about the excessive intrusion of police into the lives of Black teenagers and the intolerant—sometimes deadly—reactions that police and civilians have toward Black children. But in the end, this is also a book about extraordinary resilience. It is a story about Black youth who learn to define themselves as peaceful, talented, and intelligent despite media profiles that seek to label them otherwise. It is about strong Black families, heroic parenting, and valiant teaching that help Black youth develop affirming racial identities and learn to speak out against injustice in safe and constructive ways. It is about survival and success in the face of pervasive injustice—well beyond anything that is expected of White middle-class youth who enjoy the privileges of physical safety, public affirmation, and protracted periods of academic and social freedom.

In May 2020, once again, the nation—and the world—exploded with outrage at the brutal police killing of yet another Black American. George Floyd wasn't the first and, sadly, I am sure he won't be the last Black American to be killed by the police. But his killing was one tragedy too many, and his murder added fuel to a growing movement of Black people who are unwilling to accept the continued dehumanization of people who look like them. Young Black voices have been central to that movement. Drawing attention to the issues that impact them most, Black youth are asking elected officials to defund the police, remove police from schools, invest in health and social services to support all youth, and treat Black children with the humanity to which they are entitled. Black youth want the country to acknowledge their innocence, power, purpose, and beauty. I do too.

This book is for everyone who cares about improving the lives of Black youth in America. It is for everyone who wants to change the way Americans view and engage with Black children. And it is for everyone who is willing to radically reduce the footprint of police in the day-to-day lives of Black youth. But, most important, it is for everyone who believes that Black children are children too.

# THE RAGE OF INNOCENCE

# 1

## American Adolescence in Black and White

White clients are a rare sight in a public defender's office in a city like Washington, D.C. In my twenty-five years of practice, with hundreds of clients, I have represented only four white youth. That's it. Four—and one of them wasn't technically my client and another wasn't technically White. I remember them all well.

My first White client, "Jason," presented me with my greatest moral challenge as a Black woman and zealous defender. After getting over my surprise at seeing a White kid in the cellblock, I realized that Jason was a lot like my other clients. He was sixteen and wore a T-shirt, jeans, and sneakers. He was a nice kid who was afraid of what might happen in court. As the story unfolded, I learned that Jason had been arrested with four high school friends who crashed a Jewish fraternity party at George Washington University. The fraternity kicked the boys out and called the police. This escapade probably wouldn't have warranted police intervention, but one of the boys got mad and spray-painted a swastika outside the fraternity house. That boy ran away while Jason and the others were stopped and arrested. After a Friday night in detention, the boys were charged with burglary as a hate crime.

Jason's first hearing was on a Saturday, which meant there weren't enough marshals to escort five handcuffed youth into the courtroom at the same time. Instead, the marshals insisted on bringing the boys out in pairs. When the marshals brought the first two from the cellblock, their parents entered from the hallway. The shock in the room was palpable. The judge jerked back in his seat and exclaimed, "Why do we need marshals at all! Look at these kids and their parents! I am certainly not going to keep any of them locked up." Clearly, he was as surprised as I was to see five White teenagers in a D.C. courtroom. But at that time, he didn't know why the boys had been arrested. He didn't know if they had shot, killed, or raped someone. He didn't know if they had robbed a bank. And he didn't know if they had ever been in trouble before. He simply assumed that five White kids with parents present shouldn't be in detention. It was one of the rare moments in my career when my loyalty to my client faltered. I wanted to yell back, "Are you kidding me!" But I held my tongue. The judge let them all go home.

Days later, I visited Jason at his bucolic two-story home with a driveway and a dog. He was my first and only client in twenty-five years of practice who lived in one of the wealthy White suburbs in Virginia. The surprises didn't stop there. When we sat down at the kitchen table, he looked very nervous and said he had something to tell me. He passed me a magazine—about skinheads. He quickly followed that with "I am a skinhead, but I'm not in it because I hate Blacks or Jews." For him, it was about economics and politics. For him, it was a harmless subculture. More important, he insisted that he didn't paint the swastika on the wall and would never have done so. He was honest and transparent; he wanted me to know everything because I was Black. Unlike his friends who had hired expensive private lawyers, Jason and his mother explained that the family was in the midst of an expensive divorce and just couldn't afford to pay for another lawyer. They would be grateful if I would stay on the case.

Despite his confessed ties with the skinheads, I was still fairly convinced that Jason's party crashing was just foolish adolescent behavior. I was also convinced that we didn't need the legal system to teach these boys that it was a bad idea to crash a college party. Yes, they entered a residence without permission. And yes, it was terrible that one of them drew a swastika, but there was no indication that the rest of the boys had anything to do with that graffiti or even realized it was a Jewish fraternity. What it boiled down to was a night of reckless, impulsive behavior by a group of high school teenagers.

About two weeks after the boys were arrested, the prosecutor offered them a "consent decree"—essentially an agreement to dismiss their cases if the kids stayed out of trouble for the next six months. That was many years ago, when it was unheard of to get a consent decree for a serious felony like burglary, much less a hate crime, in D.C. Fortunately, I didn't have to talk about Jason's interest in the skinheads and answer questions about what that might mean. Instead, I joined his parents in blaming their son's late-night partying on the stress of the divorce, and I urged him to take the deal.

I learned a lot from representing Jason. First, I learned that White kids do the same stupid things that Black kids do. They hang out in packs. They do what their friends want them to do— or at least what they *think* their friends want them to do. They drink alcohol before it's legal, and they chase the next thrill. They are impulsive and reactive, and they don't think ahead to the consequences of their behavior.

Jason's case also confirmed what I had always suspected— that our judges make a lot of assumptions about our kids based on race and class. To be clear, this was a judge I had known and respected for many years. He was open-minded and creative. He had always been fair, listening carefully to both sides of an argument before making a decision. But in this moment, his response was quick, automatic, and instinctual. He didn't ask any questions and didn't wait for the prosecutor to make her case. These boys could have been violent predators for all he knew. So why was he so quick to let them go? Because he saw five boys who looked like him—five White, middle-class, educated boys with well-dressed parents who looked deeply concerned. They certainly didn't look like the vast majority of young people who normally appear before him. I can't imagine any scenario in which even this liberal, fair-minded judge would have released five Black boys who walked into his courtroom—with or without their parents—without asking a single question.

Most important, I learned that kids like Jason would be treated very differently in the courts than kids like Eric, who was arrested for the Molotov cocktail. But Jason and Eric weren't that different at all. Both had parents who loved them. Both were doing well in school. Both were arrested for some foolish adolescent activity. Yet Jason was in and out of the system in less than thirty days with no real impact on his school, reputation, or future. Eric was in court for nine months, expelled from school, and barred from his after-school activities. The judge assumed Jason was harmless. School security wouldn't even give Eric the benefit of the doubt. Jason was just being a teenager. Eric was a threat.

The second White client I ever represented, "Alex," brought me to tears. He was a poor kid, living with his single mother and brother in a very small apartment in the wealthy, mostly White upper northwest side of D.C. When I met Alex, he had been charged with aggravated assault for hitting a classmate. The prosecutor called him a bully, but I was convinced that Alex was the one being bullied. Although I failed to convince the judge that Alex was acting in self-defense at trial, Alex's story was so compelling that the judge ultimately agreed to dismiss his case "in the interest of justice," even though the prosecutor had presented enough evidence to prove his guilt. We all felt sorry for him. His classmates picked on him because he was poor, socially awkward, and physically disheveled. He didn't "belong" in "Upper Caucasia." To make things worse, he was big for his age and didn't have any friends at the school. He was both the target and the scapegoat whenever there was a fight.

My third White client, "Ted," was technically not my client. When Ted was arrested for having a rifle in his car, his father hired a big law firm in D.C. to represent him. I watched Ted's initial court hearing from the audience. Ted's lawyer was smart and certainly had the resources to hire the best investigators and law clerks money could buy, but it was clear he had no idea what happens in D.C.'s juvenile court. When the hearing was over, I walked up to the lawyer, gave him my business card, and offered to help in any way I could. The bleeding-heart defender in me couldn't let any child suffer through the mysteries of our local courthouse without guidance. The lawyer wisely took me up on the offer, and I shadowed him through the entire case for free. Ted lived in Maryland but had driven into the city and parked his car. When we reviewed the evidence, it was clear that Ted had a gun in the backseat. Like Jason, Ted eventually got a "consent decree"—an outcome that was again at the time virtually unheard of for a gun charge.

My fourth "White" client, "Mahmoud," wasn't actually White. Well, he wasn't a White American. He was an Egyptian who looked White and was repeatedly described as "White" by every adult he met in D.C.'s juvenile court. I represented Mahmoud in three separate cases from 2016 to 2018. I learned more in those two years about what White kids do in the District of Columbia than I did in my entire career. Like Alex, Mahmoud lived in "Upper Caucasia." Unlike Alex, Mahmoud had friends. Lots of them. And they were all White. He was active on social media, loved to talk, and gave us an amazing firsthand view into the lives of his friends. During the two years we investigated his cases, we were privy to photographs, Facebook and Instagram posts, Twitter tags, and phone calls about party crashing, property damage, underage drinking, skipping school, profanity, inappropriate sexual innuendos, drugs of all types, burglary (a real one), robbery, and more. All by White kids! My favorite photo was of two cute White girls standing with thumbs up as they posed next to a hole in the wall of a vacant house for sale. It was a photo from one of their many party-hopping excursions in empty houses, causing untold damage and heartache to the homeowners. At every house, empty beer cans, trash, and food were strewn about. Doors were damaged, windows were broken, and there was plenty of graffiti on the walls.

It was no coincidence that I represented only Mahmoud and none of the truly White youth. Mahmoud was an outsider. He was the fall guy for his friends. When the police interviewed the cute White girls, they snitched on Mahmoud, claiming he had planned the party and invited everyone else in. Mahmoud was baffled by their accusations, insisting that he was invited on social media like everyone else. Despite the repeated scapegoating, Mahmoud never pulled away from his friends. He was desperate to fit in and overcome his status as a foreigner.

Although Mahmoud eventually pled guilty to burglary and destruction of property, his court hearings were always quite different from the hearings I shared with my Black clients. Notwithstanding multiple violations of probation, Mahmoud was often released to his parents when my other clients would have been locked up. His probation officer and the judge accepted my argument that he wouldn't "fit in" with the other (that is, Black) kids in the detention center. Even when he couldn't stop using drugs and detention became inevitable, the judge sent him to a youth shelter house instead of the local detention facility. Mahmoud was the only "White" kid the staff had ever seen in the shelter. Predictably, the staff regularly excused him from group activities and allowed him to read in his room. Before his probation ended, Mahmoud was allowed to move to the West Coast for college. He is doing just fine.

I could write this entire chapter in anecdotes, but then you wouldn't believe me when I say that White kids are treated differently than Black kids for committing the same kinds of crimes all over the country. So let's look at the history, the science, and the data.

## THE INVENTION OF (WHITE) ADOLESCENCE

First, the history. Most of us take adolescence for granted as a distinct stage of life bridging childhood and adulthood. But it is actually a relatively new concept. The modern idea of adolescence did not appear until the late nineteenth century and didn't gain widespread traction until the 1950s or 1960s.[1] Before the Industrial Revolution (1760–1840), we thought of development in only two stages, with childhood including anyone under the age of eighteen, or sometimes twenty-one, and adulthood including everyone else.[2] As industrialization shifted the nation's economy from farming to manufacturing, the role of children also changed.[3] In 1860, 72 percent of those employed in the United States worked in agriculture.[4] By 1930, that number had decreased to 21 percent. Children raised in agrarian cultures were expected to work and contribute to the upkeep of the family just like adults. After the Industrial Revolution, the number of youth working in the field decreased, and the number of youth enrolled in high school and college increased dramatically.

Shifts in the workforce created higher-paying jobs that required skilled labor and advanced education. In response, many parents, especially those in the middle class, encouraged their children to stay in school to develop the skills they needed to succeed.[5] In 1900, 43 percent of fourteen- and fifteen-year-old boys and 18 percent of fourteen- and fifteen-year-old girls were employed in the United States.[6] By 1930, only 12 percent of boys and 5 percent of girls were working at that age. At the same time, the number of students enrolled in public high schools increased from 519,000 in 1900 to 3.9 million in 1928. In 1852, Massachusetts became the first state to pass a law requiring children to attend school.[7] By 1900, most northern and western states had passed similar "compulsory education laws." Enrollment in college and professional schools also increased after the Industrial Revolution. In the 1890s, the number of students enrolled in colleges increased by 38.4 percent, and the number of medical, law, dentistry, pharmacy, and other professional schools doubled between 1876 and 1900.

Adolescence was essentially "invented"—by White middle-class parents—to give their children an advantage in the changing Western world. Adolescence brought with it the privilege of extended education, prolonged self-discovery, and new opportunities for fun and leisure. In the transition to adulthood, society expected—or at least hoped—youth would not only develop new skills but also test boundaries, wrestle with moral dilemmas, and find their special talents. Parents and teachers taught children about the important responsibilities of family, work, and community but gave them time to think independently and shape their own identities.

This newfound adolescence wasn't always greeted with joy. Adolescence originated at a time of considerable upheaval in the United States, and some worried that this new period of freedom would weaken the family and wreak havoc on society unless young people were controlled. As workers moved from the country to the city in search of industrial jobs, families changed and society seemed less orderly. Many believed that young people were the cause of that disorder and should be regulated "at every turn."[8]

American psychologist G. Stanley Hall emerged as the "father of adolescence" in 1904 when he wrote about the physical and biological changes that begin with the "growth spurt" and conclude with the end of physical development, usually in a person's twenties.[9] Although Hall focused on the physical changes that occurred during adolescence, he was also concerned about the character and personality traits that accompanied those changes. Hall described adolescence as a time of "storm and stress" and believed that adolescents should be protected and excluded from adult activities.[10]

Responding to Hall's work, cultural anthropologist Margaret Mead argued that the characteristics of adolescence were caused by the cultural pressures of Western society, not biology.[11] Although Hall and Mead disagreed on the cause, both expressed an increasingly negative view of adolescence and advocated for new social programs that would monitor and control young people.[12] Heeding the call for increased supervision and more opportunities to teach youth moral values, states not only passed mandatory school attendance laws but also expanded laws to reduce child labor and created a special juvenile legal system to deal with delinquent youth.[13] These policies allowed states to impose middle-class values on youth and further separated adolescents from children and adults.[14]

## THE ADOLESCENT BRAIN

Now, the science. We know a lot more about the adolescent brain than we did even twenty years ago.[15] Although the brain doesn't grow in size much past age five, it does change in some very important ways between puberty and the early twenties.[16] During this period, the brain is described as "plastic"—or malleable to adapt and respond to new experiences and the environment.[17] In his book *Age of Opportunity,* developmental psychologist Laurence Steinberg teaches us that adolescence is the last period of significant flexibility in the brain.[18] It is also probably the last real opportunity we have to set individuals on a path to success.

Although most psychologists no longer talk about adolescence as a time of "storm and stress," they do remind us that it is a season of impulsivity and recklessness. During adolescence, the brain changes in ways that affect how we seek out and enjoy pleasure, how we control ourselves, and how we interact with other people.[19] Changes in the brain that accompany puberty make us more easily aroused by our emotions and more likely to become angry or upset at a time when we don't have the capacity to fully regulate our thoughts, emotions, and actions.[20] These changes also increase our willingness to take risks and chase excitement. Our desire for novel and exciting experiences increases shortly after puberty and then declines as we transition to adulthood. Many of the fears we may have developed during childhood are temporarily repressed in adolescence, only to return when we are adults.[21]

Across a wide variety of activities, adolescents take more risks than either children or adults, with the likelihood of risky and reckless behavior usually peaking sometime during the late teens. Violence also increases during this age, as do self-inflicted injuries, unintentional drownings, drug experimentation, accidental pregnancies, property crime, and deadly car crashes.[22] As Steinberg explains, the rise in testosterone during puberty makes males more reckless and aggressive and increases both accidents and deaths.[23] This science helps explain why adolescents commit more crimes per capita than children or adults in the United States and in nearly all industrialized cultures.[24]

The science also explains why the crime rate goes up when adolescents hang out in groups. Peer pressure is not a myth. Teenagers are particularly reckless when they are together.[25] They do stupid things to get attention, impress others, and win friends. Others join in so their friends won't think they are "lame" or scared. Even when teenagers like my client Jason clearly know the difference between right and wrong, they still make bad decisions in the heat of the moment, with friends, and without time to think or to talk to an adult.[26] Parts of the brain that control our most advanced thinking, like logical reasoning, planning, and complicated decision making, take longer to develop and are not fully mature until the early or mid-twenties.[27] Eventually, as we mature, we get better at controlling what we think, how we feel, and what we do. But until then, we can expect (and even forgive) the ridiculous things teenagers do.

We forgive most adolescent indiscretions precisely because experts tell us those indiscretions are normal. We forgive because all of us can recall something stupid we did as a teenager and yet managed to come out just fine. Adolescence is a time of trial and error. It is a time when teenagers learn from their mistakes, gradually resist peer pressure, and begin to think about what will happen if they do the wrong thing. The hesitation that once held them back in childhood returns as they set new goals and take on new responsibilities. Research shows that even young people who end up in court for serious crimes will age out of that behavior by late adolescence, and most will age out naturally, without significant court intervention.[28]

Developmental psychologists also teach us that adolescence looks remarkably similar all over the world.[29] Teenagers behave like teenagers wherever they live—at least in the most fundamental ways. Youth in every country take risks, chase excitement, act without thinking, and are easily influenced by their friends.[30] But of course, context does matter. Not all youth have the privilege of a prolonged and forgiving adolescence. Modern adolescence offers the greatest benefit to White, middle-class, able-bodied, heterosexual, college-bound boys—boys who have experienced little if any trauma and have few responsibilities other than pursuing their own interests and ambitions.[31] For these youth, impulsivity and mischief are a luxury, and even a rite of passage into adulthood. For Black youth, adolescent mischief can be a death sentence, or at least an excuse for police harassment and abuse. Racism and discrimination distort normal adolescent behaviors into crime and deviance among Black youth and deny them the grace and tolerance society extends to their peers. Even when the data shows that White youth are just as likely as Black youth to use drugs, carry a weapon, drink while driving, and have unprotected sex, Black youth are more likely to be stopped, arrested, and punished for whatever they do.[32]

### #CRIMINGWHILEWHITE

My 1-to-99 percent White-to-Black client ratio might lead you to believe that very few White youth live in Washington, D.C., or that very few White youth commit crimes in the city. Neither is true. Although D.C. was once affectionately known as Chocolate City, in 2019 about 24 percent of youth under the age of eighteen were White and 52 percent were Black.[33] And of course, White youth do commit crimes in D.C. They just don't end up in juvenile court.

Researchers have been collecting data about teenagers' behavior for years. Forty years of adolescent self-report studies from the University of Michigan and the Centers for Disease Control (CDC) confirm that youth of all races and ethnicities admit involvement in risky, irresponsible, and even dangerous behaviors. In 2018, 58.5 percent of high school teenagers surveyed in the United States reported that they had tried alcohol by the twelfth grade, 42.9 percent had been drunk, and 49 percent had tried marijuana.[34] More than 39 percent reported having had sex,[35] and within that group 13.8 percent reported that they had used no protection to prevent pregnancy. Nothing in this data collection suggests that Black youth are inherently more reckless, impulsive, or dangerous than White youth. In fact, notwithstanding some differences in the type of drug, type of weapon, or age at the onset of such behaviors, White youth report risky behaviors at rates similar to—and sometimes higher than—Black and Hispanic* youth. Data on adolescent drug use paints this picture well.

Although Black youth tend to report using marijuana more often and at earlier ages than White youth,[36] White youth are more likely to report using many other drugs by the eighth through twelfth grades. Hallucinogens, synthetic marijuana, and all forms of prescription drugs, such as OxyContin, Vicodin, tranquilizers, and amphetamines obtained without a doctor's prescription, are just a few of the drugs that are more popular among White youth than Black youth.[37] White youth are also more likely than Black youth to have tried or used an electronic vapor product, such as e-cigarettes, vaping pens, and hookah pens.[38] White youth also far outpace Black youth in all forms of alcohol use—including onetime experiences, binge drinking, getting drunk, and driving after drinking.[39] Similarly, although Black youth are more likely to report carrying a gun specifically or getting into some type of physical fight at school, White youth are more likely to report carrying some type of weapon overall, including a gun, knife, or club, at some point in the ninth through twelfth grades.[40]

All of these behaviors arise out of the same impulsive, short-sighted features of adolescence that are common among youth of all races. Yet we don't treat youth of all races the same. Poor Black youth who experiment with drugs and alcohol in public spaces like a park or a street corner are more visible—and appear

---

*Throughout this text, I use the word "Latinx" to describe a person of Latin American origin or descent in a gender-neutral or nonbinary way unless a particular study or data source uses the term "Hispanic."

more dangerous—than wealthier White youth who use drugs in the privacy of their own homes and clubhouses. Black youth who have greater access to more stereotypically frightening drugs like crack are demonized as violent criminals, while White youth who can afford more expensive drugs like powder cocaine are excused as impulsive and experimenting teens. Teachers and counselors who are inundated with negative images and faulty narratives about Black youth in poor, urban schools are less likely to tolerate and forgive adolescent misconduct than teachers who work with White youth in rural or wealthy communities. And police officers who are vulnerable to racial bias and stereotypes in fast-paced and stressful encounters with youth make snap judgments and racialized assumptions about what they see and how they will respond.

At every stage of the juvenile legal system, Black youth are treated more harshly than White youth. Despite years of evidence that White youth use drugs at the same rates as Black youth or higher, 19 percent of all drug cases referred to U.S. juvenile courts in 2018 involved Black youth.[41] This data is notable when we consider that only 15 percent of youth in the juvenile court age range that year were Black.[42] Black youth also accounted for 35 percent of all juvenile arrests for any crime in 2018 and 40 percent of all cases in which the youth was sent to a detention facility to await trial or sentencing.[43] Black youth accounted for 39 percent of all cases formally processed in a juvenile court, 37 percent of all cases in which the youth was found guilty, and more than 51 percent of youth whom a judge transferred from juvenile court to be tried as an adult.[44] After they were found guilty, Black youth accounted for more than 41 percent of all cases in which the youth was placed in secure or nonsecure residential settings.[45]

These differences are not lost on anyone who pays attention. Just ask the White youth. On the night of December 3, 2014, Jason Ross, a writer for *The Tonight Show Starring Jimmy Fallon,* tweeted, "Busted 4 larceny at 11. At 17, cited for booze + caught w gun @ school. No one called me a thug. Can't recommend being white highly enough."[46] He then tweeted, "OTHER WHITE PEOPLE: Tweet your stories of under-punished f-ups! It's embarrassing but important! Let's get #CrimingWhileWhite trending!"[47] Ross's Twitter campaign began the day after a New York grand jury decided not to indict Daniel Pantaleo, the police officer who killed Eric Garner in a chokehold on July 17, 2014.[48] Response to the hashtag was explosive. At one point the hashtag was being published at a rate of six hundred tweets per minute.[49] The tweets described a broad range of activity but were consistent in describing police responses that were respectful, lenient, and free from violence:

- "I dined and dashed—cop found me at the movies, I paid the bill and he left. I was rude but not arrested and not killed. #CrimingWhileWhite"[50]
- "Me & my grunge friends smoking at the mall. Mall cop tells us to move. We tell him to F off. He laughs & bums a smoke. #CrimingWhileWhite"[51]
- "Arrested for DUI, cop took me to drive through ATM so I'd have money to bail myself out. #Crimingwhilewhite"[52]
- "Friend w/ suspended license gets flat tire/pulled over in someone else's car. Cop says he will use my license (passenger) #CrimingWhileWhite"[53]

Although not independently verified, the tweets provide a trove of self-reported evidence documenting the privilege of White adolescence. So, if the science and the data tell us that White youth act a lot like Black youth, then why don't we treat Black youth the same? The answer is simple: we don't see Black children as children.

## WHITE ADDICTION, BLACK CRIME: RACE AND OPIOIDS IN AMERICA

Race lies at the heart of how we think about and respond to normal teenage behaviors. Racial stereotypes in the media, popular culture, and historical propaganda tell us which kids we should fear and which kids we should indulge and forgive. Fraternity hazing, sexual play, adolescent pranks, and drug use are sources of humor and entertainment in mainstream Hollywood movies like *Risky Business, American Pie, Fast Times at Ridgemont High, Mean Girls, Superbad,* and *Project X.* White youth benefit from the compassion and tolerance of White adults who can see themselves in those cinematic images. Even when society looked at rebellious young hippies, Goths, punks, and metalheads with skepticism and dismay, we didn't think of them as violent "thugs" and criminals. We didn't describe them as "terrorists" and "gang members." And we certainly didn't arrest them in droves. Our tortured debate about race and opioids makes this point clear.

We have seen three waves of opioid use in the United States. The first wave spanned from 1979 to the mid-1990s when heroin affected Blacks and Whites alike.[54] The second wave, spanning from the mid-1990s to 2010, brought a significant increase in opioid deaths among White Americans as aggressive marketing by the pharmaceutical industry led to the overprescription of pain relievers like codeine, morphine, hydrocodone, and oxycodone. Opioid misuse among youth quickly became one of the nation's greatest concerns as the number of deaths continued to climb. In 2018, 4,633 youth aged fifteen to twenty-four died from a drug-related overdose.[55] Approximately 78 percent of those were attributable to opioids.

The third and final wave of opioid use began around 2010 when policy makers acted to reduce access to prescription painkillers. As prescription painkillers became harder to obtain and increasingly expensive, many of those who developed an addiction to prescription drugs turned to cheaper street alternatives, such as heroin and synthetic opioids—like the illegally manufactured fentanyl. Nearly 80 percent of people who have used heroin started by misusing prescription opioids, and in 2017, 78 percent of people who died in the United States from an opioid overdose were White.[56] Ironically, racism protected Black youth from the rapid increase in opioid deaths. Motivated by fears that Black people would sell or abuse the prescription, and buying into the myth that Black people have a higher tolerance for pain than Whites, doctors were less likely to prescribe painkillers to Blacks.[57]

Racism also led politicians to take a more sympathetic response to opioid use than had ever been seen in U.S. history. Shortly after taking office, President Donald Trump, who had consistently supported tough criminal penalties for marijuana and crack,[58] established the President's Commission on Combating Drug Addiction and the Opioid Crisis.[59] In July 2017, the commission released a report urging the president to declare the opioid crisis a national emergency.[60] The president followed that recommendation in October 2017, marking the first time a drug epidemic had been labeled a public health emergency in the United States.[61] In the months that followed, the White House and the Department of Justice pledged billions of dollars for treatment, public education, and law enforcement efforts to shut down websites that sell opioids, crack down on fraudulent prescribers, and stop the production and sale of illicit fentanyl.[62]

Previous drug epidemics that have gripped communities of color were met with condemnation and punishment. The first anti-opium laws adopted in the 1870s vilified Chinese immigrants.[63] Anti-cocaine laws passed in the early twentieth century targeted Black men in the South, and anti-marijuana laws of the 1920s were aimed at Mexican migrants. In virtually every decade since the 1970s, state and federal governments have increased their law enforcement responses to drugs in poor Black communities. President Nixon's "War on Drugs" created popular hysteria about drug use in the 1970s and increased federal spending on law enforcement strategies that criminalized drug addiction. In the 1980s, President Reagan declared drugs "an especially vicious virus of crime" and continued the nation's punitive response to the crack epidemic that was ravaging Black communities.[64] Reagan enforced new drug laws that authorized sentence enhancements and imposed mandatory minimum sentences that dramatically increased the prison population, especially among Black Americans.[65]

From 1985 to 1995, the percentage of African Americans sentenced for drug offenses rose 707 percent, compared with only 306 percent for Whites.[66] President Bill Clinton continued the tough-on-drugs strategies in the 1990s and did nothing to end the wide disparity in sentencing for crack and powder cocaine.[67] By 2017, more than 2.2 million Americans were in prison or jail.[68] Nearly 60 percent of them were Black or Latinx.

Unlike the crack epidemic, which garnered little sympathy for Black Americans who became addicted to the deadly drug, the opioid epidemic has gripped the nation with compassion, drawing out White suburbanites to lobby their state officials to treat their addicted children with dignity. To justify their stark pivot from tough-on-crime punishments to a treatment-minded response, policy makers depict opioid addicts as innocent victims of corporate pharmaceutical greed. In the popular opioid narrative, the victims are rural, educated, and sometimes even affluent White youth who had no intention of acquiring a drug habit.[69] In the distorted American imagination about race and crime, Black children are deviant villains who make a calculated choice to use and sell drugs for their own profit and demise.[70]

### LIFE AFTER HOMICIDE:
### THE ULTIMATE PRIVILEGE OF WHITE ADOLESCENCE

The grace we extend to White youth doesn't stop at drug use. Even in the face of deadly violence and extreme recklessness, the media gives White youth every presumption of innocence. Judges are eager to protect whatever potential White youth have to succeed in the future. Court staff offer mental health services and drug treatment to keep White youth out of jail, and jurors accept whatever excuse the youth might offer. Consider the case of Cameron Terrell—an eighteen-year-old who lived with his family in Palos Verdes, California, a wealthy White suburb of Los Angeles. In 2017, Cameron was charged with murder for driving the getaway car in a gang-related homicide. Spoiler alert: Cameron was acquitted of all charges because the jury was convinced he was just "studying" Black gang culture.[71]

On October 1, 2017, Cameron Terrell drove two Black friends into South Los Angeles. His friends were members of the Rollin' 90s Crips gang.[72] While Cameron waited in the car, his teenage friends confronted, shot, and killed twenty-one-year-old Justin Holmes in rival gang territory. Evidence later revealed that Holmes was not involved in any gang. Cameron was arrested two weeks after the shooting when police found video showing the two teens running from the shooting directly to Cameron's car parked a few blocks away. Cameron sped away with his friends.

Cameron had a very different background from his friends. He grew up in a house valued at nearly $2 million, with parents who could afford to post $5 million in bail.[73] Cameron was out on pretrial release seven days after his arrest and was spotted at a World Series Dodgers game within days of his release. He returned to school and was allowed to live at home pending trial. Cameron's two friends lived in the south side of Los Angeles, in a poor neighborhood near Jesse Owens Park. As you may have guessed, his friends remained in custody.[74]

During police questioning, Cameron admitted to driving his friends to the Manchester Square neighborhood—a community he knew to be in the territory of the Eight-Tray Gangster Crips, a rival of the Rollin' 90s. Although he knew his friends were gang members, he claimed to be shocked that anyone had a gun that night. Cameron thought they were going to tag their rival's territory or maybe get into a fistfight, but not kill anyone. At trial, Cameron's defense attorney argued that Cameron never joined the gang. Instead, he was just fascinated by gang culture and read books about gang life.[75] His attorney explained that Cameron hung around in Jesse Owens Park because he was an only child whose parents were having "issues" at home.[76] He urged the court not to derail Cameron's education, but to instead just get him away from the negative influences.

The jury found Cameron not guilty despite overwhelming

evidence of his gang involvement. At trial, the prosecutors presented texts, Facebook messages, videos, and photos of Cameron hanging out with known gang members, flashing gang signs, and wearing gang colors.[77] Social media posts show that Cameron began socializing with Rollin' 90s members at least a year before his first police contact. Police first became aware of Cameron in the spring of 2017 when they had multiple interactions with him at the park where the Rollin' 90s were known to hang out.[78] Other witnesses spoke about Cameron's allegiance to the Rollin' 90s and his dislike for rival gangs. His gang nickname was Milk, and he had a tattoo of a W on his chest that identified the specific clique he associated with. After the murder, Cameron posted a video on social media of his Rollin' 90s friends kicking over candles at a street memorial for Holmes. Cameron also posted a rap composition on social media proclaiming, "You know what it is right / the homie got shot / I just need to kill somebody." Police found a hoodie with gang insignia and a can of spray paint in Cameron's car when they arrested him.

Let's imagine the same facts in a different color. Would a Black child ever be acquitted of murder, or even accessory to murder, for "studying" White culture in a wealthy White neighborhood? Of course not. A Black Cameron in a White community would be arrested just for being out of place. Even though Cameron had to be prosecuted as an adult at the age of eighteen, he still received all the benefits of his youth. Visually, Cameron did not fit the popular image of a "gangbanger." He was White, wealthy, and wearing a suit and had a well-groomed haircut and light blue eyes. The jurors couldn't imagine him as a threat or a "thug." At most he was a troubled teenager going through a "phase." Eager to protect his promising future and blindly accepting his claims of intellectual curiosity about Black culture, the jurors gave him the benefit of the doubt. After he was acquitted, Cameron went on to college at the University of Houston.

Cameron Terrell was not the first White youth to make national headlines with a creative excuse for his behavior. Just a few years before, there was Ethan Couch. Ethan grew up in a rural suburb of Fort Worth, Texas. His parents were divorced, and they indulged him in every way they could. On June 15, 2013, Ethan wanted to have a party, so he did—at his father's house. To get more beer for the festivities, Ethan and seven others piled into his father's red pickup truck with Ethan at the wheel. Ethan was sixteen and driving with a restricted license. Shortly thereafter, he was seen on Walmart surveillance cameras stealing two cases of beer and jumping back in the truck with his friends.[79] An hour later, Ethan lost control of the truck, moving seventy miles per hour through a forty-mile-per-hour residential zone. He swerved off the road and hit a group of people who were helping a woman with a disabled SUV. Three hours after the crash, Ethan still had a blood alcohol content of 0.24—three times the legal limit for adults in Texas.[80] He also tested positive for marijuana, Valium, and muscle relaxants.[81] Ethan killed four people in the crash and injured nine others. Two of his friends were riding in the bed of the pickup truck. One friend suffered a severe brain injury and was paralyzed when he was thrown from the truck as it flipped over and hit a tree.

Ethan was charged with four counts of manslaughter for driving recklessly and intoxicated.[82] At his sentencing hearing, his defense attorney hired a psychologist to argue that Ethan should not be sent to prison because he suffered from "affluenza." Resurrecting a term that dates back to at least the 1980s, the defense argued that because Ethan grew up in a dysfunctional wealthy family, he never learned that his actions had consequences. The defense team also initially claimed that Ethan's parents would send him to an expensive residential treatment center in California. The facility would offer substance abuse and mental health treatment, along with horseback riding, martial arts, dance, swimming, cooking, and massages. Satisfied that Ethan could be "saved" without jail time, the judge rejected the prosecutor's request for twenty years in prison and sentenced Ethan to ten years of probation and ordered that he be sent for therapy at his parents' expense for an unspecified amount of time.[83] Records later revealed that Ethan's parents paid $1,170 a month for his stay at a state-owned inpatient mental health facility in Vernon, Texas.[84]

Many criticized the judge's sentence and complained that "affluenza" set a double standard for the rich and the poor and for White and Black youth. As one psychologist asked, "What is the likelihood if this was an African-American, inner-city kid that grew up in a violent neighborhood to a single mother who is addicted to crack and he was caught two or three times . . . what is the likelihood that the judge would excuse his behavior and let him off because of how he was raised?"[85] Her answer: Not likely at all.

This wasn't the first—or last—time Ethan would be in trouble with alcohol. At the age of fifteen, he had been caught in a parked pickup truck with a naked, passed-out fourteen-year-old girl. He pled no contest to being a "minor in possession of alcohol" and was sentenced to probation, with a compulsory alcohol awareness class and twelve hours of community service.[86] Almost two years after his manslaughter sentence, in December 2015, Ethan was spotted in a video posted on Twitter playing beer pong at a party. His probation officer reported him "missing" when Ethan disappeared shortly thereafter. Ethan and his mother had fled to Mexico but were later arrested and deported back to Texas following a manhunt. Only then was Ethan sentenced to two years in jail for violating his conditions of probation.

Ethan is one of many White youth who have been sent to boarding school, drug treatment, or a mental health facility instead of prison after a violent crime. White adolescence carries with it a privilege to push boundaries, seek adventure, impress friends, and make mistakes. White youth can get high, crash a party, carry a gun, steal a car, and break into a vacant house with little risk of arrest, detention, or severe sentence. Even after the most heinous behavior, a White child is still a child—with all the promise of redemption and a future worth saving. Adolescence was truly made for them.

But the rest of this book is dedicated to the remaining 99 percent of my clients—the Black children who have been arrested, prosecuted, and even killed for doing far less than what Cameron Terrell and Ethan Couch did. It is dedicated to all of the Black youth who don't have the luxury of testing limits, talking back, or making poor decisions as other children do. It is for every Black child who has been criminalized for just being a child.

# 2

## Toy Guns, Cell Phones, and Parties: Criminalizing Black Adolescent Play

### TOY GUNS AND WAR GAMES

Toy guns are a staple of adolescent play. A quick Google search turns up several Top 10 lists for the "best toy guns of the year."[1] Water guns, paint guns, guns in virtual video games, BB guns, cap guns, dart guns, and Nerf guns are standard merchandise in Walmart, Target, Amazon, and the local dollar store. Boys—and girls—play with guns at home, in the park, and at school. Entire parks are devoted to paintball guns. Cops and robbers, cowboys and Indians, and war games are common themes at the movies and on the television screen.

Playing with guns, especially among boys, has been a common feature of American culture for centuries. It wasn't until the 1980s and 1990s that parents and teachers began to worry about the dangers of toy guns.[2] Despite sporadic attempts to ban them after high-profile school shootings, toy guns remain popular in the twenty-first century. Surveys show that about 60 to 80 percent of boys and about 30 percent of girls play with aggressive toys like guns at home.[3] Even when parents refuse to buy them, children chase after each other yelling "pow pow" and pointing their thumb and forefinger in the shape of a gun. Toy guns are inescapable. Cartoons like *Looney Tunes, Batman, The Simpsons, Family Guy, The Boondocks,* and *Pokémon* have all aired episodes with guns. The cartoon images are so plentiful that in 2014, Democrats attempted to ban gun manufacturers from using cartoon characters to market guns. The bill never passed.[4]

Contrary to common fears, research offers no scientific evidence that playing with toy guns in childhood leads to violence later in life.[5] In fact, some have argued that roughhousing, verbal dueling, playing with toy weapons, and war games might be good for children who learn to negotiate power and achieve victory in the safety of fantasy and play.[6] Of course, the toy industry has resisted any claim that toy guns themselves encourage aggressive behavior and prefers to highlight the benefits of friendly competition, exercise, and an active mind.[7]

Given the saturation of toy guns in our society, we shouldn't be surprised or even worried about a twelve-year-old boy playing with a toy gun at a local park on a lazy Saturday afternoon. But that's exactly what happened in Cleveland on November 22, 2014. Someone was very worried.

*He looked big for his age.*

—CLEVELAND COUNTY PROSECUTOR TIM MCGINTY

Shortly before 3:30 p.m., a park visitor called 911 to report that someone, "probably a juvenile," was pointing a "pistol" at random people at the Cudell Recreation Center in Cleveland.[8] Twice, the caller told dispatch the gun was "probably fake."[9] When a police car sped onto the Cudell park lawn, twelve-year-old Tamir Rice was sitting on a picnic table in a gazebo.[10] One of the officers in the car, Timothy Loehmann, jumped out and shot Tamir two times in the chest. Loehmann later said he saw a Black male pick up a black gun and put it in his waistband. The car carrying Loehmann and his partner had not come to a complete stop before Loehmann fired his weapon.[11] Within two seconds of the officers' arrival, Tamir was shot down.[12]

It turns out that Tamir had been holding an imitation pistol— or an "airsoft" replica gun,[13] popular among children and sold at places like Walmart and Dick's Sporting Goods. Surveillance video shows that Tamir had been walking around the park earlier, occasionally extending his right arm, and talking on the phone.[14] Tamir's mother said that a friend gave him the toy shortly before he went to the park.[15]

So many things went wrong that afternoon. At the outset, the police dispatcher never told officers that the 911 caller said the gun was probably fake and the person holding it was probably a child.[16] Although the officers approached the gazebo from the safety of their car, they did not take any time to assess the situation before jumping out to fire. The officers drove up at a high rate of speed, stopped less than ten feet from Tamir,[17] and did not take cover inside or behind the car long enough to ask questions and allow Tamir to respond. Contradicting the officers' claims that they had repeatedly yelled, "Show me your hands," through the open car window, several witnesses reported that they never heard any verbal warnings before the gunfire.[18] Even with a warning, two seconds is an incredibly short time for anyone—especially a twelve-year-old—to process an officer's commands and comply.

Another critical error occurred when the Cleveland police department failed to thoroughly screen Officer Loehmann before hiring him. In the aftermath of the shooting, investigators learned that Loehmann had previously worked in a Cleveland suburb called Independence. After observing him for four months in the police academy and one month in the field, Loehmann's superiors deemed him emotionally unstable and unfit for police duty. According to their reports, Loehmann was unable to follow basic instructions, demonstrated a dangerous loss of composure, had a "dismal" record of handling weapons, and became visibly "distracted and weepy" as a result of relationship problems.[19] Loehmann resigned from the Independence Police Department to avoid his certain termination. He had been employed there from March to August 2014, departing just three months before he killed Tamir Rice. Cleveland police officials did not discover Loehmann's prior personnel record until it was far too late.

Loehmann was never prosecuted for killing Tamir. Two experts on police use of force concluded that the shooting was reasonable under the circumstances.[20] The county prosecutor, Tim McGinty, blamed the shooting on human error, mistakes, and miscommunication by all involved.[21] McGinty's analysis ignored a critical variable—race. Tamir's death was much more than the sum total of administrative and procedural errors. His death draws us to the center of what it means to be Black and adolescent. It wouldn't have mattered if the officers had been told that the person in the park was probably a child or the gun was probably fake. When officers arrived on the scene, they saw a Black male with a dark object. That alone made him "dangerous." Tamir's race negated any possibility that he was a child—playing in a park, with a toy.

Loehmann lives in America—a country overwhelmed by stereotypes that associate Black males with crime and violence. The subconscious link between Blackness and criminality is so strong that regardless of which one people think of first, they automatically think of the other.[22] When people see a Black person on the street, they think about crime. When people think about crime, they see a Black person. Sometimes these thoughts cause people to see things that aren't there and to do things they wouldn't otherwise do. Research conducted over the last twenty years shows that both police officers and civilians are more likely to believe— accurately and inaccurately—that a common object, such as an everyday tool, is a lethal weapon in the hands of a Black person than when it is in the hands of a White person.[23] They are also more likely to believe that a common toy—like a baby's rattle— is a threatening object, like a gun, when it is associated with a Black child's face, even a child as young as five years old.[24] Even a brief exposure to Blackness can shatter long-standing and deeply embedded notions about the presumptive innocence and harmlessness of children.

In the weeks after Tamir was killed, police and prosecutors defended the shooting by arguing that Tamir looked much older than his mere twelve years. Prosecutors were emphatic that Tamir was "big for his age," weighing 175 pounds, standing five feet seven inches tall, and wearing size 36 pants and a man's extra-large jacket.[25] Tamir is not alone. Black youth are often perceived to be older than they really are. In 2014, researchers showed police officers a series of photographs of young White, Black, and Latino males suspected of criminal behavior and asked them to estimate the age of each child.[26] The officers overestimated the age of the Black felony suspects by five years, but underestimated the age of the White felony suspects by one year. The older an officer thought the child was, the more likely the officer was to believe the child was culpable of the suspected crime. Researchers also found that civilian study participants perceived the "innocence" of Black children aged ten to thirteen to be equivalent to that of non-Black children aged fourteen to seventeen and the innocence of Black children aged fourteen to seventeen to be equivalent to that of non-Black adults aged eighteen to twenty-one.[27]

Stereotypes and biases about Blackness and criminality help explain the high number of deadly police shootings of unarmed Black Americans. Presumptions about Tamir's likely criminality are so entrenched that even an officer who is strongly opposed to racism would have a hard time avoiding the effects of implicit bias. Tamir's death, and others like it, cannot be reduced to the conduct of one or two rogue officers who are racist, or even emotionally unstable like Loehmann. Loehmann was called in to make a split-second decision, with limited information and considerable stress. Although we know that bias thrives in these tense moments,[28] few police departments train officers to manage their biases and de-escalate encounters to minimize the use of weapons. Even fewer train officers on how to effectively engage with adolescents.[29]

## THE BENEFITS OF ADOLESCENT PLAY

In interviews after the shooting, Tamir's mother, Samaria Rice, told reporters that she felt as if prosecutors were trying to blame her for her son's death and talked to her as if she were a bad mother for letting him have the BB gun.[30] Judgments like these fail to appreciate the many difficult choices every Black parent must make. Tamir was playing outside, in a park, within walking distance of his house, at 3:30 on a Saturday afternoon. He was a child, playing with a toy given to him by an adult family friend. There was nothing unusual—and certainly nothing reprehensible—about this activity. Ms. Rice was giving her son time outside to *play*—a basic life necessity just as important as food, shelter, and sleep.

Play and recreation are such routine aspects of adolescence that most of us forget how important these activities are for healthy physical and social development. Teenagers spend as much as 40 percent of their day free from work, school, and other responsibilities.[31] Youth fill this time with sports, after-school clubs, recreation programs at the local community center, video games, television, music, and idle play. Sometimes they just sit still and reflect. At its most basic level, play helps youth relieve stress and anxiety from school and other demands on their lives. Tussling with friends in the yard and kicking a ball in the street are good for a child's physical and mental health. Excitement and adventure make life's inevitable difficulties more bearable, while joy and happiness allow us to clear our heads, put life in perspective, and give us the stamina and resilience we need to learn and achieve. Recreation is so important that schools all over the country build "free time" and physical education into the weekly curriculum.[32]

Experts tell us that playtime also builds character and social skills.[33] As youth play and compete, they learn to get along, work as a team, and resolve conflict. They come to respect other people's feelings and develop a sense of loyalty, empathy, and belonging. Over time, most youth will also develop intimate and lasting relationships with friends who will "have their back" and help them navigate the complicated spaces of school, home, and the neighborhood. Even youth who spend most of their free time on social media and the internet find community and develop interpersonal skills, leadership, and creativity.[34] At their best, social networks give youth the support and resources they need to share their opinions and speak out against injustice.

Two of the most important benefits of leisure are autonomy and self-determination.[35] Youth who find activities that are meaningful and personally rewarding are motivated to set their own goals and take initiative without their parents' prodding. Recreation allows youth to discover their talents and develop the confidence, self-esteem, and determination they need to succeed. The brain's flexibility during adolescence makes the teenage years a particularly good time to cultivate lifelong skills and passion for music, art, sports, and other recreational hobbies.[36] Teens who struggle with low self-esteem in school may experience pride as they succeed in other aspects of their life.

Of course, some youth will fill their free time with activities adults consider dangerous and unhealthy. But research suggests that even experimenting with drugs and alcohol can contribute to healthy adolescent development if it is temporary rather than addictive.[37] Similarly, even a fight on the playground can give students the courage they need to stand up for themselves in the future. As we learned in the last chapter, teenagers seek out intense and exciting experiences. They take risks and make mistakes. These experiences are both normal and instructive. As young people face the consequences of their choices, they learn to control their impulses and think before they act. As adults, many of us know our alcohol limit precisely because we can remember a night—or two—when we drank too much. Parents and teachers help teenagers reflect on these moments by imposing consequences that are not designed to criminalize or embarrass them, but instead help them make better decisions in the future. The most successful parents gradually give youth more autonomy to explore and take risks by themselves while offering just enough support and redirection to keep them safe.[38]

Notwithstanding the vast benefits of play, Black children are routinely denied the developmental advantages of leisure and recreation. While White parents encourage their children to go to parties, make friends, laugh, and be creative with little concern for their safety, Black parents like Samaria Rice live in constant fear that their sons and daughters will be stopped, arrested, or even killed for normal adolescent play. We need only read the newspaper to see how often Black children around the country are treated like criminals for just being children.

In Miami, Florida, fourteen-year-old Tremaine McMillian was forced to the ground in a chokehold by an officer who stopped him for roughhousing with a friend on the beach on Memorial Day 2013.[39] In Washington, D.C., two boys were arrested for selling water on the National Mall in June 2017.[40] In Jacksonville, Florida, eleven-year-old Fatayi Jomoh was handcuffed for dribbling a basketball in a gym after an officer told him to stop in August 2018.[41] In Binghamton, New York, four twelve-year-old Black and Latina girls were strip-searched for giggling and laughing in the hallway at their middle school in January 2019.[42] Apparently, the girls were being "hyper" and "giddy." In Canton, Michigan, ten-year-old Bryce Lindley was charged with aggravated assault after one of his classmates was injured in a playground game of dodgeball at his elementary school in July 2019.[43]

Without free and unburdened play, Black youth are at a constant disadvantage—physically, mentally, socially, and academically. Because Black youth are under the constant surveillance of the police and other adults who expect them to be criminal, play becomes a source of anxiety instead of rest and relaxation.

### CELL PHONES AND BACK TALK: SPRING VALLEY HIGH

Cell phones are even more common than toy guns. Teenagers use their phones for just about everything. They text, download apps, play games, surf the internet, do their homework, listen to music, take pictures, and communicate by live video and other social media platforms. Parents buy their children phones to stay in touch and keep them safe. According to the Pew Research Center, 95 percent of teens surveyed in 2018 reported having a smartphone or access to one.[44] The average age for getting a first phone is about ten years old.[45] Forty-five percent of teens say they are online on a near-constant basis.[46] According to a 2016 study by the Center for Gender Equity in Science and Technology, Black youth are far more likely to be daily users of smartphones than computers, and 78 percent of eleven- to seventeen-year-old Black teens have their own smartphones.[47]

Cell phones have also become a standard part of teenagers' romantic lives, friendships, and social engagement. Pew found that 50 percent of teens surveyed in 2015 let someone know they were interested in them romantically by "friending" them on Facebook or other social media sites.[48] Forty-seven percent expressed their attraction by "liking," commenting, or otherwise interacting with someone's personal social media account. Girls are even more likely to communicate with friends by phone than boys. Sixty-two percent of girls spend time with friends every day by text messaging, compared with 48 percent of boys.

Of course, adolescents do irresponsible things with their phones. Even when parents and teachers forbid children from using phones at certain times and in certain places, the temptation is too great. Cell phones have been described as an "addiction" or "dependence" for young people.[49] Students use phones in class instead of paying attention. Teenagers are distracted by phones in the car. And young people use phones to send sexually inappropriate messages or to bully and threaten others. Given what we know about adolescent development, it is unrealistic to expect youth to exercise discipline and restraint with their phones. Yet that is exactly what was expected of sixteen-year-old Shakara Murphy at Spring Valley High in South Carolina.

*But what they did was wrong. They violated the law.*
—SPRING VALLEY SHERIFF LEON LOTT

On October 26, 2015, the nation watched as news stations played and replayed cell-phone video of a Black tenth grader being dragged out of her seat by a school police officer in Richland County, South Carolina.[50] The encounter began when a teacher thought Shakara was using her phone in algebra class and escalated when she refused to put it away and leave the classroom as instructed. An officer who was stationed at the school was called in to "deal with her." Senior Deputy Ben Fields wrapped his arm around Shakara's neck and flipped her backward out of her seat and onto the floor. After pulling her from the desk, Fields threw Shakara across the floor, berated her in front of her classmates, and dragged her from the room. The attack left Shakara with a cast on her right arm, carpet burns on her forehead, and a swollen neck, back, and shoulder—all originating from her failure to follow the teacher's instructions.[51]

When Deputy Fields entered the room, one of Shakara's classmates, Niya Kenny, did what many teenagers do today. She took out her own phone and began recording. Niya knew Fields's reputation as "Officer Slam" and cried, screamed, and prayed for Shakara as she watched.[52] Most of the students seemed frozen. The teacher just stood there. Deputy Fields and other school officials told Niya to sit down, be quiet, and put her phone away. She refused. Niya was outraged. As she later told a reporter, "I had never seen nothing like that in my life, a man use that much force on a little girl . . . A big man, like 300 pounds of full muscle. I was like, no way, no way. You can't do nothing like that to a little girl."[53] Niya's heart went out to Shakara—a student she didn't know. Shakara was new to the school, and Niya kept thinking, "I know this girl don't got nobody."[54] Deputy Fields came back for Niya after dealing with Shakara. Both Niya and Shakara were arrested for misdemeanor charges of "disturbing schools," which at the time carried a fine of up to $1,000 and up to ninety days in jail.[55]

Niya spent much of the next several hours crying after Fields handcuffed her and removed her from class.[56] Shakara had been released to a guardian, but Niya was escorted out to a police van. Niya sobbed as she grasped the reality of what it meant to go to jail and worried about what her mother would say. Despite the very adolescent nature of this incident, Niya had just turned eighteen and therefore spent the next nine hours in the adult lockup at the Alvin S. Glenn Detention Center in Columbia. At the facility, she was searched, fingerprinted, photographed, and held in a cold room with about twenty adults. Shortly after 8:00 p.m., Niya was released by a judge.

Riding away from the school where she had once run cross-country track and sung in the gospel choir, Niya decided never to return to Spring Valley High. Niya's mother told reporters that before her daughter's arrest she "had a sense of pride" in her daughter's school.[57] "It's one of the better schools in Columbia. A lot of the affluent kids go there." As Niya's mother knew, Spring Valley High had earned its reputation as one of the country's most academically challenging high schools. After the arrest, Ms. Ballard-Kenny feared that the school had undermined everything she taught her daughter about justice.

Niya's arrest was not the first disciplinary controversy in the Richland County School District. In a school that was not particularly violent, Black students had long felt they had been mislabeled and treated unfairly. A group of Black parents had already created an association to help students who had been unfairly punished under school district policies and state laws criminalizing disturbing the school.[58] In the year leading up to Deputy Fields's violent response to Shakara, the school district had also set up task forces on diversity and discipline and hired a chief diversity officer to help address the concerns.

Richland County sheriff Leon Lott ultimately fired Fields for using inappropriate force and violating department policy and training. But Lott also blamed Shakara, saying "she started this" by being disrespectful and disruptive in class.[59] The sheriff made it clear in public statements that he thought physical intervention and arrest were necessary and appropriate to hold both girls accountable. His only concern was Fields's technique in removing Shakara from the chair. When pressed about the deputy's decision to arrest Niya, who only stood to protest Fields's aggressive response, Lott argued, "She still disrupted class. You saw other students that did not disrupt the class. They sat there, and they did what students are supposed to be, and that is well-disciplined."

Lott was particularly put off by Niya's profanity. Niya admitted in television interviews that she was "screaming what the F, what the F, is this really happening."

Despite the sheriff's idyllic vision of what children "should be," anybody who has a child, has ever taught a child, or has been a child themselves knows that Shakara's refusal to follow instructions was normal teenage behavior. Shakara's failure to put her phone away and complete her math assignment probably wouldn't have even drawn the other students' attention had the teacher not made such a spectacle of it. Niya, too, responded like a normal twenty-first-century teenager. She stood up, spoke out, and filmed a perceived injustice. These girls weren't involved in any violent or aggressive behavior that would threaten the physical safety of other students in the classroom. Sure, the girls were disrespectful and maybe even disruptive, but playing on a cell phone, refusing to pay attention in math class, talking back, and cursing at school administrators aren't crimes.

It is difficult, if not impossible, to imagine a scene in which any police officer would violently drag a White, middle-class child from her desk at school. Sheriff Lott outraged and offended many when he told the press that he wasn't sure race contributed to Fields's conduct—especially since Fields had been "dating an African-American woman for 'quite some time.' "[60] As is so often the case, Lott misunderstood the nature of implicit racial bias and how it operates both within and across race. Fields was no more immune from bias because he dated a Black woman than a Black officer would be immune from bias because he is Black. Stereotypes about Blackness and criminality are so strong that they operate even within the same race.[61]

Spring Valley High's pattern of disparate treatment of Black students offers strong support for claims that school officials were targeting Black youth based on racial bias and inaccurate assumptions about Black adolescence. After her own encounter with Fields, Niya joined other youth in a federal class-action suit challenging the "disturbing schools" statute and accusing Fields of unlawfully and recklessly targeting Black students.[62] South Carolina has since amended its overly broad and vague disturbing-schools law to now apply only to nonstudents who harm or threaten to harm students or teachers in a school or college.[63]

Parties are yet another important feature of adolescent play. Most of us remember the excitement that accompanied our first high school parties—house parties, tailgates, block parties, birthday parties, pool parties, sleepovers, and skate parties to name a few. Parents, on the other hand, recall the anxiety they shared watching their teenagers head out to gatherings fueled by adolescent impulsivity, bravado, and hormones. Parents of every race and class have experienced sleepless nights worrying about drugs and alcohol, unprotected sex, vandalism, and drunk driving. Parents have agonized over whether to let their children go and what to tell them.

For most parents, the benefits of a party usually outweigh the risks. For Black parents, the risks too often outweigh the benefits. Fear of drunk driving, raucous fighting, and even date rape are often surpassed by the fear of police violence against Black youth. Black parents worry about what will happen when police respond to a noise complaint or report of disorderly conduct. In these moments, even the best safety tips may not be enough. Charmaine and Odell Edwards learned this lesson in the worst way when their son Jordan was killed by Officer Roy Oliver.

In the spring of 2017, Jordan Edwards was a fifteen-year-old freshman at Mesquite High School in Mesquite, Texas. Jordan was an honor roll student who hoped to play football in college. He was trying out for his team's defensive position and was well liked by his coaches, teachers, and classmates. Jordan's coach described him as "everybody's friend—his attitude and smile, everything about him. He was excellent—3.5 GPA, never in trouble, no attendance issues. He was a kid that did everything right."[64] A parent of one of Jordan's teammates described Jordan as a "great kid" with "awesome parents."

Jordan was excited about a house party that was scheduled for Saturday, April 29. The party would be held in Balch Springs, a nearby working-class suburb with about 25,000 residents in the Dallas–Fort Worth metro area. Four out of five of its residents identified as non-White.[65] In the weeks leading up to the party, Jordan begged his stepbrother Vidal Allen to take him.[66] Vidal was sixteen and had a driver's license. When Vidal finally agreed, their parents gave the boys permission and let Vidal drive the family car.

Jordan and Vidal were joined by their brother, seventeen-year-old Kevon, and two other fifteen-year-old teens, Maximus and Maxwell Everette, who were also brothers. Kids began arriving at the party around 9:00 p.m. By 11:00 p.m., the neighbors were getting annoyed. As is so common with teenage gatherings, the crowd grew larger and the noise got louder. A neighbor called the police. Officers arrived within minutes, and teenagers began to scatter. When the partygoers heard gunshots nearby, they started to run. As Vidal began to drive away, the Balch Springs officer Roy Oliver grabbed his rifle and fired five shots into the Edwardses' car window, hitting Jordan in the head. Jordan was in the front passenger seat. The boys in the back could see Jordan slumped over with smoke coming out of his head. He was dying in front of them.

Contrary to Officer Oliver's initial claim that the family's black Chevrolet Impala was reversing aggressively toward him, videos showed that Vidal was clearly driving away when the shots rang out. Oliver approached the Impala while his partner was yelling out profanities and commanding Vidal to stop. Vidal says he was trying to shift the car into "park" when the officer fired.[67] Vidal turned on the next street and stopped to call Jordan's father for help. Instinctively, Mr. Edwards told Vidal to make sure the police could see his hands and feet. Despite these precautions, officers who arrived on the scene moments later treated the boys like criminals. They were all handcuffed and detained for interviews. Vidal was held overnight in police custody. The officers also threatened to arrest Jordan's father for "hostile behavior."[68]

The police later described Vidal as a witness, not a suspect, but Vidal and his family could hardly tell the difference. Vidal says he heard officers use the "N-word" and was afraid the police would shoot him next.[69] Maximus, Maxwell, and Kevon were equally traumatized by what they witnessed and devastated by the loss of their friend and brother.[70] It is unlikely that any of them will ever get the image of Jordan's murder out of their heads.

The similarities between Jordan's death and Tamir's death are disturbing. The differences are telling. Like Tamir, Jordan was shot soon after officers arrived on the scene. In both tragedies, the officers responded to a situation that was fluid and potentially dangerous to themselves and others. In both incidents, the officers acted with limited information, made assumptions that were ultimately contradicted by the facts, and shot hastily, giving the victim little time to respond to the officers' commands. When Loehmann saw Tamir, he assumed he was a threat. When Oliver looked into the Edwardses' Impala, he assumed the boys were the source of danger at the party. Despite any evidence to support his claim, Oliver was convinced that one or more of the boys was a gang member who had fired the shots that caused everyone to flee.[71] Oliver also interpreted Vidal's attempt to drive away as an act of aggression instead of fear. As it turns out, the gunshots had been fired into the air from the parking lot of a nearby nursing home, having nothing to do with the party or the boys who attended.[72] Unfortunately, those shots fit well within the common narrative that American streets are overrun by violent Black youth intent on terrorizing society.

Unlike Tamir, who was shot by a new officer with a record of emotional instability, Jordan was shot by an experienced six-year veteran of the local police department. Before he was hired in Balch Springs, Roy Oliver served for six years in the army, completed two tours of duty in Iraq, and worked for a year as a police officer in a small town outside Fort Worth.[73] Oliver's last firearms training was on April 22, just seven days before he killed Jordan Edwards.[74] Yet the Balch Springs police chief quickly determined that Oliver acted contrary to department protocol and that his behavior did not meet the "core values" of the department.[75] Ultimately, the officer's training and department protocols offered Jordan little protection against Oliver's innate bias and assumptions about Jordan and his brothers and friends.

Oliver responded the way so many other officers have done in similar circumstances. Researchers have used a series of simulated video games to help us understand how race affects an individual's decision to shoot a suspected offender.[76] In each of the simulated studies, participants were shown images of Black and White males holding an object and given milliseconds to "shoot" or "not shoot" if they thought the object was a gun. Participants were much more likely to shoot when the object was associated with an unarmed Black target than an unarmed White target.[77] They were also faster to shoot armed Black targets than armed White targets and slower in deciding not to shoot unarmed Black targets.[78] Studies replicated with police officers have produced the same results. Even trained officers with firearms experience are more likely to shoot Blacks than Whites.[79]

Our culture is saturated with racial stereotypes that become so hardwired in our brains that we don't realize they are there. It is these stereotypes that override even the most advanced police and military training. As Professor Joshua Correll, a leading researcher in bias and police shooting, tells us, "In the very situation in which [officers] most need their training, we have some reason to believe that their training will be most likely to fail them."[80] Consistent with the empirical research, data confirms that Black Americans are more than twice as likely as their White peers to be killed by police. In 2016, police killed Black Americans at a rate of 6.66 per 1 million people, compared with 2.9 per 1 million for White Americans.[81]

After Jordan Edwards's murder, Jordan's father blamed himself for his son's death, telling reporters that "he should never have let his son go to the party."[82] Jordan's brother Vidal also blamed himself for asking for permission to go. But Jordan's parents did everything they could to protect their son—short of locking him in the house. They sent him to the party in a group.

They allowed the boys to use the family car. And they told the boys not to drink or use drugs. The boys didn't have any weapons. They didn't fight. And they had an exit plan. Vidal told investigators that he had scanned the backyard for a way out if anything went wrong. The boys knew where to go and how to get there if there was a problem. And that's exactly what they did. They did what any parent would have wanted them to: they got in the car to leave at the first sign of trouble. Tragically, none of that kept Jordan safe.

In the end, Jordan's greatest threat was not violence at the hands of other young partygoers but violence at the hands of the police. Roy Oliver was convicted of murder and sentenced to fifteen years in prison.[83] He is one of the few officers who have been successfully prosecuted for killing an unarmed Black person. There was simply no appropriate explanation for Oliver's decision to fire a rifle into a car full of teenagers. Given the facts, the police and prosecutors couldn't vilify the boys as "thugs." They couldn't blame the shooting on an absent father or inattentive mother. And they couldn't point to any prior criminal record or other evidence to claim that Jordan and his brothers were violent, weapon-toting gang members. Contrary to some early claims, police officials conceded that no teenagers were using drugs or alcohol at the party, and Jordan's autopsy confirmed that no illegal substances were found in his system.[84]

While Black boys have borne the brunt of police brutality, Black girls are not immune from police violence. Texas was home to another party that drew national attention for police violence against Black youth. On Friday, June 5, 2015, officers were summoned after a fight between a Black teenager hosting a pool party and two middle-aged White women who didn't want her and her friends to be there. The party was held in McKinney, Texas, at a private neighborhood pool in Craig Ranch, a predominantly White subdivision north of Dallas.[85] The party was a combined end-of-the-school-year and birthday celebration. Officers arrived at the pool around 7:15 p.m., responding to a call about a "disturbance involving multiple juveniles at the location, who do not live in the area or have permission to be there, refusing to leave."[86] Event organizers told reporters that they did in fact have passes for their guests.

The physical fight started when one of the White adults slapped nineteen-year-old Tatyana Rhodes in the face. Tatyana, a Black resident of the complex and an organizer of the event, said the White resident made racist remarks such as "black f-cker" and "that's why you live in Section 8 homes."[87] Tatyana attempted to defend herself and some of the younger teens, telling the woman she couldn't speak to them that way.[88]

A thirteen-year-old girl, Jahda Bakari, who videoed the incident, said police were only targeting minorities. "I honestly believe it was about race because mostly they did nothing to the Caucasians."[89] A White youth, Brandon Brooks, who shot another video, told NBC News that an officer "was chasing after all those kids, just putting every black person he saw on the ground."[90] Fourteen-year-old Grace Stone, another White youth who was a guest of the party, confirmed these accounts and said she was the only White youth detained after she tried to defend her Black friends by giving her version of events to the police.[91]

In the seven-minute video that was widely circulated after the party, Officer Eric Casebolt approaches fifteen-year-old Dajerria Becton with a baton raised and yells at her to "get your ass down."[92] Casebolt grabs her by the wrist, drags her to the ground in her bikini, and wrestles her arm behind her back while she is begging for him to stop. Dajerria yells, "He hit me for no reason. Call my momma! Call my momma! On God!" as the officer pulls her braids and forces her face into the grass, shouting, "On your face!" As other teens race over to help Dajerria, Casebolt shoves some girls with his hands and pulls his gun on two unarmed Black boys. He later yells at other boys seated on the ground, telling them, "Get your asses down," "Stay," and "Don't make me f—ing run around here with thirty pounds of goddamned gear on in the sun because you want to screw around out here." The officers created an absurd dilemma for the teens. As Jahda pointed out, "They were trying to make us leave, but if we ran, they'd chase after us, and if we stayed, then they'd arrest us."[93]

Some White residents defended the officers' behavior, saying the officers were "just doing the right thing when these kids were fleeing and using profanity and threatening security guards."[94] One witness told reporters that he did not hear racist comments and that a DJ was blasting music that was not appropriate for children. Others complained that the pool party had been advertised on social media and some teens entered the pool area by jumping the fence. Still others sympathized with the officer, speculating that his emotions had just gotten the best of him because he had responded to two suicide calls earlier in his shift that day.[95] Casebolt was a ten-year veteran of the force and former Cop of the Year.[96] At least one White resident conceded that Section 8 housing has been a difficult issue for the residents of Craig Ranch: "We hate it. We don't want that. We moved here thinking we were moving to an upscale neighborhood."[97] But in her mind, their discomfort with public housing has "never been about race."

After considering the range of community reactions, the chief of police described Casebolt's behavior as "indefensible" and placed him on administrative leave.[98] Casebolt later resigned. A grand jury declined to indict Casebolt on any criminal charges, but the city later settled a federal lawsuit with Dajerria and other youth for the relatively small sum of $184,850.[99] Dajerria's family also asked that the police be trained on excessive force, racial sensitivity, and handling youth.[100] The city did not agree to these demands, but McKinney leaders hosted a community forum to discuss policing with the residents. Dajerria's physical injuries have healed, but the psychological damage from this incident will likely follow her for a long time to come.

Whatever they did wrong—jumping the fence, playing music too loud, listening to the wrong kind of music, using profanity, arguing with authorities, running when told to sit, staying when told to leave, or otherwise being rowdy, the Black teenagers in McKinney, Texas, didn't do anything worse than what White youth do all over the state. In fact, most of the youth were just standing, watching, crying, and pleading for the officer's sympathy.

If there is any doubt that White youth are treated differently for the same adolescent behavior, we need only look at video footage from a pool party in San Marcos, Texas. In September 2016, the Twitter user @WhiteBoy_Ejyay posted a video of a fight that broke out during a pool party at Capstone Cottages, a student housing apartment complex a few miles from Texas State University.[101] Party guests in the video appeared to be mostly White college boys, and the party devolved into an "all-out dude-brawl" between at least five young men. One of the partygoers punched another so hard he fell backward into the pool as the others heckled and cheered them on. No residents called the police. No adults intervened. And no police swarmed the complex. While the White boys in San Marcos were allowed to fight and party with reckless abandon, Black youth across the country are grieving the loss and abuse of friends, classmates, and teammates violently attacked or gunned down by police for doing what teenagers are allowed and encouraged to do all over the world.

### CURFEW LAWS: THE NEW BLACK CODES

Youth curfew laws have existed for more than a hundred years but gained popularity during President Bill Clinton's administration in the 1990s. Responding to unfounded predictions that crime would increase drastically among Black youth in the coming years, President Clinton pushed for an increase in juvenile curfew laws. By 2009, 84 percent of cities with populations greater than 180,000 had adopted curfew laws as a safety measure.[102] Since then, millions of teens have been arrested for curfew violations.[103] Philadelphia alone reported 16,079 violations in 2014, which was among the highest in the country.[104] That same year, police across the nation arrested more youth for curfew and loitering violations than for all violent crimes (murder and non-negligent manslaughter, forcible rape, robbery, and aggravated assault) combined.[105]

Lawmakers typically regulate youth with two types of curfews: nighttime curfews intended to curb youth crime and victimization; and daytime curfews intended to reduce truancy during school hours.[106] Penalties for violating curfew laws often include fines, community service, or jail time for the child and their parents.[107] Opponents of these laws cite research demonstrating that curfew restrictions are not effective at reducing youth crime and victimization and complain that no other country treats its children this way.[108] Like so many other low-level, nonviolent offenses, curfew laws strain relationships between police and youth—particularly youth of color, who tend to be disproportionately targeted by these regulations.[109] The history of youth curfew laws in Baltimore, Maryland, tells this story well.

Baltimore is known to have one of the strictest curfew laws in the country.[110] Lawmakers adopted the city's first juvenile curfew in the mid-1990s after describing youth as a "menace to the preservation of public peace, safety, health, morals, and welfare."[111] In 2014, the Baltimore City Council passed an updated curfew law, forcing young people off the street as early as 9:00 p.m. During the summer months, children thirteen and under must be inside from 9:00 p.m. to 6:00 a.m., and children fourteen to sixteen years old must be inside from 11:00 p.m. to 6:00 a.m. Although the bill eliminated incarceration as a penalty, it increased the fine to $500. The penalty can be waived if the parents and children attend counseling provided by the city.[112] Council members hoped to reduce youth crime by limiting the hours when youth could be in public places without adult supervision and wanted to ensure that youth would be well rested and focused in school.

Disparities in curfew enforcement were evident almost immediately. In 2015, there were 371 new curfew violators, 314 were Black youth and 40 were White youth.[113] In response to community protests and complaints about the racial disparity, the mayor's Office of Human Resources asked the police to modify their curfew enforcement in 2018. Prioritizing services over punishment, police began dropping young curfew violators off at home rather than at the city-run resource centers.[114] City workers could then visit the youth at home to offer support and services and address the needs of the whole family.

Youth in Austin, Texas, experienced a similar shift in curfew laws from 1990 to 2017. Lawmakers in Austin first introduced a juvenile curfew in 1990 to reduce crime by and against youth. At one point, Austin had both daytime and nighttime curfews, but in June 2017 the city ended the daytime restriction and opted for a more lenient "three strikes" citation policy. Even then, youth under seventeen were banned from being outside from 11:00 p.m. to 6:00 a.m. unless they were accompanied by a parent or in front of their house.[115] If youth were found outside during those times, they were charged with a misdemeanor and received a $500 fine.

Critics argued that the curfew restrictions were ineffective and complained of "overtly racist targeting and hyper-policing" in communities of color, while youth in wealthier areas were let off with a warning.[116] Austin police issued 528 daytime violations and 157 nighttime violations in 2016, often to fifteen- or sixteen-year-olds in the least affluent parts of the city.[117] Although Black youth made up only 8 percent of the city's population, they made up 17 percent of the nighttime and 15 percent of the daytime violations. The Austin Police Department ultimately conceded that there was no evidence that curfew laws were reducing crime against youth. In September 2017, the Austin City Council voted to end the youth curfew. Refuting the fears of some curfew proponents, crime against youth decreased by 12 percent within the year after Austin's youth curfew law was rescinded.[118]

Racial disparities in youth curfew enforcement persist all over the country. As Dr. Mike Males, a senior researcher at the Center on Juvenile and Criminal Justice, noted, "[Curfew laws] are always racially discriminatory. We have not found a single exception to that."[119] Although Black youth made up only 15 percent of the U.S. population under eighteen in 2014, they represented 46 percent of the curfew arrests nationally.[120] Black girls are especially vulnerable to being charged for nonviolent offenses such as curfew violations.[121]

In Minneapolis, the ACLU found that 56 percent of curfew charges between January 2012 and September 2014 involved Black youth compared with 17 percent for White youth.[122] Sixty-four percent of all residents in Minneapolis were White that year. Data from Dallas shows that less than 14 percent of the 11,150 curfew citations issued between 2007 and 2018 went to White children.[123] Forty-six percent went to Hispanic children, and 40 percent went to Black children. In 2018, 90 percent of Dallas curfew violations went to Black and Hispanic youth, while only 65 percent of all residents in Dallas were Black or Hispanic. Disparities exist even in cities that rarely enforce their curfew laws. Only twenty-four youth were cited for curfew violations in Richmond, Virginia, in 2018, but 98 percent of those youth were Black. Sociologist Liz Coston at Virginia Commonwealth University states, it is "highly unlikely that the only people who are actually violating curfew laws are black when less than half the city is black."[124]

Racial disparities in curfew enforcement align with the general overrepresentation of minority youth in the juvenile legal system.[125] Viewed in the most generous light, disparate curfew enforcement occurs when officers fall back on subconscious racial stereotypes to make quick, on-the-spot assessments about youth they see outside.[126] Viewed through a more pernicious lens, youth curfew laws are eerily reminiscent of the Black Codes adopted in 1865 to keep newly freed Blacks in their place after emancipation.[127] Like the old Confederate statutes that criminalized loitering, vagrancy, curfew violations, and traveling without proof of employment, contemporary enforcement of youth curfew laws derives from harmful myths about Black children and allows Whites to maintain social hierarchies that exclude Black youth from public spaces. Although the racially explicit intent may be absent from the new laws, discriminatory enforcement of youth curfews suggests that attitudes about Blacks—and Black youth in particular—have not changed.

# 3

## Hoodies, Headwraps, and Hip-Hop: Criminalizing Black Adolescent Culture

### FROM THE WHITE HOOD TO THE BLACK HOODIE

It was a typical January in Washington, D.C., when sixteen-year-old "Malik" entered a subway station on his way home. To protect his face from the cold, Malik was wearing a black ski mask popular among teenagers at the time. As he entered the station, two Metro Transit police officers told him to take it off his head. Assuming the officers just wanted to see his face, Malik immediately rolled up the mask to the top of his head. Without further warning, one of the officers grabbed the mask and ripped it off. Confused and outraged, Malik reached out to get it back as another officer grabbed him from behind and pinned him against the handrails of a moving escalator. At the top of the escalator, the officers forced Malik to the ground with his face against the concrete. One officer dug his knees into Malik's neck and back while the other handcuffed him. By the time the officers put him in a police car, Malik's ear, eye, and bottom lip were swollen, and his face was bleeding above his right eye. Officers had to take him to the hospital before he could be admitted to the juvenile lockup.

By the time I met Malik, I had been defending children in juvenile court for fifteen years. Every time I thought I had seen it all, something new would surprise me. In this case I wasn't surprised to hear how Malik had been manhandled. I had seen that before. But I had never heard of a child being charged with "wearing a hood or mask" in public. I remember standing in court the day after Malik's arrest trying to figure out what law he had broken. It turned out that Malik was accused of violating an obscure D.C. statute written in 1981 after a resurgence of the Ku Klux Klan in the neighboring states of Maryland and Virginia.[1] My law students and I were so disturbed by this case that we started researching the law's history as soon as we got back to the office. The plain language of the statute prohibited anyone from wearing a hood or mask with the intent to intimidate, threaten, abuse, or harass another person. The historical record made clear that lawmakers really wanted to prevent the Klan and other hate groups from violating the civil rights of ethnic minorities.[2] Although White nationalists certainly had a right to free speech, the city council wasn't going to let them speak behind the cloak of a white hood.

Fast-forward to 2010 when I met Malik—a Black teenager charged with wearing a hood and assaulting a police officer. The officers claimed that Malik was intimidating the other patrons by being loud and boisterous. They described his attempt to get his hat back as an assault. Fortunately, our judge disagreed. At trial, Malik and his friends insisted they were just laughing and talking as they entered the station. The officers conceded that none of the Metro riders had complained, and it was never clear why the officers were so offended by Malik's ski mask. Malik wore the mask on a cold day, in the dead of winter. At most, he got agitated when the officers snatched it away because he had already rolled it to the top of his head. As Malik's girlfriend testified so eloquently, "I don't know how we got here. One minute we were walking into the Metro station, talking and laughing, and the next thing I know there were two police officers in front of us. They went from 0 to 100 in a matter of seconds."

The racial implications were not lost on Malik. Although both officers were Black, Malik resented the officers' intrusion and complained that police were always harassing him and other Black youth in D.C. More important, he understood clearly that he had been charged with violating a law originally designed to protect him. Just as lawmakers sought to strip the white hood of its power, privilege, and violence, police and prosecutors were using the mask or hood prohibition to criminalize Malik for wearing ordinary winter attire.

Malik was arrested about two years before Trayvon Martin was gunned down in Sanford, Florida, wearing a gray hoodie—another iconic head covering. Trayvon's murder firmly established the hoodie as the contemporary symbol of Black deviance. Of course, there is nothing inherently dangerous, or even racial, about a ski mask or hoodie—that is, until it is worn by a Black youth.

The first hoodie, or hooded sweatshirt, appeared in American culture in the 1930s as a practical piece of clothing to keep high school athletes warm at a track meet or on the sidelines of a football field.[3] Reportedly designed by the company we now know as Champion, the hooded sweatshirt also became popular with blue-collar workers in factories, warehouses, and construction sites. The garment became a "hoodie" when it was donned by young graffiti artists, break-dancers, skateboarders, and B-boys in the 1970s and 1980s. It became even more popular in adolescent hip-hop culture in the 1990s when rappers like LL Cool J featured it in videos like "Mama Said Knock You Out" and the Wu-Tang Clan sported it on the cover of their album *Enter the Wu-Tang (36 Chambers)*. And yes, the hoodie has had some ties to the criminal underworld and outcast youth cultures as it provided anonymity to teenagers who were skateboarding without permission, hip-hop fans who were tired of being harassed by the cops, and "stickup boys" who were actually robbing and stealing. Ironically, the hoodie's fate as a purported camouflage for criminals probably gained its greatest notoriety in 1987 with the highly publicized sketch of the White Unabomber in a hoodie and aviator sunglasses.

But for most teenagers the hoodie is just a good hideaway. It masks anxiety and other emotions they would rather not share. It hides acne, facial hair, and other bodily imperfections. It covers headphones in study hall, allows youth to blend into the crowd, and creates a cone of solitude. It is an adolescent aesthetic. Most White youth can walk about in a hoodie without attracting much attention at all. White girls wear their hoodies to yoga class, ballet lessons, and Pilates. White boys wear theirs to lift weights, run track, or warm up for football. Black youth have no such luxury. A Black boy in a hoodie is viewed as a threat and a menace. His clothing causes shopkeepers to call 911, White women to cross the street clutching their bags, and police officers to grab their guns for protection. For many Americans, the mere mention of the word "hoodie" conjures up an image of a dangerous young Black male. Trayvon's hoodie wasn't just a fashion statement or shirt to keep him warm. It was a bull's-eye.

Those of us who live and work with Black youth have long recognized the dangers of Black adolescent fashion—the hoodie, the ski mask, sagging pants, gold jewelry, and hairstyles that irrationally threaten others and mark Black youth as criminal. For Black parents, the hoodie creates another impossible dilemma. Just as critics blamed Tamir's mother for allowing her son to play with a toy gun, others blamed Trayvon's parents for allowing him to wear a hoodie. Geraldo Rivera insisted that "the hoodie is as much responsible for Trayvon Martin's death as George Zimmerman was."[4] Rivera went on to chastise the Martins for not making their son aware of the risks and warned parents to stop letting their children wear the garment. Despite the many protests and political efforts to rehabilitate the image of the hoodie in the wake of Trayvon's death, Black parents still have little hope that their children can ever be safe in the face of unfounded assumptions about Black youth and their attire.

## SAGGING PANTS AND CITY ORDINANCES

Like the hoodie, sagging pants appeared in popular culture in the mid-1980s and early 1990s when rappers like LL Cool J opted for slightly oversized sportswear as part of their signature look.[5] Legend claims that young people adopted the sagging pants style to mimic inmates who were prohibited from wearing belts in prison to prevent suicides and injury.[6] As inmates returned to the community, they supposedly carried the look home to appear tough and earn credibility on the street. Another version of the legend contends that prisoners wore their pants low to let other inmates know they were sexually available. Some historians have questioned the validity of these myths, speculating that they may have been created to scare youth about what might happen if they committed crimes and went to jail.[7] Regardless of how the style originated, the prison narrative no longer accounts for all—or even most—of the youth who wear it.

Hip-hop spread sagging pants from the city to the suburbs and to youth all over the world.[8] Female rappers like TLC and MC Lyte adopted the trend, as did White rappers like Mark Wahlberg and Vanilla Ice. More recently, Justin Bieber took on the look as he rose to fame from 2010 to 2020. As late as January 2020, Bieber proclaimed, "My pants will stay sagging."[9] Other White celebrity saggers include Ross Lynch, Liam Payne, Zac Efron, the Janoskians, and even Taylor Swift in her "Thug Story" duo with T-Pain. For youth in and out of the criminal world, sagging pants is just a cool fashion trend that mirrors the art and music they admire.

We live in a country that usually honors and protects free speech and self-expression.[10] Despite some restrictions on public nudity and self-expression in school, even teenagers get to express their views, challenge authority, and dress however they please.[11] Our personal appearance is the quintessential expression of who we are, where we come from, and what we believe in.[12] Our clothes reflect our ethnic identity, our family tradition, and the generational trends of our schools and neighborhoods.

Fashion is especially important in adolescence. Youth adjust their styles to connect with others or set themselves apart. While some youth choose styles that blend in with the crowd, others reject the status quo in favor of creativity and flair. Still others choose clothes that express their political convictions or racial and ethnic pride. Like the tie-dye worn by hippies in the 1960s and the dashikis and military gear worn by Black Panthers in the

1960s and 1970s, sagging pants are an act of rebellion, a badge of honor, and a right of heritage. For some, sagging pants and other hip-hop styles are blatant rejections of middle-class values and mainstream clothing labels.[13]

Public reaction to the sagging trend was fast and fierce. Schools were the first to object, adopting dress codes in the 1990s that prohibited students from wearing "oversized apparel," "baggy pants . . . worn low on the waist," or "clothes that expose undergarments."[14] Police officers convinced school officials that sagging pants were an early sign that students were being lured into the gang life.[15] Principals and teachers hoped dress codes would prevent gang violence, reduce graffiti, and make students feel safer in the classroom.[16] They also hoped the codes would reduce peer pressure to buy expensive clothes and prevent students who were not involved in a gang from being mistakenly targeted because of their attire.

State lawmakers were next to challenge the sagging style. In 2004, Louisiana lawmakers introduced, but failed to pass, a bill that would have made it unlawful to wear clothing in public that intentionally exposed undergarments or any portion of the pubic hair, cleft of the buttocks, or genitals.[17] A year later, Virginia lawmakers failed to pass a bill that would have made it a crime to intentionally display below-the-waist undergarments in a lewd or indecent manner. Although neither of these bills succeeded at the state level, both proposals drew widespread media coverage and inspired local lawmakers to introduce city ordinances.[18]

The earliest sagging pants city ordinances appeared in Louisiana, with at least five cities banning the style in 2007.[19] The restrictions vary from city to city, with some cities making it illegal for anyone to appear in public in a state of nudity, partial nudity, in dress not becoming of his or her sex, or with any indecent exposure of his or her person or undergarments.[20] Although many of the laws give police officers broad discretion to decide what constitutes "dress not becoming," some cities are more meticulous in specifying the inches of skin or underwear that may show before there is a violation. Penalties for violating the laws include fines of $50 to $500, community service, trash abatement, or jail time up to six months.[21]

Beyond Louisiana, city lawmakers introduced sagging pants laws across the country with varying degrees of success from 2007 to 2018.[22] Lawmakers succeeded in Wildwood, New Jersey (June 12, 2013), Timmonsville, South Carolina (July 5, 2016), Albany, Georgia (November 23, 2010), and Opa-locka, Florida (October 24, 2007), among many others.[23] At least one county—Jasper County, South Carolina—placed the burden on parents, making it unlawful "for any custodial parent or guardian to willfully allow their minor to appear in a public place wearing his or her pants more than three inches below his or her hips and thereby exposing his or her skin or intimate clothing."[24]

Despite early state-level losses in Virginia and Louisiana, lawmakers persisted in other states. In a rare show of bipartisan agreement, five Democrats and two Republicans in South Carolina joined together in 2018 to co-sponsor a sagging pants bill that would make it unlawful for a person to wear pants "more than three inches below the crest of his ileum."[25] The ileum is the third part of the small intestine. Imagine a teenager trying to figure that out. State lawmakers proposed a similar bill in Mississippi in 2017.[26] Neither bill passed.

Although most lawmakers have been wise enough to frame their official support for these bills as an opposition to nudity and indecent exposure, the public commentary and disparate enforcement suggest there is something much more sinister at play. Sagging pants laws draw upon racial stereotypes about Black criminality and provide a ready excuse to ostracize Black youth. Lawmakers repeatedly describe the style as "thuggish," offensive, and immoral.[27] Police officers contend that the style promotes gangs and violence by allowing offenders to hide guns and drugs deep in their pockets.[28] Schools prohibit sagging pants as an explicit response to a perceived problem with gangs on campus.[29]

Deep-seated fears and assumptions about Black youth in sagging pants have been evident in court cases upholding the clothing ban. Richard Bivens, a student in the Albuquerque Public Schools, discovered this reality when he challenged his school's dress code in a federal court.[30] Although the judge agreed that Richard's sagging pants were an expression of his identity and culture,[31] he was swayed by testimonials from others who interpreted the style as a sign of gang activity or affiliation. Apparently, the people's right to be free from the fear of gangs was more important than Richard's right to express himself. Even without a specific sagging pants ordinance, police have used disorderly conduct and indecent exposure laws to regulate boys in oversized attire.[32] In 2015, four Tennessee high school students were charged with indecent exposure and two of them were jailed for wearing sagging pants.[33]

Historical contradictions in dress-code enforcement are revealing. The sagging pants style is not the only fashion to have been associated with prison life. Critics also objected to tattoos and body art that emerged with the rise in American incarceration.[34] Yet state and local lawmakers never made it a crime to have a tattoo. The threat of jail time and a criminal record clearly sets sagging pants apart from all other adolescent fashion. Lawmakers never outlawed tie-dyed shirts and bell-bottom pants in the 1960s despite their association with weed and hallucinogens. Lawmakers never authorized police to arrest teenagers solely on the basis of their morbid all-black attire, pale makeup, and solid black hair that was common in the 1980s Goth culture and later associated with high-profile mass shootings in the 1990s. And they certainly never made it a crime for young people to shave their heads and wear steel-toed Doc Martens work boots with red and white shoelaces despite their association with the violent, racist, and anti-Semitic acts of the skinheads. Sagging pants laws singularly target a style associated with Black culture and expose America's unique infatuation with criminalizing and incarcerating Black adolescents.

Sagging pants ordinances also give Whites another tool to demonize and exclude Black youth from public and private places. In 2011, the Fort Worth Transportation Authority told potential bus passengers to pull up their pants or stay away.[35] In 2014, the Greensboro Transit Authority adopted a rule that required riders to pull up their pants or risk being barred from the system.[36] Private businesses have been even more expansive than city leaders in their clothing restrictions. An Indiana nightclub not only prohibited loose-fitting pants but also banned baseball caps, hair picks, grills, and gold chains.[37] A Virginia Beach nightclub prohibited patrons from wearing braids, twists, cornrows, or dreadlocks and was fairly explicit about not wanting "hip-hoppers" in the establishment.[38] The owner admitted to reporters that his Virginia Beach club was for a "mainstream crowd," while his Newport News club was for the Black crowd.

If sagging pants are dangerous at all, that danger arises from the aggressive enforcement of clothing bans against frustrated teens and adults who resent the frivolous intrusions of police in their everyday lives. The nation watched in horror as the enforcement of a sagging pants law turned deadly in Shreveport, Louisiana, when a police officer shot a thirty-one-year-old Black man, Anthony Childs, in February 2019.[39] That encounter started when an officer tried to stop Childs because his pants fell below his waistline. When Shreveport's law was originally adopted in 2007, city council members made clear that the law would only allow police to issue a citation and summons to appear in court. It did not authorize police to arrest or search those who violated the law. Nonetheless, Shreveport records indicate that 726 people were either taken into custody or given citations for wearing sagging pants between 2007 and 2019. Of these, 699 were Black men and 12 were White. A Black council member expressed shame at having passed an ordinance that was enforced in such an unintended way.[40] Lawmakers abolished the law four months after Anthony Childs died.

Impassioned objections to sagging pants conjure up memories of the violent disapproval of zoot suits worn by young Black and Mexican American men in the 1930s.[41] Zoot Suit Riots became common sport for White sailors and police officers who went out in search of young men dressed in long boxy coats and tight-cuffed pants.[42] Angry Whites pulled Black and Mexican American youth from streetcars, pummeled them in the street, and stripped them of their clothes while crowds watched—much as they did during the lynching era. The media portrayed the zoot suit as a sign of moral depravity linked to gangs, gambling, alcohol, jazz music, premarital sex, and the threat of street violence. The most violent attacks took place in Los Angeles in June 1943, but similar, smaller riots popped up in other big cities across the country as zoot-suiters clashed with the police and angry Whites.[43] Although sagging pants haven't generated the same violent public attacks, laws banning them have exposed Black youth to unnecessary and aggressive police harassment.

In virtually every city where sagging pants laws have been proposed, local residents have protested, arguing that the provisions were racially motivated from the outset or would inevitably lead to biased enforcement.[44] NAACP and ACLU offices across the country denounced the laws as discriminatory and threatened to sue if lawmakers did not repeal them.[45] Yet the Black community remains divided. Many of the lawmakers who have introduced and supported these laws are Black.[46] While some buy into the myth that sagging pants glorify a prison mentality and lead young people to crime,[47] others complain that the style is demeaning to Black culture and disrespectful to elders. President Obama said the laws are a waste of time, but is remembered for telling Black boys to pull up their pants so their mothers and grandmothers wouldn't have to see their underwear.[48]

The intra-race debate about sagging pants reflects a much broader debate about "respectability" within the Black community. Proponents of "respectability" accept restraint and decorum as the price Blacks must pay for privilege and opportunity in a White-dominated world.[49] Black children must abandon—or at least suppress—those aspects of Black culture that Whites fear and resent in hopes of securing access to schools, careers, neighborhoods, and social opportunities.

Others teach respectability as a basic strategy for survival.[50] Elders warn that being in the wrong place, at the wrong time, with the wrong clothes will draw unwarranted attention, and even violence. Dressing conservatively is necessary to reduce the anxiety that Whites have about Black adolescence. Black youth are not persuaded. As their history lessons teach, Blacks have been beaten, whipped, and lynched in their Sunday best. As their own experiences reveal, Black youth can be arrested in fitted pants, in a button-up shirt, and while socializing with the "right" kids, at the right time, and in the right place. Black youth resent school dress codes that chill their creativity and self-expression in the very place where they are expected to learn about free speech.[51] More important, they refuse to take responsibility for the hostile and aggressive policing that has more to do with racism and bias than pants size, waistlines, and hoodies.

As cultural, class, and generational divides persist, Black leaders find themselves asking painful questions like "What could Trayvon Martin or Tamir Rice have done to avoid suspicion?" "What could their parents have done to protect them?" Regardless of how well intentioned these questions may be, they unfairly burden Black youth and their families with the responsibility of protecting themselves from racist and unwarranted abuse and deflect attention from where it should be—on fighting the dehumanization of Black adolescents.

### "DRESS CODED" FOR GIRLS

While sagging pants laws tend to target Black boys, other grooming policies disproportionately target Black girls by drawing upon old myths and stereotypes about Black women's sexuality.[52] The 1960s and 1970s ushered in a significant shift in adolescent fashion as the antiwar movement, civil rights movement, and second wave of the feminist movement gained momentum.[53] Students' clothes reflected their individual and political views and made school officials increasingly uneasy. Girls wore pants as a rejection of traditional gender-based roles and hierarchies, while schools responded with dress codes that sought to keep girls in their place and reinforce conservative values. Dress codes prohibited girls from wearing pants and slacks, as well as skirts that were too short or too tight.[54] In the 1990s, dress codes were expanded to prohibit spandex, leggings, short shorts, skinny jeans, yoga pants, halter tops, sleeveless shirts, and other clothing that school officials believed were sexually distracting to boys.[55]

Not much has changed since the 1990s. In 2018, the National Women's Law Center found that dress codes in Washington, D.C.'s public high schools continue to rely on gender-based stereotypes that give teachers and administrators broad discretion to discipline students for being "inappropriate," "unladylike," and "distracting."[56] Vague and imprecise rules require clothing to "be sized appropriately to fit the Scholar . . . What is too big or too small is determined in the sole discretion of the . . . Administration." Dress codes vary from school to school but often include rules like this: No shorts and skirts more than two inches above the knee or any shorter than the fingertips. No pants, shorts, skirts, or undershirts that have patterns, lace, polka dots, stripes, holes, or words. No sleeveless, backless, cropped, off-the-shoulder, spaghetti-strapped, or cutoff shirts, blouses, dresses, or tank tops. No ripped jeans. No makeup, lipstick, colored gloss, or nail polish.

Dress codes have been used to police girls' bodies of all races,[57] but vague and subjective standards like those in D.C. are particularly vulnerable to racial bias and stereotypes that depict Black girls as older and more knowledgeable about sex.[58] Researchers from the University of Kentucky found that dress-code violations and other minor infractions are disproportionately applied to Black girls.[59] Although Black girls made up 16 percent of girls in U.S. public schools in the 2015–16 academic year, data collected by the Department of Education shows that Black girls accounted for 39 percent of girls arrested in school that year.[60] The disparities between Black and White girls are even greater than the disparities between Black and White boys. In the 2017–18 academic year, Black boys were suspended 2.65 times more than White boys; Black girls were suspended 4.19 times more than White girls.[61] In every state in the country, Black girls are more likely to be suspended than their White peers.[62] In Washington, D.C., Black girls are 20.8 times more likely to get suspended from school than White girls.[63]

For dress-code violations, Black girls may be pulled out of class, called to the front office, sent home, shamed, or embarrassed in front of their classmates. Many girls are sent home without a formal suspension, allowing the schools to keep their suspension rates artificially low.[64] When the students aren't sent home, they may be forced to wear oversized shirts or pants to cover the offending attire. In some schools, rips and tears in the jeans are covered by duct tape or gym shorts worn over the pants. Some girls have been asked if they are wearing a bra and what kind of bra they are wearing.[65] Others are just told to go home and put on a bra.

Black girls with curvier bodies face the greatest scrutiny. Relying on rules that prohibit clothes that are "too 'tight' or 'revealing,'"[66] school staff treat curvy girls as if they were intentionally provocative and promiscuous and punish them for wearing the same thing as smaller girls.[67] Girls and their parents spend a lot of money trying to stay in compliance. Even when dress codes and uniforms are adopted under the guise of making school easier for low-income students who can't afford expensive brand-name clothes, the schools often require students to buy expensive—and exceptionally unflattering—uniforms.

Adolescents are especially preoccupied with their physical appearance. Girls even more so. Undue attention to girls' appearances leaves them feeling insecure about their bodies and prevents them from focusing on their schoolwork. Instead of addressing the boys' inappropriate treatment of girls, dress codes that focus on the ways girls distract boys make Black girls feel responsible for unwanted and unwarranted sexual harassment, leering, and bullying. The very policies that are designed to protect girls actually draw more attention to their bodies and reinforce the sexualization of Black bodies. Boys begin to think it is okay to comment on—and even touch—girls' bodies and clothes because their teachers and counselors do it too.

After the National Women's Law Center released its report in 2018, students in Washington, D.C., organized walkouts and met with school leaders to discuss the unfair enforcement of school dress-code policies. In Montgomery County, Maryland, students at Albert Einstein High School protested when the new principal sent an email saying, " 'Shorts must not expose private areas when sitting, walking, climbing stairs, or doing normal school activities.' Also forbidden: 'Bandeaus, backless tops, exposed midriffs, or visible undergarments.' "[68] Students were particularly bothered by the principal's primary focus on acceptable dress for girls and complained that it was impossible to enforce the policy fairly. In the weeklong protest that followed the email, students called attention to the issue on social media, launched a petition asking the principal to reconsider the policy, and came to school dressed in direct violation of the new rules.

## BRAIDS, LOCS, AND THE HIGH TOP FADE: POLICING THE BLACK CROWN

Even more than clothes, Black hair is a hallmark of Black identity. Black boys experiment with styles like the high or low top fade, waves, tapers, Mohawks, twists, and dreadlocks. Black girls wear their hair in cornrows, twists, buns, Afros, Bantu knots, individual braids, French braids, extensions, rods, locs, and coils. Black hairstyles hold great cultural significance. Braids, in particular, have been an integral part of African and African American culture.

In African tradition, women used braids to indicate their tribal association, marital status, or age. On the southern American plantation, braids were easier to manage in the heat and with the limited time women were allowed to care for themselves. Black women also used braids or plaits to communicate secret messages, such as the number of roads a fugitive must walk to escape into freedom. After emancipation, braids lost their power as some Black women tried to assimilate with their middle-class White peers by pressing or chemically straightening their hair. Braids remained common among Black women in domestic jobs and eventually made a comeback in the 1960s when the Black Power movement rejected Eurocentric beauty standards and restored pride in Black hair in its natural form.[69] Black was beautiful again, and Black men and women wore Afros as a sign of power in the fight for racial equality.[70]

Notwithstanding its rich historical significance, Black hair has also been a source of stigma and oppression. Anti-Black-hair sentiments date back to the North American slave trade. The word "dreadlocks" originated from the time of the slave trade when Africans' hair naturally formed into locs during the Middle Passage and were deemed "dreadful" by Whites. Stereotypes that locs are dirty, unprofessional, and unkempt persist today.[71]

Ironically, attempts to cover up Black hair with a headwrap have been met with the same disdain. Contemporary headwraps loosely resemble the wraps worn by women in the southern cotton fields to keep their heads cool in the scorching daytime sun.[72] Black women also wore headwraps to express themselves creatively and reclaim some measure of dignity in the face of dehumanizing treatment by Whites and overseers. Years later, Black men began to wear headwraps or "durags" to create waves in their hair for swag and style. Despite their multiple uses and value, critics equated the durag with a thug mentality when it was adopted by young hip-hop artists.[73]

Today, anti-Black-hair sentiments are enforced through school dress codes that unfairly target hairstyles common among Black youth.[74] Styles like dreadlocks and braids make teachers and principals uncomfortable and subject Black youth to harsh school discipline and expulsion. In August 2019, Narvie Harris Elementary School in Decatur, Georgia, prominently displayed a poster with photographs depicting "Appropriate" and "Inappropriate" hairstyles for students.[75] Photos of inappropriate styles included young Black boys with textured high tops, faded sides, and artistic shapes and designs neatly cut into their hair. Photographs of inappropriate girls' styles included braids and colorful barrettes. None of the styles were obscene, threatening, or inherently offensive. The school later removed the poster after students and parents complained that the policy was irrational and racially biased. The DeKalb County School District characterized the poster as a "miscommunication."

In August 2018, Christ the King School, a private Roman Catholic school near New Orleans, told eleven-year-old Faith Fennidy to leave class because her braided hair extensions violated the school's dress code.[76] The school's handbook broadly prohibits hairstyles that are "faddish" and otherwise "deemed inappropriate" by the administration. It specifically prohibits extensions, wigs, hairpieces, and any other style that alters the student's natural hair. Faith had worn braids for the previous two years and was not aware of any changes to the school's policy when the new year began. Even after Faith's parents spent a "considerable amount of money" to change her hair, she was told that her hair still did not comply with school policy. Faith never returned to Christ the King. The school claims that her parents withdrew Faith on their own. The Fennidys say the school told her to "not come back."

In 2017, fifteen-year-old twin sisters Mya and Deanna Cook were punished for refusing to remove their braids at Mystic Valley Regional Charter School in Malden, Massachusetts, just outside Boston.[77] The girls' braids violated the school's grooming policy prohibiting hair extensions and "drastic or unnatural hair colors or styles" that could be "distracting." The Cook twins were adopted by White parents when they were toddlers and had decided to wear braids as they learned more about Black culture. The school suggested that the sisters use chemicals or heat to straighten their hair. When they refused, they were kicked off their sports teams, banished from the prom, and received multiple detentions.

Despite the school's claim that its grooming policies were designed to emphasize education and promote equity, the policy was disproportionately enforced against Black girls. Ms. Cook and other mothers reported that the administrators abruptly began cracking down on the dress-code policy in April 2017 when they gathered twenty or so Black and biracial students to inspect their hair and question them about whether their braids contained any "fake" hair. About half the girls received detentions.[78] The state attorney general's office agreed that the policy might violate state and federal law and instructed the school to immediately stop enforcing it and reverse any discipline imposed on the students, including the Cook twins.[79]

In each of these schools, disparate enforcement of the grooming policies sends the message that something is wrong with African hair and African-descended identity. It suggests that "good students" will abide by traditional Eurocentric beauty standards. School officials either didn't care or failed to realize how denigrating and damaging it was to ask Mya and Deanna to straighten their hair. They might as well have asked the girls to lighten their skin, wear colored contact lenses, or have cosmetic surgery to alter their noses.[80] The school effectively asked the girls to change the essence of who they are.

For Black girls, hairstyles are more than aesthetics and identity. Braids, locs, twists, and Afros are often healthier, more manageable, and less expensive than chemically straightened hair. Hair straightening requires extreme heat and chemicals that have been linked to an increased risk of uterine fibroids among Black women. The chemicals can also cause permanent or temporary scalp damage and hair loss, as well as the emotional distress that follows. These losses are especially traumatic for a teenage girl who is self-conscious and acutely aware that others are watching and judging her.

Girls who don't have time or money to get their hair done hide their hair in headwraps—violating other school rules. The National Women's Law Center found that almost 70 percent of school dress codes in Washington, D.C., prevent students from wearing cultural items like headwraps, scarves, and bandannas unless they are for religious purposes.[81] Even the hijab was considered a violation of the policy. When students at Washington, D.C.'s Duke Ellington School of the Arts noticed that Black students were being singled out for headwraps in 2019 even though they weren't explicitly prohibited by the school's policy, students planned a protest in which they wore headwraps, bonnets, and durags to school.[82]

Black girls aren't the only ones who have been victimized by hair grooming policies in school. In January 2020, administrators at Barbers Hill High School, a public school in Mont Belvieu, Texas, told DeAndre Arnold and his parents that he could receive an in-school suspension and be banned from his graduation ceremony if he did not cut his dreadlocks. DeAndre had been wearing his hair in locs since seventh grade as an expression of his Trinidadian heritage. School district officials insisted that while there is a rule covering hair length, there is no rule banning dreadlocks. DeAndre's mother said her son had always followed the policy on length by keeping his hair off his shoulders, above his earlobes, and out of his eyes. The problem began when the handbook was abruptly amended in December 2019 to forbid boys from wearing "adornments" in their hair. School officials told DeAndre that he was no longer allowed to keep his hair tied up with clips and rubber bands. As is true with so many dress-code disputes, the school insisted that DeAndre was never forbidden from attending school. DeAndre said school officials told him not to come back until he cut his hair.[83]

In April 2019, staff at Berry Miller Junior High School in Pearland, Texas, used a jet-black Sharpie to color in a Black teen's faded haircut that violated the school's dress code.[84] "J.T." was a thirteen-year-old seventh grader who got a fade with a design cut into the hairline. According to the code, "Hair must be neat, clean, and well groomed. Extreme hair styles such as carvings, mohawks, spikes, etc. are not allowed." J.T.'s design resembled an *M* and did not depict anything that was violent, offensive, or obscene. His parents did not know the style violated the dress code. Yet the principal forced J.T. to choose between having his scalp colored in or an in-school suspension that would make him miss class and jeopardize his position on the track team.

The three White staff involved in the incident laughed as they drew on J.T.'s head. To add insult to injury, the black ink did not match J.T.'s brown skin and made the design stand out even more. Other students made fun of him, called him a "thug," and created memes mimicking him. After a lawsuit filed by J.T.'s parents, the school district changed its dress code to remove any "perceived racial, cultural and religious insensitivities." The restrictions on fade cuts were removed.

In December 2018, a White referee forced sixteen-year-old Andrew "Drew" Johnson to cut his dreadlocks right before a wrestling match.[85] Drew was a varsity high school wrestler from Buena Regional High School in New Jersey. He describes himself as part Puerto Rican and part Black. The referee said Drew's hair was "unnatural" and gave him ninety seconds to cut it or forfeit the match.[86] The video of Drew's haircut has been viewed more than 15.3 million times, including by many Black youth and celebrities who have had their own humiliating experiences with hair discrimination.[87] After a coach cut his hair, Drew walked onto the mat with tears in his eyes and half of his locs gone. Meanwhile, his White opponent's hair continued to flop below his eyebrows in violation of the same policy. The school's next two matches were canceled as the referee continued to insist that Drew's hair did not satisfy the rules. On December 19, 2019, New Jersey's governor signed a law making it illegal to discriminate against people based on hairstyles associated with race.[88]

Recent publicity about youth like Mya, Deanna, Drew, J.T., and DeAndre has prompted public demonstrations, social media protests, and legal challenges. Professor Wendy Greene launched a social movement—#FreeTheHair—to advocate for people of color who want to wear their hair as it freely grows.[89] Efforts to repeal these rules and regulations have begun to educate the public about bias and discrimination, but unfortunately the attitudes that underlie them remain strong. Dress-code enforcements continue to stigmatize and isolate Black students from other children and deny them an opportunity to learn at a critical time in their development.

WHEN PLAYING HIP-HOP GETS YOU SUSPENDED . . . OR KILLED

As is true with other forms of play and leisure, most of us underestimate the importance of music in healthy adolescent development.[90] Music is both social and personal. Teenagers unite around music at concerts, parties, rallies, dates, and dinners. Sometimes teenagers choose music to fit in and enhance their social status. Others choose music in protest and resistance. Like our clothes, our musical preferences reflect who we are, where we come from, and what we believe in. Even as youth develop their own tastes, they are naturally drawn to music that validates their racial, cultural, religious, and family tradition. Youth who feel marginalized often find power and comfort in music that challenges the dominant social and political order. Music also encourages creativity, skill, and passions.

Biological benefits have also been associated with music. Music has been shown to relieve pain, help patients relax before surgery, improve sleeping patterns in premature infants, and reduce tension and anxiety in people with depression.[91] Listening to music is an emotional experience that helps young people cope and relax during times of distress and instability. Neurologists explain that music activates hormones and neurotransmitters that increase pleasure, reduce stress, and help people bond with others.[92] Even sad music makes teens feel better as they immerse themselves in their emotions and are able to work through a problem faster.[93]

It should be no surprise that teenagers spend a great deal of time and money listening to music. With such easy access to streaming services like YouTube, Apple Music, Spotify, Tidal, and Pandora, adolescents listen to music about four hours a day.[94] Young people learn to appreciate music in early adolescence and develop a lasting preference for various types of music by late adolescence.[95] They listen to music on their phones, on their computers, in their cars, with their friends, and alone. They listen when they are multitasking and when they are doing nothing else. And contrary to the fears of many adults, music often keeps teenagers out of trouble by keeping them safely occupied as they stop to listen.

Notwithstanding its value, music of all genres can be problematic. Music can glorify drugs, alcohol, and sexual promiscuity or reinforce violent, profane, demeaning, and misogynistic messages in society. Despite the recurrence of these themes across the musical spectrum, rap music generates fear and harsh opposition like no other genre. The very word "rap" affects how listeners interpret a song's lyrics.[96] In 1996 and 1999, psychologist Carrie Fried found that listeners interpreted lyrics from a 1960s folk song differently depending on whether they were explicitly or implicitly told that the lyrics came from a 1990s country song or a 1990s rap song.[97] Those who believed the lyrics were rap described them as more threatening and offensive and advocated for warning labels or outright bans. Researchers from the University of California, Irvine, replicated this study in 2016 and observed the same results.[98]

While rap continues to draw intense public criticism, pop music remains one of the most popular genres. In 2019, researchers found that pop music lyrics contain the same amount of violent content as rap and hip-hop.[99] Yet songs like Gwen Stefani's "Hollaback Girl," Maroon 5's "Wake Up Call," and Robin Thicke's "Blurred Lines" reached the pop charts without backlash from conservatives despite their focus on girls fighting in the schoolyard, a man shooting his girlfriend's lover, and a man pressuring a woman into sex against her will.

The double standard is equally evident in country music. In 2019, sociologist Braden Leap analyzed the lyrics of country songs that topped the *Billboard* charts for more than 836 weeks from 1983 to 2016.[100] More than 80 percent of those songs were performed by male artists. By the 2010s, country hits increasingly objectified women and focused on men providing women with alcohol, transportation, and places to "hook up." The subgenre of "dirty country" is particularly known for its subtle use of sexual and sexist innuendos that demean and objectify women.[101] From Conway Twitty's 1973 hit "You've Never Been This Far Before" to David Allan Coe's 1982 "Pick 'Em, Lick 'Em, Stick 'Em" and Eric Church's 2014 "Like a Wrecking Ball," dirty country is rich with toxic masculinity, sexual conquest, and graphic images of young girls losing their virginity. Country lyrics also have their share of White pride and racism. With nostalgic allusions to an idyllic American past, not so subtle references to the beauty of blond hair, blue eyes, and freckles, and outright racial slurs, country artists appeal to an overwhelmingly White audience and define and celebrate masculinity as Whiteness.[102]

While pop and country artists have managed to escape the ire of politicians and lawmakers, rap artists and their fans have been treated like pariahs in the media and by the police who track them on social media and stake them out at concerts. Instead of acknowledging the social conditions that inspire the violent lyrics that are common in rap, critics make exaggerated claims about rap's role in causing crime and violence in society.

Rappers, on the other hand, have been outspoken, both in lyrics and in public commentary, about the poverty and joblessness that lured young Black men into selling crack and the violence that accompanied it. The artists have also used their music to condemn racial injustice, White supremacy, and the American government as a whole.[103] Unlike country musicians who honor their White identity with little resistance, rap artists draw intense public criticism for asserting Black power and commenting on America's racist past and present.

Rappers have had an especially contentious relationship with the police, particularly since N.W.A's 1989 battle with the FBI over their song "Fuck tha Police" and Ice-T's 1992 controversy with politicians over "Cop Killer," which challenged police brutality and racial profiling.[104] In the weeks after the release of "Cop Killer," police threatened to withhold emergency protection from retailers who continued to sell the album that featured the song, and President George H. W. Bush denounced Warner Records for releasing the song. Because rap lyrics often reinforce racial stereotypes about Black males' hypersexuality, violence, and profanity, rap music has not always generated political support from the Black middle class. Black leaders who describe the genre as thuggish, criminal, gangsta, and the devil's music are reluctant to defend it with the same fervor they mount against other forms of racial discrimination.

In local communities, rap has been the target of school regulations and government prohibitions. In some school districts, officials explicitly ban rap and hip-hop. In others, school rules include broad prohibitions on "loud and vulgar music" and give school staff discretion to decide what is appropriate or not. In Portland, Oregon, public school officials faced backlash in 2016 when the district declared rap music "inappropriate" for buses.[105] In a memo to bus drivers, school officials provided a list of "acceptable" radio stations within three genres—pop, country, and jazz. All other genres were excluded. In its effort to mitigate outrage over the memo, school officials argued that the policy was meant to shield students from religious teachings, profanity, and violent lyrics.

In 2019, a junior high school in Batesville, Mississippi, canceled a speaking engagement with a local rapper, Fly Rich Double.[106] School officials decided he was not a good "role model" for the students, although he was one of the school's most successful alumni. His critics complained that his music glorified thugs, killers, gangbangers, drug smugglers, and even terrorists. Students interviewed after the announcement described Fly Rich as an inspiration and were disappointed with the school's decision to disinvite him. With his own success reflected in nine million views of his videos at the time, Fly Rich insisted that he was planning to encourage the children to set goals, work hard, and be whatever they want to be. Fly Rich's mother was especially disappointed that the school bought into stereotypes about rap and maintained that although his lyrics are explicit, her son knows what is appropriate for children.

The media's inflammatory portrayal of rap music has terrified the nation and led to some deadly results. In July 2019, seventeen-year-old Elijah Al-Amin was killed by a White man, Michael Paul Adams, who said rap music made him feel unsafe.[107] Adams approached Elijah inside a Circle K gas station in Peoria, Arizona, and slit his throat with a pocketknife when he heard rap blaring from his car. Elijah had done nothing wrong. In 2012, seventeen-year-old Jordan Davis was killed by a White man, Michael David Dunn, who complained about the loud "thuggish" music blaring from the SUV Jordan was riding in with three friends.[108] Dunn parked next to the SUV at a gas station in Jacksonville, Florida, and demanded that the boys turn it down. When Jordan balked at Dunn's request, Dunn fired four shots, killing Jordan. Michael Dunn and Michael Adams might be outliers as killers, but their attitudes about Black youth and rap music are not uncommon at all.

In their 2019 book, *Rap on Trial: Race, Lyrics, and Guilt in America,* Erik Nielson and Andrea Dennis detail the criminalization of rap music in the legal system. Prosecutors treat rap music like autobiographical accounts of the artists' lives instead of the hyperbole and bravado that it obviously is. Recognizing that rap lyrics evoke an intense negative reaction among many, prosecutors rely on rap songs to convict Black artists of murder and other violent crimes in the absence of other, more direct forms of evidence.[109] Prosecutors craft stories that capitalize on fears and racial stereotypes about the genre and quote from or play songs that inflame the jurors and increase the likelihood of conviction. Nielson and Dennis remind us that if the criminal legal system treated other kinds of music the way it treats rap, many more legendary artists would be prosecuted for murder. Johnny Cash would have been among the first on that list with his fictionalized confession in "Folsom Prison Blues": "But I shot a man in Reno just to watch him die." While our criminal courts routinely deny rap its status as artistic expression, no one would expect a judge or prosecutor to view Johnny Cash's lyrics as anything other than a creative and melancholy narrative he imagined after watching the movie *Inside the Walls of Folsom Prison.*

Like any good businessman or woman, rappers write the songs that sell. They write the songs that speak to the plight of their young fans and take creative license to convince their audience that they, too, share a lived experience. The most successful rappers learn to play their part well. By taking on a persona that convinces others that they are hard, dangerous, and not to be messed with, many rappers don't have to be violent in their real lives. The same is true with their listeners.

Research contradicts claims that listening to extreme music causes anger, aggression, or delinquency.[110] Although violent lyrics may resonate with vulnerable youth, the music itself doesn't cause the violence. And in some cases, the music may even replace or reduce violence by providing troubled youth with an outlet for their anger and an opportunity to play out the violent themes in the safety of fantasy.[111] In the case of rap, playing the music with friends allows youth to hide behind a facade of bravado that prevents them from ever having to act out in real life. Critics also ignore the many positive messages evident in rap, including resilience, self-esteem, coping, self-determination, and cultural pride.

## FRIENDS, GANGS, AND SOCIAL MEDIA: GROWING UP BLACK IN THE AGE OF INTERNET SURVEILLANCE

Every high school has its cliques. The jocks, nerds, tomboys, cheerleaders, mean girls, gamers, punks, preps, geeks, and skaters, among others. Cliques are a normal part of adolescent development. Teenagers sort themselves into groups that provide comfort, security, and support.[112]

As youth begin to assert their independence from parents, they naturally gravitate toward peers who are most like them.[113] To cope with the anonymity and intimidation that often accompany the transition to middle and high school, teens tend to hang out in groups of five or six, but sometimes as few as two or three. To reduce anxiety about difference, their friends are usually about the same age, gender, race, class, and social status. Teenagers signal their loyalty to their clique by sitting together at school, hanging out after class, dressing alike, and giving themselves nicknames and symbols. For most kids, these behaviors are considered normal and even encouraged for healthy social engagement. For Black youth, these behaviors earn them the label of "gang" or "crew" and put them at risk of arrest—just for being in the group. Jelani Henry and his brother, Asheem, shared this experience.

The Henry brothers were born in Harlem in 1991 and 1992.[114] They grew up watching their neighborhood split into small and informal crews that coalesced around various blocks and street corners in the city. Each crew was made up of a dozen or so teens from the local community, and none of them was connected to a national gang like the Bloods or the Crips. When Jelani and Asheem were twelve and thirteen, they began to run with a crew called the Goodfellas. The Goodfellas provided the boys with camaraderie, status, and cachet with the girls. The crew started as a neighborhood clique that never intended to get involved in crime. Eventually, the crew became a source of protection after the boys were robbed and attacked by other crews in the neighborhood. Asheem became deeply involved in the crew, while Jelani remained at the periphery, leaving the neighborhood daily to attend school in Yonkers and staying out of the neighborhood beefs and rivalries. Jelani thought of the crew as his family, not a "gang."

Like so many adolescent cliques, the boys who called themselves Goodfellas grew up together all of their lives. They played basketball, had sleepovers, celebrated each other's birthdays, listened to music, were proud of their crew, and wore shirts and jackets to prove it. The Goodfellas were also active on social media. Jelani and Asheem appeared in rap videos on YouTube, had accounts on Myspace and Facebook, and posted about themselves and their crew in images tagged with "Goodfellas" and "GF." The boys developed their social media profiles for fun and for survival. Jelani's profile was more persona than real. Jelani knew that "liking" a song or fight on Facebook or YouTube would show his loyalty and affiliation with the Goodfellas and give him the credibility and the reputation of his set without requiring him to participate in the crime and conflict.[115]

In 2008, Asheem was arrested for possession of a gun—a gun that didn't work and that he had never shot. Asheem admitted that he carried it for protection and was sentenced to five years of probation. He was sixteen at the time. A few years later, after he graduated from high school and moved to New Jersey for college, Asheem's mother called to tell him the police were looking for him. Apparently, his old gun charge, combined with a series of photographs of himself standing with the Goodfellas when he was fourteen and fifteen, made him a suspect in a criminal enterprise. He was charged with conspiracy. By then—November 2011—Asheem was twenty and prosecuted as an adult.

Five months after his brother was charged with conspiracy, Jelani was next.[116] The police had been tracking him too. But this time the charges were much worse. Although Jelani had never been convicted of a crime and had nothing more serious than a citation for jumping a subway turnstile, prosecutors described him as a known and violent gang member responsible for two murders. The judge refused to release him on bail and instead sent him to New York's notorious Rikers Island, where he would wait for nineteen months before prosecutors would finally dismiss his case.

In the months that followed his arrest, Jelani and his lawyer learned how little evidence the prosecutors had. Without reliable and consistent eyewitness accounts, the police and prosecutors relied on photographs, postings, and "likes" they compiled from Facebook. Like so many others, Jelani was on New York City's list of youth being tracked—and sometimes actively engaged—by police through fake accounts on Twitter, Facebook, YouTube, Myspace, and Instagram. Jelani became the target of police attention because of his relationship to Asheem, his residence near 129th Street and Lenox Avenue, and his friendship with the Goodfellas. It didn't matter that Jelani had chosen to remain at the periphery of his crew's violence. His association with the clique was enough to earn him the label gangbanger.

Gangs have been present in America since before the turn of the nineteenth century.[117] Early twentieth-century studies treated gangs as normal social groups of adolescent males.[118] In these first studies, criminality was not identified as the defining feature of a gang, and gangs weren't intrinsically negative.[119] Early youth gangs involved mostly White and European immigrant boys who were regarded as adventurous, fun loving, and spirited, despite occasional acts of delinquency.[120] Researchers identified the gangs' main activity as "mere loafing together" but noted that the gang was also capable of collective action and generally attached to a local territory.[121]

Although White youth gangs in the nineteenth and early twentieth centuries annoyed adults with their cursing, drinking, fighting, stealing, and rowdiness, they also had the political support of adults who rewarded them for defending the neighborhood turf—especially by keeping Blacks away.[122] Local politicians legitimized the gangs by sponsoring neighborhood athletic clubs and providing them with a clubhouse for their recreation. To prove their Whiteness and superiority and to expedite their assimilation into America, White youth gangs of European descent often terrorized free Blacks and their businesses throughout the nineteenth century. White gang violence against Black youth took on even greater vigor as more Blacks migrated to northern cities in the middle of the twentieth century.

The earliest Black youth gangs formed in response to obvious race and class inequities in the city and frustration about the lack of jobs and other opportunities. Youth gangs gave marginalized youth an opportunity to belong and achieve status and offered them an outlet for their frustration—through protests, race riots, and even delinquent acts.[123] Black gangs that emerged from the 1940s through the 1970s refused to be the passive victims of White violence.[124]

As isolation and extreme poverty increased in urban ghettos in the 1950s and 1960s, Black youth gangs began to turn on each other. By the early 1970s, new definitions of "gang" began to focus on the youth's criminal activities and the community's negative reaction toward them.[125] Youth who caused trouble were far more likely to be viewed as a "gang" if they were poor, urban, and Black. Black gang violence reached a high point in the 1980s and 1990s with easy access to guns and deadly battles over control of the crack cocaine market.[126] The temporary spike in gang violence in the 1990s forever branded street gangs as a violent terror in American society. Unfortunately, that image was uniquely tied to Black youth.

Today, "gang" is a pejorative term reserved almost exclusively for Black and Latinx youth. Responding to the public hysteria around youth violence in the late 1980s, federal and state governments passed new laws that made it a crime for an individual to be in a gang, regardless of whether they committed any other criminal act.[127] State lawmakers and federal agencies define "gang" in the broadest terms. Federal entities like the National Gang Center classify a group as a youth gang if it has three or more members, generally aged twelve to twenty-four; the members share an identity, typically linked to a name or other symbols; the members view themselves as a gang and are recognized by others as a gang; the group has some permanence and a degree of organization; and the group is involved in an elevated level of criminal activity.[128] As written, almost every college fraternity, sorority, sports fan club—and many police departments—would fit this definition.

Fraternities have plenty in common with a typical street gang. Not only do they share a common name, dress in matching attire, and use symbols and hand signs, but they are also notorious for their criminal behavior. With rampant drug and alcohol abuse, vandalism, violent initiation rituals, and rape, frat boys give the Crips, Bloods, and Latin Kings a run for their money. Even if we don't think of fraternity brothers as violent gun-toting gangbangers, the victims of their sexual assaults and violent hazing experience that conduct as a distinction without much difference.

Contemporary antigang laws and regulations draw arbitrary distinctions between Black and White youth groups and capitalize on racialized stereotypes about Black adolescence. In September 2020, President Trump told the White nationalist Proud Boys to "stand back and stand by," signaling his solidarity with the far-right extremist group and urging them to be ready to defeat antifa and the left. The New York Police Department admits that the Proud Boys, who describe themselves as a gang, are not included in the city's gang database.[129] The National Gang Center explicitly exempts White supremacist hate groups from its annual youth gang survey by instructing participants to exclude ideological groups, motorcycle gangs, and organized crime.[130] Although its own definition of a gang calls for some evidence of "permanence and a degree of organization," the center seems to ignore evidence that crews like Asheem and Jelani's Goodfellas are far less organized than the Mafia and the skinheads. As Asheem told reporters after his conviction for conspiracy, "We were just young dumb kids running around, and we just happened to run under one name. There wasn't no hierarchy, there wasn't order." More often than not, the government's extreme and discriminatory responses to Black youth groups evolve out of fear and ignorance about race and adolescence rather than a careful study of the social, political, and economic roots of gang activity.[131]

Although gang activity and involvement have decreased considerably since the 1990s, fears and stereotypes about Black youth remain deeply entrenched in the American psyche. Data collected from the mid-1990s through 2017 shows a significant decline in the percentage of youth involved in gangs, the number of students reporting the presence of gangs in their schools, and the frequency of gang activity reported in local jurisdictions.[132] Particularly noteworthy, the percentage of students aged twelve to eighteen who reported the presence of gangs at their school decreased overall from 20 percent to 9 percent between 2001 and 2017.[133] Notwithstanding these declines, law enforcement agencies continue to expand and monitor gang databases that are overwhelmingly populated with Black and Latinx youth.

Gang databases exist in at least sixteen states and several major cities across the country.[134] Approximately 20,000 people were added to New York City's gang database between August 2003 and August 2013.[135] Ninety-nine percent were Black or Hispanic. An additional 17,000 were added to the database from December 2013 through February 2018. Ninety-eight percent were Black or Hispanic. As of November 2015, there were 150,000 people in California's Gang Database.[136] Of those, 64.9 percent were Hispanic; 25 percent were Black; 8 percent were White. In August 2016, Portland, Oregon, police listed 359 people as gang members, with 81 percent identified as a racial or ethnic minority.[137]

Researchers at the University of Illinois studied the demographics of more than 128,000 adults in Chicago's gang database in 2018.[138] Seventy percent were Black, 25 percent were Latinx, and less than 5 percent were White. Researchers also believe that an additional 28,000 to 68,000 youth are included in the database and that 95.3 percent of those who were added before they turned eighteen are Black or Latinx. The Chicago Police Department has collected its own gang data and found that of the 134,242 individuals designated as gang members over the last twenty years, 91.3 percent of them were Black or Latinx males.[139]

The overrepresentation of minorities in gang databases is largely a product of racial stereotyping and police surveillance methods that focus heavily on inner-city neighborhoods.[140] Contemporary gang suppression tactics give law enforcement virtually unlimited discretion to collect information and add youth to a database. As requirements for inclusion in the data set become more permissive, racial disparities become more pronounced.[141]

Youth in California can be added to the database if they have been seen associating with known gang members, including family, friends, and classmates; are known to have a gang tattoo; are frequently seen in a police-designated "gang" area, even if they happen to live there; have been seen wearing clothing associated with a gang; have been arrested for offenses consistent with typical gang activity; have been seen displaying gang symbols or hand signs; have admitted to being in a gang; or have been identified as a gang member by a reliable source.[142] Law enforcement agencies need evidence of only two of these criteria to enter a youth into the database. Most people added to the databases have been added without having been arrested or accused of a crime, and many database entries include photographs taken without the person's knowledge.[143]

Gang documentation starts early. Notwithstanding data showing that only 1.7 percent of individuals in California's gang database are under eighteen, local public defenders and youth advocates report that police begin tracking kids as young as ten.[144] Police question people of all ages, including children in early elementary school, about their nicknames, their family members and friends, and where they live or hang out.[145] In New York City, 30 percent of individuals added to the database between 2003 and 2013 were children when they were added.[146] One New York City gang indictment revealed that police and prosecutors arrested several fifteen-year-olds after tracking them for four and a half years of suspected crew activity in Manhattan.[147] Young people have been swept into gang databases for appearing in photographs with friends or family believed to be associated with a gang, scribbling gang-related signs in the margins of a school notebook, living in a neighborhood known for gangs, getting a tattoo, or drawing gang-related graffiti on a wall, desk, or subway.[148] By the time a child is finally arrested and has access to a lawyer, there may be years of police contact, photographs, phone records, and social media information on file. Police often construct an elaborate network of relationships, associations, neighborhood affiliations, and alleged grudges by and against a child before the child is ever suspected of an identified crime.

Schools have also been closely involved in the identification of suspected gang members. Again targeting adolescent fashion most associated with youth of color, school districts across the country revised their dress codes in the 1990s to ban jewelry, insignias, baseball caps, gloves, colored shoestrings, certain colors of clothes, and any other symbol of gang life in the school.[149] Some schools prohibited male students from wearing earrings and "expensive clothes" that might have been purchased with the proceeds of gang crimes.[150] In 1994, the Office of Safety and Youth Development within New York City's Department of Education created the Gang Prevention and Intervention Unit to combat gangs in New York City's public school system.[151] In guidelines that read much more like a parents' checklist for the early signs of puberty than a strategy for eliminating gangs, school safety officers were instructed to look for warning signs of gang involvement like "changes in behavior," "alcohol/drug use," "staying out late," "interest in certain colors and clothing," "use of hand signals, slang, and graffiti," "poor attendance at school," and "hanging out with gang members." Officers and educators were also advised to watch for clues of gang affiliation on book bags, hats, bandannas, and notebooks. These guidelines are still in effect for the more than 5,500 school safety agents who work in New York City's public schools and give school officers broad discretion to monitor, exclude, and add youth to New York's gang database.[152] Students in New York report that police expelled more than a dozen students from a Bronx school in 2017 for suspected gang involvement.[153]

Inclusion in the gang database guarantees that children will be subject to heightened police scrutiny. Police install surveillance cameras and facial recognition technology to track and monitor suspected gang activity in Black neighborhoods.[154] Police stop and frisk Black youth based on nothing more than suspected gang attire, even when there is no reason to believe the child has been involved in a crime.[155] Police treat emoji, hashtags, "likes," and Facebook friendships as an admission of gang membership, and target teenagers for boasting about crimes they didn't commit, making threats against rival groups they have no intention of pursuing, and posting rap lyrics that glorify guns and violence.[156] Unfortunately, police and prosecutors who lack the cultural competencies to accurately interpret urban communication often misinterpret—or intentionally misconstrue—"signifying" and bravado as more nefarious than they really are.[157]

# 4

## Raising "Brutes" and "Jezebels": Criminalizing Black Adolescent Sexuality

On October 10, 2018, Jeremiah Harvey walked past a White woman in a convenience store in Flatbush, Brooklyn.[1] As the woman was bending over the counter, Jeremiah's book bag grazed her butt. The woman, Teresa Klein, immediately accused him of grabbing her "ass." Jeremiah was nine years old. Jeremiah's mother, Someko Bellille, was outraged by the accusation and exchanged heated words with Ms. Klein. Ms. Klein called 911 as bystanders filmed her on the phone saying, "That's right, the son grabbed my ass, and she decided to yell at me . . . and I would be more than happy to submit the security tapes for evidence . . . I was just sexually assaulted by a child." Onlookers, mostly Black, berated her for calling the police on a child. A White woman chastised her as well. Ms. Klein ridiculed the onlookers in return, telling them they could not "shame" her for "being a White woman who called the police on a Black child." Eventually they all walked away. Fortunately, the police did not come, and Jeremiah, his mother, and his sister went home.

Cell-phone recordings of Ms. Klein calling the police went viral. Finding herself in the national spotlight, Klein reviewed the store's surveillance footage showing that Jeremiah never touched her and apologized to Jeremiah through a news interview, saying, "Young man, I don't know your name, but I am sorry." By then the damage had been done. Jeremiah and his sister did not initially understand why Ms. Klein had called the police and cried hysterically believing their mother was about to get locked up. Ms. Bellille recalled that as they were walking away, Jeremiah was crying and pointing to the patrol cars on the street and asking, "Mommy, are they here to take you away from us?"

In the days after the encounter, Jeremiah spoke first at a community meeting and then in an interview with his mother on *Good Morning America*. In tears at the community meeting, he told the audience, "I don't forgive this woman, and she needs help."[2] After thinking about it for a few days, Jeremiah and his mother accepted the apology. Jeremiah decided that "friendship is the key." His mother hoped that people would learn from the incident.

In the heart-wrenching interview with *Good Morning America*, Jeremiah cried again as he recounted his experience. Ms. Bellille spoke about the difficulty of explaining what happened to her son. "To be having a conversation with your son about sexual assault at the age of 9—I never thought I'd be having this conversation." She recalled asking her son, "Do you know what sexual assault is?" "Do you know what rape is?" He did not. She asked, "Do you know what hate is?" "Do you know what racist is?" He did. To help him understand that he was not the only Black child who had been falsely accused of sexually accosting a White woman, Ms. Bellille told Jeremiah the story of Emmett Till, who was brutally murdered in 1955 for allegedly whistling at a White woman. "You are here today in 2018. Time has changed, but people's hatred has not." Jeremiah also remembered their conversation, saying, "I started to tear up because she was giving me all these examples that I didn't know about and that were emotional to me and that she had to sit down and explain to me about as I was going to bed."

Ms. Bellille is certain the only reason her son is not dead, in jail, or living with the stigma of a sexual assault is that the video showed what really happened. Yet she is still worried that he will be scarred for a long time by this incident. During the interview, Jeremiah said, "It's still hard because lately on my mind, like, I can't think nothing more but this." Jeremiah was not only humiliated by Ms. Klein's reaction and accusation in the moment, but he is now also traumatized by his new understanding of what it means to be Black and sexualized in America. Before Jeremiah could even think of himself in sexual terms, Ms. Klein identified him as a sexual deviant based on his race.

## THE SEX TALK: BLACK PARENTS AND THEIR SONS AND DAUGHTERS

Sexuality is a normal, healthy, and necessary part of adolescent development. Most of us remember our first sexual encounter—usually involving some experimentation with a friend or acquaintance, not the person we were destined to marry. Maybe we fantasized about kissing the cool guy or popular girl at school. Maybe we were interested in someone of the same sex or refused to be locked into the binary male-female dichotomy that society presses upon us. Maybe we watched sexually explicit movies or looked at magazines with naked bodies. And at some time, we probably talked to our friends about our newest love interest.

Adolescent romance looks a little different in the digital age. "Sexting" is the new normal in courting rituals. Instead of hand-made notes and cards, teenagers send sexually inviting text messages, "selfies," and video links of themselves by cell phone.[3] In 2016, the Cyberbullying Research Center reported that about 12 percent of adolescents aged twelve to seventeen had sent some explicit image of themselves to another person.[4] About 19 percent said they had received a sexually explicit image from someone else.[5] However the romance starts, sooner or later most young people start thinking about having sex, and many will have their first sexual encounter in their teen years. CDC data from 2011 to 2015 reveals that 42 percent of girls and 44 percent of boys between fifteen and nineteen reported that they had had sex.[6] A 2017 report from the CDC's National Center for Health Statistics found that about 55 percent of teenagers had sexual intercourse by age eighteen.[7]

Puberty usually starts between ages eight and thirteen for girls and between nine and thirteen for boys.[8] Puberty is accompanied by hormones like testosterone and estrogen that transform children into sexual beings.[9] With their libidos activated and their bodies capable of reproduction, teenagers begin to ask questions and think about sex. It is quite normal for children aged nine to twelve to start looking at themselves naked in the mirror, comparing genital size in the school bathroom, touching themselves in secret, and maybe even touching each other with permission.[10] Between ages fourteen and seventeen, it is normal for young people to look at nude pictures for sexual arousal, have explicit and detailed conversations about sex with friends, and try sexual activity with a partner of a similar age.[11]

Teenagers learn a lot about sexuality from their friends and the internet, but at some point parents will have to step up to prepare their children for the inevitable changes in their bodies. Parents will talk to their girls about their period and to their boys and girls about masturbation, pregnancy, and the risk of sexually transmitted diseases. They will set curfews and other rules for dating, and they might look for a book or video with the latest advice on "how to talk to your kids about sex." Parents who are the most progressive will talk to their children in terms that are respectful and accepting of the full range of sexual identity. Black parents will explore all of these issues and more.

For Black parents like Someko Bellille, the Black Sex Talk must include a tutorial on America's irrational fears of a hyper-sexed Black "Brute" and a wildly promiscuous Black "Jezebel." Black boys learn that White girls have been taught to fear them. Black girls learn that their teachers and classmates will assume they are more sexually experienced than they are.[12] Black parents are terrified to let their teenage boys date White girls. "What if her parents don't approve? What if her feelings get hurt?" The fallout is real. A White girl who is hurt by a Black boy or confronted by her parents might lie for revenge or cover and convert her initial excitement about interracial sex, dating, and flirtation to an accusation of rape or misunderstanding.

## FEARMONGERING AND MANIPULATION OF
### BLACK ADOLESCENT SEXUALITY

The Brute and Jezebel stereotypes have been manipulated to advance important economic and political interests favoring Whites in American history. After the Civil War, Whites resented Blacks' freedom and were terrified of their fight for civil rights. Distorting Black sexuality became a powerful tool to justify lynching, induce fear, and put Blacks in their place.[13] Whites manufactured images of Blacks as savages, brutes, and monsters naturally prone to violence and aggression to protect White power and prevent others from seeing Black children as children. Black males were depicted as lewd, sexually insatiable, and a particular threat to White women. The 1915 film *The Birth of a Nation* stoked fears of Black men savagely attacking White women. The legacy of the violent, sexualized Black male is one of the most durable tropes of White supremacy.[14] When Dylann Roof killed nine people at an African Methodist Episcopal church in Charleston, South Carolina, in 2015, he told his victims that he just had to do it because "you rape our women, and you're taking over our country, and you have to go."[15]

Many of the most publicized allegations of Black sexual violence have involved adolescents. In 1931, nine Black boys aged thirteen to nineteen were falsely accused of raping two White women on a train in Scottsboro, Alabama. The boys spent many years in prison while their cases were tried and retried. In 1955, Emmett Till was fourteen when he was accused of harassing a White woman in Mississippi. He was shot and mutilated. In 1958, James Hanover Thompson was nine when an eight-year-old White girl kissed him and his seven-year-old friend David Simpson on the cheek in North Carolina.[16] Later that night, James and David were arrested and charged with molestation after the boys were hunted down by the girl's father and neighbors. The boys were beaten, detained for six days without access to a lawyer or their parents, and then sentenced to indefinite terms in a reform school with the possibility of release at age twenty-one. The boys were finally released after three months in detention and international outrage.

The youngest person ever executed in twentieth-century America was a Black boy, George Stinney. He was fourteen when he was accused of murdering two White girls, aged eleven and seven, in 1944. Despite scant evidence that George had the strength, motive, or opportunity to kill one, much less two girls, George was convicted and sentenced to die in the electric chair. In keeping with American folklore about Black deviant hypersexuality, the police were convinced that fourteen-year-old George wanted to have sex with the eleven-year-old.[17] There was no evidence that either of the girls had been sexually assaulted. George was executed three months after his arrest.

The criminalization of Black adolescent sexuality extends beyond the South. Yusef Salaam, Kevin Richardson, Antron McCray, Korey Wise, and Raymond Santana ranged in age from fourteen to sixteen when they were accused of raping a White woman in New York City's Central Park in 1989.[18] Four of the boys were Black and one was Latino. Ava DuVernay's Netflix miniseries *When They See Us* offers a vivid and painful account of the prosecutors' and police officers' racist dehumanization of the suspects during their investigation of the rape.

The five boys were just kids at the time, doing kid things—hanging out in a group and doing what their friends do. Korey had been hanging out with his girlfriend at an ice cream shop when his friend Yusef stopped by to persuade him to go to the park. There were dozens of kids in the park. The kids were loud and silly. They were reckless and impulsive, and a few of them were intimidating and assaulting others in the park.[19] But most of them were just being kids. The public's willingness to believe the police narrative that the boys were "animals" "wilding" and raping in the park highlights an important link between race, adolescence, and sexuality.

Police and prosecutors persisted in the case even when the evidence against the boys didn't match the allegations. The timelines didn't match. The DNA didn't match. And other than Korey and Yusef, none of the boys knew each other. The police and prosecutors ignored the boys' initial denials and made their case only by manipulating the boys to falsely confess.

Inside the courtroom, the boys were dehumanized. They were charged with rape, assault, robbery, and rioting. Yusef, Kevin, Antron, and Raymond were tried in juvenile court and sentenced to five to ten years in a youth prison. Although Korey was only sixteen at the time, he was considered an adult under New York law. He was sentenced to fifteen years in prison, where he spent much of his time in solitary confinement. Each of the boys was ordered to register as a sex offender.[20] Each spent seven to thirteen years in prison before they were all exonerated. Thirteen years after the rape, Matias Reyes—completely unconnected to the boys—confessed to the crime. His DNA matched.

Media hype and public fear of the five boys—and others who looked like them—were palpable outside the courtroom. News clips, including an advertisement by the future president Donald Trump calling for the death penalty,[21] fed the 1990s public hysteria over youth crime, especially involving Black and Latinx youth. Like Emmett Till and so many others falsely accused after him, the Central Park Five found themselves at the center of conservative politicians' efforts to control and manipulate public opinion about Black youth.

The Central Park rape occurred at a time when Americans were anxious about an increase in violent and deadly crime by young men between the ages of fourteen and twenty-four.[22] The 1990s ushered in the most vile and explicit attack on Black adolescence in America to date. In a series of articles and television interviews, Princeton professor and criminologist John DiIulio Jr. incited terror among the public and policy makers, claiming that "a new generation of street criminals is upon us— the youngest, biggest and baddest generation any society has ever known . . . America is now home to thickening ranks of juvenile 'superpredators'—radically impulsive, brutally remorseless youngsters, including ever more preteenage boys, who murder, assault, rape, rob, burglarize, deal deadly drugs, join gun-toting gangs and create serious communal disorders."[23]

DiIulio racialized his "superpredator" myth in explicit and unapologetic ways in a 1996 *City Journal* article headlined "My Black Crime Problem, and Ours." DiIulio predicted that "not only is the number of young black criminals likely to surge, but . . . as many as half of these juvenile superpredators could be young black males."[24] DiIulio's predictions were accepted as fact despite the lack of scientific foundation. Fortunately, his fictitious band of violent young Black superpredators never materialized, ultimately disproving his predictions. Aside from a momentary increase in crime in the mid-1990s, crime decreased considerably among youth in the years that followed.[25] Notwithstanding the clear evidence of DiIulio's error, the now Exonerated Five and many Black children like them have spent their adolescent years in cages on the heels of this vicious narrative.

Little has changed in the intervening twenty-five years. Black boys still get arrested, sent to prison, and forced to register as sex offenders for both consensual and fabricated sexual contact with White girls. Even as the form of sexual engagement continues to evolve, Black boys are viewed as predators. In 2016, Levar Allen was charged with possession of child pornography and contributing to the delinquency of a minor after exchanging nude pictures with a White friend.[26] He was seventeen. She was sixteen. Levar was an award-winning three-sport athlete at Parkway High School in Bossier City, Louisiana. He had never been in trouble with the law. Although his mother had warned him about the consequences of sexting, Levar did what millions of teenagers do: he acted impulsively without thinking through the consequences. His classmate sent him a nude photo, and he sent her one in return. The exchange may have been crass, but it wasn't predatory, abusive, or degrading. It was a consensual exchange between two teens. Yet her parents called the police, and Levar was arrested.

Louisiana law says that a seventeen-year-old can be charged with child pornography for sending nude pictures to anyone sixteen and younger, even if they consent. A sixteen-year-old can be charged for sending nude pictures to anyone of any age. The police said both youth would be charged, but their focus was clearly on Levar, who they claim had other sex-related videos on his phone. Many wondered whether police and prosecutors would have pursued any of this if Levar had not been Black or if his classmate had not been White. His mother, Chasity Washington, thinks not. Ms. Washington told reporters that her son's worst mistake was to reply to a nude video his White classmate sent to him: "I think because she's white, the parents got upset that she's been doing what she's been doing."[27] And therein lies the heart of the matter. Even in 2016, Levar's arrest reflects the long legacy of fears of Black sexual deviance. Levar's case was eventually dismissed in 2017.[28] Contrary to earlier claims, the girl was never charged.

It was against this same historical backdrop that Teresa Klein accused Jeremiah Harvey of sexual assault in Flatbush in 2018. Of course, Ms. Klein was adamant that her accusation had nothing to do with race. According to her, she was standing at the counter in a convenience store. She felt something or someone touch her butt. She turned around and Jeremiah was walking past. Voilà. He must have touched her. When the story is told that way, she's right: it doesn't sound as if race had anything to do with it. But let's revisit this. It is one thing to assume that Jeremiah was the one who touched her. It's quite another to assume that he did so intentionally, and with some desire to gratify himself sexually. He was nine. And he looked nine. How many times have we been jostled in a store, on a bus, or at a ball game? How many times have we passed someone in a doorway? When one enters and another exits, people touch. Most of us recognize that contact as meaningless, accidental, and harmless. But Ms. Klein immediately assumed the worst. And to make matters worse, she didn't believe him when he denied the accusation.

This is exactly how subconscious bias works. Our biases let us fill in missing pieces of information so we can process and react to what is happening around us.[29] We do this all the time. We encounter a stranger, and we make snap decisions about whether he is safe or dangerous. Sometimes this is a lifesaving instinct. Sometimes it is just harmful and degrading to others.

Left to draw a conclusion without all of the facts, Ms. Klein subconsciously created meaning out of the information she did have. If Ms. Klein had seen a girl or woman—of any race—chances are she would have assumed the touching was accidental. If Ms. Klein had seen a White nine-year-old boy, it is unlikely she would have assumed the child's touch was sexual. But Jeremiah was both Black and male, and after fifty years of exposure to racist stereotypes about Black men Ms. Klein was not moved by his young age. When researchers studied this very question—would a child's young age reduce the impact of racial bias on perceptions of criminality—the answer was no.[30] In school, Ms. Klein probably read about the lynching of Black men in retaliation for the alleged rape of White women. Living in New Jersey, she certainly would have heard news accounts of the Central Park jogger. And for years thereafter, she would have watched media reports that repeatedly portrayed Black men and boys as violent sexual predators. Regardless of whether Ms. Klein actively recalled any of those events in the moment, research teaches us that any one or more of these stereotypes would have contributed to her subconscious thinking about Jeremiah in the bodega.

## (WHITE) BOYS WILL BE BOYS

The stereotypes and risks associated with Black sexuality leave Black children confused about what normal, healthy sexual development looks like—especially when they see and hear how different their experiences are from White boys'. While most agree that adolescence begins with the onset of puberty, there is less consensus on where adolescence ends.[31] We usually talk about adolescence from age ten to eighteen, but for some it may extend to age twenty-five.[32] Adulthood is typically tied to certain milestones like marriage, financial independence from parents, completing high school and college, getting a full-time job, and having children.[33] Delays in these milestones have extended the length of adolescence for many youth in America. For example, in 1950 the median age at first marriage was 22.8 for men and 20.3 for women.[34] By 2017, that age was 29.5 for men and 27.4 for women. The average age at which mothers give birth to their first child has also continued to rise. In 1970, women had their first child at an average age of 21.4; by 2015, that age was 26.4.[35]

Psychologist Jeffrey Arnett coined a new term for these trends: "emerging adulthood."[36] Generally spanning from the late teens through the mid-twenties, emerging adulthood is a time when adult responsibilities are delayed while adolescent experimentation continues and even intensifies. Although many young people think they have reached adulthood when they leave home for college, experts tell us that young people continue to develop socially, emotionally, intellectually, and sexually well beyond their teen years. Certain types of risky behaviors such as unprotected sex and substance use may even peak during this period as young people spend more time away from parents, with friends, and without obligations to a spouse or child.

Emerging adulthood is as much a cultural phenomenon as a developmental stage. In his book *Guyland: The Perilous World Where Boys Become Men*, sociologist Michael Kimmel lays out the code of conduct for males—mostly White and relatively wealthy—who are suspended between late adolescence and early adulthood.[37] In "guyland," guys socialize in packs, engage in excessive drinking, and watch pornography. Masculinity is demonstrated by sex and sexual prowess. Guys prove their manhood by hazing and degrading other males, mistreating women, and blaming their victims. The "guy code" frees them to pursue fun without accountability, while cultures of "entitlement," "silence," and "protection" allow them to be gross, offensive, and misogynistic without concern for how their behavior impacts others.

The boys in *Guyland* are rarely held accountable for their drunken revelry, promiscuity, and derogatory attitudes toward women. Sex is a rite of passage, and boys are expected to prove their manhood at the expense of women. For young White boys living in the space between boyhood and manhood, society seems to condone misogyny, violence, and other misconduct with the excuse that "boys will be boys." Sometimes the excuse is explicit. Other times it is implicit in society's willingness to pardon young White men for their words, actions, or attitudes, especially about women.

"Boys will be boys" originated from a Latin proverb: "Children (boys) are children (boys) and do childish things."[38] Although the original proverb was meant to explain why a boy said or did something immature or childish, the phrase has been used to trivialize the misbehavior of males at all stages of development. What started as a harmless quip has now morphed into a catch-all excuse for men and boys who behave in ways that are rough, aggressive, and improper.[39] The mantra also suggests that boys are predisposed—maybe even biologically hardwired—to engage in violent and predatory sexual behavior.[40]

America's willingness to excuse sexual violence committed by elite White boys captured national attention in 2018, when Brett Kavanaugh was nominated to the Supreme Court by President Donald Trump. A former acquaintance of Kavanaugh's, Dr. Christine Blasey Ford, alleged that he sexually assaulted her at a party in the early 1980s when he was seventeen and she was fifteen.[41] Ford described Kavanaugh as "stumbling drunk" and said that he and his friend Mark Judge trapped her in a room and pinned her to a bed. Kavanaugh tried to remove her clothes and covered her mouth when she tried to scream. Ford was afraid he might accidently kill her.[42] Meanwhile, his friend Judge laughed "maniacally" as he watched,[43] egging Kavanaugh on at times but also telling him to stop at other times.[44] Kavanaugh vehemently denied Ford's allegations.

Additional women came forward, accusing Kavanaugh of sexually abusive and physically aggressive behavior toward women. One woman accused Kavanaugh of thrusting his penis against her face when they were both students at Yale. Another said

Kavanaugh frequently touched women without their consent at house parties and tried to remove their clothes to expose their private parts. At those same parties, Kavanaugh and Judge tried to get girls drunk and disoriented so they could be "gang raped" by a "train" of boys.[45]

Notwithstanding these traumatic accounts, scholars, journalists, and politicians believed that Kavanaugh's youthful indiscretions should not bar him from a Supreme Court appointment. Although he disagreed with Kavanaugh's conservative politics, University of Pennsylvania professor Jonathan Zimmerman argued that Kavanaugh's sexual past was not disqualifying, because "of course he was different then; he was a third of the age he is now. And teens do stupid, dangerous and destructive things."[46] *The Washington Post*'s Kathleen Parker said, "So here we are debating an adolescent boy's qualifications to become a Supreme Court justice. What's next, his potty training?"[47] Retired federal judge Nancy Gertner said, "Teenage boys are nuts," and she has seen how allegations, even when found to be false, can unfairly tarnish young men.[48] Many others, mostly men, expressed concern that if Kavanaugh could be accused of something like this, all men were in danger of being put on the stand. Instead of denying the incidents ever happened, Kavanaugh's supporters tended to chalk up the assaults to adolescent folly—a prime example of how "boys will be boys."

Of course, "boys will be boys" has its fair share of critics. Unfortunately, too many of those critics have fallen into the trap of debating the validity of the adolescent development research instead of keeping the attention focused on the privilege and power that undergird the phenomenon that gives boys a pass for behaving badly in adolescence.[49] "Boys will be boys" is not just a shorthand summary of the developmental research showing that young people are reckless during their adolescent years. It is an excuse that is deeply embedded in privilege, power, race, gender, and entitlement. It is a mantra that creates a double standard not only between boys and girls but also between White boys and boys of color. Truth-telling about race and privilege doesn't invalidate the developmental research; it just explains how the science is applied differently across race and class.

White boys behave badly because they can. Society teaches White boys that even predatory sex is acceptable. It teaches Black boys that normal sexual behavior is criminal. Let's compare the experiences of two well-known student athletes—Brock Turner and Marcus Dixon.

### BLACK BOYS CAN'T BE BOYS: MARCUS DIXON

In 2003, Marcus Dixon was an eighteen-year-old Black senior, one class away from graduation at Pepperell High School in the Lindale suburb near Rome, Georgia.[50] Marcus was adopted at the age of twelve by his White parents, Kenneth and Peri Jones. He was raised in a largely White community in the northwest corner of the state, and his high school was 94 percent White at the time. With a 3.96 grade-point average, Marcus was a star in the classroom and on the football field. Teachers and students loved him and were elated that he earned a football scholarship to Vanderbilt University—that is, until he was charged with rape.

On February 10, 2003, Marcus's fifteen-year-old White classmate Kristie Brown accused him of forcing her to have sex in a classroom trailer. Marcus was charged with forcible rape, statutory rape, and child molestation. Critics complained that the charges were motivated by race. At trial, Marcus testified that the encounter was consensual and recalled Kristie saying, "My dad can't find out about us having sex because he'll kill both of us."[51] He understood that in his hometown Black boys having sex with White girls is "not something you do."

Although the jury agreed that the sex was consensual and found Marcus not guilty of rape and false imprisonment, they did convict him of statutory rape and aggravated child molestation due to Kristie's age. At the time, it was a felony offense in Georgia to have sex with a minor under the age of sixteen.[52] Kristie was three months shy of her sixteenth birthday. The judge sentenced

Marcus to ten years in prison, shocking the jurors and much of the public. The president of the Children's Defense Fund, Marian Wright Edelman, called the case a legal lynching.[53] Alvin Jackson, the former president of the Rome chapter of the NAACP, said the case had turned up long-hidden veins of racism in Rome, Georgia.[54]

Although both of her sons were excellent students and promising athletes, Marcus's mother recalls that "racism just underlies the whole thing. If that had been [her White son] Casey, instead of Marcus, they would have said, 'OK, this is a good kid—they wouldn't have done that.' But they didn't do that with Marcus."[55] Marcus's privilege of attending a White school and being adopted by White parents didn't shield him from the stereotypes that vilify Black boys. His status as a beloved football player didn't protect him either. Ironically, athletes have been notoriously excused for their sexual indiscretions relying on the "boys will be boys" retort.[56] But Black athletes who get lured into the permissiveness of the mantra soon realize they aren't entitled to the same grace and forgiveness as their White teammates. The detective investigating Marcus's case dug up every prior suggestion of sexual misconduct he could find—including a claim that Marcus had exposed himself in a prank and that he had inappropriately touched another girl.[57] White boys can be boys. Black boys cannot.

Marcus's story ends better than those of most Black youth in his position. Although this case almost ruined Marcus's life and career, the media coverage caught the attention of a corporate lawyer, David Balser, who offered to represent Marcus on appeal for free. On May 3, 2004, the Georgia Supreme Court ruled that Marcus should have been prosecuted only for the misdemeanor statutory rape, not the more serious aggravated child molestation.[58] Because Georgia lawmakers clearly intended for "sex between teenagers less than three years apart" to be punished with a maximum sentence of one year in prison, the court vacated Marcus's ten-year sentence and allowed him to go home.[59] By the time he was released, Marcus had already served more than a year in prison. The Georgia legislature later changed the statute used to convict Marcus. It is no longer a felony when teenagers agree to have sex.

After his release from prison, Marcus was able to go to Hampton University, where he became team captain on the football team and a star athlete. Although he described being in prison like "being dead,"[60] he exhibited extraordinary resilience in college, excelling in the classroom and earning the 2008 Arthur Ashe Jr. Male Sports Scholar of the year. Marcus went on to play in the National Football League for the Dallas Cowboys, New York Jets, and Kansas City Chiefs and in the Canadian Football League. Most Black boys are not so fortunate. Black boys without the grades, athletic scholarship, interest from college recruits, support and resources from White parents, and national media attention aren't likely to fare as well. They certainly aren't likely to fare as well as Brock Turner.

In 2016, twenty-year-old Brock Turner was a freshman at Stanford University. He was a champion swimmer with goals of competing at the Olympics. Brock was arrested after two students found him on top of an unconscious, partly clothed woman behind a dumpster outside a fraternity party.[61] The students intervened and held Brock until the police arrived. Unlike the jurors in Marcus's case, Brock's jury did not believe his behavior was consensual. Brock was convicted of three felony counts for sexual assault of an unconscious person, sexual assault of an intoxicated person, and sexual assault with intent to commit rape. The maximum sentence he could receive for his convictions was fourteen years in prison. The prosecutors requested six years. The judge sentenced him to six months in jail. Brock went on to serve only half that jail time, followed by three years of probation.

In justifying his six-month sentence, Judge Aaron Persky (a Stanford alumnus) spoke of Brock's positive character, lack of criminal history, and future and discussed the role alcohol played in the incident.[62] The judge was convinced that Brock would not be a danger to others and worried that a prison sentence would "have a severe impact on him."[63] "I think you have to take the whole picture in terms of what impact imprisonment has on a specific individual's life," Persky said at the sentencing.[64] Brock's father, Dan Turner, leveraged an implicit "boys will be boys" excuse when he trivialized Brock's crime as just "20 minutes of action out of his 20 plus years of life."[65] Mr. Turner argued that the media attention, loss of an athletic scholarship, and sex offender registration were more than enough punishment for his son. In his own letter to the judge, Brock blamed his conduct on the culture of partying and drinking at Stanford. Like the boys described in Kimmel's *Guyland,* Brock and his father expected Brock to benefit from the privilege of adolescence well into his early twenties.

More recently, a New Jersey judge, James Troiano, found himself in the headlines after he opted in July 2018 for leniency for a sixteen-year-old White boy who filmed himself raping an intoxicated sixteen-year-old girl, "Mary."[66] We don't know this New Jersey boy's name because he was tried in juvenile court and given all the protections of confidentiality. Court records list his initials as "G.M.C."[67] The sixteen-year-old boy assaulted his victim in a dark basement during a pajama party at a school gym. The boy filmed himself penetrating her from behind, with her head hanging down and her chest exposed. He later shared the video with friends and sent a text that said, "When your first time having sex was rape." Evidence also showed that before the assault a group of boys sprayed Febreze on the girl's behind and slapped her so hard she still had hand marks the next day. During the assault, the lights in the gym remained off, and the door was barred by a foosball table. Mary was later found on the floor vomiting with torn clothes and bruises. She was driven home by a friend's mother.

Judge Troiano declined the prosecutor's request to try the sixteen-year-old as an adult, noting that he was "clearly a candidate for not just college, but probably for a good college." He went on to highlight that the boy came from a good family, attended an excellent school, had good test scores, and was an Eagle Scout.[68] He reprimanded prosecutors for not telling the girl and her family that pressing charges would destroy the boy's life.[69] The judge even mused that the behavior wasn't rape at all, describing rape as something reserved for an attack at gunpoint by strangers. He dismissed the text messages as "just a 16-year-old kid saying stupid crap to his friends."[70] The judge's bias toward this White privileged teenager was so apparent that the appellate court issued a scathing fourteen-page opinion vacating the judge's ruling and criticizing the judge for deciding the case based on his own views rather than on the legal standard established for waiving children to adult court.

Of course, Judge Persky's and Judge Troiano's lenience toward Brock Turner and G.M.C. does not mean they would have punished a Black youth more severely. In fact, a group of public defenders who represented clients in front of Judge Persky defended Brock's sentence and believed he would have done the same for their similarly situated Black and Latinx clients.[71] And indeed, Black youth would benefit from a judge like Persky—a judge who is willing to consider both the nature of the offense and the promising future of the defendant. Unfortunately, the barriers to wealth and privilege for many minorities mean that few Black youth are "similarly situated" to Brock.

Even when material similarities do exist—as they did for Marcus Dixon—judges across the country are rarely as sympathetic as Judge Persky. Our country's long history of bias prevents judges, prosecutors, and probation officers from seeing Black youth with the same promise and potential as Brock. Data and research bear this out. A 2016 study of sentencing in one midwestern state showed that Black people were 78 percent more likely to receive a prison sentence than Whites for the same or similar offenses.[72] Defendants with darker skin tones and more Afrocentric features received the harshest sentences. A 2017 U.S. Sentencing Commission report found that Black men received 19.1 percent longer sentences for the same federal crimes as White men between 2012 and 2016.[73] Children transferred for prosecution in adult court face similar disparities, with reports showing that Black youth receive harsher and longer sentences than White youth in criminal courts.[74]

Research confirms that race has a significant impact on our perceptions of adolescent culpability and assessment of punishment for youth who commit serious crimes.[75] In one study of implicit bias in the criminal legal system, researchers provided participants with a factual summary of a recent Supreme Court case involving a violent young offender along with policy arguments in support of and in opposition to life without parole sentences for youth in non-homicide cases. Participants were asked to read about the brutal rape of an elderly woman by a fourteen-year-old male with seventeen prior convictions and take a position on youth sentencing policy. In half of the case summaries, study participants were told the child was Black. In the other half, they were told the child was White. Even among those who explicitly embraced a liberal political ideology, study participants who believed the offender was Black were more likely to favor harsher sentences, such as life without the possibility of parole, for serious youth offenders. Participants who believed the offender was White were more likely to agree that adolescents should be considered less culpable—and sentenced less harshly—than adults who committed the same crime.[76] Remarkably, a simple one-word manipulation of the race of the perpetrator shifted public opinion about how young offenders should be treated in the courts.

Stereotypes and presumptions about Black adolescent sexuality are so entrenched in our court systems that they can sometimes lead to absurd conclusions. In Washington, D.C., a sixteen-year-old boy pled guilty to a misdemeanor sexual assault. Before the sentencing hearing, the judge ordered the child to complete a sexual violence risk assessment with the court's mental health clinic. The assessment was designed to predict whether the child would present a "high," "medium," or "low" risk of harm to the community in the future and help judges, prosecutors, and probation officers make important decisions about the child, including whether he should be released back to his family after the offense. Unfortunately, the sixteen-year-old showed up to his evaluation with his pants sagging below his waistline, upsetting the psychologist, who was offended by his boxer shorts. The evaluator expressed significant concern about the youth's inappropriate attire and identified him as a high risk to the community. Although the child was before the court on a sexual assault charge, he otherwise had little prior contact with the court, was doing well in school, had a supportive family, and spent most of his time with well-behaved friends. These positive factors did little to allay the evaluator's concerns about his potential threat to others. Bias, stereotypes, and cultural ignorance fed the psychologist's belief that the youth's sagging pants were evidence of his sexual deviance and warranted a punitive sentence and all of the collateral consequences that would likely follow.

### OVERCOMING THE JEZEBEL MYTH: BLACK TEENAGE GIRLS

So much of the debate about sexual deviance among adolescents has centered on boys. But Black girls have been equally harmed by the historical stereotypes that overstate and criminalize Black sexuality to serve the political and economic interests of Whites. Like their fathers and brothers, Black women and girls have been portrayed as immoral, erotic, and seductive.[77] To fuel the institution of slavery that depended on Black women to produce more Black bodies for Whites to sell and control, White men used Black women as breeders and concubines. From slavery to Jim Crow, White men concocted hyper-sexualized images of a Black "Jezebel" to justify their abuse and oppression of Black women and girls.

Even as the first juvenile court opened its doors and other "benevolent" institutions were formed to save and rehabilitate troubled and neglected children in the early twentieth century, progressive child savers viewed Black girls as beyond redemption and did not believe that Black mothers could raise moral, well-behaved, and sexually restrained daughters.[78] Black women who resisted this narrative fought to prevent Black girls from being sent to reform schools where they might be involuntarily sterilized and subject to physical and sexual abuse by staff and guards who saw them as promiscuous.[79] Today, stereotypes that portray Black girls as "easy" and sexually mature lead to unwarranted and excessive discipline in school and harsh treatment by the police.

In 2017, researchers at Georgetown Law's Center on Poverty and Inequality surveyed a sample of adults about their perceptions of girls' development in the twenty-first century and found that adults view Black girls as less innocent and more like adults than White girls.[80] Survey participants perceived Black girls to behave older than their stated age, to be more knowledgeable about adult topics, including sex, and to be more likely to take on more adult roles and responsibilities than White girls of their age. These findings help explain why Black girls face more severe and more frequent discipline in school, greater use of force by school resource officers, and harsher penalties in the juvenile legal system. In her book *Pushout* (2016), Monique Morris takes a closer look at sexual stereotypes that cause educators to discipline or exclude Black girls from school.[81] Morris recounts stories from Black girls who are punished for being unladylike, inappropriate, and otherwise violating the traditional norms of femininity. Her narratives document the verbal and physical harassment Black girls experience from classmates and school staff and reflect the persistent sexualization of Black girls' bodies. Hyper-sexualized images of Black girls have followed girls from school to the juvenile legal system. In Washington, D.C., the percentage of young Black girls entering juvenile court has risen dramatically, even as that of young Black boys has decreased.[82] Our client "Mia" really helped me understand how Black girls are objectified and sexualized by the police.

My colleagues and I met Mia one summer when she was charged with burglary and theft. Mia had been arrested when she was found in the closet of an abandoned apartment. The police believed she had helped her boyfriend and his friends break into and steal from another apartment nearby. A White male detective from the Metropolitan Police Department (MPD) took Mia into a small interrogation room at the police station. Mia sat on a metal chair. The detective sat directly in front of her. Their knees were barely a foot apart. The detective initially appeared to be concerned about her, telling her that she had been reported missing and he was there to help. But the tone of the interview changed quickly as the detective got more aggressive—vacillating between sexually explicit come-ons, threats, scare tactics, and promises to help her if she would just confess. The shift started with "You are so lucky you're not my daughter . . . because where I grew up, guess what you'd be getting now? You'd be getting the belt." He then spent several minutes painting a grotesque image of Mia's likely future. He said, "I don't want to come into an apartment one day that's vacant, 'cause they said something smells real bad in there. And I see your dead body in there . . . Or you get hung up with the wrong guy, and like I said, next thing you know you're in Alaska somewhere being a prostitute and he's pimping you out. Or you get raped." The detective came back to this theme again and again. He seemed worried that Mia was being trafficked or taken advantage of by her boyfriend or the older men with whom she hung out.

Throughout the interview, the detective preyed on Mia's vulnerabilities as a young girl. At times, he employed the very techniques that pimps use to groom girls into sex trafficking—flattery, promises of protection, isolating the girl from her community, and getting to know the girl's interests in order to build trust. The detective pressed Mia about what she liked to do—modeling, school, dance, and the many possibilities for her future. At one point he commented on Mia's looks: "You're a pretty girl, you're tall . . . let's say you're a pretty young lady. If I were your age, I would date you. Seriously. You know? But you're running around with the wrong crew." The implication was clear. If Mia wasn't running around with the Black boys she was with, she could date someone like the detective.

Mia was especially vulnerable to the detective's tactics. She was only sixteen and had not begun the tenth grade. Her great-aunt took her in when she was young because her mother was in and out of her life due to an ongoing drug addiction. Mia had run away before, and there were public records indicating that she had been assaulted by her boyfriend—the same boyfriend with whom she was arrested. Understanding how much Mia would value his praise and validation, the detective manipulated and exploited her with the very sexual tropes he claimed to protect her from. His ploy worked. Mia even laughed and smiled when the detective suggested he would date her. Like the many other boys and men who saw her as sexually available and easy prey, the detective used her for his own gain—to close a criminal investigation. Toward the end of the interrogation, the detective offered her leniency if she confessed. "Like I said, you ain't gonna get in trouble, most likely. I mean, you'll probably go home." He kept Mia in the room for forty-five minutes until she began to talk about how the boys entered and stole from the apartment.

Sexual stereotyping is particularly damaging for Black girls like Mia who are trying to navigate their sexual identities.[83] Recent changes in the onset of puberty for Black girls have only complicated this process. Data from the 1960s shows that girls generally began to develop breasts at about age thirteen. In the 1990s, that age dropped to ten. By the mid-2000s, data showed that 25 percent of Black girls began developing breasts by the age of seven, while only about 10 percent of White girls develop breasts by that age.[84] Research suggests that changes in the age of puberty have been caused by the negative effects of chemicals that are increasingly common in American consumer products such as plastic, furniture, pesticides, hair care, and many meat and dairy items.[85] Developmental shifts also stem from obesity, family stress, premature birth, and changes in sleep patterns.

While boys often get an ego boost from early maturation that makes them more confident and popular, girls who begin puberty earlier are more likely to experience psychological trauma including depression, anxiety, panic attacks, and eating disorders. Early maturing girls stand out from the crowd and attract attention from boys who expect them to make decisions about sex before they are ready and from parents and teachers who judge them for being "fast" and acting older than their age.[86] Some youth who feel self-conscious around peers their own age hang out with older kids to fit in and gradually venture into activities they wouldn't otherwise try until later, including sex, truancy, smoking, drinking, and drugs.[87] These behaviors are especially common among girls who have been physically, sexually, and emotionally abused or abandoned by their families.[88] A child like Mia, who was both neglected by her family and described as "tall" and "pretty" by the detective, was particularly vulnerable to the seemingly positive attention of older boys and men, as well as the negative influence of delinquency.

Unfortunately, a child like Mia is also more likely to be punished as a criminal than supported as a victim or survivor of abuse and neglect. Like the Progressive Era courts of the early twentieth century, contemporary child welfare and juvenile legal systems are ill-equipped to effectively serve Black girls. The detective in Mia's case only pretended to care about her history of trauma and abuse and ultimately did nothing to help her. In court, the prosecutor treated Mia's case like any other, expressing no concern about the detective's investigative tactics and offering no leniency for her involvement in the boys' criminal scheme. When we highlighted Mia's history of domestic abuse and manipulation by older men, the prosecutor responded, "Well, if you are worried about your client, call the abuse and neglect division." In her mind, Mia was a felon because she helped her boyfriend enter and steal from a neighbor's apartment. Anything else was beyond her concern. Such narrow thinking, lack of interagency collaboration, and poor police training exacerbate the trauma girls like Mia experience and contribute to the unnecessary criminalization and sexualization of Black girls.

Even Black girls who commit less serious offenses to cope with abuse and trauma often face the harsh intervention of the court. The most common crimes for which girls are arrested—running away, truancy, and substance abuse—are also the most common symptoms of abuse.[89] Yet, despite the obvious signs of trauma, educators, police officers, and juvenile justice staff invest little time and resources into understanding and meeting their unique needs.[90] Girls who are victims of sex trafficking are arrested on prostitution charges, curfew violations, and incorrigible behavior. Girls who have been forced into criminal activity by their boyfriends face harsh sentences and little compassion from prosecutors and judges who lack the expertise, skill, and resources to address the trauma that motivates these behaviors.

In detention, girls are re-traumatized by the use of restraints, strip searches, the loss of privacy, and the emotionally isolating and punitive environment of the facility.[91] Worse, many girls experience additional physical and sexual abuse from other youth and staff in the facility. According to a 2018 survey released by the Bureau of Justice Statistics, over 7 percent of those in state juvenile facilities and large non-state facilities reported sexual victimization by staff or other youth in the twelve months preceding the survey.[92] And 5.8 percent reported abuse by staff charged with supervising them.

The proportion of girls arrested and incarcerated has continued to grow over the last two decades, especially for minor, nonviolent offenses. Girls of color are particularly affected by this trend.[93] Black girls, specifically, are 3.5 times more likely than White girls to be incarcerated.[94] In 2015, Black girls accounted for 15 percent of the female youth population in the U.S. but made up 35 percent of female delinquency cases and 34 percent of girls in residential placements, including detention and other secure and nonsecure out-of-home placements.[95] We should expect this trend to continue until adults release Black girls from the false and degrading stereotypes about Black sexuality and meaningfully appreciate the cultural, economic, and developmental factors that cause them to perceive Black adolescent girls as more promiscuous and delinquent than their White peers.

# 5

# Policing Identity: The Politics of Adolescence and Black Identity Development

In the spring of 2018, "Jamal" stopped by to visit his cousin who lived in an apartment in Northeast Washington, D.C. Just as he was leaving, Jamal noticed a police car drive up slowly behind him and stop in the middle of the street. The car was carrying three uniformed officers—two White, one Black. A White officer, in full uniform, with his gun visible on his waist, got out of the car and began walking rapidly in Jamal's direction. The officer yelled out, "Hey, sir, may I talk to you real quick? Did you just come out of the building there?"

Jamal stopped and turned to face the officer. "Yeah, I was trying to call my cousin."

"You live there?"

"No."

"Let me check you out. Do you have any weapons on you? You think I can pat you down real quick?"

Angered by the request, Jamal turned to leave just as the officer reached out to touch him. The officer grabbed Jamal's jacket, pulled him back, and tackled him to the ground. Another officer joined in to hold Jamal's face down in the dirt with a knee in his back.

"What you run for?"

"Cuz y'all just . . ." The officer cut him off, saying, "No, he told you to stop and he tried to grab you and you took off running."

"Cuz every time . . . I get locked up for nothing."

Unfortunately, this time Jamal had a gun in his jacket. Jamal was eventually taken to the juvenile detention center and charged the next day with possession of a firearm. My law fellow was appointed to represent him. When we interviewed Jamal, we weren't surprised that he had been locked up for the gun, but we were very confused about why the officer had stopped and searched him in the first place.

Jamal insisted that he had just been walking down the side-walk, texting on his phone, when the officer accosted him. At the detention hearing, an officer who had been on the scene admitted they weren't responding to any report of crime. They weren't responding to a citizen complaint. There had been no call for service. There was no lookout for a "suspicious" Black male in the neighborhood. And at no point prior to the search did the officers see Jamal do anything illegal. The only explanation the officer gave was that the building where Jamal had been visiting was a "known drug area." Even then, the officer admitted that Jamal didn't appear to be involved in any drug transaction. He didn't appear to be using drugs. And he wasn't holding anything that looked like drugs or a weapon. In fact, the officer admitted that he had not been called to that building in months.

From the very beginning, the prosecutors knew they would have trouble with this case. The law is pretty clear. Police officers can't stop and search someone just because they live, work, or visit in what the police have deemed a high drug area. The police must have a specific reason to believe that Jamal was committing or had committed some crime. There was no such reason in this case. About four weeks after Jamal's arrest, we filed a motion asking the judge to prohibit the prosecutors from introducing the gun as evidence against Jamal as a remedy for the officers' illegal intrusion. The prosecutors dismissed the case before the judge could even decide.

As we got to know Jamal in the short time we represented him, it became clear that in his mind everything in this case was about race. Jamal was tackled, handcuffed, and forced to the ground within twenty-five seconds of the officers' arrival in the block. Jamal repeatedly asked the officers to pick him up and get him out of the dirt. With his body contorted as he tried to keep his face off the ground, Jamal yelled out, "Can y'all just pick me up?"

One officer responded, "No."

"Y'all got cuffs on me. Where am I going to go?"

"It don't matter if we got cuffs on you. We don't know what you were running for."

"Can I just sit on the curb?"

"No."

"I'm trying to sit on the curb, what the fuck . . ."

"Sit your ass on the ground and shut up, all right?"

"You're a bitch ass, bruh. You got me sitting in dirt . . . can't even sit on the fucking curb."

As soon as Jamal scoots himself up to sit on the curb, the officer grabs him by his ankles and yanks him back into the dirt.

"Bruh, where the fuck is I'ma go to, bruh? Let me sit on the curb."

"Sit down, stop. You wanted to run before. Stop acting like a child now."

"But I am a child." Jamal was sixteen.

"Sit there and take it."

A few minutes later, the officer says, "You need to act like an adult."

"How can I act like an adult? I don't know how to act like an adult. I act like what I am, a child."

"Okay, you're no child."

Within a minute, at least two additional police cars, each with several more uniformed officers, come to the scene. The conversation continues antagonistically for several more minutes as Jamal repeatedly asks the officers to call his mother. The officers refuse to call until Jamal gives his full name, date of birth, and address. When Jamal finally offers his birth date, the White officer who initially stopped him continues to press him for his age.

Perturbed at the absurdity of the question, Jamal asks the officer in thick sarcasm, "Well . . . if I was born in 2001, how old am I? . . . Look, Black people are smarter than White people, so just shut up." A Black officer nearby chuckles.

Jamal continues, "You know I'm right . . . Oh, you ain't going to say nothing because you are in front of your Black friend."

The White officer grabs him by the arm and turns him around. "Just stop talking please."

With even more exaggerated sarcasm, Jamal says, "Oh, you getting offended? My bad. I apologize. I apologize."

"I'm not offended. It's just for someone who claims to be so smart, you make such dumb decisions."

"I don't make dumb decisions; I'm just worried about my life. Y'all ain't worried about my life, is y'all? No. Y'all worried about y'all life and y'all jobs . . . Y'all have plans."

Other officers jump in with equal sarcasm and no apparent sympathy for Jamal's plight. "Same way you planned to put that gun in your coat, right? No different. You got it all worked out. It's like one big puzzle you put together." Another officer, clearly taking a jab at Jamal's hairstyle, said, "Yeah. Everything matched together like your fade, like it just all came together today." Yet another officer followed with "You need to wipe that tear, man."

Later, as the officers were collecting his property for inventory, Jamal again became agitated as he asked the officers to give his money to a friend standing nearby instead of taking it to the police property division. "You do Black people wrong. Yeah, can y'all give me my money, yeah, that's why I only fuck with Black people. You see how he acting, you see."

At some point, Jamal sees a Black woman in her yard nearby and calls out, "Hey, excuse me, miss, can you call this number for me?"

She responds, "I'm not getting in none of y'all stuff. I'm just making sure everything is fair."

"You ain't seen it was fair how they were throwing me on the ground, though."

Again, for Jamal, everything in this case was about race. Race explained why the officers were always in his neighborhood— harassing and searching him—whether he did something wrong or not. It explained why the officers assumed the worst about him and why he always assumed the worst about the officers. It explained why the officers kept him in the dirt even after they had him in handcuffs. It explained why the neighbor came out of her home to make sure the police were "fair." It explained what his mother had taught him about Whites in comparison to Blacks. And it even explained why Jamal thought he had to carry a gun that day. It was clear that Jamal's understanding of who he was and what it means to be a Black teenager in America had been shaped by the many moments he had experienced or witnessed just like this. His very "identity" was developed in conversations with and about police officers like the ones who stopped him that day.

## RACE AND ADOLESCENT IDENTITY DEVELOPMENT

Although we are always evolving, a child's image of him- or herself becomes relatively fixed between childhood and early adulthood.[1] Adolescence is a time when young people develop the intellectual capacity to see themselves through the lens of others and begin to care about what others think of them.[2] It is a time when adolescents begin to think about how they fit into society and relate to other people.[3] Psychologists refer to this evolution as adolescent "identity development." It is one of the most important things that happens in this developmental stage.

The experiences we have during adolescence have a profound impact on how we see ourselves in the future. What adults and peers say to and about young people today affects how they will see themselves tomorrow.[4] How adults respond to adolescent behaviors now affects the way young people will behave later.[5] As to be expected, positive feedback helps youth feel better about themselves and improves their overall health and well-being. Negative feedback tends to reduce a child's self-esteem and contributes to mental health problems like anxiety and depression.[6]

In America's politically charged and racially divided society, race plays a central role in how adolescents think about themselves and their identities.[7] Even infants are able to recognize physical differences in skin color, but at that stage color is just a physical fact.[8] Race is neutral or insignificant. Most children are born to parents who look like them and don't understand what race means until much later. Youth only begin to think about race when they are "caught off guard" by some experience that exposes them to the importance of race in society.[9] White children are often able to live and flourish in a state of race neutrality for many years. Their Whiteness gives them privilege, opportunity, and a naïveté that shields them from what it means to have a racial identity. Their race rarely creates controversy for them in their early years, and many will make it to—and even through—adolescence without ever being challenged about their Whiteness.

Black children, on the other hand, are confronted by race almost from birth.[10] Some Black youth are intentionally caught off guard in the safety of their own homes by parents who try to prepare them for the discrimination they are likely to face outside. Others are exposed to race when they notice that Blacks are underrepresented in some activity they would like to join, excluded from some place they would like to be, or overrepresented in some experience they don't want to have, like school suspensions or arrests. In the most painful moments, Black youth are confronted by race through some violent or traumatic encounter with "Whiteness" that makes them realize their very lives and freedom are threatened by racial hatred.

Identity development is a daunting task for any child. It is even more daunting for Black youth who are forced to figure out who they are and what they want to be within the bounds of racial categories that were created to benefit some at the expense of others.[11] By the time they reach adolescence, Black youth are keenly aware of how other cultures view and devalue Blackness.[12] They grow up witnessing stark segregation in virtually every sector of society and observe Blacks portrayed in the most negative and stereotypical ways in the news and popular media.[13]

A 2006 study showed that 92 percent of Black youth surveyed

in Iowa and Georgia had experienced some racial discrimination by the age of ten.[14] A 2020 study found that Black teens aged thirteen to seventeen who were surveyed in Washington, D.C., faced an average of five racially discriminatory experiences per day.[15] These experiences occurred in person, online, individually, and vicariously through the shared experiences of friends and family. Some discriminatory experiences were subtle, while others were overt, including teasing about their skin tone and hair texture. As is common across the country, examples of racially discriminatory experiences in D.C. included unwarranted police accusations, being watched closely or followed around by security guards in a store or mall, being verbally abused by police, and noticing people lock their car doors, cross the street, or look at them as if they were criminal when they approached. In every setting, Black youth are made to believe they are out of place, out of order, or speaking out of turn.

In neighborhoods like Northeast D.C., where our client Jamal grew up, policing plays a central role in Black identity development. By the time he was seventeen, Jamal had survived many encounters with the police—each of which confirmed his sense that police would always see him as criminal. Jamal's resentment was palpable, and his guard was always up. Jamal spoke about his own identity in direct contrast to the officers' identity. That is, "Black people are smarter than White people." His affirmation of Black intelligence was part of his survival strategy to resist racist labeling. He both anticipated and experienced racism in every encounter with the police. Even the officer's teasing about his hairstyle was a subtle critique of his cultural identity. More important, Jamal sensed that the police didn't care about his people—Black people. Jamal's very decision to carry a gun rose out of his sense that Black people would never be protected by the police. Jamal's experiences were clearly shared by his friends and neighbors and became a source of bonding among complete strangers. Even when the neighbor was unhappy about Jamal's criminal activity in her community, she clearly wanted the police to know she was "watching" them too.

While many youth develop coping strategies as Jamal did to resist faulty narratives about their race, others struggle to disentangle those narratives from the positive messages they receive from their families and communities. It is quite normal for teenagers to experiment with different identities during adolescence.[16] In one season, they may strive for academic success. In another, they may be eager for attention from the popular yet delinquent crowd. In yet another, they may be politically outspoken about injustice and discrimination. Youth are more likely to settle on a negative identity when they have been rejected or ignored after trying their best to receive positive feedback from adults who are important to them. Students who are smart yet never acknowledged in class may eventually stop trying to get positive attention in the classroom and instead behave inauthentically to please or impress others, feel included, or hide some aspect of their personality that others don't appreciate.[17] Some students who believe they are not valued may disengage from school altogether and find support and community with other youth who are delinquent.[18]

For some, the onslaught of negative images is overwhelming. Without parents and other adults to help them navigate the many conflicting messages they receive about their identity, young people may subconsciously incorporate those negative images into their own perception of who they are.[19] Youth who are treated like criminals regardless of what they do often have a hard time seeing themselves any other way.

### IN MY PARENTS' HOUSE: RACIAL SOCIALIZATION AND BLACK IDENTITY DEVELOPMENT

Black parents cannot afford to ignore race. Society is not fair and just, and Black youth cannot count on the promise of meritocracy and "color blindness."[20] Adolescents need space to talk openly and candidly about race and what it means in their lives. After their first jarring encounter with race, young people begin to ask questions and sometimes even immerse themselves in learning about their heritage.[21] Black youth may adopt African names, become intensely interested in African or African American history, and find inspiration in Black culture. Youth tend to develop positive feelings about their own ethnic group during early and middle adolescence.[22]

For Black youth, racial identity is often framed as a liberation from Whiteness and a need to confront oppression.[23] Race begins to drive important decisions about religion, career, politics, family, marriage, values, and goals.[24] Race influences the music young people listen to, the television shows they watch, the clothes they wear, the books they read, the classmates they sit with, and the views they form about the police and the law. Frequent contact with youth who look like them improves adolescents' positive feelings about themselves and their ethnicity.[25] For many youth, racial identity becomes the most important organizing principle in their lives, often surpassing gender, religion, and socioeconomic class.[26]

Adolescence is the first time youth have the intellectual capacity to think ahead and consider what their lives might look like in the future.[27] To thrive, Black youth must transcend harmful racial ideas and stereotypes that seek to limit them.[28] Black youth benefit from counter-narratives like "Black Pride" and "Black Lives Matter."[29] Race pride helps Black youth like Jamal see themselves in counter-stereotypical ways and reduces stress by helping them resolve conflicting information about their race and culture.[30]

Relying on their newly acquired intellectual skills, adolescents can understand that other people may see them differently than they see themselves. Youth with a healthy sense of who they are learn to distinguish between their own opinions of themselves and the structural conditions that suggest something different.[31] A Black child may believe that "Black is beautiful" and at the same time understand that "White is powerful."[32] Despite their frequent encounters with racism and prejudice, Black teenagers can overcome barriers to success with the support and affirmation of adults in the Black community.[33] Approval from loved ones—like parents, teachers, and mentors—is much more important to adolescents' self-esteem than the opinion of the broader society.[34] Well-adjusted youth ultimately find their own sense of self and remain confident that they will become who they want to be.[35]

Parents often play the most important role in adolescents' racial identity development.[36] Parents may speed up racial identity formation with deliberate strategies to introduce and give meaning to race in every aspect of the family life.[37] This process of "racial socialization" requires a delicate balance. Parents walk a tightrope between preparing their children for the potential for bias and discrimination, on the one hand, and teaching them to distrust everyone who doesn't look like them, on the other.[38]

Parents' messages about racial identity are sometimes as basic as the lifesaving, matter-of-fact advice that keeps children safe in police encounters.[39] In much the same way parents teach their children to "stop, drop, and roll" in a fire, Black parents teach their children to "move slowly," "keep your hands out," "shut your mouth," and "just do what they say" when stopped by the police.[40] Unfortunately, at times, parents can create more stress and anxiety by over-preparing youth for the possibility of discrimination or by engaging in the conversation too early. When parents and other relatives describe their experiences with racism, youth may relive that trauma with nightmares, flashbacks, irritability, and anger of their own.[41] While it is important to help youth recognize and manage the more subtle signs of genuine racial bias, these lessons also make some youth more sensitive to the emotional pain of discrimination and hypervigilant to the possibility of threat from others.[42]

Parental messages about race can also make it difficult, and sometimes impossible, for Black youth to have any positive experiences with Whites.[43] Black youth who are only exposed to Whiteness as racist may develop an overly rigid view of race. When Black youth encounter a White person—or anyone who represents Whiteness—they may be confused, depressed, or angry at those they believe are responsible for their predicament.[44] They

can't imagine that a White person might ever be an ally or provide resources, support, and opportunity. Similarly, they can't
imagine that a police officer might ever help or care about their
safety. Youth who grow up in segregated schools and housing
have little opportunity to engage with Whites other than the
police. And because policing has been so closely aligned with
Whiteness in America, distrust of the police cuts across race lines.
Black youth like Jamal believe that Black officers are working to
preserve and enforce White power. Jamal was hostile to the Black
officers because he had not seen them stand up to their White
colleagues or speak out against injustice. His own experiences
with Whiteness through policing culminated in a complex blend
of anger, pride, and despair.

We should not be surprised, or even alarmed, when youth
like Jamal express anger or initiate conflict with White peers,
teachers, or police officers. These reactions are often psychologically healthy and even necessary as they construct their racial
identities.[45] Even as Whites experience these confrontations as
threatening and offensive, Black youth may need them to maintain their dignity and self-respect. Problems may occur, however,
when Black youth can't move beyond this stage.

Black youth may get stuck in anger, despair, and isolation
if they don't learn to balance the need to resist with the need
to function in a multiracial world. Adolescents whose parents
focus on the affirming aspects of racial identity are better at
navigating racism than those whose parents emphasize only the
dangers of Whiteness and racism.[46] Youth who can move beyond
simplistic Black-and-White thinking become less defensive and
learn to establish meaningful relationships with Whites who
are conscious of their own race-based privileges and behaviors.
As youth become more nuanced in their thinking and development, they can hold positive and negative messages about race
in healthy tension at the same time. They can feel secure in
their own identity as Black youth while also forming trusting
relationships with White allies.[47] They can also learn to turn

their rage at White people into anger at oppressive systems and racist institutions.

Black youth also learn to "act out" different identities in different contexts.[48] They may choose to act, talk, or dress differently in predominantly White settings than in Black settings. This "code switching" can be healthy and appropriate if it is the child's intentional and authentic choice. It is less affirming and less effective when it is imposed by parents and other adults who insist upon "respectable" Black behavior. As long as Black youth recognize that "Black respectability" can never fully protect them against the violence of racism, code switching can be an important temporary strategy to avoid unwanted attention and protect themselves against violence and harassment. Of course, not every child wants to code switch. In fact, many will construct their primary identities around protest and resistance. Black pride becomes the anchoring feature of their identity. It also presents another opportunity for police to criminalize Black adolescence.

### PROTEST OR RIOT? CRIMINALIZING RACE PRIDE

Just as young people begin to think about who they are individually, they must also think about who they are in society. Our identities are inextricably tied to the larger communities in which we live. Jamal is not just Black; he is Black American. He achieves his most authentic identity through the freedom, equality, and opportunity that America is supposed to offer him. Jamal's verbal resistance to the officers was something much more than "back talk." It was a form of activism and civic engagement—albeit nonconventional and mildly offensive. Jamal was validating his identity and insisting on his right to be treated with dignity and fairness.

Research suggests that youth activism plays an important role in healthy adolescent development. An individual's capacity to challenge, resist, and change their suffering is important in any democratic process.[49] We all need to feel heard and valued within our communities, and adolescents are no different. Organized social and political movements create a sense of belonging for youth—especially youth of color—who otherwise feel excluded from society.[50] Youth who are engaged in activism tend to feel better about society and themselves and tend to have more hope than those who sit on the sidelines.[51] Youth groups offer community, solidarity, and friendships and teach valuable leadership skills such as strategic thinking, effective decision making, and persuasive communication. Young activists learn to navigate bureaucracies and appreciate the power of collective action. Some youth find a lifelong purpose and meaning in organizing.

Many schools have recognized the value of civic engagement and now incorporate some form of civic participation in the academic curriculum.[52] Civic engagement can take many forms. Most often students are encouraged to volunteer in a soup kitchen or other charitable organization, raise money for a cause, or participate in electoral politics by campaigning for a local politician, voting, writing letters to elected officials, or petitioning. The unifying objective is to teach students to identify and address some issue of public concern.[53] Unfortunately, not all youth have the resources, opportunity, or even desire to participate in these more traditional forms of civic engagement. Youth who have been ignored and excluded from conventional politics may "act out" in ways that are socially unacceptable to dominant society. Black youth like Jamal may lash out at police officers, teachers, and others who stereotype and mistreat them.

Just as schools are teaching civic responsibility and encouraging youth to find their voice, police are responding in ways that tolerate some forms of activism and criminalize others. From the civil rights era to the contemporary Black Lives Matter movement, America has a long history of criminalizing activities that promote Black identity and demand civil rights. In July 1963, seven "Negro juveniles," aged sixteen to eighteen, were arrested and charged with trespass for sitting at a segregated lunch counter in a local pharmacy in St. Augustine, Florida.[54] The juvenile court judge offered to let the youth off with probation if they stopped protesting and stayed away from further demonstrations. The parents of three children agreed. The others refused. The judge sent the remaining four teenagers to the state reform school, where they stayed for six months. In 1968, Barbara Burrus and about forty-five other Black youth, aged eleven to fifteen, were arrested for willfully impeding traffic in Hyde County, North Carolina, after walking along Highway 64 singing, shouting, and clapping.[55] The youth, accompanied by adults, were protesting school assignments and a school consolidation plan.

Police today continue to criminalize Black youth for individual and collective protests against perceived injustice. In February 2019, an eleven-year-old Black boy was arrested in Lakeland, Florida, for refusing to recite what he described as the "racist" Pledge of Allegiance.[56] The arrest report claimed the boy was disruptive, didn't follow commands, called school staff racist, and threatened to beat up the teacher and get the school resource officer and principal fired. The boy insisted that he didn't threaten anyone. He was taken to a juvenile detention center and charged with disrupting a school function and resisting arrest. He was also suspended for three days.

Many of the recent mass protests have evolved in response to police and civilian brutality against Black Americans. Spontaneous rallies and mass protests in defense of Black lives are viewed as an affront to Whiteness and American civil order. Black youth who participate—or speak out on their own—are called "angry," "rude," "disrespectful," "volatile," or "dangerous."[57] Police are particularly sensitive to civic protests against police violence. Instead of engaging young activists in meaningful dialogue, police often criminalize protests, marches, demonstrations, hunger strikes, boycotts, and civil disobedience related to racial injustice. Black youth have risked retaliation, harassment, and violence to participate in protests after the killings of Black Americans like Tamir Rice, Rekia Boyd, Eric Garner, Michael Brown, Freddie Gray, Breonna Taylor, and George Floyd. Youth in Ferguson, Baltimore, Cleveland, and Minneapolis have been arrested for disorderly conduct, disrupting the peace, and rioting.

Often giving short shrift to the brutality that sparked the protests, politicians have villainized protesters in the media to justify
aggressive tactics such as teargassing, beatings, and the use of
riot gear. In 2020, President Trump described protesters in Minneapolis as "thugs" in a tweet about public demonstrations after
the killing of George Floyd.[58] Just four weeks prior, the president
had described a contingent of armed White men who stormed the
Michigan statehouse as "very good people" who "just want their
lives back."[59] Although it is illegal to bear firearms inside the
statehouse, the Michigan demonstrators openly carried weapons
in the senate gallery.[60] In stark contrast, even unarmed activists
in the Black Lives Matter network have been accused of domestic
terrorism, reverse racism, and bigotry.

In January 2017, Garry McCarthy, former superintendent of
the Chicago Police Department, accused the Black Lives Matter movement of promoting a "state of lawlessness," encouraging youth not to comply with law enforcement, and increasing
both civilian-on-civilian violence and civilian shootings of police
officers.[61] In July 2017, a police officer who was injured during a protest organized after a deadly police shooting in Baton
Rouge, Louisiana, sued Black Lives Matter and its local movement leaders.[62] The suit accused the movement and activists of
inciting violence against police. In August 2017, the FBI coined
a new designation, "Black Identity Extremists" (BIE), to warn
police departments across the country of a growing threat of
premeditated violence against law enforcement.[63] Using language
so broad that it would apply to almost anyone who challenges
racism,[64] the FBI defined a BIE as anyone who uses force or violence in response to perceived racism and injustice in America
and seeks to establish separate or autonomous Black social institutions, communities, or governing organizations.[65]

In December 2017, Rakem Balogun discovered that police had
been monitoring him for years when he was arrested for "domestic terrorism" in part because of his Facebook posts criticizing
the police.[66] Armed FBI agents stormed his house in tactical gear,
dragging him and his fifteen-year-old son out into the cold in

their underwear. Balogun has long been an activist, co-founding two groups to fight police brutality and advocate for the rights of Black gun owners. Investigators began monitoring Balogun after he participated in a rally in Austin, Texas, in March 2015. Balogun was angry and vented on social media about the police killing innocent Black men and women in America. He was locked up for five months and denied bail. He lost his home, his car, and his job with an information technology company. His son was forced to move and transfer schools. His newborn daughter spent much of her first year without her father before the U.S. attorney's office dropped the charges.

The message to Balogun's son and other Black teenagers was clear. Black identity expression is a threat to civil society. Just when we want adolescents to be thinking about who they are and how they can contribute to society, police officers teach Black youth that race pride and opposition to racial injustice can get them expelled from school, arrested, or even killed by the police.

# 6

## Cops in School

"Sharice" and "Mike" had been dating off and on for a year. They lived in the same neighborhood and went to the same high school. They were seventeen and loved each other in that intense teenage sort of way. But they had a lot of challenges. Sharice had a learning disability and emotional distress that caused her to overreact when she felt as if things were out of her control. Mike was a typical teenage boy. He was charming and attractive and liked attention from girls. Together they had a lot of fun, but they were also a ticking time bomb waiting to explode. And they did explode—a lot—and often at school.

Sharice was particularly frustrated with Mike one Friday after lunch. She yelled. They argued. And then, convinced that Mike was cheating on her, Sharice grabbed his phone out of his hand and began scrolling through his texts as she walked away. A school resource officer standing nearby knew the couple well and walked over to intervene. His "intervention" was to arrest Sharice—in the hallway, between classes, in front of other students. Sharice was picked up by the D.C. Metropolitan Police Department and charged with robbery for "taking the property of another without permission by stealth or force." Sharice spent the night in detention, appeared in court the next day, and had to meet with a probation officer for two months before her case was finally dismissed. Our defense strategy was largely to convince the prosecutor that this was an excessive and inappropriate—if not absurd—use of the juvenile legal system.

The officer who arrested Sharice defended his decision by arguing that this wasn't the first time Sharice and Mike had argued at school. He had seen Sharice in several other outbursts and wanted her to stop. Like so many other students in public schools around the country, Sharice attended a school without enough counselors.[1] When she got upset, she didn't know how to control her emotions, and there was no one there to help her. In this case, the officer believed he had "no choice" but to arrest her.

#### COPS AT THE GATE: RACE AND
#### DESEGREGATION BEFORE COLUMBINE

When I was in high school, my school looked like a school. Teachers were in the classrooms. Our principal was in the front office. We had a guidance counselor who helped us think about where to go to college or how to get a job. We had a gym, a basketball court, and a football field. Today, when I meet my clients at school, I can barely distinguish a school visit from a legal visit to the local youth detention center. At the front door, I am greeted by a phalanx of uniformed police officers, some of whom have guns at their side. In schools, these officers are called school resource officers, or SROs.[2] They are sworn police officers who patrol schools all over the country. In D.C., the officers tell me to take everything out of my pockets, put my items in a plastic bin, and run them through a metal detector. I am then instructed to walk through a full-body scanner, and if I wear big jewelry or have metal in my shoes, the officer will "wand" me again with a handheld detector on the other side.

I watch as students all around me are treated the same. There is a lot of verbal banter between the students and the officers— some of it playful, some of it hostile. At one school, an officer tells a child, "You know you're not supposed to have a cell phone in school. You need to sign that into the front office." The student lets out a loud sigh and drops the f-bomb. Another student yells out, "Man, I'm going to be late to class, let me go through." At least one student is asked to remove his shoes. As I look up, I can see security cameras in the lobby. And when I head to a classroom on the third floor, I am escorted to the elevator by an officer who wants to make sure I am okay. To put it mildly, the schools my clients attend look like prisons at the front door.

School resource officers appear in all fifty states.[3] They are visible in both urban meccas and small towns. In 1975, only 1 percent of U.S. schools reported having police stationed on campus.[4] By the 2017–18 school year, 36 percent of elementary schools, 67.6 percent of middle schools, and 72 percent of high schools reported having sworn officers on campus routinely carrying a firearm.[5] In raw numbers, there were ninety-four hundred school resource officers in 1997.[6] By 2016, there were at least twenty-seven thousand.[7] Because police operate under many different titles in schools, these numbers are surely low. Tallies often miss private security guards and neighborhood officers assigned by the local police department to patrol several schools without any formal agreement with the school district.[8]

According to a survey of school resource officers in 2018, more than half worked for local police or sheriff's departments.[9] Twenty percent worked for school police departments, and the remaining worked for some "other" category including the school district, an individual school, school security employers, private companies, and fire departments. Some school systems, like those in Baltimore, Indianapolis, Los Angeles, Miami, Oakland, and Philadelphia, have their own independent police departments.[10] The Los Angeles School Police Department has more than four hundred sworn police officers and one hundred non-sworn school safety officers.[11]

School resource officers often patrol with guns, batons, Tasers, body cameras, pepper spray, handcuffs, K-9 units, and handheld and full-body metal detectors like those found at an airport.[12] Some are even equipped with military-grade weapons such as tanks, grenade launchers, and M16s. In 1990, Congress authorized the transfer of excess Department of Defense property to federal and state agencies to fight drug activity. As of September 2014, almost two dozen public schools, including schools in Los Angeles, Florida, and Texas, had received military-grade equipment through the program.[13] Students in Los Angeles's Unified School District (LAUSD) were outraged to learn their schools had received the same types of military weapons that were used to suppress protests in Ferguson, Missouri, after Michael Brown was killed. The LAUSD Police Department returned those weapons in 2016.[14]

So what happened to cause such a shift in school culture since I was in high school thirty-five years ago? For far too long I accepted the simple and often repeated explanation that parents were terrified to send their children to school after the deadly mass shooting at Columbine High School in 1999. Although Columbine certainly played a role in the rapid expansion of school resource officers in the early twenty-first century, the National Association of School Resource Officers (NASRO) had already formed in 1991, eight years before the tragedy in Colorado.[15] Our nation's obsession with policing in public schools began long before Columbine. That story began in the mid-twentieth century, with the fight for—and against—racial desegregation.

The first law enforcement officer appeared in public schools as early as 1939 when the Indianapolis Public Schools hired a "special investigator" to serve the school district from 1939 to 1952.[16] In 1952, that investigator began to supervise a loosely organized group of police officers who patrolled school property, performed traffic duties, and conducted security checks after hours. The group was reorganized in 1970 to form the Indianapolis School Police. It is significant that the Ku Klux Klan controlled both the state legislature and the Indianapolis Board of School Commissioners from the 1920s through the formation of the early school police force.[17] The Klan had segregated Indianapolis schools by 1927 and kept them that way until the federal government intervened in the 1960s.

Other school districts began hiring police in the mid-twentieth century—more explicitly in response to the evolving racial dynamics in the country.[18] American cities had become more diverse after World War II as Blacks left the Jim Crow South in search of opportunities in industrial centers like Los Angeles and Flint, Michigan. Whites who were uncomfortable with the exploding populations and shifting demographics blamed the new migrants for emerging social problems such as poverty, racial and ethnic tension, and crime.[19] Teachers in Flint planted the seed—maybe inadvertently—for a law enforcement presence in schools during a 1953 workshop, when they expressed concerns about growing student enrollments and the potentially negative impacts of overcrowding, including delinquency.[20] Seeking to address these concerns, Flint educators, police, and civic leaders collaborated in 1958 to implement the nation's first Police-School Liaison Program and ultimately developed the framework for school resource officers as we know them today.[21]

Schools across the country followed Flint's lead. In April 1967, almost a decade after the first police-school alliance, approximately 150 educators, judges, and police officers from the East Coast to the West attended the first national Police-School Liaison Workshop in Flint.[22] The next year, police interns enrolled in the Mott Institute for Police-School Liaison Officers to learn how to implement similar programs in their local communities.[23] Programs sprang up in cities like Anchorage, Atlanta, Baton Rouge, Boise, Chicago, Cincinnati, Los Angeles, Miami, Minneapolis, New York City, Oakland, Seattle, and Tucson.

These programs emerged on the heels of the U.S. Supreme Court's 1954 decision in *Brown v. Board of Education* to end legal segregation in public schools. This landmark ruling came after years of advocacy by those who rallied against the separate and unequal school systems set aside for Black youth. In the years that followed, school districts across the country refused to integrate. In 1956, 101 White congressmen issued the Southern Manifesto, urging southerners to exhaust all "lawful means" to resist the "chaos and confusion" that school desegregation would bring.[24] As the mayor of Montgomery, Alabama, declared, "Every right-thinking white person in Montgomery, Alabama and the South . . . must make certain that Negroes are not allowed to force their demands on us."[25] In response, Presidents Eisenhower and Kennedy sent in federal military troops to force integration in Arkansas, Mississippi, and Alabama and fend off White residents who used violence and vandalism to prevent their children from having to commingle with Blacks.[26]

State and local governments also sent police into schools under the pretense of protecting Black youth. The real motives, however, likely had more to do with White fear, privilege, and resentment. Municipal leaders in the North and South claimed that Black children lacked discipline and feared they would bring disorder to their schools. In 1957, representatives from the New York City Police Department described Black and Latinx students in low-income neighborhoods as "dangerous delinquents" and "undesirables" capable of "corroding school morale."[27] Policing in schools also gave school administrators a mechanism for preserving resources for White middle-class students and keeping Black youth in their place.

Tensions escalated the following decade as Black students balked at Whites' opposition to racial equality and schools' bold refusals to integrate. In cities like Greensboro, North Carolina, and Oklahoma City students organized protests, walkouts, and marches to demand equal resources and opportunity.[28] Students also insisted upon culturally relevant curricula and basic dignity in the classroom. In November 1967, thirty-five hundred Philadelphia students walked out of school and marched to the board of education, demanding Black history courses, more Black educators, and the freedom to express their culture.[29] In October 1967, violence erupted between Black and White students in a Cincinnati high school.[30] Cincinnati newspapers blamed the unrest on the emerging Black Power movement and argued that activist groups like the Student Nonviolent Coordinating Committee and the Congress of Racial Equality were inciting violence. White middle-class Americans equated civil rights action with crime and delinquency, inflaming—and sometimes manufacturing—fears of a growing youth crime problem. In this turbulent climate, cities implemented school-police partnerships to combat a "problem" that police and educators explicitly and implicitly blamed on Black and other marginalized youth.

Policing in the schoolhouse grew in lockstep with civil rights protests and gradually became a permanent fixture in integrated schools. In 1966, the police department in Tucson, Arizona, assigned officers to six junior high school campuses as Mexican American students protested inequitable practices, advocated for a Chicano studies program, and resisted bans on bilingual education.[31] In 1967, eight armed and twenty-five unarmed policemen were assigned to conduct random "check-ins" in Washington, D.C.'s 136 elementary schools as part of their routine patrol.[32] Also in 1967, Thomas D'Alesandro III was elected mayor of Baltimore after campaigning on a school integration plan. That same year, the Baltimore City School District created a security division with more than twenty full-time police to govern its public schools.[33] By 1972, urban school districts in forty states had some form of policing in their schools.[34]

While most school-police partnerships started as local initiatives like the one in Flint, these programs began to draw federal support in 1965 when President Lyndon B. Johnson established the Commission on Law Enforcement and Administration of Justice to "inquire into the causes of crime and delinquency" and provide recommendations for prevention.[35] In its 1967 report, the commission predicted that youth would be the greatest threat to public safety in the years to come. The report drew a tight connection between race, crime, and poverty and frequently reminded readers that "Negroes, who live in disproportionate numbers in slum neighborhoods, account for a disproportionate number of arrests."[36] The commission referred to young people in racially charged language like "slum children" and "slum youth" from "slum families" and noted that many Americans had already become suspicious of "Negroes" and adolescents they believed to be responsible for crime.[37]

The commission devoted considerable attention to the problem of "ghetto riots." Although the commission rightly acknowledged the riots' role in protesting poor living conditions in the "ghettos," it also legitimized the more nefarious and popularly held beliefs about these upheavals. The commission described riots as giving "moral license to compulsively or habitually criminal members of the ghetto community to engage in their criminal activities, and to ordinarily law-abiding citizens to gratify such submerged tendencies toward violence and theft as they may have."[38] The commission's analysis aligned with television and newspaper reports that stoked fears by depicting civil rights protests as criminal acts instead of political demonstrations against oppression.[39]

Local and national media wrote about "roving bands of Negro youth"[40] taking over certain areas and "terrorizing residents" and engaging in "continual youth warfare."[41] The racial unrest, social disorder, and increase in youth crime during those years led many politicians to call for "law and order" reforms in the schools. Against this backdrop, local and state law enforcement agencies applied for federal grants through the Department of Justice's newly created Office of Law Enforcement Assistance (LEA) to fund new crime prevention plans like school-police partnerships.[42] Cities like Tucson and Cincinnati took advantage of LEA opportunities and received funds to expand their partnerships.[43]

Concerns about discrimination in school-based policing surfaced almost immediately, including in Flint, the birthplace of the school-police partnership. Notwithstanding initial concerns about delinquency in school, Black teachers and parents began to complain that Flint's Police-School Liaison Program targeted students of color. As reported in a 1971 review of the initiative, some teachers said the program was "aimed specifically at the black community" and was "anathema to black people" because it enforced "middle class white ethics and mores."[44] Other teachers described the police presence as a form of racist intimidation and recommended that officers be screened for racial and religious prejudice. Community leaders from civil rights organizations, such as the Michigan Civil Rights Commission and the Flint Urban League, also viewed the police force as intimidating and argued that "the program, as it operates, creates abrasiveness between the school administration and the black students."[45]

Claims of racial disparities in police enforcement showed up in other parts of the country. In 1979, White students rioted in the hallways of South Boston High School in opposition to mandatory desegregation.[46] While police allowed the White students to protest uninterrupted, they refused to allow ten Black students they identified as "potential troublemakers" to enter the school. Stories like these suggest that police were not assigned to protect Black youth and enforce integration but to control Black students and protect White youth and White-owned property.

The race-baiting and fearmongering that motivated the first school-police partnerships during the civil rights era were followed by the mythic lies of the "superpredator" craze in the 1990s. With crime on the rise and the crack epidemic at full throttle by the end of the 1980s, White fears reached epic proportions.[47] State and federal politicians accepted John DiIulio's highly publicized yet unscientific predictions of the coming band of Black teenage superpredators with reckless abandon and passed legislation to increase police presence in every aspect of Black adolescent life. Schools were a natural focus.

Congress passed both the Gun-Free Schools Act and the Violent Crime Control and Law Enforcement Act in 1994.[48] The Gun-Free Schools Act was passed to keep drugs, guns, and other weapons out of schools. The Violent Crime Control Act created the Office of Community Oriented Policing Services (COPS), radically increased federal funding for policing in communities, and laid the foundation for a new wave of federal funding for police in schools. States took additional steps to shore up school safety. For example, in 1998, the New York City Board of Education voted to transfer school safety from educators to the New York Police Department.[49]

And then there was Columbine. On April 20, 1999, the nation was rocked by a mass shooting at Columbine High School in Littleton, Colorado.[50] Two twelfth graders, Eric Harris and Dylan Klebold, murdered twelve students and one teacher. Twenty-one additional people were injured by gunshots. Another three were injured trying to escape the school. At the time, Columbine was the deadliest school shooting in U.S. history. Harris and Klebold had hoped to inflict even greater harm with several homemade bombs in the school cafeteria and in their cars parked in the school parking lot. Fortunately, the bombs did not detonate. The shooters were two eighteen-year-old White boys. The boys' journals and schoolwork suggest they had been planning the massacre for a year before it occurred. Some say the boys were infatuated with Adolf Hitler and planned the killing spree as an expression of their social and political beliefs. Others say the boys planned the attack to get revenge against the school and students who had mistreated them.

Whatever the motive, Columbine was the twelfth in a spate of school shootings committed by students between 1996 and 1999.[51] These deadly tragedies terrified parents and teachers all over the country and prompted increased funding for school safety everywhere. In October 1998, just months before the shooting at Columbine, Congress had already voted to allocate funding for the COPS in Schools grants program.[52] Days after the shooting, in April 1999, President Clinton promised that the COPS office would release $70 million to fund an additional six hundred police officers in schools in 336 communities across the country.[53] In 1998 and 1999, COPS awarded 275 jurisdictions more than $30 million for law enforcement to partner with school systems to address crime and disorder in and around schools.[54] Between 1999 and 2005, COPS in Schools awarded more than $750 million in grants to more than 3,000 law enforcement agencies to hire SROs.[55] At least ten states created their own grant programs to fund school police.[56] Years later, state and federal agencies renewed and increased their police in schools funding after the mass shootings at Sandy Hook Elementary School in Connecticut in 2012 and the Marjory Stoneman Douglas High School in Parkland, Florida, in February 2018.[57]

Although these shootings do explain the immediate increase in funding for police in schools, the shootings do not explain the disproportionate surge of police in schools serving mostly Black and Latinx students. Although the vast majority of the school-based shootings in the 1990s—and again in 2012—occurred in primarily White suburban schools, school resource officers are more likely to be assigned to schools serving mostly students of color. National data from the Department of Education's Office for Civil Rights reveals that youth of color are more likely than White youth to attend schools that employ school police officers.[58] In the 2015–16 school year, 54.1 percent of middle and high schools serving a student body that was at least 75 percent Black had at least one school-based law enforcement or security officer on campus. By contrast, only 32.5 percent of schools serving a student body that was 75 percent or more White had such personnel in place.

Not only are Black students more likely to attend schools with police on-site, but they are also more likely to be referred to law enforcement and arrested at school. Black students were three times more likely to get arrested at school in the 2015–16 school year than White students.[59] Although they made up only 15 percent of the school population, Black students accounted for 31 percent of students arrested or referred to law enforcement across the country.[60] That disparity was even greater for Black girls, who made up 17 percent of public school enrollment but represented 43 percent of girls arrested at school. In the 2017–18 school year, Black boys were 2.44 times more likely than White boys to be arrested at school, while Black girls were 3.66 times more likely than White girls.[61] These disparities persist notwithstanding evidence that Black students are no more likely than White youth to engage in the risky and impulsive behaviors that lead to arrest.[62]

The Columbine narrative is both too narrow and too broad to explain racially discriminatory policing in America's public schools. It is too narrow in its conscious and subconscious attempts to divorce contemporary school policing from the super-predator craze of the 1990s and the civil rights backlash that preceded it three decades earlier. It is too broad in its effort to capitalize on Columbine's violent tragedy as an easy and politically acceptable "cover story" for the continued proliferation of police in inner-city schools. Occurring on the heels of a decade or more of political efforts to demonize Black youth, the Columbine shooting arguably gave state and federal agencies a socially defensible and seemingly unassailable justification to increase funding for an infrastructure of police in schools that would criminalize Black adolescence and propel the mass incarceration of Black students.

CRIMINALIZING SCHOOL DISCIPLINE

The 1990s brought a rapid increase in both school suspensions and school-based arrests as police officers remained confused about their roles on campus and new laws were passed to criminalize normal adolescent behavior.[63] Administrators in the first school-police partnerships viewed school resource officers as part teacher, part counselor, and part law enforcement officer only when necessary.[64] The partners in Flint hoped to foster a positive relationship between youth and police, prevent youth crime, and provide counseling services for students believed to be at risk of delinquency.[65] As police became more entrenched in schools, students, parents, and civil rights advocates complained that police officers weren't trained to be counselors and worried about the potential for conflicts of interest when police tried to serve multiple functions.[66] Civil rights groups worried that police were violating students' rights through unsupervised interrogations, harassment, and surveillance.

Thirty years later, police still haven't figured out what schools want them to do, and schools haven't figured out what they want police to do. Only fifteen states require schools and law enforcement agencies to develop memoranda of understanding (MOUs) to specify the scope and limits of the officers' authority on campus.[67] When school districts do have an MOU, they usually focus on the cost-sharing aspects of the agreement and offer few details about when, where, and how police can intervene with students.

Guidance from the local police department is usually equally vague and overly broad. In Maryland, for example, Baltimore City School Police receive the same basic academy training as Baltimore City police officers, have "all the powers of any peace or police officer in the state," and operate with a full slate of general orders that govern the investigation of crimes within and beyond the schools.[68] In Oakland, the school security officers' policy and procedure manual described the officers' main role as providing a "calming presence" to the school community.[69] Officers were also authorized to enforce school rules, restrain and detain individuals, and search people and their property if they had reason to believe they were involved in a crime. The Oakland school board eventually voted to remove security officers from schools in June 2020.

Even when school resource officers are expressly hired to respond to emergencies and protect students from guns and serious threats of violence, they are quickly drawn into the more routine activities of law enforcement on campus. Forty-one percent of school resource officers surveyed in 2018 reported that "enforcing laws" was their primary role on campus.[70] Police often arrive with little or no training on how their traditional law enforcement roles should differ within the school context and even less training on developmental psychology and adolescent brain development. A 2013 study found that police academies nationwide spend less than 1 percent of total training hours on juvenile justice topics.[71] In the 2018 survey, roughly 25 percent of school police surveyed indicated they had no experience with youth before working in schools.[72] Sixty-three percent reported they had never been trained on the teen brain; 61 percent had never been trained on child trauma; and 46 percent had never been trained to work with special education students. Without better training and guidance, police in schools do what they always do. They detain, investigate, interrogate, and arrest. They also intervene with force—sometimes violent and deadly force. Policing has become such an integral part of the school setting that many schools have offices or other spaces set aside specifically for police to detain and interrogate students and conduct other police business. In Illinois, the police department set up "booking rooms" where officers can process students arrested on campus.[73]

Ultimately, more police in schools means more arrests—three and a half times more arrests than in schools without police.[74] And it means more arrests for minor infractions that teachers and principals used to handle on their own. When I was in high school in the mid-1980s, we were sent to the principal's office when we acted out. Sometimes we had to stay after school for detention. I even got suspended once for "play fighting" with one of my classmates, but I was never arrested. Today, children like my client Sharice get arrested regularly at school, and mostly for things kids do all the time: fighting or threatening a classmate, breaking a window in anger, vandalism and graffiti, having weed, taking something from someone on a dare, arguing in the hallway when they are supposed to be in class.

Data from across the country mirrors what I see in D.C. Although only 7 percent of officers surveyed in 2018 described their duties as "enforcing school discipline," evidence shows that educators routinely depend on police to handle minor misbehaviors such as disobedience, disrespectful attitudes, disrupting the classroom, and other adolescent behaviors that have little or no impact on school safety.[75] State lawmakers have even passed laws making it a crime to disturb or disrupt the school. As of 2016, at least twenty-two states and dozens of cities and towns outlaw school disturbances in one way or another.[76]

The Maryland state legislature adopted its "disturbing schools" law back in 1967, shortly after the Baltimore City School District created its school security division.[77] During the 2017–18 school year, 3,167 students were arrested in Maryland's public schools.[78] About 14 percent of those arrests were for "disruption." Until May 2018, students in South Carolina could be arrested for disturbing the school if they "loitered about," "acted in an obnoxious manner," or "interfered with or disturbed" any student or teacher at school.[79] The penalty was a $1,000 fine and a possible ninety-day sentence in jail. In the 2015–16 academic year, 1,324 students were arrested or cited in South Carolina for disturbing schools, making it the second most common delinquency offense referred to the family court.[80] Black students were almost four times more likely than White youth to be deemed criminally responsible for disturbing schools.[81] South Carolina lawmakers finally eliminated the crime in 2018, three years after the nation watched the sheriff's deputy yank sixteen-year-old Shakara Murphy from her seat in her Spring Valley math class.

In McKinney, Texas—the city now famous for the police assault on bikini-clad Black girls at a pool party—disorderly conduct and disruption of class were the two most common offenses charged by SROs from 2012 to 2015.[82] Although Black students made up only 13 percent of the city's school population, they accounted for 53 percent of the disorderly conduct arrests and 43 percent of the disruption of class offenses charged. In Florida, 50 percent of school arrests in 2018–19 were for misdemeanor offenses like disorderly conduct and minor assaults associated with a school fight.[83] A thousand Florida students were arrested for school-related disorderly conduct alone, which was the most common reason for the arrest of Black and Latina girls in Florida public schools.[84] While Black girls made up 22 percent of Florida's total female student population, they accounted for 74 percent of female students arrested for disorderly conduct.

Most kids who get arrested at school aren't the violent teenagers we worry about. Instead, they are Black teenagers like my seventeen-year-old client Sharice, who grabbed her boyfriend's cell phone to see whom he had been texting, or my fifteen-year-old client Eric, who put liquid in a bottle that looked like a

Molotov cocktail. Even teenagers who have been arrested for what sound like serious violent offenses are often still just being teenagers. Remember Sharice was charged with robbery, making her a "serious felon" in the FBI crime statistics. Eric was charged with attempted arson, another serious crime. Another one of my clients, "Renee," became a serious felon after grabbing her teacher's hat on a bus.

Renee was sixteen and enrolled in a school for students with special needs. One afternoon, she was riding a public bus with five classmates when she recognized her teacher's aide seated at the back of the bus. Seeking attention from her friends, Renee snatched the aide's hat and tossed it to one of her classmates. After playing a game of catch through peals of laughter, the children dropped the hat and got off the bus. Unfortunately, the hat got lost in the melee. Still angry the next morning, the aide called the police when the students arrived at school. Renee was charged with robbery, forever branding her a "dangerous felon" and conjuring up fears that far exceed anything she actually did. Renee's behavior—albeit unfair to the teacher—wasn't that different from the pranks and teasing that children of all races participate in all over the world.

Renee and her classmates all had intellectual and emotional disabilities that made it hard to learn and even harder to sit still and behave in school or on the bus. Data suggests that one in five students in the United States will develop mental health difficulties significant enough to warrant a diagnosis.[85] Because the majority of mental health concerns first emerge during adolescence, school staff are often the first to see children who are distressed or traumatized, especially in low-income districts.[86] Youth today are experiencing record levels of depression, anxiety, and trauma.[87] Approximately 72 percent of children in the United States will have experienced at least one major stressful event, such as witnessing violence, experiencing abuse, or suffering the loss of a loved one by the age of eighteen.[88] One in ten students will be affected by their mental health needs enough to require support services from their school. Unfortunately, most schools don't have the resources to help students deal with these challenges. Policing only makes them worse.

Despite this disturbing data, we continue to spend more money on law enforcement than on mental health supports. According to a report prepared by the American Civil Liberties Union in 2019, 1.7 million students attend schools with police but no counselors.[89] Six million students attend schools with police but no school psychologist. Ten million students attend schools with police but no social workers. Black students are three times more likely to attend a school with more security than mental health personnel. Almost 21 percent of middle and high schools serving mostly Black students had more security on campus in 2016 than staff available to support students' mental health needs.[90] Among predominantly White schools, this number was only 2.5 percent.

With so few resources to support and manage students with special needs, disabilities, and related behavioral problems, teachers frequently turn to law enforcement for help. Students with disabilities are nearly three times more likely to be arrested than students without disabilities.[91] That risk is multiplied for Black and Latinx students with disabilities. In the 2015–16 school year, Black boys with disabilities were arrested at five times the rate of all students. Although Black and Latino boys with disabilities together made up only 3 percent of student enrollment nationally, they accounted for 12 percent of all student arrests.

As parents, students, and teachers have long feared, police officers are not well suited to navigate the range of emotional and psychological issues students exhibit in school. And in many cases, police do more harm than good. The officer who arrested Sharice for snatching her boyfriend's phone didn't do anything to help her, her boyfriend, or the school. Mike didn't need the officer's help. He wasn't afraid of Sharice, and he wasn't worried about getting his phone back. He knew Sharice would eventually calm down. The school also wasn't any safer, quieter, or more conducive to learning in Sharice's absence. Sharice's quarrel with Mike barely caught anyone's attention until the officer put her in handcuffs and dragged her away. In the days and weeks that followed, our juvenile court didn't do anything to improve Sharice's coping skills or her relationship with Mike. In fact, it only created more stress.

### TELLING THE COPS FROM ROBBERS: MORE GUARDS, LESS SAFETY

Police in schools are symbolic. They provide an easy answer to fears about violence, guns, and mass shootings. They allow policy makers to demonstrate their commitment to school safety. And for a time, they make teachers and parents "feel" safe. But those who have studied this tell us this is a false sense of security.

Schools with school resource officers are not necessarily any safer. An audit from North Carolina, for example, found that middle schools that used state grants to hire and train SROs did not report reductions in serious incidents like assaults, homicides, bomb threats, possession and use of alcohol and drugs, or the possession of weapons.[92] And many advocates for police in schools forget that school resource officers were widely criticized for their failures to intervene in the shootings at both Columbine and Parkland. The officer in Columbine followed local protocol at the time and did not pursue the shooters into the building.[93] Many speculated that if he had, there was a good chance the gunmen would not have reached the library, where so many students were targeted. Instead of immediately confronting the threat, school police secured the scene and waited for SWAT teams to arrive. The sheriff's deputy who was assigned to the Marjory Stoneman Douglas High School in Parkland also never went in the building despite an active-shooter policy that instructed deputies to interrupt the shooting and search for victims after a cease-fire.[94] Students later complained that they saw the armed deputy standing outside in a bulletproof vest while school security guards and coaches were running in to shield the students.

Police don't make students feel safer—at least not Black students in heavily policed communities. To the contrary, police in schools increase psychological trauma, create a hostile learning environment, and expose Black students to physical violence. For students who have already been exposed to police outside school, negative encounters with police in school confirm what their parents and neighbors have told them. Black students enter their schools to be accosted by the same officers who stop, harass, and even physically assault their family and friends on the street. In much the same way they resent aggressive and racially targeted policing in their communities, students resent inconsistent and unfair school discipline. Black students don't feel welcome or trusted at school and are less likely than White students to report that school police and security officers have treated them with respect.[95]

For many students, schools have become a literal and figurative extension of the criminal legal system. As schools increasingly rely on police officers to monitor the hallways and control classroom behavior, students feel anxious and alienated by the constant surveillance and fear police brutality.[96] Over time, students transfer their distrust, resentment, and hostility toward the police to school authorities. Teachers become interchangeable with the police, principals become wardens, and students no longer see school staff as educators, advocates, and protectors. Students often talk about school discipline as if it were a criminal case. In a survey of students, parents, and teachers in a suburban midwestern high school, Black parents expressed concern about racial bias in the way their children were disciplined, while Black students spoke about suspension, expulsion, and other disciplinary proceedings with words like "crime," "self-defense," "guilty," "prisoner," "offender," "assault," "felony," and "misdemeanor."[97] Teachers used words like "charged," "locked up," and "trespass."

Racially disparate policing and discipline affect how students think about themselves and their behavior at a critical time in their development. Black youth are made to believe their teenage behaviors are criminal and unalterable; White students are treated as if those same behaviors are fleeting and normal for their age. Black students who feel devalued by unfair disciplinary practices are more likely to withdraw and become delinquent.[98]

Policing in schools creates a vicious vortex. Students in heavily policed environments are less likely to be engaged and more likely to drop out.[99] Youth who drop out are more likely to be arrested. There is a reason that children who drop out end up in the juvenile legal system. It's not just that they have more time on their hands; it's that they have more time on their hands at a stage in life when they are most impulsive and least likely to exercise self-control.[100]

School resource officers often measure their success by arrest rates and rarely consider the negative impact of policing on an adolescent's development, educational prospects, and future. Hostility between students and the police creates a negative school environment that makes learning very difficult. Research in brain science shows that stress can disrupt learning by preventing the brain from retrieving and retaining long-term memories and from updating old memories in light of new information.[101] Stated simply, students who are scared, anxious, and hurting don't learn well.

Students who don't learn well perform poorly on tests. This might help explain the results of a recent study finding that increased police presence in New York City neighborhoods reduced the test scores of Black male students.[102] It might also help explain why researchers in Texas found that an increase in funding for law enforcement in schools was followed by a 6 percent increase in school discipline, but a 2.5 percent decrease in high school graduation rates and a 4 percent decrease in college enrollment.[103] In California, schools with a higher security-staff-to-student ratio also report an increased loss of instruction for Black students, suggesting that police in schools are directly involved in routine discipline or contribute indirectly to a harsher, more exclusionary climate.[104]

Not only do students *feel* less safe in school, but they *are* less safe. Policing in schools puts Black children at risk of physical harm. Deputy Ben Fields attracted national attention when he dragged Shakara from her desk, but he is not an outlier. Far too often, police contact with youth involves physical violence, verbal abuse, and psychological trauma. Students have been sent to the hospital for lacerations, broken noses, bruises, bleeding, severe brain hemorrhaging, bone fractures, broken jaws, stitches, concussions, blurry vision, and broken wrists.[105] Although schools rarely track police-student contact and use-of-force data,[106] news reports and anecdotal student accounts are far too prevalent to dismiss them as the actions of a few rogue officers.

Organizations like the Alliance for Educational Justice (AEJ) have been tracking police assaults in schools across the country for many years.[107] Since 2009, AEJ has recorded numerous stories from students of color, as young as twelve years old, who have been hit on the head, choked, punched repeatedly, slammed to the ground, kneed in the back, dragged down the hall, pepper sprayed while handcuffed, shocked with a stun gun, tased, struck by a metal nightstick, beaten with a baton, and even killed by police at school.[108] In one particularly vicious encounter in Tampa, a school resource officer grabbed a Black female student by the ankles and snatched her legs out from under her. In another, a school resource officer in Houston, Texas, flipped a fifteen-year-old Black girl to the ground and pinned her down with his elbow on her throat. Most recently, in January 2021, sixteen-year-old Taylor Bracey was knocked unconscious and suffered from headaches, blurry vision, and depression after being body-slammed on a concrete floor by a school resource officer in Kissimmee, Florida.[109]

Students with disabilities feature prominently in many of these stories. In Dallas, an officer tased a seven-year-old Latino boy with a mood disorder and attention deficit and hyperactivity disorder (ADHD) after responding to a report that the student was banging his head against a wall.[110] In Louisiana, an officer dragged a ten-year-old Black girl with autism by the ankles after she left her classroom and tried to climb a tree.[111] The officer knelt on her back and pinned her face into the ground, making it difficult for her to breathe.

Most often, police violence is inflicted in response to nonviolent student behaviors. Students have been physically assaulted for wearing a hat indoors, not tucking in their shirts as required by the dress code, being late to class, going to the bathroom without permission, participating in school demonstrations, fighting in school, having marijuana, being emotionally distraught, cursing at school officials, refusing to give up a cell phone when asked, arguing with a parent on campus, and throwing an orange at the wall. After Michael Brown was murdered in Ferguson, Missouri, investigators from the Department of Justice found that officers in the local school district often used force against students of color for minor disciplinary violations like "peace disturbance" and "failure to comply with instructions."[112] In one instance, a fifteen-year-old girl was slammed against a locker and arrested for not following an officer's orders to go to the principal's office.

In 2015, a school resource officer in Baltimore pled guilty to three counts of second-degree assault for hitting a middle school student in the head with a baton and pepper spraying two others while they were restrained.[113] Criminal convictions like this are rare. Police are seldom held accountable for discrimination, assault, or using excessive force. The lack of clarity about the scope and limits of the officer's role in school makes it difficult if not impossible for parents and students to sue or take other action against the police. Student and parent handbooks provide little information about grievance procedures and the role of officers in schools. In many jurisdictions, students have no clear mechanism through which to file a complaint with the school or the police department.[114] Even when there is a formal complaint process, students find it difficult to prove that police acted with a discriminatory intent.[115] Absent an extended pattern of discriminatory behavior, courts typically find police to be acting reasonably and within the scope of their authority.

Students who attempt to record and challenge police brutality on their own have been physically assaulted, disciplined, and arrested in response.[116] Niya Kenny's arrest after she recorded the school deputy in Spring Valley is well known, but there are others. When high school junior Brian Burney was assaulted by a school police officer at Benjamin Franklin High School in Philadelphia, a classmate started recording.[117] Another officer demanded that the student delete the footage or risk arrest. A teacher later seized the phone and deleted the footage herself. A fourteen-year-old student who recorded the principal at Woodland Hills High School in Pittsburgh was arrested for "wiretapping" after he exposed the principal for making violent threats against students.[118]

At its worst, aggressive and unfair policing can initiate rather than reduce crime and misconduct among students who have lost trust in school officials and feel anxious and angry with the police.[119] Students who resent police intrusion have less respect for the rules and the officers who enforce them and may act out with physical and verbal aggression.[120] Instead of ensuring safety and fostering cooperation, police often heighten disorder among students and diminish the authority of school staff.[121]

Students of color have characterized policing in schools as a coordinated and intentional effort to control and exclude them.[122] Ironically, proponents of the federally funded COPS in Schools grant program hoped that sending police to schools would improve the image of police generally and increase the level of respect that young people have for the law and the role of law enforcement.[123] Even Flint's first school-police partnership was framed as an attempt to "improve community relations between the city's youth and the local police department."[124] To date, these efforts have failed. Police in schools remain deeply entrenched in their traditional law enforcement roles and have been unable to dislodge youth's negative opinions and attitudes about them.[125] The more recent and highly visible incidents of discrimination and brutality against students of color only reinforce historical images of the police as a tool of racial oppression.

THE PAST AS PROLOGUE: SEPARATE AND STILL UNEQUAL

Now, sixty-five years after the Supreme Court ruled that racial segregation in public schools is illegal, Black youth are still systematically denied free, safe, and appropriate education. School segregation is now achieved and maintained through school-based arrests and exclusions that deny Black youth access to a high school diploma and all of the opportunities that diploma can provide. In modern America, where formal education is the primary gateway to college, employment, and financial independence, policing in school puts Black youth at a severe disadvantage.

Adolescence is the worst time to stop or delay the learning process with extreme and unnecessary discipline. Adolescence is the last significant stage of brain development and the time when we acquire the final set of skills and abilities we need to function independently in society.[126] The adolescent brain has a remarkable ability to adapt as long as we keep young people engaged in novel, challenging, and cognitively stimulating activity.[127] Forcing students out of schools and into the regimented schedule of a juvenile or adult prison narrows the brain's opportunity to evolve in ways that help them think critically and make good decisions. People who are bad at reasoning, planning, and regulating their emotions and behaviors have a hard time excelling in contemporary society.[128] Even for youth who commit serious crimes, pushing them out of school is the worst thing we can do. Most youth will age out of delinquent behavior naturally with little or no intervention.[129] But even those who need more accountability will benefit from the emotional support and guidance of teachers, counselors, coaches, and positive peers who can help them set new goals and identify new opportunities.

Given how little school-based arrests achieve, current policing strategies can no longer be justified as necessary for school safety. The unnecessary and extreme discipline of Black youth has little to do with the school-based massacres of the 1990s. Columbine can't explain police involvement in routine school discipline, dis-criminatory enforcement of school rules, or massive spending on the police infrastructure in American schools. And it certainly can't explain the violent force that is used to control children of color and manage children with disabilities. It is about time we admit that our infatuation with policing Black children in schools was never about Columbine.

7

## Contempt of Cop

"Marquette" and "Shanna" have lived in Washington, D.C., all of their lives. One lives in Southeast D.C., and the other lives in Northwest. Both are Black teenagers who had similar encounters with the police in the fall of 2018. Marquette's encounter began when he met his two older brothers after school at a Rita's Italian Ice. Conveniently located near a bus stop down the street from Marquette's high school, Rita's is a popular hangout for kids heading home after class. On this day there were at least ten other students at the shop, most of whom were standing outside near the take-out window.

About twenty minutes after Marquette arrived, an officer who worked at the school walked up and ordered everyone to leave. The officer said the group was blocking the entrance. Marquette insisted he was not. Marquette also heard the officer say, "If y'all are smoking, move." Marquette wasn't smoking and didn't move. He assumed the warning didn't apply to him. For that, he was handcuffed and hauled away while his brothers watched, confused about what he had done. There had been no physical altercation. No argument. No call for help from the shop. And no opportunity for Marquette to explain why he was standing there. In fact, Marquette was good friends with the take-out clerk and had already asked her if he was in the way. She assured him that he was not.

At the age of sixteen, Marquette spent the night in the juvenile detention center and was charged the next day with "incommoding"—a charge I had never heard of in twenty-four years of practice in D.C.'s juvenile court. Basically, it means blocking passage. In her report, the arresting officer said she told Marquette to move and he refused. She also described his behavior as "disorderly." Fortunately, the prosecutor disagreed and did not add disorderly conduct to his charges. Marquette was supervised by a probation officer for almost two months before he agreed to participate in a mediation with the arresting officer in exchange for dismissal of his case.

Like Marquette, Shanna was arrested at a popular after-school hangout. Shanna left her high school in Northwest D.C. and walked three blocks to a McDonald's where her classmates usually met in the afternoon. Fifteen to twenty teenagers were on the sidewalk, laughing, talking, and being silly. At some point, one of the McDonald's employees called the police to get the kids to quiet down and move away from the door. When three marked police cars and six uniformed officers arrived, the children were visibly agitated and annoyed by the extreme show of authority. One of the boys flipped the officers off with his middle finger. Several others cursed and yelled. Almost all refused to move. The incident escalated quickly when Shanna began threatening the officers, saying she would spit on them and "beat their asses." Shanna called one of the officers a "bitch," and police described her as "aggressive" and "combative."

Shanna describes her experience with the police quite differently. She says she was just asking the police for help because one of the McDonald's employees had taken her cell phone. The officers refused to listen and kept telling her to leave. Shanna felt angry and defeated and remembers being surrounded by four officers—three men and one woman—in uniform with guns at their waists. She felt trapped and admits that she "kirked out" when one of the officers grabbed her arm. What the officers didn't know was that Shanna had been removed from her mother's home just weeks before, after allegations of physical abuse. Shanna was living in a foster home and separated from her mother for the first time ever. She was fifteen. No one stopped to figure out why she was so emotionally distraught. No one gave her time to calm down. Instead, the police wrestled her to the ground and put her in handcuffs, leaving bruises on her hands and arm. She was five feet tall and 120 pounds. Like Marquette, Shanna was arrested and detained overnight. She was charged the next day with threats, resisting arrest, and unlawful entry for refusing to move from in front of the McDonald's. She was also charged with assault on a police officer because the officers said she kicked one of them during the takedown.

Marquette's and Shanna's experiences were remarkably similar. They were both doing what teenagers do—hanging out with friends and maybe being rowdy after school. Neither had drugs or weapons. Neither had been accused of any serious crime. Even Shanna's "combative" stance didn't involve physical aggression until the officers put their hands on her. Although McDonald's asked the police to move the teenagers out of the way, no one complained of any crime on the property. Rita's didn't even call the police.

So why were these two children stopped, arrested, and physically assaulted for such minor misbehavior? They had the audacity to disobey and disrespect an officer. They were guilty of "contempt of cop."

### CONTEMPT OF COP: A.K.A. DISSIN' THE POLICE

Disrespecting a police officer is not a crime. Our Constitution protects people who question, rudely speak to, or even yell at the police—at least until their words become "fighting words." Fighting words are intentional. They are meant to harm others or truly frighten others about the possibility of getting hurt.[1] Short of that, we live in a country that allows us to talk back to, criticize, and curse at the police without getting arrested. These are the benefits of living in a free state.[2] We expect properly trained officers to have "thicker skin" and exercise more restraint than the average citizen. We don't expect them to retaliate or respond belligerently to verbal attacks or provocation. And we certainly don't expect them to lose their cool in response to adolescent emotion and bravado. Yet that is exactly what happens far too often.

"Contempt of cop" is a phrase commonly used by judges, attorneys, the public, and even officers themselves to describe arrests for disrespecting the police.[3] The phrase is a play on the term "contempt of court," which is an actual offense for being discourteous or defiant of a court's rulings or decorum. Contempt of cop arrests typically involve the arbitrary and unlawful detention of individuals who express their views about the law and law enforcement or who otherwise assert their rights as guaranteed by the Constitution. As one might expect, many of these arrests occur after an individual's claim of racial bias or resistance to some perceived racial injustice. The arrests rarely serve a legitimate law enforcement purpose and often involve excessive force or brutality as a retaliation for the individual's challenge to the officer's authority.[4] Department of Justice investigators in Ferguson, Missouri, found a pattern of such arrests after civilians complained about unfair treatment. In most cases, an officer would stop someone—often for some racially motivated suspicion—and when the individual became frustrated and asked why he was being stopped, he was punished with arrest for "resisting" or some other assaultive behavior.[5]

Of course, there is no national data on "contempt of cop" arrests. Police have little incentive to track such information. But one way to tease this data out is by studying common "cover charges," particularly in cases where a low-level offense is the only offense charged. Officers arrest their critics for disorderly conduct, threats, resisting arrest, fleeing from the police, assault on a police officer, and obstructing justice or failing to obey. Data compiled by local investigators and journalists documents this pattern at the city level. In Durham, North Carolina, researchers analyzed all cases in which the arrestee was charged only with resisting arrest or resisting coupled with a minor offense like trespassing.[6] Only 23 percent of such arrests led to convictions, suggesting that the great majority of the arrests were unwarranted. Ninety percent of those arrests involved people of color. A study in Seattle looked at cases in which the only charge was "obstructing a public officer" and found that obstructing arrests often began with some verbal criticism of the officer, frequently followed by an order to "back off" or "leave the area."[7] When the individual refused, they were arrested. The study also found that half of the arrestees were Black in a city that is mostly White. Prosecutors dismissed nearly half of the obstruction cases. Investigators who reviewed arrest data in Baltimore over a few months in 2009 found that prosecutors declined to prosecute more than 6,000 people who had been arrested for disorderly conduct. More than 98 percent of those arrestees were Black.[8]

In Washington, D.C., where Marquette and Shanna were arrested for equally minor charges, the police department has a long history of contempt of cop arrests. In 1998, *The Washington Post* published a five-article series after a study of more than 750 lawsuits filed against the D.C. Metropolitan Police Department, including those involving "contempt of cop."[9] As journalist Sari Horwitz reported, "The triggering offenses are typically minor, but the officer often perceives a challenge to authority and acts to regain control." Like their peers in other parts of the country, officers in D.C. don't like to be questioned about why they are doing what they do, and they don't like crowds to gather and watch. Questions are viewed as a sign of disrespect and refusals to cooperate are tantamount to sin.

While obstruction of justice and disorderly conduct are the most common cover charges in other cities, assault on a police officer (APO) has been a favorite among D.C. police. In the nineteenth and early twentieth centuries, APO was narrowly defined to prohibit physical assaults against an officer. In 1953, during the Great Migration of Blacks into cities like Washington, Congress broadened the statute to include "resisting, opposing, impeding, intimidating, and interfering."[10] The law was amended again in the 1970s in response to civil rights and antiwar marches to make it a crime to resist an illegal arrest. In 2007, the D.C. Council added a misdemeanor option to the statute, and APO arrests increased again. In 2015, a five-month investigation revealed that D.C. residents had been charged with APO for as little as "wiggling while handcuffed" and yelling at an officer.

There were almost 2,000 cases of APO between 2012 and 2014 in Washington, D.C.[11] In nearly two-thirds of those cases, APO was the only charge. The D.C. police were arresting residents for APO almost three times more often than police in other similarly sized cities, and 90 percent of the people they arrested were Black. Prosecutors declined to bring charges against more than 40 percent of those who were arrested. Concerned about the racial imbalance and overuse of the charge, lawmakers finally amended the APO statute in 2016 to narrow its scope and adopted a new statute solely for resisting arrest.[12] Even after this change, 565 people were arrested in 2018 for assault on a police officer.[13]

Concerns about contempt of cop arrests have been so widespread in D.C. that the American Civil Liberties Union has been able to secure thousands of dollars in damages for victims who could establish false arrest and free speech violations.[14] In one case, the jury found the District of Columbia responsible for a false arrest for disorderly conduct after the city had been on notice of the troubling pattern of arrests but failed to take steps to fix it. Unfortunately, civil suits like these have not curtailed the practice, and recent changes to the law did not prevent Shanna from being arrested and charged with both resisting arrest and assault on a police officer in 2018.

Most of the contempt of cop studies track adult arrests.[15] If we replace the adults with teenagers, the opportunities for "contempt of cop" increase exponentially. Any parent, teacher, coach, or counselor who works with youth knows that teenagers can be emotional and irrational. They yell. They talk back. They refuse to do what they are told. The best teachers and parents learn how to manage these verbal tirades. They listen and let the child blow off steam. They wait patiently for the child to calm down and then offer a firm and measured response. Most of the time, an argument can be resolved without touching the child. It can almost always be resolved without intervention by the police.

Some officers learn how to manage youth well. Maybe they have kids of their own. Maybe they coached a sports team or worked in a school before joining the police department. Maybe they are just patient. Unfortunately, far too few police departments provide the training officers need to work with adolescents.[16] Despite our desire for police to have thicker skin, the reality is that police are people too, and they bring their own emotions to every encounter. Some take it personally when a young person is hostile, aggressive, or profane—especially when the officer is only there to help. What many officers perceive as disrespect is often just teenagers showing off, enjoying the thrill of a new risk, or deflecting stress, anxiety, and other emotions.[17]

Teenage boys in particular are deeply concerned with their social status and care a lot about fairness and respect.[18] The battle for street credibility begins when the officer and the child are equally invested in affirming and asserting their status.[19] The battle between Black boys and the police is especially tortured. Research shows that Black adolescent males are more likely to develop a "hypermasculine," or aggressive, persona to cope with what they perceive as negative experiences and risks with teachers, police officers, salespeople, and others who don't seem to value them.[20] Because adolescents are especially sensitive to social and emotional cues at a time when they have less ability to calm their emotions and contain their reactions, they have a particularly hard time remaining quiet in response to an officer's angry glare or aggressive tone.

Even when children know it is dangerous to talk back to the police, they often can't help it, especially in fast-paced, emotionally charged situations like those that occur on the street.[21] In the heat of the moment—in front of their peers and in the face of a perceived injustice—adolescents have a hard time thinking about the likely consequences of their actions and making rational choices. Adolescents are more likely than either children or adults to respond impulsively rather than retreat or remain silent, even when specifically instructed not to respond.[22] The stress, fear, and anger commonly associated with police contact undermines adolescents' capacity to control their responses, especially when they have been victimized by or threatened with police violence.[23]

As is true with adults, we don't have a perfect way to count adolescent "contempt of cop" arrests. But we do have data showing that youth were accused of "disorderly conduct" in 48,000 cases in 2018. We also know that Black youth were significantly overrepresented in those numbers. Black youth were accused in 44 percent of disorderly conduct cases that year,[24] and were three and a half times more likely to be accused of that offense than White youth.[25] Youth were accused of "obstruction of justice" in 90,500 cases in 2018, accounting for 12 percent of all juvenile court referrals that year.[26] Although Black youth as a whole made up 16 percent of the youth population,[27] they accounted for 36 percent of the youth accused of obstruction that year.[28]

We also have plenty of anecdotal evidence from across the country to show that Black teenagers are arrested and physically abused for being rude, giving attitude, and not submitting to an officer's authority. In Miami-Dade County, Florida, an officer took fourteen-year-old Tremaine McMillian down in a chokehold when he purportedly made "dehumanizing stares" and clenched his fists after an officer told him to stop roughhousing with his friend on the beach.[29] Tremaine was arrested for resisting arrest and disorderly conduct. In Stockton, California, an officer pinned sixteen-year-old Emilio Mayfield to the ground with a billy club at 8:00 in the morning when he refused the officer's order to sit down after he was stopped for jaywalking in a bus lane on his way to school.[30] Four additional officers piled on top of him as he lay on the ground. Emilio was arrested for trespassing and resisting arrest.

In New York City, a fifteen-year-old Black boy was holding a deli bag and walking to a homeless shelter when a plainclothes detective and sergeant in an unmarked vehicle ordered him to stop without announcing they were police.[31] The boy was tackled and handcuffed when he ran. The bag contained a cheese roll and a piece of cake. In Tamarac, Florida, police slammed fifteen-year-old Delucca Rolle's head to the ground as he was trying to pick up a cell phone dropped by another student who was being arrested.[32] The officers claimed Delucca had taken an "aggressive stance" and was interfering with the officer. Delucca was arrested for resisting arrest, trespass, and assault. In Portland, Oregon, Thai Gurule was wrestled to the ground and physically beaten by multiple officers after talking back and cursing at one of them.[33] Thai was arrested for disorderly conduct, criminal threats, interfering with public safety, resisting arrest, and aggravated assault. Police claimed he balled up his fist and tried to choke one of them. Video footage contradicted that account. The list goes on and on. YouTube videos and news reports throughout the country show police encounters with Black youth that escalate from adolescent back talk to an all-out beatdown in a matter of seconds.

The similarities in these stories are striking. In no case had the police been called to the scene to investigate a physical or violent offense. In each case, the child was involved in some adolescent posturing or disobedience. In each case, the child's adolescent defiance was met with some physical attack by the police. And almost every contact led to a resisting arrest charge. But only one of these youth—Thai Gurule—appeared before a judge who actually understood what happens to Black youth who disrespect the cops.

Thai's encounter with the police began a little after midnight on September 14, 2014, when police were looking for a group of seven to nine African American men, including one shirtless man who had been walking the streets and reportedly damaging property and yelling profanities.[34] Although Thai, his brother, and their friend didn't match the description in any way other than race and gender, the officers approached and ordered them to stop. When officers yelled out, "Hey," and clapped their hands at Thai, Thai turned around and yelled, "Don't fucking clap your hands at me." Thai was sixteen. Officers quickly wrestled him to the ground.

One officer held him by the hair. Others pummeled him multiple times with their fists and knees. Another officer tased him.

Thai's judge, Diana Stuart, clearly understood what happened that night and publicly and explicitly admonished the officers for their "contempt of cop" arrest for Thai's failure to pass the "attitude test."[35] The judge also ruled that the police had no lawful reason to stop Thai, acquitted him of all criminal charges, and described the officers' conduct as a "senseless and aggressive use of excessive force."[36] Unfortunately, most judges don't intervene as Black teens continue to rack up criminal charges, endure physical abuse by the police, and face lengthy periods of probation or even jail time for doing what teenagers do—making police officers mad. With rare judicial reprimands and even rarer successful police brutality claims, police attitudes and behaviors are not likely to change. Even after Thai's judge dismissed the charges, the local police union maintained that the officers did nothing wrong and accused the judge of "Monday morning quarterbacking."[37]

Officers continue to blame youth for police use of force. In the days after Emilio Mayfield was stopped for jaywalking, a spokesperson for the Stockton Police Department told the media, "If everyone would just learn to comply with lawful orders from police officers and not try to hold or grab any of our weapons, force would never have to be used."[38] Videos posted on the internet after his arrest show that Emilio touched the officer's baton only after the officer forced it up against his body and shoved him with it. In the days after Tremaine McMillian was put in a chokehold, a Miami-Dade detective told the media that the physical intervention was justified because Tremaine was stiffening up and pulling away. "All of that body language alone is already letting the officers know that this is a person that now is obviously getting agitated and can become violent . . . Of course we have to neutralize the threat in front of us."[39] Responses like these ignore everything we know about adolescent development. They also ignore everything we believe about a child's right to live without unnecessary police intrusions in their lives.

## RESISTANCE: THE REVOLUTION STARTS HERE

A child's response to the police is not always an uncontrolled adolescent outburst. Sometimes it is an intentional act of resistance. Fear and resentment have socialized a generation of Black youth to challenge and resist the police.

In a civil society, it is important to help young people develop a healthy respect for authority and discourage them from breaking the law.[40] We achieve this goal over time by making sure our children are treated fairly in their daily interactions with people in charge.[41] Studies show that when parents, teachers, police officers, and other role models enforce rules and make decisions in a way that is fair, young people are more likely to respect them and obey their rules.[42] Adults demonstrate fairness by giving youth an opportunity to express their opinions and concerns before decisions are made, making decisions that are neutral and consistent across the school or community, treating young people with dignity and respect, and demonstrating that adults can be trusted to do what they say they will do.[43]

The opposite is equally true. Children's negative experiences with the police can undermine their respect for the law and law enforcement as they transition to adulthood.[44] By the time they reach adolescence, most Black youth have been warned about the dangers inherent in any police contact. For many Black youth, these lessons save their lives. But for some, these lessons also transfer animosity and resentment about the police from one generation to the next.[45] Children grow up watching their friends and family accosted for minor infractions like not wearing a seat belt, having the windows too tinted, and playing the radio too loud.[46] Black youth describe their neighborhoods as overrun by police who stop them multiple times a day just to pat them down and ask questions.[47]

Black youth resent pedestrian stops, vehicle stops, and the specialized units and detectives who are assigned to patrol their neighborhoods.[48] Black boys and girls say that officers treat them as if they are always "criminal" and complain that police are mean and disrespectful and do not know how to talk to Black people.[49] They describe the police as hostile and rude, and are especially offended by the officers' use of racial slurs, profanity, and other inflammatory and demeaning terms like "punk" and "sissy."[50] Black youth are angered by strip searches, genital touching, and being told to "lift your shirt" or "put your hands on the wall."[51] Youth interviewed in St. Louis reported that the vast majority of their contacts with the police occurred when they weren't doing anything wrong.[52] Frustrated by the "officers' apparent inability to distinguish law-abiding residents from those engaged in crime,"[53] the youth resented stops that seemed arbitrary and unfair and quickly learned that obeying the law did little to protect them from police intrusion and physical violence. In fact, as the researchers in St. Louis concluded, being innocent could actually increase a child's chance of being assaulted because they are more likely to challenge the officers' actions.[54]

Community resentment is high and respect for the police is at an all-time low among Black youth.[55] Youth in general have less favorable attitudes toward the police than adults.[56] Black youth have even less favorable attitudes about the police than White youth. Unlike White youth who tend to see police misconduct as an aberration, Black youth experience that misconduct as pervasive.[57] In Black communities where most police encounters with youth occur outdoors in the public view, almost every negative encounter is witnessed by several other youth who go home to tell their friends and family or post the incident on social media. The net result is that Black youth come to expect unfair treatment and carry these feelings and expectations into adulthood.[58] Over time, their resentment and resistance to the police become unconscious and automatic.[59]

Black youth also come from a long tradition of speaking out against injustice. Today, Colin Kaepernick and other Black athletes "take a knee" and refuse to sing the national anthem to call attention to racism and police brutality. Rappers like Jay-Z and Nas take on the police in their lyrics, and music icons like Beyoncé feature public resistance to the police prominently in their videos.

Young Black activists join Black Lives Matter marches, and newly elected Black leaders use their public office to address police corruption. Unfortunately, most Black youth don't have access to these platforms and opportunities. Even fewer have faith in formal grievance procedures for police misconduct.[60] These youth learn to protest in other ways, like recording and posting police violence on social media, speaking directly and explicitly about racism when they encounter officers on the street, and refusing to report crimes or cooperate with the police in criminal investigations. Black youth no longer see police as a legitimate source of authority.[61] Black teens routinely run from police to avoid face-to-face contact and refuse to seek police assistance even when they have been injured or otherwise aggrieved.[62] The ripple effects are felt throughout the legal system when Black Americans refuse to testify as witnesses in criminal trials, reject jury service, or decline to convict Black defendants who are clearly guilty.[63]

In cities like Washington, D.C., almost every arrest is accompanied by some video footage. Sometimes there is video from the police department's vast network of surveillance cameras throughout the city. Other times there is video from a government building, a private business, or a personal cell phone. Most often there is video from police body-worn cameras. While the cameras do little to curtail police abuses, they provide incredible insight into the thoughts and opinions Black children have about the police. Black youth frequently accuse the police of stopping them because they are Black; they angrily protest physically invasive searches; and they occasionally remind the police that "D.C. is not Trump's city." Some children are more direct in their vehement dislike for the police, calling the officers derogatory names and hurling the f-bomb and other profanities at the police.[64]

Resistance is part of the vicious cycle that plays out between the police and Black children. Just as Black youth have been conditioned to resent the police, police have been conditioned to expect hostility from Black youth. Suspicion and distrust are mutual.[65] These expectations are exacerbated by the stereotypes and biases police have about Black children. Police expect youth in general to be antiauthoritarian.[66] They expect Black youth to be dangerous.[67] Unfortunately, Black youth's visible hostility toward the police confirms what police expect. As hostility grows on both sides, the risk of violence—even deadly violence—increases.

Of course, not all police violence against Black youth involves resistance. Remember that Officer Timothy Loehmann shot Tamir Rice within seconds of his arrival at the park.[68] Had Tamir been given a chance to respond to instructions, there is little reason to believe he wouldn't have complied. Killings like this remind us that Black youth are at risk no matter what they do.

## TOTAL SUBMISSION: "COPS SHOT THE KID"

In 2018, the American rapper Nas released a heartrending and evocative song, "Cops Shot the Kid," featuring Kanye West and samplings from Slick Rick's 1989 "Children's Story" and Richard Pryor's 1973 film *Wattstax*. The music video was poignant, and the lyrics captured what every Black child knows: "White kids are brought in alive / Black kids get hit with like five."[69] That is five bullets for normal summer adolescent fun like "Slap-boxin' in the street / Crack the hydrant in the heat." As the boys say, "I don't wanna hurt nobody / We just came here to party / See a few dames, exchange some names." The message is clear—Black kids just want to be kids, and yet they know their lives are profoundly limited by the constant surveillance and persistent threat of police violence.

It is impossible to forget the images of Michael Brown Jr.'s bloody corpse lying on the sweltering asphalt, Eric Garner being choked out by an officer on a Staten Island sidewalk, and Tamir Rice falling to the ground after he was shot at the recreation center. These tragic images are revisited time and again in music, videos, and social media and serve as a constant reminder that Black youth are always at risk of summary execution. The long and growing list of Black youth who have been killed by the police operates much like lynchings did in the segregated Reconstruction South. Highly publicized killings teach Black children that it is futile to speak up, ask questions, and voice their displeasure at being harassed for doing what White kids are free to do all over the world. They learn that it is futile—even suicidal—to tell an officer no and walk away.

Our Constitution protects us from officers who stop and search us based on stereotypes and assumptions, on implicit racial biases, or for no reason at all. The right to privacy is so important in our country that we would rather let an offender go free after an illegal stop than allow the police to search us at will.[70] Of course, we can always give up that right and voluntarily agree to be searched. But let's consider what happened to my client "Andre."

Andre was a fifteen-year-old Black boy who was walking down the street with a friend, James. There was no report of crime, and Andre and James weren't doing anything out of the ordinary. They weren't loud. They weren't smoking. They weren't drinking. They weren't roughhousing. Yet the police drove up next to them and asked if they had heard any gunshots. When the boys said no, the police asked them to "show me your waist." Both boys complied by lifting their shirts. Still unsatisfied, the officers asked the boys for permission to search them, at which point Andre and his friend said yes. Four uniformed officers jumped out of their police car, forced the boys against the wall, and frisked them. The police found a gun on Andre.

Our first reaction might be to praise the officers for getting a weapon off the street, but a deeper analysis should cause us to think twice about the other consequences. It is far from clear that recovering Andre's gun improved our public safety enough to outweigh the harm done to racial equity, fundamental privacy, community respect for law enforcement, and the psychological well-being of Black youth.

The chances are great that had Andre and James been White, the police would never have asked them to "show me your waist" and agree to a full body search. The officers' requests grew out of racialized assumptions and undermined the very democratic principles of our country. The police admitted there had been no gunshots and conceded they had no specific reason to believe that

Andre or James had a gun. But they were adamant that the boys had "consented" to a search. What they failed to appreciate is that "voluntary" isn't quite so voluntary if a child thinks he will get shot if he refuses. When we asked Andre why he agreed, he said, "Wouldn't you? They were going to frisk us anyway. And if we ran, they were just going to shoot us in the back."

Pick any day, in any month, in a city like Washington, D.C., and you will hear stories like this—stories about Black youth who comply with the unlawful "requests" of the police to avoid worse outcomes. Consider the fate of Black youth who run from the police in Baton Rouge, Louisiana. In an investigation spanning 2017 to 2019, the Marshall Project examined the use of police dogs across the nation. Baton Rouge stood out from all the rest.[71] Police dogs bit a child an average of once every three weeks, and all but two of the fifty-three children attacked by a police dog were Black in a city where just over half of the population was Black. In nearly every case, the child was suspected of a nonviolent property crime but said to be hiding or running from the police. In every instance, the officer responsible for the dog was White. Some bites required stiches or left scars, and most youth were deprived of immediate treatment for their injuries despite the high risk of infection. Conjuring up memories of canines used to chase runaway slaves in the antebellum South or to break up protests in the civil rights era, police dogs create terror in Black communities and demand compliance with authority.

Given the everyday fears and trauma that Black boys experience with the police, Andre's acquiescence in the moment can hardly be described as consent. Research shows that few adults have the psychological strength to refuse an officer's request to search.[72] Youth have even less capacity to evaluate their options wisely in these moments. For youth who don't know their rights and have always been taught to obey those in authority, a police request sounds a lot like a demand. For those who understand they have a right to refuse, the officer's request presents an impossible choice—refuse and get shot or maimed, or comply and be arrested, or at least psychologically depleted from the encounter.

It is important that although Andre had a gun, his friend James did not. The vast majority of stops don't lead to a gun, or any contraband at all. In Washington, D.C., 412 children were stopped by the police in a thirty-day window from July 22 to August 18, 2019.[73] Of those, 371 were Black and 26 were Latinx. A gun was found in only four of those stops. Drugs were found in only one of those stops. Ninety-six percent of the stops turned up no contraband at all. In New York City, out of more than 500,000 police stops in 2009, officers found a gun in only 1.1 percent of those encounters. Out of 4.4 million police stops in New York between 2009 and 2012, police ultimately released 90 percent of the targeted persons after no evidence or other wrongdoing was discovered.[74]

We can't dismiss James's contact with the police as a necessary evil for the good of the whole. Even if Andre's submission to the police search gets one gun off the street, it is not without significant cost. The collateral damage from over-policing Black youth not only includes a loss of respect for law and law enforcement, but it also imposes a significant emotional and physical tax on Black bodies. As detailed in chapter 9, the mental health implications are severe. Black children live in a perpetual Catch-22. They are beaten or killed if they have the audacity to stand their ground and resist. They are presumed guilty if they exercise their right to run or walk away. They are emotionally debilitated if they submit or comply. And none of this makes us any safer because Black youth are rarely as dangerous as police think they are.

## LOOKING GUILTY: STEREOTYPE THREAT AND THE "STUTTER STEP"

There is almost nothing Black youth can do to rid themselves of the stereotypes and assumptions that automatically brand them as dangerous. Black teenagers always "look" guilty no matter what they do. And they know it.

My client "Tarik" knew he looked guilty when he walked out of his apartment building one Saturday morning in October

2019. Tarik lived in an apartment complex with his mother and two siblings in Northeast D.C. At the time, he was sixteen and liked to visit friends and family in the buildings next door. Tarik walked out of his building, headed down the walkway, and turned left at the sidewalk. Just as he turned, he saw a police car with two officers staring at him. The officers' presence caught him off guard and caused him to hesitate, creating the slightest break in his stride. The officers described that break as a "stutter step."

Police followed Tarik in their cruiser, pulled up on the curb, and jumped out to follow him on foot as he continued to walk away. Instinctively, Tarik took off running, and then hid behind a bush when he couldn't get in the building next door. When the police grabbed him, they kept asking, "Why are you running? Why are you running?" Tarik replied, "Because you are chasing me!" Police later said he had been "acting strangely" and described his flight as "unprovoked."

This is a classic exchange between Black youth and police in America. A child sees the police. The child is convinced the police are looking at him and gets nervous that he is about to be accused of something he didn't do. The child's nervousness makes him *look* as if he did something he didn't do. When the police approach to ask questions, the child gets scared and runs. The police say his running confirms the child's guilt. It is an impossible conundrum.

Our country's highest court has said that it is okay for police to consider an individual's nervousness and flight from the police when deciding whether there is enough suspicion to stop and frisk them.[75] The Supreme Court based its decision on the widely held belief that people only get nervous around the police when they are guilty. The Court was just wrong about this. People are nervous around the police for all kinds of reasons. Black people are nervous not only because they are afraid of getting killed but also because they are afraid the police will think they are guilty—no matter what they do.

People who believe they will be judged and treated unfairly because of their race face what researchers call "stereotype threat."[76] Blacks—and especially Black boys and men—who have grown up with demonizing stereotypes about their purported criminality, are much more likely than Whites to worry that they will be accused of crimes they did not commit. Blacks who think they are being stereotyped often experience high blood pressure, rapid heart rate, and heightened anxiety.[77] That anxiety causes other involuntary reactions like fidgeting, twitching, blinking, frightened facial expressions, nervous smiling, and a stiff posture. In other words, people who are anxious about being stereotyped look anxious.

Adding to the list of perverse outcomes, the fear of being accused also causes people to become self-conscious about whether they are acting in ways that confirm the stereotypes.[78] Black men who anticipate being stopped or investigated by the police do things to try to make themselves look less guilty. They might smile, avoid eye contact, whistle classical music, or otherwise try to control their behavior and speech to avoid looking guilty. To avoid attention, they go out of their way to control behaviors that would otherwise be automatic—like how close they stand to others, where they hold their hands, whom they look at, and for how long. Unfortunately, the more Black men try to deflect attention away from themselves, the more attention they draw. The more they try to appear innocent and nonthreatening, the more threatening they seem. It's a no-win situation.

The work of managing stereotype threats is exhausting. When individuals think others have negative beliefs about them, they use a lot of mental energy trying to disprove those beliefs.[79] The energy they spend looking for and reacting to clues about what others are thinking impairs their ability to do other things they need to do—like processing, retaining, and recalling information.[80] Thus, people who are anxious about being stereotyped often take longer to speak, speak more slowly, stutter or hesitate as they talk, and take too long to make a point—again making them look more guilty.[81]

Police training only reinforces this endless loop. Police are trained to look for and protect themselves against those who might be dangerous.[82] A recent study of police training materials found a significant overlap between common "indicators" of danger and common responses to stereotype threat. Fidgeting, empty stares, avoiding eye contact, scratching, hesitant or partial responses, tight jaw, touching the face, looking around, clenched fist, heavy breathing, repetitive phrases, and sweating all feature prominently in both lists. Yet none of the police materials discuss—or even mention—stereotype threat.

### POLICING LANGUAGE AND DISABILITY

Considering what we know about normal adolescent development, we can see how hard it would be for a teenager to navigate the complicated landscape of a police stop. Black youth who are stopped will cycle through a range of emotions from resentment at being unfairly targeted, fear of getting hurt or killed, anxiety about getting in trouble, embarrassment at being harassed in front of friends, confusion about what the officer wants them to do, stress about whether they might have done something wrong, and exhaustion at the repetition and futility of it all. Just as these youth have a hard time understanding all they are feeling and why, they have an even harder time finding the words to express it.

In 2018, my student and I were appointed to represent seventeen-year-old "Kwame," who was charged with assault on a police officer, unlawful entry, and multiple counts of destruction of property. Kwame was arrested when he entered a Metro station after having been barred for "jumping the turnstile," or entering without paying, earlier that morning. Having no other way to get back home, Kwame returned to the station with his girlfriend later that afternoon, hoping he could slip through the emergency gate unnoticed. As soon as an officer approached him, Kwame knew he had been caught and immediately put his hands behind his back as if in faux cuffs.

In the first few moments, Kwame engaged calmly with one officer who was standing off to his side speaking with little emotion. It appeared that everything would be okay until moments later when another officer walked up, put his arm on Kwame's shoulder, and began pulling him toward the door. At that moment, Kwame lost all control—screaming, kicking, and flailing his arms as multiple officers joined the fray. It appeared that one officer was banging Kwame's head on the turnstile. The officers say Kwame was banging his own head. When officers finally handcuffed him and dragged him outside, Kwame kicked a metal newspaper stand and was wrangled into a police car. In the car, Kwame stretched out on his back and kicked the door violently, knocking it off its hinges.

Kwame's story is remarkable both for how quickly the incident escalated and for how little training the officers had to deal with this child. If the officers had continued to talk to him calmly without touching him, it is unlikely the encounter would have exploded the way it did. As one of the officers told Kwame's aunt shortly after the arrest, it was immediately apparent that something was "off" about him. Kwame's body tensed up as soon as the first officer walked up, and his expression appeared distant, as if he were thinking about something else. Kwame also told the officer not to touch him.

Kwame's reaction to the officer's physical contact was certainly far out of proportion to anything that was happening at the moment. But even then, it could have been controlled with a little patience and redirection. Instead, the police did what police do. They arrested him. They arrested him without trying to understand why he was "off" and without considering other viable options, like calling the mobile crisis unit operated by the local mental health department or waiting for his girlfriend to call his guardian as she told them she was doing.

Kwame was held in detention overnight and charged with assault on a police officer the next day. One of the officers said Kwame had stomped on his foot and kicked him in the leg. Kwame was supervised on probation for almost a year—in a court system that was not designed to care for children with disabilities as severe as Kwame's.

When we met Kwame, he was attending a full-time school for students with severe learning disabilities. He had a therapist and was taking eight different medications for ADHD, mood disorder, anxiety, and sleep disruption. He was also scheduled to be tested for autism in the following weeks. After meeting with a local speech and language pathologist, I began to understand what happened to Kwame in the Metro station that day.[83]

Children like Kwame often have sensory deficit disorders that make loud noises, police lights, buzzing sounds, and physical touch by a stranger terrifying and traumatic. Touching a person with autism may cause him to fight or flee—likely explaining why Kwame lost control when the second officer emerged out of nowhere and touched his shoulder. Children like Kwame also often have limited memory and recall, making it difficult for them to follow instructions—especially the rapid-fire, multistep instructions that are often given by the police. "Stand up, take your hands out of your pocket, step back, put your hands up where I can see them, be quiet." Instead, children like Kwame need directions simplified and repeated. And indeed, Kwame's aunt told us that she had to guide him every morning with individual instructions to brush his teeth, take a shower, and get dressed for school.

Kwame sounded a lot like another Black child who made the national news—Stephon Watts. Tragically, Stephon's encounter with the police had a deadly outcome. In February 2012 in Calumet City, Illinois, just south of Chicago, officers shot and killed fifteen-year-old Stephon Watts in the basement of his own home. Stephon was diagnosed with Asperger's syndrome, a developmental disorder characterized by social and communication difficulties, eccentric behavior, and often singular, intense interests.[84] Stephon was prescribed at least one of the same drugs as Kwame—Abilify, for concentration and aggression.

When Stephon didn't take his medicine, he often became angry, refused to listen to others, fought with family members, and re-treated into mental solitude. Stephon's parents—Danelene Powell and Steven Watts—relied on emergency services when he became agitated or wandered off. Social workers and doctors advised the family to contact the police when Stephon needed immediate psychiatric care. Stephon's mother followed that advice, but his father, who grew up in Chicago and had an intense distrust of police, resisted. Ms. Powell told reporters after Stephon's death that "Steven would tell me, 'Stop calling the police. They're going to murder Stephon one day.'"

On the day Stephon was killed, his father did exactly what he told his wife not to do: he called the police. Mr. Watts immedi-ately regretted it and called the police back to tell them not to send help. Unfortunately, the police were already on the way. When Officers William Coffey and Robert Hynek arrived, Mr. Watts initially lied. Hoping the officers would just leave, he told them that Stephon had left the house. When Stephon called out from the basement, officers went downstairs. Within seconds, Stephon was dead. As the officers got to the bottom of the steps, Stephon appeared, "waving a knife." Officer Hynek yelled, "Knife," and immediately fired his gun, hitting Stephon under his right arm-pit. Officer Coffey also fired, striking Stephon in the back. The second shot killed him. Neither officer asked Stephon to drop the knife. Neither used any of the de-escalation or crisis intervention techniques they were taught in training. And neither used pepper spray, Mace, or a Taser.

Stephon's death was completely avoidable, maybe even more so than most. Stephon was well known to the Calumet Police Depart-ment, and the department had taken several precautions to make sure something like this did not happen. Most significantly, the department had flagged Stephon's address with a code to alert officers that someone with a mental disability lived there. The two officers who ended up killing him had even been to the house the year before. In one visit, the officers had been able to observe a trained negotiator work successfully with Stephon on the scene. In another visit, the officers had been able to use a Taser to get

Stephon to drop the knife he had been swinging. Unfortunately, none of those precautions were sufficient to protect Stephon in 2012.

Without extensive training and multiple opportunities to practice, police are not well suited to respond to children like Stephon and Kwame. The Calumet Police Department required their officers to take "roughly two hours" of training on autism and Alzheimer's disease. Hynek reported that he had autism-related training once in the seventeen years he had been on the force.[85] Coffey had the training once in his six years on the force. I am astonished that our client Kwame wasn't also shot, given how much more volatile, fast-paced, and unpredictable his encounter with the police was. Unlike the officers in Stephon's case, the police in D.C. weren't on notice that Kwame had a disability and had never seen a mental health professional engage with him.

Asperger's syndrome is a type of autism, and the experts who reviewed Stephon's case said a lot of the same things we learned about Kwame. Adolescents are impulsive. Autistic children are even more so. Autistic children have poor "executive functioning," which affects their problem solving, reasoning, working memory, and task-management skills.[86] People with autism have trouble following commands and are easily overwhelmed by encounters with the police. Because youth with cognitive disabilities often behave and respond in ways that appear aggressive, noncompliant, and violent, police who are not trained to identify and manage the signs of mental illness or disability can misinterpret those behaviors as mean, malicious, and threatening. Encounters escalate quickly when officers have little patience to deal with an emotional outburst from a child.[87]

Violent and aggressive encounters between police and children with a range of disabilities occur regularly nationwide. Estimates from the U.S. Department of Education tell us that a high percentage of youth in the juvenile legal system have cognitive and language deficits. Although data is difficult to obtain, estimates of incarcerated youth who have a learning disability range from as low as 30 percent to as high as 85 percent. Common disabilities include emotional or behavioral disorders, intellectual disability, and attention deficit hyperactivity disorders.[88] In 2016, the Centers for Disease Control and Prevention estimated that one in fifty-four children under the age of twenty-one have been diagnosed with autism.[89] A study published in February 2017 shows that nearly 20 percent of young people on the autism spectrum have had some sort of "run-in" with the police by age twenty-one, and about half of those occurred by age fifteen. About 5 percent of youth on the spectrum are arrested by the time they are twenty-one.[90]

Although Black and White children are diagnosed with autism at roughly the same rates,[91] we can expect that Black children with autism will be arrested more often than White youth with that diagnosis given what we know about implicit bias and how it affects police perceptions of Black youth.[92] As we examined in the last chapter on school-based arrests, Black boys with disabilities were arrested at five times the rate of all students in the 2015–16 academic year.[93] Data on police killings is similar. In a 2015 *Washington Post* analysis of nearly four hundred police-involved deaths, a quarter of which involved someone with a mental illness, Black people were killed three times more often than Whites or other minorities.[94]

At face value, Stephon's and Kwame's behaviors appeared to confirm the stereotypes police already have about Black youth and violence. Youth with language impairments may curse at the police because they cannot process emotions like frustration and anxiety and do not have the words to express themselves in more appropriate ways. Youth may also use aggressive language as a defense mechanism against those who confront or tease them. It is likely no coincidence that my client Shanna, who wrestled with officers in front of McDonald's, was dealing with the emotional trauma of being removed from her mother's care. It is also likely no coincidence that Marquette, who was adamant that the officer's instructions to move from in front of Rita's did not apply to him, was diagnosed with ADHD and had not been able to take his medicine. Children with cognitive communicative disorders have difficulty understanding, processing, and responding to "WH" questions like who, what, where, when, and why, and may appear to be suspicious or hiding something.[95] In response, they might stutter, talk fast, clutter their words, or jump from topic to topic when they get upset or excited. These responses begin to sound a lot like the police indicators for attack.

Even Black youth who don't have cognitive and language disorders are often at a severe disadvantage when police misunderstand their colloquial dialect, idioms, and slang—sometimes to the point of absurdity. Early in my career as a defender, I was appointed to represent a small fourteen-year-old boy, "Robert," who was arrested for threatening a police officer. The police report alleged that my client threatened to "smoke" a female officer when she told him she would arrest him if he didn't move. The officers interpreted that language as a threat to kill. When I interviewed Robert in the cellblock, he burst out laughing and said, "Ms. Henning, I told her I was going to smoke her! Meaning I could outrun her in a flash!" And indeed, he did just that. The police report stated that my client took off running and was only stopped when he was tackled by another officer. Clearly all common sense went out the window when the prosecutor charged him with threats. In the moments before he ran away, Robert hadn't done anything that would suggest he was threatening, dangerous, or in any way hostile toward the officer. He simply failed to obey her instructions and then ran away. In hindsight, I can't help but wonder if the officer arrested Robert for disrespecting her—that is, for "contempt of cop."

# 8

## Policing by Proxy

On April 12, 2018, fourteen-year-old Brennan Walker knocked on a door in a quiet residential neighborhood in Rochester Hills, Michigan.[1] It was 8:30 on a Thursday morning, and Brennan was hoping to get directions to the local high school. He and his family had just moved to the area and Brennan overslept, missing his bus to school. Thinking he could remember the four-mile bus route, Brennan started walking but soon realized he was going in circles and stopped for help. He picked a door with a Neighborhood Watch sticker, assuming that would be a safe bet. Unfortunately, the White woman who answered didn't think that was safe at all. Dana Zeigler began screaming, "Why are you trying to break into my house?" and wouldn't listen as Brennan tried to explain why he was there. In the meantime, her husband—a fifty-three-year-old retired firefighter—came running down the stairs, grabbing a 12-gauge shotgun on the way. Brennan ran away while Jeffrey Zeigler bolted out of his house, firing at Brennan from behind. Fortunately, Mr. Zeigler forgot to take the safety off the gun, so Brennan is still alive. Brennan kept running until he found somewhere to hide and broke down crying.

With the limited facts we have, it is almost impossible to understand why the homeowners would have assumed so quickly that Brennan was there to rob them. It is even more difficult to fathom why Mr. Zeigler fired his gun at the fourteen-year-old. It was broad daylight at 8:30 a.m. There was a child at the door—by himself. It was a quiet neighborhood not known for crime, and Brennan wasn't engaged in any behavior that was particularly suspicious. Children knock on residential doors all the time—selling cookies and candy to raise money for the local football team, hoping to make money cutting grass or shoveling snow, and gathering signatures for a political action campaign. Even if Mrs. Zeigler wanted to exercise caution before answering the door to a stranger, she could have greeted him, asked for his name, and found out what he needed through the closed door. She could have asked him to "hold on" while she got her husband to come down and join her. Instead, Mr. Zeigler woke up to hear his wife screaming. The Oakland County sheriff described the homeowners' reactions as "absurd" and "disgusting."[2]

Brennan and his mother, Lisa Wright, will remember this experience for a lifetime. We can only imagine Ms. Wright's fear when the police called her at work to tell her that someone had shot at her son. Ms. Wright dropped everything and rushed to be with him. Like so many Black mothers, Ms. Wright had told Brennan that he would always have to take extra steps to keep himself safe: "Don't wear hoodies. Be open and approachable. Take your hands out of your pockets."[3] According to the security footage from the Rochester Hills home, Brennan appeared to have been doing everything his mother taught him. Unfortunately, that wasn't enough.

"Vigilante" shootings of innocent and unarmed Black teens occur far too often. In the last decade alone, we have lost Trayvon Martin, Darius Simmons, Jordan Davis, and Renisha McBride to name just a few. The year 2012 was remarkable. In February 2012, local Neighborhood Watch captain George Zimmerman shot seventeen-year-old Trayvon Martin as he was on his way home from a convenience store in Sanford, Florida. In May 2012, seventy-six-year-old John Henry Spooner killed his thirteen-year-old neighbor Darius Simmons, whom he wrongly suspected had broken into his home to steal guns. In November 2012, forty-five-year-old White software developer Michael David Dunn shot seventeen-year-old Jordan Davis after an argument over loud music at a gas station. And in November 2013, a fifty-four-year-old White man, Theodore Wafer, shot nineteen-year-old Renisha McBride in Dearborn Heights, Michigan, after she knocked on his door for help after a car accident at 4:40 a.m.

But long before then, there was fifteen-year-old Latasha Harlins, who was shot in March 1991 by the South Korean store owner Soon Ja Du, who thought Latasha was trying to steal a bottle of juice. And in December 1984, there were four Black teenagers—Barry Allen, Troy Canty, Darrell Cabey, and James Ramseur—who were shot on a New York subway by Bernhard Goetz, a thirty-seven-year-old White man who thought they were robbing him. And even before then, there was fourteen-year-old Emmett Till, who was lynched in 1955 by four White vigilantes who said he whistled at a White woman.

In each case, the shooter was a civilian—either a vigilante, self-appointed to protect an entire community, or a lone ranger, protecting his or her own home or property from the perceived threat of Black youth. Each case sparked national debate about the presumptive dangers of Black adolescence and the rights of citizens to defend themselves.

### WHEN THE VIGILANTES BECOME HEROES: FROM BERNHARD GOETZ TO GEORGE ZIMMERMAN

Batman, Superman, and Spider-Man. These are just a few of our nation's comic book vigilantes. They are American heroes who take the law into their own hands when the police have failed. They stand ever ready to intercept a robbery in progress, wrestle a mugger to the ground, or save a woman from the threat of imminent attack. They protect and serve for the good of society.

America has also always had its share of real-life vigilante "heroes." From the lynch mobs of the nineteenth and twentieth centuries to the masked Klansmen who have periodically reemerged from Reconstruction to the civil rights era and beyond, self-proclaimed vigilantes have fought to protect White women from rape, White property from theft, and White men from violent uprisings by Blacks. In the years after emancipation, White men took it upon themselves to round up and hang Black men, women, and children who defied racial conventions or were falsely accused of sexual assault, insurrection, or treason. Hooded Klansmen in the 1950s and 1960s bombed churches, burned crosses, and threw bricks in windows to suppress Black activists who were too outspoken. As lynchings and bombings drew international outrage, a new form of vigilantism emerged in the 1980s and 1990s. The new vigilantes operated under the legal facade of self-defense.

On December 22, 1984, Bernhard Goetz shot and wounded four Black teenagers when one of them, nineteen-year-old Troy Canty, asked him for $5 on the New York subway.[4] Goetz had been mugged in 1981 by three Black youth who smashed him through a plate-glass door. After helping the police arrest one of those youth, Goetz was angry that the boy had been charged only with "criminal mischief" for ripping Goetz's jacket. Convinced that he could not count on the police for protection in the future, Goetz bought a five-shot .38-caliber handgun and carried it illegally after being denied a permit.[5]

Goetz fired all five shots when he encountered Troy Canty and his friends in the subway. Despite the boys' later insistence that they were only panhandling for money, Goetz was convinced they were going to rob him. Goetz responded to Troy's request by pulling out his gun and firing four shots in rapid succession. The bullets hit Troy in the chest above the heart, nineteen-year-old Barry Allen in the back, and eighteen-year-old James Ramseur in his arm on the way into his left side. Goetz fired a fifth shot, hitting nineteen-year-old Darrell Cabey in the side and paralyzing him from the waist down. Goetz turned himself in to the police after hiding out for nine days.

Bernhard Goetz emerged as a hero to many as rising crime rates and exaggerated predictions of violence by Black youth left civilians feeling as if the police weren't doing enough to protect them. Goetz was celebrated in newspapers across the country as the "Subway Vigilante."[6] New Yorkers wore T-shirts branded with "Thugbusters," "Acquit Bernhard Goetz," and "Goetz Four, Crooks Zero."[7] Movie producers and publishing companies offered movie deals and book contracts. Among critics and supporters alike, Goetz became a household name in popular culture. At least one cartoon strip, *Doonesbury,* and several songs, including those by Billy Joel, Lou Reed, and the Beastie Boys, featured Goetz in their story lines and lyrics.[8]

Although many people were offended by the racist overtones in Goetz's assumptions about the boys, there was no clear racial divide between those who opposed and those who supported him. Black and White citizens found themselves on both sides of the debate. Neighbors of the four youth spoke of how the boys had frequently terrorized their community and thought they got what they deserved.[9] Black citizens wanted to protect their communities from Black children they believed were out of control. One group, the Guardian Angels, a volunteer patrol group, which included Black and Latinx teenagers, raised money to support Goetz.[10] One National Rifle Association member described Goetz as "the avenger for all of us" and called for a volunteer force of armed civilians to "patrol the streets."[11] On the other side of the debate, Black civil rights leaders like Al Sharpton and then director of the NAACP Benjamin Hooks, denounced Goetz's actions as racist and far beyond the realm of self-defense.[12]

A jury acquitted Goetz of attempted murder and first-degree assault charges in June 1987 but convicted him of carrying a loaded, unlicensed weapon in a public place.[13] In deciding the case, the jury was allowed to consider Goetz's prior experience of being robbed and agreed that a reasonable person in Goetz's situation was justified to act in self-defense. Goetz was ultimately sentenced to one year in jail without probation.[14] He served eight months of that sentence. Darrell Cabey won a civil judgment of $43 million against Goetz in 1996.[15] He never received any money.

Many saw the jury's acquittal on the murder charges as an endorsement of vigilantism.[16] Benjamin Hooks described the jury verdict as "inexcusable." Congressman Floyd Flake agreed, say-ing, "I think that if a black had shot four whites, the cry for the death penalty would have been almost automatic."[17] In the aftermath, the media sensationalized the incident and stoked fears about the potential dangers of Black youth running wild. Politicians latched onto the incident in their promise to crack down on crime and make the city safe. Goetz became a symbol of fear—especially White fear.

The key question in Goetz's trial was whether he "could have reasonably believed that he was about to be robbed or seriously injured and whether it was reasonably necessary for him to shoot four youths to avert any such threat."[18] Researchers focused on Black crime rates to argue that it was reasonable and rational for Whites to be afraid of Black youth. In 1987, Marvin E. Wolfgang, a criminologist at the University of Pennsylvania, claimed that Blacks commit homicide, rape, robbery, and aggravated assault at rates at least ten times higher than Whites. Commenting on Goetz's shooting, Wolfgang said, "The expectation that four young black males are going to do you harm is indeed greater than four young whites . . . I can understand the black posi-tion that this is a racist attitude, but it's not unrealistic."[19] He also argued that people "can be very intimidated by young black males or people who seem to represent this so-called underclass by their dress or comportment, very intimidated."

A formal investigation into the impetus for Goetz's shooting, commissioned by then U.S. attorney Rudolph Giuliani, concluded that fear, not race, was the motive for Goetz's actions.[20] Goetz had stated in taped statements that it was the youth's mannerisms that led him to pull his pistol and shoot.[21] Finally, years after the trial and after public outrage and sensation had subsided, Goetz himself admitted in an interview with Stone Phillips of *Dateline NBC* that he had been more afraid of the boys because they were Black.[22] A resident of Goetz's apartment building also said Goetz made racial slurs at a tenants' association meeting, most notably, "The only way we are going to clean up these streets is to get rid of the spics and niggers."[23]

Marvin Wolfgang would not be the last academic to use demographic calculations to justify White fears of Blacks and dismiss claims of racism in the criminal legal system as unreasonable paranoia by Blacks. In the 1990s, Princeton professor John DiIulio Jr. argued, "If blacks are overrepresented in the ranks of the imprisoned, it is because they are overrepresented in the criminal ranks—and the violent criminal ranks, at that . . . Especially in urban America, white fears of black crime—like black fears of black crime—are rational far more than reactionary or racist."[24] Those fears of Black crime likely motivated the killing of fifteen-year-old Latasha Harlins in 1991.[25]

Shortly before 10:00 a.m. on Saturday, March 16, 1991, Latasha entered a store in South-Central Los Angeles to purchase juice. Latasha put a $1.79 bottle of orange juice in her backpack while holding money in her hand to pay. Without seeing the money, Korean store owner Soon Ja Du assumed Latasha was planning to steal. After a verbal exchange and physical altercation, Latasha turned to leave the store. Du reached under the counter, grabbed a revolver, and shot Latasha in the back of the head, killing her instantly. After speaking with two eyewitnesses and viewing the videotape from the store security camera, the police concluded that Latasha intended to pay for the beverage and Du had not acted in self-defense.[26]

Although Du did not emerge as a hero like Goetz, she certainly garnered sympathy from the public and the judge who sentenced her.[27] People understood that tensions between Blacks and Koreans were high in Los Angeles and Koreans were just as afraid of Black youth as Whites were. A jury found Du guilty of voluntary manslaughter, and the local district attorney asked for the maximum prison sentence of sixteen years.[28] At sentencing, the judge exhibited extraordinary compassion for Du. Concluding that Du shot Latasha under extreme provocation and duress, Judge Joyce Karlin stated, "Did Mrs. Du react inappropriately? Absolutely. But was that reaction understandable? I think that it was."[29] The judge sentenced her to five years of probation, 400 hours of community service, and a $500 fine.[30]

Fast-forward twenty years and another "hero" emerges in the debate about the people's right to defend themselves against the threat of Black adolescence. In February 2012, then twenty-eight-year-old George Zimmerman and his wife at the time rented a town house in a gated community called the Retreat at Twin Lakes in Sanford, Florida.[31] Zimmerman was the watch coordinator for the Twin Lakes Neighborhood Watch program registered with the local police department.[32] Zimmerman was on his way to Target when he saw Trayvon Martin, a Black boy he didn't recognize. Zimmerman called 911 to report a "suspicious person."

Disregarding the 911 operator's directive to stay in his car and leave Martin alone, Zimmerman chased, confronted, and then shot Trayvon after a physical struggle. Zimmerman says he shot in self-defense. Critics say he racially profiled Trayvon. Trayvon was seventeen years old. At the time he was accosted by Zimmerman, Trayvon was talking to his girlfriend on the phone and walking back from a convenience store. He was later found dead with his cell phone, an Arizona watermelon tea, a bag of Skittles, $40.15 in cash, a cigarette lighter, and some headphones.[33]

Police took Zimmerman into custody for questions after the shooting but ultimately released him because they found no evidence to disprove his claim of self-defense. Police told the media they were prohibited from arresting Zimmerman under Florida's Stand Your Ground laws that allowed him to defend himself with deadly force.[34] Intense public pressure eventually led to Zimmerman's arrest and prosecution for attempted second-degree murder and manslaughter.[35]

In the days and weeks after Trayvon's death, public reaction divided along racial lines, with more Blacks than Whites believing that Zimmerman was guilty of murder and had acted with racial bias.[36] After his arrest, Zimmerman was able to raise more than $200,000 for his defense and living expenses through a website he created for donations from his supporters.[37] By May 2012, reporters discovered that Zimmerman had raised twice as much as the charity established by Trayvon's parents. In late

2013, Zimmerman began selling paintings, including a painting of a Confederate flag in honor of a Florida gun store that refused to do business with Muslims.[38] One of his paintings sold for more than $100,000 on eBay. Trayvon's murder and public support for George Zimmerman tell us a lot about how vigilantes become heroes in the "White space."[39] A jury ultimately decided that Zimmerman was not guilty.[40]

### STAND YOUR GROUND: JORDAN DAVIS

Our laws have always allowed us to act in self-defense. If we believe we are in immediate danger of bodily harm, we can defend ourselves. We can even take another's life to save our own. Our country has also recognized the home as a special place. Laws allow us to use whatever force we need to defend our homes, even if it means killing someone to block out a dangerous intruder. But our right to defend self and property is not without limits. Because we value life, many states require us to try to get to a place of safety to avoid taking a life. We call these requirements "duty to retreat" laws.

Beginning around 2005, many states began eliminating the duty to retreat requirement.[41] Vigilantes like George Zimmerman now have legal protections that were not available to Goetz in 1984. New "Stand Your Ground" laws greatly expand an individual's right to defend themselves and their personal property. These laws allow us to stay put wherever we are, as long as we have a right to be there and aren't involved in illegal activities ourselves. Through laws, court rulings, or a combination of both, more than thirty states have adopted a Stand Your Ground rule allowing the use of deadly force against an attacker with no duty to retreat.[42]

Stand Your Ground laws have sparked heated debate, especially in Florida, one of the first states to adopt such a law. When Trayvon Martin was killed, many thought Stand Your Ground would be at the center of George Zimmerman's defense. Zimmerman's defense team avoided that debate by arguing that

Zimmerman was pinned in by Trayvon and had no opportunity to retreat, making Stand Your Ground irrelevant to the case. But later that year, another Florida court was presented with that very question. On November 23, 2012, Michael Dunn shot seventeen-year-old Jordan Davis at a gas station in Jacksonville, Florida.[43] Dunn's attorney said they planned to mount his defense squarely on the Stand Your Ground law.[44]

Dunn's defense reveals just how expansive—and misunderstood—the Stand Your Ground principle has become. Michael Dunn was not at home. He was not even in his hometown. He was visiting Jacksonville for a wedding. When he stopped at a gas station with his fiancée, he parked next to a red SUV that was already in the lot and asked the Black teenage occupants to turn down their music.[45] One of the boys immediately complied, but Jordan was not so charitable. When Jordan told his friend to turn the music back up, Dunn and Jordan got into a heated debate that led to Jordan's death.

When Jordan in effect stood his own ground and asserted his right to listen to whatever music he wanted at whatever volume, Michael Dunn took his life, firing multiple shots into the SUV, hitting Jordan in the legs, lungs, and heart. As the SUV backed up to avoid the gunfire, Dunn got out of his car and fired four more shots head-on at the SUV. In his defense, Dunn claimed that Jordan threatened him with "a gun or a stick" through the open window while yelling obscenities at him, including "You're dead, bitch. This is going down now." Dunn insisted that he was afraid for his life even as the driver of the SUV backed away to avoid the attack.

Jordan's death led to several state and federal legislative debates about the dangers of Stand Your Ground laws.[46] On one side of the debate, advocates argue that these laws are necessary to protect victims' rights over a criminal's life. On the other side, opponents argue that the laws expand self-defense too far, creating dangerous conflicts in the community and giving too much weight to racial biases that often underlie the perceived threats. Data confirms that instances of fatal violence increased significantly after states adopted Stand Your Ground laws and Black communities have been disproportionately affected by the use of deadly force against unarmed citizens in those states.[47]

Opponents also complain that the laws promote vigilantism and make it more difficult to prosecute individuals who commit a crime and then claim self-defense.[48] States with Stand Your Ground laws have statistically higher rates of "justifiable" homicides than states without those laws.[49] In Florida, the justifiable homicide rate increased more than 200 percent after the law was passed. Whites who rely on a Stand Your Ground defense against Black attackers are more successful than Blacks who rely on the defense against White attackers.[50] According to the Urban Institute, White-on-Black homicides in Stand Your Ground states are 354 percent more likely to be ruled justified than White-on-White homicides.[51] Others worry that misinterpretation of harmless activities and behaviors can lead to deadly force, especially against racial and ethnic minorities, when in fact there is no danger.[52] Stand Your Ground laws can be dangerous for trick-or-treaters, children who accidentally cross into their neighbor's yard while playing or mowing the lawn, a drunk person stumbling into the wrong neighborhood, or a teenager who knocks on the door for directions.

## UNLEASHING THE VIOLENCE:
### THE POLICE MODEL FOR VIGILANTE "JUSTICE"

Throughout American history, police silence in the face of civilian brutality against Blacks has implicitly sanctioned vigilantism as an acceptable form of "law enforcement." Because Blacks were viewed as property during slavery, Whites could punish Blacks however they wished without risk of interference from the state. In the years that followed abolition, police feigned ignorance in their efforts to identify the perpetrators of highly visible lynchings despite photographs clearly depicting the culprits and their large crowds of eager onlookers. Lynchings persisted as sport and entertainment well into the twentieth century and were largely tolerated by everyone in power, from the local sheriff to U.S. senators.[53] In some cases, lynchers were even aided by law enforcement officers who would leave an inmate's cell unguarded after rumors of a mob forming.[54]

The modern-day Zimmerman-Dunn form of vigilante justice might have been birthed from a newer wave of public spectacle— that of Black bodies in the street after police shootings. Emboldened by the recurring exonerations of police officers who kill and buoyed by laws that expand their right to self-defense, civilians do what they see police do. Like lynchings, police-on-Black killings have several common components. One, they are often unjustified by any real threat or danger from the victim. Two, the killers usually take great pains to sully the victim's character as they defend their own violent actions. Three, the killers are rarely held accountable by the public or the legal system. Four— and maybe most important—the killings reinforce implicit and explicit stereotypes about Blackness and incite unwarranted public fears of Black youth.

News accounts of police shootings of unarmed Black teenagers are growing. Cedrick LaMont Chatman, William L. Chapman, Michael Brown Jr., Kendrec McDade, Tamir Rice, Ramarley Graham, Laquan McDonald, Jordan Edwards, and Tony Robinson are just a few of the most well publicized. About 1,144 unarmed Black people were shot by the police between January 2015 and August 2019.[55] Although Blacks make up only 13 percent of the entire population, about 36 percent of all unarmed persons killed by the police in the United States between 2015 and 2019 were Black. Police violence analysts also tell us that 21 percent of Black victims of police shootings were unarmed compared with 14 percent of White victims between 2013 and 2018.[56] Thirteen of the hundred largest U.S. city police departments killed Black men at higher rates than the U.S. murder rate in that same time span, and those killings are not always determined by the prevalence of violent crime in each city. Some cities with higher rates of violent crime have fewer police shootings than cities with lower rates of violent crime.

While Americans of all races are increasingly outraged by the killing of unarmed Black youth, police narratives about who those youth are keep the nation more divided than ever. Those who don't want to believe we live in a nation that kills innocent children because of the color of their skin must convince themselves that police stories about dangerous Black youth are true. Police officers who kill must convince the public that the slain youth aren't innocent and, more important, that they aren't children at all. After every police shooting of a Black teenager, the killer, their supporters, and sometimes the media vilify the slain victims by focusing on physical features that made the youth look older, the youth's purported resistance to police instructions, and the youth's delinquent past—which was rarely, if ever known, to the officer at the time of the shooting. The police response after Michael Brown's death demonstrates this strategy well.

On August 9, 2014, Ferguson, Missouri, police officer Darren Wilson spotted two Black males walking in the middle of the road and told them to move to the sidewalk.[57] One of the males was eighteen-year-old Michael "Mike" Brown Jr., who replied, "Fuck what you have to say."[58] Wilson's account of what happened next is laden with dehumanizing and animalistic imagery.

Wilson said Mike came to his car window, enraged, hitting him in the face and grabbing for his gun. Wilson and Mike struggled, and Wilson fired two shots. Wilson compared Mike to a professional wrestler, saying, "When I grabbed him, the only way I can describe it is I felt like a five-year-old holding onto Hulk Hogan." Mike then took off down the street. Wilson followed. Mike stopped running at a light pole and turned toward Wilson. When Wilson told the teenager to get on the ground, Wilson said Mike "looked at me, he made a grunting, like aggravated sound and he starts, he turns and he's coming back towards me," with his left hand in a fist and his right hand in his waistband. Wilson raised his weapon and shot to kill.

Wilson fired twelve shots in total, two from his car and ten outside. In explaining why he shot, Wilson described a look of anger and intense aggression that came across Mike's face—an expression that made him "look like a demon." Wilson contin-ued, "He was almost bulking up to run through the shots, like it was making him mad that I'm shooting him. And the face that he had was looking straight through me, like I wasn't even there, I wasn't even anything in his way." Although Mike was shot sixty-one seconds after the police dispatch noted that Wilson had just stopped two men,[59] Mike's body lay in the street for four hours before he was transported to the St. Louis County Medical Examiner's Office.[60]

In the days and weeks after the shooting, Wilson, the pros-ecutors, and reporters talked a lot about Mike's alleged theft of cigarillos from a convenience store earlier that morning.[61] As if it justified the killing, Wilson and his supporters treated the theft as a sign of Mike's moral failings and spent a great deal of time trying to obtain information about his prior juvenile and criminal record. At the extremes, Mike was described on social media as "a sorry assed, criminal, hoodlum, n*****" with a "criminal record a mile long."[62] Others inaccurately claimed that he was "known for numerous assaults and robberies." Mike had turned eighteen three months before he was killed, and a representative from the St. Louis Family Court reported that he had no serious felony charges or convictions in juvenile court.[63] A documentary released two and half years after Mike was killed also cast doubt on claims that Mike stole cigarillos the day he was shot.[64] Ana-lyzing store surveillance cameras from earlier that morning, the filmmakers contend that Mike had purchased or bartered for the cigarillos several hours before the shooting and left them with the cashier for pick up later.

By contrast, Officer Darren Wilson emerged as a hero. By No-vember 2014, Wilson's supporters had raised $500,000 from the Shield of Hope charity, GoFundMe, and Facebook pages called "We Are Darren Wilson," "I Support Officer Wilson," and "Sup-port Darren Wilson."[65] His friends and allies bought T-shirts and wristbands that said "I Stand By Darren Wilson." Even the Fer-guson prosecutor seemed to be among Wilson's top fans.[66] Acting more like a defense counsel than the St. Louis County prosecutor,

Bob McCulloch and his team "challenged" and "confronted" their own witnesses in the grand jury and pointed out previous inconsistent statements and other evidence that discredited their accounts. Given that approach, few could be surprised that Wilson was not indicted.

The pattern of vilifying the victim and putting the shooter on a pedestal is evident in many other cases. On January 7, 2013, Chicago police officer Kevin Fry shot and killed seventeen-year-old Cedrick LaMont Chatman.[67] In defense of his shooting, Fry emphasized that Cedrick jumped out of a stolen car and ran when instructed to stop. The officer focused on Cedrick's size, noting that he was five feet seven and 133 pounds, and claimed that he turned back to look at the officers while he was running. Fry also told investigators he believed Cedrick was armed and pointing a gun at his partner.

The head of the Independent Police Review Authority at the time, Lorenzo Davis, saw things differently. After reviewing surveillance footage from nearby cameras, Davis concluded that Cedrick was running for his life and never turned or pointed at the officers. Video also showed that Cedrick was killed less than ten seconds from the time he jumped out of the car. No gun was found on the scene, and officers later acknowledged that Cedrick was carrying a box with an iPhone. Davis was fired from the Police Review Authority, and another investigator reversed his findings.

In their extreme effort to sully Cedrick's character and deflect blame away from Fry for Cedrick's death, prosecutors charged the two boys who had been involved in the earlier car theft with Cedrick's murder. Relying on a "felony murder" theory, the prosecutors argued that if the boys had not robbed a man and stolen his car in the first place, the police would never have killed their friend. Those charges were later dismissed. Cedrick's friends were ten blocks away when Cedrick was shot.

On October 20, 2014, Chicago police officer Jason Van Dyke shot and killed seventeen-year-old Laquan McDonald.[68] Van Dyke and other officers on the scene claimed that Laquan was behaving erratically, refused to put down a knife he was carrying, and lunged at them. Police dashcam video released thirteen months later shows that Van Dyke was approaching Laquan and that Laquan had been walking away when he was shot. Van Dyke was on the scene for less than thirty seconds before opening fire. He began shooting approximately six seconds after exiting his car, and he fired sixteen shots in fifteen seconds.[69] Most of the shots hit Laquan in his back while he was on the ground.[70]

The first responding officer said he didn't see the need to use force, and none of the other eight officers on the scene fired their weapons.[71] Nonetheless, initial police accounts of the incident, consisting of about 400 pages of typed and handwritten reports,[72] prompted police supervisors to rule the case a justifiable homicide.[73] The reports omitted the number of shots Van Dyke fired and focused on the officers' claims that Laquan was acting "crazed" and carried a knife.[74] The police also claimed that McDonald's knife was in the open position, but that was later contradicted by evidence that the knife was found folded at the scene.[75]

Few of these cases are easy. Police have a hard job and need to protect themselves. Prosecutors and juries who can't possibly know what the officers were thinking at the time of the killings are reluctant to second-guess an officer's "split-second" decision to shoot—especially when confronted with an "oversized" and imposing Black child.[76] Postmortem attacks on the victim's character with prior criminal acts allow the public to identify with the shooter over the victim and breed intolerance of even the most normal adolescent behaviors and low-level crimes. Worse, they confirm stereotypes that portray Black youth as violent and dangerous.

In the weeks after Laquan's death, reporters dug into his early life—probably in an attempt to humanize him, but ultimately providing fodder for those who wanted to vindicate the officer's claim that he was protecting himself from a dangerous Black threat. A story in the *Chicago Tribune* reported that "few were surprised when he [McDonald] grew into an often-angry teen who embraced the drugs and gangs that made up the brutal landscape of his West Side neighborhood. McDonald had learning disabilities and was diagnosed with complex mental health problems, including post-traumatic stress disorder. He had school suspensions, expulsions, truancies and drug possession arrests and was in and out of juvenile detention."[77] Every police shooting gives the media an opportunity to tell a story like this—a story that focuses attention on the youth's troubled past instead of the officer's decision to shoot an unarmed teenager. Even in its sympathetic portrayal of a Black child who grew up with a hard life, this account gives the public every reason to fear that a wallet, a phone, a toy, or a bulge in a pocket might be a gun.

Demonizing the victims has served its purpose well. Darren Wilson was never indicted for killing Mike Brown. Kevin Fry was never indicted for killing Cedrick LaMont Chatman. Officer Timothy Loehmann was never charged with killing Tamir Rice. Madison, Wisconsin, officer Matthew Kenny was never prosecuted for killing nineteen-year-old Tony Robinson Jr. New York police officer Richard Haste was never prosecuted for killing eighteen-year-old Ramarley Graham. And Pasadena, California, officers Jeffrey Newlen and Mathew Griffin were never prosecuted for killing nineteen-year-old Kendrec McDade.

Police officers who kill are rarely held accountable through the criminal courts. Ninety-nine percent of police killings between 2013 and 2019 did not result in an officer being charged with a crime.[78] The few officers who have been prosecuted either were captured on videos that contradicted their original reports, became the target of intense public scrutiny that forced the prosecutor's hand, or killed a child for whom no criminal record could be fabricated and no other possible justification for the shooting could be concocted. Jason Van Dyke became Chicago's first patrolman in almost fifty years to be convicted of murder.[79] Prosecutors asked the judge to sentence him to at least eighteen years in prison for killing Laquan McDonald. The judge sentenced him to seven. Without the video that was released more than a year after the shooting, many would have accepted Van

Dyke's account of Laquan's danger without question.[80] With the increase in cell-phone footage and public outrage, maybe more officers will be held accountable.

Against this backdrop, it is not unreasonable to conclude that contemporary police-on-Black violence has unleashed—or at least condoned—a new wave of vigilante violence against Black youth. Vigilantes like George Zimmerman and Michael Dunn sound a lot like the police when they explain why they killed Trayvon Martin and Jordan Davis.

Although he was not on duty that night as Neighborhood Watch captain, Zimmerman stopped and called 911 when he saw someone who looked as if he did not belong. Zimmerman told the operator, "This guy looks like he's up to no good or he's on drugs or something."[81] He also expressed his resentment about people he felt had gotten away with break-ins in the neighborhood, referring to them as "these fucking punks" and "these assholes, they always get away."[82] Zimmerman later told reporters, "I felt he was suspicious because it was raining. He was in-between houses, cutting in-between houses, and he was walking very leisurely for the weather . . . It didn't look like he was a resident that went to check their mail and got caught in the rain and was hurrying back home. He didn't look like a fitness fanatic that would train in the rain."[83] Providing Zimmerman with further "justification" for his suspicion, Trayvon ran after seeing him, causing Zimmerman to get out and follow him.[84] When the two met, they fought and Zimmerman fired his weapon. Zimmerman told police he fired in self-defense. Apparently, unknown Black boys must be killed to save lives and keep the neighborhood safe.

Zimmerman decided Trayvon was "suspicious" the moment he saw him. Zimmerman's supporters reinforced that narrative by latching onto reports that Trayvon had been sent to stay with his father in Sanford, Florida, after being suspended from high school for ten days.[85] School officials say he had marijuana residue in his book bag, suggesting that he had at some point been in possession of weed—a drug that 49 percent of high school teenagers report having tried by the twelfth grade.[86] Both Zimmerman's supporters and the media put Trayvon on trial instead of Zimmerman. Investigators tracked down Trayvon's school records and found that he had also been suspended once for graffiti and another time for tardiness and truancy. He had also been questioned for having jewelry and a screwdriver in his backpack. Trayvon's family blamed the police for "trying to kill his reputation."[87] His family's lawyer, Benjamin Crump, described the reports as "irrelevant" and "demonizing."

Trayvon's family later worked with sympathetic media outlets to share an alternative narrative about Trayvon. From them, we learned that Trayvon was a seventeen-year-old junior attending Krop Senior High in Miami, Florida.[88] He was looking forward to his junior prom and senior year. Trayvon planned to go to college and talked about going to the University of Miami or Florida A&M University. One of his teachers described him as a sweet kid who loved math and usually made As and Bs. Trayvon also hoped to one day fly or fix planes and attended the George T. Baker Aviation Technical College in the afternoons. He responded to the nicknames Slimm and Tray and had a girlfriend with whom he spent hours talking and texting. Tray still loved Chuck E. Cheese and baking chocolate chip cookies for his young cousins, and he had just been horseback riding with his mother eight days before his death. George Zimmerman couldn't imagine or accept this image of Trayvon.

Michael Dunn's fear and disdain for Black youth was even more explicit than Zimmerman's. In phone calls to his girlfriend from the jail after his arrest, Dunn kept saying that Jordan Davis and his friends were "bad" and frequently referred to them as "thugs" and "gangsta rappers."[89] Despite Jordan's suburban upbringing and very close relationship with his father, Dunn assumed Jordan and his friends had no male role models and asked his girlfriend questions like "Where are their dads?" He bought into other stereotypes with questions like "What is it about the subculture that makes them feel entitled?" and "It is a surprise that more folks don't tell them to pull up their pants." As one of Jordan's friends told reporters after Dunn's trial, "thug" is the new n-word. In Dunn's mind hip-hop music is synonymous with gang violence.

In case after case, since Bernhard Goetz became the Subway Vigilante in 1984, the killers and their supporters highlight the criminal records of their victims as if their prior misdeeds confirm the present threat and justify the killings. Investigators looking to validate or discredit Dunn's claims of self-defense were no different. Drawing attention away from whether Dunn actually saw a weapon in the moments before he fired his gun, news outlets reported that the driver of the SUV was on probation and violating his 7:30 curfew at the time of the shooting.[90]

But, of course, self-defense has to be based on something more. We can't presume that someone who has committed a crime in the past will do so in the future. We also don't kill people because they smoke marijuana or drink alcohol. We don't kill teenagers because they get suspended from school, disobey their mothers, or play hip-hop music. And we don't kill people because their friends have criminal records. We don't even kill people who have done heinous things like carjacking—especially not without trial in a court of law. Ultimately, it doesn't matter whether these kids were good or "bad," but making them look bad is what justifies the violence and gets other Black kids killed.

What else could have made Dana Zeigler as scared as she was when a fourteen-year-old knocked on her door at 8:30 a.m.? At her husband's trial for shooting at Brennan Walker, Mrs. Zeigler testified, "I saw a black person standing at my door and I screamed at him and I asked him what he was doing there." Responding to skepticism about her fears of such a young child, she said, "He didn't look like a child. He was rather large."[91] Her image and fears about Brennan were deeply ingrained and subconscious.

### POLICING BY PROXY: SECURING THE WHITE SPACE

But what was the real threat? Jordan Davis was on Thanksgiving break when he was hanging out with three friends, "mall hopping and girl shopping," in a red SUV.[92] The boys were listening to "Beef," a hip-hop song by Lil Reese, Lil Durk, and Fredo Santana, when they stopped at a gas station to buy gum and cigarettes. Although one of his friends initially thought it was wise and polite to turn the music down as Dunn requested, Jordan was offended and didn't hold his tongue. Reactive, emotional, and impulsive as teenagers often are, Jordan yelled out, "Fuck that nigga."[93] For that, he got two bullets in his legs and one in his side.

This case was much less about fear than about privilege and entitlement. At least one eyewitness reported that Michael Dunn began shooting through a closed door immediately after telling Jordan, "You're not going to talk to me like that." And there was little evidence to support Dunn's claim that he thought he saw a stick or gun in the window. There was no weapon of any type ever found in the SUV or the area nearby. Jordan's friends testified that Jordan never got out of the car, and Dunn's own fiancée, Rhonda Rouer, undermined much of Dunn's story. Rouer testified that Dunn never mentioned seeing a weapon in the SUV and told her, "I hate that thug music," as they pulled up next to the SUV.[94]

Further undermining his claim of fear, Dunn didn't call the police after the shooting.[95] He didn't drive to a police station. He didn't call out for help, and he didn't alert anyone that four "dangerous" Black youth might be roaming the streets of Jacksonville. Instead, he and his fiancée drove to a bed-and-breakfast in St. Augustine, Florida, ordered pizza, took the dog for a walk, poured a rum and Coke, and watched a movie. The next day they drove home to Satellite Beach after hearing news reports that Jordan Davis had died.

This case was about Michael Dunn's desire to live freely without the intrusion of Black youth and their "thug" music. It didn't matter that Jordan and his friends were already parked at the gas station before Dunn pulled up next to them, or that Jordan and his friends were at home in Jacksonville, while Dunn was

in from out of town. It didn't matter that the music was playing from inside a private vehicle. Michael Dunn wanted to park
in that spot, at that moment, without that music, and Jordan
was in the way. Worse, Jordan challenged the unwritten rules
of White space, power, and privilege. That is why Jordan Davis
was murdered.

Dunn's language and behavior during and after the shooting
revealed too much about his motives and gave the jury little choice
but to convict him of first-degree murder.[96] Much like the vigilantes of the nineteenth and early twentieth centuries, Michael
Dunn killed Jordan to protect a valued interest—Whiteness.[97]
Being White, looking White, and sometimes even aligning oneself
with Whiteness have value worth protecting. In the most tangible
sense, Whiteness carries with it certain legal, social, financial,
and political advantages that arise from increased access to the
workforce, marketplace, academy, and residential spaces. But
Whiteness also has psychic value—a feeling of superiority that
comes from the reputation and status of being or aligning with
Whites.[98]

Professor Cheryl Harris describes the inherent value of Whiteness as a "treasured property" in a society based on racial caste.[99]
Because the benefit of Whiteness derives from not being Black,
even poor Whites enjoy this value as they remain at the bottom of the class hierarchy and get relatively few of the material
benefits.[100] Throughout American history, Whites have collaborated across class lines to protect power, privilege, and space
through slavery, lynching, legalized racial segregation, and mass
incarceration. In their earliest iterations, cross-class collabora-
tions were obvious and intentional in their efforts to subordinate
Blacks. White overseers helped White plantation owners control
enslaved Blacks, and poor Whites later joined the southern ruling
class to create violent groups like the Ku Klux Klan to enforce
segregation.[101] In their current iterations, cross-class coalitions
are less defined, and their racial intent is less explicit. For most
Whites today, the power of Whiteness is not consciously held,
but instead unconsciously adopted and sustained by racial ste-

reotypes, images, and implicit biases that have been internalized about Black people.[102] Even Whites who reject explicitly racialized messages subconsciously accept narratives that criminalize Blackness and incite fear. In this way, Whiteness continues to thrive in contrast to Blackness.

Today, Whites keep Blacks in place—literally and figuratively— through false, exaggerated, or irrational claims of danger. Brennan Walker, Trayvon Martin, and Renisha McBride were obviously and literally "out of place" when they were shot in neighborhoods where they weren't expected to be. On November 2, 2013, Theodore Wafer heard nineteen-year-old Renisha McBride banging loudly on his door at 4:40 a.m.[103] Wafer, who lived in the predominantly White suburb of Dearborn Heights, Michigan, opened his door and shot her in the face.[104] Renisha had been involved in a car accident about four hours earlier. Disoriented and intoxicated, she roamed away from the car and was not seen again until she arrived on Wafer's front porch. Wafer called 911—after he shot her. He says he was home alone, scared, and thought someone was breaking in. He described Renisha as drunk, belligerent, and suffering from a head wound caused by the car crash.[105]

To explain his failure to call the police before firing his shotgun, Wafer said he couldn't find his cell phone at first and peeped out of the window to see a shadowy figure move from the side to the front of his house. Evidence suggests that Wafer opened the front door before he fired through the closed and locked screen. There was no sign of forced entry, and there was no damage to any locks on his home. At trial, Wafer said he honestly and reasonably believed he was in danger. The jury disagreed and convicted him of second-degree murder.[106] In the days and weeks after Renisha's death, media reports highlighted that she had been drinking alcohol and smoking marijuana and took the car without her mother's permission after an argument about her chores.[107] They also noted that she had been speeding, hit a parked car, and then walked off after the accident.

Trayvon Martin was also killed in a place others thought he

shouldn't be. Trayvon's death occurred after a downturn in the economy, which caused a significant devaluation of homes and an influx of renters into the Twin Lakes community.[108] Zimmerman and other Neighborhood Watch volunteers were on the lookout for unknown Black males who were potential thieves and trespassers in their "White" space. Because the benefit of Whiteness comes from not being Black, even Zimmerman could capitalize on his White skin and downplay his identity as both a renter and a Latino. Zimmerman, whose mother was born in Peru and whose father was of German American descent,[109] had every incentive to protect his interest in Whiteness by setting himself apart from the "dark" intruders and aligning himself with his White neighbors. Tellingly, in the moments before his death, Trayvon described Zimmerman as a "creepy-ass cracker"—a term typically used to refer to a poor White person in the South.[110] Trayvon clearly saw little if any distinction between Zimmerman and other "Whites" who sought to demonize and exclude him.

The vigilante shootings of Black youth like Brennan, Jordan, Renisha, Trayvon, and Emmett Till before them also play a symbolic role in society. Emmett Till was lynched in 1955, one year after the Supreme Court ruled that racial segregation in public schools was illegal. His murder coincided with White backlash across the country and reminded Blacks that integration was not going to come easy, if at all. Emmett Till was killed to preserve Whiteness, both in the immediate need to protect the White woman who accused him of whistling at her and in the much broader political need to prevent Blacks from claiming their rightful place in society.[111] Decades later, vigilante killings send an unmistakable message that Black youth should not overstep the boundaries of Whiteness preserved by iron gates, suburban dividing lines, and requests to turn down their music. Vigilante violence is particularly effective against adolescents as it seeks to impose limits and boundaries before their identities are fully formed.

## SEE SOMETHING, SAY SOMETHING:
### THERE'S AN APP . . . OR A LINDA . . . FOR THAT

Most White people won't shoot a Black child who knocks on their door or walks through their neighborhood. But many will call the police to report a "suspicious" Black youth lurking in the neighborhood, mowing the lawn, shopping at the mall, swimming in a pool, brushing a woman with a book bag, or getting in a car at the carnival.[112] We have all been trained to report suspicious activity to prevent crime and protect ourselves. But Whites have also been implicitly trained to keep Black youth out of White spaces.

In June 2018, an industrious twelve-year-old, Reggie Fields, made national news after a White family called the police to report that he was cutting part of their lawn.[113] Reggie, who operates Mr. Reggie's Lawn Cutting Service in Maple Heights, Ohio, had been hired by Linda Krakora's neighbor to cut their grass. Apparently, he cut too much. The Krakora family called the police again, two weeks later, complaining that Reggie and his friends were playing on a Slip 'n Slide in the yard next door. Ms. Krakora told reporters, "We have always been told by the police that if we feel threatened, don't confront these people, just call us." And the Krakoras have done just that. They have called the police sixty times on their Black neighbors. As they say, "If we feel it's going to be more of an issue to go over trying to talk to somebody, for our safety, we just call the police." It's not at all clear what the threat could have been in June 2018. When the police investigated, they identified both incidents as a civil matter and left without issuing any citations.

In May 2018, high school seniors Eric Rogers II and Dirone Taylor needed something to wear to prom.[114] They met their friend Mekhi Lee, a college freshman, around 1:00 p.m. at the Nordstrom Rack in Brentwood, Missouri. When they noticed several store employees watching and following them around, they left but returned moments later to get a hat one of them had left behind. An elderly White woman who was a customer in the store confronted the teens, calling them "punks" or "bums" and asking them, "Are your parents and grandparents proud of what you do?" The boys asked to speak to a store manager, only to be told by store employees that they could not meet with anyone. As they left a second time, a manager waved them back in. The elderly woman who confronted them was rung up separately by a White manager and escorted to her car.

After making a purchase and exiting the store for the final time, the boys were met in the parking lot by Brentwood police, who told them that Nordstrom Rack employees had accused them of shoplifting "handfuls of products." Fortunately, the police let the boys go after looking at their receipts and searching their bags. Unfortunately, as Dirone told reporters, he felt embarrassed and agitated, with "mixed emotions with the whole situation" because they didn't deserve to be treated the way they were. Like so many Black youth who have been in this situation, Dirone and his friends bought something from the store just "to show them that we are equal and didn't have to steal anything." The president of Nordstrom Rack admitted that his company did not handle the situation well and apologized to their families.

In June 2018, a White San Francisco businesswoman, Alison Ettel, called 911 on an eight-year-old Black girl who was selling water outside her home.[115] She claimed the girl was being too loud. Ettel later apologized for how she handled the situation and stepped down as CEO of a local medical marijuana company. In September 2018, a couple flagged down police when they saw an eighteen-year-old Black male riding in the backseat of a car with two White women in Wauwatosa, Wisconsin.[116] These Good Samaritans were worried that the women were being robbed. The police pointed their guns, ordered Akil Carter from the car, and told him to drop to his knees. Akil was detained in handcuffs until police realized he was the grandson of one of the women who were on their way home from Sunday church services. Maybe the saddest part of the incident is that the couple who called the police were Black themselves, further demonstrating how entrenched stereotypes about Black adolescent criminality have become.

Each of these incidents ended without physical injury or arrest. Unfortunately, not all police calls end this way, especially when teenagers are involved. On March 24, 2012, Oscar Carrillo called the police to report that his computer had been stolen in Pasadena, California.[117] Hoping to get the police to respond more quickly, Carrillo lied. Contradicting his claim that he had been robbed at gunpoint, security cameras showed a young man taking Carrillo's computer from his parked car. When Officers Jeffrey Newlen and Mathew Griffin arrived in response to the report, they saw nineteen-year-old Kendrec McDade running and appearing to clutch the right side of his waistband. Fearing for his life, Officer Griffin fired four times through the open driver's side window of his patrol car.

Investigation revealed that Kendrec was not armed and had been carrying only a cell phone in his pocket. Video surveillance also showed that Kendrec had not stolen the computer, but had been standing at the rear of Carrillo's car at the time it was taken. In the aftermath of the shooting, Pasadena police arrested Carrillo, saying his false report led to Kendrec's death. Prosecutors later dismissed the charges related to the shooting, concluding that the officers acted reasonably in killing Kendrec and that Carrillo's lie was just "one in a series of acts . . . that culminated in the fatal shooting."[118] Carrillo pled guilty to two misdemeanor false reporting charges.[119]

Calling the police is a privilege that many Black youth and their families have long since relinquished. As Stephon Watts's father used to tell his wife before their autistic son was killed, calling the police will get you killed.[120] Tragically, he was right. Given what we know about how quickly police encounters with adolescents escalate to violence, it is irresponsible—and maybe even criminal—to call the police for the trivial acts of mowing the lawn, selling water, or even shoplifting when the loss prevention officer on-site can check bags and receipts.

Lying or exaggerating about any detail of a crime is reprehensible. White lies kill. Even those who call the police with integrity bear some responsibility for the fatal police encounters, psychological harm, and unnecessary arrests and criminal records that Black youth face. The recent storm of police violence against Black youth has created a Hobson's choice for White business owners, homeowners, and neighbors who want to protect their space but don't want the police to kill.

We live in a "see something, say something" culture that has lured civilians into the hyper-surveillance of Black children. If we see a suspicious character lurking around our neighborhood or local store, there is now an app for that. SketchFactor and Good Part of Town—originally called Ghetto Tracker—were independently created user-friendly smartphone applications that claimed to help people avoid unsavory parts of New York City and Washington, D.C.[121] Each app allowed users to rate a neighborhood based on whether it appeared "safe" or "ghetto." Residents interested in protecting the sanctity and safety of their communities were invited to report "sketchy" people in the vicinity. People all over the country can also use Nextdoor.com, a social network site that allows its users to cite "suspicious activity" about their Black neighbors.

Both SketchFactor and Nextdoor.com came under intense fire for promoting racial profiling. Nextdoor.com posted on its corporate blog that it was implementing a series of changes intended to diminish user bias, including a prohibition on racial profiling in the site's guidelines and new reporting forms that emphasize the suspicious act rather than the person. SketchFactor has been discontinued, but there are many other apps and services that achieve the same goals with more innocent-sounding names.[122] Most recently, Amazon has been criticized by civil rights organizations for capitalizing on racial fears and developing dangerous partnerships with local police to support its Ring technology, which provides homeowners with high-speed doorbell cameras that allow them to observe, record, and report a potential threat at their front doors.[123]

Many of the crime watch services and apps have been inspired by or developed in partnership with local police departments or other government agencies like San Francisco's Bay Area Rapid Transit (BART). Intentionally drawing civilians into everyday surveillance, the BART Watch app allows riders to report suspicious activity, crimes, and other unwanted behaviors to authorities instantly. Like the private apps, BART Watch took complaints of racial profiling seriously, and its sponsors pledged to implement changes to reduce reports of noncriminal behavior.[124]

In February 2014, the Georgetown Business Improvement District partnered with the Metropolitan Police Department in Washington, D.C., to launch an initiative, using a real-time mobile messaging app called Operation GroupMe.[125] The app allowed Georgetown businesses, police officers, and community members to surreptitiously send each other thousands of messages with descriptions and pictures of customers acting suspiciously. According to data collected from the app between March 2014 and July 2015, more than 90 percent of the images shared were of African Americans. Consider the following examples:

American Apparel employee: *"Suspicious shoppers in store, 3 female. 1 male. Strong smell of weed. All African American. Help please."*
True Religion employee: *"What did they look like?"*
American Apparel employee: *"Ratchet." "LOL."*[126]

"Ratchet" is a slang term for trashy that often has racial connotations. In another exchange, a Hu's Wear employee took a photo of a tall, elegantly dressed African American man wearing distressed jeans, a gray scarf, and a long brown coat:

*"AA male. He just left. Headed towards 29th street. About 6 foot. Tats on neck and hand. Very suspicious, looking everywhere."*
Suitsupply employee: *"He was just in Suitsupply. Made a purchase of several suits and some gloves."*

Like SketchFactor and Ghetto Tracker, Operation GroupMe was discontinued after public backlash. Yet these apps continue to grow in popularity in other cities and states with few systematic studies of their racial impact. Connecticut launched CT Safe in November 2018 to allow the general public to anonymously report unusual activity and upload photos.[127] Among the suspicious activities people should look for are trespass, theft, vandalism, recruiting, weapons-related and cyber-related crimes, human tracking, and "any activity believed to be suspicious." In 2018, the Florida Department of Law Enforcement created FortifyFL as part of its efforts to make schools safer after the shooting at Marjory Stoneman Douglas High School.[128] While the app's focus is on school safety, it allows students and school officials to report the same kinds of suspicious activities as the other apps.

No data regarding the racial impact of either of these apps is available. User instructions in apps like these often identify suspicious factors to include odors and fluids, groups operating in an "orchestrated or rehearsed manner," and people in "bulky" or "inappropriate" clothing.[129] Given what we know about adolescents and public perceptions of Black youth, we can be sure that Black youth are regularly targeted on these platforms.

Most of us are not consciously racist. And most of us believe that race has nothing to do with our suspicions. Linda Krakora insisted that race had nothing to do with her decision to call the police when Reggie Fields mowed her lawn. Teresa Klein said race had nothing to do with her 911 call to report that Jeremiah Harvey had sexually touched her in a Brooklyn convenience store.[130] Alison Ettel said race had nothing to do with her call to report the eight-year-old for selling water.[131] But a few hidden cameras demonstrate just how much race does affect our decisions to call the police.

John Quiñones, host of the ABC TV show *What Would You Do?*, uses hidden cameras to observe how ordinary people behave when they are confronted with dilemmas that require them to make split-second decisions in various scenarios involving race and gender. In one of the most compelling episodes, producers chain a bicycle to a pole in a public park.[132] In the first segment of the experiment, a White teenage male wearing a T-shirt and baseball cap on backward uses tools to cut through the chain. For over an hour, many people walk by and speculate about what he might be doing. Virtually all keep walking.

After a while, the producers alter the experiment, replacing the White male with a Black teenage boy also dressed in a T-shirt and cap on backward. Within minutes of the Black boy hovering over the bike, people begin to stop and ask him what he is doing. "Is this your bike?" "Are you trying to steal it?" People call the police and yell for help, and one brave man even walks over and takes the boy's tools while a crowd begins to gather and yell at the Black teen.

In a third and final variation of the experiment, the bike thief is a beautiful White woman with blond hair. Not only does no one call the police, but several men—even one riding a bike alongside his appalled wife—stop to ask her if she needs help. One gentleman tells her with tongue in cheek that he has "some experience stealing bikes" in his childhood.

When people were interviewed about their responses to the young Black male, they all insisted that their decision to call the police or intervene to prevent the theft had nothing to do with race. When others were asked about their decision not to stop the beautiful blond woman, they said, "Well . . . we wouldn't expect a beautiful woman to be stealing." The participants were not actors. The scenarios were not scripted. Each witness was a civilian unwittingly caught in a reality TV show demonstrating that Black youth are presumed criminal.

# 9

## Policing as Trauma

We got a strange phone call in December 2019. One of our clients, "Kevin," called to say, "I have been in the house all day because the police are waiting for me out front."

We could hear Kevin's mom in the background yelling, "No, they are not! They're not out there for you, boy."

Kevin and his mom have lived in Washington, D.C., all of their lives. They have moved a lot, but they have spent most of their time in Southeast D.C. At the time of this call, they were renting a house in the northeast part of town. Their living room window looked out to the street, and Kevin could see a police car parked directly in front of his house. A marked cruiser with two White officers had been sitting there for hours. Kevin was convinced they were waiting for him to come out so they could arrest him.

The police have been a constant presence in Kevin's life. They crisscross through his neighborhood multiple times a day. They appear in marked and unmarked police cars. They come in uniform and in T-shirts emblazoned with "Metropolitan Police." They park on the street corner and at the local gas station. Sometimes they roll into the neighborhood fast and "jump out" on Black men and boys as they are walking down the street, talking on the phone, or sitting in front of their apartment buildings. Sometimes the police come in response to a call from the owner of a local convenience store who is tired of the boys selling weed in front of his market. Sometimes the police come "undercover" to buy weed in plain clothes and arrest the unsuspecting seller. But more often than not, they are just on routine patrol, passing through to watch the families come and go. Officers are present at all times of the day or night. Kevin is just as likely to see an officer at 8:00 a.m. or noon as he is to see one at 5:00 p.m. or midnight. Kevin suffers from insomnia, so he likes to walk to the twenty-four-hour mart a block up from his house. He has run into officers as early as 3:00 in the morning.

I represented Kevin for about three years with the support of three different law students. Kevin should have graduated from high school in 2020, but he doesn't like school. He has been diagnosed with depressive disorder and attention deficit hyperactivity disorder, making it hard for him to concentrate in class. When I last spoke to him, he was planning to enroll in a vocational program and study for his general equivalency diploma.

Kevin is very talented. He writes lyrics and records rap videos. His videos have a huge following, and he would love to make a career in music. Awaiting that success, Kevin started selling weed. A lot of it. And he made good money doing so. Kevin started smoking weed at the age of ten. He started selling at fifteen. When he started selling, it was a crime to possess or sell marijuana in the District of Columbia. In 2015, D.C. decriminalized marijuana, making it legal for anyone over twenty-one to possess up to two ounces of marijuana for personal use. Dispensaries popped up in D.C., and business owners began to offer weed in exchange for gifts.[1] The change in marijuana laws didn't change the way the police dealt with Kevin. Kevin was a minor, so he still wasn't supposed to have or sell weed. The police kept him under close surveillance.

Kevin has been stopped no fewer than fifty times, mostly in the three-block radius of his home. Of course, at times, the police stops were fair and justified. Kevin has sold weed to an undercover officer; he has sold weed in the presence of an officer; and he has sold weed in front of an eyewitness who told officers he was selling weed. But Kevin has been stopped far more times for no reason at all. He has been stopped when there was no call for service, no sale of drugs, and no criminal activity at all. He has been stopped alone and with friends. He has been stopped on his way in to buy chips at the convenience store and sometimes on his way back out. He has been stopped when he was texting his girlfriend and when he was just waiting at the bus stop or sitting in a folding chair outside his building.

Kevin has been to court more times than I can count. He has pled guilty to some charges, and he has fought others at trial. Many of his cases have been dismissed by the prosecutor or thrown out by a judge who reviewed evidence of police violating his rights. Kevin describes his contact with the police over the years as hostile, unnecessary, and at times quite violent. He has been to the hospital at least three times as a result of police force. Once he was shoved against a wall and then dragged backward down the street by his wrists, which were handcuffed behind his back. Another time he ended up in an ankle brace after officers tackled him to the ground. Another time he complained of chest pains after an officer climbed on top of him to search his pockets for drugs. On that occasion, the officer realized he had forgotten to search Kevin before putting him in a squad car. Instead of pulling Kevin back out of the cruiser, the officer climbed into the backseat, forced Kevin onto his back, and held him down with a knee in his rib cage while he finished the search. Kevin was still in handcuffs and yelling for the officer to "get off." Kevin is five feet four and 120 pounds.

More than anything, Kevin really hates being strip-searched. On one occasion, he became unhinged in a cellblock when a male officer reached down with little warning and tried to search his underwear. Convinced that Kevin was hiding pills in his rear, the officer was going to search underneath his testicles and between his butt cheeks. Kevin recoiled and backed up against the wall. Two other officers watched—one male, the other female. Kevin kept telling the officer not to touch his "dick" and called the officer a "bitch." He screamed and hollered and tightened his body against the wall so no one could touch him. All three officers then forced him to the ground, shackled him by his arms and feet, and carried him like a hog down the hall to an even smaller cell.

The officers knew they had touched a nerve with Kevin. Not only was he hysterical, but he had also called out for his "lawyer" several times in the encounter. The officers called for an internal investigation within the police department. When the investigator arrived, Kevin tried to explain how "the officer made me feel uncomfortable" during the search. The investigator twisted his words, discredited his complaint, and stomped out of the cell, slamming the door behind him. Kevin didn't have better words to explain what happened, and the investigator didn't have the patience to deal with a teenager who was yelling, cursing, and unable to give a clear and orderly account of the facts. The investigator was there less than five minutes.

When Kevin called in December to say the police were waiting for him outside, his mom thought her son was being "paranoid." I thought Kevin was traumatized. Yes, Kevin's mom was right: the police probably weren't actually "waiting" for him when he called that day. We weren't aware of any warrants, and if the police had one, they would have just come inside to arrest him. But Kevin's fear wasn't irrational. Someone who doesn't live in Kevin's neighborhood might think, "Well, if he wasn't doing anything wrong, he wouldn't be so worried." But most of us can't imagine seeing the police every day, multiple times a day— whether we have done anything wrong or not. Most us can't imagine walking to a convenience store and having police stare at us—no matter what we wear, with whom we make eye contact, or how fast or slow we walk. In Kevin's world, the officers are always there waiting for him to stumble. No, Kevin wasn't being paranoid. He was experiencing what so many Black youth experience in cities like Washington, D.C. He was dealing with the traumatic effects of over-policing.

## "I CAN'T BREATHE": DIRECT AND VICARIOUS TRAUMA

Trauma is any distressing or disturbing experience that causes significant fear, helplessness, confusion, or other disruptive feelings intense enough to have a lasting negative effect on a person's attitudes, behaviors, and social, emotional, or spiritual well-being.[2] Trauma can result from physical or emotional injuries or the threat of either. Adolescents may experience trauma from physical abuse, the loss of someone they love, community violence, disasters, grief, or bullying. For many young people, policing helps relieve trauma. Police might arrest an abusive parent, break up a fight, respond to a natural disaster, or reduce crime in the community. But for some youth, policing itself is traumatic. Black youth like Kevin experience trauma from direct acts of police aggression, witnessing or hearing about police aggression toward someone they know, or repeated exposure to the details of police aggression—even involving people they don't know.[3] For some, the cumulative stress caused by the daily, gratuitous, and discriminatory encounters with police becomes overwhelming and paralyzing.

In the Black community, the traumatic effects of policing often begin with word-of-mouth or media accounts of police violence. More than 500 civilians were fatally shot by the police in the first six months of 2020; 105 of them were Black. If police killings continue at this pace, they will likely reach or surpass the number of killings in 2018 and 2019. In 2018, 994 people were fatally shot by the police; 209 of them were Black. In 2019, 1,004 people were shot by the police; 234 were Black.[4] The rate of fatal police shootings among Black Americans is much higher than that of any other ethnicity. Black Americans were killed by the police at a rate of 31 per million of the population between 2015 and June 2020. White Americans were killed at a rate of 13 fatal police shootings per million of the population.[5] Black youth accounted for a significant number of those deaths. Between 2015 and 2020, approximately 16.8 percent of Black people fatally shot in police encounters were twenty-one and under.[6] Only 5.17 percent of

White people fatally shot in police encounters were twenty-one and under.

It is hard, if not impossible, for parents to shield their children from the graphic and disturbing images of police violence. Ninety-five percent of teens aged thirteen to seventeen reported having access to a smartphone in 2018.[7] Forty-five percent say they are online "almost constantly." This is double the number of teens who responded that way just three years before. Another 44 percent of teens say they go online multiple times per day. In 2018, the most popular website among teens was YouTube, with Instagram and Snapchat a close second and third. The use of smartphones, video sharing, and social media platforms allows for unprecedented access to information on police brutality.

Black youth can't avoid the traumatic images of police violence as videos become permanently available and play automatically as youth scroll through news feeds on their various social media accounts.[8] Black youth heard Eric Garner yell, "I can't breathe," over and over as he was choked by police in New York. They watched Walter Scott being chased and falling to the ground after he was shot in the back by police in North Charleston, South Carolina. They watched Sandra Bland as she was harassed and ridiculed in an unnecessary confrontation with the police after a traffic stop in Prairie View, Texas. They watched Philando Castile bleeding and dying in a car as his girlfriend and her daughter watched the police kill him in Falcon Heights, Minnesota. They watched as Stephon Clark was shot in his grandmother's backyard in Sacramento, California. And they watched as George Floyd was murdered in Minneapolis, Minnesota, by an officer who held his knee on his neck for nine minutes and twenty-nine seconds until he could no longer breathe.

Researchers have described "viral videos" of police killings as one of the most traumatic events facing adolescents of color.[9] Videos have been posted by bystanders, families of the victims, and police departments that were ordered to release body-worn and dashcam footage in response to public outcry and investigation. The videos are graphic and appalling. They are played over and over on the news and social media long after the killings. They become fixed in a child's mind and cause grief and anxiety. Research suggests that watching police violence is similar to watching the Twin Towers collapse on 9/11, people stranded on roofs and bridges during Hurricane Katrina, and people killed or injured during the Boston Marathon and Oklahoma City bombings.[10]

Repeated exposure to high-profile police killings is particularly detrimental to the mental health of Black youth. In 2019, researchers analyzed data collected from a national sample of Black and Latinx youth aged eleven to nineteen and found that youth with more frequent exposure to traumatic experiences while online reported higher levels of post-traumatic stress disorder and depressive symptoms.[11] Youth described depressive symptoms as being sad, feeling like crying, and feeling alone. PTSD symptoms included reexperiencing the traumatic event, hyperarousal, and numbing. Girls in this study reported even higher levels of symptoms in each category than the boys.

These national results mirror more localized studies in cities and states across the country. In a series of focus groups convened with Black boys aged fourteen to eighteen in Hartford and New Haven, Connecticut, researchers identified several recurring themes among youth who had witnessed high-profile police killings in the media.[12] These youth expressed an acute awareness that young Black men are seen as a threat and have to be careful to get home alive.[13] The boys also expressed fear about being profiled by the police, becoming the victim of police violence, and knowing other kids who might be targeted by the police for what they wear and how they act. Many of the boys could "identify" with the victims of the high-profile shootings and understood that police killings could happen to them in their own communities. Those who had personally experienced unpleasant encounters with the police were even more likely to be anxious about the national police cases.

To get home safe, the boys in Connecticut learned to change what they say, how they dress, and what they do—including avoiding certain streets at night, taking down their hoods, and explaining their actions if stopped by the police. The boys essentially learned to "be what [the police] wouldn't expect you to be."[14] These strategies resonate with Black youth across the country. Black youth now automatically pull their hands out of their pockets, put their hands on the dashboard, or put their hands up and yell, "Don't shoot," when confronted by the police. Black youth routinely run at the sight of police—not because they are hiding something or doing anything wrong, but because they are terrified of getting shot, choked, or maimed. Black youth learn these safety measures from their parents, construct them with friends, or develop them instinctively to survive. But the need for survival strategies is itself a source of trauma.

Just having to worry about becoming a victim is as frightening and stressful as being a victim.[15] Even when the anticipated violence doesn't happen, youth often suffer from the same psychological effects that would normally accompany such an encounter. Survival strategies are also embarrassing and demeaning. Having to placate or acquiesce to the police—especially when innocent of any crime—steals the youths' dignity and undermines their self-esteem.

Even as outrage continues to mount as more Black people are callously murdered by the police, the day-to-day brutalities of American policing remain largely hidden from public view. While a small percentage of Black youth will actually die at the hands of police, many more will experience some form of degrading or invasive police encounter multiple times in their lives. Youth in general have more frequent contact with the police than adults because they play outside, congregate in public spaces, hang out late, play loud music, and engage in risky behaviors.[16] Black youth in urban cities like Chicago, Cincinnati, New York, and Washington, D.C., see police as a constant, inescapable, and unwelcome presence in their communities.[17]

Even in New York City, where the number of stops and frisks plummeted after national publicity and civil rights litigation against the police department in 2011, racial disparities have persisted. Between 2014 and 2017, Black and Latino males between the ages of fourteen and twenty-four accounted for only 5 percent of the city's population, yet made up 38 percent of reported stops. In 2018, 57 percent of all people stopped by the police in New York City were Black, 31 percent were Latinx, and 10 percent were White.[18] In 2019, 59 percent of the people stopped were Black, 29 percent were Latinx, and 9 percent were White.

Consistent with what we learned from Kevin, Black and Latino boys are just as likely to be stopped by the police when they are not involved in crime as they are when they have been involved in crime.[19] In New York City, 80 percent of young Black and Latino males stopped between 2014 and 2017 were innocent of any crime. More than 93 percent of those who were frisked for weapons during the stop didn't have a weapon. Black and Latinx people were more likely to be frisked than Whites and, among those frisked, were less likely to be found with a weapon. They were also significantly more likely to experience police use of force.[20]

In a 2016 wellness survey, youth from five cities—Boston, Chicago, Denver, St. Paul, and Philadelphia—were asked to identify the leading barriers to adolescent health.[21] With remarkable agreement, the participants, who were mostly Black, cited poor police-youth relations as a key impediment to their health and well-being. Across the five sites, youth said they were over-policed, undervalued, marginalized, and living under siege. They spoke candidly about their fear and mistrust of police, which caused anxiety and led them to avoid public spaces. They complained that stereotyping and police bias made them feel unsafe and unwelcome in their own schools and communities, and observed that Blacks were most likely to be targeted. They also believed that young people engage in risky behaviors to cope with pervasive stress—including stress caused by racial tension and police brutality. Even when the youth identified gentrification, unemployment, and the lack of community resources as other significant contributors to poor adolescent health, they often tied those concerns to policing. While gentrification worsened already poor relations with local police, unemployment was both a cause and a result of increased policing in Black communities.

## COLLATERAL DAMAGE:
### POLICING AND ADOLESCENT MENTAL HEALTH

Often my client Kevin is laid-back and relaxed. He is funny and creative. He wears his hair in twists and likes nice clothes. His style is artistic and unique. Although Kevin hasn't gone to school much past the eighth grade, he is clearly much more intelligent than his grade level reflects. Despite his learning disabilities, he reads and writes well, and in some of his darkest moments, including those at the youth detention facility, he has written rap lyrics that keenly reflect on his life. Kevin is quite talented, and his mother often gets emails and calls from artists interested in collaborating with him. When he was locked up, he asked us to bring him books and blank writing journals. When I last spoke to him, he was reading a romance novel—maybe because he was in love himself and excited about the anticipated birth of his first child. Kevin also loves his mother and is rarely too far away from her. He smiles and will give you a hug if you ask for one. On a good day, I know he likes me and the young lawyers who work with me.

But Kevin is not always easy. He is often tense and withdrawn. He is anxious and stressed. He is defensive and almost always on guard. He doesn't sleep at night, and he never feels safe. He asks a lot of questions and gets angry easily. When he is really worked up, he yells and curses. He yells at his mom. He yells at the police. He yells at me and the lawyers who work with me. He walks away and slams down the phone when he doesn't want to talk anymore. He doesn't like disappointment and doesn't have the skills to manage his emotions. There are days when he thinks everyone is out to get him—especially the police. His anger and resentment at the police are palpable. Kevin has all the signs of trauma.

Like so many other young Black men and boys, Kevin has been

watched, followed, questioned, manhandled, and told to lift his shirt by the police more times than he can remember. Young black men who experience physically and emotionally invasive police encounters report considerable signs of trauma and anxiety.[22] Those signs increase with the frequency of the police contact, the intrusiveness of the contact, and the young men's perception that the contact was unfair. Encounters involving harsh language, racial insults, or taunts about sexuality create the most stress and are perceived as the most offensive.[23]

In 2019, researchers analyzed data collected from 918 at-risk youth, with an average age of fifteen, who had been stopped by the police over a three-year period.[24] Thirty-nine percent of the youth stopped were thirteen years old or younger at the time of their first stop. Most had been stopped on the street, but 24 percent were stopped at school and 29 percent were stopped at other locations. Youth who were stopped more frequently were more likely to report feeling angry, scared, and unsafe and more likely to experience stigma and shame. Those who experienced more invasive stops like searches, frisks, harsh language, and racial slurs were more likely to report both emotional distress during the stop and post-traumatic stress after the stop. Youth experienced stress regardless of whether they were engaged in delinquent behavior or not. Even youth who had an extensive history of delinquency were not immune from the emotional distress, trauma, and stigma associated with the most intrusive stops.

In 2018, another team of researchers looked at the impact of routine police stops on the psychological well-being of a sample of Latino and Black boys in the ninth and tenth grades in a large southern city.[25] Youth in that study reported on the effects of those stops six, twelve, and eighteen months after they occurred. As in other studies, youth who experienced more frequent police stops reported greater psychological distress, which they described as finding it hard to wind down, feeling downhearted and blue, and being close to panic.[26] That research made me think about Kevin's anxiety and insomnia. And indeed, in 2020, researchers looked specifically at the connection between exposure to police stops and adolescent sleep patterns.[27] Analyzing data from 3,444 U.S. youth who reported on their experiences of social stigma, post-traumatic stress, and sleep quality after direct and vicarious exposure to police stops, researchers found that youth who had been exposed to police stops exhibited significantly greater odds of sleep deprivation and low sleep quality. Even when the youth were only bystanders to the stops or witnessed more subtly abusive police behaviors, they still experienced trauma that lowered both the quality of their sleep and the number of hours they slept. These findings are consistent with other studies that list nightmares, flashbacks, and insomnia as symptoms commonly associated with police trauma.[28]

The mere presence of an officer in a heavily policed and racially targeted neighborhood can be toxic for an adolescent's health.[29] Young people who have witnessed or experienced invasive police encounters often recall and relive those experiences whenever they see the police. They may have vivid flashbacks and revisit the same physical and psychological reactions, such as sweating, difficulty breathing, and nausea.[30] To avoid triggering memories and reduce the emotional effects of prior police contact, some Black youth stay inside or limit their use and enjoyment of public and recreational spaces.[31] Others just go out of their way to avoid contact with the police and are always on guard against the possibility of abuse.[32]

Police presence also evokes all of the fears and emotions associated with stereotype threat—the fear of being stereotyped as criminal simply because of one's race. As we learned in chapter 7, stereotype threat makes young people feel distressed, guilty, hostile, irritable, ashamed, nervous, jittery, and afraid. For some, the effects of police trauma are not immediately evident. At first, the effects of an individual encounter with the police may seem subtle or temporary, but over time—especially with long-term or repeated exposure—policing can affect adolescent well-being for days, weeks, and even a lifetime after a traumatic event.

The time and location of a police stop have a significant impact on how Black youth experience those encounters. Emotional distress, stigma, and other post-traumatic symptoms are more pronounced when a child is stopped at school.[33] Youth who are arrested at school may be removed from class, handcuffed, and paraded down the hall in front of friends and teachers. Niya Kenny described her experience with the deputy in her South Carolina school as "embarrassing" and frightening.[34] School encounters with police are particularly stigmatizing as teachers, staff, and classmates label and exclude the targeted youth from after-school activities and other opportunities. Black youth have to navigate the added stress of trying to convince their parents and teachers they are not to blame for some unwarranted stop or arrest by the police. Students who worry that others will judge them negatively may hide their police contact from friends and family and avoid others to prevent them from using the contact to hurt their feelings.

Many youth who have frequent contact with the police already suffer from the stress and trauma associated with poverty, social isolation, discrimination, crowding, underemployment, violence, and victimization.[35] It is difficult to know how many youth have preexisting mental health disorders and trauma before they encounter the police. One way to estimate that number is to determine how many of the youth referred to the juvenile legal system have previously diagnosed mental health disorders when they enter the system. Recent data estimates that 40 to 70 percent of detained or incarcerated youth have some mental health disorder. Even the conservative estimate is much higher than the estimated 10 to 20 percent of the general adolescent population that report such disorders.[36] Another study found that 51 percent of youth in correctional facilities—typically used for long-term placement after sentencing—reported having problems with anxiety.[37] Seventy percent of those youth also reported having experienced at least one traumatic event in their lifetime.

Police contact during and after arrest can trigger previous stress and depressive symptoms, especially if the youth believe their arrests were motivated by racism. Youth who live in heavily policed and under-resourced communities are significantly more likely to report post-traumatic stress after a police encounter.[38] Black youth who have experienced early traumas often resist being touched by the police and don't want to be dominated or controlled.

### #SAYHERNAME: BLACK GIRLS AND TRAUMA

Although Black men and boys are more likely to be stopped, frisked, and killed than Black women and girls,[39] the data and stories shared throughout this book demonstrate that Black girls have every reason to be afraid of the police.[40] According to 2015 data from the Police-Public Contact Survey (PPCS), Black women were about 17 percent more likely to be in a police-initiated traffic stop than White women, and 34 percent more likely to be stopped than Latina women.[41] Collectively, less than 1 percent of White, Black, and Latina women surveyed experienced a police-initiated street stop in 2015, with little disparity across race. However, once stopped, Black women were roughly three times more likely to be arrested than White women and twice as likely to be arrested as Latina women. Black women were at least as likely as White men to be arrested during a police-initiated stop, while White women were about half as likely as White men to be arrested during those stops.

Analysts from the Prison Policy Initiative concluded that racial disparities among women who were arrested after a street stop appear to be related to what happens during those stops. This analysis resonates with Sandra Bland's experience in Texas when she was pulled over for a frivolous traffic stop, expressed her outrage at being stopped and ticketed, and was then arrested for talking back and "resisting" the officer's instructions. Although police use of force was relatively low among all 2015 PPCS survey participants, use-of-force rates were higher for Black women than White or Latina women. Black women experienced police force during a stop at about the same rate as White men, while White women were significantly less likely to experience use of force than White men.

Black women and girls living in over-policed neighborhoods have similar experiences with trauma as Black males.[42] Black girls suffer from the trauma of watching siblings, partners, fathers, and uncles being stopped, assaulted, and killed. They and their mothers grieve the loss of companionship and intimacy from those who have been incarcerated and often struggle to compensate for the loss of income and support. And like their brothers, Black girls are afraid of being stopped, accosted, searched, and assaulted by the police.

In August 2020, Brittney Gilliam was on her way to the nail salon with her six-year-old daughter, twelve-year-old sister, and fourteen- and seventeen-year-old nieces when she was pulled over and accused of driving a stolen car in Aurora, Colorado.[43] Officers pulled up with guns drawn and yelled for the girls to put their hands out of the window and get out of the car. In a video captured by an onlooker, the children can be heard wailing and calling out for their mothers as they are handcuffed and forced to lie facedown on the pavement for over two hours with their hands behind their backs. The police eventually realized they had made a mistake. Gilliam's license plate did not match that of a stolen out-of-state motorcycle, which the officers should have been looking for. Ms. Gilliam later told reporters that she felt powerless and dehumanized by the experience. The girls, who could barely eat and sleep in the days after the encounter, started weekly therapy.

In January 2021, a nine-year-old girl experienced similar trauma when she was pepper sprayed by police officers in Rochester, New York, after refusing to get in a police car.[44] Officers were initially called to the nine-year-old's home in response to a domestic dispute between her parents and were told that the girl "wanted to kill herself and wanted to kill her mom."[45] Videos from the officers' body-worn cameras show the girl screaming while an officer holds her head down on the snow-covered ground and handcuffs her. Later the officers try to wrestle her into a police car and threaten to put pepper spray "in her eyeballs" as she repeatedly cries out "I want my dad." A male officer can be heard saying, "Just spray her already." At one point, an officer scolds the nine-year-old by telling her she is "acting like a child," to which she responds, "I am a child." After she was pepper sprayed, the girl continued to sob in the back of the police car, telling the officers that her eyes were burning and the handcuffs were painfully tight.

Black women and girls have every reason to fear the police as evident by the #SayHerName campaign, which has worked to lift up the names of girls and women who have been killed by the police. Atatiana Jefferson, Sandra Bland, Rekia Boyd, Breonna Taylor, and Ma'Khia Bryant are among the most visible. Other victims include Charleena Lyles, Korryn Gaines, Natasha McKenna, Pearlie Golden, Yvette Smith, Michelle Cusseaux, Tanisha Anderson, Miriam Carey, Shelly Frey, Kathryn Johnston, and Eleanor Bumpurs.[46] Black transgender girls have the added trauma of witnessing the police killings of Black transgender women, such as Mya Hall, Kayla Moore, and Duanna Johnson.

Many of these women and girls were killed in response to mental health calls, nonemergency 411 calls, and calls they made themselves. Black girls and women are also at risk of being shot as bystanders when police are in pursuit of Black men. India Kager, Tarika Wilson, and Aiyana Stanley-Jones were all killed this way. In one of the most tragic cases, seven-year-old Aiyana Stanley-Jones was asleep in her bed when Detroit police raided her family's apartment looking for her uncle who was suspected in a murder.[47] Officers lobbed a flash-bang grenade into the apartment, catching Aiyana's blanket on fire, and then began shooting as they entered. An officer shot Aiyana in the head as she was sleeping on the couch. The police refused to provide help to the dying girl and forced her parents and grandmother to sit in her blood for hours. Two juries failed to reach a verdict in the case against the Detroit police officer Joseph Weekley.

## FROM TRAUMA TO HUMILIATION

Police brutality extends beyond physical force to include emotional as well as verbal assault and psychological intimidation.[48] Black children are stopped and frisked in public, forced to sit on the sidewalk while neighbors watch, and humiliated by police who tease, berate, or question their manhood. Kevin says his most embarrassing encounter with the police occurred when he was standing outside in his neighborhood with twenty other kids when the police drove up fast, pulled their car onto the sidewalk, jumped out, and tossed him against the wall. The other kids stood there in shock. This wasn't a neighborhood sweep. This wasn't a routine stop and frisk. The police weren't responding to any complaints from a local business. The kids hadn't run at the sight of the police. In fact, the officers had already circled through the block about ten minutes earlier, and nothing was out of the ordinary. Yet the officers stopped Kevin—and Kevin alone—and refused to tell him why.

We later learned that the police had taken a "visual inventory" of the kids standing outside during their first pass through the block. The officers parked around the corner to discuss what they had seen. The officers recognized Kevin and said they had seen him coming out of the convenience store from which he had been barred. They also knew he would probably have weed. For that, they circled back to pick him up—in the middle of the day, in front of twenty people. Kevin's alleged unlawful entry and marijuana possession hardly justified the embarrassing takedown he experienced that day.

At times, police contact goes beyond embarrassing to be humiliating, degrading, and dehumanizing. In May 2019, police officers in Sacramento, California, covered a Black twelve-year-old's face with a mesh sack after he reportedly ran away from a security guard who claimed he was panhandling and asking people to buy things for him.[49] Two nearby Sacramento officers saw him running and stepped in to help the guard. Cell-phone video captured the twelve-year-old boy detained by the police and calling for his mom. When the boy struggled, an officer forced him to the ground on his stomach with a knee in his back. Another officer placed his knee on the boy's thigh. The officers later put a "spit sack" on his head when they say he was trying to spit on them. The boy's fifteen-year-old sister arrived at the scene and called their mother, who panicked because her son suffers from an upper respiratory disease. His mother described the incident as "every parent's nightmare." The officers cited the boy for battery on a peace officer.

It is hard to imagine the police arresting a twelve-year-old, but it is more common than we might think. In fact, Kevin was first arrested at age twelve—for arguing with the police. The officers thought he should be charged with "assault on a police officer" under an old version of the law that defined assault to include interfering and resisting an officer.[50] Prosecutors decided not to charge that case, but a few months later Kevin was arrested for shoplifting, removed from his home, and committed to the department of youth services for two years. Whenever we ask him about that time in his life, Kevin gets visibly agitated and tells us that we will never understand how "it fucks you up" to be committed at such a young age for some "stupid shit" like shoplifting. That was before our prosecutors and judges became more enlightened in D.C. Fortunately, I am convinced that Kevin would never be committed—and probably not even prosecuted—for shoplifting at the age of twelve today, but I am not so convinced that our police will ever stop arresting twelve-year-olds for theft.

On April Fools' Day 2019, in Washington, D.C., police handcuffed a Black ten-year-old boy after another child said he had been assaulted and robbed of his cell phone by several youth with a pellet gun.[51] Police arrested the ten-year-old and his friend as the lead suspects, and videos of the two boys went viral. When a friend called the ten-year-old's mother to come to the scene, she arrived to find her son handcuffed in police custody. She later told reporters, "It was hurting me. There were so many people out there, I didn't know what to do. My mind was just blown from the situation. I see my son on the ground with three police around him at just 10-years-old."[52] The boy's mother also said the experience traumatized her son so much that "he couldn't even sleep last night. His mind was just so rumbling." Four days later, prosecutors reported that surveillance cameras showed the ten-year-old had nothing to do with the robbery and publicly announced that he was innocent.[53]

Just three weeks later, on April 24, 2019, D.C. police came under fire again when they handcuffed a nine-year-old Black boy on another public street. This time the incident began when the boy was leaning against a car and an officer told him to get off. The officer got annoyed when the nine-year-old talked back and didn't move. Other children watched and laughed as police chased the child in circles around the parked cars. When the officer finally caught up to the boy, he grabbed him by his jacket and brought him to the ground. Within an instant, the boy's silly banter with the police turned to hysteria as the officer handcuffed him and pulled him away from his friends. The boy screamed and cried and eventually soiled his pants. When his mother found out about the incident from a family friend, she was "devastated" and told a reporter, "I was traumatized for my son having to go through that. His use of force was unnecessary. My son was not a threat. He was not committing a crime. He was not harming anyone. It should have never been to that."[54] The nine-year-old told the reporter that the handcuffs hurt and he was "scared" because he thought he was going to get locked up.[55]

Both of these cases outraged the public and led the Metropolitan Police Department to adopt a new policy prohibiting officers from handcuffing children twelve years old and younger except in the most dangerous situations. While the new regulation was an important procedural response, it might have missed the real point: that we just need to treat children like children.

Sadly, the regulation didn't do enough to change all law enforcement attitudes about Black children. Less than a year later, another D.C. police agency faced public outrage when a thirteen-year-old was arrested for "horseplay" at a Metro station.[56] It all started when two boys were "grabbing onto each other . . . as if they were fighting." When two Metro Transit Police officers asked if they were fighting, the boys said they were just playing. The boys were classmates and friends. Still not satisfied, the officers ordered the boys to sit on a bench and asked for their parents' names and contact information. The thirteen-year-old refused, insisting that "we told him we wasn't fighting and that should have been the end of it. But then he's talking about, he wants my information. 'No, I don't have to do it. I didn't commit a crime.'" When the boy stood up from the bench, an officer yanked him by his arm and pushed him to the ground. Two officers held him against the floor while he was crying and screaming, "It hurts." The officers claim the boy had pushed one of them and said, "Back up from me." Bystanders expressed outrage at how quickly the police escalated the incident and how much force they used.

### POLICING AS RACISM: "POLICE DON'T LIKE BLACK PEOPLE"[57]

Black youth feel the effects of racism in every aspect of their lives.[58] At school, they are viewed as intellectually inferior and treated like second-class citizens.[59] In the community, Black youth are regarded with suspicion and forced to deal with the implicit and explicit assumptions others make about their abilities, motives, and intentions.[60] Data shows a stark increase in hate crimes against Black youth since the 2016 presidential election.[61] Researchers in one 2020 study found that Black teenagers aged thirteen to seventeen in Washington, D.C., faced an average of five racially discriminatory experiences per day, with little differences between boys and girls.[62] Some experiences were subtle and unintentional. Others were overt and deliberate. Black youth experienced discrimination individually, in groups, and vicariously through the shared experiences of friends and family.

Racism appears in many forms, including verbal name-calling, subtle slights by others, and physical violence. Some Black youth are teased and harassed by their peers or adults about their hair texture, skin tone, language, or accent.[63] Others are treated poorly in public accommodations as they watch youth of different races receive preferential treatment. Black youth face discrimination in person and online. Racial discrimination is particularly common online as the internet allows for anonymous self-expression with little consequence.[64] Black youth are exposed to racial epithets, written posts, digital images, and videos on social media.

Policing mirrors and expands other experiences with racism and discrimination. Black youth experience policing as discriminatory when it assigns more officers, allocates more surveillance technology, enforces more criminal laws, and endorses more aggressive practices in Black communities than in White communities. Not only are youth frustrated by what they perceive to be countless unfair and unwarranted encounters with the police, but they are also bothered by what they see as slow response times and an outright failure of police to respond to and investigate crimes reported by Black victims.[65]

Black youth also understand that police have always been a significant barrier to their success and an essential partner in other structures of oppression. Youth who are targeted by the police are assigned to court systems that continue to explicitly and implicitly discriminate against their race.[66] With a conviction—and sometimes just an arrest—Black youth may be barred from schools, housing, jobs, and professional licenses they need to compete in America's economy. Law enforcement decisions about whom to watch and whom to stop contribute to enduring racial inequities in the legal system and have been linked to poor academic outcomes, reduced job prospects, and poor mental and physical health in Black communities.[67]

Kevin's experiences with racism may help explain his poor performance in school despite his obvious intelligence. Several studies have found a link between persistent racism and decreased academic achievement.[68] Like other victims of trauma who have difficulty focusing on and completing everyday tasks,[69] many youth who have been the targets of discrimination find it difficult to pay attention in school, complete their work successfully, and engage respectfully with teachers, administrators, and school resource officers they believe are racist. Even worse, Black youth who repeatedly observe or experience bigotry lose faith in the possibility of a long life and successful future.

The lack of accountability for police violence is another form of racism. Just as young people cannot escape news accounts of police killings, they also cannot ignore the public's apathetic response to racial profiling, blatant racism, and systemic biases that have contributed to the reckless and sometimes intentional police violence against Blacks.[70] White silence in the face of police brutality is tantamount to consent.[71] Black youth are troubled by officers who cover for their colleagues' misconduct, prosecutors who refuse to indict police who kill, and jury verdicts that exonerate even the most egregious acts of police brutality. Public reactions that demonstrate support for police shootings of Blacks cause hurt, anger, and stress.[72] At best, unchecked police violence signals to Black youth that Black lives don't matter. At worst, it represents a state-sanctioned attack on Black Americans.[73]

Racism in all of its forms has a significant impact on the mental and physical health of children and adolescents.[74] While not everyone who experiences racism will develop symptoms of race-based trauma, repeated exposure to high levels of discrimination and prejudice interrupts the cognitive, social, and emotional development of Black children.[75] Even teasing that appears playful at first may later impact important aspects of adolescent development, including racial identity formation and self-esteem.[76] More than twenty-five years of research has documented a strong link between experiences of racism and depressive symptoms in Black youth.[77] Black adolescents who report frequent experiences of being insulted, excluded, and teased about their race or ethnicity develop symptoms such as hypervigilance, panic, distrust, increased aggression, substance abuse, shame, self-harm, emotional detachment, and depression.[78] As with other forms of trauma, the effects of racism occur through both direct and vicarious experiences. Adolescents don't have to be personally involved for the discriminatory event to impact their psychological adjustment.[79] Although children and adolescents who are the targets of racism experience the most significant impact, watching perceived racist acts is almost as traumatizing as experiencing them.[80]

Black youth who are afraid of being targeted tend to avoid eye contact with strangers, and are often reluctant to take risks and enter new situations. Youth who have experienced discrimination are particularly suspicious of government agencies, social workers, and mental health providers. This was especially true for Kevin. Kevin rarely showed up for appointments with new service providers and vocational opportunities without multiple attempts and extensive prodding. We were most successful at getting Kevin to attend when one of our lawyers or staff would pick him up and go with him. While Kevin's limited transportation explained part of the problem, our conversations with him in the car revealed something much more challenging at work. Kevin was always convinced the providers were going to set him up to fail and never believed that anyone but close friends and family could ever have his best interest at heart.

## THE KIDS ARE NOT "ALRIGHT"

*It is easier to build strong children*
*than to repair a broken man.*

—ATTRIBUTED TO FREDERICK DOUGLASS

I worry about my clients. And I worry about the link between police violence and early deaths among Black Americans.[81] Violent and aggressive policing not only increases the risk of fatal injuries but also reduces life expectancy among Black youth and adults who live with chronic stress and extended trauma.[82] When faced with a threat, the body activates defense systems and produces stress hormones, such as cortisol, that are necessary for survival.[83] The "fight-flight-freeze" response, which is the body's natural reaction to danger, is often accompanied by an accelerated heartbeat, inflammation, and rapid and shallow breathing.[84] When the threat is persistent or recurring—such as with racial discrimination, police violence, or the fear of such violence—the survival process causes rapid wear and tear on body organs and can lead to diabetes, strokes, ulcers, cognitive impairment, autoimmune disorders, high blood pressure, accelerated aging, and death.[85]

Sometimes fight-flight-freeze responses can become overactive, triggering reactions to nonthreatening situations, especially among youth who have an extensive history of direct and vicarious trauma. Data tracking the health of youth by race shows that Black youth fare much worse than White youth across many indicators of health, including obesity, teen pregnancy, suicide, and morbidity.[86] The chronic stressors caused by policing put teenagers at greater risk for these and other long-term health problems.

That risk is only exacerbated by evidence that Black youth are significantly less likely than White youth to seek, receive, and complete treatment for depression and other mental health disorders.[87] Kevin has a strong objection to mental health services. At one appointment, he got tired of waiting to see the doctor and got up to talk to the lady at the front desk. When he asked her what they were going to "do to him" in the appointment, she mentioned that the doctor might decide he needs medication. All of a sudden Kevin started screaming about not wanting to be there anymore and stormed out of the building. When we caught up with him outside, he eventually said he didn't want to take any medicine that was going to "alter his brain." As is so often the case when he doesn't know how to articulate his fears, Kevin flipped out. By then we had learned to let Kevin go, allow him to cool down, hear out his concerns, and answer his questions patiently and without judgment. Unfortunately, most people don't have time for that—especially not those who work for overextended and under-resourced government-funded mental health providers.

Some Black youth avoid treatment because they don't trust health-care providers or are afraid of the stigma associated with treatment. Black youth are particularly afraid their friends will ridicule them and their families won't support them if they ask for mental health support. Others receive inadequate treatment due to conscious and unconscious racism by treatment providers or are denied treatment altogether because they don't have the money or insurance to pay.

Youth who receive culturally inappropriate services engage poorly and leave early. Black youth, in particular, may express their depressive symptoms differently than White youth.[88] Black teens often talk about their symptoms as headaches, stomachaches, and insomnia without explicitly connecting them to depression or other mental health problems. This language gap makes it less likely they will get the help they need.[89] This might also explain why Kevin had such a hard time talking to the investigator who asked if he wanted to make a sexual assault complaint against the officer who searched him. Kevin couldn't explain why the search made him uncomfortable.

Youth of any race who live with undiagnosed and untreated mental health concerns may act out with aggression.[90] When youth suffer inside or feel as if their lives are out of control, they may put up a tough facade and appear unapproachable to keep people away and cope with anxiety. Some youth become defiant or violent with adults. Black youth who act out as a symptom of their mental health challenges are often punished, excluded from school, or arrested.[91]

Trauma is harmful at any age, but it is especially harmful in adolescence. As we explored in chapter 1, our potential in life is shaped not only by the genes we inherit from our parents but also by the experiences we have in adolescence.[92] Because the adolescent brain has the remarkable capacity to change and adapt in response to positive or negative experiences, trauma can have a significant and lasting effect on how a child's brain develops and life unfolds.[93] The adolescent brain is particularly vulnerable to damage from physical and psychological harms like trauma and stress.[94] Research shows that the link between stressful events and trauma symptoms is even stronger during adolescence than childhood. Puberty makes the brain more sensitive to a range of environmental influences, including the way people treat us. Adolescents are not only more attentive to their encounters with the police but also more likely to be influenced by those encounters in negative and enduring ways.[95]

Abuse and trauma arising out of perceived racism during adolescence can affect the brain's prefrontal cortex, which helps us think logically, process our emotions, and control our behaviors.[96] It may also contribute to mental illnesses and addictions that make it difficult to succeed as adults.[97] Statistics show that most serious mental health problems and major psychological disorders—including disorders relating to mood, substance abuse, anxiety, impulse control, and eating—begin somewhere between ages ten and twenty-five. Mental health problems that emerge in adolescence become more entrenched as people get older, and the fears that young people develop in their teen years are especially difficult to get rid of later in life.[98]

At the extreme, the toll of persistent chronic stress may end in suicide. Suicide is the second leading cause of death among youth aged ten to nineteen. Reversing previous evidence that Black youth were among the least likely to commit suicide, recent data shows that there has been an alarming increase in the number of Black youth who have committed suicide, attempted suicide, or been injured from an attempted suicide in the last several years.[99] Although there has been little research specifically examining suicide risk among Black teens, the few studies that do exist suggest that depression, delinquency-system contact, poor family support, substance abuse, and trauma arising out of racism and discrimination are all risk factors for suicidal thoughts and attempts among Black youth.[100] Consistent with research showing that Black youth are reluctant to seek treatment when they need it, a 2019 study of parents and other caregivers found that half of caregivers were unaware their child had thoughts about suicide.[101] This was particularly true among Black families and other racial minority groups.

A LIFE IN BALANCE

*If you can, help others, and if you can't*
*at least don't harm them.*

—DALAI LAMA[102]

At some point, the police—and all of the people who hold them accountable—have to decide whether the goals they hope to achieve can ever be accomplished through aggressive and repeated police interventions. The longer I worked with Kevin, the clearer it became that the police were wasting a lot of time and money trying to get him to stop selling weed. They weren't reducing overall marijuana use in the community. They weren't making D.C. streets any safer. And they weren't even making D.C. residents *feel* any safer. Worse, they were doing a lot of damage to Kevin's psyche and hope for the future.

D.C. should have learned from New York's history with stops and frisks. From at least 2006 to 2011, the New York Police Department alienated, terrorized, and infuriated generations of Black and Latinx people with their rampant stop and frisk policy.[103] Yet, as the data reveals, the police were rarely successful in achieving their goal of getting guns and drugs off the street.[104] Equally telling, the end of stop and frisk didn't lead to a drastic increase in crime as predicted. Quite to the contrary, crime in New York City dropped significantly between 2011 and 2018, when the city recorded the lowest number of homicides in nearly seventy years.[105]

Police in D.C. like to say they don't "stop and frisk" like the police in New York. Our former police chief even testified before the city council in February 2019 that the D.C. Metropolitan Police Department "has never had a stop and frisk program."[106] The rebuttals were fast and furious. It turns out that is not exactly what the chief meant. He probably just meant to say that D.C. has never publicly and intentionally adopted an explicit policy of policing Black communities the way New York City did in the first decade of the twenty-first century. But even that isn't quite right.

In the weeks that followed the chief's testimony, D.C. residents were quick to point out that D.C. practices were just as racist and traumatizing as those in New York. They were quick to highlight local data showing that courts dismissed about 40 percent of all gun possession cases in D.C. from 2010 to 2015, supporting anecdotal claims of pervasive illegal stops by the police.[107] It is hard to get good data on how often police stop people unlawfully in D.C. Cases get dismissed for all kinds of reasons, including poor witness credibility, plea bargains, and the prosecutors' inability to determine who actually possessed a particular gun. But many cases get dismissed by judges and prosecutors who recognize that police have violated the rights of a person who was stopped. That was certainly true for Kevin.

By the time Kevin turned eighteen, the prosecutors had dismissed more of his cases than they had prosecuted. Police body-worn cameras showed time and time again that the police stopped Kevin with no clear and legitimate reason to believe he was involved in a crime. The police stopped him without seeing a crime, without the report of a crime, and without reason to believe a crime had even been committed. Most often the police reports just said that Kevin looked nervous and agitated or that police had seen a "glimmer" of drugs or paraphernalia in some bag or pocket. More often than not, videos contradicted the officers' claims. Kevin was rarely doing anything out of the ordinary when he was stopped, and the police could almost never see anything "glimmering" from his person or property.

In almost every case, the reports say the area in which Kevin was stopped was "known for drugs" and that Kevin himself was "known to sell drugs." That is probably the real reason police kept stopping him, but neither of those facts gives the police a lawful basis to stop anyone. The police don't get to stop Kevin every time they see him just because he sold marijuana in the past. On those occasions, the prosecutors often dismissed the charges to avoid the time and hassle of trying to litigate our opposition in court. When the prosecutors couldn't or wouldn't dismiss, we sometimes asked a judge to review the videos and decide. Fortunately for Kevin, the officers' testimony rarely held up against the cameras. It seems that everyone but the police realized that Kevin has the right to live and walk freely in his neighborhood without being harassed.

Ultimately, the chief's blunder about stop and frisk practices in D.C. actually did some good. It made the chief acknowledge that his department had been underreporting stop and frisk for years and led to the first comprehensive release of MPD stop and frisk data in September 2019.[108] Of course, the data confirmed what my clients have been saying for years: police stop far more Blacks than Whites, and they do so at rates that far exceed the percentage of Blacks in the city. In the first round of data—which included only a four-week period from July 22 to August 18, 2019—police officers stopped more than 11,600 people across the city, including motorists, pedestrians, and others. Seventy percent of those stopped were African American, 15 percent were White, and 7 percent were Hispanic.[109]

When analysts dug more deeply, data showed that 1,470 of those stops involved a frisk, and 93 percent of those who were frisked were Black. This data is especially remarkable in a city where only 46.4 percent of its residents are Black. Black people were frisked seven times more often than Whites who were stopped by the police. Police made an arrest in only 20 percent of the 11,600 stops and in only 43 percent of the 1,470 frisks.[110] Less than 9 percent of the frisks led to any weapons-related charges. As one D.C. Council member predicted months before she had the data to back it up, "Stop and frisk traumatizes our neighbors without making our neighborhoods safer."[111]

As an attorney who has represented Black youth in the District of Columbia for twenty-five years, I am confident these numbers are still low and incomplete. Police don't count the number of times they walk by and tell a child to "lift your shirt," nor the number of times they ask a child, "Where are you coming from?" and "Where are you going?" They don't include the number of times police tell a child to move off a public street, sidewalk, or park. More important, they don't tell us anything about how those police contacts make young people feel—about themselves, about the police, or about the city in which they live.

Infographics and talking points released by MPD in the days after the stop and frisk data was published repeatedly talk about how "short" the stops were, noting that "three out of four stops were resolved in about fifteen minutes."[112] The police chief also liked to refer to frisks as a "protective pat down"—as if that were a distinction that made a difference.[113] The police clearly have no idea how traumatic and destructive even a brief physical or non-physical encounter with the police can be—especially for Black youth like Kevin who have been the lifetime targets of repeated, unnecessary, and aggressive intrusions by the police.

It turns out that D.C. is not that different from New York after all. D.C. police have violated Kevin's civil rights. They have traumatized Kevin and his family. And they have created a toxic environment for his entire community. The very strategies MPD uses to deter crime among Black youth have the opposite effect.[114] Police encounters that increase psychological distress among adolescents cause anger, resentment, and coping strategies that lead to more delinquent behavior.[115] Some youth turn to alcohol and drugs to cope with anxiety and manage the pain of perceived injustices.[116] Others turn to gangs and delinquency to protect themselves and compensate for what they see as an ineffective, untrustworthy, and illegitimate police department.[117] The 2018 survey of boys in a large southern city found that Black and Latinx boys who had experienced the acute stress associated with police stops were more likely to engage in delinquent behavior in the weeks and months after those stops.[118] This was true even among those youth who had never engaged in delinquent activity before their first police stop. Thus, while law-abiding behaviors did not prevent Black boys from being stopped, being stopped did cause Black boys to commit crimes thereafter.

Delinquency also increases as Black youth retaliate against the police with verbal and physical aggression. It should be no surprise that most of Kevin's marijuana arrests have been accompanied by some "assault on a police officer" or "resisting arrest" charge. Kevin has a penchant for spitting on the officers or kicking them after he is in handcuffs. It is just unrealistic to expect young people like Kevin to go about their lives as if their traumatic experiences with the police don't affect them. Police pile on more stress than youth can handle and then get angry and punish them when they break. Once in the legal system, the youth's distrust of the police spills over to probation officers, judges, advocates, teachers, and other state actors who might want to help them. Yet youth like Kevin rarely get the support and treatment they need to address the trauma and depression associated with policing.[119]

To be clear, questions about policing and public safety are rarely easy. Black people care a lot about their safety and sometimes need help.[120] Kevin's own internal conflicts about calling the police bear that out. Not too long ago, Kevin and his pregnant girlfriend were robbed at gunpoint. Kevin was furious that someone had taken their phones and money and had been terrified the assailants would hurt his girlfriend. But he refused to call the police. In his mind, the police would be useless at best and harmful at worst. He was certain the police wouldn't be able to get their stuff back, and he was convinced—rationally or irrationally—that the police would figure out a way to spin his report back to blame him for something he didn't do. At the end of the day, he blamed himself for walking with his girlfriend in a neighborhood too far from home. He never saw the police as a source of help and protection.

But Kevin's greatest dilemma with the police came when a close friend was shot right in front of him. Several boys were present, but none of them were willing to call for help. When the others ran, Kevin couldn't bear to let his friend die. He stayed but agonized for several minutes before calling 911—"for an ambulance." He emphasized "ambulance" but knew the police would come too. He tells us that saving the life of a close friend or family member would be the only reason he would call the police.

As Kevin passes his eighteenth birthday, I am hopeful. I have every reason to believe that Kevin will "age out" of crime naturally—just as the developmental research says he will. He has a girlfriend. He is expecting a baby. He has applied for a new vocational program, and he has learned from trial and error. Kevin has more at stake now and knows he can't keep selling weed. About two months after his last case closed, Kevin's mom called to tell us that he had moved out of town to live with an aunt and get a new start. He wants to learn a trade, probably be an electrician, and take care of his girlfriend and baby. Kevin decided that he couldn't do any of that in D.C. with the police always watching, so he left the only city he has ever known. We will see what happens. Maybe he will come back. Maybe he will love his new home. In the meantime, D.C. has lost a really smart and talented kid.

# 10

# The Dehumanization of Black Youth:
# When the Children Aren't Children Anymore

## GEORGE AND WILLIE MUST DIE: KILLING BLACK INNOCENCE

On March 23, 1944, police officers came to find fourteen-year-old George Stinney at his home in Alcolu, South Carolina. The police were convinced he had brutally murdered two young girls by beating them over the head with a metal spike and dumping them in a muddy ditch.[1] George and his seven-year-old sister, Aime, were said to be the last ones to have seen the girls alive. George and Aime were Black. The murdered girls were White. The girls were last seen riding their bicycles looking for flowers. George was barely five feet tall and did not yet weigh a hundred pounds.

Alcolu was a small, racially segregated sawmill town. Whites and Blacks lived on opposite sides of the railroad tracks and attended separate schools and churches. George lived with his parents and four siblings. The Stinneys lived in housing provided by George Sr.'s employer at the sawmill. George's parents weren't home when the police came, but his seventeen-year-old brother, Johnny, was. The police took them both away in handcuffs. The police eventually released Johnny, but they held on to George.

Police questioned George alone in a small room without his parents and without an attorney. The officers claimed he confessed to killing eleven-year-old Betty June Binnicker and eight-year-old Mary Emma Thames. Consistent with the pervasive stereotypes

about Black boys in the 1940s, the police, the politicians, and the public were convinced that George killed Mary Emma to have sex with Betty June.[2] Police later claimed he admitted as much in a confession. None of this was supported by the medical evidence or the officer's initial recounting of the confession. There was no written record of any admission, and there was no evidence that the girls had been sexually assaulted.

Prosecutors charged George with two counts of first-degree murder. The court appointed Charles Plowden, a tax commissioner campaigning for election to local political office, to represent George. The trial lasted two and a half hours on April 24, 1944, with six witnesses and no transcript of the proceedings. The courtroom was packed with more than 1,000 people, but Blacks were not allowed inside. George's attorney did not cross-examine the prosecutor's witnesses and did not call any witnesses on George's behalf. The all-White jury decided George was guilty in ten minutes.

George was executed at 7:30 p.m. on June 16—less than three months after he was accused. George was the youngest person in America to be put to death by the electric chair. News accounts at the time reported that the straps on the chair were too big for George's tiny body and that he had to sit on books to reach the headpiece.[3] When the switch was flipped, the convulsions knocked down the mask and exposed George's tears. He was pronounced dead within four minutes of the initial shock.

According to George's former cellmate, Wilford Hunter, George denied the charges until his execution and couldn't understand why they would kill him for something he didn't do.[4] George's sister Aime also insisted that she and George had nothing to do with the girls' deaths. Aime and her family had been terrified to speak to the police back in 1944. After George's arrest, his father was fired from the sawmill, and the Stinneys fled their home. George was held in jail in Columbia, South Carolina, fifty miles from Alcolu, and did not see his parents until after his trial and conviction. He saw them once, in the Columbus Penitentiary, shortly before he was executed.

Civil rights lawyers, activists, and historians have kept George's memory alive. At a new trial in December 2014, new witnesses testified, including George's siblings and a witness from the search party that discovered the girls' bodies. A child forensic psychiatrist testified that George's "confession" was likely false and coerced and should never have been trusted. Seventy years after George was killed, South Carolina judge Carmen Mullen threw out his conviction, calling it a "great and fundamental injustice."[5]

Just five months after George's death, another series of events began to unfold, leading to the execution of another Black child, Willie Francis. This time, the execution would occur about 850 miles southwest of Alcolu in St. Martinville, Louisiana. In November 1944, the White owner of Thomas's Drug Store, Andrew Thomas, was shot five times in his home. For nine months his murder remained unsolved, and rumors of potential suspects were rampant.[6] Residents of St. Martinville noted that Thomas was a lifelong bachelor and often spent time with married women. It was popularly suspected that he had been killed by a jealous husband.[7] However, rumors also circulated that Thomas was in a sexual relationship with sixteen-year-old Willie, who worked for Thomas at the drugstore. These accounts implied that Willie was sexually abused by Thomas and that Willie's vague reference to a "secret" in one of his written confessions would support that theory.[8]

On August 3, 1945, Willie was stopped by police in Port Arthur, Texas, while visiting his sister. Suspecting Willie of trafficking drugs because he had a suitcase, the officers took him into custody and questioned him. Willie had a stutter and was barely literate. At the time, St. Martinville had the lowest literacy rate in Louisiana and no high schools for Black children.[9] Willie was often described as a boy with a low level of emotional maturity for his age and was always trying to please people.[10] Even after he convinced the officers he was not trafficking drugs, the police continued to question him about other crimes. They believed his stutter was evidence of a guilty conscience.

Despite the absence of any notes or records of the interroga-

tion, the Port Arthur chief of police reported that Willie confessed to the murder "in a matter of minutes."[11] Officers also claimed to have found an ID with Thomas's name on it in Willie's wallet. During the month after his arrest and before he was indicted, Willie was questioned in jail many times and was described as accommodating. Willie's written confessions stated that he planned Thomas's murder by stealing a .38 pistol from the deputy sheriff of St. Martinville. It also stated that he stole and later pawned Thomas's wallet and its contents. Willie then supposedly led law enforcement officers to the murder weapon.[12] Several details undermined Willie's confession. The sheriff never reported that his gun was stolen. The pawnshop's owner did not recognize Willie during the investigation. And most important, the sheriff had previously threatened to kill Thomas for having an affair with his wife.[13]

Willie did not meet his defense lawyers until one week before his trial.[14] At trial, the prosecution's case relied solely on the confessions. All of the bullets that had been recovered from the scene of the crime had been "mysteriously lost"—along with the murder weapon—on their way to the FBI for analysis.[15] No fingerprints had been taken from the weapon or the victim's wounds, leaving no physical evidence that could tie Willie or anyone else to the crime. After the state closed its case, defense counsel stated they "had no evidence to offer on behalf of the accused."[16] The trial lasted just two days, and a jury of all White men found Willie guilty after fifteen minutes of deliberation. Despite the district attorney's claim that no juror was from St. Martinville, later investigation showed that at least three jurors were from there, and several others were from a neighboring town. Nine jurors also shared surnames with members of the judge's family tree.[17] The judge sentenced Willie to death, but Willie did not die easily.[18]

On May 3, 1946, Willie could be heard screaming, "I'm not dying. Take it off! Take it off!" as he wrestled against the heat and shock of Louisiana's electric chair, commonly referred to as Gruesome Gertie.[19] Apparently, the two technicians responsible for preparing the chair for Willie's execution were drunk and botched the wiring during setup. Louisiana's governor ordered that Willie be executed again six days after the debacle.[20] During the next year and a half, two lawyers who agreed to take Willie's case for free worked with the NAACP to appeal the second execution. Without challenging Willie's guilt or the inadequacy of his trial, the lawyers argued that a second execution would be cruel and unusual punishment. The U.S. Supreme Court disagreed, stating that "accidents happen for which no man is to blame."[21] Willie was killed by electrocution on May 9, 1947, at 12:01 p.m., a little more than a year after the state's first attempt.

Although George Stinney is most widely known as the youngest person to be executed in twentieth-century America, Willie Francis was only two years older than George when he was first sentenced to die. Willie is best known for having lived through the first failed execution by electrocution in the country. Both of their trials demonstrated an appalling disregard for justice. In each case, the time from suspicion to execution was absurdly short. Investigation was deemed unnecessary, contradictions were ignored, the child's dying claims of innocence were disregarded, and mere accusations were accepted without challenge. Because the trials were so inadequate, and their legal representation so deficient as to seem purposeful, the proceedings provided little more assurance of fairness and accuracy than a lynching by mob violence. Each child was isolated from his family and given no meaningful opportunity to defend himself. At the ages of fourteen and sixteen, neither boy could understand what was happening to him or how to respond to the charges. If these proceedings were unfair for an adult, they were depraved for a child.

## SUMMARY EXECUTION AND BODIES IN THE STREET: THE DEHUMANIZATION OF BLACK CHILDREN

Executing children is now considered barbaric, uncivilized, and inhumane all over the world. Because most countries understand that children are less culpable for their crimes and more likely to reform than adults, youth executions have always been rare. At least four international human rights agreements prohibit nation-states from executing people who committed crimes before the age of eighteen.[22]

Children are special. On our good days—when we are not angry or afraid of our children for taking risks and failing to live up to our high moral standards—we are patient and forgiving. Western notions of childhood also cloak most children with a presumption of innocence. Even when they make mistakes and commit crimes, we treat them with grace and compassion. Recent studies of the adolescent brain make us even more forgiving. We understand now more than ever why young people have such a hard time controlling their behaviors and making wise and responsible choices. And because most of us believe that young people can and will change with time and intervention,[23] we choose not to punish most youth as severely as adults for their misdeeds.

So why were George and Willie executed at such a young age? The most likely answer is they were born Black in a country that did not see them as children. Since 1642, when the first child was put to death in an American colony, 365 people have been executed in the United States for crimes they committed when they were still children.[24] Black youth like George and Willie were the most likely targets of those executions. In the contemporary era from 1976 to 2005, 22 people were executed in the United States for crimes they committed as children. Half of them were Black. One was Latino.

Between 1990 and 2004, the United States was one of only seven countries known to have executed people for crimes committed when they were a minor. The other nations were the Democratic Republic of the Congo, Iran, Nigeria, Pakistan, Saudi Arabia, and Yemen.[25] All nations have since outlawed the juvenile death penalty. The mandate against killing children is so strong that the Inter-American Commission on Human Rights ruled in 2002 that executing those who committed crimes while under the age of eighteen is a violation of "jus cogens"—a sort of universal human rights standard—making it akin to genocide, slavery, and apartheid.[26] Yet it was not until 2005 that our Supreme Court finally joined the rest of the international community in deciding that it was cruel and unusual to execute a child.[27]

In the United States, human rights abuses like slavery, lynching, and Jim Crow persisted as long as they did because Whites did not see Blacks as human. Southern Whites killed, punished, dominated, and enslaved those they saw as inferior and immoral. But George Stinney and Willie Francis were more than just the collateral damage of Jim Crow politics, and their stories are not just relics of a racist and segregated past. The attitudes that precipitated their executions have endured well beyond the 1940s and extend much farther north than the Mason-Dixon Line. Although George and Willie wouldn't be sent to the electric chair today, they could still be "executed" by the police without investigation, trial, or mitigation hearing.

Far too many Black youth who have been killed by the police or the state are innocent. In all likelihood, George didn't kill Betty June Binnicker and Mary Emma Thames. Willie probably didn't kill Andrew Thomas. Tamir Rice didn't have a real gun and wasn't going to shoot the police. Jordan Edwards wasn't riding in a stolen car and didn't have anything to do with the gunshots heard at the party he attended in Balch Springs, Texas. And Cedrick Chatman was carrying an iPhone box, not a gun, when he was shot by police in Chicago. Even evidence uncovered fifty years after Emmett Till's lynching suggests that Emmett likely didn't even whistle at a White woman.[28]

But factual innocence is largely irrelevant in the summary executions of most Black children. Narratives crafted to justify Jim Crow segregation and lynching made George and Willie natural scapegoats in the deaths of two White girls and a pharmacist. The rather absurd claim that George Stinney "killed the smaller girl to rape the larger one"[29] fit the narrative that Black men and boys were sexual deviants who posed a constant threat to White women. It didn't matter that there was no physical evidence of sexual abuse or that George didn't have the physical strength to kill the girls. And it certainly didn't matter that George was only fourteen. In Willie's case, it didn't matter that the evidence pointed to the local sheriff as the real killer. Willie was just a pawn in a battle between two White men who wanted the same woman. He was ultimately sacrificed for the sheriff's freedom and reputation.

In the days and weeks leading up to George's death, hundreds of people urged South Carolina's governor to block the execution.[30] Some reminded the governor of a sixteen-year-old White boy who had been sentenced to twenty years for rape and murder near the time of George's conviction. The governor was not moved.[31] Even today, not everyone believes that George should have been cleared of the allegations. As late as December 2014, White Alcolu residents resisted posthumous efforts to overturn George's conviction despite the weakness of the state's case. Earlier that year, members of Betty June Binnicker's family gathered with friends at a restaurant to challenge what they believe is now a "false impression" of George as a "shy" and "bashful" little Black boy who was railroaded by the White people.[32] Instead, they recounted old narratives to paint George as a violent bully who was mean and threatening. Although a few expressed reservations about the state's decision to execute a child, they all insisted there was no racial element to George's trial and conviction. None of them had any doubt about George's confession. The crime fit every stereotype they had—and still have—about Black boys.

## "PERENNIAL LOST CAUSE": BLACK CHILDREN IN THE COURTS

In 2021, George Stinney and Willie Francis could still be prosecuted as adults and sentenced to die in prison. Before 1899, children accused of crimes were sent to criminal courts to be tried and prosecuted like adults. In the nineteenth century, progressive child savers became concerned about the welfare of youth in the criminal legal system.[33] Arguing that children were different from adults, reformers fought to remove young people from adult prisons and create new specialized courts that would "treat" instead of punish them. The child savers established work farms and reform schools for children convicted of crimes and helped establish the first juvenile court in Chicago in 1899.

Yet, from the outset, early juvenile justice reformers were not interested in treating or rehabilitating Black youth. Instead, the first child welfare homes focused their efforts on "normaliz[ing]" or "whiten[ing]" European immigrants who were drawn to America as it transformed into a modern industrialized society.[34] The upper- and middle-class Anglo-Protestant Europeans who had come a few generations earlier sought to assimilate newly arrived immigrant youth into "sober, virtuous, middle-class Americans like themselves."[35] Black children were never seen as worthy of these efforts. During slavery, southern plantation owners whipped enslaved Blacks and used other forms of physical abuse to discipline and punish disobedience. After emancipation, Black children accused of crime in the South faced convict leasing, lynching, and other forms of punishment.

Progressive reformers viewed Black children as a "perennial 'lost cause' . . . lacking the physical, moral, and intellectual capacity on which normalization would depend."[36] When some child welfare institutions finally opened their doors to Black children, they didn't even pretend to rehabilitate them. Black children were relegated to the "colored section" and denied the rehabilitative services that were seen as a waste of resources for Black youth.[37] While these homes educated and trained White youth to be farmers and skilled artisans, Black youth received little if any recreation, education, or moral instruction. Black boys were trained to meet the agricultural and other manual labor needs of the day.[38] Black girls were trained to be cooks, maids, and seamstresses.

Less friendly readings of the child savers movement argue that the Progressives deliberately constructed juvenile courts to limit and control the freedom and success of poor immigrants, and thereby protect their own middle-class existence.[39] As European immigration came to an end after World War I,[40] Black youth eventually replaced poor White immigrants as the disproportionate target of juvenile court proceedings. What arguably started as a means to control poor White children later morphed into a racially motivated system of isolation and control as immigrant youth assimilated into society and recently freed Blacks continued to assert their place in the new social order.[41]

A second wave of juvenile court reform coincided with the civil rights movement of the 1960s and lasted until the late 1990s, when politicians rejected rehabilitation in favor of "law and order" responses to adolescent offending.[42] Responding first to the social unrest caused by racial tension and increased youth crime during the civil rights era, lawmakers passed new laws such as the Omnibus Crime Control and Safe Streets Act of 1968 to militarize the police force and prevent further disruption.[43] Responding later to an increase in violent and deadly crime among young Black males who had easy access to guns and drugs in the 1980s and 1990s, lawmakers again took aggressive measures to protect the public.[44] In both waves, Black youth were demonized by the media and conservative politicians and portrayed as the chief villains in the war on crime.[45]

In the wake of dehumanizing narratives about Black youth in the 1990s, many states passed laws that would allow judges to impose harsher penalties on young offenders. States adopted mandatory minimum sentences, authorized lengthy periods of incarceration in state facilities, and crafted blended-sentencing schemes that require youth to spend additional time in an adult prison after completing their initial sentence in a youth facility.[46] Policy makers also adopted civil penalties—often called collateral consequences—to further punish and control youth who commit crimes. A child who is convicted of a crime can now be evicted from public housing, expelled from school, and forced to register as a sex offender or submit DNA samples for inclusion in a state database.[47] Most important, almost every state added to or changed its laws to allow—and in some cases require—prosecutors and judges to send even more children to adult courts at younger ages, for more offenses, and for longer periods of time.[48] As a result, between 1993 and 1999 the number of youth under the age of eighteen held in adult jails more than quadrupled.[49]

In 2015, at least 75,900 youth under the age of eighteen were prosecuted as adults in the United States.[50] A staggeringly disproportionate number of those youth were Black. Although Black youth made up only 15 percent of all youth under juvenile court jurisdiction in the United States in 2018,[51] they accounted for more than 51 percent of all youth who were transferred by a judge from juvenile court to a criminal court that year.[52] These disparities were true even among children who committed similar types of crimes.

Although Black youth were charged in only 38 percent of cases involving crimes against a person in 2018, they accounted for almost 57 percent of youth who were transferred from juvenile to adult court for those same offenses.[53] Similarly, although Black youth were accused in only 19 percent of drug cases in 2018, they made up more than 26 percent of all youth transferred in drug cases that year.[54] These numbers only include youth who were transferred to adult court by a judge. No federal law requires states to collect data on the other ways children may be sent to adult courts. There is no national record of how many youth are sent to adult court by a prosecutor who has unreviewable discretion and authority to make that decision, or by state laws that automatically treat minors as "adults" when they commit certain crimes at certain ages.

Racial disparities in juvenile transfer are even more pronounced in state records.[55] Florida has the dubious distinction of prosecuting and incarcerating the highest number of children as adults in the country. The vast majority of those youth are Black. Of the 1,169 Florida children transferred to adult court from 2017 to 2018, 771 were Black.[56] Prison sentences were also 7.8 percent longer for Black youth in Florida than White youth sentenced for the same type of offense.

In Missouri, 72 percent of the children transferred to adult court by a juvenile court judge in 2015 were Black, even though they accounted for only 14.8 percent of the state's youth population and only 40 percent of youth charged with a felony offense.[57] In New Jersey, 68 percent of the youth that prosecutors wanted to try as adults between 2011 and 2016 were Black; 19 percent were Hispanic. Judges granted the prosecutors' request to transfer in more than half of those cases. Ultimately, 80 percent of all youth prosecuted in adult courts were Black in a state where only 17.9 percent of youth were Black in that time frame.[58] In Oregon, 139 youth were prosecuted in adult courts in 2017.[59] Of that number, 15.8 percent were Black in a state where only 2.3 percent of all youth were Black. County-level data in Pennsylvania reveals that Black youth accounted for more than 80 percent of youth charged as adults by the prosecutor's office in Allegheny County in 2016 and 2017, but made up only about 20 percent of the youth population in that county.[60]

Once transferred to adult court, youth face the same harsh penalties as an adult. Despite recent legal challenges to lengthy and severe sentences for all young people,[61] twenty-five states still allow judges to sentence children to die in prison.[62] These "life without parole" sentences require youth to spend the rest of their natural lives in prison without any opportunity to demonstrate they have been rehabilitated. They will never be able to tell a parole board about their good behavior, academic achievements, religious conversion, or time to reflect in prison. Most will never attend a high school prom or graduation ceremony, and most will never get married, have children, own a home, or care for their aging parents. Many of them will lose contact with an intimate partner and lose custody of children they had before their conviction. Black children will be impacted the most.

In a 2016 review of youth sentences in the United States, there were more than twice as many Black youth serving juvenile life without parole sentences as White youth.[63] Even when comparing youth arrested for the same offense, Black children arrested for murder from 1992—the height of the "superpredator" panic—to 2013 were twice as likely to be sentenced to life without parole as White children arrested for murder.[64] Racial disparities are even worse within some states. In 2016, 81 percent of people serving life without parole in Louisiana for crimes committed when they were under eighteen were Black.[65] The youth population of the state was about 39 percent Black at the time.[66] In Arkansas, 70 percent of the youth serving life sentences in 2016 were Black in a state where the youth population was less than 20 percent Black.[67] In Texas, thirteen of the seventeen people serving juvenile life without parole sentences in 2015 were Black; the other four were Hispanic.[68]

Racial differences in sentencing result from a series of decisions by prosecutors, judges, probation officers, and juries. In most cases, judges will determine the sentence, but prosecutors decide what charges to bring and whether to bring those charges in juvenile or adult court. Jurors decide guilt or innocence, and probation officers help judges decide what sentence to impose by reviewing a youth's social history and assessing the child's prospect for rehabilitation. Widely held stereotypes that depict Black youth as violent and threatening overshadow our shared cultural beliefs that adolescents are capable of change. Although the Supreme Court has reduced the total number of youth sentenced to die in prison by declaring mandatory juvenile life without parole sentences illegal,[69] racial disparities remain high in discretionary juvenile life sentences.

Implicit racial bias affects every stage of the criminal legal system, including decision makers' views about the appropriate punishment for Black youth.[70] In 1998, in one of the earliest studies on racial bias in youth sentencing, researchers reviewed 233 narrative reports written by probation officers in anticipation of a youth's disposition in juvenile court.[71] The narratives revealed that probation officers were more likely to blame crime on external influences, such as dysfunctional families, drug and alcohol use, difficulties at school, and the influence of delinquent peers, when White youth were involved.[72] Probation officers were significantly more likely to blame crime on internal personality traits, such as lack of remorse, lack of cooperation with the probation officer, and failure to take the proceedings seriously, when Black youth were involved. Interpreting behaviors in this way made probation officers more likely to predict that Black youth would re-offend in the future and recommend sentences longer than the sentencing guideline range.[73] These differences held true even when Black and White youth committed similar crimes and had similar past criminal behavior.

In 2004, another team of researchers studied the impact of unconscious racial stereotyping on police officers' and probation officers' perceptions of whether youth were culpable, deserved to be punished, and were likely to re-offend by asking participants to read a vignette of a crime allegedly committed by a teenager.[74] Although none of the participants received information about the race of the youth in the vignettes, some were subtly prompted with a series of words commonly associated with Black Americans. Those who had been prompted to think about Blacks judged the alleged offender to be more mature and "adult like," more violent, more culpable, and more likely to re-offend than those who had not been prompted. Those who were primed to think about Blacks also endorsed harsher punishment. These views were consistent across the ethnicity and gender of the participants and persisted even when the decision makers consciously desired to avoid prejudice.

More recent studies confirm that racialized assumptions and attitudes about Black youth continue to inflame irrational fears and reduce public sympathy for those who have been accused.[75] As we discussed in chapter 2, researchers from the University of California, Irvine, and the University of Pennsylvania found that police and civilians were more likely to perceive Black youth as older, less innocent, and more responsible for their behaviors than either White or Latinx youth.[76] Demonstrating the real-world consequences of these biases, researchers from Stanford University found in 2012 that study participants were more likely to support severe sentences like juvenile life without parole when they believed a violent adolescent offender was Black.[77] Those same participants were willing to accept less punitive sentences when they believed the young offender was White.

Ironically, we tend to believe that the threat of a lengthy prison sentence will deter youth from committing serious crimes. But as we considered in chapter 1, that logic is faulty. Teenagers rarely think ahead to anticipate what will happen before they act—especially when they are with their friends in the fast-paced, emotionally charged moments that typically characterize even the most serious adolescent crime. Teens act impulsively, with little reflection on what the consequences might be—for themselves, their families, or their victims. It is only later that they look back and realize their mistakes and commit to change. This is why we usually spare young people the most severe punishments. But tragic stories about youth like Niecey Fennell and Kalief Browder suggest that society isn't willing to extend the same reprieve to Black youth.

### ARRESTED DEVELOPMENT:
### NIECEY FENNELL AND ADULT JAILS AND PRISONS

Once children are prosecuted as adults, people seem to forget they are still children. Youth in criminal courts can be sent to live with adults in jails and prisons. They can be shackled, chained, or forced into labor on a work gang. They can be locked in cells that include little more than a bed and a lidless toilet that sits right next to the bed. If there is a window at all, it usually allows in only a sliver of light and doesn't permit the child to see anything outside. Although the child can usually see out the front of the cell, they can rarely see other inmates in cells to the left or the right. The cells are often freezing in the winter and smothering in the summer. Youth are locked in these cages for the majority of the day, and staff control when and how much they can sleep, eat, or read. If they are not in solitary confinement or under some other special watch, they might leave the cell for meals and an hour or two of exercise. When they are allowed to work, they earn pay well below minimum wage, and what they do make is typically added to a "commissary" account for food and toiletries the jail or prison fails to provide. Youth are isolated from family and friends, locked in tight, crowded spaces with strangers, and get little uninterrupted time to sleep. Physical and sexual abuse are common.[78]

As reported in 2019, on any given day, approximately 935 children under the age of eighteen are locked up in adult prisons.[79] An additional 3,600 are held in adult jails where they wait for trial, sentencing, or a decision about whether they should be tried as a child or an adult. Although federal law incentivizes states to protect youth from the harms of adult prisons under the Prison Rape Elimination Act (PREA), only nineteen states are in full compliance with that law.[80] Unfortunately, PREA requirements apply only to state-run correctional facilities, leaving the vast majority of children unprotected in adult jails and other pretrial detention facilities run almost exclusively by county governments.[81]

PREA restricts children from having any contact—sight, sound, or physical—with adult prisoners within their housing units. Outside the housing units, youth and adults may commingle in the presence of prison staff.[82] Staff routinely violate these requirements.[83] Children may not be separated at all, or they may sleep in separate cells but risk abuse by adults every time they enter an unsupervised common area to eat a meal or take a shower. Children who are physically separated from adults may still be bullied and abused by adults who taunt them across the hall or verbally harass them as they pass by at a distance. Even in prisons that meet the PREA standards, guards and adult inmates still manage to physically and sexually abuse youth.[84] In many facilities—especially those with fewer youth—staff may create "sight and sound separation" by sending youth to solitary confinement for twenty-three hours a day, severely restricting their freedom and denying them any opportunity for human contact and educational programming.

Uniece "Niecey" Fennell was one of the thousands of youth who were held in an adult jail in 2016. Niecey and her twin brother, Demoraea, were born in Southern California but moved to Durham, North Carolina, in 2015. Niecey had a traumatic childhood with her father, who was addicted to drugs, involved in a gang, and abused her mother, Julia Graves. Julia eventually removed Niecey's father from their home, but Niecey was depressed and missed a fair amount of middle school as a result of the family turmoil. Julia later moved her children to Durham for a new start. The night before they moved, Demoraea ran away and the family was forced to leave him behind. For months, Niecey woke up in the middle of the night, hyperventilating, after dreaming of her twin brother being killed in California. Even when Demoraea later joined them in Durham, Niecey never settled in. While at school one day, she was slammed to the floor by a school resource officer and suspended for fighting. Although she was forced to complete a mental health evaluation before she could return to school, Niecey never received any services after the evaluation.

On July 16, 2016, Niecey was accused of driving a car that was involved in a drive-by shooting.[85] She was sixteen. Her family and friends say she was forced to drive and had no idea there would be violence. Niecey was sent to the Durham County jail and held on a $5 million bail. Although the jail had written policies prohibiting youth from having any contact with incarcerated adults, in practice children like Niecey were routinely assigned to an adult unit where they had constant verbal and physical contact with older inmates.[86] The jail housed 800 to 900 people at a time on eight floors in "pods" that housed 48 inmates in a cluster. Niecey's cell had one exterior window—a horizontal slit positioned above her bunk with bars covering it. Her cell door had a small window, allowing the guards to look in. Niecey was one of the youngest detainees at the jail. Although she slept in a cell by herself, she was housed in a pod with thirty-six women and had constant contact with all of them. Niecey did not attend school and received no counseling or other mental health support. Jail staff received no specific training or protocol on how to treat or supervise an adolescent in the facility.

For eight months, Niecey was the victim of physical violence, verbal threats, and bullying by older women in the jail. Inmates taunted and harassed her with names like "bitch" and "murderer" and threatened her with physical violence. Some of the women would push her, slam her against the wall, or put their hands in her face as she walked down the hall to the shower. Niecey's primary antagonists were women affiliated with the Bloods street gang, some of whom were facing murder and accessory to murder charges. The Bloods were particularly suspicious of Niecey's California roots and wrongly assumed she was involved in a gang herself. One of her antagonists struck her in the face because she could not name a Durham "set" of the Bloods.[87] To maximize her sense of hopelessness, other detainees told her, "You're never going home," and actively encouraged her to kill herself.

Jail staff were aware of the violence and did nothing to protect Niecey. Some guards even joined in the harassment, telling her that although she was just a "little girl," her life was over and she would "die in prison." Niecey cried often and expressed distress about the bullying. One correctional officer who had personal and family ties with several of the adult inmates was particularly hostile toward Niecey. Niecey became so afraid that she eventually stopped coming out of her cell when the others were allowed to gather in the common areas twice a day.

Adult jails and prisons are particularly dangerous places for teenagers. Incarcerated youth face verbal and psychological intimidation and are the frequent victims of physical attacks with fists and handmade weapons. Staff rarely do enough to prevent or stop violence among inmates, and sometimes even orchestrate that violence by smuggling in weapons for inmates to use in a fight.

Youth may also be beaten by staff in adult correctional facilities.[88] For reasons varying from punishment to retaliation to no reason at all, staff attack children by tackling them to the ground, punching or kicking them in the head and face, or beating them with a baton, radio, or broomstick while they are handcuffed.[89] In everyday interactions, staff use unnecessary and excessive physical restraints like shackling and restraint chairs that keep youth strapped in position for extended periods of time.[90] Guards also use various forms of psychological trauma, including unwarranted discipline and extended periods of isolation, to taunt and bully youth in their care.[91] In one particularly egregious instance of abuse, guards at Florida's Palm Beach County jail forced youth to drink sewage water from the sink attached to the toilet in their cells.[92] Youth rarely report any of these violations out of fear of retaliation and the seeming futility of the effort.[93]

Youth detained with adults are especially vulnerable to sexual abuse. Guards and adult inmates take advantage of the youth's relative size and powerlessness to physically overpower or psychologically coerce them into sexual acts.[94] The most violent rapes and assaults occur in cells and other "blind spots" hidden from camera surveillance. Guards coerce youth by threatening them with consequences like time in solitary confinement or the loss of family visits, or by offering special privileges like meals from their favorite restaurant.[95] Adult inmates use similar strategies to coerce youth, threatening to get them in trouble or reveal information they don't want revealed or promising to protect them from other inmates if they cooperate.[96]

Even youth who are not the direct victims of physical or sexual abuse while incarcerated experience trauma from witnessing or anticipating that violence. Adolescents, whose brains are still developing, are particularly vulnerable to the ongoing psychological trauma they experience in adult jails and prisons. The daily violence, stress, and chaos common in these facilities can also permanently compromise the immune system and lead to serious health conditions, ranging from chronic headaches and sleep disorders to heart problems.[97] One study found that youth who were prosecuted in the adult system had a mortality rate nearly six times higher than the general population.[98] Another study found that each additional year an inmate spent in prison reduced life expectancy by two years.[99] A youth's overall health and mortality are further compromised by communicable diseases, such as HIV, hepatitis C, and tuberculosis, which are more prevalent in prisons and jails.[100]

Despite the prevalence of mental health problems among incarcerated youth, mental health services, psychotherapy, and medication available in adult facilities are rarely adequate and appropriate for the developmental needs of young people.[101] Many youth enter prisons with preexisting mental health conditions that are exacerbated by the stressful experience of incarceration.[102] Other youth develop post-traumatic stress disorder and other symptoms of distress while incarcerated.[103] A study of more than 1,800 youth tried as adults found that youth sentenced to adult prisons are significantly more likely to suffer from psychiatric disorders than youth who remained in youth facilities.[104] Another study found that one-third of incarcerated youth experiencing depression developed their symptoms after they entered the correctional facility.[105] Youth of color are less likely than White youth to receive mental health treatment before they enter the system and while they are incarcerated.[106]

Like so many other incarcerated youth, Niecey did not receive the mental health services she needed in the Durham County jail despite numerous signs that she was suffering. Her personal traumas were well known in the facility but met with little or no compassion. In November 2016, while Niecey was still detained, her twin, Demoraea, was shot to death in Durham. Officials refused to allow her to attend his funeral. She took his death hard and fell into depression without any outlet to grieve. Initially concerned that Niecey might hurt herself, staff placed her on suicide watch but returned her within three or four days to the women's unit, where the other inmates continued to taunt her. Around the time of her brother's death, Niecey saw another inmate on her pod try to take her life by hanging herself from the bars on the window. Niecey watched the guards cut the woman down and the medical personnel take her away. Four months later, Niecey did the same. In the early morning hours of March 23, 2017, staff found Niecey hanging from a bedsheet attached to a bar in front of her window.[107]

In the days leading up to her death, Niecey told the adults around her that she was going to end her life, but no one took her seriously.[108] Hours before Niecey died, her lawyer sent an email to jail staff, expressing concern about the harassment. Jail staff responded but dismissed the lawyer's concerns. That same night, at least one other inmate also told staff about Niecey's distress. Nineteen-year-old Dominic Jackson was Niecey's confidant from the cell directly below hers. Dominic and Niecey spoke regularly through the plumbing fixtures connecting their cells. Shortly before she killed herself, Niecey told Dominic that she wanted to "go be with [her] brother." Alarmed by her question "How would you feel if I hung myself?," Dominic told one of the guards on his own pod.

Other correctional officers had also observed Niecey crying loudly in her cell that evening. At one point, a sergeant stopped by to tell her, "If you don't stop all that crying, we'll put you on suicide watch." After a short conversation, the sergeant left Niecey's cell and took no further action. He didn't call a mental health professional for advice. He didn't have Niecey transported to a hospital for a psychiatric evaluation. And he didn't check on her in the fifteen-minute intervals that would have been required had she been returned to suicide watch.[109] Niecey died in a place no teenager should be. Shortly after her death, prosecutors dismissed all charges against the two men Niecey had been driving at the time of the shooting. The prosecutors had asked the judge to keep Niecey locked up because they wanted her to testify against the shooter. Without her, they had no case.

Odds are that if prosecutors had treated Niecey like a child—and a witness—instead of a calculated murderer, they would have been more successful. Odds also are that if we left most teenagers alone and did nothing at all in response to crime, we would get better results than we do by locking them up with adults. Treating children like adults increases crime. Treating children like children is both more humane and more effective. With meaningful opportunities to succeed and support from caring adults, most youth will naturally "age out" of both minor and serious criminal behavior by late adolescence.[110] As their brains mature, teenagers get better at making decisions, controlling their impulses, and saying no to their friends' dumb ideas.[111] Treating kids like adults before they are ready prevents them from developing the cognitive and social skills they need to mature into law-abiding citizens.

Few environments pose a greater risk to healthy adolescent development than the toxic and isolating setting of an adult prison or jail. Incarcerated youth rarely participate in activities that give them the opportunity to think critically and independently or to make decisions that have real-world consequences.[112] Unlike classrooms that offer novel, challenging, and cognitively stimulating activity, prisons and jails operate by rigid rules and repetitive schedules that deny youth the opportunities they would otherwise have to solve problems, build resilience, practice responsible judgment, and socialize with peers who are positive.[113] Research confirms that incarceration slows development and hinders adolescents' capacity to control their impulses, suppress their aggression, take personal responsibility, and resist negative peer influence.[114] Youth prosecuted as adults have few opportunities to complete school and participate in vocational training that would allow them to become financially independent. They have even fewer opportunities to participate in extracurricular activities that teach interpersonal skills, collaboration, and civic responsibility. Youth returning home after incarceration rarely have the academic and social skills they need to succeed as adults.[115]

Incarceration also deprives youth of important relationships and emotional support when they need it most. Youth who have intimate relationships with a girlfriend or boyfriend, a sibling, close friends, or even their own children tend to be more resilient and hopeful.[116] Youth who have the support of caring adults are better equipped to overcome trauma and develop coping strategies they need to handle disappointments and manage anxiety.[117]

Demoraea Fennell's death was so traumatic for Niecey precisely because he was the one person who could calm her down when she was sad or angry. Niecey lost significant contact with Demoraea and the rest of her family when she was arrested. Although her mother and sister were able to speak with her by phone and visit her through a Plexiglas window at the jail, at some point her mother moved to Las Vegas and was no longer able to visit. Niecey never told her mother how bad things were at the jail, and the jail never told her mother she had been put on suicide watch after her brother's death. Without these essential relationships, life seemed bleak for Niecey. The physical and verbal attacks from the older inmates only made it worse.

## OUT OF SIGHT, OUT OF MIND:
### KALIEF BROWDER AND SOLITARY CONFINEMENT

Niecey isn't the only Black youth to have committed suicide in an adult jail. In October 2016, jail staff found fifteen-year-old Jaquin Thomas hanging from a window bar in his cell at the Orleans Justice Center.[118] Family reported that Jaquin was abused by older inmates who stole his food and beat him. The sheriff's department that managed the facility confirmed that Jaquin had been beaten by another young inmate weeks before his suicide. Jaquin's grandmother described him as "scared out of his wits."[119] On the day Jaquin took his life, a sheriff's deputy passed by his cell four times without looking in, despite protocol requiring staff to check on inmates in that section of the jail every fifteen minutes. Jaquin hung by a rolled bedsheet for ninety minutes before anyone even noticed his body hanging limp under the window.

For decades, data has shown that court-involved youth like Niecey and Jaquin are more likely to commit suicide than youth in the general population.[120] Youth in adult jails are thirty-six times more likely to die by suicide than youth in juvenile detention facilities.[121] Teenagers in adult prisons are twice as likely to commit suicide as adults in adult prisons.[122] Those risks are even greater for youth who enter jails and prisons with a history of trauma and untreated psychiatric disorders. Those risks might be greatest among incarcerated youth who endure days, weeks, and even months in solitary confinement.

Kalief Browder was raised in the Bronx, New York, by Venida

Browder, who adopted him after he was placed in Child Protective Services.[123] On May 15, 2010, Kalief was stopped by police in connection with a robbery of a backpack that occurred two weeks earlier. The victim's brother Roberto Bautista reported simply that "two male Black guys" took his brother's book bag. Bautista identified Kalief and his friend as the culprits while observing them from the back of a police car. Kalief insisted he was innocent, and the police never found a bag. Nonetheless, prosecutors charged him as an adult for second-degree robbery, grand larceny, and assault.

At court, a judge sent him to await trial on Rikers Island and initially set bail at $3,000. Kalief was just sixteen at the time. Unfortunately, he and his family couldn't afford the bail. A few weeks later, on July 10, 2010, the judge ordered that Kalief remain in detention without bail because he was already on probation for a previous "joyriding" offense.[124] The Department of Probation said this new felony arrest was a violation of his conditions of probation. Kalief would stay in Rikers for three years.

The Rikers Island jail complex is operated by the New York City Department of Correction and houses about 10,000 inmates on any given day. Kalief was placed in the Robert N. Davoren Complex (RNDC) that housed boys aged sixteen to eighteen.[125] During one of his first nights on the island, Kalief and several other teenagers were lined up against a wall and repeatedly punched in the face, one at a time, by the guards. They accused Kalief of being involved in a fight he had nothing to do with. Kalief quickly learned that this type of aggression was an everyday occurrence in Rikers and lived in constant fear of violence from both the guards and the inmates who beat him mercilessly.[126] The guards told him, "We're gonna break you," and they did.[127]

Verbal disputes with the guards often escalated quickly into a physical altercation, even when Kalief was in the most vulnerable locations like the shower. When he wasn't beaten, Kalief was starved and denied a shower for two weeks. Even in solitary confinement, a guard challenged Kalief to a fight, knocking him to the ground and pinning his face to the floor while he beat him. On another occasion, video footage shows guards beating Kalief while he was handcuffed.[128] Kalief suffered the same fate at the hands of other inmates. In October 2010, he was beaten by ten boys in his gang-controlled unit after he got into a fight with a gang leader who spit in his face.[129] Violence among youth in the facility was routine, and gang members would regularly beat Kalief up for something as simple as refusing to give up his seat and sit on the floor while watching TV.[130] Kalief often worked out to gain physical strength to defend himself from the violence.

Kalief was one of many children to suffer from the brutality of Rikers. Although he was separated from adult inmates in a unit set aside for teenagers awaiting trial as adults, the adolescent center had long been recognized as the most violent unit on the Rikers complex. Investigators found that boys often entered the RNDC with a host of mental health problems at the peak of adolescence and were much more violent and impulsive than the adults on other parts of the island.[131] In 2014, the Department of Justice released a report and filed a lawsuit alleging that Rikers had a "deep-seated culture of violence" and that teenage boys like Kalief experienced extreme violence daily at the hands of guards and inmates.[132] The report found that guards routinely used unnecessary and excessive force against adolescents, including punching and kicking them in the face, as a way to control and punish them. It was not uncommon for the teenagers to have broken bones, jaws, and noses, or cuts and wounds requiring stitches.

Kalief spent two of his three years in solitary confinement—most often for fights with other adolescent males. These were usually the types of fights one would expect to see among teenage boys forced to live together in a close setting with little supervision and a lot of stress. When Kalief wasn't in total isolation, he slept in an open room with fifty other boys.[133] Inmates washed their own clothes with soap and a metal bucket that left rust stains on their garments. To prevent theft by other inmates,

Kalief slept on top of his clothes. Tensions were high and conflict was frequent. One fight started when Kalief asked an inmate to stop throwing shoes at people.[134] When the boy refused, Kalief took the boy's sneakers and threw them back at him. The fight that followed landed Kalief in isolation.

Mirroring its record of executing children, the United States remains woefully behind the rest of the world in curtailing its use of solitary confinement for youth. In facilities across the country, youth can be held in a room smaller than a parking space—often without bedding, soap, or natural light—and isolated from any human contact for twenty-two to twenty-four hours a day.[135] They receive meals through the door and are not allowed to buy additional food through the commissary, causing many to lose weight and stunting their growth at a critical time in their development. If they were enrolled in school, youth in solitary confinement may receive a work packet shoved through the door but no instruction. Perhaps most devastatingly, these youth will be denied visits, calls, and letters from family and friends.[136]

The United Nations special rapporteur on torture described solitary confinement as "cruel, inhumane, [and] degrading treatment" and called for a prohibition on the solitary confinement of children under eighteen years old.[137] Other leading youth organizations have condemned the practice, including the American Academy of Child and Adolescent Psychiatry, which declared that any youth subjected to solitary confinement for more than twenty-four hours must be evaluated by a mental health professional.[138]

Despite several national campaigns to end the practice,[139] no state has completely eradicated the use of solitary confinement for youth. While twenty-nine states and the federal prison system prohibit solitary confinement as a form of punishment,[140] these policies still allow guards to send youth to solitary cells for other purposes such as suicide watch, protection from other inmates, and medical attention. Because most adult facilities are not equipped to protect and treat young inmates, youth in adult prisons are at greater risk of being isolated "for their own good."[141] As is true at every stage of the juvenile and criminal legal systems, Black youth are at greater risk of severe sanctions like isolation.[142]

Solitary confinement is devastating for adolescent development. Young people like Kalief, who have limited experience managing their disabilities, anxieties, fear, and trauma, suffer the most from prolonged segregation.[143] The trauma and stress of indefinite seclusion may irreparably damage an adolescent's brain and permanently impact their ability to make calm and well-reasoned decisions.[144] Even a short stay in solitary confinement can have lasting, negative impacts on youth. Hallucinations, severe depression, extreme anxiety, uncontrollable rage, paranoia, suicidal thoughts, and self-harm have all been reported by youth in isolation.[145] Children who suffered abuse and neglect prior to solitary confinement are more likely to experience these symptoms.[146]

While some facilities will screen youth for suicide risk when they first arrive, most will never screen them again unless they say they are thinking about hurting themselves.[147] Even then, staff will often ignore the cries and obvious signs of depression from youth like Niecey Fennell and Kalief Browder. Kalief tried his best to stay afloat in jail, reading and studying for his General Educational Development (GED) examination. Yet, despite his best effort to stay focused, depression got the best of him on numerous occasions. Kalief tried to take his own life at least three times while at Rikers. He tried first in 2010, and twice more in 2012. In 2012, he tried to hang himself using strips of a sheet tied to a ceiling light in the cell. Kalief later said the correctional officers goaded him to commit suicide.[148] Ten days after this attempt, Kalief was transported to the courthouse but never brought into the courtroom. He was told that his case would again be delayed. That night, Kalief made a sharp instrument from the bucket in his cell and started to slit his wrists before an officer intervened.[149]

Kalief's scars lasted long after he was finally released from Rikers. When Kalief walked out of Rikers Island on May 29,

2013, he had endured three years of abuse, isolation, and terror, which his attorney equated to torture.[150] Kalief initially approached his release and the dismissal of his charges with optimism and purpose. He reunited with family, passed his GED exam, and enrolled in Bronx Community College. In the first semester, he earned eleven credits and a 3.562 GPA. Unfortunately, Kalief could not escape the trauma he had endured. His depression returned, and panic attacks crippled him in class. His mother, Venida Browder, said he was angry and paranoid in a way he never was before Rikers.[151] She lamented that his life "spiraled" from that experience.

Six months after his release, Kalief tried to hang himself and was admitted to a psychiatric hospital where he would return several times in the next two years.[152] The torment was so great that he stopped attending school for a time and became an advocate for reform, telling his story to journalists, celebrities, and politicians who might prevent other youth from suffering the way he did.[153] In interviews and conversations with his family, Kalief described himself as "mentally scarred," "paranoid," and "robbed of his happiness."[154] When he returned to college, he wrote a paper called "A Closer Look at Solitary Confinement in the United States."[155] In the paper, Kalief cited research on the physical and psychological effects of solitary confinement, including chest pains, weight loss, diarrhea, dizziness, and fainting, as well as poor concentration, confusion, memory loss, paranoia, psychosis, violent fantasies, anxiety, depression, lethargy, and insomnia. Kalief was likely familiar with all of these symptoms.

On June 6, 2015, two years after his release, Ms. Browder found her son hanging from a noose made of his own bedsheets. He hanged himself from an air conditioner outside his bedroom window. Kalief's trauma was too much to bear even when he had opportunities for school and advocacy. Kalief wanted to work and succeed as a businessman, but depression prevented full recovery.

Kalief's story is not unusual. Suicide is one of the leading causes of death after release from prison or jail.[156] Youth returning from incarceration not only carry a psychological burden of trauma but also face little hope of completing school, finding stable housing, and getting a job.[157] Even when they do find a job, they earn less than those who have not been incarcerated.[158] Youth incarcerated as adults also frequently lose the right to vote, access to public housing, driving privileges, and professional licenses they need for work. They may be automatically removed from Medicaid rolls and required to reenroll through a lengthy reapplication process upon release.[159] Children in many states must register as sex offenders, even for offenses that look a lot like normal adolescent behaviors.[160] And unlike youth tried in the juvenile system, young people convicted in adult courts have records that are publicly available to anyone with a computer or access to the local courthouse.[161]

Unfortunately, none of these punitive responses to adolescent crime make us any safer. Multiple studies have found that youth incarcerated with adults are more likely to commit new crimes in the future, more likely to do so sooner, and more likely to commit more serious crimes than those who are handled in the juvenile system.[162] The abysmal ineffectiveness of prosecuting youth as adults suggests that the practice is meant to achieve some goal other than public safety. Kalief's story reflects an extraordinarily callous disregard for the basic humanity of Black children. Kalief spent the final years of his childhood insisting on his innocence and waiting for a trial that never came. The prosecutors requested and the courts granted thirty-one continuances from May 2010 to May 2013. Kalief refused to accept the government's first plea offer, which would have sent him to prison for three and a half years, as well as its second plea offer, which would have reduced that time to two and a half years. On March 13, 2013, Kalief again refused to plead guilty, even to an offer of two misdemeanors and time served. The prosecutor was finally forced to dismiss his case.

Kalief's family later hired former Brooklyn prosecutor Paul V. Prestia to sue the Bronx district attorney and other system actors for malicious prosecution and intentionally misleading the court about their readiness for trial.[163] Kalief's lawyer argued that prosecutors knew very early they would have no witness when Mr. Bautista returned to his home in Mexico. It is hard to imagine anyone allowing a White youth to languish in jail for three years without a trial. While we no longer execute Black children like George Stinney and Willie Francis, we effectively end their lives when we rob them of their childhood, humanity, and innocence in adult prisons and jails.

# 11

### Things Fall Apart: Black Families in an Era of Mass Incarceration

A PARENT'S AGONY AND OUTRAGE

*It was a Saturday morning. It was just me and Kalief. I heard him upstairs—doing all of this moving around. I thought he was moving furniture. I didn't pay it much attention because when Kalief is upset, he paces. Then all of a sudden I heard this boom. I raced upstairs, and I saw the air conditioner kicked out of the window. I race back downstairs and outside. As I opened the backyard door. Kalief was hanging there.*[1]

This is how Venida Browder remembered the horrendous day she found her son dead at their home on June 6, 2015. It was two years and seven days after his release from Rikers. The night before he died, Kalief told her, "Ma, I can't take it anymore."[2] She tried her best to talk him through it. Nothing she said would help. His paranoia had become so intense that he would not talk about his case or his time at Rikers inside their house.[3] If they needed to talk, he would insist they go outside and past the front gate. Standing outside on the evening of June 5, he tried to explain that he had received a threatening message on Facebook, leading him to believe "they" were watching him: "They said they warned me and I didn't listen." Venida never fully understood what Kalief was afraid of that night, but she could see the tears in his eyes and knew her son was terrified and hurting. The next night, Kalief's brother helped Venida access Kalief's computer. They could not find the messages Kalief had been worried about.

Just sixteen months later, on October 14, 2016, Venida died from a heart attack. She was sixty-three. Like her son, she died far too early. Kalief's brother Deion Browder believes the pain over Kalief's death and the stress of fighting for justice literally broke their mother's heart. In a 2019 op-ed, Deion wrote, "Over the past few years, the country has heard the harrowing story of my brother Kalief Browder . . . However, what the country doesn't really know is the impact my brother's detention and death had on my family, especially my mother."[4] Deion is right. Most of us can't imagine the agony of having a child arrested for something he didn't do, watching him languish in jail for three years without recourse, visiting him weekly to hear about the physical and psychological torture, and not being able to do anything about it. Even fewer of us can imagine the torment that must come with finding our son hanging from a noose outside our home. Ms. Browder is one of many parents who have faced the agony of losing a child in a country that criminalizes Black adolescence.

Trayvon Martin's parents did not find out their son had been killed until the day after he was shot.[5] Trayvon's father, Tracy, became worried when Trayvon didn't come home on February 26, 2012. Tracy Martin went to bed figuring his son must have gone to the movies with his cousin. When Trayvon still wasn't back the next morning, Tracy called the police. Shortly thereafter, three cars pulled up at his home. None of them was carrying Trayvon. After getting a description of the missing child, a detective showed Tracy a picture of Trayvon's body—dead at the scene of the shooting—"his eyes rolled back, a tear on his cheek, saliva coming from his mouth."[6]

Tracy describes the days and months that followed as a "nightmare." When Trayvon's mother, Sybrina Fulton, heard the news, she could not eat, sleep, or get out of bed.[7] As she told reporters,

"I just started to cry and cry," and asked Tracy to go see Trayvon's body. "I needed to know if that was my baby, dead."[8] "I cried every day. There was nothing else I could do as a mother."[9] For weeks, the local police chief resisted requests to release the 911 emergency calls to the public, but he was eventually overruled by the mayor. The mayor invited Trayvon's parents and their lawyers to his office to listen to the calls. When they heard a voice cry, "Help! Help!" Sybrina burst into tears and yelled, "That's Trayvon. That's our son!" and ran out of the room.

Jordan Davis was also living with his father when he was murdered in Jacksonville, Florida, on November 23, 2012. Jordan's mother, Lucy McBath, who was battling her second round of breast cancer, had just talked to him the day before.[10] It was Thanksgiving, and he thanked her for always believing in him and being his biggest supporter. The next day, Jordan's father, Ron Davis, called to say Jordan had been murdered by a man who thought Jordan and his friends were playing their music too loud. Describing her son's murder as "the worst thing that could happen to a mother," Lucy was devastated.[11] Before his death, Lucy and Jordan had talked about what happened to Trayvon just nine months earlier.[12] Lucy warned him that because he was Black, the same thing could happen to him. Ron said he never thought Black Friday 2012 would be the last time he hugged his son. His last words to Jordan were "Goodbye, have a good time. I will see you tonight," as he headed out the door.[13] That was the last time he would see Jordan alive. Years after his death, Ron described November 23 as the worst day of his life and said he stills thinks about his son every day.

Tamir Rice would have been eighteen years old on June 25, 2020, six years after the police killed him in November 2014. His mother, Samaria, recalls vivid details from that day—the turkey sandwich she fed him before he left, the money she gave him and his sister Tajai to buy snacks at the store, and the knock on the door from neighborhood boys who told her the police had shot her son.[14] She remembers telling the boys they didn't know what they were talking about and running out to find police surrounding her son's body when she arrived at the park gazebo where he lay. She remembers the police threatening to put her in the back of a police car if she didn't calm down and being told to stop holding Tamir's hand at the hospital because his body was evidence.[15] Worse, she remembers sensing that her son was already gone before he was pronounced dead.

Samaria still keeps some of Tamir's favorite things—his teddy bears, his drawings, his Hot Wheels cars.[16] As her lawyers say, Tamir's death has "shattered the life of the Rice family."[17] In an interview with USA Today, Samaria Rice described holidays as hard—not joyful—Mother's Day as not the same, and his birthday as tough.[18] She says that being a Black mother in America is stressful and she is "nervous and scared all the time."[19] Like so many other mothers who have lost their sons or daughters to police brutality or racist civilian violence, Samaria relives Tamir's death every time she hears about another killing. "I'm sick mentally, physically, emotionally," she tells reporters as she tries to explain why she couldn't eat or sleep after the deaths of Ahmaud Arbery, George Floyd, and Breonna Taylor.[20] "When I hear there's a new victim of police brutality or a hate crime, it's just this numbing feeling."[21] A month after George Floyd's murder, Samaria said, "You don't ever get over nothing like this. It's an empty feeling of loss when you don't have your puzzle complete."[22]

Mike Brown's mother, Lezley McSpadden, was at work when she received the call from a friend that someone had been shot in the street near Canfield Green Apartments in Ferguson.[23] Lezley was worried, knowing that Mike was staying with his grandmother in Canfield so he could use the makeshift music studio in her home to write rap lyrics.[24] Within minutes, her cell phone rang again. It was her sister telling her that Mike had been shot. Lezley ran back into the grocery store where she worked screaming, "I need to get to my son! The police just shot my son!"[25] A co-worker drove her to Canfield Drive, where Mike's body lay, but the police would not let her through.[26] In her book, *Tell the Truth and Shame the Devil,* Lezley recounts seeing his body and wailing, "Naw, naw, naw, that ain't my child! It can't be!"[27] All she could see was a yellow sock peeking out from a sheet on the ground and a red St. Louis Cardinals cap nearby. She recognized both as "Mike-Mike's." She begged the officers, "Let me see my son! Why ain't he off the ground yet? Do anybody hear me?" She also demanded to know which officer did this, but they wouldn't answer and told her to be quiet and settle down.[28] One officer, posted up with an assault rifle, was rude and gave her the middle finger when she got in his face.[29] In an interview with *The Washington Post,* Michael Brown Sr. recalled that officers had pushed them back at the scene, "sicced dogs" on them, and treated them like "trash."[30] "There was no concern" for how the family was feeling.

Videos from Canfield Drive show Lezley distraught and crying, "Why? Why? Why did you have to shoot my son?" and "You took my son away from me."[31] Photos of her at the scene evoke memories of the iconic images of Mamie Till-Mobley collapsed on the floor the first time she saw Emmett's body shipped to her from Mississippi, and later images of Mamie crying inconsolably at the burial. In the weeks and months after Mike was killed, Lezley McSpadden and Michael Brown Sr. talked openly about their pain. "Living is a struggle, just as a black person," Lezley said. "It's even harder to get out of bed to think about going to work."[32] "When you lose a child, it isn't something that just sits in your heart. It's in your mind. It darkens your spirit."[33] Photos from Mike's funeral show Michael Brown Sr. drenched in sweat and overcome with grief. Defying any myth that brave Black men don't cry, Michael Sr.'s anguish was unmistakable as he sat with his head cocked back and mouth wide open in a tormented scream.[34]

There is a unique and unenviable bond among the parents who have lost children in these tragic ways. The week after Jordan died, Ron Davis got a text from Trayvon's father: "I just want to welcome you to a club that none of us wants to be in."[35] Ron

Davis then became a primary source of support for Michael Sr.[36] Venida Browder said, "I've met a lot of people, judges, politicians. I've even met Sandra Bland's mom. And out of all the people I met, she is the one that really understands my pain, because she lost her child. When we met, her hug really hit me. And I could not control my tears."[37] But these parents are as outraged as they are heartbroken.

From Emmett Till to Kalief Browder, Black families have been outraged by the injustice of what happened to their children and furious about how police, prosecutors, jurors, and many of the White public responded. Venida Browder blamed Rikers and the entire criminal legal system for her son's suicide: "He may have hung himself, but the strings were pulled by the system. They destroyed my family, and they definitely destroyed me. And I've lost faith in the judicial system, the police."[38] Lezley McFadden and Michael Brown Sr. were angered by the officers' horrific insensitivity in the hours after their son was killed, the media's complicity in helping the police vilify Mike, and the public's persistent support for Officer Darren Wilson, who killed their child. On the day Mike died, Lezley screamed into the TV cameras, "You took my son away from me . . . You know how hard it was for me to get him to stay in school and graduate? You know how many black men graduate? Not many. Because you bring them down to this type of level, because they feel like they don't have much to live for anyway."[39] Lezley's angry outcries continued months later when a jury decided not to indict Wilson for the killing.

In their painful and provocative documentary, *Rest in Power,* and book of the same name, Trayvon's parents share their outrage at George Zimmerman's claim of self-defense, after he got out of his car and followed Trayvon when the dispatcher told him not to. They were furious that it took forty-four days for police to arrest Zimmerman; angered that Trayvon's body was immediately subjected to a drug and alcohol test, but Zimmerman was not; and appalled that Zimmerman's trial judge prohibited the prosecutors from using the term "racial profiling."[40]

They were devastated that a jury of six women, five of whom were White, found Zimmerman not guilty of second-degree murder or manslaughter. Tracy Martin said, "As a parent and an African American man, I lost hope and faith in our justice system on the day the killer of our son was acquitted."[41] Jordan Davis's parents expressed similar outrage when a first jury agreed that Michael Dunn was guilty of three counts of attempted murder for firing into the car where Jordan's friends were sitting, but deadlocked on whether Dunn acted in self-defense in killing their son.[42] Ron Davis said that ultimate justice would not come until Dunn's claim of self-defense was completely rejected and he was forced to admit his guilt in murdering Jordan. They didn't get that justice until the conclusion of a second trial, seven months later on October 1, 2014.

Through their pain, these parents transformed their sorrow into advocacy. Following the lead of Mamie Till-Mobley, who opened her son's casket and released photos of Emmett's brutalized body to expose the racism of white America, black parents still refuse to accept their trauma in silence. Determined to make sure her son was not forgotten and the abuse he suffered in detention would never happen to another child, Venida Browder threw herself into the role of activist—a role she never expected or wanted.[43] Venida advocated fiercely to end cash bail, created the Kalief Browder Memorial Scholarship to assist students at Bronx Community College, and partnered with Jay-Z and the Stop Solitary for Kids campaign to tell her son's story and bring attention to the injustices of the criminal legal system.[44] The public outcry after Kalief's death led New York City to reform the city's cash bail system, ban the use of solitary confinement for sixteen- and seventeen-year-olds, and later remove minors from Rikers.[45]

Tracy Martin and Sybrina Fulton also never wanted a life of activism.[46] Yet, in addition to their book and documentary, Trayvon's parents formed the Trayvon Martin Foundation and launched a STEM (science, technology, engineering, and mathematics) camp and medical-career mentorship program for Black youth. They also supported other grieving parents through the

Circle of Mothers and the Circle of Fathers.[47] When Jordan Davis was murdered, Lucy McBath became determined to work toward a world in which Black parents would no longer have to warn their children about racism and refused to let Jordan be vilified by the public the way other Black youth were after their murders.[48] Lucy became a spokesperson for Everytown for Gun Safety and Moms Demand Action and spoke at the Democratic National Convention in 2016.[49] Her biggest feat was winning a state congressional seat that had been held by Republicans since 1979, making her the only Black woman in Georgia's congressional delegation.[50] Ron Davis testified at the Florida capital for the repeal of Stand Your Ground laws, gave a TEDx Talk, and is the founder and CEO of the Jordan Davis Foundation, offering scholarships and financial assistance to disadvantaged youth.[51]

Lezley McSpadden has become a powerful advocate against police violence. She and Michael Brown Sr. have spoken internationally, including an address to the United Nations, to bring awareness to their son's story.[52] She also created the Michael O. D. Brown We Love Our Sons and Daughters Foundation, which provides support and resources to mothers who have lost children to police brutality.[53] Like Sybrina Fulton, Lezley joined Mothers of the Movement and wrote a book about her son and the aftermath of his death. Like Lucy McBath, she also ran for public office in Ferguson, though she lost that bid.[54] Samaria Rice founded the Tamir Rice Foundation and has toured the country to advocate for police reform.[55] Most recently, she created the Tamir Rice Afrocentric Cultural Center, which will provide mentoring, art programming, and other resources to children. Speaking of her activism, Samaria has said, "God is using me in a way that's much bigger than all of us."[56]

Black parents lead the way for justice even as they grieve the murders, abuse, false accusations, and unnecessary incarceration of their children. While we praise their advocacy, we must also honor and acknowledge their pain by resisting the dehumanization and criminalization of Black children.

### BOUND AND CHAINED:
#### SHACKLING A GENERATION OF BLACK CHILDREN

Venida Browder agonized over Kalief long before he committed suicide. That agony began the day he was arrested for the stolen book bag.[57] Parents rarely find out about an arrest directly from the police. Instead, they are more likely to get a call from a neighbor, friend, or relative telling them their child was last seen stopped, chased, or worse—beaten—by a police officer or attacked by a police dog. Some parents will be close enough to get to the scene in time to see their child in handcuffs on the ground, in the back of a police car, or crying out in fear and pain. Others won't see their child until the next day, in shackles and a detention center jumpsuit.

When police do call parents, the calls are usually perfunctory, with little more than notice that their child will appear in court the next day. Parents regularly complain that officers won't tell them what their child was arrested for, where their child is being held, how badly they have been injured, whether they need a lawyer, or even what time the court hearing will be. In my own work, I can't count the number of times I have received a frantic call from a mother or grandmother asking if I can find out whether her child has been locked up or sent to the hospital. Most often, the child didn't come home, and other kids in the neighborhood say they saw him with the police.

Very few parents can forget the first time they saw their child in shackles—on the street, at the police station, or in a courtroom. The attorneys, police, staff, and judges who work in these spaces take handcuffing for granted. But it is not normal. There is something especially horrifying and unnerving about a child in chains. I certainly remember the first time I saw a child in shackles as a college intern in Durham, North Carolina, but my own reaction pales in comparison to the pain Black mothers feel seeing their own children in restraints. I got a glimpse of that pain early in my career when I stood at defense counsel's table waiting for one of my clients to be escorted in for his arraignment. As the marshals brought him into the courtroom, I could hear his mother crying softly next to me. As I turned to hand her a tissue, she told me it was like watching her child in slavery. Since then, I have seen far too many Black mothers weep at the sight of their children bound at the hands and feet.

Shackling is just as traumatic for the child as the parent. Children are embarrassed to have their parents see them in custody but at the same time desperate to have their parents' love and support in that moment. Because most handcuffs are too big for an average child, police will often attach the cuffs at the elbow or upper arm. Children who are terrified of the experience may wiggle, pull away, or stiffen up, causing the handcuffs to tighten and make the pain worse.[58] Teenagers like my client Kevin complain about being dragged backward by their arms or forced to lie in a car or on the ground faceup with handcuffs jabbing into their backs. Experts tell us that shackling can trigger memories and symptoms of prior traumas and cause anger, anxiety, mistrust, and animosity toward the police.[59] Given data showing that the vast majority of adolescent offenses are not violent, shackling children is rarely necessary to keep the public safe or prevent children from running away. Yet it remains a routine part of the criminal process.

Once a child is brought before the court, a judge must decide whether to keep them in detention or let them go home to await trial. The judge may release the child with a promise to appear, set bail to incentivize the child and their family to return to court, or detain the child without bail if the judge is concerned the child won't return or will be a danger to others in the community. Bail is a standard feature of the adult criminal legal system, but many people are surprised to learn that it is also common in many juvenile courts. As of April 2019, nineteen states had laws or court rules that expressly allow courts to set bail for children.[60] Nine states prohibit the practice. In many states, judges have broad discretion to set bail based on the severity of the charge, the child's criminal history, and the child's past failures to appear at scheduled court hearings.

Implicit racial bias might cause a judge to make incorrect assumptions about the child's potential danger to others and thus set higher bail amounts or deny bail altogether for Black youth. Judges regularly set high bail amounts without meaningfully considering what the family can afford. Courts most often set bail for children between $100 and $500, but in seven states courts set bail in excess of $10,000. Even low bail amounts result in poor youth being detained until trial, or induce them to plead guilty in exchange for release. Youth who do not have family who can afford the bail often remain in detention for a long time awaiting trial.

In adult jails, like the ones where Niecey Fennell and Kalief Browder were held, research shows that Blacks are often required to pay a higher bail amount than Whites. A recent but limited review of data from eleven states across the country shows that Black defendants are more likely than White defendants to be detained without bail, and when they do receive bail, that bail is more than twice as high as that for White defendants.[61] An older 2011 study in five large counties found that bail was $7,000 higher for Blacks than Whites for violent crimes, $13,000 higher for drug charges, and $10,000 higher for crimes related to public order.[62] A study in Delaware found that the average bail amounts were $5,000 higher for Blacks than Whites,[63] and a study in the Miami-Dade and Philadelphia areas found that the average bail for Black defendants was $7,281 higher than for White defendants.[64]

White youth like Cameron Terrell get to go home to await trial on a gang-related murder charge, not only because they have more resources, but also because their bail is often lower than that of their Black peers. Black youth like Kalief Browder remain in jail on less serious charges because judges set higher bail amounts or no bail at all and their families can't afford to get them out. Venida Browder spoke often of her agony and guilt about not being able to afford Kalief's initial $3,000 bail.[65]

## VISITING DAY: LOVING CHILDREN FROM A DISTANCE

Visitation presents another major challenge for families who cannot afford bail. Family who want to visit a child in detention or jail often have to travel long distances, at great costs, with few visiting hours and limited access by public transportation. Venida Browder described her visits to Rikers as an all-day trip. "I'm in the Bronx, and it took about two and a half hours on a good day. It's a job. But I went every weekend for three years. If he was in a facility in the Bronx, I could have went on a weekday . . . If he was closer, I could have been more support to him."[66] Yet Venida did what she could—taking Kalief clean clothes and snack money each week.

For many families, juggling work schedules to make room for a weekly visit can be impossible. Even when a family member can take time away from school or work, the facilities can make visitation difficult by limiting the number of visitors per day or enforcing arbitrary and unpublished rules about the dress code and contraband.[67] Many facilities withhold visitation privileges as a sanction for minor disciplinary infractions. Some jails, like the Durham County jail where Niecey took her life, replaced their in-person visits with phone and video calls. In many facilities, youth may only call during limited hours at exorbitant phone rates. Calls and videos may also be recorded, leaving youth with no privacy to report abuse at the facility or talk about their legal case. Even when the calls aren't recorded, detention staff and other children are often nearby, making private conversations virtually impossible.

When young people plead guilty or are found guilty after trial, they may be sent to an adult prison or youth residential treatment center that is even farther away than the local jail. Because Washington, D.C., does not have any long-term prisons or youth facilities within the city, my clients who are sentenced for extended periods of time are automatically sent away from their families, friends, and mentors. Youth who are "committed"—or sentenced to our city's youth services agency—are sentenced for an "indeterminate" period of time up to their twenty-first birthday. This practice is common across the country and means that children and their families don't have a clear, predetermined end date for the sentence. Children essentially have to "earn" their way back home by demonstrating they have been rehabilitated and are no longer a danger to the public.

For youth in D.C., the closest long-term youth facility is in Laurel, Maryland, about twenty-five miles outside the city, but the local youth services agency sends many of its children to treatment facilities hundreds of miles from home. Over the years, I have represented young people who have been sent to Iowa, Florida, Pennsylvania, and New Jersey. Some youth leave home for years at a time. Families can rarely, if ever, afford to fly or drive out to visit. If requested, the youth services agency may provide transportation to a facility one time during a child's stay, but unfortunately many parents can't take advantage of this opportunity due to work, childcare responsibilities for other children, or a fear of flying. In many cases, neither the child nor the family has ever been on a plane before the child is incarcerated out of state.

Despite evidence that youth who maintain strong relationships with loved ones fare better in prison and are more likely to succeed in rehabilitation, the juvenile and criminal legal systems have done little to make sure parents and families can stay engaged.[68] In 2012, the Vera Institute of Justice found that youth who were never visited had significantly higher incidents of misbehavior compared with youth who received regular or even infrequent visits.[69] That same year, Justice for Families, an organization founded by parents and families committed to ending youth incarceration, found that 86 percent of family members surveyed wanted to be more involved in their child's treatment in correctional facilities and residential placements.[70] Three-fourths of those family members reported serious barriers to visiting their children, including difficulties with transportation, distance, time, cost, insufficient visiting hours, restrictive visitation rules, or having visitation rights taken away as a disciplinary measure.[71]

Too often, the juvenile legal system has treated families as a primary cause of adolescent delinquency rather than a source of protection and support.[72] The very foundation of the juvenile legal system was rooted in a *parens patriae,* or "the state as parent," philosophy, which assumed that parents—especially Black parents—had failed when their children committed a crime.[73] The state believed it needed to step in when the parents were incapable of providing appropriate supervision and guidance.

This deficit-based view of Black families persists today in juvenile and family courts across the country and is evident in police and public efforts to vilify Black children as "wild" and unsupervised. These views not only reinforce false and demeaning narratives about Black youth but also fail to recognize the important role Black parents play in promoting healthy adolescent development. As youth navigate the difficult transition from childhood to adulthood, they need their parents more than ever. Even as teenagers forge their own independent identities, parents continue to play a significant role in shaping adolescent responses to peer pressure, answering difficult questions about race and discrimination, and helping youth understand the consequences of their risky and impulsive behaviors. Parents provide both a "secure base" from which to explore and a "safe haven" for support, redirection, and protection.[74] Youth who have strong bonds with their parents or guardians tend to engage in less risky behaviors and have fewer mental health problems and better social skills and coping strategies.[75] Even with the usual tensions that emerge between teens and their parents, youth still rely on their parents for emotional support and guidance.[76]

Venida Browder remembered going through Kalief's things after he died and finding a questionnaire that asked whom he wanted to talk to when he was angry. She was the first person he listed. "Do you know how it felt that he put me?" she asked through tears.[77] "He put me down first, and there was nothing I could do to stop him."

## PARENTS AS LAWYERS: THE CENTRAL PARK EXONERATED FIVE

Parents feel helpless at every stage of the legal system. There are few things more confusing and daunting than being a parent in an interrogation room with a child. In most states, police can question children without parental consent.[78] But in a few states, like New York, laws require the police to notify parents before an interview and give them an opportunity to be present.[79] Sometimes it is hard to tell which is worse—a child interrogated alone or a child interrogated with a parent. Although the laws were intended to protect children during police interviews, parents rarely know more than a child about the challenges and pitfalls of an interrogation. Even when they do understand the rights to remain silent and get a lawyer, they seldom have the psychological strength to withstand the officers' grueling and prolonged pressure to waive those rights.

Parents also have their own internal conflicts. Some parents are embarrassed by their child's involvement in the system and are eager to get out with minimal disruption and publicity. Others struggle between the desire to discipline and the desire to protect. Parents who fear their child might be guilty of some crime or adolescent mischief may be swayed by an officer's claim that the evidence is overwhelming and urge the child to take responsibility for what they have done. Parents seldom appreciate how difficult it is to undo a false confession and how easy it is for police to distort the facts. Parents who do appreciate the gravity of the situation try to protect their children but find it impossible to navigate police interrogation strategies. The impossibility of this moment is best told by the parents of the five, now exonerated, boys arrested after the Central Park rape in April 1989.

In the hours after Trisha Meili was raped, officers began rounding up young boys from the park and calling their parents to come to the police station.[80] Although New York law required detectives to have a parent present during the interrogation of a child under sixteen, the detectives understood just how important it was to separate the boys from their families. The officers used trickery, coercion, subtle deception, and outright lies to get parents out of the room for critical parts of the interviews. At times, they downplayed the seriousness of the accusations, leading some parents to believe their boys were only being investigated for disorderly conduct, and repeatedly assured them they would be able to take their children home after the interviews.

Kevin Richardson's mother, Grace Cuffee, was the first to arrive at the station that night at around midnight.[81] After waiting for about thirty minutes without seeing her son or receiving any new information, she asked about the delay. An officer told her they were waiting for all of the parents to arrive. This was likely the first step in a larger ploy to make the parents exhausted, anxious, and eager to return to other obligations like their jobs and families. The ploy worked on many of them. After more than two hours, Grace was feeling weak and tired from the lingering effects of a stroke she had seven years earlier and asked again about when she could take her son home.[82] Eleven hours after fourteen-year-old Kevin was arrested, he and his mother followed two detectives into a cramped room with four desks and a few filing cabinets.

After advising Kevin of his rights, the detectives began a grueling multi-hour interrogation that became increasingly intimidating and aggressive. At various intervals, other officers called Grace out of the room, leaving Kevin to be grilled alone and surrounded by as many as five detectives. Due to her weakened condition, Grace could not stay through the entire ordeal and after nearly twelve hours signed a consent form allowing her twenty-four-year-old daughter, Angela, to take her place. Neither Angela nor Kevin's father, who arrived a little while later, had any idea how much trouble Kevin was in. At 1:00 p.m., Kevin signed a statement he had written by hand, falsely confessing to a rape he knew nothing about. His father and sister signed as well.

Raymond Santana's father, Raymond Sr., and grandmother Natividad Colon encountered a similar ordeal when they went to find Raymond at the Central Park Precinct.[83] Although both arrived at around 5:00 a.m. on Thursday, Raymond was not interviewed until around 1:40 that afternoon. By the time the interview started, Raymond Sr. had left for work after being led to believe the situation was not as serious as it truly was. Raymond's grandmother stayed behind to serve as his guardian for the interview. Knowing that Natividad spoke limited English, the detectives interrogated Raymond entirely in English and took turns coming in and out of the room, sometimes pulling Natividad out with them so they could be more aggressive in their tactics.

The detectives employed the same divide-and-conquer strategy to lure a false confession from Antron McCray at the Twentieth Precinct when they urged his mother, Linda McCray, to leave the room and persuaded his stepfather, Bobby McCray, to get Antron to confess.[84] Linda McCray was Antron's best advocate. Convinced her son was being railroaded into giving details about a crime he didn't commit, Linda cried and screamed and tried to assure the police Antron was telling them everything he knew. Understanding how important it was to isolate Antron from his mother's support, the detectives persuaded her to leave the room by telling her that Antron may be afraid to tell the truth in front of her.

Meanwhile, another detective pulled Bobby McCray aside and told him that Antron needed to confess if he didn't want to go to jail. Although Bobby believed Antron was not involved in the rape, he was equally convinced the police would never let Antron leave until he told them what they wanted to hear. Like the other parents, Bobby still believed Antron would go home if he gave the detectives a statement. At first, Antron resisted, saying he wasn't going to lie, but his stepfather became frustrated and threw a chair across the room, eventually persuading him to cooperate with the police. Antron and his parents signed his written statement. Although most people believe they would never confess to a crime they didn't commit, police interrogation tactics create such intense psychological pressure that only the strongest can resist it.[85] Antron and his stepfather were both demoralized by the inquisition.

These encounters have a devastating impact on the parent and the child. Before his arrest, Antron had been very close to his stepfather. Bobby McCray had coached Antron's baseball team and made Antron feel like his best friend.[86] That relationship was forever changed on April 20, 1989. Bobby faced an impossible dilemma and only wanted to help. When he realized that Antron would not be coming home, Bobby was heartbroken that he had encouraged his stepson to lie and had a hard time facing him after that. Bobby withdrew physically and emotionally and lost touch with Antron when he was incarcerated. Linda McCray stood by her son throughout his trial and traveled by train, bus, or car every weekend to visit him wherever he was incarcerated.

Yusef Salaam's mother was probably the most fiercely protective. Sharonne Salaam arrived at the Twentieth Precinct around 11:45 p.m. demanding to see her son.[87] Thinking Yusef was sixteen, the detectives were already interrogating him alone. Linda Fairstein, chief of Manhattan's sex crimes prosecution unit, told Sharonne that she could see her son after the interview was over. Sharonne protested, saying he was only fifteen. The prosecutor refused to take her word for it and demanded proof of his age. Ms. Salaam did not have any documentation with her, but continued to object to the interrogation until the detectives finally stopped—but not before they had questioned him for an hour and a half. The damage had been done. Although Yusef never signed a written statement, the stalling and delay bought the police valuable time to put him on the scene and get him to falsely implicate himself and his friends in the attack.

Korey Wise's mother—who was five months pregnant—got the runaround. Having already been to the Central Park Precinct and to central booking in search of her son, Deloris Wise finally found him at the Twenty-Fourth Precinct. When she asked to see Korey, a detective said, "Why would you want to see a scumbag like him?"[88] Korey was actually sixteen, and thus not entitled to have his mother present in the interview room. Alone under the detectives' intense pressure and promises that he would go home if he admitted to a rape, Korey also confessed to crimes he did not commit and was tried and convicted as an adult for sexual abuse and assault. He served thirteen years in an adult prison. Like so many other children who are forced to "grow up" with adults behind bars, Korey was beaten multiple times, held in solitary confinement, and abused and harassed by inmates and prison guards. He did not see his family nearly enough and rarely had money for extra food and basic necessities like toiletries from the commissary. Ava DuVernay's four-part miniseries *When They See Us* highlights the anguish that parents experience as their children suffer and languish in jails and prisons. DuVernay's final episode is devoted almost exclusively to the mental and physical duress that Korey endured.

Parents like Deloris Wise feel helpless. Not only was it difficult for her to visit her son, but like so many mothers with children in jail, there was little she could do when she got there. Kalief Browder's mother explained this feeling powerfully: "Sometimes I would cry because there was nothing I could do. He used to tell me, 'Mom, stop crying,' 'cause people would notice. But as his mother, I'm supposed to protect him. But there was nothing I could do with him being in there. When he first told me how he was being beat, I said, 'Well, Kalief, I can go over their heads and I can go tell.' And he said, 'No, mom. Don't do that.' Because he was afraid of what would happen to him."[89] Incarcerated youth like Kalief, Niecey Fennell, and Korey Wise often internalize their pain to shield their parents from the heartache.

### *BROTHERS AND KEEPERS:*[90] SIBLINGS BEHIND BARS

Many of us have reflected on the trauma any parent must experience with the arrest, incarceration, or death of a child. But few of us stop to think about the equally devastating effects of policing and incarceration on siblings. I know those effects well because my own brother died in prison.

In April 2013, I was attending an end-of-the-year outing with my law students when my phone rang. It was a number I didn't recognize, so I didn't answer. The phone rang two more times, and I knew I should take the call. It was the Department of Correction calling from Whiteville, Tennessee, to tell me that Dustin Henning had a double aneurysm. He was in a coma. I was listed as the first point of contact, and prison medical staff suggested that I come out to the facility immediately. I caught a plane the next day, accompanied by my younger brother, Kyle.

The next two weeks were torturous. It was infuriating to see our brother handcuffed to the bed and under the constant surveillance of a prison guard when it was clear he could never run away or threaten anyone in the hospital. We stayed in Tennessee for a few days but returned to D.C. after medical staff assured us that it was unlikely Dustin even knew we were there. Back at home, I received almost daily calls from the hospital about whether they should do this procedure or that procedure to keep him alive. He never came out of the coma. Two weeks after the first call, Kyle and I had to make the agonizing decision to pull him off life support.

I was an adult by the time my brother died, but I was a teenager when he was first arrested. We were living in North Carolina, and I was in my ninth-grade English class when my White teacher walked over to my seat and said, "I was sorry to read about your brother in the paper yesterday." I had no idea what she was talking about. My parents had tried to shield us from my brother's arrests as long as they could. But in our small town, everybody knew everybody, and apparently my English teacher had taught my brother two years before me. The paper reported that my brother had been arrested for theft. Clearly failing to appreciate the many reasons why a child might steal or be accused of stealing, my teacher asked me, "Why did he steal? Don't you have enough?"

On another occasion a local preacher stopped by our home to talk to my parents about how he could help my brother. As I let him in and led him to the living room, he could tell that I was put off by the odd way he kept looking around our house. He finally said, "I'm sorry. I am just surprised. I didn't expect Dustin to come from a family like this." He was referring to our relatively middle-class existence in our small southern town. He was shocked that a child could be caught up in the criminal courts if he lived in a house "like ours." We still lived on the Black side of town, on the "other side of the railroad tracks," and we still went to public schools, but we had a nice house, two cars, and all of the kids—including Dustin—were on track for college.

Before we moved to North Carolina, my brothers and I had spent several years in an elite private school in Tennessee, courtesy of my grandparents, who paid the bill. Everybody always wanted to know what my parents did "wrong" to raise a child who had so much contact with the police. I remember days listening to my brother and father argue. I remember nights hearing my mother cry. I remember my brother running away from home and not coming back for days at a time. And then those days stretched into years. When he finally "resurfaced" about three years after one mysterious departure, we found out he was in prison. For some reason, he had made his way back to our birthplace, Nashville. I remember crying uncontrollably when I came home during my freshman year of college to find out that he would be in prison for a long time. When he was released, he continued to struggle with a heroin addiction and eventually went back to prison after assaulting his wife and taking her car in a drug-induced rage. His wife said his rampage came out of nowhere. He was sentenced to seven to ten years for carjacking and aggravated battery.

Class and education obviously didn't shield my brother from policing and incarceration. We grew up in Black neighborhoods, with Black friends, doing all of the silly things teenagers do. When he wasn't at home, the rest of the world had no reason to think he was any more privileged or educated than his friends. There is no clear answer for why my brother ended up in prison for the last eight years of his life, but I can assure you that he started off just like any other teenager—making impulsive decisions to be cool with his friends, experimenting with drugs, and testing boundaries and limits. I can also assure you that he didn't start off doing anything more dangerous and reckless than the

White kids in our high school did. But the White kids didn't fill the courthouses in our hometown. I can't help but wonder if my brother's path would have been different if he had been treated like a typical teenager instead of a deviant criminal when he made his first mistakes. Maybe there was nothing "wrong" with him until the system responded as if everything about him was wrong.

Eventually, my brother and I began to write to each other. I wrote sporadically while I was in college, consumed with my own life's journey. I wrote more often after I became a defense attorney in 1995. Visiting prisons as a defender made me realize how awful his experience must be, and I couldn't imagine being in a place like that without family writing and checking in. I put my last letter in the mail, including a money order, four days before he died. I am certain he didn't receive it before his stroke. The prison didn't send the letter or the money order back. As the prison guard reminded us when we visited the hospital, Dustin had been scheduled for release from prison just two months after his death.

While entire books have been devoted to the impact of parental incarceration on children,[91] there is very little research on how young people experience the loss of a sibling to jail or prison.[92] Courts rarely track the number of youth in custody who have siblings, and few police officers and judges think about how their decision to arrest and detain one child might affect other youth in the child's family. The little research that does exist confirms my own experience and that of my clients and other young people we hear about in the media. Professionals who work with incarcerated youth and their families explain that children experience considerable trauma from the complex array of feelings they have about their sibling's arrest and absence from the home.[93] Emotions include concern about their sibling's safety, sadness about the loss of a friend and companion, anxiety about having to visit a brother or sister in prison, shame and embarrassment about having a sibling in the "system," and sometimes resentment about the disruption the sibling's arrest has caused to the family.

Young people who have seen their siblings in police custody may have nightmares and periodically relive vivid images of their brother or sister in handcuffs or a police car. Others are left to imagine and worry about what life must be like inside a detention facility. Because parents can rarely tell the child how long a sibling will be gone, especially in the early stages of a case, a child's anxiety may continue unresolved for extended periods of time.[94] Incarceration is a confusing type of loss for young people. Although the sibling is physically absent from everyday activity, they are still alive and psychologically present in the child's life through memory, visitation, or conversation. This ambiguity often leaves the child confused about whether it is appropriate to grieve.[95] The shame associated with incarceration also prevents some young people from openly discussing, mourning, or otherwise coping with that loss or absence.

Visitation creates one of the greatest dilemmas for parents and the children involved. Young people are often torn between their desire to see and check on a sibling and their own fears and anxieties about visiting a prison.[96] Visitation is traumatic for anyone who doesn't want to be searched, patted down, or otherwise touched by strangers as they enter the facility.[97] Some youth are embarrassed to be seen in a prison and resent the real and perceived insults from the guards and other correctional staff. Youth who feel bad about not wanting to visit may withdraw and stop writing or calling their sibling to avoid questions and guilt about their absence. In some families, the incarcerated youth may refuse the visits and contact, leaving siblings on the outside feeling hurt, angry, or saddened by the rejection. Other youth are disappointed when their siblings miss a major milestone in their lives, like a first date, graduation, or wedding. Even when youth are eager to see their siblings, some facilities may restrict visitation to parents and adult relatives, and few judges consider the potential impact on siblings when deciding whether and for how long to send a child to a distant prison or residential treatment center. Like my own parents, adult guardians agonize about whether and how much to tell other children about a sibling's arrest and are often unwilling to let a child miss school to attend court hearings or visit the sibling in jail.

Stigma, shame, and isolation are recurring themes in many families with incarcerated children. Young people may be bullied by other youth who taunt them about their sibling's status or just find it difficult to relate to peers who don't understand their situation. Young people who are nervous about what others might think may keep the sibling's incarceration a secret, adding to their feelings of loneliness and isolation. Some even pretend their sibling died or just never existed. Many youth—especially in Black communities where children are under constant police surveillance—discover they have become the target of police scrutiny as a result of their sibling's arrest. Police in the family's neighborhood assume the child must be destined for a life of crime because *"this is what your family does."*[98]

Unfortunately, some siblings do turn to crime and delinquency as they become withdrawn or angry or develop low self-esteem and other mental health problems associated with their sibling's incarceration.[99] The stress of having a sibling in jail can also lead to academic challenges as young people become preoccupied about the well-being of their sibling or find it difficult to navigate the new demands created by their sibling's absence. Almost every incarceration leads to some restructuring of the family's day-to-day routine. Youth who are left at home often have to take on new household responsibilities when siblings are no longer available for chores and parents are forced to spend more time handling the sibling's legal affairs. These children sometimes feel neglected when parents have less time to spend with them and begin to miss important events like school plays, sports games, and parent-teacher conferences. Resentment grows as siblings believe "the problem child" is sucking up all the attention.

In 2016, journalist Juleyka Lantigua-Williams wrote a six-part series for *The Atlantic* about siblings in prison.[100] The magazine also collected stories from readers who anonymously described their feelings and experiences of having a brother or sister behind bars.[101] Several contributors wrote about the challenges of living with a grieving parent, while others highlighted the financial toll the sibling's incarceration put on families who had to cover attorneys' fees and prison visits. One contributor who wrote about the incarceration of her brother when she was nine years old noted that "holidays and his birthday—in December—always left my mother depressed . . . No one cared to ask how I felt or how I currently feel." Unfortunately, few courts provide services for the siblings of young people involved in the legal system.[102] Even outside the system, there are few if any support groups or other services uniquely tailored to help young people cope with the emotional stress associated with a sibling's arrest and custody.

The effects of a child's incarceration rarely end when the child returns home. Those who return often bring their anger, anxiety, and depression from the experience, and siblings who have been home are rarely equipped to handle the increased tension that comes with life after custody. Kalief's mother told journalists that Kalief was angry all the time. "He got in a verbal altercation with one of his brothers, and next thing you know, they started fighting. I was looking at Kalief, and a look came over him that wasn't Kalief. And it terrified me. And his brother had to go to the hospital because he threw him onto a glass table, and his brother cut his foot. Kalief later apologized and told me, 'Ma, I don't know what happened, but I was back at Rikers and I had to fight.'"[103]

Siblings of Black youth who die in or after prison or who are killed by the police or vigilantes are forced into the national spotlight with little time to grieve.[104] Siblings may be drawn in to testify as a witness at trial, forced to defend their sibling's character, or asked to make public appearances to plea for police accountability and criminal justice reform. Kalief Browder had five siblings, several of whom have written op-eds, appeared in documentaries and news programs to share Kalief's story, and sued New York City for the wrongful death of their brother.[105]

Tamir Rice had three siblings. His older sister, fourteen-year-old Tajai Rice, was inside the Cudell Recreation Center when she heard gunshots and another child told her that Tamir had been shot.[106] Video footage shows Tajai running to her brother moments after the shooting.[107] Less than ten feet from where her brother lay, officers tackled her to the ground, handcuffed her, and put her in the back of a police car.[108] Because a sibling is both friend and family, their death often causes a deep and unique sense of loss and guilt. Samaria Rice told reporters that Tamir and Tajai were "very, very close. It's like two peas in a bucket. They have a lot of similar ways . . . She told me that she did not know what she was going to do without her brother . . . They did everything together. You did not see one without the other."[109] In her own emotional comments at a rally two days after Tamir was killed, Tajai thanked everyone for coming and told the crowd that Tamir was loving and would love them all.[110] Tajai and Samaria filed a complaint with the Cleveland police oversight board, arguing that officers forced Tajai to watch her brother die after they shot him and handcuffed her.[111] Tajai's complaint said, "I did not do anything wrong. I was not treated with respect or decency." Her sentiment is one shared by many in her shoes.

The public heard from Trayvon Martin's brother Jahvaris many times in the weeks and months after Trayvon was killed. Jahvaris was called to testify at George Zimmerman's trial to say he recognized his brother's voice on the 911 call. He should know the voice well because he grew up sharing a room with Trayvon. In an April 2012 interview with CNN, Jahvaris described Trayvon as smart, good at sports, and eager to follow Jahvaris to college.[112] Jahvaris had just seen him eight days before he was killed, during a horseback ride to celebrate their mother's birthday. To him, Zimmerman's claim that Trayvon was violent that night "didn't sound right": "He is not a violent person." Five years later, in May 2017, Jahvaris said his emotions still flowed heavy, at even the slightest hint of sadness.[113] Trayvon's killing has forever changed the way he processes stories of racism or race-related crimes. "It's not until it happens to you that it opens you up, and you pay way more attention. Once your eyes are open, you have to do more." Of course, Jahvaris doesn't want to be defined by the tragedy his family endured, but Trayvon's death certainly influenced his own decision to get involved in community organizing and activism.

### EVICTED:[114] FAMILIES IN PERIL

Although I am convinced that class and education offer little protection against the criminalization of Black adolescence, I am equally convinced that poverty makes the experience much worse. My brother's arrests and incarceration were emotionally overwhelming and traumatic for all of us, but they never caused us to lose our home or our parents to lose their jobs. My clients and their families tell a different story about their encounters with the legal system in Washington, D.C.

I met "David" when he was fifteen. I represented him for three years. David's life was complicated. He was a very smart kid. He was kind and had a lot of potential. Sadly, other obligations prevented him from doing his best in school and succeeding in ways that were lawful. David's mother had cerebral palsy and was confined to a wheelchair. She was paralyzed from the waist down. David had two brothers, one older and one younger. Despite her physical limitations, David's mother was strong, determined, and very involved in her sons' lives. She insisted that her boys go to school, secured public housing for the family, and learned to navigate the government's bureaucracy so she could provide for them all. They were a close-knit family and cared a lot about each other. But life was a struggle.

David's family always had food and a roof over their heads, but they didn't have anything extra. David and his older brother managed to take care of themselves, but their nine-year-old brother, "Jerrod," suffered the most. Jerrod was anxious and depressed. He wet the bed and didn't always have clean clothes for school. He couldn't focus on his schoolwork and didn't make friends. David and his brother felt responsible for Jerrod. They both began selling drugs to try to make things better for their family. And things were a little better—for a while. David could provide clothes for himself and Jerrod. He could buy extra food for the house, and he never thought he would have to worry about his family being evicted, homeless, or torn apart. Sadly, he was wrong.

David's family had long been under the "care" and supervision of the D.C. government. With his mother's disability, various city agencies were always involved and watching—the D.C. Housing Authority, the Child and Family Services Agency, and the Department on Disability Services, to name just a few. For a long time, David's family lived in a two-story public housing unit. His mother was confined to the bottom floor while the boys took over the second floor, largely unsupervised. The second floor was a real concern for social workers and other city representatives who visited. Visitors often observed drug paraphernalia in various parts of the house and reported the smell of marijuana emanating from the upper level. David's mother asked the Housing Authority to move her family to a one-story home so she could better supervise the boys. Instead, agency officials called the police, had the boys arrested, and threatened to evict the entire family based on public housing rules that prohibit drug use on the property. In the meantime, the Child and Family Services Agency opened a neglect investigation and threatened to remove Jerrod from the home because his mother was unable to supervise him.

This experience nearly tore David's family apart—physically and emotionally. After multiple arrests over the next two years, David's older brother ended up in prison, and David was placed on probation in juvenile court. The family court judge responsible for David's delinquency case and Jerrod's neglect case initially presented David's mother with an unbearable choice. The judge wanted to know if she should send Jerrod to a foster home or David to the local detention facility. Either way, the judge was determined to protect Jerrod from the negative influences of his siblings. No parent should be asked or expected to make that choice. Ultimately, the judge decided on her own to send Jerrod to a group home for neglected children.

Until then, David had been one of my toughest clients. Not hard. Not mean. Not angry. Just strong. But when the judge decided to remove his little brother from their home, David collapsed on the floor, crying inconsolably. He understood that his actions—selling drugs to make things better for his family—caused the judge to take Jerrod away. But Jerrod was doomed for tragedy from the moment city officials decided to treat the older boys as criminals instead of victims of their mother's unfortunate medical challenges. Instead of providing the boys with meaningful alternatives to selling drugs, they punished them. That strategy didn't help anyone—least of all Jerrod, who was depressed about his mother's illness, devasted by the loss of one and possibly two brothers to prison, and terrified about his own removal from the only home he knew. It was David's story, even more than my own, that really helped me understand the impact of arrest and incarceration on siblings.

David was not my only client to risk losing or to lose public housing. Several years ago, I arrived at the courthouse to represent "Isaiah" in what I thought would be a routine juvenile probation review hearing. Isaiah had pled guilty to drug possession and had been doing pretty well on probation. He was going to school, meeting with his probation officer weekly, and not using drugs at the time. As soon as I entered the courthouse, Isaiah's mother walked over to tell me she had just received a notice to vacate their apartment. Somehow the D.C. Housing Authority had learned about Isaiah's drug case.

With Isaiah's home in jeopardy, the review hearing quickly turned into an argument about alternative housing. Isaiah's probation officer asked the judge to consider revoking Isaiah's probation so he could live in a youth shelter house. After listening to my arguments about the inappropriateness of detention as a solution to homelessness, the judge decided not to revoke probation at that time but instructed my client to stay in close contact with his probation officer. We all agreed that Isaiah was a pretty quiet kid who had not been in trouble aside from this one offense. Shortly after the hearing, my client, his mother, and his sister were indeed evicted and began moving between friends and family as they could. With no stable address and no consistent phone number,

Isaiah soon lost contact with his probation officer. A few months later, the judge finally revoked his probation and sent him to the detention center for thirty days. Isaiah's probation ended when he was released.

As is true for so many youth in the legal system, the consequences of Isaiah's drug conviction far outweighed the severity of his crime. Detention served no meaningful purpose for Isaiah, his family, or the general public. For a time, detention made the judge and probation officer feel better because they knew Isaiah had a safe space to sleep, but the temporary sleeping arrangement did nothing to address the family's housing crisis and likely wasn't any safer than the friends and family who took him in. The detention facility also didn't provide drug treatment, vocational programming, or counseling to prepare him for his return to the community. The eviction converted a case of adolescent drug use into a major, long-term crisis for an otherwise stable family.

In Washington, D.C.—and cities all across the country—a child and his entire family can be denied access to or evicted from public housing when the child has been charged, convicted, or even suspected of a crime.[115] These evictions are supported by federal law known as the "One Strike" housing policy.[116] To avoid eviction, the family may instead remove the "offending" child from the home.[117] While there is no formal count of the number of people affected by the "One Strike" policy, the effects are clear. The policy has increased the number of evictions in urban cities exponentially. An informal study of records from one New Orleans court revealed that 20 percent of the eviction actions filed by the local public housing authority were based on the conduct of a child.[118] In Chicago, about 25 percent of One Strike evictions in the city resulted from a child's arrest. Normal adolescent behaviors like a teen fight, vandalism, or drug possession can leave a child and all of their siblings homeless, disrupting the children's education and causing anxiety and depression in response to the new circumstances and environment.[119]

Even when they don't lose their housing, families face the financial burden of juvenile courts that require parents to pay fines and fees for just about everything—diversion programs, counseling, drug testing, mental health evaluations, treatment and rehabilitation programs, probation, custody, and court costs.[120] As of 2016, twenty states charge fees for juvenile probation or supervision.[121] Twenty-two states charge fees for diversion. Thirty-one states charge fees for evaluation or testing. Eleven states charge to seal or expunge a record. Twenty-five states impose generic "court costs."Forty-seven states charge parents for the care of youth while in the system—including the cost of placement, programming, food, clothes, shelter, and health care. Judges also routinely order children and their families to pay restitution regardless of whether they can afford to pay.

Many youth who are released pending trial are required to wear electronic GPS monitors that track their movement. Although these monitors are attached to the "offending" child, they affect the entire family, especially those family members who already feel targeted and surveilled by police. Electronic monitoring often requires the family to have a landline phone, and if the electricity or phone is disconnected because the family can't pay the bill, some jurisdictions will return the child to detention. Although electronic monitoring was developed as an alternative to incarceration, it comes at a steep cost for poor, mostly Black and Latinx families who often can't afford the initial application and enrollment fees, ongoing administrative costs, or moving fees if the child changes residence.[122] Many cities and counties also require the youth to pay for lost or damaged equipment, potentially burdening the family with thousands of dollars in costs. When families fail to pay the fines or fees, the state can send collection agencies after them, tack on interest, garnish their wages, seize their bank accounts, intercept their tax refunds, suspend their driver's licenses, or charge them with contempt of court.[123] If wages can't be garnished, a child may be kept on probation or incarcerated longer.[124] Dequan Jackson was one of those children.

*The New York Times* wrote about Dequan in 2016.[125] Dequan is from Duval County, Florida. When he was thirteen years old, he was charged with battery for crashing into a teacher while fooling around at school. He met most of his probation conditions—working forty hours in a food bank, meeting with an anger management counselor, and keeping curfew—but his mother was unable to make the final $200 payment for his court and public defender fees. The court added fourteen months to Dequan's initial one year of probation while it waited for the payment. After his mother finally pulled together the $200, Dequan's family received a bill for an additional $868. The family had been charged $1 per day for Dequan's probation supervision. For a family like Dequan's, living paycheck to paycheck in public housing, even the smallest fee can be out of reach. The consequences of criminalizing Black adolescence are steep while the benefits are few.

## 12

---

# #BlackBoyJoy and #BlackGirlMagic: Adolescent Resilience and Systems Reform

In the introduction, I promised to offer a bit of hope at the end of the book. My hope lies in the persistence and resilience of Black youth like Eric, whom I represented ten years ago. Writing this book has made me want to find all of my clients to see how they are doing. I am still in touch with some. Others have long since put their court experience behind them and don't want to be reminded of it by me. But I knew a few might be happy to hear from an old advocate. Eric was at the top of my list. Remember Eric was my thirteen-year-old client who was arrested at school for possession of a Molotov cocktail. I have thought about Eric, his mother, and his sister "Jalen" many times over the years, so I was eager to track them down.

Years later, now the summer of 2020, I still had their numbers in my phone contacts. His mother's number rang to a voice mail with no identifier. I was afraid to leave a message. His sister's number rang twice and she answered.

"Is this Jalen?" I asked.

"Yes."

"You aren't going to believe this, but this is Kris Henning from Georgetown Law. Remember me?"

"No way! No way!! We were just talking about you last month!" I could hear screaming in the background as she yelled out, "This is Kris Henning!" A male voice answered, "My lawyer Kris Henning?" And she replied, "Yes, your lawyer!"

Jalen turned her attention back to me. "I am on another phone with Eric, and I am on the way to see my mom. She isn't going to believe it's you." I could hear her tell Eric goodbye and that she would see him in a minute.

Amazed, I asked, "What made you think of me last month?"

"Well, Eric got arrested for protesting, so we thought we were going to need your help again, but he got released. So everything is okay."

"Well, I can't be mad at him for protesting!"

"Me either," Jalen said. "I'm kind of proud of him. He has become a real activist!"

Jalen got home and put Eric and their mom on the speakerphone. We talked for more than two hours. Eric was thirteen when I last saw him. He is twenty-two now. Jalen had moved away to North Carolina and just happened to be visiting her family in D.C. when I called.

I asked them what they remembered about the day Eric got arrested in middle school. They remembered the details just as I did. Jalen started off by recalling how she ran up to me when I walked into the courthouse to ask if I could represent her brother. We rehashed old stories, including our outrage at how much everyone overreacted that day—the school resource officer, the teacher, the principal, other students, and the local news stations. All for nothing. Eric had a glass bottle with liquids that would never catch on fire and a piece of toilet paper that would burn out before the fire ever reached the glass. Eric reminded us that he didn't even have a lighter and that it never occurred to him to try to light the paper wick. He was a thirteen-year-old boy playing with a new "toy."

We spent most of our time talking about how Eric was doing now. Eric graduated from high school, lived with one sister in South Carolina for a couple of years, and then with Jalen for another year in North Carolina. Along the way, he developed a love for cooking—like his mom, who used to cater on the side. In each state, he worked at restaurants, honing his culinary skills and paying attention to what it takes to run a restaurant. Eric eventually returned to D.C., where he worked first at a restaurant and then in retail. And then George Floyd was killed.

Eric's retail job was located in the heart of the protest zone and had to close for a while. At first Eric watched the protests on TV, but then he saw President Trump threaten military action against the protesters and hold up a Bible in front of St. John's Episcopal Church. He watched D.C. police officers dressed in riot gear use tear gas, flash grenades, and rubber bullets to force protesters away from the church.[1] Eric couldn't stay home anymore. He went out to protest.

Almost immediately, Eric found a passion and a purpose he didn't know he had. On his first day of protesting, he met a group of five women holding signs. They looked tired, and he couldn't imagine how much longer they would last. He and a friend left and came back with five folding chairs. It was a gift to help the women stay strong. On his second day of protesting, he noticed that people were hungry but making do with granola bars, trail mix, and an occasional sandwich donated by a church. His restaurant experience made him think about the alternatives. On his third day of protesting, Eric caught an Uber and showed up in the protest zone with a grill and $50 worth of burgers and hot dogs. His plan was to give it all away for free. And he did—that day, and for many weeks to follow.

Eric's $50 investment quickly turned into six grills, a generator, two tables, a tent, and several chairs—all donated by people who were inspired by what he was doing. Eric also attracted multiple volunteers, gathering daily in the newly named Black Lives Matter Plaza. Eric's new team launched a social media campaign and drew a lot of public support. Eric was back in the news, but this time as an activist. Eric moved into a protest camp near the White House and stayed in a tent until the police tore it down and made all of the campers leave without time to gather their things.

Eric didn't cook to make money or satisfy his own personal

agenda. He did it to make people strong enough to stay outside and speak their minds. He did it to create a safe space for people to "dialogue" and "decompress" during the protests. He met people of every race and class, from all over the country. He spent time with the homeless and with the wealthy. He got on the megaphone, he taught, and he learned.

Eric's mother had been a strong and persistent advocate from the day I met her in 2011, so I wasn't surprised to hear about all that Eric was doing despite his early challenges in the juvenile court. When I asked him what made him thrive, Eric said his mother never gave up on him and was serious about education. Eric has four siblings, all of whom have excelled. Two have college degrees, one is in college, and the fourth is in the military.

After our first two-hour call, I knew I had to see Eric in person. We were still bound by the restrictions of the COVID-19 pandemic, so we planned a "socially distant" outing on his front porch for the next weekend.

Eric is intellectually curious, politically aware, and very well read. We talked about art, religion, history, law, and literature. He reads George Orwell, Stokely Carmichael, Huey Newton, and Angela Davis. He loves to read and write poetry and recited one of his poems for me. His poem was a powerful reflection on race, history, and politics in America. His favorite poets are Robert Frost, Edgar Allan Poe, and Langston Hughes. We talked about D.C. politics, term limits for Supreme Court appointments, the 2020 presidential election, and what it means to be an American. He pulled out a law dictionary and asked me questions about the First Amendment, the law of protests, and search and seizure. I came up with a list of books he might like to read. He was far wiser and more knowledgeable than I ever was at age twenty-two.

Of course, we also talked about race, crime, and incarceration. When his mom sat with us, she said "the system" was designed to keep Black families broken but was happy to see folks finally waking up with the protests. When I asked Eric how he thinks about the police now, he summed up his strategy in a word— "avoidance." To demonstrate, he recalled a recent occasion when he encountered the police on his way home from work. He was riding a skateboard and wearing his work uniform. Apparently, there had been a crime nearby. As he began to approach the front door of his house, he realized the police were watching him. Instinctively, he turned around to head into the alley to enter his house from the back door. The police stopped him and patted him down. He pointed to his house, explained that he was just coming home from work, and reminded them that he had just skated past them on a skateboard. They let him go.

Police cars and motorcycles drove down Eric's street four times as we sat outside. On the fourth time, he told me, "This is what policing looks like here. There is no reason for them to ride down our street." Pointing half a block up the road, he said, "The main road is right there. This isn't a shortcut. They can get to their district without coming this way. I think they just come through to watch us. Police make me not want to go outside. They make me angry." He also wondered out loud, "And I don't know if Black police are 'with it' [meaning the racism] or just not aware."

I learned so much from Eric in the time we spent together. And I found the hope I was looking for. Notwithstanding his distrust of the police and his concerns about politics and injustice in America, Eric turned his outrage into action. Before I left, I asked him if he was happy. He said, "The better word is 'excited.' I am excited about what is happening right now. I am excited to be a part of it. I don't know what is going to happen with my grill, but I have a lot of ideas about how to keep it going." Eric's excitement for the future and his insistence on building a better way forward for all of us are shared by countless other youth leading protests and advocating for change across the country. This is what gives me hope.

### HELP THEM HEAL: PROMOTING BLACK ADOLESCENT RESILIENCE

For young Black people like Eric, racism—in all of its subtle and overt forms—is a given. The vast majority of Black youth will experience some form of racial discrimination in their lifetime.[2]

I can't prevent that with this book. But I can identify strategies to help Black youth thrive in the face of structural inequities and targeted racism, and I can help us think about how to disrupt the bad habits, wrong thinking, and misguided policies and practices that continue to hurt them.

The good news is that young people are resilient. They can "bounce back" and function well even after significant disruption, stress, and adversity.[3] While we continue on the long journey toward decriminalizing Black adolescence and fixing what is wrong with American policing, we must act now to repair the harms of racial trauma and create new opportunities for Black youth to succeed in the face of demonizing stereotypes that cause others to fear and devalue them.[4] Black children like Eric have a good chance of thriving as adults even if they have experienced difficult life circumstances, but usually only if we help them get there. "We" means all of us—parents, teachers, mentors, social workers, pediatricians, mental health experts, faith leaders, athletic coaches, community activists, lawmakers, government officials, and the media.

Fortunately, we have good research on how to improve adolescent resilience before, during, and after a traumatic event. We prepare youth for resilience almost from birth by ensuring that every child has at least one "irrationally caring adult" in their lives—that is, one adult who will show them unconditional love and support no matter what they do.[5] A network of caring adults is even better. Resilience is cultivated through strong family relationships, community support, religious and spiritual connections, and basic necessities such as stable housing, family income, education, and recreational opportunities.[6] Parents and mentors improve adolescent resilience by nurturing personal attributes like positive self-esteem and teaching good problem-solving skills to help youth resolve conflicts with others. Young people who have sustained contact with a community of advocates who keep them safe and make them feel as if they belong have a much better chance of fighting off self-defeating attitudes and navigating real and perceived threats in society.[7]

Adults lay the foundation for resilience by helping youth develop a strong racial identity.[8] Researchers who study risk and resilience tell us that racial and ethnic identity help youth overcome adverse childhood experiences and set higher expectations for what they can achieve in school and their careers.[9] Youth with a strong racial identity are less likely to drop out of school or turn to crime to cope with racial adversity.[10] Racial identity seems to create a buffer against discriminatory experiences and prepare youth to handle the stress and other psychological harms associated with oppression.[11] It also helps youth cultivate a healthy sense of self, which is one of the most important factors in improving and sustaining good adolescent mental health and overall well-being.[12] Positive self-esteem is especially important for Black girls who are devalued based on their race and their gender.[13]

Racial identity development is part of the broader "racial socialization" we studied in chapter 5. Racial socialization does more than teach children how to anticipate and survive experiences of racial trauma. It also helps them find a safe and effective way to confront injustice and bring about change. Parents can teach and model coping strategies that help youth change undesirable situations, manage their emotions about situations they cannot change, and adapt to situations when there is no other alternative.[14] Although parents usually have primary responsibility for helping children navigate the daily stressors in their lives, every adult in a child's network must understand how racial trauma impacts adolescent health and be prepared to help young people cope and heal.[15]

Schools can help students develop healthy adolescent identities by incorporating and affirming race history in the curriculum. Black history not only educates Black youth about race and racism in America but also empowers them with the knowledge of Black contributions, achievements, and resources that can help them thrive in the face of oppression.[16] Black history essentially "liberates" Black youth from the negative messages they receive about their worth and abilities and gives them the "psychological strength" they need to resist or rebound after encounters with racism.[17]

Religion and spirituality play a similarly important role in resilience. Racial socialization often includes elements of faith and other cultural traditions that provide meaning, purpose, hope, and a sense of community.[18] In a study of almost 1,600 Black youth aged twelve to eighteen, researchers found that religious activities such as personal prayer and reflection and social engagement with others through church services and youth activities increased optimism and reduced depressive symptoms such as restless sleep, poor appetite, and feeling lonely or disliked.[19] Black youth involved in religious activities also tend to be more engaged in school and have lower rates of delinquency, drug use, and risky sexual behaviors.[20]

Unfortunately, our window of opportunity may be short with all of these strategies for resilience. As we discussed in chapter 1, developmental experts tell us that adolescence is our last great chance to make a difference in how young people will think and behave as adults.[21] Research on the link between religion and resilience, for example, suggests that religion is most important in early adolescence and gradually becomes less influential by the time youth are seventeen or eighteen years old.[22] Any public health agenda committed to racial equity should take affirmative steps to support youth in adolescence before they turn to more negative coping strategies like substance abuse and other risky behaviors to manage race-related stressors.

Ultimately, Black children are resilient because Black families are resilient.[23] If we want to serve Black youth better, we have to reduce the barriers that prevent them from accessing mental health treatment and empower parents and caregivers with the resources they need to support children who have been directly and indirectly impacted by the criminalization of Black adolescence. This work must start with culturally competent tools designed to assess and meet the unique mental health needs of Black youth.[24] Contrary to historical views that Black parents lack the capacity to raise moral and resilient children, Black families have long succeeded in guiding their children through the worst of America's racial tragedies to produce smart, healthy, and dynamic young leaders. Instead of asking how parents have "failed" their children when they end up in the criminal legal system, we should ask how society has failed our families.

### LET THEM LEAD: YOUTH ACTIVISM AND REFORM

If you want to know how to make the world a better place for Black children, then ask them. I didn't really appreciate the importance of youth activism until 2003, when the D.C. Council considered a proposal that would significantly overhaul the juvenile legal system and make juvenile court records more accessible to the public.[25] More than three hundred students from D.C. schools showed up to testify in opposition to critical parts of the proposal. I was mesmerized, and more important, the council members were persuaded not to adopt the most extreme provisions of the bill.

I was again reminded of how powerful youth voices can be in April 2019, when students from a local youth activist organization, Pathways 2 Power, convened a roundtable called "Creating a Seat at Our Table." At the roundtable, youth leaders from across the metropolitan area met with the police chief, a representative from the mayor's office, and members of the D.C. Board of Education and D.C. Council to express their concerns about educational inequities, negative and ineffective police engagement with youth, and the lack of resources and opportunities for youth in the area. Young advocates told city officials they were tired of not being invited to weigh in on matters of most importance to them and argued that the root causes of violence are poverty, gentrification, inadequate housing and education, and untreated mental health challenges. Since that event, I have continued to watch other local youth-led organizations like Black Swan Academy and Mikva Challenge make their voices heard on issues such as the school dress code, police in schools, and immigration policy.

Youth activism is vibrant all over the country. Some of the most vocal youth activists emerged after the tragic shootings at Sandy Hook Elementary and Parkland's Marjory Stoneman Douglas High School. Students were clear they wanted the violence to end at their schools, but they were equally clear they didn't want more police and more guns to make that happen. Students rallied for commonsense gun safety laws and organized the first national school walkout on March 14, 2018—a month after the Parkland shooting.[26]

Students of color immediately noted that advocacy from Black and Latinx students rarely gets the same attention as the majority-White students' calls for gun control did after the rallies in Parkland.[27] They insisted that any campaign to reduce gun violence in schools must also address violence in communities of color. Students at Booker T. Washington High School in Atlanta weren't allowed to leave the building for the walkout but made their views known by kneeling in the hallways, following the lead of Colin Kaepernick. Students in Baltimore and Chicago asked for programs to address poverty and mental health services. Students in Brooklyn demanded police reforms.

A second national school walkout was held on the anniversary of the Columbine High School massacre, April 20, 2018, with more than 2,000 events and at least one event in every state across the nation.[28] The second walkout incorporated guest speakers and voter registration to increase turnout in the November midterm elections. Beyond issues of school safety, students across the country have coordinated rallies, protests, marches, walkouts, petitions, and social media campaigns to draw attention to the Black Lives Matter movement, DACA (Deferred Action for Childhood Arrivals), global climate change, the police-free schools movement, and President Trump's travel ban against several majority-Muslim countries.[29]

Speaking truth to power isn't just a cliché. It is an important part of healthy adolescent development. As explored in chapter 5, youth who organize and protest develop valuable leadership skills and are more likely to vote and stay involved in politics when they are older. Civic activism also improves the emotional, spiritual, and physical well-being of Black youth by helping them heal from racial trauma and become agents of their own destiny.[30] Young activists who challenge social, political, and economic injustice learn to envision better alternatives for themselves and their friends and reduce their risk of depression, despair, anger, apathy, fear, and self-destructive behaviors.[31] Civic activism also helps young people resist harmful narratives about their race.[32] More than anything, activism teaches young people that life doesn't always have to be this way. Young people like my client Eric are speaking out because they are convinced that police don't have to harass and abuse Black people. They are convinced that no more Black children like Tamir Rice and Michael Brown have to die. That kind of attitude and activism can be encouraged in young people by parents, teachers, and mentors. Teachers are uniquely positioned to partner with students on politically charged issues like racial oppression and to work with youth to design a culturally diverse curriculum and lead other antiracist reform initiatives at school.[33]

We must listen to our young people—not only because it makes them healthier and wiser adults, but also because listening helps us find better solutions to the social inequities in our communities. Communities thrive when lawmakers, school administrators, and community leaders treat young people as partners and problem solvers rather than troublemakers.[34] Although some youth will speak out in ways that adults find offensive, policy makers do well to listen with respect and implement their suggestions with genuine commitment and adequate resources. Highly visual protests—good, bad, or ugly—educate the public, energize voters, and often create a sense of civic renewal for the entire community. More important, protests hold schools, police departments, and youth service agencies accountable for meaningful change. City lawmakers can create more opportunities for Black youth to be heard by creating internships, meeting with students in schools, inviting students to testify at rule-making and agency oversight hearings, and engaging youth in campaign debates.

## LET THEM LEARN: POLICE-FREE SCHOOLS

On July 7, 2020, the D.C. Council voted to end the Metropolitan Police Department's management of the largest school security contract in the District.[35] This vote effectively reversed the 2004 law that gave MPD responsibility for school safety and transferred that responsibility back to the D.C. Public Schools (DCPS).[36] In the 2019–20 academic year before this vote, MPD had a School Safety Division that managed 325 contract security guards as well as an additional 116 of its own sworn officers who served as school resource officers in D.C.'s public schools.[37] In addition, patrol officers from each of MPD's seven patrol districts are expected to serve schools by ensuring students' safe travel to and from school, responding to schools in the case of emergency, and assisting schools in reducing truancy. The 2020 vote reauthorized DCPS to develop its own approach to school security, but noted that the agency should still coordinate its safety plan with the police and local homeland security agency. The new law also requires schools to replace school security training practices with a "positive youth development philosophy" for any security personnel with whom the schools contract.[38]

The council's vote came after a campaign spearheaded by Black Swan Academy, a youth-led nonprofit organization that focuses on empowering Black youth through civic leadership and engagement.[39] Youth advocates complained that school police were driving the school-to-prison pipeline and highlighted data showing that 92 percent of school-based arrests during the 2018–19 school year were for Black youth, although Black students make up only 66 percent of D.C.'s public school population.[40] The campaign was also supported by Black Lives Matter DC, local teacher advocacy groups like D.C. Area Educators for Social Justice and the Washington Teachers' Union, and a host of other local and national civil rights organizations like the Advancement Project, the D.C. Fiscal Policy Institute, the Alliance for Educational Justice, the Communities for Just Schools Fund, and the Center for Popular Democracy.[41] In a June 2020 poll by the D.C. Fiscal

Policy Institute, two-thirds of D.C. voters surveyed supported removing police from schools and using the funds for "mental health and student support programs."[42]

Council member David Grosso, who co-chaired the Committee on Education and introduced the resolution, expressed concern that DCPS had one contracted security guard or special police officer for every 129 students, but only one social worker for every 217 students, one psychologist for every 402 students, and one counselor for every 408 students.[43] Mr. Grosso recommended that DCPS use the reallocated funds to implement DCPS's mission of "academic success and social-emotional development of [its] young people."[44] Advocates have asked that funds be reallocated from the security contract to hire social workers, counselors, community violence interrupters, mental health professionals, and "credible messengers" who are neighborhood leaders with relevant life experience and skills to help youth transform their attitudes and behaviors around violence.[45]

Of course, the D.C. police-free schools campaign has its opponents. The DCPS chancellor, Lewis D. Ferebee, and Mayor Muriel Bowser have opposed the campaign, expressing concerns about the school system's capacity to manage the school security contract on its own and arguing that D.C. has worked hard to ensure school resource officers and security guards support students.[46] Although the July 7 change in law was an important step in reducing the role and power of MPD in D.C. schools, the law itself does not mandate police-free schools. The chancellor will retain considerable authority to decide how to implement the changes required. As of this writing, the chancellor has not indicated whether or how he would scale back the current security program or reallocate funds to other student support services. Only time will tell.

The police-free schools movement is a national movement with international support.[47] As of June 2020, at least thirteen cities had active campaigns, with hashtags like #CounselorsNotCops and #PoliceFreeSchools.[48] Given the movement's deep commitment to racial justice, it is no surprise that many of these campaigns gained additional momentum and success in the days after George Floyd was killed. The Minneapolis Board of Education passed a resolution to terminate its contract with the Minneapolis Police Department on June 2, 2020.[49] Just weeks later, on June 24, 2020, the Seattle School Board voted to suspend the partnership between Seattle Public Schools and the Seattle Police Department.[50] The suspension was part of a larger proposal to improve the school climate for Black students, who made up only 14 percent of the district's student body but accounted for nearly 50 percent of students referred to the police by school employees in the 2019–20 academic year. The proposal also directed the superintendent to create a Black studies curriculum and will replace armed police with unarmed security at school district events like dances and basketball games.[51]

Nearly a decade ago in 2011, the Black Organizing Project began advocating for the elimination of police from the Oakland Unified School District (OUSD) after a school police officer shot and killed twenty-year-old Raheim Brown outside Skyline High School.[52] In 2015, the Black Organizing Project and other community organizers successfully pressured OUSD to remove "willful defiance," an ambiguous rule enforced disparately against Black students, from the list of permissible reasons for suspension and expulsion, but it wasn't until June 2020 that advocates saw real movement on their demand for police-free schools.[53] On June 24, 2020, the Oakland School Board voted unanimously to eliminate the OUSD Police Department from school campuses three weeks after a student-led protest against police brutality drew a crowd of 15,000 people.[54] Removing police from schools is both transformative and symbolic for Black students. Removing police not only prevents educators and administrators from relying on police for routine discipline but also communicates to Black students that Black lives and Black minds matter.[55]

Teachers, students, and parents do not fall neatly on one side of the police-free schools debate or the other. Students have led campaigns to remove police from schools in cities like Durham, Columbus, Milwaukee, Phoenix, and Seattle.[56] Educators have been just as vocal in favor of the movement in cities like Chicago, Los Angeles, Racine, and Seattle.[57] The Chicago Teachers Union has been working with community groups, grassroots organizations, and students since 2015 to advocate for the removal of police from the Chicago Public Schools.[58] On June 11, 2019, United Teachers Los Angeles (UTLA) published a statement titled "Imagine Police-Free Schools with the Supports Students Deserve," calling for the end of L.A. school police.[59] UTLA succeeded in getting the board of education to eliminate security searches using metal detectors and discriminatory "wanding" of students in the 2019–20 school year. In March 2021, the Los Angeles board of education voted to cut 133 school police positions, ban the use of pepper spray on students, and divert $25 million from school police to programming to support the education of Black students.[60]

From Los Angeles to Boston, youth advocates are calling for the reallocation of school police funds to restorative justice, mental health, and academic supports that help students reach their fullest potential. In Chicago, the #CopsOutCPS coalition is advocating for the reallocation of the $33 million currently spent on 180 SROs to hire 317 social workers, 314 school psychologists, and 322 nurses.[61] In Portland, the school board vice-chair, Rita Moore, said that resources should be reallocated for developmentally appropriate, trauma-informed, and culturally sensitive restorative justice practices.[62] In cities like Racine and Miami, advocates have pushed for the expansion of ethnic studies and antiracist curricula.[63]

These advocates are not interested in having "trained" officers mimic counselors and educators, or school boards replace sworn police officers with security staff or "sentries" employed by the school.[64] They want real investment in nurses, librarians, counselors, and mental health professionals who not only keep the peace but also help young people thrive socially, emotionally, and academically.[65] They want more teachers and smaller class sizes to improve student achievement and prevent misconduct, and they want school districts to hire professionals who help students think critically and solve problems.[66] Most important, they want school boards and community leaders to engage students and parents in redefining what school discipline looks like.[67]

### KEEP THEM SAFE: EFFECTIVE STRATEGIES
### FOR SCHOOL SAFETY AND STUDENT DISCIPLINE

"Police-free schools" doesn't mean that schools can never call the police. It just means that police will not be involved in the day-to-day lives of our children and that money previously spent on law enforcement will be redirected to strategies better equipped to keep our schools safe.[68] Schools will still call the police to address guns or significant violence on campus, but administrators and educators will also be forced to think more creatively about the alternatives for routine discipline. Two organizing principles should guide our search for alternatives: first, Black children are children too; second, the most successful strategies for ensuring student safety rarely involve policing.[69] Once we accept these truths, every school and every police department should radically reduce the footprint of police in the lives of Black youth.

School safety starts with healthy, well-adjusted students. Given the high and increasing rates of trauma among America's school-age youth, any effective school safety plan must include a robust mental health staff. School-based mental health services reduce suspension and expulsion and improve attendance, academic achievement, career preparation, and graduation rates by removing emotional and psychological barriers to learning.[70] To ensure early interventions before more significant mental health concerns and disruptive behaviors emerge, Mental Health America—a leading voice for the mental health and wellness of children—recommends universal screening for mental health problems in schools by pediatricians or primary care physicians, in much the same way schools screen students for hearing and vision problems.[71]

Of course, if we are not careful, mental health labels can be just as racially biased and stigmatizing as school discipline and arrests. Many schools will need to hire medical personnel, clinicians, social workers, and other mental health providers who have been trained in antibias, anti-oppressive, and gender equity practices and who can address the unique needs of Black students.[72] Schools will also need to collaborate with community-based mental health treatment providers, child welfare departments, and health insurers to supplement school-based services.[73]

School safety requires a developmentally appropriate approach to behavior management and school discipline. Effective frameworks for behavior management include positive behavior interventions and support, restorative justice, and social emotional learning. Positive behavior supports replace zero-tolerance and other exclusionary policies like suspension and expulsion with a three-tiered support system that focuses on student expectations and achievements.[74] In the first tier, instructors provide universal supports for all students by setting positive expectations for appropriate behavior—like respect and responsibility—throughout the school.[75] In the second tier, instructors provide targeted supports for students who have shown mild signs of misbehavior and may benefit from more structure, such as peer mentoring or team building.[76] The third tier is designed to provide intensive supports for students who frequently misbehave, have experienced trauma, or need one-on-one supports based on their individual needs.[77] Recent studies show that positive behavior interventions and supports have been effective in decreasing office referrals and bullying, improving the school climate, and increasing academic achievement and perceptions of school safety.[78] Research also suggests that this framework may be especially useful for students with disabilities.[79]

Restorative justice focuses on improving interpersonal relationships and resolving conflicts. Restorative practices include "proactive circles" that set behavioral expectations or "ground rules" for all students; small impromptu conferences to resolve low-level disagreements and repair harm between two students; "responsive circles" to address tensions or behaviors affecting a larger group of students or an entire class; and "restorative conferences" led by a trained facilitator to address more serious incidents or a cumulative pattern of repeated but less serious incidents.[80] Restorative justice makes students aware of the positive and negative impacts of their behaviors, while avoiding labels and punishments that stigmatize and shame them. Restorative practices should be fair and provide students with an opportunity to be heard before decisions are made, explain why decisions have been made, and clarify expectations and sanctions for not meeting those expectations.[81] Sanctions include apologies, community service, letters, and restitution. Restorative practices have been linked to improved school climate, better attendance, and lower suspension rates, which in turn reduce the racial and economic disparities in suspension.[82] Restorative practices may also engage family members in a student's academic achievement and positive behavior and help parents feel more connected to the school.[83]

Social and emotional learning (SEL) has been particularly effective among youth from kindergarten through eighth grade. SEL equips students with the knowledge, attitudes, and skills they need to understand and manage their emotions, maintain positive relationships, and make responsible decisions.[84] Skills include self-awareness, self-management, social awareness, and interpersonal skills.[85] Social emotional learning reduces students' emotional distress and helps students feel safer and more emotionally secure with school administrators, classmates, and family.[86] SEL also incorporates intensive interventions for aggressive behavior[87] and teaches skills that help students avoid drug use, interpersonal violence, bullying, and other problem behaviors.[88] Research suggests that social emotional learning contributes to a more positive social environment by reducing disciplinary referrals, out-of-school suspensions, violence, and other aggressive incidents.[89]

Each of these approaches will take time, money, and real commitment by school administrators and state and local lawmakers. Our children are worth that investment. We can't keep doing what we have been doing—policing Black children as if they are to be feared, isolated, and denied access to meaningful educational opportunities. We have the tools we need to build healthy students, successful learners, and safe schools. Now we just need to treat Black children as if they belong and remember that we don't need police to save our schools.

## SET NEW STANDARDS:
### LIMITING AND TRAINING POLICE IN SCHOOLS

Although the police-free schools movement has won over several new converts, police are likely to remain in many schools. If school boards and elected officials will not remove police from schools, then we must set new standards and hold them accountable.

In 2017, the American Civil Liberties Union of Washington released a report addressing the increased reliance on school resource officers within the state and its impact on students.[90] The report began with the chilling story of a thirteen-year-old Black student named Tucker who was arrested and sent to juvenile detention after a teacher heard him curse under his breath and told him to sit outside. When Tucker refused to sit out in the cold, the teacher called the school resource officer to deal with him. The officer slammed Tucker to the ground, put his knee on the back of his head, and arrested him. Tucker was charged with "disturbing school" and "disrupting a law enforcement officer." At the time of the report, eighty-four of Washington's hundred largest school districts had police assigned to schools on a daily basis with little or no substantive guidance on the scope and limits of the officers' authority. There were no state laws or policies that directly addressed the use of police in schools and no state agency to track police placement, program structure, or the impact of school resource officers on the students.

The report captured the attention of state lawmakers. In 2019, the Washington state legislature passed a comprehensive law to regulate school resource officers and articulate a clear statement of values, intent, and standards.[91] The new law does not require or encourage school districts to employ school resource officers, but instead establishes minimum training requirements when officers are present and requires each district to adopt an agreement between the district and the local law enforcement agency. The agreements must clearly articulate the officers' duties and responsibilities and explicitly prohibit school resource officers from becoming involved in school discipline that should be handled by school administrators. The agreements must also clarify the circumstances in which a teacher or school administrator may ask a school resource officer to intervene.

The Washington law is a model for other states to follow. Every state or city with police in schools should require schools to establish a clear memorandum of understanding, limiting the officers' authority within the school to serious violent offenses and clearly excluding school resource officers from routine school discipline.[92] Police should not be called for public order offenses such as disorderly conduct, trespassing or loitering, dress-code violations, insubordination, profanity, vandalism, petty thefts, most school fights, or other similar offenses. Police should be a last resort for serious criminal conduct.[93] MOUs should include minimum training requirements and detail how legal issues, such as searches, seizures, and interrogations, will be handled.[94] MOUs should be periodically reassessed to determine if the relationship or goals should be redefined, and school districts should provide students and community members with an opportunity to annually review the school resource program and develop a process for families to complain about abuses by school resource officers.[95]

Other cities have limited the authority of school police through school board directives or police department regulations. In 2013, Denver Public Schools signed a memorandum of understanding with the Denver Police Department to prevent officers from writing tickets for minor misbehavior such as bad language and to require officers to participate in training on topics such as teenage psychology and cultural competence.[96] In 2014, the Philadelphia police chief instructed his officers to stop arresting youth for minor infractions, such as schoolyard fights and possession of small amounts of marijuana, which together accounted for approximately 60 percent of all school-based arrests.[97] In June 2020, San Francisco's mayor announced that the city's police officers will no longer respond to noncriminal activities like school discipline.[98]

As schools reimagine the role and limits of police in schools, they should reduce the number of officers on campus, eliminate police uniforms, and move officers from the main school buildings to satellite offices to reduce the teachers' and administrators' reliance on the police. School districts should be included in the recruitment and selection of school resource officers and engage the community in the oversight of those officers.[99] Ideal candidates should have experience working with youth and an interest in working in an education setting.[100]

Police can no longer engage with children using the same guidelines and philosophy they use for adults. There is now significant consensus on developmental principles that must guide training for school-based officers.[101] Strategies for Youth—an organization whose sole mission is to reduce harm and improve relations between police and youth—has developed a national training curriculum to teach officers about the teen brain and help them understand that youth perceive, process, and respond differently than adults to social cues and interpersonal interactions. Courses like Policing the Teen Brain and Policing the Teen Brain in School help police de-escalate tense encounters inside and outside school and teach officers to engage youth with empathy, patience, and age-appropriate techniques.[102] Trainings also focus on trauma and other common mental health challenges among youth, such as depression, autism, and attention deficit hyperactive disorder. Youth volunteers engage the police in role plays and help them understand why young people are more or less likely to comply in police encounters.

Strategies for Youth has documented success in training officers in Boston and Cambridge, Massachusetts, and in at least one county in Indiana. Boston's Massachusetts Bay Transportation Authority saw an 80 to 84 percent decline in youth arrests after the training from 1999 to 2009. Youth arrests declined by 65 percent after Strategies for Youth trained officers in Cambridge and by 31.7 percent after trainings in one Indiana county.[103]

Adolescent development and de-escalation training must be paired with information about the short- and long-term harms of arrest and incarceration and guidance on mental health resources that provide alternatives to police intervention. In schools, police must also be educated on the constitutional and civil rights of children, including student privacy, search and seizure, youth interrogation, and the educational rights of students with disabilities.[104] In 2019, Strategies for Youth released a report analyzing state laws regarding the regulation of school police.[105] At the time of the report, only twenty-four states and the District of Columbia had passed laws specifically to address training for school resource officers. Two of those states, Georgia and Utah, did not make the training mandatory. Only three states, Kansas, Nebraska, and Virginia, had laws that required training with a developmentally appropriate, trauma-informed, and racially equitable curriculum. Only Illinois required the involvement of adolescent experts, psychologists, or education specialists in the development of its curricula. Washington State's law was adopted after the Strategies for Youth report and now appears to have the most comprehensive requirements for an MOU and police training of any state in the country.[106]

Washington's law appears to fall short in one regard—its description of the officers' role as teacher, informal counselor, and law enforcement officer. Even as well-meaning school resource officers embrace much-needed child-centered reforms, it is important that they not try to do too much. The National Association of School Resource Officers endorses a "triad model" that assigns officers these same responsibilities—that of teacher, counselor, and enforcement officer.[107] Under this model, school resource officers might mentor students and teach classes related to policing, civics, government, and responsible citizenship.[108] Although NASRO explicitly states that the triad model does not involve officers in school discipline,[109] critics argue that school resource

officers with multiple roles receive either inconsistent or no specific training prior to entering a school, spend most of their time
in law enforcement activities rather than teaching and counseling, and still act as disciplinarians in schools even when policies
dictate otherwise.[110] Others worry that conflating the mentoring
and law enforcement roles robs students of essential protections
against self-incrimination by creating a deceptively friendly perception of school resource officers during investigation and interrogation.[111] Without clear limits and narrow authority, confusion
is inevitable for everyone.

Finally, police should not be called to handle situations they
are not equipped to handle. Police don't want to be first respond-
ers in a mental health or drug induced crisis. That should be left
to social workers, medical professionals, and trained mediators.
Eugene, Oregon, has a program that other cites might replicate.
CAHOOTS, which stands for Crisis Assistance Helping Out on
the Streets, is operated by a community health clinic and funded
through an allocation of 2 percent of the police department
budget.[112] CAHOOTS has been around for more than thirty
years, and Eugene's residents know that when they call 911 or
the city's nonemergency number to report a mental health crisis,
drug-related episode, or threat of suicide, CAHOOTS will send
unarmed outreach workers and medics—usually an EMT or a
nurse—who are trained in crisis intervention and de-escalation.

Although CAHOOTS teams are prohibited from responding
when there is "any indication of violence or weapons," or a crime
involving "a potentially hostile person" or "a potentially dangerous situation," the program estimates it responds to 17 percent of
all calls handled by dispatchers. Other cities are starting to take
notice of CAHOOTS' success. Pilot programs are beginning in
San Francisco, Oakland, and Portland. Programs like this only
work if they are adequately funded and everyone is trained to
use the service—teachers, counselors, 911 dispatchers, and the
officers. Mobile mental health crises units like these may be an
effective alternative for intervening with youth who are dealing
with trauma in school.

REPAIR THE HARM: COMMUNITY ENGAGEMENT,
PROCEDURAL JUSTICE, AND BIAS REDUCTION

School-based reforms provide a foundation for how we should reimagine police engagement with Black youth in the community. The same guiding principles apply: Black children are children too, and the most successful strategies for responding to adolescent behaviors rarely involve policing.

State and local law enforcement agencies have been under considerable scrutiny in response to high-profile police-involved deaths in the last ten years. In March 2015 and August 2016, respectively, the U.S. Department of Justice completed extensive investigations of the police departments in Ferguson, Missouri, and Baltimore, Maryland.[113] Each report prepared in connection with those investigations provides important suggestions for police reform generally and for policing youth in particular. President Obama also convened the Task Force on 21st Century Policing in 2014 to identify best practices and offer recommendations on how policing could reduce crime while building public trust.[114] Since then numerous campaigns have been launched across the country to demand and outline strategies for police reform.

Most notably, We the Protesters, a national organization committed to ending racism and police violence in the United States, launched Campaign Zero to promote a comprehensive set of policy recommendations informed by data, research, and human rights principles to change the way police serve the community.[115] Several themes emerge across each of these reports and initiatives, including the elimination of unconstitutional and racially targeted stops, searches, and arrests; accountability for excessive use of force that undermines public safety and community trust; and the need to repair the broken relationship between police and the Black community.

There have also been some targeted efforts to restore community trust in the police. Community policing is a philosophy that encourages law enforcement agencies and their officers to partner with the people they serve to solve problems that lead to crime, social disorder, and fear.[116] Community engagement helps police departments disrupt racial stereotypes and biases, understand community concerns about local policing practices, and repair the antagonistic relationship between police and the community.[117] In the two Department of Justice reports prepared after the killings of Michael Brown in Ferguson and Freddie Gray in Baltimore, the agency urged police to develop and implement a comprehensive community policing agenda that encourages police to be transparent with data; consult with the community before adopting or amending department policies; regularly assess community satisfaction; and engage the community in the oversight of routine policing, use of force, and racial disparities.[118]

Procedural fairness is another important framework for building trust and establishing the legitimacy of law enforcement.[119] Procedural justice seeks to improve police-civilian contacts and enhance public trust and confidence in the police by teaching officers to treat people with dignity and respect in every interaction, make decisions based on facts instead of racialized assumptions, give people a voice, and act in ways that convince the community they will be treated fairly and with goodwill in the future. Procedural justice is now one of the most studied methods for improving public perceptions of fairness in police actions and building legitimacy in law enforcement.[120] Police departments that employ these principles should see higher levels of civilian cooperation in face-to-face encounters, greater compliance with the law, more public support for the police, and greater willingness of civilians to assist the police in solving crime.[121]

Given research showing that adolescents care a lot about fairness, procedural justice is particularly important with young people.[122] Simple changes like explaining the reasons for a stop and responding respectfully to a youth's questions may help improve a youth's perception of justice—especially among Black youth who frequently complain about officers' refusal to give them even basic information before, during, and after a stop.[123] But procedural justice is more than just being nice to kids who ask questions.

Deep and lasting improvements in police-community relations will require police to publicly acknowledge the role of policing in past and present racial injustices and to abandon false and harmful narratives about Black youth.

Police departments must also implement strategies to identify and reduce racial bias. Studies suggest that well-intentioned actors can overcome automatic or implicit biases, at least to some extent, when they are made aware of the stereotypes and biases they hold, have the cognitive capacity to self-correct, and are motivated to do so.[124] This means that implicit bias trainings will do little to decriminalize Black adolescence in a police department with officers who become defensive whenever racial disparities are raised or with leaders who are not willing to take a courageous stance against racism. Trainings that are intermittent and merely reactive to some public relations crisis will never be sufficient to bring about meaningful and lasting change.

To achieve permanent organizational reform, all trainings and the principles they teach should be incorporated into periodic performance reviews and promotion criteria and translated into policy, general orders, and protocols for which officers can be held accountable. Psychologists who study implicit racial bias and policing tell us that broad discretion, ambiguous decision-making criteria, and little oversight lead to racially disparate outcomes.[125] When decisions and behaviors are regulated by clear and binding rules and norms, police and other decision makers are more likely to apply them fairly and without bias. When there are no rules, or the rules and norms are vague and not clearly applicable, decision makers are more likely to act in ways that favor Whites and disfavor people of color.

Implicit bias training cannot be abstract and theoretical but must instead be grounded in the experiences of the participating officers and tailored to the unique issues that arise in policing Black youth. One study found that individuals can reduce their implicit racial bias over time by relying on strategies like stereotype replacement, counter-stereotypic imaging, individuation, perspective taking, and increasing opportunities for positive contact with people of color.[126] Stereotype replacement would require officers to replace stereotypical responses to Black youth with non-stereotypical responses. Thus, instead of responding in anger to a child's hostility during a police encounter, the officer would calmly explain the reason for a stop, genuinely listen to and acknowledge the child's frustration, and patiently answer the youth's questions. Counter-stereotypic imaging would require officers to imagine Black youth in counter-stereotypic ways. Police departments might periodically identify and share stories about Black youth who have served their community well, enrolled in college, secured employment, or excelled in academics, arts, and sports. Police should also be encouraged to draw upon images of their own children when they encounter Black youth in the street and ask themselves how they would respond to their children in similar circumstances.

Individuation would require officers to obtain more specific information about a child before inferring anything about the youth or the youth's behavior. In practice, officers need to observe, inquire, and investigate more thoroughly before deciding to stop or arrest a child. When a stop cannot be avoided, the officers should reduce their risk of subconsciously overestimating a Black child's age by asking the child how old they are and looking for other evidence of the child's age—such as clothing, language, and presence in a place frequented by children.

Perspective taking would require officers to understand and appreciate what a Black child must be thinking and feeling during any police encounter. Tension between Black youth and the police is at an all-time high, and Black youth are anxious, afraid, and even angry at the police. When Black youth are hostile, rude, or aggressive, the adults have to be adults. Police have the greater responsibility to defuse conflict in one-on-one contacts with youth and a broader obligation to repair the real and perceived harms caused by policing in the Black community. Failure to account for these realities can lead to rapidly escalating conflicts that emerge from misunderstandings or actual discriminatory acts.[127] As a more systemic statement of values, police leaders should explicitly acknowledge and prohibit "contempt of cop" arrests that punish youth who are only disrespectful to an officer.

If we want real and sustained improvement in the relationship between police officers and Black youth, at some point the two groups will have to sit down and talk to each other. A range of initiatives have emerged in the last decade to facilitate meaningful youth-police dialogues.[128] Some of these initiatives were formed in response to calls for more community-oriented policing, while others have grown out of the protests, media attention, and public criticism surrounding recent officer-involved shootings of unarmed Black youth. These programs seek to build trust between police and Black youth and improve the officers' capacity to interact safely with young people.[129] Youth-police dialogues allow young people to share their concerns about police behaviors, give them an opportunity to offer suggestions for reform, and help them understand the officers' intentions, concerns, and perspectives.

Participants should expect that initial dialogues about race and policing will cause discomfort, fear, sadness, and anger—especially with adolescents who are grappling with these issues at a critical time in their development.[130] In any honest conversation about race, multiple truths may coexist, and all participants should work to uncover and examine their own preconceived notions about the other.[131] The best youth-police dialogues will be led by facilitators who work separately with each group before the dialogues begin. The dialogue itself should be youth centered, allowing the youth to explain how they have understood and been impacted by their experiences with the police.[132] Facilitators should steer the conversation away from adolescent criminality and help participants focus on establishing healthy interactions between youth and police without blaming youth for their mistrust of authority and lack of skills to resolve conflicts peacefully. Ultimately, a structured dialogue should conclude with points of agreement and identify some collective action and concrete steps both parties can take to bring about change. Like many other police reforms, youth-police dialogues have not yet been rigorously evaluated, but greater trust between youth and police should make policing easier and safer for the officers and the youth.

### POLICE THE POLICE: HOLDING POLICE ACCOUNTABLE

It will take more than standards, training, and facilitated dialogues to prevent the kind of physical abuse and inappropriate use of force that Tucker experienced when he was slammed to the ground in Washington or that Shakara experienced when she was yanked from her chair in South Carolina. This kind of change will come only with accountability and a real shift in culture.

Stories of police accountability are hard to come by. In 2017, a Baltimore school police officer was charged and ultimately pled guilty to one count of second-degree assault after cell-phone footage emerged on social media showing him slapping a sixteen-year-old in the face three times and then kicking him while another officer egged him on because the child had "too much mouth."[133] The officer was placed on probation for eighteen months and forced to resign from his job. In 2019, in Broward County, Florida, a police officer was arrested when school district officials found security footage of him slamming a fifteen-year-old female student to the ground at a school for children with emotional and behavioral disabilities.[134] Arrests and prosecutions like these are few and far between. Prosecutors are reluctant to bring criminal charges against the police who are crucial to their work, and police officers who fear retaliation from their department rarely speak out against their comrades. The absence of criminal accountability signals to students that while their own misconduct will often have severe legal consequences, the adults can do as they wish.

School resource officers are also rarely fired for using force against children.[135] In September 2019, a school resource officer in Orlando, Florida, was fired when he arrested two six-year-old children—in two separate incidents—without proper approval and against the principal's request that he not do so.[136] In December of that same year, a school resource officer in North Carolina was fired when he was caught on surveillance video repeatedly slamming an eleven-year-old student to the ground.[137] These are the outliers. Far too many officers are allowed to remain in place even after multiple reports of abuse or inappropriate use of force with children.

School boards and police departments that want to eliminate the culture of abuse must adopt rules and standards that lay the foundation for subsequent accountability. Interagency rules should explicitly limit the types of force officers may use with youth and require officers to give a clear warning, attempt to de-escalate the encounter, and exhaust all alternatives before using force.[138] When force is used, school officials must notify the youth's parent or guardian as soon as possible and establish clear and accessible procedures for submitting, resolving, and tracking complaints against the officers.[139]

Lawmakers and judges should also make it easier for young people to hold officers accountable in civil lawsuits. Young people rarely succeed in civil claims due to the "qualified immunity" doctrine that protects officers from liability when they are acting in the line of duty. A child may overcome the officer's immunity only if she can show that the officer's conduct violated "clearly established" constitutional standards or rights of the child.[140] In one rare finding of liability, a federal court determined that a school resource officer acted unreasonably in handcuffing a nine-year-old elementary school student to punish her for telling a gym coach she was going to "bust [him] in the head."[141] Although the coach had already reprimanded the child, the officer overheard the interaction and injected himself into the situation. The court concluded that the school resource officer violated the student's "clearly established" rights and was not entitled to immunity because "every reasonable officer would have known that handcuffing a compliant 9-year-old child for purely punitive purposes is unreasonable." Although it could never relieve the child's trauma from being handcuffed before her tenth birthday, the court's decision was an important public statement that what happened was wrong.

Our nation's high court can reduce the barriers to civil liability by either eliminating the qualified immunity doctrine altogether or identifying constitutional violations and articulating clear standards of reasonableness in police encounters with youth in future cases.[142] Both Justices Sonia Sotomayor and Clarence Thomas, who sit at opposite ends of the Supreme Court's ideological spectrum, have called upon the Court to revisit qualified immunity.[143] In June 2020, U.S. representatives Ayanna Pressley and Justin Amash introduced a bill to end qualified immunity, specifying that police officers who violate the civil rights of civilians like George Floyd should not be exempt from liability.[144] If passed, the bill could reduce violence by officers who wish to avoid the financial cost of their abuses.

While the risk of criminal prosecution, civil liability, and discharge from employment should incentivize significant reform, the most effective accountability will come from officers who immediately intervene to prevent their colleagues from using unnecessary and excessive force with youth. As Christy Lopez, one of the leading advocates for police reform, noted, if any one of the other officers at the scene had forced Minneapolis police officer Derek Chauvin to take his knee off George Floyd's neck, George might still be alive, and the public reaction might have been quite different.[145] Ironically, the Minneapolis Police Department changed its use-of-force policy in 2016 to require officers to intervene if they see another officer using excessive force.[146] The Minnesota attorney general's Working Group on Police-Involved Deadly Force Encounters also released a report in February 2020 recommending that all law enforcement officers in Minnesota be required to intervene to prevent unreasonable force.[147] Yet, as George Floyd's death underscores, peer intervention, like any worthwhile reform, will not work unless individual officers have the courage to speak up and leaders in the department publicly encourage and reward intervention.

Police can develop peer intervention skills and strategies through programs like the Ethical Policing Is Courageous (EPIC) program, created in 2014 by Dr. Ervin Staub and the New Orleans Police Department,[148] and the Active Bystandership for Law Enforcement Project (ABLE) at Georgetown Law.[149] Both programs provide practical, scenario-based training, technical assistance, and research to prevent police misconduct, reduce police mistakes, and improve officer health and wellness.

### REWRITE THE LAWS: DECRIMINALIZING BLACK ADOLESCENCE

If police won't change, then lawmakers have a responsibility to make them change—both by decriminalizing normal adolescent behaviors and by writing laws that set limits on what police can and cannot do to children. Police arrest children for "disturbing schools" and "disrupting class" because the law says they can. Police put eight- and nine-year-old Black children in handcuffs because we don't tell them not to. From "sagging pants" to "resisting arrest" and "disorderly conduct," lawmakers have been both intentional and complicit in criminalizing Black adolescence. If we are serious about reducing the hyper-surveillance and over-criminalization of Black youth, then we must rewrite state and federal laws that make it a crime to be a Black child in America.

In the Jim Crow era, it was easy to see how laws like the Black Codes were written to limit and punish Black people for being Black. Our laws aren't so blatantly racist today, but they certainly have the same harm and effect. Even when a law doesn't say anything about race, lawmakers often know it will impact one race more than another. Sagging pants laws provide an obvious example. A law that singles out a style that is most common among young Black males doesn't have to say anything about race in its text to intentionally increase the chance that Black teenage boys will be stopped, harassed, arrested, and even injured by the police. While other laws are less obviously biased, it is usually not that difficult to anticipate which youth will be most impacted by a new law. Laws that make it a crime to "disturb schools" were written to make schools quieter and safer places for children. But they were also written to help teachers punish and exclude students they identify as unmanageable and unruly. Long before those laws were adopted, school discipline data provided lawmakers with ample evidence that Black students would be the most frequent targets of arrests for disturbing schools.

One way to figure out whether a law will disproportionately affect Black youth is to require lawmakers to provide a "racial impact statement" before they pass any new law or regulation. Racial impact statements look a lot like fiscal and environmental impact statements that ask lawmakers to predict how much money it will cost to enforce a new law or how much harm a new law will cause to our water or air quality. Racial impact statements rely on statistical forecasts to help lawmakers predict how a proposed law will impact different races.[150] The Sentencing Project provides extensive guidance and up-to-date examples on the use of "racial impact statements" to help lawmakers evaluate the potential harm and disparities of a proposed policy. Iowa, Connecticut, and Oregon have already passed laws requiring racial impact statements when new criminal justice policies are introduced, and the Minnesota Sentencing Guidelines Commission routinely produces racial impact statements, even though it is not required to do so by law.[151] Arkansas, Illinois, Kentucky, Mississippi, New York, Oklahoma, and Wisconsin have also proposed new laws that would require lawmakers to prepare and consider racial impact statements.

Armed with statistical evidence and anecdotal examples of harm from the community, state lawmakers can ensure that it is not a crime to be and act like a child. In 2013, Texas lawmakers decided that students could no longer be charged with "disrupting class" in their own schools.[152] They also decided that students under twelve could no longer be charged with any low-level misdemeanor offenses at school. To charge an older child with such an offense, an officer would have to write up a formal complaint with sworn witness statements. The results were instantaneous. The number of charges for minor offenses like disrupting class went down by 61 percent that year, saving hundreds of youth from being arrested, embarrassed, and possibly assaulted at school.

Lawmakers clearly have the power to decriminalize adolescence and reduce the presence of police in the lives of Black youth—both in and outside of school. Lawmakers should excuse teenagers from criminal responsibility for offenses like disorderly conduct, trespass, simple drug possession, disregard of police commands, disturbing schools, petty thefts, fare evasion or "turnstile jumping" on public transportation, curfew violations, sagging pants, school fights that do not involve serious injuries to others, and adolescent aggressive speech, including profanity and threats. These are matters better left to counselors in schools and parents in the community—just as they are for many White youth.

Our elected officials should also abandon gang designations and gang databases that label Black youth as gang involved for doing what most kids do—dressing alike and hanging out with their friends. A few states and cities have already taken steps to eliminate or reduce the use of gang databases.[153] New York City reduced the number of people in its database from 34,000 to 17,441 in 2019, after several years of culling the database for accuracy.[154] The Police Bureau in Portland, Oregon, abandoned its gang designations altogether in 2017 after explicitly acknowledging that its database had unintended racial consequences.[155] Instead of relying on outdated and racially biased gang labels and penalties, state lawmakers and agency administrators should invest in gang prevention strategies that have proven to reduce crime and violence among young people. The National Institute of Justice maintains a CrimeSolutions database to identify, screen, and evaluate existing gang prevention strategies.[156] The Institute of Behavioral Science at the University of Colorado Boulder also maintains a registry called "Blueprints for Healthy Youth Development" to identify and rate research-driven interventions that are effective in promoting healthy adolescent development and reducing antisocial behaviors like gang activity.[157]

Lawmakers can further decriminalize Black adolescence by reducing racial profiling. According to a recent poll conducted by *Reason* magazine, 70 percent of Americans oppose the practice of racial profiling by law enforcement agencies and officers.[158] Recognizing that racial profiling is both degrading to those who are targeted and ineffective as a law enforcement strategy, community leaders and lawmakers have lobbied for explicit anti-racial-profiling laws.[159] In its 2014 report *Born Suspect,* the NAACP provided a comprehensive review of existing anti-profiling laws and identified several key components of a model law.[160] An effective law would provide a detailed definition of racial profiling and explicitly ban profiling by all law enforcement agencies and officers across a broad range of investigatory activities, including all forms of stop and frisk in public and private transportation, immigration enforcement, and surveillance practices.[161] An effective law would also require law enforcement agencies to collect and report data on racial profiling and provide a complaint process and legal remedies for violations.

To date, at least thirty states have passed at least one anti-racial-profiling law, while lawmakers in several other states have introduced similar provisions without success.[162] The U.S. Congress failed to pass the End Racial and Religious Profiling Act (ERRPA) when it was first introduced by Senator Ben Cardin in 2017.[163] Senator Cardin has repeatedly sought support for this legislation and reintroduced the bill in March 2021.[164] ERRPA was included as a key component of the George Floyd Justice in Policing Act of 2021, which was passed by the House of Representatives on March 3, 2021. If passed by the Senate, the act would also end qualified immunity, lower legal standards to convict police officers of misconduct, and provide grants to help states investigate constitutional abuses by police departments.[165]

Police aren't the only people who need to be regulated. Advocates have lobbied policy makers to punish civilians who use frivolous 911 calls to criminalize and harass Black people for #LivingWhileBlack.[166] In October 2018, in the weeks after a White woman called the police on nine-year-old Jeremiah Harvey for accidentally touching her butt with his book bag, New York state senators Jesse Hamilton and Kevin Parker renewed efforts to establish criminal consequences for those who make 911 calls when there is no public threat.[167] Governor Andrew Cuomo ultimately signed a different version of Senator Parker's bill into law in June 2020, making the misuse of 911 calls a civil rights violation that might require offenders to pay damages to their victims.[168] Those who worried that Senator Parker's bill did not go far enough favored Senator Hamilton's bill, which would have classified the misuse of these biased, nonemergency phone calls as a hate crime.[169]

California lawmakers Rob Bonta and Shamann Walton also introduced bills in the summer of 2020 to deter frivolous, racially motivated 911 calls. Assemblyman Bonta's bill would make discriminatory 911 calls a hate crime across the state and expose offenders to both criminal sanctions and civil fines.[170] His bill is still pending in the state Senate Public Safety Committee. San Francisco lawmaker Walton introduced a bill, the Caution Against Racially Exploitative Non-Emergencies, or CAREN, Act, to make it illegal to knowingly make false and harassing 911 calls on a racially targeted group and allow victims to sue for damages of at least $1,000.[171] Despite criticism from some California women who believe the proposal was sexist and vilified individuals with the name Karen, the ordinance was endorsed by all eleven members of the San Francisco Board of Supervisors in October 2020 and signed into law by the mayor thirty days later.[172]

In 2019, Grand Rapids banned racially motivated 911 calls with a human rights ordinance that imposes a $500 fine for such calls.[173] The Oregon Senate passed a law in 2019 giving victims of discriminatory 911 calls a private right of action.[174] Although this law does not impose criminal sanctions, it does give victims a right to sue wrongdoers and receive up to $250 in damages.[175] The law took effect on January 1, 2020. While false police reports have long been illegal in New Jersey, state lawmakers voted in October 2020 to increase the penalties for those who make or threaten to make frivolous or harassing 911 calls with the purpose of intimidating others on the basis of their race, religion, or other protected trait.[176] A person who is guilty of knowingly placing a racist or otherwise-biased 911 call for the purpose of intimidation will be subject to three to five years in prison, a fine of up to $15,000, or both.

### TREAT BLACK CHILDREN LIKE CHILDREN: REGULATING AND INCENTIVIZING HUMANE CONTACT WITH YOUTH

The police have to treat children like children. That means remembering that their brains are still forming and they are still learning to manage their emotions and control their impulses. It also means protecting them from physical harm and reducing unnecessary and traumatic encounters with the police. Lawmakers should prohibit strip searches, Tasers, chokeholds, police dogs, body slams, and other physical maneuvers on children. Lawmakers should also prohibit police officers from handcuffing the youngest children.

At the investigative stage, laws should prohibit officers from relying on a child's purported "consent" for a search, and instead require police to have specific reasons to believe a child is committing or has committed a crime before conducting any search or frisk.[177] Lawmakers can write laws that prohibit officers from considering a child's "flight" from the police as a reason for a stop and prohibit officers from interrogating children without a lawyer.[178] They can also require the police to call a child's parents immediately after arrest with detailed information about the child's health and location. The possibilities are myriad and improvements are feasible with a little creativity from our elected officials.

Although the juvenile legal system falls largely within the purview of state and local governments, federal laws can be used to inspire state reform and model America's values and commitment to the humane treatment of Black youth. In 2016, for example,

President Obama's administration banned solitary confinement of youth in federal prisons, recognizing its devastating and long-term impact on adolescent development.[179] Although very few youth are held in federal prisons, the law allowed the president to educate state lawmakers on the destructive and racially dispro-portionate consequences of isolation on Black youth like Kalief Browder.

The power of federal law lies primarily in incentivized fund-ing. The federal government has demonstrated its extraordinary influence over policing in America's schools by pouring billions of dollars into police departments and school districts that agree to hire school resource officers and invest in school security equip-ment like metal detectors and surveillance cameras. The federal government can now reshape the nation's approach to school safety by reallocating funds from the COPS in Schools programs to mental health services, counselors, and other alternatives to policing. Federal funding may also incentivize data collection on racial disparities in school discipline and law enforcement and improve outcomes for all youth in the juvenile legal system.[180]

The Juvenile Justice and Delinquency Prevention Act (JJDPA), originally passed in 1974, is the most comprehensive federal law aimed at youth justice issues. Congress has amended the JJDPA several times to offer funding to states that agree to take steps to decrease the disproportionate confinement of youth of color in juvenile and adult jails and prisons.[181] In 1992, and again in 2002, Congress reinforced its commitment to racial equity by making the effort to reduce disproportionate minority confine-ment a "core requirement" of the JJDPA and tying states' eligi-bility for funding to the states' compliance with efforts to track and reduce disparities in the system. The law also expanded its data collection from disproportionate minority *confinement* to disproportionate minority *contact,* requiring states to collect data at all points of the juvenile legal system, from arrest through transfer to adult court.[182]

The JJDPA was last reauthorized in December 2018, despite efforts by the Trump administration to reduce the burden of data collection on the states.[183] With the reauthorization, the JJDPA reduces the detention and confinement of youth for minor offenses like skipping school, violating curfew, and running away from home. It also requires states to assess and address racial and ethnic disparities in every aspect of their juvenile legal systems and limits the circumstances in which youth may be held in adult jails.[184]

### DO NO (FURTHER) HARM: COURTS, JAILS, AND PRISONS

The criminalization of Black youth may start with policing, but it certainly doesn't end there. When youth are policed in their schools and communities, they are sent to courts where prosecutors, probation officers, and judges can "just say no." At every stage of a juvenile or criminal case, key decision makers have an opportunity to decline prosecution, dismiss cases, and recommend that youth be diverted from the court system and released back to their families. Every state actor who does not take an active stance against racial inequities is at least complicit—and at worst active—in perpetuating the criminalization and over-policing of Black youth.

Prosecutors are the most powerful gatekeepers in the juvenile and criminal legal systems.[185] Prosecutors had an opportunity to stop every inappropriate, racially biased, and unnecessary prosecution described in this book. My client Eric should not have been charged with attempted arson and possession of a Molotov cocktail. Malik should not have been charged with the KKK-targeted offense of "wearing a hood or mask" in public for wearing a ski mask in the dead of winter. Shanna should not have been charged with robbery for snatching her boyfriend's cell phone. Marquette should not have been charged with "incommoding" for failing to move from in front of an ice cream shop, and Sharice should not have been charged with assault on a police officer for having an emotional breakdown down in front of McDonald's. Prosecutors could—and sometimes did—dismiss Kevin's drug cases after they watched video clearly showing police violating his right to be free from an unlawful stop and frisk. Every one of these cases could have been interrupted by prosecutors who have the power to insist upon the humane and equitable treatment of all youth.

As a matter of policy, prosecutors should decline to prosecute youth for low-level, nonviolent offenses, especially stemming from school-based incidents where there is a pattern of unnecessary arrests and court referrals for Black youth. Prosecutors should refuse to charge minor street offenses like loitering and disorderly conduct, especially when investigation suggests that the arrest is an officer's retaliation for the youth's disrespect. Prosecutors should minimize the use of felony charges when less serious offenses or noncriminal interventions more appropriately reflect the adolescent nature of the child's behavior.[186] Prosecutors should never prosecute children as adults or ask for lengthy punitive sentences when rehabilitative alternatives would be more effective and equitable across race and class. Prosecutors should be trained in adolescent development and racial bias and track their own charging decisions by race, age, gender, and any other demographic that may lead to disparities. Prosecutors should closely review police body-worn camera and other surveillance footage and rigorously interview police officers about their specific justifications for a stop, frisk, and arrest. Prosecutors should also critically interview civilian witnesses to determine if there is explicit or implicit bias in the witnesses' recollections of the facts, identification of perpetrators, and interpretations of "suspicious" behaviors.

Much of this book has been about the criminalization of normal adolescent behaviors—those things that all kids do and that don't cause much physical or lasting harm to other people. But there are times when court intervention may be a necessary response to serious youth crime. Even then, Black youth who commit a serious crime are entitled to the same grace, dignity, and rehabilitative interventions that White youth receive. Kalief Browder, Niecey Fennell, and Korey Wise should never have been prosecuted or detained in the adult system—regardless of their guilt or innocence. Kalief certainly shouldn't have languished in

Rikers for three years waiting for a trial prosecutors knew would not happen without their key witness. Prosecutors have to be courageous in resisting the traditional law enforcement responses that disproportionately harm Black youth. I don't imagine that any of this will be easy. Prosecutors may face considerable backlash from those who cling to deeply entrenched fears of Black children. Prosecutors will have to educate the community on the traumatic effects of incarceration and identify effective alternatives to prosecution.

Judges are no less complicit in the criminalization and mass incarceration of Black youth. Judges set standards and communicate values through their decisions at every stage of a case. Even though they don't decide which children will be arrested and prosecuted, judges wield extraordinary influence over police behavior and prosecutorial discretion by refusing to consider evidence collected by officers who rely on biased and inaccurate stereotypes and assumptions to stop and harass Black children. Police won't keep violating the rights of Black youth if judges tell them not to. Judge Shira Scheindlin became a household name in criminal justice circles when she agreed with a group of Black and Latinx New Yorkers who sued the City of New York, the mayor, and named and unnamed New York police officers for implementing and sanctioning a pattern and practice of unlawful police stops and frisks on the basis of race or national origin.[187] Her courageous opinion led to significant changes in New York and beyond.

Judges are vulnerable to the same biases as the rest of us and must learn to evaluate every police stop from the lens of history and oppression. They must understand that Black children run from the police not because they are guilty and suspicious but because they are terrified and traumatized.[188] At trial, judges should be as courageous as Judge Diana Stuart, who found that sixteen-year-old Thai Gurule had done nothing to warrant the senseless "contempt of cop" arrest and beatdown he received when he disrespected a Portland police officer.[189]

It wasn't just the prosecutor who let Kalief Browder languish in jail for three years. It was also every judge who accepted the prosecutors' repeated excuses for delay, set a bail amount that Kalief's family could not pay, and eventually held Kalief without any opportunity to post bail. Multiple judges could have prevented the needless suicides by Black children like Niecey Fennell and Jaquin Thomas by refusing to send Black fifteen- and sixteen-year-olds to adult jails and prisons and offering Black youth an opportunity to receive mental health and social services instead of lengthy periods of incarceration at sentencing. Niecey and Jaquin wouldn't have been the first children to go home to their parents after being accused of a serious crime. Remember that the wealthy White Cameron Terrell went home with parents who could afford a $5 million bail when he was charged with murder after driving the car that sped away with two shooters in Palos Verdes. Niecey Fennell was given no such luxury when she drove away with two shooters in Durham. Until there is significant policy reform in bail practices,[190] judges must vigorously guard against their own racial biases and avoid risk assessment tools that rely on risk factors that are seemingly race neutral but repeatedly disadvantage Black youth and their families.[191]

It wasn't just the prosecutors and police officers who let Korey Wise suffer in solitary confinement in an adult prison until he was exonerated in the Central Park jogger case. It was also the judge who sentenced him to up to fifteen years in prison. Korey wouldn't have been the first child to get rehabilitative treatment instead of incarceration after a serious offense. Some will recall Ethan Couch, the wealthy White teen who was allowed to go to an expensive rehabilitative treatment center after a night of drunken revelry that killed four and injured nine others. Others will recall the Wisconsin teenagers Morgan Geyser and Anissa Weier, who were found not guilty by reason of mental disease or defect and sent to a mental institution instead of prison after brutally stabbing their twelve-year-old friend because they believed the fictional character Slender Man told them to.[192]

In most cases, city and state officials have access to rehabilitative interventions that have been proven to reduce crime even among the most serious and chronic young offenders.[193] Multisystemic therapy, which has been particularly successful with violent and aggressive youth, is a community-based model that seeks to empower families with the skills and resources they need to advocate on behalf of their children in school and the community and to help their children cope with family challenges and resist negative peer influences.[194] Functional family therapy provides therapists who work with families to improve the emotional connection between youth and their parents and helps parents learn to impose structure and limits on children.[195] Other effective intervention models include aggression replacement therapy, which seeks to develop social skills, emotional control, and moral reasoning among chronically aggressive and violent adolescents, and trauma-focused cognitive behavioral therapy, which is designed to help children from three to eighteen years old overcome serious emotional problems such as post-traumatic stress, fear, anxiety, and depression.[196] Each of these programs adopts a public health approach to violence prevention and relies on research to test and identify successful prevention strategies.[197]

Finally, it is disturbing to contemplate the possibility of racial bias among juvenile and criminal defense attorneys. It is even more disturbing to think that Black youth might be harmed by the very people assigned to protect them. Yet there is plenty of evidence that defenders harm Black youth through unchecked biases, benign neglect, unrealistic commitments to color blindness, and outright discrimination. Bias affects defenders' case triage decisions and assessments of witness credibility, client culpability, and the value of plea offers.[198] In some parts of the country, criminal defense attorneys thought Trayvon Martin looked just as suspicious as George Zimmerman said he did and Mike Brown looked just as terrifying as Officer Darren Wilson claimed.

At its best, the attorney-client relationship can help buffer youth from the harmful effects of the legal system. At its worst, it can undermine youth's respect for the law and law enforcement.[199] Defenders cannot effectively serve Black youth without understanding the traumatic effects of policing in Black communities and the racist history of the juvenile court movement. As defenders confront their own biases and learn more about the nature and scope of racial inequities in the system, hopefully they will be even more outraged and motivated to challenge them head-on.[200] Every actor in the criminal legal system—the lawmakers, police officers, probation staff, prosecutors, judges, and defenders—has an opportunity and a responsibility to resist the criminalization of Black adolescence.

### TELL THEIR STORIES

Stories like Eric's are incredibly powerful, especially at a time when the media and the public seem to relish in stock narratives that focus on tragedy and violence in the Black community. Eric's story tells us something quite different. It tells us that Black children are just children—with all of the same virtues and growing pains as any other child. In adolescence, Black children act impulsively, respond emotionally, test the limits, wrestle with their identity, and worry about what others think. But at the same time, they are intensely curious, wildly creative, and deeply loyal to their friends and family. They also care passionately about justice and society and want the world to be a better place for themselves and everyone who looks like them. We owe it to them to tell the whole story—a story that includes both the trauma and injustice they experience in America and the power of their resilience despite the odds.

In 2013, Washington, D.C., native CaShawn Thompson created the hashtag #BlackGirlMagic in response to hateful articles published online about Black women.[201] The hashtag soon morphed into a powerful movement with millions of people using it to counter negativity and uplift Black women. In 2016, the musician Chance the Rapper tweeted photos of himself with the hashtag #BlackBoyJoy.[202] He wasn't the first to use the tag, but he drew a huge following, with thousands of others posting photos of Black men and boys happy, smiling, and reveling in childlike joy. The hashtag has been used to remind the world that

Black men and boys work and play, dance and create, love and laugh, marry and have children, and just enjoy life in ways that others seem not to expect them to do.

Black Americans have learned to author their own identities and craft their own narratives as a form of resistance and healing. Artists, activists, Congress members, clergy, athletes, and media icons are still trying to reclaim the "hoodie" from its oppression of Black children. In the months following the killing of Trayvon Martin, protesters across the country wore hoodies in solidarity with Trayvon and other Black youth at risk of violence. In her 2016 "Formation" music video, Beyoncé featured a young Black boy in a hoodie standing boldly in front of riot police. In 2017, nineteen-year-old photographer Myles Loftin launched a video and photography project that depicted Black boys in colorful hoodies laughing and having fun as an affront to the stereotypical depiction of Black boys as thugs and superpredators.

Yet, just as Black Americans are committed to sharing their stories of joy and success, they also refuse to remain silent while others try to bury the truth about racial injustice in America. Athletes, journalists, artists, and advocates have been equally persistent in their challenge to police brutality, racial inequities, and the dehumanization of Black children. Los Angeles Rams players started an NFL game with "Hands Up, Don't Shoot" in 2014. WNBA Lynx stars donned shirts in 2016 that said "Change Is Us," with pictures of Philando Castile and Alton Sterling. Colin Kaepernick took a knee during the national anthem to protest police brutality in 2016, and LeBron James spoke out in April 2019 when fifteen-year-old Delucca Rolle was pepper sprayed, slammed, and punched in the head by Florida police who said he had taken an "aggressive stance."[203]

Rap lyrics have become the anthem of Black social protest with Grammy Award–winning Kendrick Lamar leading the way with his single "Alright" and others resurrecting N.W.A's 1988 "Fuck tha Police." The rapper Lil Baby released the song "The Bigger Picture" and joined Atlanta city councilman Antonio Brown in June 2020 to address the state of the nation and its impact on Black people, including police brutality, public protests, and COVID-19. The song quickly became the most streamed protest track of this pivotal moment.[204] Lil Baby plans to donate all proceeds to the National Association of Black Journalists, Breonna Taylor's legal team, the Bail Project, and Black Lives Matter.[205] Media mogul Viola Davis and her husband, Julius Tennon, produced a four-part docuseries revisiting the deaths of Eric Garner, Ezell Ford, John Crawford, and Sandra Bland,[206] while Ava DuVernay's documentary *When They See Us* looked back to the Central Park jogger case to call attention to solitary confinement, coercive interrogation, and police officers' rush to judge and condemn Black youth. Producer Kenya Barris has used his popular sitcom *Black-ish* to examine almost every topic relevant to Black America, including police brutality and racial discrimination in schools.

So this book does end with hope, but also with a call for justice. When I told Eric and his family about my book project, their first reaction was "These are stories that need to be told!" And they are right, these are stories that need to be told. And I will keep telling them until there are no more stories like this to tell.

# Acknowledgments

I have a photo of Emmett Till and Tamir Rice on my wall. This book is for them and about them. This book is also for all of the Black children I have worked with over the last twenty-five years. It is for the children I have represented in court, the children who shared their stories with me and with the public, and for all of the young advocates who have raised their voices for reform. They inspire me and fuel my passion for justice.

I have never represented a child alone. There is always a team of defenders, investigators, and law clerks. Early in my career, I had the privilege of working with a phenomenal team of lawyers and advocates at the D.C. Public Defender Service, where we launched a specialized unit to meet the multidisciplinary needs of youth in the legal system. Now that team includes the extraordinary staff in the Georgetown Juvenile and Criminal Justice Clinics. Thanks to Wally Mlyniec for giving me my first legal job as a Prettyman-Stiller Fellow in the Juvenile Justice Clinic and then guiding me back to Georgetown several years later. The book would never have been completed without the tireless commitment of my colleagues Rebba Omer and Olajumoke Obayanju, who researched, edited, brainstormed, and then researched some more. It would not have been completed without Eduardo Ferrer, who helped manage the clinic when I needed time to write, and Katrecia Banks, who encouraged me, supported me, and made our office run more smoothly.

Because I teach a law clinic, I now represent all of my clients with a cadre of students and law fellows who are just as outraged as I am about racial injustice. Many of the client stories in this book are shared stories—stories shared by wonderful young lawyers like Ryan Gephardt, Jessica Gingold, Lula Hagos, Jamie Hospers, and many more.

The ideas for systemic reform were drawn from the collective wisdom of a much larger community of juvenile defenders across the country. Thank you to Patti Puritz and Mary Ann Scali for creating the National Juvenile Defender Center and bringing us all together. Special thanks to Mary Ann for being a close friend and relentless partner in the fight for racial justice. Your encouragement, emotional support, and wisdom sustained me. Thank you to my defender friends who have made me a better advocate: Amy Borror, Tim Curry, Ebony Howard, Kristina Kersey, Amanda Powell, and Sherika Shnider. Our community includes young advocates who inspire me to stay in the fight and make sure their voices are heard: Black Swan Academy, Pathways 2 Power.

The juvenile defender community is buttressed by an all-star cast of criminal justice advocates and scholars who read and commented on drafts, taught me how to stop writing like an academic, and challenged me to grapple with the most difficult parts of criminal justice reform and racial equity. I have learned so much from Paul Butler, Sheryll Cashin, Angela J. Davis, James Forman Jr., and Christy Lopez. Special thanks to Angela, who allowed me to join *Policing the Black Man*, introduced me to Erroll McDonald and Pantheon Books, and guided me through the publication process from beginning to end. But my most persistent readers and allies have been the members of the Mid-Atlantic Criminal Law Research Collective: Kami Chavis, Andrea Dennis, Roger Fairfax, Renée Hutchins, Sherri Keene, Michael Pinard, Yolanda Vázquez.

This book is full of science and data—neither of which I knew anything about when I started my first job as a public defender. The world has changed. We can now advocate for evidence-based, data-driven reforms because of the important work of developmental psychologists like Laurence Steinberg and Jennifer Woolard and the nation's best juvenile justice data analyst, Melissa Sickmund. Thank you all for answering my questions, making sure I didn't overstate the science, and teaching me to be hyperprecise in how we describe the data. More important, thank you for helping us think about how science intersects with practice.

A book that incorporates as much news, science, and data as this one does requires many research assistants. Chief among them were Kara Dunovant, Grace Lee, and Emma Mlyniec. Special thanks to Emma, who worked on this book long after she graduated, just because she cared about the mission. Thanks to the many students and fellows who provided research for this book: Isaiah Boyd III, Vitória Castro, Lauren Dollar, Landon Harris, Heather Hu, Joe Johnson, Isaiah Jones, Erin Keith, Elizabeth Miller, Darryn Mumphrey, Malcolm Morse, Jenadee Nanini, Mirabella Nwaka, Victoria Brown, Janelle Sampana, Drew Smith, and Andre Tulloch. Georgetown Law has the most extraordinary professional library team on the planet. My library liaison, Andrea Muto, was as invested in this project as I was for the last two years. Her colleagues Yelena Rodriguez, Thanh Nguyen, and the entire library team were equally supportive.

After the research comes the publication. Thank you to my outstanding editor, Erroll McDonald, for fighting for the book at so many stages along the way. Thank you for your wisdom, your guidance, and your passion for giving voice to Black authors and Black issues.

I didn't write this book out of intellectual curiosity. I wrote it for action. It is my hope that every chapter will help guide practice, training, and policy. Special thanks to Bill Treanor and Georgetown Law for providing the support and funding to make that a reality through the Ambassadors for Racial Justice, the Juvenile Defense and Racial Justice Fellow, JTIP Summer Academy, and so many other initiatives that allow us to try out these ideas.

Then there are all of my family members and friends who endured hours and hours of my talking about the book. To my road dog, Jill Morrison, thank you for being my ally, my thought partner, and my honest critic. This book is ours. Thank you to Robert Pierre for your extraordinary wisdom and guidance all along the way. Thank you to my collective sisterhood from Lambda Omega Spring 1990 for your support and encouragement. You pulled me through. And thank you to my Takoma Park crew Abby Beckel, Marco and Priya Konings, Orla Oconner, Jay Schwarz, and Andrew Yew for brainstorming, encouraging, and supporting this endeavor during the pandemic.

This book was birthed through the emotional support and the prayers of Rose and Kirk Gaskins, who checked on me every day for two years when I hit rock bottom and wanted to give up. Only you and God know what you did for me. Your wisdom transcended the personal and helped me think through race equity and juvenile justice. Thank you to Thedford Collins for your love and persistence when I tried to shut everyone out. You and Doris brought light, love, and encouragement throughout this journey.

The Hennings are a very tight-knit family. This book would not be without my brother Kyle Henning and my sister-in-law Justine, who spent hours helping me think through everything from the book title to the cover to the audience and just checking in to make sure I was okay. I love you both. My aunts and uncles have been my surrogate parents since my parents left this earth far too early: My aunt Yvonne Parks has been my teacher, caretaker, and cheerleader. My aunt Anne Henning Byfield planted the seed for this project many years ago by asking me, "So when are you going to write a book?" Thank you for being my fiercest advocate. Thank you to my brilliant uncles Herman, Garnett, JP, and Ainsley for sharing your wisdom over the years. Special thanks to my uncle Herman, who passed away before this was finished, but not before letting me know how proud he was about the manuscript. Thank you to my aunts Mita and Ernestine and all of my cousins, including Andra, Antoinette, Armintry, Audra, Carma, Michael, and Pam, who have raised Black children, shared their stories, and helped me brainstorm about multiple aspects of the book. Thank you to Jahbrielle for your creativity and wisdom.

And most important, thank you to my parents, George and Rita Henning, both of whom instilled in me a fire for justice, a passion for race equity, and commitment to service. Their values supported my work in juvenile justice. This book helped me rally back from a tragic season of love and loss of both parents, my brother Dustin Henning, and my husband, Marcus Scott. They all appear in these pages.

# Notes

INTRODUCTION: MOLOTOV COCKTAIL OR SCIENCE EXPERIMENT?

1. Office of Juvenile Justice and Delinquency Prevention, Statistical Briefing Book: Arrests by Offense, Age, and Race, 2018 (Washington, D.C.: U.S. Department of Justice, 2019).

2. Office of Juvenile Justice and Delinquency Prevention, Statistical Briefing Book: Juvenile Arrest Rates by Race, 1980–2018 (Washington, D.C.: U.S. Department of Justice, 2019).

3. Charles Puzzanchera, "Juvenile Arrests, 2018," Juvenile Justice Statistics National Report Series Bulletin, June 2020.

4. Namita Tanya Padgaonkar et al., "Exploring Disproportionate Minority Contact in the Juvenile Justice System over the Year Following First Arrest," *Journal of Research on Adolescence* (Dec. 2020); Joshua Rovner, *Disproportionate Minority Contact in the Juvenile Justice System* (Washington, D.C.: Sentencing Project, May 2014).

5. Melissa Sickmund, A. Sladky, and W. Kang, "Easy Access to Juvenile Court Statistics: 1985–2018," Office of Juvenile Justice and Delinquency Prevention and the National Center for Juvenile Justice, 2020. The total number of judicial waivers in 2018 was 3,624 compared with 6,530 in 2005.

1. AMERICAN ADOLESCENCE IN BLACK AND WHITE

1. Frank Fasick, "On the 'Invention' of Adolescence," *Journal of Early Adolescence* 14 (Feb. 1994): 6–23; Laurence Steinberg, *Adolescence* (New York: McGraw-Hill Education, 2017), 72–73

(arguing that the concept of adolescence did not exist until the Industrial Revolution); Philippe Ariès, *Centuries of Childhood: A Social History of Family Life* (New York: Random House, 1962) (concluding that the modern concept of adolescence did not appear until the late nineteenth century based on wide-scope survey of Western texts); American Psychological Association, "Developing Adolescents: A Reference for Professionals," Jan. 2002.

2. Ariès, *Centuries of Childhood,* 30.
3. Richard A. Settersten Jr., Frank F. Furstenberg Jr., and Ruben G. Rumbaut, *On the Frontier of Adulthood: Emerging Themes and New Directions* (Chicago: University of Chicago Press, 2005).
4. U.S. Census Bureau, *Bicentennial Edition: Historical Statistics of the United States, Colonial Times to 1970, Part I* (Washington, D.C.: Bureau of the Census, 1975).
5. Kent Baxter, *The Modern Age: Turn-of-the-Century American Culture and the Invention of Adolescence* (Tuscaloosa: University of Alabama Press, 2008), 26.
6. Joseph Kett, "Reflections on the History of Adolescence in America," *History of the Family* 8 (Jan. 2003): 355.
7. Baxter, *Modern Age,* 26, 27.
8. Ibid., 29.
9. Ibid., 44; G. Stanley Hall, *Adolescence: Its Psychology and Its Relation to Physiology, Anthropology, Sociology, Sex, Crime, Religion, and Education* (New York: D. Appleton, 1904); Kett, "Reflections on the History of Adolescence," 355, 358.
10. Kett, "Reflections on the History of Adolescence," 355, 358; Hall, *Adolescence,* 1.
11. Margaret Mead, *Coming of Age in Samoa* (New York: William Morrow, 1928); Margaret Mead, *Growing Up in New Guinea: A Comparative Study of Primitive Education* (New York: William Morrow, 1930); Margaret Mead, *Sex and Temperament in Three Primitive Societies* (New York: William Morrow, 1935).
12. Stefanie DeLuca, Susan Clampet-Lundquist, and Kathryn Edin, *Coming of Age in the Other America* (New York: Russell Sage Foundation, 2016).
13. Kett, "Reflections on the History of Adolescence," 355, 361; Baxter, *Modern Age,* 26, 29.
14. Baxter, *Modern Age,* 24.
15. Laurence Steinberg, *Age of Opportunity: Lessons from the New*

*Science of Adolescence* (Boston: Houghton Mifflin Harcourt, 2014) (noting that the study of the adolescent brain was about fifteen years old as of 2014).

16. Ibid., 5, 8.

17. Ibid., 22, 25.

18. Ibid., 10, 17.

19. Ibid., 37.

20. Ibid., 15; Elizabeth Cauffman and Laurence Steinberg, "(Im)maturity of Judgment in Adolescence: Why Adolescents May Be Less Culpable Than Adults," *Behavioral Science and Law* 18, no. 6 (Feb. 2001): 741, 748–49, 754 table 4; Laurence Steinberg et al., "Age Differences in Sensation Seeking and Impulsivity as Indexed by Behavior and Self-Report: Evidence for a Dual Systems Model," *Developmental Psychology* 44, no. 6 (Nov. 2008): 1764, 1774–76.

21. Steinberg, *Age of Opportunity*, 43–44.

22. Ibid., 68–69.

23. Ibid., 49.

24. Michael Dreyfuss et al., "Teens Impulsively React Rather Than Retreat from Threat," *Developmental Neuroscience* 36, no. 3–4 (2014): 220–27.

25. Margot Gardner and Laurence Steinberg, "Peer Influence on Risk Taking, Risk Preference, and Risky Decision Making in Adolescence and Adulthood: An Experimental Study," *Developmental Psychology* 41 (July 2005): 625–35 (discussing a study that found that teens took more risks in a driving game when their peers were in the room than adults in the same situation); Laurence Steinberg and Kathryn Monahan, "Age Differences in Resistance to Peer Influence," *Developmental Psychology* 43, no. 6 (Nov. 2007): 1531–43 (discussing a study finding that individuals' capacity to resist peer pressure grows linearly between ages fourteen and eighteen, but after eighteen there is not much evidence of further growth).

26. Cauffman and Steinberg, "(Im)maturity of Judgment in Adolescence," 741, 748–49, 754 table 4; Steinberg et al., "Age Differences in Sensation Seeking and Impulsivity as Indexed by Behavior and Self-Report," 1764, 1774–76; Steinberg, *Age of Opportunity*, 15.

27. Steinberg, *Age of Opportunity*, 26.

28. Laurence Steinberg, Elizabeth Cauffman, and Kathryn C. Monahan, "Psychosocial Maturity and Desistance from Crime in a

Sample of Serious Juvenile Offenders," *Juvenile Justice Bulletin,* March 2015; Edward P. Mulvey et al., "Trajectories of Desistance and Continuity in Antisocial Behavior Following Court Adjudication Among Serious Adolescent Offenders," *Development and Psychopathology* 22, no. 2 (May 2010): 453–75.

29. Laurence Steinberg et al., "Around the World, Adolescence Is a Time of Heightened Sensation Seeking and Immature Self-Regulation," *Developmental Science* 21, no. 2 (March 2018).

30. Steinberg and Monahan, "Age Differences in Resistance," 1538–39 (finding that although some patterns in resistance to peer influence vary slightly by ethnicity and socioeconomic status, generally all groups follow the same basic pattern in developing resistance to peer pressure as age increases); Laurence Steinberg et al., "Age Differences in Future Orientation and Delay Discounting," *Child Development* 80 (Jan./Feb. 2009): 29–44 (finding that youth of similar ages exhibited a weak ability to think ahead and appreciate the future regardless of class and ethnicity); Cauffman et al., "Age Differences in Affective Decision Making as Indexed by Performance on the Iowa Gambling Task," *Developmental Psychology* 46 (Jan. 2010): 193–207 (finding that youth as a class prefer risks that produce short-term rewards over long-term gain, with no significant differences among ethnicities).

31. Jeffrey J. Arnett, "Does Emerging Adulthood Theory Apply Across Social Classes? National Data on a Persistent Question," *Emerging Adulthood* 4 (Oct. 2015): 227–35; Jeffrey J. Arnett, "Emerging Adulthood: A Theory of Development from the Late Teens Through the Twenties," *American Psychologist* 55 (May 2000): 469–80.

32. Joshua Rovner, *Racial Disparities in Youth Commitments and Arrests* (Washington, D.C.: Sentencing Project, April 2016) (citing the Centers for Disease Control and Prevention, *2013 Youth Risk Behavior Survey* (2016)); Sentencing Project, *Fact Sheet: Black Disparities in Youth Incarceration* (Washington, D.C.: Sentencing Project, Sept. 2017).

33. Annie E. Casey Foundation, "Child Population by Race in District of Columbia," National KIDS COUNT Data Center, Sept. 2020.

34. Lloyd Johnston et al., *Monitoring the Future: National Survey Results on Drug Use, 1975–2018,* Institute for Social Research, University of Michigan, Jan. 2019.

35. Centers for Disease Control and Prevention, "Trends in the Prevalence of Sexual Behaviors and HIV Testing National YRBS:

1991–2017," National Center for HIV/AIDS, Viral Hepatitis, STD, and TB Prevention, 2017.

36. Ibid.; Johnston et al., *Monitoring the Future*.

37. Johnston et al., *Monitoring the Future*.

38. Laura Kann et al., "Youth Risk Behavior Surveillance—United States, 2017," *Surveillance Summaries* 67 (June 2018): 34–35 (The prevalence of having ever used an electronic vapor product was higher among White (41.8 percent) and Hispanic (48.7 percent) than Black (36.2 percent) students. The prevalence of current electronic vapor product use was higher among White (15.6 percent) and Hispanic (11.4 percent) than Black (8.5 percent) students.).

39. Ibid., 46 (The prevalence of having driven a car or other vehicle when they had been drinking alcohol was higher among Hispanic (7.0 percent) than White (5.0 percent) and Black (4.1 percent) students. Prevalence of having ever drunk alcohol was higher among White (61.7 percent) and Hispanic (64.7 percent) than Black (51.3 percent) students.).

40. Ibid., 13 (The prevalence of having carried a weapon was higher among White (18.1 percent) than Black (10.8 percent) and Hispanic (12.7 percent) students and higher among White male (29.0 percent) than Black male (15.3 percent) and Hispanic male (18.4 percent) students.); Ibid., 34 (In 2017, more White youth than Black youth reported carrying some type of weapon within the thirty days leading up to the survey).

41. Sarah Hockenberry and Charles Puzzanchera, *Juvenile Court Statistics 2018* (Pittsburgh: National Center for Juvenile Justice, 2020), 21.

42. Ibid. (noting that Black youth make up 15 percent of the U.S. population under juvenile court jurisdiction). See also Charles Puzzanchera, "Juvenile Arrests, 2018," *Juvenile Justice Statistics National Report Series Bulletin,* June 2020, 8, 11 (noting that 16 percent of the U.S. population aged ten to seventeen is Black, and the arrest rate of Black youth for drug offenses is 1.4 times the White rate).

43. Office of Juvenile Justice and Delinquency Prevention, *Statistical Briefing Book: Arrests by Offense, Age, and Race, 2018* (Washington, D.C.: U.S. Department of Justice, 2019); Hockenberry and Puzzanchera, *Juvenile Court Statistics 2018*, 21, 33.

44. Hockenberry and Puzzanchera, *Juvenile Court Statistics 2018*, 52, 58.

45. Ibid. (noting "placed" includes secure and nonsecure out-of-home placements).

46. Jason Ross (@jasonjross), Twitter, Dec. 3, 2014, 1:05 p.m.

47. Jason Ross (@jasonjross), Twitter, Dec. 3, 2014, 1:42 p.m.

48. Zachary A. Goldfarb, "#Crimingwhilewhite: White People Are Confessing on Twitter to Crimes They Got Away With," *Washington Post*, Dec. 4, 2014.

49. Drew Harwell and Danielle Paquette, "The Surprising Origins of the Crimingwhilewhite Movement," *Washington Post*, Dec. 4, 2014.

50. Robyn Kopp (@filmfixation), Twitter, Dec. 3, 2014, 2:30 p.m.

51. Brian Wisti (@brianwisti), Twitter, Dec. 3, 2014, 2:29 p.m.

52. @Dr24hours, Twitter, Dec. 3, 2014, 3:36 p.m.

53. McCallister Crowley (@EstelleSweaty), Twitter, Dec. 3, 2014, 5:36 p.m.

54. Monica Alexander, Mathew Kiang, and Magali Barbieri, "Trends in Black and White Opioid Mortality in the United States, 1979–2015," *Epidemiology* 29, no. 5 (Sept. 2018): 707.

55. National Institute on Drug Abuse, *Number of National Drug Overdose Deaths Involving Select Prescription and Illicit Drugs, Ages 15–24 Years Old* (Washington, D.C.: National Institute of Health, U.S. Department of Health and Human Services, 2019).

56. Kaiser Family Foundation, "Opioid Overdose Deaths by Race/Ethnicity," KFF.org, 2018.

57. Keturah James and Ayana Jordan, "The Opioid Crisis in Black Communities," *Journal of Law, Medicine, and Ethics* 46, no. 2 (June 2018): 404, 408; Anjali Om, "The Opioid Crisis in Black and White: The Role of Race in Our Nation's Recent Drug Epidemic," *Journal of Public Health* 40, no. 4 (Dec. 2018).

58. Om, "Opioid Crisis in Black and White," e615.

59. James G. Hodge et al., "Redefining Public Health Emergencies: The Opioid Epidemic," *Jurimetrics* 58 (Nov. 2017); White House, "President Donald J. Trump Is Taking Action on Drug Addiction and the Opioid Crisis," Oct. 26, 2017.

60. Hodge et al., "Redefining Public Health," 1.

61. Taleed El-Sabawi, "Defining the Opioid Epidemic: Congress, Pressure Groups, and Problem Definition," *University of Memphis Law Review* 48 (2018).

62. Jeff Sessions, "How Law Enforcement Is Taking Action on the Opioid Crisis," *Boston Globe,* Aug. 13, 2018; White House, "How We Will Win the War on Opioids," March 1, 2018.

63. Drug Policy Alliance, "A Brief History of the Drug War," Sept. 15, 2016, drugpolicy.org.

64. Ronald Reagan, "Radio Address to the Nation on Federal Drug Policy," Oct. 2, 1982.

65. Deborah Vagins et al., *Cracks in the System: Twenty Years of the Unjust Federal Crack Cocaine Law* (Washington, D.C.: American Civil Liberties Union, 2006).

66. Om, "Opioid Crisis in Black and White."

67. Drug Policy Alliance, "Brief History of the Drug War."

68. Betsy Pearl and Maritza Perez, *Ending the War on Drugs* (Washington, D.C.: Center for American Progress, 2018).

69. Jack Hubbard, Samuel Hodge, and Rachel Rempel, "Opioid Abuse: The Fall of a Prince," *Quinnipiac Health Law Journal* 21 (2018): 159.

70. Julie Netherland and Helena B. Hansen, "The War on Drugs That Wasn't: Wasted Whiteness, 'Dirty Doctors,' and Race in Media Coverage of Prescription Opioid Misuse," *Culture, Medicine, and Psychiatry* 40, no. 4 (Dec. 2016): 664.

71. Nicole Santa Cruz, "Jury Acquits Palos Verdes Estates Man of Murder in Suspected Gang Killing in South L.A.," *Los Angeles Times,* July 23, 2018.

72. Dennis Romero, "A Black Man Was Fatally Shot in the Back. A Wealthy, White Teen Suspect Is Free," *LA Weekly,* Nov. 13, 2017.

73. Ibid.; Dennis Romero, "Palos Verdes Teen Charged in Gang Murder Was a South L.A. Fixture," *LA Weekly,* Nov. 20, 2017.

74. Romero, "Black Man Was Fatally Shot in the Back."

75. Ibid.

76. Nicole Santa Cruz, "A Wealthy Teen Was Cleared in a South L.A. Killing. Critics Say His Race and Privilege Helped Him Win," *LA Weekly,* Sept. 22, 2018.

77. Ibid.

78. Santa Cruz, "Jury Acquits Palos Verdes Estates Man."

79. Manny Fernandez and John Schwartz, "Teenager's Sentence in Fatal Drunken-Driving Case Stirs 'Affluenza' Debate," *New York Times,* Dec. 13, 2013.

80. Alissa Zhu, "'Affluenza' Case Highlights Socioeconomic, Racial

Disparities in Justice," *Juvenile Justice Information Exchange,* March 18, 2014.

81. Tristan Hallman, "Attorney Defends Probation for Teen in Burleson DWI Crash That Killed 4," *Dallas Morning News,* Dec. 12, 2013.

82. Gary Strauss, "No Jail for 'Affluenza' Teen in Fatal Crash Draws Outrage," *USA Today,* Feb. 5, 2014.

83. Zhu, "'Affluenza' Case Highlights Socioeconomic, Racial Disparities in Justice"; Daniel Victor, "Ethan Couch, 'Affluenza Teen' Who Killed 4 While Driving Drunk, Is Freed," *New York Times,* April 2, 2018.

84. Deanna Boyd, "Troubled Teen Is Being Treated at a State Hospital in Vernon," *Fort Worth Star-Telegram,* April 11, 2014.

85. Ramit Plushnick-Masti, "'Affluenza' Defense Draws Criticism in Ethan Couch Sentence for Fatal DWI Wreck," *HuffPost,* Dec. 12, 2013.

86. Teresa Woodward, "Teen Driver Involved in Deadly Crash Had Prior Alcohol Citations," WFAA, June 21, 2013; CNN Wire, "Profile of Ethan Couch's Parents, Who Attorneys Argued Spoiled Him, Made Him Irresponsible," Fox 4 Kansas City WDAF-TV, Dec. 21, 2015.

## 2. TOY GUNS, CELL PHONES, AND PARTIES: CRIMINALIZING BLACK ADOLESCENT PLAY

1. Michelle Ullman, "The Best Nerf Guns and Super Soakers You Can Buy," *Business Insider,* July 25, 2018; Bobby Bernstein, "101 Best Cool Gifts for Boys: The Ultimate List," *Heavy,* April 2020, heavy.com; Kay Braeburn, "10 Best Amazon Prime Day Toys Deals," *Heavy,* July 2018, heavy.com; Bobby Bernstein, "16 Best Toy Guns: The Ultimate List," *Heavy,* Feb. 2020, heavy .com.

2. Jay Mechling, "Gun Play," *American Journal of Play* 1 (2008): 192, 201; Robert H. Wood, "Toy Guns Don't Kill People—People Kill People Who Play with Toy Guns: Federal Attempts to Regulate Imitation Firearms in the Face of Toy Industry Opposition," *City University of New York Law Review* 12 (2009): 263 (noting that the first federal toy gun law was tacked onto the end of the Federal Energy Management Improvement Act of 1988).

3. Lisa Zamosky, "Toy Guns: Do They Lead to Real-Life Violence?," WebMD, Dec. 2011, webmd.com.

4. F. Riehl, "Democrat's Bill Bans Use of Cartoon Characters to Market Guns," AmmoLand Gun News, July 17, 2014.

5. Sven Smith, "Learning to Blast a Way into Crime, or Just Good Clean Fun? Examining Aggressive Play with Toy Weapons and Its Relation with Crime," *Criminal Behavior and Mental Health* 28 (Aug. 2018): 313; Elissa Strauss, "Why Boys Love Guns, and What to Do About It," CNN, March 12, 2018; Michael G. Thompson, *It's a Boy! Your Son's Development from Birth to Age 18* (New York: Ballantine Books, 2009).

6. Mechling, "Gun Play," 192; Karen Ellen Goff, "The Relation of Violent and Nonviolent Toys to Play Behavior in Preschoolers" (PhD diss., Iowa State University, 1995).

7. "Toy Industry Association Statement on Toy Guns and Violence," Toy Association, Oct. 2016.

8. Brandon Blackwell, "Cleveland Police Officer Shot Tamir Rice Immediately After Leaving Moving Patrol Car," *Plain Dealer,* Jan. 12, 2019.

9. "Tamir Rice: US Police Kill Boy, 12, Carrying Replica Gun," BBC News, Nov. 24, 2014.

10. Ryllie Danylko, "Protests Break Out in Cleveland over Tamir Rice Shooting, Ferguson Grand Jury Decision," Cleveland.com, Jan. 12, 2019.

11. Judge Ronald B. Adrine, Judgment Entry on Tamir Rice Case, *In Re: Affidavits Relating to Timothy Loehmann and Frank Garmback,* Cleveland Municipal Court, June 2015.

12. Elahe Izadi and Peter Holley, "Video Shows Cleveland Officer Shooting 12-Year-Old Tamir Rice Within Seconds," *Washington Post,* Nov. 26, 2014; German Lopez, "Cleveland Just Fired the Cop Who Shot and Killed 12-Year-Old Tamir Rice More Than 2 Years Ago," *Vox,* May 30, 2017.

13. Emma G. Fitzsimmons, "12-Year-Old Boy Dies After Police in Cleveland Shoot Him," *New York Times,* Nov. 23, 2014.

14. Danylko, "Protests Break Out."

15. Richard A. Oppel Jr., "National Questions over Police Hit Home in Cleveland," *New York Times,* Dec. 8, 2014.

16. "Cleveland Cop Who Killed 12-Year-Old Tamir Rice Not Told Boy's Age, That Gun Might Be Fake: Union," *New York Daily News,* Dec. 13, 2014.

17. "Video Shows Cleveland Cop Shoot 12-Year-Old Tamir Rice Within Seconds," NBC News, Nov. 26, 2014.

18. Ida Lieszkovsky, "Tamir Rice Investigation Released: The Big Story," *Plain Dealer*, June 13, 2015.

19. Christine Mai-Duc, "Cleveland Officer Who Killed Tamir Rice Had Been Deemed Unfit for Duty," *Los Angeles Times*, Dec. 3, 2014.

20. Steve Almasy, "Tamir Rice Shooting Was 'Reasonable,' Two Experts Conclude," CNN, Oct. 12, 2015 (citing Kimberly A. Crawford, "Review of Deadly Force Incident: Tamir Rice," Cuyahoga County Office of the Prosecutor, Oct. 10, 2015, and S. Lamar Sims, "Investigation into the Officer-Involved Shooting of Tamir Rice Which Occurred at Cudell Park, 1910 West Boulevard, Cleveland, OH, on November 22, 2014," Cuyahoga County Office of the Prosecutor, Oct. 6, 2015).

21. Cory Shaffer, "Grand Jury Hearing Evidence in Tamir Rice Shooting," Cleveland.com, Oct. 27, 2015.

22. Jennifer L. Eberhardt, "Seeing Black: Race, Crime, and Visual Processing," *Journal of Personality and Social Psychology* 87 (Aug. 2004): 876, 881.

23. Ibid., 876, 881; Andrew R. Todd, Kelsey C. Thiem, and Rebecca Neel, "Does Seeing Faces of Young Black Boys Facilitate the Identification of Threatening Stimuli?," *Psychological Science* 27 (Feb. 2016): 384.

24. Todd, Thiem, and Neel, "Does Seeing Faces of Young Black Boys," 384.

25. Christopher Ingraham, "Why White People See Black Boys Like Tamir Rice as Older, Bigger, and Guiltier Than They Really Are," *Washington Post*, Dec. 28, 2015.

26. Phillip Atiba Goff et al., "The Essence of Innocence: Consequences of Dehumanizing Black Children," *Journal of Personality and Social Psychology* 106 (Feb. 2014): 526–45.

27. Ibid., 529.

28. Kimberly Kahn et al., "How Suspect Race Affects Police Use of Force in an Interaction over Time," *Law and Human Behavior* 41, no. 2 (April 2017): 117–26.

29. Lisa H. Thurau and Lany W. Or, *Two Billion Dollars Later: States Begin to Regulate School Resource Officers in the Nation's Schools* (Cambridge, Mass.: Strategies for Youth, 2019).

30. Sean Flynn, "The Tamir Rice Story: How to Make a Police Shooting Disappear," *GQ*, July 14, 2016.

31. Linda L. Caldwell and Peter Witt, "Leisure, Recreation, and

Play from a Developmental Context," *New Directions for Youth Development* 130 (2011): 13.

32. SHAPE America and Voices for Healthy Kids, *2016 Shape of the Nation: Status of Physical Education in the USA* (Annapolis Junction, Md.: SHAPE America–Society of Health and Physical Educators, 2016) (noting that thirty-nine states require elementary students to take physical education, thirty-seven states require junior high school students to take physical education, and forty-four states require high school students to take physical education).

33. Caldwell and Witt, "Leisure, Recreation, and Play," 13–27.

34. Ibid., 20.

35. Ibid., 18.

36. Ibid., 23, 36.

37. Ibid., 14, 23.

38. Laurence Steinberg, *Age of Opportunity: Lessons from the New Science of Adolescence* (Boston: Houghton Mifflin Harcourt, 2014); Caldwell and Witt, "Leisure, Recreation, and Play," 17.

39. "Tremaine McMillian, 14-Year-Old with Puppy, Choked by Miami-Dade Police over 'Dehumanizing Stares,'" *HuffPost,* May 30, 2013.

40. Janice Williams, "Police in Washington D.C. Arrest Black Teens for Selling Water Bottles, Because 'Safety,'" *Newsweek,* June 24, 2017; Steve Nelson, "Undercover Police Handcuff Teens Selling Water on National Mall," *U.S. News & World Report,* June 23, 2017.

41. James Hetherington, "Jacksonville Woman Says Her Son Was Handcuffed for Bouncing a Basketball in a Gym," *Newsweek,* Aug. 9, 2018.

42. Erik Ortiz, "Four Girls at N.Y. Middle School Subjected to 'Dehumanizing' Strip Search, Lawsuit Says," NBC News, April 30, 2019.

43. Kamilah Newton, "10-Year-Old Boy Charged with Assault over Dodgeball Game: 'Our Kids Are Racially Targeted,'" Yahoo, July 29, 2019.

44. Monica Anderson and Jingjing Jiang, "Teens, Social Media, and Technology 2018," Pew Research Center, May 31, 2018.

45. Influence Central, "Kids & Tech: The Evolution of Today's Digital Natives," *Influence Central Trend Report,* 2016.

46. Anderson and Jiang, "Teens, Social Media, and Technology."

47. Victoria J. Rideout et al., *The Digital Lives of African Ameri-*

*can Tweens, Teens, and Parents: Innovating and Learning with Technology* (Tempe: Arizona State University Center for Gender Equity in Science and Technology, 2016).

48. Amanda Lenhart, Monica Anderson, and Aaron Smith, "Teens, Technology, and Romantic Relationships," Pew Research Center, Oct. 1, 2015.

49. José De-Sola Gutiérrez, Fernando Rodríguez de Fonseca, and Gabriel Rubio, "Cell-Phone Addiction: A Review," *Frontiers in Psychiatry* 7 (Oct. 2016): 175.

50. Sarah Aarthun and Holly Yan, "Student's Violent Arrest Caught on Video; Officer Under Investigation," CNN, Oct. 2015; "Violent School Incident Sparks Debate," CBS7, Oct. 2015.

51. Desire Thompson, "ATTORNEY: Teen from Spring Valley Video Didn't Obey Orders Because 'Punishment Was Unfair,' " *NewsOne,* Nov. 2, 2015.

52. Amy D. Sorkin, "What Niya Kenny Saw," *New Yorker,* Oct. 30, 2015.

53. Amanda Ripley, "How America Outlawed Adolescence," *Atlantic,* Nov. 2016.

54. Khaleda Rahman and Snejana Farberov, "Sheriff Claims Officer Who Manhandled Black Female Student Isn't Racist Because His Girlfriend Is African American—as Her Classmate Says She's Been Arrested for Filming the Shocking Scene," *Daily Mail,* Oct. 28, 2015.

55. South Carolina Code of Laws § 16-17-420, Disturbing Schools (2015) (The amended disturbing schools law increases the penalty from ninety days in jail to one year, and from a $1,000 fine to $2,000).

56. Ripley, "How America Outlawed Adolescence."

57. Ibid.

58. Ibid.

59. Sorkin, "What Niya Kenny Saw."

60. Erik Ortiz and Craig Melvin, "South Carolina Deputy Ben Fields Fired After Body Slamming Student: Sheriff," NBC News, Oct. 28, 2015.

61. Luca Guido Valla and Davide Rivolta, "Stereotypical Biases in Black People Toward Black People," *Society for Personality and Psychology: Character and Context,* May 28, 2019; Luca Guido Valla et al., "Not Only Whites: Racial Priming Effect for Black

Faces in Black People," *Basic and Applied Social Psychology* 40, no. 4 (July 2018): 195–200; Rob Voigt et al., "Language from Police Body Camera Footage Shows Racial Disparities in Officer Respect," *Proceedings of the National Academy of Sciences* 114, no. 25 (June 2017): 6521–26 (finding that "officers speak with consistently less respect toward black versus white community members, even after controlling for the race of the officer, the severity of the infraction, the location of the stop, and the outcome of the stop").

62. Complaint, *Kenny v. Wilson*, No. 2:16-cv-2794-CWH (D.S.C. Aug. 11, 2016), ECF No. 157; Sorkin, "What Niya Kenny Saw."

63. H.R. Res. 5045, Sess. of 2019–20 (S.C. 2020).

64. Liam Stack and Christine Hauser, "Police Account Changes in Killing of Texas 15-Year-Old," *New York Times,* May 1, 2017.

65. Jennifer Emily, Ray Leszcynski, and Marc Ramirez, "Balch Springs Police Fire Officer Roy Oliver, Who Fatally Shot Jordan Edwards with Rifle," *Dallas News,* May 2, 2017 (noting that eight out of ten Balch Springs police officers are white).

66. Julieta Chiquillo, "Flashback: Jordan Edwards' Stepbrother Recounts Harrowing Night, Hearing Cop's Fatal Shots," *Dallas News,* Aug. 28, 2018.

67. Ibid.

68. Emily, Leszcynski, and Ramirez, "Balch Springs Police."

69. Terence Cullen, "Jordan Edwards' Brothers Say Cops Used N-Word After Pulling Them Over Moments After Texas Teen's Fatal Shooting," *New York Daily News,* May 18, 2017.

70. Michael Edison Hayden, "Twin Brothers Describe Police Officer's Fatal Shooting of Friend," ABC News, May 8, 2017.

71. Terrence Cullen, "Fired Texas Cop Roy Oliver Claims Sound of Breaking Window Made Him Shoot Unarmed Teen Jordan Edwards," *New York Daily News,* July 19, 2017.

72. Jennifer Emily, "Gunfire Before Officer Killed Jordan Edwards Came from Nursing Home Parking Lot, Investigators Find," *Dallas News,* May 11, 2017.

73. Manny Fernandez and Matthew Haag, "Police Officer Who Fatally Shot 15-Year-Old Texas Boy Is Charged with Murder," *New York Times,* May 5, 2017.

74. Emily, Leszcynski, and Ramirez, "Balch Springs Police."

75. "Jordan Edwards Shooting: Texas Police Officer Fired," BBC

News, May 3, 2017; German Lopez, "The Police Officer Who Killed 15-Year-Old Jordan Edwards Has Been Charged with Murder," *Vox,* May 5, 2017.

76. Timothy Pleskac, Joseph Cesario, and David Johnson, "How Race Affects Evidence Accumulation During the Decision to Shoot," *Psychonomic Bulletin and Review* 25 (Oct. 2017): 1301–30 (summarizing studies).

77. Joshua Correll et al., "The Police Officer's Dilemma: Using Ethnicity to Disambiguate Potentially Threatening Individuals," *Journal of Personality and Social Psychology* 83, no. 6 (2002): 1314–29; Joshua Correll et al., "The Influence of Stereotypes on Decisions to Shoot," *European Journal of Social Psychology* 37, no. 6 (July 2007): 1102–17; Joshua Correll et al., "Across the Thin Blue Line: Police Officers and Racial Bias in the Decision to Shoot," *Journal of Personality and Social Psychology* 92, no. 6 (2007): 1006–23.

78. Correll et al., "Police Officer's Dilemma"; Anthony Greenwald, Mark Oakes, and Hunter Hoffman, "Targets of Discrimination: Effects of Race on Responses to Weapon Holders," *Journal of Experimental Social Psychology* 39, no. 4 (July 2003): 399–405; Ashby E. Plant and Michelle Peruche, "The Consequences of Race for Police Officers' Responses to Criminal Suspects," *Psychological Science* 16, no. 3 (March 2005): 180–83, 141–56.

79. Correll et al., "Across the Thin Blue Line"; Jessica Sim, Joshua Correll, and Melody Sadler, "Understanding Police and Expert Performance: When Training Attenuates (vs. Exacerbates) Stereotypic Bias in the Decision to Shoot," *Personality and Social Psychology Bulletin* 39, no. 3 (Feb. 2013): 291–304; Correll et al., "Influence of Stereotypes."

80. Lopez, "Police Officer Who Killed 15-Year-Old Jordan Edwards."

81. Ibid.; "The Counted: People Killed by Police in the US," *Guardian,* 2015–16.

82. Daniella Silva, "White Texas Police Officer Found Guilty of Murder for Fatally Shooting Black Teen in Car," NBC News, Aug. 28, 2018.

83. "Jury Sentences Former North Texas Officer to 15 Years in Prison for Murder," CBS Local DFW, Aug. 29, 2018.

84. Jennifer Emily, "Police Found No Alcohol or Drugs at Party Where Cop Shot Jordan Edwards," *Dallas Morning News,* June 28, 2017.

85. "McKinney, Texas Population 2020," World Population Review, 2020 (Data shows that McKinney residents were 76.31 percent

White, 11.56 percent Black or African American, 6.71 percent Asian, 2.86 percent two or more races, 2.04 percent other race, 0.48 percent Native American, and 0.04 percent Native Hawaiian or Pacific Islander).

86. Abby Phillip, "'Go Back to Your Section 8 Home': Texas Pool Party Host Describes Racially Charged Dispute with Neighbor," *Washington Post,* June 8, 2015.

87. David Mack, "This Man Speaking Out About the McKinney Pool Party Isn't Telling the Full Story," *BuzzFeed News,* June 10, 2015.

88. E. Johnson Photography, "McKinney Pool Party Teen Interview (ORIGINAL)," YouTube, June 7, 2015.

89. "Girl at Texas Pool Party: 'It Was About Race,'" CBS News, June 8, 2015.

90. Jacquellena Carrero and Alex Johnson, "McKinney, Texas, Cop Placed on Leave After Pulling Gun on Teens at Pool Party," NBC News, June 7, 2015.

91. "Witness, Resident Sound Off on the Texas Pool Party Incident," Fox News Video, June, 2015; Mack, "This Man Speaking Out."

92. "Witness, Resident Sound Off."

93. "Girl at Texas Pool Party."

94. "Witness, Resident Sound Off"; Mack, "This Man Speaking Out."

95. Bill Chappell, "'His Emotions Got the Best of Him' at Pool, Officer's Attorney Says," NPR, June 10, 2015.

96. "Witness, Resident Sound Off."

97. Mack, "This Man Speaking Out."

98. Carol Cole-Frowe and Richard Fausset, "Jarring Image of Police's Use of Force at Texas Pool Party," *New York Times,* June 8, 2015.

99. Tom Uhler, "Settlement Reached in Viral Video Case of McKinney Police Breaking Up Pool Party," *Fort Worth Star-Telegram,* May 29, 2018.

100. Julieta Chiquillo, "Girl Pinned Down at McKinney Pool Party Sues Ex-cop, City for $5 Million," *Dallas Morning News,* Jan. 5, 2017.

101. Michael Barajas, "A Tale of Two Texas Pool Parties," *San Antonio Current,* Sept. 14, 2016.

102. Ivonne Roman, "The Curfew Myth," Marshall Project, July 31, 2018 (citing the most recently available statistic).

103. Tom Dart, "Austin Votes to End Its Youth Curfew amid Racial Bias Concerns," *Guardian,* Sept. 29, 2017.

104. Tik Root, "Life Under Curfew for American Teens: 'It's Insane, No Other Country Does This,'" *Guardian*, May 28, 2016.

105. Sana Johnson, "What City Leaders Should Know About Curfews for Minors," Coalition for Juvenile Justice, May 4, 2016.

106. Johnson, "What City Leaders Should Know."

107. "Curfew Laws by State," National Youth Rights Association, 2020.

108. Root, "Life Under Curfew."

109. Roman, "Curfew Myth."

110. Root, "Life Under Curfew."

111. Luke Broadwater, "Baltimore Summer Youth Curfew Begins Friday; Police Will Take Kids Home Instead of to City-Run Centers," *Baltimore Sun*, May 25, 2018; Andrew Middleman, "In the Street Tonight: An Equal Protection Analysis of Baltimore City's Juvenile Curfew," *University of Baltimore Law Forum* 46 (2015): 10, 29–30.

112. Broadwater, "Baltimore Summer Youth Curfew."

113. Middleman, "In the Street Tonight."

114. Broadwater, "Baltimore Summer Youth Curfew."

115. Dart, "Austin Votes to End Its Youth Curfew."

116. Elizabeth Welliver, "UPDATED: City's Curfew Criminalizes Young People of Color—It's Time to End It for Good," *Grassroots Leadership Blog*, Sept. 29, 2017.

117. Dart, "Austin Votes to End Its Youth Curfew."

118. Roman, "Curfew Myth."

119. Root, "Life Under Curfew."

120. Johnson, "What City Leaders Should Know."

121. Ibid.; Monica Rhor, "Pushed Out and Punished: One Woman's Story Shows How Systems Are Failing Black Girls," *USA Today*, May 15, 2019.

122. Root, "Life Under Curfew."

123. Shawn Shinneman, "Youth Curfew Takes Center Stage at City Council," *D Magazine*, Feb. 6, 2019.

124. Mallory Noe-Payne, "In Richmond, Virtually All Juveniles Stopped for Curfew Violations Were African-Americans," WVTF, Aug. 12, 2019.

125. Johnson, "What City Leaders Should Know,"

126. Roman, "Curfew Myth."

127. "Black Codes," History, Oct. 10, 2019, history.com.

## 3. HOODIES, HEADWRAPS, AND HIP-HOP:
### CRIMINALIZING BLACK ADOLESCENT CULTURE

1. Karlyn Barker, "A Resurgence by the Klan," *Washington Post,* June 2, 1980.

2. Code of the District of Columbia, Wearing Hoods or Masks § 22-3312.03 (1983).

3. Dennis Wilson, "The History of the Hoodie," *Rolling Stone,* April 3, 2012; Troy Patterson, "The Politics of the Hoodie," *New York Times,* March 2, 2016.

4. Linton Weeks, "Tragedy Gives the Hoodie a Whole New Meaning," NPR, March 24, 2012.

5. Niko Koppel, "Are Your Jeans Sagging? Go Directly to Jail," *New York Times,* Aug. 30, 2007; Elizabeth Wellington, "A Fashion Firestorm over Pants That Sag: New Jersey Proposals Target Hip-Hop Style," *Philadelphia Inquirer,* Oct. 4, 2007; Guy Trebay, "In Jailhouse Chic, an Anti-style Turns into a Style Itself," *New York Times,* June 13, 2000 (noting that "the history of style in the late 20th century is substantially the history of hip-hop," and any survey of fashion in the last two decades could not omit the importance of "track suits, sweat clothes, wrestling, boxing or soccer shoes, designer sneakers, outsize denims, prison-style jumpsuits, underwear worn above the trouser waistband, do-rags, cargo pants, messenger bags, dreadlocks, cornrows, athletic jerseys, Kangol caps").

6. Trebay, "In Jailhouse Chic"; Koppel, "Are Your Jeans Sagging?"

7. Gene Demby, "Sagging Pants and the Long History of 'Dangerous' Street Fashion," NPR, Sept. 11, 2014.

8. Guy Trebay, "Taking Hip-Hop Seriously, Seriously," *New York Times,* May 20, 2003; Trebay, "In Jailhouse Chic."

9. Rosario Harper, "Justin Bieber Drops New Yummy Banger and Vows He'll Never Stop Sagging His Pants," *SOHH,* Jan. 4, 2020, sohh.com; Shyla Watson, "Justin Bieber Will Never Pull Up His Pants!!!," *BuzzFeed,* Jan. 4, 2020.

10. The First Amendment provides that "Congress shall make no law respecting an establishment of religion, or prohibiting the free exercise thereof; or abridging the freedom of speech, or of the press; or the right of the people peaceably to assemble, and to petition the Government for a redress of grievances." The Supreme Court has established that the First Amendment protects

symbolic speech and expressive conduct as well as written and spoken speech. See, e.g., *Tinker v. Des Moines Independent Community School District,* 393 U.S. 503, 506 (1969) (recognizing that the wearing of black armbands to protest the Vietnam War was protected speech). See also *Kelley v. Johnson,* 425 U.S. 238, 244 (1976) (assuming that "the citizenry at large has some sort of 'liberty' interest within the Fourteenth Amendment in matters of personal appearance").

11. *Barnes v. Glen Theatre Inc.,* 501 U.S. 560, 569–70 (1991) (plurality opinion) (holding that the government has a strong interest in protecting order and morality); *Hazelwood School District v. Kuhlmeier,* 484 U.S. 260, 266 (1988) (finding that the "special characteristics of the school environment" allow for restrictions on student expression that would be unconstitutional if the government were to make similar restrictions on society at large); *Tinker,* 393 U.S. at 506 (holding that students do not shed their constitutional rights to freedom of speech or expression at the schoolhouse gate).

12. Gowri Ramachandran, "Freedom of Dress: State and Private Regulation of Clothing, Hairstyle, Jewelry, Makeup, Tattoos, and Piercing," *Maryland Law Review* 66 (2006): 18–26, 46.

13. Trebay, "In Jailhouse Chic"; Anthony Westbury, "Saggy Pants Symbolize What's Gone Wrong in Black Community, Kids Say," *TCPalm,* Oct. 21, 2010.

14. Amy Wilson, "Public School Dress Codes: The Constitutional Debate," *BYU Education and Law Journal* 147 (1998); Wendy Mahling, "Secondhand Codes: An Analysis of the Constitutionality of Dress Codes in the Public Schools," *Minnesota Law Review* 80 (1996): 715–42; *Chalifoux v. New Caney Independent School District,* 976 F. Supp. 659, 664 (S.D. Tex. 1997) (discussing challenge to school dress code); *Bivens v. Albuquerque Public Schools,* 899 F. Supp. 556, 558 (D.N.M. 1995) (same); *Jeglin v. San Jacinto Unified School District,* 827 F. Supp. 1459, 1463 (C.D. Cal. 1993).

15. Bob Baker, "Dressing for Death: Officers Help Parents Understand What Gangs Are All About," *Los Angeles Times,* May 11, 1988.

16. Mahling, "Secondhand Codes," 718–20.

17. William Vandivort, "I See London, I See France: The Constitutional Challenge to 'Saggy' Pants Laws," *Brooklyn Law Review* 667 (2009).

18. Mike Ward and Colby Rogers, "Sagging Support," *Richmond Times-Dispatch,* Feb. 11, 2005.

19. Gonzales, La., Code of Ordinances § 8-145 (2007); Abbeville, La., Code of Ordinances § 13-25 (2007); Shreveport, La., Code of Ordinances § 50-167 (2007); Port Allen, La., Code of Ordinances § 54-13 (2007); Alexandria, La., Code of Ordinances § 15-128 (2007); Koppel, "Are Your Jeans Sagging?" (discussing Delcambre, Louisiana, passing a law in June 11, 2007); Jeff Moore, "Sagging Bagged by Town," *Daily Iberian,* June 12, 2007 (noting that the ordinance in Delcambre, Louisiana, reads: "It shall be unlawful for any person in any public place or in view of the public to be found in a state of nudity, or partial nudity, or in dress not becoming to his or her sex, or in any indecent exposure of his or her person or undergarments, or be guilty of any indecent or lewd behavior").

20. Moore, "Sagging Bagged by Town."

21. Gonzales, La., Code of Ordinances § 8-145 (2007) (fines $50–$500); Abbeville, La., Code of Ordinances § 13-25 (2007) (jail up to six months).

22. Vandivort, "I See London," 667.

23. Sarah Figalora, "Meet the Passionate 'Driving Force' Behind Florida City's Saggy Pants Ban," ABC News, July 22, 2014; Demby, "Sagging Pants"; Opa-locka, Fla., Code of Ordinances No. 07-19 (2007); Koppel, "Are Your Jeans Sagging?"

24. Jasper County, S.C., Ordinance 08-15 (Dec. 2015); Onika Williams, "The Suppression of a Saggin' Expression: Exploring the 'Saggy Pants' Style Within a First Amendment Context," *Indiana Law Journal* 85 (2010): 1169.

25. Mary Elizabeth Williams, "Are Sagging Pants Laws Making a Comeback?," *Salon,* Feb. 21, 2018.

26. R. L. Nave, "Sagging Pants Could Draw Fine," *Mississippi Today,* Jan. 24, 2017; H. B. 1353, Sess. of 2017 (Mississippi 2017).

27. Marjorie Esman, "Saggy Pants Legislation: A New Look for Racial Profiling," *Louisiana Weekly,* July 8, 2013.

28. "Police Chief Refuses to Yield on Saggy Pants Crackdown," *Guardian,* July 21, 2008; William Lee, "Village Cracks Down on Exposed Undies," *Chicago Sun-Times,* Aug. 14, 2008 (stating that the proposal for a saggy pants ordinance in Midlothian, Illinois, was "fueled by residents' concerns that sagging pants is indicative of a gang problem in the village").

29. *Bivens,* 899 F. Supp. at 558.

30. Ibid., 556.

31. Ibid., 560–61.

32. Bryn Mickle, "ACLU: Florida Ruling Cuts Holes in Flint's Low-Pants Ban," *Flint Journal,* Sept. 18, 2008.

33. Ed Mazza, "Tennessee Teens Arrested and Jailed for Wearing Saggy Pants," *HuffPost,* Dec. 14, 2015.

34. Demby, "Sagging Pants."

35. Jim Forsyth, "Saggy Pants Mean No Ride on One Texas Bus System," Reuters, June 2, 2011.

36. Greensboro Transit Authority, "Policy and Procedures Manual, 1.A.20 Proper Attire Policy," April 17, 2014.

37. Charlton McIlwain, "Trayvon Martin: The Crime of Being Black, Male, and Wearing a Hoodie," *Christian Science Monitor,* March 27, 2012.

38. Ibid.; Tim McGlone, "Two Patrons Sue Virginia Beach Nightclub Alleging Discrimination," *Virginian-Pilot,* Jan. 19, 2007.

39. Sara MacNeil, "After Shooting of Black Man, Louisiana City Votes to End Sagging Pants Law," *USA Today,* June 12, 2019; Sara MacNeil, "Councilwoman Seeks to Abolish Sagging Pants Law, Questions Remain in Officer-Involved Shooting," *Shreveport Times,* May 22, 2019.

40. MacNeil, "After Shooting of Black Man."

41. Koppel, "Are Your Jeans Sagging?"

42. Demby, "Sagging Pants."

43. "Zoot Suit Riots," History, Sept. 27, 2017, history.com.

44. Moore, "Sagging Bagged by Town."

45. Vandivort, "I See London," 667; Eric Stirgus, "Critics Say Ban on Saggy Pants a Racial Trigger," *Atlanta Journal-Constitution,* Jan. 17, 2008; Ben Schmitt and Michele Munz, "Saggy-Pants Suit? Chief Will Press on Pants," *St. Louis Post-Dispatch,* July 21, 2008; ACLU, "ACLU Reminds Iberville Parish That Clothing Is Protected Expression," media release, March 17, 2014; "Florida City Repeals Saggy Pants Ordinance: Move Comes After NAACP Threatened Legal Action," ClickOrlando.com, Sept. 17, 2014.

46. Wellington, "Fashion Firestorm"; Koppel, "Are Your Jeans Sagging?"; Figalora, "Meet the Passionate 'Driving Force' " (noting that first African American councilwoman in Ocala, Florida, was driving force behind saggy pants law); MacNeil, "Councilwoman Seeks to Abolish."

47. Koppel, "Are Your Jeans Sagging?" (quoting the Georgetown pro-

fessor Michael Eric Dyson, author of *Know What I Mean? Reflections on Hip-Hop*).

48. Demby, "Sagging Pants"; Koppel, "Are Your Jeans Sagging?"

49. Erin Kerrison, Jennifer Cobbina, and Kimberly Bender, "'Your Pants Won't Save You': Why Black Youth Challenge Race-Based Police Surveillance and the Demands of Black Respectability Politics," *Race and Justice* 8 (2017): 9.

50. Ibid., 26.

51. Ibid.

52. P. R. Lockhart, "Black Girls Are Disciplined More Harshly in School. Dress Codes Play a Big Role," *Vox,* April 26, 2018.

53. Deanna J. Glickman, "Fashioning Children: Gender Restrictive Dress Codes as an Entry Point for the Trans* School to Prison Pipeline," *Journal of Gender, Social Policy, and the Law* 24, no. 2 (2016): 263–84; David Crockett and Melanie Wallendorf, "Sociological Perspectives on Imposed School Dress Codes: Consumption as Attempted Suppression of Class and Group Symbolism," *Journal of Macromarketing* 18 (1998): 115–31; Natalie Smith, "Eliminating Gender Stereotypes in Public School Dress Codes: The Necessity of Respecting Personal Preference," *Journal of Law and Education* 41 (2012): 251–59.

54. Mary Whisner, "Gender-Specific Clothing Regulation: A Study in Patriarchy," *Harvard Women's Law Journal* 5 (1982): 73–119; see *Breese v. Smith,* 501 P.2d 159, 161 (Alaska 1972); *Johnson v. Joint School District No. 60,* 508 P.2d 547, 548–49 (Idaho 1973); *Scott v. Board of Education,* 305 N.Y.S.2d 601, 603, 606 (N.Y. Sup. Ct. 1969); Crockett and Wallendorf, "Sociological Perspectives on Imposed School Dress Codes"; Glickman, "Fashioning Children," 268.

55. Mahling, "Secondhand Codes" (citing Margaret Trimer, "Weather Is Warm and School Clothes Hot: Sizzling Spandex Barred by Dress Code," *Detroit Free Press,* April 25, 1990).

56. Alexandra Brodsky et al., *Dress Coded: Black Girls, Bodies, and Bias in D.C. Schools* (Washington, D.C.: National Women's Law Center, 2019).

57. Hayley Krischer, "Is Your Body Appropriate to Wear to School?," *New York Times,* April 17, 2018; Meredith Harbach, "Sexualization, Sex Discrimination, and Public School Dress Codes," *Richmond Law Review* 50 (2016); Li Zhou, "The Sexism of School Dress Codes," *Atlantic,* Oct. 20, 2015.

58. Lockhart, "Black Girls Are Disciplined"; Rebecca Epstein, Jamilia J. Blake, and Thalia González, *Girlhood Interrupted: The Erasure of Black Girls' Childhood* (Washington, D.C.: Georgetown Law Center on Poverty and Inequality, 2017).

59. Amir Whitaker et al., *Cops and No Counselors: How the Lack of School Mental Health Staff Is Harming Students* (New York: American Civil Liberties Union, 2019), 30 (citing U.S. Department of Education, "2015–16 Civil Rights Data Collection," Office for Civil Rights (April 2018)).

60. Mary Ellen Flannery, "Pushed Out: The Injustice Black Girls Face in School," *National Education Association Today,* Sept. 9, 2016.

61. Rebecca Epstein et al., *Data Snapshot: 2017–2018 National Data on School Discipline by Race and Gender* (Washington, D.C.: Georgetown Law Center on Poverty and Inequality's Initiative on Gender Justice & Opportunity and the RISE Research at New York University, 2020) (analyzing U.S. Department of Education, "2017–18 Civil Rights Data Collection," Office for Civil Rights (October 2020)).

62. Lockhart, "Black Girls Are Disciplined."

63. Brodsky, *Dress Coded,* 16.

64. Alejandra Matos and Emma Brown, "Some D.C. High Schools Are Reporting Only a Fraction of Suspensions," *Washington Post,* July 17, 2017.

65. Brodsky, *Dress Coded,* 14; Lockhart, "Black Girls Are Disciplined."

66. Lockhart, "Black Girls Are Disciplined"; Harbach, "Sexualization," 1039–40; Gail Sullivan, "New Kid at School Forced to Wear 'Shame Suit' for Dress Code Violation," *Washington Post,* Sept. 5, 2014.

67. Lockhart, "Black Girls Are Disciplined"; Monique Morris, *Pushout: The Criminalization of Black Girls in School* (New York: New Press, 2016).

68. Joe Heim, "The Long and Short of a Maryland School's Dress Code Sparks Protest," *Washington Post,* Sept. 15, 2019.

69. Siraad Dirshe, "Respect Our Roots: A Brief History of Our Braids," *Essence,* June 27, 2018.

70. Chanté Griffin, "How Natural Black Hair at Work Became a Civil Rights Issue," *JSTOR Daily,* July 3, 2019.

71. Alexia Fernández Campbell, "A Black Woman Lost a Job Offer Because She Wouldn't Cut Her Dreadlocks. Now She Wants to Go to the Supreme Court," *Vox,* April 18, 2018.

72. Brian Josephs, "Who Criminalized the Durag?," *GQ*, March 2, 2017.
73. Ibid.; Taylor Bryant, "Did Tom Ford Just Send Durags Down the Runway?," *Nylon*, Sept. 6, 2018; Sandra Garcia, "The Durag, Explained," *New York Times*, May 15, 2018.
74. Jabari Julien, "Leveraging Title VI and the Administrative Complaint Process to Challenge Discriminatory School Dress Code Policies," *Columbia Law Review* 119 (2019): 2211–12.
75. Michelle Lou, "A Georgia Elementary School Was Criticized for a Poster Dictating Hairstyles for Black Students," CNN, Aug. 2, 2019.
76. Julia Jacobs and Dan Levin, "Black Girl Sent Home from School over Hair Extensions," *New York Times*, Aug. 21, 2018.
77. Katie Mettler, "Black Girls at Massachusetts School Win Freedom to Wear Hair Braid Extensions," *Washington Post*, May 22, 2017.
78. Kay Lazar, "Black Malden Charter Students Punished for Braided Hair Extension," *Boston Globe*, May 11, 2017.
79. Mettler, "Black Girls at Massachusetts School."
80. D. Wendy Green et al., "To Alex Dan, Interim School Director, Mystic Valley School," June 20, 2017. On file with author.
81. Brodsky, *Dress Coded*, 11; Lockhart, "Black Girls Are Disciplined."
82. Samantha Schmidt, "Black Girls Say D.C. School Dress Codes Unfairly Target Them. Now They're Speaking Up," *Washington Post*, Sept. 5, 2019.
83. Chelsey Cox, "Texas Teen Banned by High School from Attending Graduation After Refusing to Cut Dreadlocks," *USA Today*, Jan. 24, 2020.
84. Elisha Fieldstadt, "Texas School Staffers Colored in Black Teen's Haircut with Sharpie, Lawsuit Claims," NBC News, Aug. 19, 2019.
85. Mariel Padilla, "New Jersey Is Third State to Ban Discrimination Based on Hair," *New York Times*, Dec. 20, 2019.
86. Jesse Washington, "The Untold Story of Wrestler Andrew Johnson's Dreadlocks," *Undefeated*, Sept. 18, 2019.
87. Janelle Griffith, "When Hair Breaks Rules: Some Black Children Are Getting in Trouble for Natural Hairstyles," NBC News, Feb. 23, 2019.
88. Padilla, "New Jersey Is Third State."
89. Wendy Greene, "#FreeTheHair," freethehair.com.
90. Dave Miranda, "The Role of Music in Adolescent Development:

Much More Than the Same Old Song," *International Journal of Adolescence and Youth* 18 (2013): 5–22.

91. Ibid.; Spectrio, "The Healing Power of Music for Hospital Patients," *Spectrio Healthcare Blog,* 2020; Amy Novotney, "Music as Medicine," *American Psychological Association* 44, no. 10 (2013).

92. Miranda, "Role of Music" (citing Vinod Menon and Daniel J. Levitin, "The Rewards of Music Listening: Response and Physiological Connectivity of the Mesolimbic System," *NeuroImage* 28 (2005): 175–84 (noting that music activates neurotransmitters involved in pleasure, such as dopamine)); Stephanie Khalfa et al., "Effects of Relaxing Music on Salivary Cortisol Level After Psychological Stress," *Annals of the New York Academy of Science* 999 (2003): 374–76; Ulrica Nilsson, "Soothing Music Can Increase Oxytocin Levels During Bed Rest After Open-Heart Surgery: A Randomized Control Trial," *Journal of Clinical Nursing* 18 (2015): 2153–61.

93. Zoe Papinczak et al., "Young People's Uses of Music for Wellbeing," *Journal of Youth Studies* 18 (2015): 1119–34.

94. "Teens Blast Music Through Streaming Services," eMarketer, Feb. 5, 2015.

95. David Hargreaves, Adrian C. North, and Mark Tarrant, "Musical Preference and Taste in Childhood and Adolescence," in *The Child as Musician: A Handbook of Musical Development,* ed. G. E. McPherson (Oxford: Oxford University Press, 2006).

96. Rodolfo Mendoza-Denton, "Why Rap Gets a Bad Rap," *Greater Good Magazine,* May 31, 2011.

97. Carrie Fried, "Bad Rap for Rap: Bias in Reactions to Music Lyrics," *Journal of Applied Social Psychology* 26, no. 23 (1996): 2135–46.

98. Adam Dunbar et al., "The Threatening Nature of 'Rap' Music," *Psychology, Public Policy, and Law* 22 (2016): 288.

99. Cynthia Frisby and E. Behm-Morawitz, "Undressing the Words: Prevalence of Profanity, Misogyny, Violence, and Gender Role References in Popular Music from 2006–2016," *Media Watch* 10 (2018): 5–21.

100. Braden Leap, "A New Type of (White) Provider: Shifting Masculinities in Mainstream Country Music from the 1980s to the 2010s," *Rural Sociology* 85 (2020): 165–89.

101. Kelsey Spigelmire, "A Bad Rap for Rap Music," *Lumberjack,* Feb. 16, 2018; Amy McCarthy, "The Ten Raunchiest Songs in Country Music History," *Houston Press,* Nov. 18, 2015.

102. McCarthy, "Ten Raunchiest Songs"; Leap, "New Type of (White) Provider"; Tom Jacobs, "Country Hits Increasingly Objectify Women and Glorify Whiteness," *Pacific Standard,* May 7, 2019.

103. Frank Williams, "How Rap Music Got Its Bad Rap: Violence Experts Blame the Change in the Genre Partly on Newer Performers' Lifestyles," *Los Angeles Times,* Jan. 13, 1995; Emma Lalley, "Amerikaz Most Wanted: The Criminalization of Gangsta Rap and the Misunderstood Motives of Tupac Shakur," American Crazy: Four Myths of Violence and National Identity, Wesleyan University, Jan. 1, 2015.

104. Asawin Suebsaeng, "The FBI Agent Who Hunted N.W.A," *Daily Beast,* April 14, 2017; Tim Scott, "25 Years of Killing Cops with Ice-T," *Vice,* June 2, 2017.

105. Bethany Barnes, "Portland Public Schools 'Rap Music' Ban Sparks Allegations of Racism," *Oregonian,* Aug. 24, 2016.

106. Jonathan Marshall, "Local Rapper Deemed Not a Good Role Model, Not Allowed to Speak at Junior High School," Fox13 Memphis, April 2, 2019.

107. Natasha Alford, "Teen Killed by White Man Who Says Rap Music Made Him Feel 'Unsafe,' " *Grio,* July 8, 2019.

108. Elliot C. McLaughlin and Devon Sayers, "Defendant Tells Police He Had Spat over Loud Music, Opened Fire, Ordered Pizza," CNN, Feb. 6, 2014; *3½ Minutes, Ten Bullets,* directed by Marc Silver (New York: Candescent Films, 2015).

109. Charis Kubrin and Erik Nielson, "Rap on Trial," *Race and Justice* 4 (2014): 201.

110. Ehud Bodner and Moshe Bensimon, "Problem Music and Its Different Shades over Its Fans," *Psychology of Music* 43 (2014): 641–60 (finding that fans of "problem music" were able to internalize emotions and were less likely to externalize negative emotions that led to antisocial behaviors).

111. Miranda, "Role of Music"; Bodner and Bensimon, "Problem Music." See also Stuart Forrest, "Code of the Tweet: Urban Gang Violence in the Social Media Age," *Social Problems* 67, no. 2 (2020) (contending that youth engage in bravado on social media to avoid having to be violent in real life).

112. Stephen Johnson, "The 12 High-School Cliques That Exist Today, and How They Differ from Past Decades," *Big Think,* Jan. 9, 2019.

113. Derek Thompson, "Why Cliques Form at Some High Schools and Not Others," *Atlantic,* Nov. 10, 2014.

114. Ben Popper, "How the NYPD Is Using Social Media to Put Harlem Teens Behind Bars," *Verge,* Dec. 10, 2014.

115. See Daniel Alarcón, "How Do You Define a Gang Member?," *New York Times Magazine,* May 27, 2015; Victor Rios, *Punished: Policing the Lives of Black and Latino Boys* (New York: New York University Press, 2011); Stuart Forrest and Ava Benezra, "Criminalized Masculinities: How Policing Shapes the Construction of Gender and Sexuality in Poor Black Communities," *Social Problems* 65, no. 2 (May 2018): 174–90.

116. Popper, "How the NYPD Is Using Social Media."

117. Christopher Adamson, "Defensive Localism in White and Black: A Comparative History of European-American and African-American Youth Gangs," *Journal of Ethnic and Racial Studies* 23 (2000); Irving Spergel et al., *Gang Suppression and Intervention: Problem and Response* (Washington, D.C.: U.S. Department of Justice, 1993).

118. Zachariah Fudge, "Gang Definitions, How Do They Work?: What the Juggalos Teach Us About Inadequacy of Current Anti-gang Law," *Marquette Law Review* 97 (2015): 979 (citing J. Adams Puffer, *The Boy and His Gang* (New York: Houghton Mifflin, 1912)).

119. Fudge, "Gang Definitions," 979 (citing Richard A. Ball and G. David Curry, "The Logic of Definition in Criminology: Purposes and Methods for Defining 'Gangs,'" *Criminology* 33 (1995): 225, 227 (citing Puffer, *Boy and His Gang*)).

120. Spergel et al., *Gang Suppression.*

121. Frederic M. Thrasher, *The Gang: A Study of 1,313 Gangs in Chicago* (Chicago: University of Chicago Press, 1927), 55, 57.

122. Adamson, "Defensive Localism in White and Black," 144–46, 148–50.

123. Albert K. Cohen, *Delinquent Boys: The Culture of the Gang* (Glencoe, Ill.: Free Press, 1971); Adamson, "Defensive Localism in White and Black," 143–69.

124. Adamson, "Defensive Localism in White and Black," 153–54, 158–61.

125. Fudge, "Gang Definitions," 991 (citing Malcolm W. Klein, *Street Gangs and Street Workers* (Englewood Cliffs, N.J.: Prentice-Hall, 1971), 13).

126. Adamson, "Defensive Localism in White and Black."

127. California Penal Code, Gang Enhancements §186.22(b) (West 1999 and Supp. 2014).

128. The National Gang Center is a coordinated project of four federal agencies: the U.S. Department of Justice, the Office of Justice Programs, the Bureau of Justice Assistance, and the Office of Juvenile Justice and Delinquency Prevention.

129. Josmar Trujillo and Alex Vitale, *Gang Takedowns in the de Blasio Era: The Dangers of "Precision Policing,"* Policing and Social Justice Project, Brooklyn College, 2019.

130. National Gang Center, "Frequently Asked Questions: About Gangs."

131. Fudge, "Gang Definitions," 1001–2 (citing C. Ronald Huff, "Denial, Overreaction, and Misidentification: A Postscript on Public Policy," in *Gangs in America* (Newbury Park, Calif.: Sage, 1990), 310–13); Michael Welch, "Moral Panic, Denial, and Human Rights: Scanning the Spectrum from Overreaction to Underreaction," in *Crime, Social Control, and Human Rights: From Moral Panics to States of Denial: Essays in Honour of Stanley Cohen,* ed. David Downes et al. (Devon Cullumption, U.K.: Willan, 2007) (discussing moral panic over street and youth crime in the early 1990s).

132. National Gang Center, "National Youth Gang Survey Analysis, 1996–2012" (noting that in the study population, which included smaller and larger cities as well as suburban and rural counties, reported gang activity went down from 39.9 percent in 1996 to 29.6 percent in 2012); Lauren Musu et al., *Indicators of School Crime and Safety 2018* (Washington, D.C.: National Center for Education Statistics, U.S. Department of Education, 2019) (noting that for students from urban areas gang presence went down from 29 to 11 percent, suburban areas from 18 to 8 percent, and rural areas from 13 to 7 percent).

133. Musu et al., *Indicators of School Crime and Safety* (relying on the School Survey on Crime and Safety's broad definition of gang to include any ongoing loosely organized association of three or more persons, whether formal or informal, that has a common name, signs, symbols, or colors, whose members engage, either

individually or collectively, in violent or other forms of illegal behavior).

134. National Gang Center, "Criminal Intelligence Information and Systems (Including Gang Databases)" (laws updated July 2020) (listing the sixteen states as Arizona, California, Colorado, Florida, Georgia, Illinois, Indiana, Minnesota, North Carolina, North Dakota, South Carolina, Tennessee, Texas, Virginia, Washington, and West Virginia).

135. Trujillo and Vitale, *Gang Takedowns,* 6.

136. California State Auditor, *The CalGang Criminal Intelligence System* (Sacramento: California State Auditor, 2016), 11.

137. Dave Cansler, Mark Graves, and Melissa Lewis, "Portland's Gang List," *Oregonian,* 2019.

138. Policing in Chicago Research Group, *Expansive and Focused Surveillance: New Findings on Chicago's Gang Database,* University of Illinois at Chicago Policing in Chicago Research Group et al., 2018.

139. Office of Inspector General, "Review of the Chicago Police Department's 'Gang Database,'" City of Chicago Office of Inspector General, 2019.

140. Linda Beres and Thomas D. Griffith, "Gangs, Schools, and Stereotypes," *Loyola of Los Angeles Law Review* 37 (2004): 949.

141. Fudge, "Gang Definitions," 998–99 (citing K. Babe Howell, "Fear Itself: The Impact of Allegations of Gang Affiliation on Pre-trial Detention," *St. Thomas Law Review* 23 (2011): 653–54).

142. California State Auditor, *CalGang.* See also RealSearch Action Research Center, *Tracked and Trapped: Youth of Color, Gang Databases, and Gang Injunction,* Youth Justice Coalition, 2012.

143. RealSearch, *Tracked and Trapped.*

144. Max Rivlin-Nadler, "How Philadelphia's Social Media–Driven Gang Policing Is Stealing Years from Young People," *Appeal,* Jan. 19, 2018.

145. RealSearch, *Tracked and Trapped,* 4.

146. Alice Speri, "New York Schools Gang Unit Pushes the Criminalization of Children," *Intercept,* Feb. 13, 2020.

147. Popper, "How the NYPD Is Using Social Media."

148. RealSearch, *Tracked and Trapped;* Emily Galvin-Almanza, "California Gang Laws Are Normalized Racism," *Appeal,* Oct. 4, 2019.

149. Paul D. Murphy, "Restricting Gang Clothing in Public Schools:

Does a Dress Code Violate a Student's Right of Free Expression?," *Southern California Law Review* 64 (1991): 1323–24; Judy Pasternak, "Gang Tension: At School, Survival Comes First," *Los Angeles Times,* Feb. 5, 1989.

150. *Olesen v. Board of Education of School District No. 228, 676 F. Supp. 821* (N.D. Ill. 1987); Katherine Bishop, "Schools Order Students to Dress for Safety's Sake," *New York Times,* Jan. 22, 1992.

151. Speri, "New York Schools."

152. Trujillo and Vitale, *Gang Takedowns,* 8.

153. Speri, "New York Schools."

154. Mike Hayes, "New Orleans Police Appear to Use Surveillance to Initiate Investigations," *Appeal,* June 3, 2019.

155. *Arizona v. Johnson,* 555 U.S. 323, 327–28 (2009) (upholding stop and frisk based on gang attire and unspecified behavior).

156. Rivlin-Nadler, "How Philadelphia's Social Media–Driven Gang Policing Is Stealing Years from Young People."

157. Forrest, "Code of the Tweet"; Rios, *Punished;* Forrest and Benezra, "Criminalized Masculinities."

## 4. RAISING "BRUTES" AND "JEZEBELS": CRIMINALIZING BLACK ADOLESCENT SEXUALITY

1. Karma Allen, "'I Felt Humiliated': 9-Year-Old Boy in 'Cornerstore Caroline' Video Speaks Out," *Good Morning America,* Oct. 19, 2018.

2. Enjoli Francis and Bill Hutchinson, "'I Don't Forgive This Woman, and She Needs Help': Black Child Wrongly Accused of Grabbing 'Cornerstore Caroline,'" ABC News, Oct. 16, 2018.

3. *Merriam-Webster,* s.v. "sexting," last modified June 1, 2020.

4. Teresa Nelson, "Minnesota Prosecutor Charges Sexting Teenage Girl with Child Pornography," ACLU, Jan. 5, 2018.

5. Justin Patchin, "New Teen Sexting Data," Cyberbullying Research Center, Feb. 24, 2017.

6. "Over Half of U.S. Teens Have Had Sexual Intercourse by Age 18, New Report Shows," Centers for Disease Control and Prevention, June 22, 2017.

7. Joyce Abma and Gladys Martinez, *Sexual Activity and Contraceptive Use Among Teenagers in the United States* (Hyattsville, Md.: National Center for Health Statistics, 2017), 5.

8. Laurence Steinberg, *Age of Opportunity: Lessons from the New Science of Adolescence* (Boston: Houghton Mifflin Harcourt, 2014), 50.

9. Ibid., 56–57.

10. "Sexual Development and Behavior in Children: Information for Parents and Caregivers," National Child Traumatic Stress Network, April 2009; "Normative Sexual Behavior," National Center on the Sexual Behavior of Youth, June 1, 2020.

11. Paediatric Society of New Zealand, "Sexual Behaviour in Children & Young People," *KidsHealth*, Sept. 29, 2017.

12. Rebecca Epstein, Jamilia J. Blake, and Thalia González, *Girlhood Interrupted: The Erasure of Black Girls' Childhood* (Washington, D.C.: Georgetown Law Center on Poverty and Inequality, 2017).

13. Martha Hodes, "The Sexualization of Reconstruction Politics: White Women and Black Men in the South," *Journal of the History of Sexuality* 3 (Jan. 1993): 402–17; Robyn Wiegman, "The Anatomy of Lynching," *Journal of the History of Sexuality* 3 (Jan. 1993): 445–67; Sandra Gunning, *Race, Rape, and Lynching: The Red Record of American Literature, 1890–1912* (New York: Oxford University Press, 1996), 22; Karlos K. Hill, *Beyond the Rope: The Impact of Lynching on Black Culture and Memory* (New York: Cambridge University Press, 2016), 10.

14. Calvin John Smiley and David Fakunle, "From 'Brute' to 'Thug': The Demonization and Criminalization of Unarmed Black Male Victims in America," *Journal of Human Behavior in the Social Environment* 26 (Jan. 2016): 350–66.

15. Jessica Glenza, "Dylann Roof: The Cold Stare of a Killer with a History of Drug Abuse and Racism," *Guardian*, June 18, 2015.

16. "'The Kissing Case' and the Lives It Shattered," NPR, April 29, 2011.

17. Lindsey Bever, "It Took 10 Minutes to Convict 14-Year-Old George Stinney Jr. It Took 70 Years After His Execution to Exonerate Him," *Washington Post*, Dec. 18, 2014.

18. Sarah Burns, *The Central Park Five: The Untold Story Behind One of New York's Most Infamous Crimes* (New York: Random House, 2011); *The Central Park Five*, directed by Ken Burns, Sarah Burns, and David McMahon (New York: Public Broadcasting Service, 2012); Natalie Byfield, *Savage Portrayals: Race, Media, and the Central Park Jogger Story* (Philadelphia: Temple University Press, 2014).

19. Gabrielle Bruney, "An Excruciating Timeline of the Central Park Five Tragedy," *Esquire,* May 31, 2019.

20. Riya Saha Shah and Marsha Levick, "The Central Park Five's Other False Label: Sex Offender," Juvenile Law Center, July 9, 2019.

21. Donald Trump, "Bring Back the Death Penalty. Bring Back Our Police," advertisement, *New York Daily News,* May 1989; Amy Davidson Sorkin, "Donald Trump and the Central Park Five," *New Yorker,* June 23, 2014.

22. Barry C. Feld, *Bad Kids: Race and the Transformation of the Juvenile Court* (New York: Oxford University Press, 1999).

23. Elizabeth Becker, "As Ex-theorist on Young 'Superpredators,' Bush Aide Has Regrets," *New York Times,* Feb. 9, 2001.

24. John J. DiIulio Jr., "My Black Crime Problem, and Ours," *City Journal* (Spring 1996).

25. Vincent M. Southerland, "Youth Matters: The Need to Treat Children Like Children," *Journal of Civil Rights and Economic Development* 4, no. 27 (Winter 2015): 765, 776 (Both the juvenile crime rate and the juvenile arrest rate declined by half between 1994 and 2009, reaching their lowest levels since the 1980s. The youth arrest rate for murder fell even more dramatically in that time frame, with the number of youth arrested for murder in the three years preceding the superpredator craze exceeding the number of youth arrested for murder in the entire decade from 2000 to 2009. Youth crime has continued to decline since 2009. Youth arrests for robbery in 2015 were 70 percent lower than their peak in the mid-1990s, aggravated assault arrests also fell by 70 percent, other assaults were down 49 percent, and the rate of youth arrests for weapon offenses was 73 percent lower than the previous peak.); Jeffrey A. Butts, "Total Youth Arrests for Violent Crime Still Falling Nationwide," *Research and Evaluation: DATA BITS,* National Juvenile Justice Network, Sept. 27, 2016; Office of Juvenile Justice and Delinquency Prevention, *Statistical Briefing Book: Juvenile Arrest Rate Trends* (Washington, D.C.: U.S. Department of Justice, 2017).

26. Shaun King, "17-Year-Old Black Boy Sexting with 16-Year-Old White Girl and Guess Who's Charged with Child Pornography," *New York Daily News,* April 28, 2016; Jeff Ferrell, "Mom Claims Foul After Teenage Son Arrested on Sexting-Related Charges," KSLA News 12, April 22, 2016.

27. Ferrell, "Mom Claims Foul After Teenage Son Arrested on Sexting-Related Charges."

28. Law Offices of Howard E. Conday, "After much work, Levar Allen's charges have been dismissed!!," Facebook, Aug. 22, 2017.

29. L. Song Richardson and Phillip Atiba Goff, "Self-Defense and the Suspicion Heuristic," *Iowa Law Review* 98 (2012): 293, 297–301; Jennifer L. Eberhardt et al., "Seeing Black: Race, Crime, and Visual Processing," *Journal of Personality and Social Psychology* 87 (2004): 876, 877.

30. Andrew R. Todd, Kelsey C. Thiem, and Rebecca Neel, "Does Seeing Faces of Young Black Boys Facilitate the Identification of Threatening Stimuli?," *Psychological Science* 27 (Feb. 2016): 384.

31. Steinberg, *Age of Opportunity*, 46.

32. American Psychological Association, *Developing Adolescents: A Reference for Professionals* (Washington, D.C.: American Psychological Association, 2002).

33. Steinberg, *Age of Opportunity*, 5–6, 46–47, 59–60.

34. U.S. Census Bureau, "Historical Marital Status Tables: Table MS-2. Estimated Median Age at First Marriage, by Sex: 1890 to the Present," Nov. 2019.

35. T. J. Matthews and Brady E. Hamilton, "Mean Age of Mother, 1970–2000," *National Vital Statistics Reports* 51 (2011): 2; Joyce A. Martin et al., "Births: Final Data for 2015," *National Vital Statistics Reports* 55 (2017): 5.

36. Jeffrey J. Arnett, "Emerging Adulthood: A Theory of Development from the Late Teens Through the Twenties," *American Psychologist* 55, no. 5 (May 2000): 469–80.

37. Michael Kimmel, *Guyland: The Perilous World Where Boys Become Men* (New York: HarperCollins, 2008).

38. "Why We Say 'Boys Will Be Boys' but Not 'Girls Will Be Girls,' " Dictionary.com, June 23, 2019.

39. *Merriam-Webster*, s.v. "boys will be boys."

40. Bronwen Clune, "It's Time We Stopped Using the 'Boys Will Be Boys' Line," *Guardian*, April 1, 2014.

41. Kate Zernike, "On Kavanaugh, a Changed America Debates an Explosive Charge," *New York Times*, Sept. 18, 2018.

42. Megan Garber, "Brett Kavanaugh and the Revealing Logic of 'Boys Will Be Boys,' " *Atlantic*, Sept. 17, 2018.

43. Courtney Enlow, "The Truth About 'Boys Will Be Boys,' " *HuffPost*, Sept. 18, 2018.

44. Suzanne Moore, "What Brett Kavanaugh Teaches Us About Teenage Boys and Male Power," *Guardian,* Sept. 26, 2018.

45. Ibid.; Joanna Walters and Lauren Gambino, "Brett Kavanaugh: Third Woman Accuses Supreme Court Nominee of Sexual Misconduct," *Guardian,* Sept. 26, 2018.

46. Nsikan Akpan, "In Kavanaugh Debate 'Boys Will Be Boys' Is an Unscientific Excuse for Assault," *PBS NewsHour,* Sept. 20, 2018.

47. Enlow, "Truth About 'Boys Will Be Boys.' "

48. Zernike, "On Kavanaugh."

49. Akpan, "In Kavanaugh Debate"; Ashwini Tambe, "A History of Using the Phrase 'Boys Will Be Boys' to Dismiss Sexual Misconduct Allegations," *Business Insider,* Sept. 28, 2018.

50. Ellen Berry, "Georgia's Supreme Court Reverses 10-Year Sentence," *Los Angeles Times,* May 4, 2004; Rich Cimini, "Dixon Making Most of Second Chance," ESPN, Nov. 22, 2011.

51. Jelani Scott, "Years Later, HU's Dixon Still a Cautionary Tale," *Hampton Script,* Feb. 15, 2016.

52. Code of Georgia, Child Molestation, Aggravated Child Molestation § 16-6-4 (2010).

53. Scott, "Years Later, HU's Dixon."

54. Berry, "Georgia's Supreme Court Reverses 10-Year Sentence."

55. Scott, "Years Later, HU's Dixon."

56. Matt Pearce, " 'Boys Will Be Boys' No Excuse; Feds Target Montana Handling of Rapes," *Los Angeles Times,* Feb. 18, 2014 (discussing investigation that began in 2012 after allegations of rapes and gang rapes of University of Montana students, including some involving university football players, were not prosecuted and noting that only 16 percent of the cases that police officers referred to the prosecutor's office between 2008 and 2012 resulted in charges); Emily Yoffe, "The Question of Race in Campus Sexual-Assault Cases: Is the System Biased Against Men of Color?," *Atlantic,* Sept. 11, 2017.

57. Scott, "Years Later, HU's Dixon."

58. *Dixon v. State,* 596 S.E.2d 147, 148 (2004).

59. "Georgia Supreme Court Overturns Conviction in Martin Dixon Case," Children's Defense Fund, May 3, 2004. See also *Dixon,* 596 S.E.2d at 150.

60. Marty O'Brien, "HU Student Puts Past Behind Him," *Daily Press,* Aug. 12, 2005.

61. Liam Stack, "Light Sentence for Brock Turner in Stanford Case Draws Outrage," *New York Times,* June 6, 2016.

62. Elle Hunt, "'20 Minutes of Action': Father Defends Stanford Student Son Convicted of Sexual Assault," *Guardian,* June 5, 2016.

63. Stack, "Light Sentence for Brock Turner in Stanford Case Draws Outrage."

64. Elena Kadvany, "Brock Turner Sentencing Draws Strong Reaction Across Country," Palo Alto Online, June 6, 2016.

65. Hunt, "'20 Minutes of Action.'"

66. Luis Ferré-Sadurní, "Teenager Accused of Rape Deserves Leniency Because He's from a 'Good Family,' Judge Says," *New York Times,* July 2, 2019.

67. *In re G.M.C.,* No. A-0223-18T4, 2019 WL 2486221, at *1–14 (N.J. Super. Ct. App. Div. June 14, 2019).

68. Ibid.; Ferré-Sadurní, "Teenager Accused of Rape."

69. *In re G.M.C.*

70. Ferré-Sadurní, "Teenager Accused of Rape."

71. Maurice Chammah, "Could Removing Brock Turner's Judge Hurt Poor and Minority Defendants?," Marshall Project, June 16, 2016.

72. Ryan D. King and Brian D. Johnson, "A Punishing Look: Skin Tone and Afrocentric Features in the Halls of Justice," *American Journal of Sociology* 122 (July 2016).

73. U.S. Sentencing Commission, *Demographic Differences in Sentencing: Update to the 2012 Booker Report* (Washington, D.C.: U.S. Sentencing Commission, 2017), 6.

74. Michael Leiber and Jennifer Peck, "Race in Juvenile Justice and Sentencing Policy: An Overview of Research and Policy Recommendations," *Law and Inequality: A Journal of Theory and Practice* 31, no. 2 (2013): 358; Peter Lehmann, Ted Chiricos, and William Bales, "Sentencing Transferred Juveniles in the Adult Criminal Court: The Direct and Interactive Effects," *Youth Violence and Juvenile Justice* 15, no. 2 (2017): 172–90; Peter S. Lehmann, "Sentencing Other People's Children: The Intersection of Race, Gender, and Juvenility in the Adult Criminal Court," *Journal of Crime and Justice* 41, no. 5 (2018): 553–72.

75. George S. Bridges and Sara Steen, "Racial Disparities in Official Assessments of Juvenile Offenders: Attributional Stereotypes as Mediating Mechanisms," *American Sociological Review* 63, no. 4

(Aug. 1998): 554, 557–84; Sandra Graham and Brian S. Lowery, "Priming Unconscious Racial Stereotypes About Adolescent Offenders," *Law and Human Behavior* 28, no. 5 (2004): 483, 499.

76. Aneeta Rattan et al., "Race and the Fragility of the Legal Distinction Between Juveniles and Adults," *PLoS ONE* 7 (May 2012) (discussing the results of 735 white American study subjects who are overrepresented in jury pools, the legal field, and the judiciary).

77. Lisa Rosenthal and Marci Lobel, "Stereotypes of Black American Women Related to Sexuality and Motherhood," *Psychology Women Q* 40, no. 3 (Sept. 2016): 414–27.

78. Cheryl Nelson-Butler, "Blackness as Delinquency," *Washington University Law Review* 90 (2013): 1335, 1388–89.

79. Ibid., 1386.

80. Epstein, Blake, and González, *Girlhood Interrupted,* 8.

81. Monique Morris, *Pushout: The Criminalization of Black Girls in Schools* (New York: New Press, 2016), 120–32.

82. Tanvi Misra, "The Rising Criminalization of Black Girls," *Bloomberg CityLab,* March 22, 2018.

83. Nelson-Butler, "Blackness as Delinquency."

84. Steinberg, *Age of Opportunity,* 51.

85. Ibid., 52–56, 173–74.

86. Ibid., 57.

87. Ibid., 56–57.

88. Malika Saada Saar et al., *The Sexual Abuse to Prison Pipeline: The Girls' Story* (Washington, D.C.: Human Rights Project for Girls, Georgetown Law Center on Poverty and Inequality, Ms. Foundation for Women, 2015), 12.

89. Ibid., 9.

90. Ibid., 5.

91. Ibid., 14–15.

92. Erica L. Smith and Jessica Stroop, *Sexual Victimization Reported by Youth in Juvenile Facilities,* 2018 (Washington, D.C.: Bureau of Justice Statistics, Dec. 2019).

93. Saar et al., *Sexual Abuse to Prison Pipeline.*

94. "Fact Sheet: Incarcerated Women and Girls," Sentencing Project, June 2019.

95. Samantha Ehrmann et al., "Girls in the Juvenile Justice System," U.S. Department of Justice, April 2019.

5. POLICING IDENTITY: THE POLITICS OF
ADOLESCENCE AND BLACK IDENTITY DEVELOPMENT

1. Laurence Steinberg, *Adolescence* (New York: McGraw-Hill Education, 2017), 213–14.
2. Michael J. Nakkula and Eric Toshalis, *Understanding Youth: Adolescent Development for Educators* (Cambridge, Mass.: Harvard Education Press, 2006), 130; Steinberg, *Adolescence*, 209–12.
3. Steinberg, *Adolescence*, 209–10.
4. Nakkula and Toshalis, *Understanding Youth*, 119; Steinberg, *Adolescence*, 213–14.
5. Nakkula and Toshalis, *Understanding Youth*, 130.
6. Steinberg, *Adolescence*, 218; Devin English et al., "Daily Multidimensional Racial Discrimination Among Black U.S. American Adolescents," *Journal of Applied Development Psychology* 66 (Feb. 2020).
7. Nakkula and Toshalis, *Understanding Youth*, 132.
8. Maria Trent, Danielle G. Dooley, and Jacqueline Dougé, "The Impact of Racism on Child Health," *Pediatrics* 144, no. 2 (Aug. 2019).
9. Nakkula and Toshalis, *Understanding Youth*, 136–37.
10. Akilah Dulin-Keita et al., "The Defining Moment: Children's Conceptualization of Race and Experiences with Racial Discrimination," *Ethnic and Racial Studies* 34 (Jan. 2011): 662–82.
11. Nakkula and Toshalis, *Understanding Youth*, 123–24.
12. Steinberg, *Adolescence*, 230.
13. Nakkula and Toshalis, *Understanding Youth*, 120.
14. Gene H. Brody et al., "Perceived Discrimination and the Adjustment of African American Youths: A Five-Year Longitudinal Analysis with Contextual Moderation Effects," *Child Development* 77 (Oct. 2006): 1170–89.
15. English et al., "Daily Multidimensional Racial Discrimination."
16. Steinberg, *Adolescence*, 220–21.
17. Ibid., 212, 222.
18. Misa Kayama et al., "Use of Criminal Justice Language in Personal Narratives of Out-of-School Suspensions: Black Students, Caregivers, and Educators," *Children and Youth Services Review* 51 (April 2015): 26–35.
19. Laurence Steinberg, *Age of Opportunity: Lessons from the New Science of Adolescence* (Boston: Houghton Mifflin Harcourt, 2014), 21.

20. Nakkula and Toshalis, *Understanding Youth,* 125.

21. Steinberg, *Adolescence,* 226.

22. Ibid., 227.

23. Nakkula and Toshalis, *Understanding Youth,* 129.

24. Ibid., 121, 128.

25. Steinberg, *Adolescence,* 227.

26. Nakkula and Toshalis, *Understanding Youth,* 122–23.

27. Steinberg, *Adolescence,* 210.

28. Nakkula and Toshalis, *Understanding Youth,* 127–28.

29. Valerie N. Adams, "Messages in the Medium: The Relationships Among Black Media Images, Racial Identity, Body Image, and the Racial Socialization of Black Youth" (PhD diss., University of Pennsylvania, 2010).

30. Steinberg, *Adolescence,* 226, 230; Nakkula and Toshalis, *Understanding Youth,* 128–31.

31. Steinberg, *Adolescence,* 211.

32. Nakkula and Toshalis, *Understanding Youth,* 131 (citing Margaret Spencer and Sanford Dornbusch, "Challenges in Studying Minority Youth," in *At the Threshold: The Developing Adolescent,* ed. S. Shirley Feldman and Glen R. Elliott (Cambridge, Mass.: Harvard University Press, 1990), 123–46).

33. Steinberg, *Adolescence,* 217. See also Trent, "Impact of Racism on Child Health" (Prosocial identity is critical during adolescence, when young people must navigate the impact of social status and awareness of interracial discrimination).

34. Steinberg, *Adolescence,* 217.

35. Ibid., 219.

36. Riana E. Anderson and Howard C. Stevenson, "RECASTing Racial Stress and Trauma: Theorizing the Healing Potential of Racial Socialization in Families," *American Psychologist* 74 (Jan. 2019): 63–75; Nakkula and Toshalis, *Understanding Youth,* 124.

37. Steinberg, *Adolescence,* 227.

38. Diane Hughes and Lisa Chen, "When and What Parents Tell Children About Race: An Examination of Race-Related Socialization Among African American Families," *Applied Developmental Science* 1, no. 4 (1997): 200–214. See also Steinberg, *Adolescence,* 227.

39. Erin M. Kerrison, Jennifer Cobbina, and Kimberly Bender, "'Your Pants Won't Save You': Why Black Youth Challenge Race-Based

Police Surveillance and the Demands of Black Respectability Politics," *Race and Justice* 8 (Oct. 2017): 7, 26.

40. Ulysses Burley III, "A Letter to My Unborn [Black] Son," *Salt Collective*, Aug. 13, 2014.

41. Steinberg, *Adolescence*, 227.

42. Ibid., 230.

43. Ibid., 227.

44. Nakkula and Toshalis, *Understanding Youth*, 131.

45. Ibid., 141.

46. Steinberg, *Adolescence*, 227, 230.

47. Nakkula and Toshalis, *Understanding Youth*, 135.

48. Ibid., 119.

49. Shawn Ginwright and Taj James, "From Assets to Agents of Change: Social Justice, Organizing, and Youth Development," *New Directions for Youth Development* 96 (2002): 27–46.

50. Shawn Ginwright, "Hope, Healing, and Care: Pushing the Boundaries of Civic Engagement for African American Youth," *Liberal Education* 97 (Spring 2011): 38–40.

51. Ibid., 34–40.

52. Elizabeth C. Matto et al., eds., *Teaching Civic Engagement Across the Disciplines* (Washington, D.C.: American Political Science Association, 2017).

53. Michael Delli Carpini, "Civic Engagement," American Psychological Association, 2009.

54. Shirley Bryce, "St. Augustine Movement, 1963–1964," Civil Rights Movement Archive, 2004.

55. *In re Burrus*, 4 N.C. App. 523 (N.C. Ct. App. 1969).

56. Louis Casiano, "Florida Boy, 11, Arrested After Refusing to Recite 'Racist' Pledge of Allegiance: Report," Fox News, Feb. 17, 2019.

57. Nakkula and Toshalis, *Understanding Youth*, 141.

58. Donald Trump (@realDonaldTrump), "These THUGS are dishonoring the memory of George Floyd, and I won't let that happen," Twitter, May 29, 2020, 12:53 p.m.

59. Donald Trump (@realDonaldTrump), "The Governor of Michigan should give a little, and put out the fire. These are very good people, but they are angry. They want their lives back again, safely! See them, talk to them, make a deal," Twitter, May 1, 2020, 8:42 a.m.

60. "Coronavirus: Armed Protesters Enter Michigan Statehouse," BBC News, May 1, 2020.

61. Chris Sommerfeldt, "Ex-Chicago Top Cop Blames Black Lives Matter for Skyrocketing Murder Rates," *New York Daily News,* Jan. 3, 2017.

62. Jon Herskovitz, "Black Lives Matter Leaders Sued over Baton Rouge Police Shooting," Reuters, July 7, 2017; Derek Hawkins, "Black Lives Matter Cannot Be Sued by Louisiana Police Officer, Federal Judge Rules," *Washington Post,* Sept. 29, 2017.

63. Jana Winter and Sharon Weinberger, "The FBI's New U.S. Terrorist Threat: 'Black Identity Extremists,' " *Foreign Policy,* Oct. 6, 2017.

64. Lincoln A. Blades, "Why the FBI's 'Black Identity Extremist' Classification Is Dangerous," *Teen Vogue,* April 30, 2018.

65. FBI CounterTerrorism Division, *(U///FOUO) Black Identity Extremists Likely Motivated to Target Law Enforcement Officers,* Federal Bureau of Investigation, Aug. 3, 2017.

66. Sam Levin, "Black Activist Jailed for His Facebook Posts Speaks Out About Secret FBI Surveillance," *Guardian,* May 11, 2018.

### 6. COPS IN SCHOOL

1. Amir Whitaker et al., *Cops and No Counselors: How the Lack of School Mental Health Staff Is Harming Students* (New York: American Civil Liberties Union, 2019), 52 (noting that 77 percent of students in D.C. attend schools that are failing to meet the recommended counselor ratio requirement). In the 2019–20 school year, there were 347 contracted security guards and special police officers inside DCPS schools and 98 MPD SROs outside DCPS schools. *School Safety Report: School Year 2019–2020,* D.C. Metropolitan Police Department, 8–10, 13. There were only 235 budgeted social workers, 127 budgeted psychologists, and 125 budgeted counselors. *Responses to FY2019 Performance Oversight Questions,* D.C. Public Schools, 2020, Q16.

2. Code of the District of Columbia, Definitions § 5-132.01 (2020).

3. Megan French-Marcelin and Sarah Hinger, *Bullies in Blue: The Origins and Consequences of School Policing* (New York: American Civil Liberties Union, 2017), 11.

4. Advancement Project and the Alliance for Educational Justice, *We Came to Learn: A Call to Action for Police-Free Schools* (Washington, D.C.: Advancement Project, 2019); Chongmin Na and Denise Gottfredson, "Police Officers in Schools: Effects on School Crime and the Processing of Offending Behaviors," *Justice Quarterly* 30, no. 4 (2013): 619, 620.

5. Melissa Diliberti et al., *Crime, Violence, Discipline, and Safety in U.S. Public Schools: Findings from the School Survey on Crime and Safety, 2017–2018*, U.S. Department of Education, National Center for Education Statistics, July 2019, table 12.
6. Advancement Project, *We Came to Learn*, 26.
7. Lisa H. Thurau and Lany W. Or, *Two Billion Dollars Later: States Begin to Regulate School Resource Officers in the Nation's Schools* (Cambridge, Mass.: Strategies for Youth, 2019).
8. Advancement Project, *We Came to Learn*, 22, 47.
9. Holly Kurtz et al., *School Policing: Results of a National Survey of School Resource Officers* (Bethesda, Md.: Education Week Research Center, 2018).
10. Ben Brown, "Understanding and Assisting School Police Officers: A Conceptual and Methodological Comment," *Journal of Criminal Justice* 34, no. 6 (2006).
11. Los Angeles School Police Department, "About Us."
12. Kurtz et al., *School Policing*, 7.
13. Advancement Project, *We Came to Learn*, 24, 49; Niraj Chokshi, "School Police Across the Country Receive Excess Military Weapons and Gear," *Washington Post*, Sept. 16, 2014.
14. Advancement Project, *We Came to Learn*, 28.
15. National Association of School Resource Officers, "About NASRO."
16. Brown, "Understanding and Assessing School Police Officers," 592; John R. Coy, *IPS Police History*, Indianapolis Public Schools, 2004.
17. Reginald Stuart, "Indianapolis Black School Preserves 50-Year Identity," *New York Times*, Jan. 29, 1977.
18. French-Marcelin, *Bullies in Blue*.
19. Isabel Wilkerson, *The Warmth of Other Suns: The Epic Story of America's Great Migration* (New York: Vintage Books, 2010).
20. Kenneth A. Noble, "Policing the Hallways: The Origins of School-Police Partnerships in Twentieth Century American Urban Public Schools" (PhD diss., University of Florida, 2017) (citing Richard R. Glasson, "Workshop Studies Flint School Problems," *Flint Journal*, May 17, 1953).
21. Noble, "Policing the Hallways" (citing Tom V. Waldron, *Police-School Liaison Program: A Report*, Flint Police Department, Flint, Mich., 1962).

22. Noble, "Policing the Hallways" (citing "First National Police-School Workshop Set," *Flint Journal*, April 23, 1967).

23. Noble, "Policing the Hallways" (citing "Policemen from Varied Locales Discuss School Liaison Programs," *Flint Journal*, Sept. 26, 1968).

24. U.S. House of Representatives, "The Southern Manifesto of 1956," History Art & Archives.

25. Stanford University Martin Luther King Jr. Research and Education Institute, "White Citizens' Councils" (citing Joe Azbell, "Council Official Says Negro 'Bloc' No Longer Threat in Elections Here," *Montgomery Advertiser*, Jan. 26, 1956).

26. John F. Kennedy Presidential Library and Museum, "Civil Rights Movement"; Advancement Project, *We Came to Learn*, 17.

27. French-Marcelin, *Bullies in Blue*, 3 (citing Lawrence Fellows, "Jansen Opposes Police in Schools; Calls Proposal 'Unthinkable'—Leibowitz Backs Idea," *New York Times*, Nov. 27, 1957).

28. Advancement Project, *We Came to Learn*, 17; Jimmie L. Franklin, "African Americans," in *The Encyclopedia of Oklahoma History and Culture*.

29. Advancement Project, *We Came to Learn*, 20.

30. Noble, "Policing the Hallways" (citing "Rallies Student Power," *Cincinnati Enquirer*, Oct. 13, 1967).

31. Elizabeth Hinton, *From the War on Poverty to the War on Crime: The Making of Mass Incarceration in America* (Cambridge, Mass.: Harvard University Press, 2016), 92.

32. Lawrence Feinberg, "Board Acts to Keep Police in Schools," *Washington Post*, Feb. 15, 1970.

33. Julia Craven, "Baltimore School Cops' Abuse of Kids Is Rooted in City's Racist History," *HuffPost*, Aug. 16, 2016.

34. Lynette Barnes, *Policing the Schools: An Evaluation of the North Carolina School Resource Officer Program* (New Brunswick, N.J.: Rutgers University Press, 2008).

35. Nicholas deB. Katzenbach, foreword to *The Challenge of Crime in a Free Society: A Report by the President's Commission on Law Enforcement and Administration of Justice*, by Nicholas deB. Katzenbach et al. (Washington, D.C.: U.S. Government Printing Office, 1967).

36. Katzenbach et al., *Challenge of Crime in a Free Society*, 37, 57.

37. Ibid., 56–66, 59 (noting that "delinquency in the slums . . . is a dis-

proportionately high percentage of all delinquency and includes a disproportionately high number of dangerous acts"). See examples on ibid., 57, 59–60, 70, 74.

38. Ibid., 37–38.

39. Advancement Project, *We Came to Learn,* 20.

40. "New Violence Erupts in San Francisco," *Washington Post,* Sept. 29, 1966.

41. "Big Cities Never Free of Violence," *Los Angeles Times,* Nov. 26, 1967.

42. Noble, "Policing the Hallways" (citing U.S. Department of Justice, Office of Law Enforcement Assistance, "Grant #52: Police-Teacher Curriculum Units for Junior High and Police Academy Use" (Washington, D.C., 1966)).

43. *School Resource Program–Tucson, Arizona,* U.S. Department of Justice, Office of Law Enforcement Assistance, July 1996; *The Cincinnati Police-Juvenile Attitude Project: A Demonstration in Police-Teacher Curriculum Development to Improve Police-Juvenile Relations* ([Washington, D.C.]: U.S. Department of Justice, Office of Law Enforcement Assistance, 1968).

44. Noble, "Policing the Hallways" (citing Tom V. Waldron, *Police-School Liaison Program: A Report,* Flint Police Department, Flint, Mich., 1971).

45. Ibid., 16.

46. "Boston Stations Police in Schools to Prevent Walkouts," *Sun,* Oct. 23, 1979.

47. Barry Feld, "Race, Politics, and Juvenile Justice: The Warren Court and the Conservative 'Backlash,'" *Minnesota Law Review* 87 (2003): 1447, 1507, 1523.

48. U.S. Code, Gun-Free Schools Act of 1994 § 7151 (1994); Violent Crime Control and Law Enforcement Act (H.R. 3355), 1994; U.S. Department of Justice, Office of Community Oriented Policing Services, "About."

49. Randal C. Archibold, "New Era as Police Prepare to Run School Safety," *New York Times,* Sept. 16, 1998.

50. "Columbine Shooting," History, March 30, 2020, history.com.

51. U.S. News Library Staff, "Timeline of School Shootings," *U.S. News & World Report,* Feb. 15, 2008.

52. School Resource Officers Partnership Grant Act, Pub. Law No. 105-302, 112 Stat. 2841 (1998).

53. Statement of President William J. Clinton, "Actions to Help Keep Our Schools Safe," April 23, 1999.
54. Rita Varano and Veh Bezdikian, *Addressing School-Related Crime and Disorder,* U.S. Department of Justice, Office of Community Oriented Policing, Sept. 2001.
55. Brad Myrstol, "Public Perceptions of School Resource Officer (SRO) Programs," *Western Criminology Review* 12, no. 3 (2011).
56. French-Marcelin, *Bullies in Blue.*
57. "Police in Schools: Arresting Developments," *Economist,* Jan. 9, 2016; Nathan James and Gail McCallion, *School Resource Officers: Law Enforcement Officers in Schools,* Congressional Research Service Report for Congress, June 26, 2013; Brittany Wallman, "The Parkland Shooting One Year Later," *South Florida Sun Sentinel,* Feb. 11, 2019.
58. Kristen Harper and Deborah Temkin, "Compared to Majority White Schools, Majority Black Schools Are More Likely to Have Security Staff," *Child Trends Blog,* April 26, 2018; Aaron Kupchik and Geoff Ward, "Race, Poverty, and Exclusionary School Security: An Empirical Analysis of U.S. Elementary, Middle, and High Schools," *Youth Violence and Juvenile Justice* 12 (2014): 337–38.
59. Whitaker et al., *Cops and No Counselors,* 24; U.S. Department of Education, "2015–16 Civil Rights Data Collection: School Climate and Safety," Office for Civil Rights, April 2018.
60. U.S. Department of Education, "2015–16 Civil Rights Data Collection."
61. Rebecca Epstein et al., *Data Snapshot: 2017–2018 National Data on School Discipline by Race and Gender* (Washington, D.C.: Georgetown Law Center on Poverty and Inequality's Initiative on Gender Justice & Opportunity and the RISE Research at New York University, 2020) (analyzing data from U.S. Department of Education, "2017–18 Civil Rights Data Collection," Office for Civil Rights (October 2020)).
62. Lloyd Johnston et al., *Monitoring the Future: National Survey Results on Drug Use, 1975–2018,* Institute for Social Research, University of Michigan, Jan. 2019.
63. Advancement Project, *We Came to Learn,* 21.
64. Noble, "Policing the Hallways" (citing Craig D. Carter, "Lawmen's Role in Schools Debated: Police First? Counselor First?," *Flint Journal,* June 25, 1972).

65. Waldron, *Police-School Liaison Program* (1962), 1.
66. Noble, "Policing the Hallways," 135 (citing Carter, "Lawmen's Role in Schools Debated").
67. Strategies for Youth, *Two Billion Dollars Later,* 7.
68. Baltimore City Public Schools, "School Police."
69. Antwan Wilson and Jeff Godown, *School Security Officer Policy and Procedures Manual* (Oakland: Oakland School District, June 29, 2016).
70. Kurtz et al., *School Policing,* 14.
71. Strategies for Youth, *If Not Now, When?: A Survey of Juvenile Justice Training in America's Police Academies* (Cambridge, Mass.: Strategies for Youth, 2013).
72. Kurtz et al., *School Policing,* 14.
73. Autry Phillips, "Police to Get Rid of 'Booking Rooms' in Illinois Schools," CBS Chicago, Sept. 28, 2017.
74. Whitaker et al., *Cops and No Counselors,* 23.
75. Shabnam Javdani, "Policing Education: An Empirical Review of the Challenges and Impact of the Work of School Police Officers," *American Journal of Community Psychology* 63 (2019): 260 (noting that the increasing presence of school police officers creates "a climate in which teachers and staff increasingly call on SPOs for minor disciplinary issues and classroom management in general"). In one study, 76 percent of principals reported using SROs to address student discipline issues. Jennifer Counts et al., "School Resource Officers in Public Schools: A National Review," *Education and Treatment of Children* 41 (2018): 408 (citing Na and Gottfredson, "Police Officers in Schools").
76. Amanda Ripley, "How America Outlawed Adolescence," *Atlantic,* Nov. 2016.
77. Craven, "Baltimore School."
78. Karen Salmon et al., *Maryland Public Schools Arrest Data: School Year 2017–2018,* Maryland State Department of Education, 2019.
79. South Carolina Code of Laws, Offenses Against Public Policy § 16-17-420 (2010 Act No. 273, § 12, eff. June 2, 2010) (amended by 2018 Act No. 182 (S.131)); Harriet McLeod, "'Disturbing Schools' Law Criticized After South Carolina Student's Arrest," Reuters, Oct. 30, 2015; Ripley, "How America Outlawed Adolescence."
80. South Carolina Department of Juvenile Justice, *Annual Statisti-*

*cal Report 2015–2016,* South Carolina Department of Juvenile Justice, June 2017.

81. Sarah Hinger, "South Carolina Legislature Repeals Racist 'Disturbing School' Law for Students," National Juvenile Justice Network, June 28, 2018.

82. "Data Analysis: Most Commonly Charged Offenses by McKinney Police Department's School Resource Officers, Disaggregated by Student Race, January 2012–June 2015," Texas Appleseed, 2015.

83. Whitaker et al., *Cops and No Counselors,* 23; Florida Department of Juvenile Justice, "Delinquency in Florida's Schools, FY 2014–15 Through FY 2018–19," 2019.

84. Florida Department of Juvenile Justice, "Delinquency in Florida's Schools, FY 2014–15 Through FY 2018–19."

85. Whitaker et al., *Cops and No Counselors,* 6 (citing Shannon Stagman and Janice L. Cooper, *Children's Mental Health: What Every Policymaker Should Know,* National Center for Children in Poverty, April 2010).

86. Laurence Steinberg, *Age of Opportunity: Lessons from the New Science of Adolescence* (Boston: Houghton Mifflin Harcourt, 2014), 37–38; Whitaker et al., *Cops and No Counselors,* 4.

87. Whitaker et al., *Cops and No Counselors,* 6 (citing Susanna Schrobsdorff, "There's a Startling Increase in Major Depression Among Teens in the U.S.," *Time,* Nov. 15, 2016); National Association of School Psychologists, "Brief Facts and Tips" (2015).

88. Whitaker et al., *Cops and No Counselors,* 6.

89. Ibid., 4.

90. Harper and Temkin, "Compared to Majority White Schools, Majority Black Schools Are More Likely to Have Security Staff."

91. Whitaker et al., *Cops and No Counselors,* 24; Amanda Merkwae, "Schooling the Police: Race, Disability, and the Conduct of School Resource Officers," *Michigan Journal of Race and Law* 21 (2015).

92. Whitaker et al., *Cops and No Counselors,* 6–7.

93. Emily Shapiro, "20 Years After Columbine, What's Changed—and What Hasn't—for School Shootings in America," ABC News, April 20, 2019.

94. Nicole Chavez, "This Is What Scot Peterson Did During the Parkland School Shooting," CNN, June 4, 2019.

95. Advancement Project, *We Came to Learn*, 54.

96. Ibid., 31.

97. Misa Kayama et al., "Use of Criminal Justice Language in Personal Narratives of Out-of-School Suspensions: Black Students, Caregivers, and Educators," *Children and Youth Services Review* 51 (2015): 26–35.

98. Jacinta M. Gau and Rod K. Brunson, "Procedural Injustice, Lost Legitimacy, and Self-Help: Young Males' Adaptations to Perceived Unfairness in Urban Police Tactics," *Journal of Contemporary Criminal Justice* 31, no. 2 (2015).

99. Brian Saady, "Throwing Children Away: The School-to-Prison Pipeline," Justice Policy Institute, Aug. 2018.

100. Steinberg, *Age of Opportunity*, 61–62.

101. Susanne Vogel and Lars Schwabe, "Learning and Memory Under Stress: Implications for the Classroom," *NPJ Science of Learning,* June 29, 2016.

102. Joscha Legewie and Jeffrey Fagan, "Aggressive Policing and the Educational Performance of Minority Youth," *American Sociological Review* 84 (2019).

103. Emily K. Weisburst, "Patrolling Public Schools: The Impact of Funding for School Police on Student Discipline and Long-Term Education Outcomes," *Journal of Policy Analysis and Management* 38 (Oct. 2018); Denise C. Gottfredson et al., "Effects of School Resource Officers on School Crime and Responses to School Crime," *Criminology and Public Policy* 19 (2020): 930.

104. Daniel J. Losen and Paul Martinez, *Is California Doing Enough to Close the School Discipline Gap?* (Los Angeles: Civil Rights Project, 2020); Daniel J. Losen and Paul Martinez, *Lost Opportunities: How Disparate School Discipline Continues to Drive Differences in the Opportunity to Learn* (Los Angeles: Civil Rights Project, 2020), 33–34; Benjamin W. Fisher and Emily A. Hennessy, "School Resource Officers and Exclusionary Discipline in U.S. High Schools: A Systematic Review and Meta-analysis," *Adolescent Research Review* 1, no. 3 (Aug. 2016); Weisburst, "Patrolling Public Schools."

105. Advancement Project, *We Came to Learn*, 71–74.

106. Ibid., 49.

107. Ibid., 31, 55, 77.

108. Ibid., 31, 32, 71–74.

109. Meredith Deliso, "Florida Teen Body-Slammed by School Resource

Officer 'Traumatized,' Family Says," ABC7NY.com, January 31, 2021.

110. Artemis Moshtaghian, "Dallas School Police Use Handcuffs to Restrain 7-Year-Old Boy," CNN, May 19, 2017.

111. Amanda Merkwae, "Schooling the Police: Race, Disability, and the Conduct of School Resource Officers," *Michigan Journal of Race and Law* 21 (2015): 147–81 (citing Letter from Sara H. Godchaux & Eden B. Heilman, S. Poverty Law Center, to Office for Civil Rights, U.S. Dep't of Educ. 15 (May 7, 2015)).

112. Civil Rights Division, *Investigation of the Ferguson Police Department*, U.S. Department of Justice, March 2015.

113. Saliqa Khan, "School Police Officer Pleads Guilty to Assault of 3 Students," WBAL-TV, Sept. 25, 2015.

114. Advancement Project, *We Came to Learn*, 50.

115. Ibid., 51; U.S. Constitution, Amend. 14.

116. Advancement Project, *We Came to Learn*, 49–50; Victor Fiorillo, "Video Captures Violent Encounter Between School Cop and Benjamin Franklin Senior," *Philadelphia Magazine*, May 10, 2016; Julia Craven, "The Girl Who Was Assaulted by a Cop on Camera at Spring Valley High Is Now Facing Charges," *HuffPost*, Dec. 17, 2015.

117. Philadelphia Student Union, "Assault at Ben Franklin," May 12, 2016; Fiorillo, "Video Captures Violent Encounter"; Advancement Project, *We Came to Learn*, 41, 49–50.

118. "Attorney for Woodland Hills Principal Speaks Out as Protestors Call for His Firing," CBS Pittsburgh KDKA 2, Dec. 6, 2016.

119. Advancement Project, *We Came to Learn*, 31 (citing Randall R. Beger, "The Worst of Both Worlds," *Criminal Justice Review* 28 (2003): 340; Kathleen Nolan, *Police in the Hallways: Discipline in an Urban High School* (Minneapolis: University of Minnesota Press, 2011)).

120. Myrstol, "Public Perceptions," 21; Nicole Bracy, "Student Perceptions of High-Security School Environments," *Youth and Society* 43 (2011); Lawrence Travis and Julie K. Coon, *The Role of Law Enforcement in Public School Safety: A National Survey* (Washington, D.C.: National Institute of Justice, 2005).

121. Advancement Project, *We Came to Learn*, 31 (citing Matthew J. Mayer and Peter E. Leone, "A Structural Analysis of School Violence and Disruption: Implications for Creating Safer Schools," *Education and Treatment of Children* 22 (Aug. 1999): 352).

122. Advancement Project, *We Came to Learn,* 42; Emma Eisenberg, "The Voice They Were Born to Use," *Philadelphia Citizen,* June 13, 2016.

123. Arrick Jackson, "Police-School Resource Officers' and Students' Perception of the Police and Offending," *Policing* 25 (2002): 633.

124. Noble, "Policing the Hallways."

125. Advancement Project, *We Came to Learn,* 42; Jackson, "Police-School Resource Officers," 637, 645–46; Myrstol, "Public Perceptions," 35.

126. Steinberg, *Age of Opportunity,* 44.

127. Ibid., 61–62.

128. Ibid., 30–31.

129. Laurence Steinberg, Elizabeth Cauffman, and Kathryn C. Monahan, "Psychosocial Maturity and Desistance from Crime in a Sample of Serious Juvenile Offenders," *Juvenile Justice Bulletin,* March 2015; Edward P. Mulvey et al., "Trajectories of Desistance and Continuity in Antisocial Behavior Following Court Adjudication Among Serious Adolescent Offenders," *Development and Psychopathology* 22, no. 2 (2010): 453–75.

## 7. CONTEMPT OF COP

1. *Elonis v. United States,* 575 U.S. (2015) (holding that the prosecution must show the defendant had subjective intent to threaten).

2. *City of Houston v. Hill,* 482 U.S. 451, 462–63 (1987); *Hill v. City of Houston,* 789 F.2d 1103 (5th Cir. 1986) (stating "They are expected to be disciplined and not so thin-skinned as to arrest bystanders for remarks that pose no danger to them or the execution of their duties.").

3. Christy E. Lopez, "Disorderly (Mis)Conduct: The Problem with 'Contempt of Cop' Arrests," *American Constitution Society* (2010): 4.

4. Deborah Sontag and Dan Berry, "Challenge to Authority: A Special Report: Disrespect as a Catalyst for Brutality," *New York Times,* Nov. 19, 1997.

5. Scott Holmes, "Resisting Arrest and Racism—the Crime of 'Disrespect,'" *UMKC Law Review* 85 (2017): 625.

6. Ibid., 632.

7. Lopez, "Disorderly (Mis)Conduct," 5–6.

8. Ibid., 7.

9. Sari Horwitz, "When Officers Go Too Far Confrontations Lead

to Beatings, Complaints, Lawsuits," *Washington Post,* Nov. 19, 1998.

10. Christina Davidson and Patrick Madden, "In DC, Wiggling While Handcuffed Counts as Assaulting an Officer," *Reveal News,* May 2015.

11. Ibid.

12. Code of the District of Columbia, Resisting Arrest § 22: 405.01(b) (2020).

13. Metropolitan Police Department, *Metropolitan Police Department: 2018 Annual Report* (Washington, D.C.: Government of the District of Columbia, 2018), 27.

14. American Civil Liberties Union, "ACLU Challenges Another 'Contempt of Cop' False Arrest: Transit Police at Fault, Suit Says, in 2011 U Street Incident," *ACLU DC News Update,* Jan. 26, 2012; American Civil Liberties Union, "Jury Awards $97,500 Against D.C. Police in 'Contempt of Cop' Arrests," *ACLU DC News Update,* March 26, 2011.

15. Holmes, "Resisting Arrest and Racism," 625.

16. Strategies for Youth, *If Not Now, When?: A Survey of Juvenile Justice Training in America's Police Academies* (Cambridge, Mass.: Strategies for Youth, 2013) (finding that police academies nationwide spend less than 1 percent of total training hours on juvenile justice topics); Holly Kurtz et al., *School Policing: Results of a National Survey of School Resource Officers* (Bethesda, Md.: Education Week Research Center, 2018) (finding that many school resource officers had not received training on the teen brain, childhood trauma, or youth with special needs).

17. Michael Cunningham, Dena P. Swanson, and Demarquis M. Hayes, "School- and Community-Based Associations to Hypermasculine Attitudes in African American Adolescent Males," *American Journal of Orthopsychiatry* 83 (2013): 244; Charles S. Corprew III and Michael Cunningham, "Educating Tomorrow's Men: Perceived School Support, Negative Youth Experiences, and Bravado Attitudes in African American Adolescent Males," *Education and Urban Society* 44, no. 5 (2011): 571–89; Martha-Grace Duncan, "'So Young and So Untender': Remorseless Children and the Expectations of the Law," *Columbia Law Review* 102, no. 6 (2005): 1469, 1493, 1500.

18. Jennifer L. Woolard, Samantha Harvell, and Sandra Graham, "Anticipatory Injustice Among Adolescents: Age and Racial/Eth-

nic Differences in Perceived Unfairness of the Justice System," *Behavioral Sciences and the Law* 26, no. 2 (2008): 207, 209; Norman J. Finkel, "But It's Not Fair! Commonsense Notions of Unfairness," *Psychology, Public Policy, and Law* 6, no. 4 (2000): 898, 903–4 (finding children and teens twice as concerned with procedural justice as college-age or older adults).

19. Phillip Atiba Goff and Hilary Rau, "Predicting Bad Policing: Theorizing Burdensome and Racially Disparate Policing Through the Lenses of Social Psychology and Routine Activities," *The Annals of the American Academy of Political Science* 687(1) (2020): 67–88, 74–76 (discussing importance of masculinity in police culture and the impact of ego threat and masculinity on aggressive and abusive behavior).

20. Cunningham, Swanson, and Hayes, "School- and Community-Based Associations," 244–51.

21. Dustin Albert and Laurence Steinberg, "Judgment and Decision Making in Adolescence," *Journal of Research on Adolescence* 21, no. 1 (2011): 216–20; Laurence Steinberg et al., "Are Adolescents Less Mature Than Adults? Minors' Access to Abortion, the Juvenile Death Penalty, and the Alleged APA 'Flip-Flop,'" *American Psychologist* 64, no. 7 (2009): 586.

22. M. Dreyfuss et al., "Teens Impulsively React Rather Than Retreat from Threat," *Developmental Neuroscience* 36, no. 3–4 (2014): 220–27.

23. Dylan B. Jackson, Alexander Testa, and Michael G. Vaughn, "Low Self-Control and the Adolescent Police Stop: Intrusiveness, Emotional Response, and Psychological Well-Being," *Journal of Criminal Justice* 66 (2020).

24. Office of Juvenile Justice and Delinquency Prevention, *Statistical Briefing Book: Characteristics of Delinquency Cases Handled by Juvenile Courts, 2018*, U.S. Department of Justice, March 31, 2020.

25. Office of Juvenile Justice and Delinquency Prevention, *Statistical Briefing Book: Juvenile Arrest Rates by Offense and Race, 2018*, U.S. Department of Justice, Oct. 31, 2019.

26. Office of Juvenile Justice and Delinquency Prevention, *Statistical Briefing Book: Characteristics of Delinquency Cases Handled by Juvenile Courts, 2018*.

27. Charles Puzzanchera, "Juvenile Arrests, 2018," *Juvenile Justice Statistics National Report Series Bulletin*, June 2020, 8.

28. Office of Juvenile Justice and Delinquency Prevention, *Statistical Briefing Book: Characteristics of Delinquency Cases Handled by Juvenile Courts, 2018.*

29. "Tremaine McMillian, 14-Year-Old with Puppy, Choked by Miami-Dade Police over 'Dehumanizing Stares,' " *HuffPost,* May 30, 2013.

30. "Teen Who Was Brutally Beaten and Arrested by 9 Cops for Jay-walking Speaks Out," *Counter Current News,* Sept. 21, 2015.

31. Bill Hutchinson, "Black Youth Have Most Complaints Against NYC Police, Including 8-Year-Old Arrested for Playing with Sticks," ABC News, June 8, 2020.

32. Ellie Hall, "Florida Police Officers Who Slammed a 15 Year-Old Black Boy's Head to the Ground in Viral Arrest Video Said He Was Acting 'Aggressive,' " *BuzzFeed News,* April 22, 2019.

33. Tim Cushing, "Judge Calls Out Portland Police for Bogus 'Contempt of Cop' Arrest/Beating," *Tech Dirt,* March 27, 2015.

34. Ibid.; Aimee Green, "Judge Rules Portland Teen Not Guilty of Resisting Arrest, Has Stern Words for Police," *Oregonian/OregonLive,* Jan. 9, 2019; Aimee Green, "Read for Yourself: Judge's Ruling That Portland Police Used Excessive Force, Offered Contradictory Testimony," *Oregonian/OregonLive,* Jan. 9, 2019.

35. Cushing, "Judge Calls Out Portland Police."

36. Green, "Read for Yourself"; Circuit Court Multnomah County, Oregon, Findings and Order, *In re Gurule, Thai* (Case No. 14JU02757, Petition No.140916138) (2015).

37. Maxine Bernstein, "Portland Police Union President Decries Judge's Findings in Case of 16-Year-Old Boy's Arrest," *Oregonian/OregonLive,* Jan. 9, 2019.

38. Margaret Sessa-Hawkins, "Video Shows California Police Striking Teenager After Allegedly Jaywalking," *PBS NewsHour,* Sept. 18, 2015.

39. Peter D'Oench, "Teen Says Police Overreacted to Incident," CBS Miami, May 28, 2013; "Tremaine McMillian, 14-Year-Old with Puppy."

40. Rick Trinkner and Ellen S. Cohen, "Putting the 'Social' Back in Legal Socialization: Procedural Justice, Legitimacy, and Cynicism in Legal and Nonlegal Authorities," *Law and Human Behavior* 38, no. 6 (2014): 602.

41. Amanda Geller and Jeffrey Fagan, "Police Contact and the Legal Socialization of Urban Teens," *RSF: The Russell Sage Foundation Journal of the Social Sciences* 5, no. 1 (Feb. 2019): 26–49;

Trinkner and Cohen, "Putting the 'Social' Back in Legal Socialization," 602; Jeffrey Fagan and Tom R. Tyler, "Legal Socialization of Children and Adolescents," *Social Justice Research* 18, no. 3 (Sept. 2005): 222.

42. Trinkner and Cohen, "Putting the 'Social' Back in Legal Socialization," 603–8; Erika K. Penner et al., "Procedural Justice Versus Risk Factors for Offending: Predicting Recidivism in Youth," *Law and Human Behavior* 38, no. 3 (2014): 225–34; Geller and Fagan, "Police Contact," 27; Fagan and Tyler, "Legal Socialization of Children," 221.

43. Fagan and Tyler, "Legal Socialization of Children," 222.

44. Lyn Hinds, "Building Police-Youth Relationships: The Importance of Procedural Justice," *Youth Justice* 7, no. 3 (Nov. 2007): 196; Geller and Fagan, "Police Contact," 27; Fagan and Tyler, "Legal Socialization of Children," 218–19.

45. Ronald Weitzer and Rod K. Brunson, "Strategic Responses to the Police Among Inner-City Youth," *Sociological Quarterly* 50 (April 2009): 235, 250.

46. Rod K. Brunson and Jody Miller, "Gender, Race, and Urban Policing: The Experience of African American Youths," *Gender and Society* 20, no. 4 (Aug. 2006): 543.

47. Rod K. Brunson, "Police Don't Like Black People: African-American Young Men's Accumulated Police Experiences," *Criminology and Public Policy* 6, no. 1 (Feb. 2007): 74; Weitzer and Brunson, "Strategic Responses to the Police," 241.

48. Weitzer and Brunson, "Strategic Responses to the Police," 241.

49. Brunson and Miller, "Gender, Race, and Urban Policing," 539.

50. Weitzer and Brunson, "Strategic Responses to the Police," 240; Brunson and Miller, "Gender, Race, and Urban Policing," 539.

51. Brunson, "Police Don't Like Black People," 81, 85; Brunson and Miller, "Gender, Race, and Urban Policing," 540.

52. Jacinta M. Gau and Rod K. Brunson, "Procedural Injustice, Lost Legitimacy, and Self-Help: Young Males' Adaptations to Perceived Unfairness in Urban Policing Tactics," *Journal of Contemporary Criminal Justice* 31, no. 2 (2015): 141.

53. Ibid., 142.

54. Brunson, "Police Don't Like Black People," 96.

55. Ibid., 81; Brunson and Miller, "Gender, Race, and Urban Policing," 534.

56. Terrance J. Taylor et al., "Coppin' an Attitude: Attitudinal Dif-

ferences Among Juveniles Toward Police," *Journal of Criminal Justice* 29, no. 4 (2001): 298, 300, 302; Brunson, "Police Don't Like Black People," 74; Yolander G. Hurst, James Frank, and Sandra Lee Browning, "The Attitudes of Juveniles Toward the Police: A Comparison of Black and White Youth," *Policing: An International Journal of Police Strategies and Management* 23 (2000): 44–46.

57. Weitzer and Brunson, "Strategic Responses to the Police," 252.

58. Hurst, Frank, and Browning, "Attitudes of Juveniles," 41.

59. Samantha A. Goodrich, Stephen A. Anderson, and Valerie LaMotte, "Evaluation of a Program Designed to Promote Positive Police and Youth Interactions," *OJJDP Journal of Juvenile Justice* (Jan. 2014): 87.

60. Weitzer and Brunson, "Strategic Responses to the Police," 246, 248.

61. Ibid., 244.

62. Ibid., 241–43.

63. Susan A. Bandes et al., "The Mismeasure of Terry Stops: Assessing the Psychological and Emotional Harms of Stop and Frisk to Individuals and Communities," *Behavioral Sciences & the Law* 37 no. 2 (2019) (describing the robust social science literature showing that stop and frisk causes a wide range of emotional and psychological harms that likely interfere with the ability of law enforcement to prevent and investigate crime); Paul Butler, "Racially Biased Jury Nullification: Black Power in the Criminal Justice System," *Yale Law Journal* 105 (1995): 677–725.

64. *L.A.T. v. State,* 650 So.2d 214 (Fla. Dist. Ct. App. 1995) ("You fucking cops, what the hell do you think you're doing? You are full of bull shit."); *In re Welfare of S.L.J.,* 263 N.W.2d 412 (Minn. 1978) ("fuck you pigs"); *C.J.R. v. State,* 429 So.2d 753 (Fla. Dist. Ct. App. 1983) ("motherfucker"); *D.C.E. v. State,* 381 So.2d 1097 (Fla. Dist. Ct. App. 1979) ("fucking pigs"); *L.J.M. v. State,* 541 So.2d 1321 (Fla. Dist. Ct. App. 1989) ("you pussy-assed mother fucker"); *State v. John W.,* 418 A.2d 1097 (Me. 1980) ("you fuckin' kangaroo"); *K.S. v. State,* 697 So.2d 1275 (Fla. Dist. Ct. App. 1997) ("Fuck this . . . I didn't do anything.").

65. Gau and Brunson, "Procedural Injustice," 144; Arrick Jackson, "Police-School Resource Officers' and Students' Perception of the Police and Offending," *Policing: An International Journal of Police Strategies and Management* 25, no. 3 (2002): 638–39.

66. Goodrich, Anderson, and LaMotte, "Evaluation of a Program," 87.

67. Brunson and Miller, "Gender, Race, and Urban Policing," 532, 534. See also Andrew R. Todd, Kelsey Thiem, and Rebecca Neel, "Does Seeing Faces of Young Black Boys Facilitate the Identification of Threatening Stimuli?," *Psychological Science* 27 (2016): 384; Jason Okonofua and Jennifer Eberhardt, "Two Strikes: Race and the Disciplining of Young Students," *Psychological Science* 26, no. 5 (2015); Phillip Atiba Goff et al., "The Essence of Innocence: Consequences of Dehumanizing Black Children," *Journal of Personality and Social Psychology* 106 (Feb. 2014): 526; Aneeta Rattan et al., "Race and the Fragility of the Legal Distinction Between Juveniles and Adults," *PLoS ONE* 7, no. 5 (2012).

68. Ashley Fantz, Steve Almasy, and Catherine E. Shoiceht, "Tamir Rice Shooting: No Charges for Officers," CNN, Dec. 28, 2015.

69. Nas, "Cops Shot the Kid: Lyrics," genius.com.

70. *Terry v. Ohio,* 392 U.S. 1, 21 (1968).

71. Bryn Stole and Grace Toohey, "The City Where Police Unleash Dogs on Black Teens," The Marshall Project, February 12, 2021.

72. Tracey Maclin, "Decline of the Right of Locomotion: The Fourth Amendment on the Streets," *Cornell Law Review* 75 (1990): 1258, 1301.

73. Eric Flack and Jordan Fischer, "DC Police Search and Frisk Black People 6 Times More Often During Stops, Data Shows," WUSA9, June 15, 2020; Metropolitan Police Department, *Stop Data Report* (Washington, D.C.: Government of the District of Columbia, 2020).

74. Bob Herbert, "Jim Crow Policing," *New York Times,* Feb. 1, 2010.

75. *Illinois v. Wardlow,* 528 U.S. 119 (2000).

76. Cynthia J. Najdowski, Bette L. Bottoms, and Phillip Atiba Goff, "Stereotype Threat and Racial Differences in Citizens' Experiences of Police Encounters," *Law and Human Behavior* 39, no. 5 (2015): 463–77.

77. Cynthia J. Najdowski, "Stereotype Threat in Criminal Interrogations: Why Innocent Black Suspects Are at Risk for Confessing Falsely," *Psychology, Public Policy, and Law* 17, no. 4 (2011): 562–91; Kimberly Barsamian Kahn, Jean M. McMahon, and Greg Stewart, "Misinterpreting Danger? Stereotype Threat, Pre-attack Indicators, and Police-Citizen Interactions," *Journal of Police and Criminal Psychology* 33 (2018): 45–54; Brenda Major and

Laurie T. O'Brien, "The Social Psychology of Stigma," *Annual Review of Psychology* 56 (2005): 393–421.

78. Najdowski, "Stereotype Threat in Criminal Interrogations."

79. Ibid.

80. Kahn, McMahon, and Stewart, "Misinterpreting Danger?"; Najdowski, "Stereotype Threat in Criminal Interrogations"; Najdowski, Bottoms, and Goff, "Stereotype Threat and Racial Differences," 463–77.

81. Najdowski, "Stereotype Threat in Criminal Interrogations" (citing Toni Schmader, Michael Johns, and Chad Forbes, "An Integrated Process Model of Stereotype Threat Effects on Performance," *Psychological Review* 115 (Oct. 2008): 336–35).

82. Kahn, McMahon, and Stewart, "Misinterpreting Danger?"

83. Dr. Shameka Stanford, interview by author, Washington, D.C., May 21, 2019.

84. Adrienne Hurst, "Black, Autistic, and Killed by Police," *Chicago Reader,* Dec. 17, 2015.

85. Ibid.

86. Ibid.

87. Michele Lavigne and Gregory J. Van Rybroek, "Breakdown in the Language Zone: The Prevalence of Language Impairments Among Juvenile and Adult Offenders and Why It Matters," *UC Davis Journal of Juvenile Law and Policy* 15 (2011): 37.

88. "Supporting Youth with Disabilities in Juvenile Corrections," Office of Special Education and Rehabilitative Services, U.S. Department of Education, May 2017. See also Lavigne and Van Rybroek, "Breakdown in the Language Zone," 37.

89. Centers for Disease Control and Prevention, "Autism Spectrum Disorder (ASD): Autism Data Visualization Tool," March 25, 2020.

90. Julianna Rava et al., "The Prevalence and Correlates of Involvement in the Criminal Justice System Among Youth on the Autism Spectrum," *Journal of Autism and Developmental Disorders* 47 (Feb. 2017): 340–46.

91. Centers for Disease Control and Prevention, "Autism Spectrum Disorder."

92. Najdowski, Bottoms, and Goff, "Stereotype Threat and Racial Differences." See also Todd, Thiem, and Neel, "Does Seeing Faces of Young Black Boys," 384; Okonofua and Eberhardt, "Two Strikes," 5; Goff et al., "Essence of Innocence," 526; Rattan et al., "Race and the Fragility of the Legal Distinction."

93. Amir Whitaker et al., *Cops and No Counselors: How the Lack of School Mental Health Staff Is Harming Students* (New York: American Civil Liberties Union, 2019), 52. See also Amanda Merkwae, "Schooling the Police: Race, Disability, and the Conduct of School Resource Officers," *Michigan Journal of Race and the Law* 21 (2015).

94. Kimberly Kindy et al., "Fatal Police Shootings in 2015 Approaching 400 Nationwide," *Washington Post,* May 30, 2015; Abigail Abrams, "Black, Disabled, and at Risk: The Overlooked Problem of Police Violence Against Americans with Disabilities," *Time,* June 25, 2020 (noting "there is no reliable national database tracking how many people with disabilities, or who are experiencing episodes of mental illness, are shot by police each year, but studies show that the numbers are substantial—likely between one-third and one-half of total police killings").

95. Stanford, interview by author.

### 8. POLICING BY PROXY

1. Mihir Zaveri, "Man Who Fired at a Black Teenager Asking for Directions Is Convicted," *New York Times,* Oct. 13, 2018; James Doubek, "Black Teenager Shot at After Asking for Directions," NPR, April 15, 2018; Eli Rosenberg, "A Teen Missed the Bus to School. When He Knocked on a Door for Directions, a Man Shot at Him," *Washington Post,* April 14, 2018; Sheena Jones, Amanda Watts, and Steve Almasy, "Teen Says He Was Asking for Directions, but Homeowner Shot at Him," CNN, April 14, 2018.

2. Jacey Fortin, "A Black Teenager Asked for Directions. A Man Responded with Gunfire," *New York Times,* April 14, 2018.

3. Ibid.

4. Suzanne Daley, "Man Tells Police He Shot Youths in Subway Train," *New York Times,* Jan. 1, 1985; Myra Friedman and Michael Daley, "My Neighbor Bernie Goetz," *New York,* Feb. 18, 1985.

5. *People v. Goetz,* 68 N.Y.2d 96, 117 (N.Y. 1986).

6. Jennifer Latson, "Two Shootings, 30 Years Apart, Linked by Fear," *Time,* Dec. 22, 2014.

7. "Bernhard Goetz," Biography, May 12, 2020, biography.com; "Individual Wearing a 'Thug Buster T-Shirt,'" gettyimages.com.

8. "Bernhard Goetz," Biography; Billy Joel, "We Didn't Start the Fire"

(Columbia, 1989); Lou Reed, "Hold On," *New York* (Sire Records, 1989); Beastie Boys, "Stop the Train," *Paul's Boutique* (Capitol Records, 1989); Gary Langer, "'Doonesbury' Draws Criticism for Subway Shooting Satire," Associated Press, Feb. 1, 1985.

9. Joseph Berger, "Goetz Case: Commentary on Nature of Urban Life," *New York Times,* June 18, 1987.

10. United Press International, "Guardian Angels Honor Goetz," *Chicago Tribune,* Dec. 23, 1985; Rian Dundon, "Pictures of the Controversial Vigilantes Who Protected the Streets in 1980s New York," Timeline, April 21, 2017.

11. John Leo, "Behavior: Low Profile for a Legend Bernard Goetz," *Time,* Jan. 21, 1985.

12. David E. Pitt, "Blacks See Goetz Verdict as Blow to Race Relations," *New York Times,* June 18, 1987.

13. Kirk Johnson, "Youth Shot in Subway Says He Didn't Approach Goetz," *New York Times,* May 20, 1987.

14. Ronald Sullivan, "Goetz Is Given One-Year Term on Gun Charge," *New York Times,* Jan. 14, 1989.

15. Tina Kelley, "Following Up; Still Seeking Payment from Bernard Goetz," *New York Times,* Sept. 10, 2000.

16. Berger, "Goetz Case."

17. Pitt, "Blacks See Goetz."

18. *Goetz,* 68 N.Y.2d at 117.

19. Berger, "Goetz Case."

20. Sarah Lyall, "N.A.A.C.P. Leader Seeks Federal Case on Goetz," *New York Times,* June 20, 1987.

21. Johnson, "Youth Shot in Subway."

22. Stone Phillips, "Stone Phillips: 15 Years of Dateline," *Dateline NBC,* July 2, 2007.

23. "Man Admits Shooting 4 in Subway," *Chicago Tribune,* Jan. 1, 1985; Friedman, "My Neighbor Bernie Goetz."

24. John J. DiIulio Jr., "My Black Crime Problem, and Ours," *City Journal* (Spring 1996).

25. Associated Press, "Merchant Charged in Girl's Fatal Shooting," *New York Times,* March 22, 1991.

26. "A Senseless and Tragic Killing: New Tension for Korean-American and African-American Communities," *Los Angeles Times,* March 20, 1991.

27. Brenda Stevenson, "Latasha Harlins, Soon Ja Du, and Joyce Kar-

lin: A Case Study of Multicultural Female Violence and Justice on the Urban Frontier," *Journal of African American History* 89 (Spring 2004): 152–76.

28. *People v. Superior Court (Du)*, 5 Cal. App. 4th 822 (Cal. Ct. App. 1992); Valerie Kuklenski, "Korean Grocer Gets Probation for Killing Black Teen," United Press International, Nov. 15, 1991.

29. Associated Press, "U.S. Looks into Korean Grocer's Slaying of Black," *New York Times,* Nov. 26, 1992.

30. *Superior Court (Du)*, 5 Cal. App. 4th at 822.

31. Chris Francescani, "George Zimmerman: Prelude to a Shooting," Reuters, April 25, 2012.

32. Campbell Robertson and John Schwartz, "Shooting Focuses Attention on a Program That Seeks to Avoid Guns," *New York Times,* March 22, 2012.

33. Angela Onwuachi-Willig, "Policing the Boundaries of Whiteness: The Tragedy of Being 'out of Place' from Emmett Till to Trayvon Martin," *Iowa Law Review* 102 (2017).

34. Miami Herald, "Sanford Cops Sought Warrant to Arrest George Zimmerman in Trayvon Martin Shooting," *Tampa Bay Times,* March 28, 2012.

35. CNN Wire Staff, "From Coast to Coast, Protesters Demand Justice in Trayvon Martin Case," CNN, March 27, 2012; Bill Chappell, "Zimmerman Arrested on Murder Charge in Martin Case; Will Plead Not Guilty," NPR, April 11, 2012.

36. Frank Newport, "Blacks, Nonblacks Hold Sharply Different Views of Martin Case," Gallup, April 5, 2012.

37. "George Zimmerman Has Raised Twice as Much as Trayvon Martin's Family," *Metro US,* May 14, 2012.

38. Michael Walsh, "George Zimmerman Paints Confederate Battle Flag to Raise Money for 'Muslim-Free' Gun Store,'" *Yahoo News,* Aug. 18, 2015.

39. Onwuachi-Willig, "Policing the Boundaries of Whiteness," 1113.

40. Arian Campo-Flores and Lynn Waddell, "Jury Acquits Zimmerman of All Charges," *Wall Street Journal,* July 14, 2013.

41. Ben Montgomery, "Florida's 'Stand Your Ground' Law Was Born of 2004 Case, but Story Has Been Distorted," *Tampa Bay Times,* Feb. 7, 2013.

42. Cynthia Ward, "'Stand Your Ground' and Self-Defense," *American Journal of Criminal Law* 42 (2014–15): 89, 90.

43. Eliott C. McLaughlin and Devon Sayers, "Defendant Tells Police

He Had Spat over Loud Music, Opened Fire, Ordered Pizza," CNN, Feb. 6, 2014.

44. Charlotte Alter, "Florida Man Who Killed Teen over Loud Music Dispute Due in Court," *Time,* Feb. 3, 2014; but see David Kopel, "Stand Your Ground Had Nothing to Do with the Dunn Verdict in Florida," *Washington Post,* Feb. 17, 2014; Patrik Jonsson, "Michael Dunn Loud-Music Life Sentence: A Corrective on Stand Your Ground Laws?," *Christian Science Monitor,* Oct. 18, 2014 (judge noting that Stand Your Ground has been misunderstood).

45. McLaughlin and Sayers, "Defendant Tells Police He Had Spat."

46. *"Stand Your Ground" Laws: Civil Rights and Public Safety Implications of the Expanded Use of Deadly Force,* Senate Hearing on S. 113-626 Before the Subcommittee on Constitution, Civil Rights, and Human Rights, Committee on the Judiciary, 113th Cong., 1st Sess., 2013.

47. Arkadi Gerney and Chelsea Parsons, *License to Kill: How Lax Concealed Carry Laws Can Combine with Stand Your Ground Laws to Produce Deadly Results* (Washington, D.C.: Center for American Progress, 2013); Christina Coleman, "Kill at Will: Stand Your Ground Laws Contribute to 600 Additional Homicides a Year," *Philadelphia Sunday Sun,* Feb. 23, 2014; David K. Humphreys, Antonio Gasparrini, and Douglas J. Wiebe, "Evaluating the Impact of Florida's 'Stand Your Ground' Self-Defense Law on Homicide and Suicide by Firearm," *JAMA Internal Medicine* 177, no. 1 (2017).

48. Evelyn Reyes, "Florida's Stand Your Ground Law: How to Get Away with Murder," *Intercultural Human Rights Law Review* 12 (2017): 147, 158.

49. Shahabudeen Khan, "One Decade Later: Florida's Stand Your Ground Law Alive and Well," *Intercultural Human Rights Law Review* 12 (2017): 115, 137.

50. Patrik Jonsson, "Racial Bias and 'Stand Your Ground' Laws: What the Data Show," *Christian Science Monitor,* Aug. 6, 2013; John K. Roman, "Race, Justifiable Homicide, and Stand Your Ground Laws: Analysis of the FBI Supplementary Homicide Report Data," Urban Institute, July 2013, 1–14; Khan, "One Decade Later," 115, 137.

51. Nicole Flatow and Rebecca Leber, "5 Disturbing Facts About the State of Stand Your Ground on the Second Anniversary of Trayvon's Death," *Think Progress,* Feb. 26, 2014.

52. Steven Jansen and M. Elaine Nugent-Borakove, *Expansions to the Castle Doctrine: Implications for Policy and Practice* (Alexandria, Va.: National District Attorneys Association, 2007).

53. Reed Karaim, "Ida B. Wells' Fight Against the Lynching of Blacks," *American History,* Feb. 2012.

54. Jamiles Lartey and Sam Morris, "How White Americans Used Lynchings to Terrorize and Control Black People," *Guardian,* April 26, 2018.

55. Joe Fox et al., "What We've Learned About Police Shootings 5 Years After Ferguson," *Washington Post,* Aug. 9, 2019; Samuel Sinyangwe, Mapping Police Violence, mappingpoliceviolence.org.

56. Sinyangwe, Mapping Police Violence.

57. *Department of Justice Report Regarding the Criminal Investigation into the Shooting Death of Michael Brown by Ferguson, Missouri Police Officer Darren Wilson,* U.S. Department of Justice, March 4, 2015, 8–9; Terrence McCoy, "Darren Wilson Explains Why He Killed Michael Brown," *Washington Post,* Nov. 25, 2014; Robert Patrick, "Darren Wilson's Radio Calls Show Fatal Encounter Was Brief," *St. Louis Post-Dispatch,* Nov. 14, 2014.

58. McCoy, "Darren Wilson Explains."

59. Patrick, "Darren Wilson's Radio Calls."

60. *Department of Justice Report Regarding the Criminal Investigation,* 8–9.

61. Thomas Barrabi, "Michael Brown Robbed Convenience Store, Stole Cigarillos Before Darren Wilson Shooting, Dorian Johnson Says," *International Business Times,* Nov. 25, 2014; David Mikkelson, "Mike Brown's Arrest Record," Snopes, May 22, 2015.

62. Mikkelson, "Mike Brown's Arrest Record."

63. Associated Press, "Judge: Lawyers Can Have Michael Brown Juvenile Records," *Seattle Times,* June 24, 2016; "No Top Felony Convictions on Michael Brown's Juvenile Record: Court," NBC News, Sept. 3, 2014.

64. Mitch Smith, "New Ferguson Video Adds Wrinkle to Michael Brown Case," *New York Times,* March 11, 2017.

65. Lauren Barbato, "Darren Wilson Is Still Doing Alright Financially," *Bustle,* Nov. 29, 2014.

66. Dana Milbank, "Bob McCulloch's Pathetic Prosecution of Darren Wilson," *Washington Post,* Nov. 25, 2014.

67. Wayne Drash and Rosa Flores, "Chicago Police Killing of Unarmed Teen Unjustified, Fired Investigator Says," CNN, Dec. 9, 2015.

68. Errol Louis, "Chicago Politics: How Justice Was Delayed for Laquan McDonald," CNN, Dec. 2, 2015.

69. Dan Good, "Chicago Police Officer Jason Van Dyke Emptied His Pistol and Reloaded as Teen Laquan McDonald Lay on Ground During Barrage; Cop Charged with Murder for Firing 16 Times," *New York Daily News,* Nov. 24, 2015.

70. Louis, "Chicago Politics: How Justice Was Delayed."

71. "Laquan McDonald: How a Chicago Teenager Was Shot Dead by Police," BBC News, Nov. 24, 2015.

72. John Medina, "New Discrepancies in Laquan McDonald Case," *Dispatch Times,* Jan. 30, 2016.

73. Sophia Tareen, Associated Press, "Chicago Cops' Versions of Laquan McDonald Killing at Odds with Video," *Herald-News,* Dec. 5, 2015.

74. Sam Levine, "Chicago Police Really Didn't Want to Release Video of a Cop Shooting Laquan McDonald 16 Times," *HuffPost,* Nov. 27, 2015.

75. Medina, "New Discrepancies"; Tareen, "Chicago Cops' Versions."

76. Phillip Atiba Goff and Hilary Rau, "Predicting Bad Policing: Theorizing Burdensome and Racially Disparate Policing Through the Lenses of Social Psychology and Routine Activities," *The Annals of the American Academy of Political Science* 687(1) (2020): 67–88, 74–75 (theorizing that disparate policing is most likely to occur in situations that promote feelings of threat or disgust, rooted in cultural stereotypes, in police officers in the absence of sufficient self-regulation by the officer); Roger Fairfax, "The Grand Jury and Police Violence Against Black Men," in *Policing the Black Man: Arrest, Prosecution, and Imprisonment,* ed. Angela J. Davis (New York: Pantheon Books, 2017), 209–33.

77. Christy Gutowski and Jeremy Gorner, "The Complicated, Short Life of Laquan McDonald," *Chicago Tribune,* Dec. 11, 2015.

78. Sinyangwe, Mapping Police Violence.

79. Mitch Smith and Julie Bosman, "Jason Van Dyke Sentenced to Nearly 7 Years for Murdering Laquan McDonald," *New York Times,* Jan. 18, 2019.

80. Gutowski and Gorner, "Complicated, Short Life of Laquan McDonald."

81. "Trayvon Martin Case to Go to Grand Jury, Fla. State Attorney Announces," NBC News, March 20, 2012.

82. "State of Florida vs. George Zimmerman: Affidavit of Probable

Cause," *New York Times,* April 12, 2012; CNN Wire Staff, "Affidavit Says Zimmerman 'Profiled' Martin," CNN, April 12, 2012; Corey Dade, "Affidavit Reveals New Details Against George Zimmerman," NPR, April 12, 2012.

83. Joy-Ann Reid, "Zimmerman Tells Hannity: 'No Regrets' over His Actions in Trayvon Martin Shooting," *Grio,* July 18, 2012; "Revising Zimmerman's Side of the Story," Fox News, July 19, 2012.

84. Seni Tienabeso, Matt Gutman, and Beth Loyd, "George Zimmerman Jury Hears Key 911 Tapes in Start of Trial," ABC News, June 24, 2013.

85. Jeff Burnside and Brian Hamacher, "Trayvon Martin Suspended from School Three Times: Report," NBC Miami, Feb. 23, 2020; Brian Hamacher, Lisa Orkin Emmanuel, and Jeff Burnside, "Trayvon Martin Suspended from Miami High School for Possession of Empty Marijuana Baggie," NBC Miami, March 26, 2012; CNN Wire Staff, "Police: Trayvon Martin's Death 'Ultimately Avoidable,'" CNN, May 18, 2012.

86. Lloyd Johnston et al., *Monitoring the Future: National Survey Results on Drug Use, 1975–2018,* Institute for Social Research, University of Michigan, Jan. 2019.

87. Burnside and Hamacher, "Trayvon Martin Suspended."

88. Miami Herald, "Trayvon Martin, a Typical Teen with Dreams of Flying or Fixing Planes," *Tampa Bay Times,* March 26, 2012.

89. *3½ Minutes, Ten Bullets,* directed by Marc Silver (New York: Candescent Films, 2015).

90. Elliot McLaughlin, "Did Jordan Davis Have a Weapon? Attorneys Spar in Loud Music Murder Trial," CNN, Feb. 11, 2014.

91. "Wife, Husband Who Shot at Black Teen Asking for Directions to School Testify," Fox2 Detroit, Oct. 11, 2018.

92. McLaughlin, "Did Jordan Davis Have a Weapon?"

93. Jacob Sullum, "Will Michael Dunn's Trial, Unlike George Zimmerman's, Have Something to Do with 'Stand Your Ground'?," *Reason,* Feb 7, 2014.

94. Ibid.; McLaughlin and Sayers, "Defendant Tells Police He Had Spat."

95. McLaughlin, "Did Jordan Davis Have a Weapon?"

96. Ray Sanchez, "Man Gets Life Without Parole for Murdering Florida Teen over Loud Music," CNN, Oct. 17, 2014.

97. Onwuachi-Willig, "Policing the Boundaries of Whiteness," 1113.

98. Ibid., 1126.
99. Ibid., 1125; Cheryl I. Harris, "Whiteness as Property," *Harvard Law Review* 106 (June 1993): 1707–91.
100. Onwuachi-Willig, "Policing the Boundaries of Whiteness," 1122, 1126. See also Isabel Wilkerson, *Caste: The Origins of Our Discontent* (New York: Random House, 2020).
101. Onwuachi-Willig, "Policing the Boundaries of Whiteness," 1124.
102. Ibid., 1127.
103. Kate Abbey-Lambertz, "Opening Statements Reveal Shooter's State of Mind in Renisha McBride Case," *HuffPost,* July 23, 2014.
104. Jelani Cobb, "The Killing of Renisha McBride," *New Yorker,* Nov. 16, 2013.
105. Abbey-Lambertz, "Opening Statements Reveal Shooter's State of Mind"; "Report: Renisha McBride Was Drunk, Possibly High When Fatally Shot," CBS Detroit, Nov. 15, 2013; Lena Jakobsson, "Man Who Shot Unarmed Michigan Teen Convicted of Second-Degree Murder," CNN, Aug. 7, 2014.
106. Jakobsson, "Man Who Shot Unarmed Michigan Teen."
107. Abbey-Lambertz, "Opening Statements Reveal Shooter's State of Mind."
108. Onwuachi-Willig, "Policing the Boundaries of Whiteness," 1121.
109. Francescani, "George Zimmerman."
110. Amanda Sloane and Graham Winch, "Key Witness Recounts Trayvon Martin's Final Phone Call," CNN, June 27, 2013; Elspeth Reeve, "New Talking Point: Trayvon Was the Bigot, as He Thought Zimmerman Was Gay," *Atlantic,* July 16, 2013; Dictionary.com, s.v. "cracker," 2020.
111. Onwuachi-Willig, "Policing the Boundaries of Whiteness," 1135–38.
112. "Why White Americans Call the Police on Black People in Public Spaces," *All Things Considered,* NPR, May 15, 2018.
113. P. R. Lockhart, "A White Neighbor Called Police on a Kid Mowing a Lawn. Later, They Called as He Played in a Yard," *Vox,* July 9, 2018.
114. Anne Branigin, "Nordstrom Rack Calls Cops on Three Black Teens Shopping for Prom, Wrongly Accuses Them of Stealing," *Root,* May 8, 2018.
115. Snejana Farberov and Hannah Parry, "'Permit Patty' DID Call the Cops: Newly Released 911 Call Confirms White CEO of a Marijuana Company Reported Eight-Year-Old Black Girl to

Police for Selling Water After Claiming She Was Only Pretending," *Daily Mail,* June 29, 2018; Niraj Chokshi, "White Woman Nicknamed 'Permit Patty' Regrets Confrontation over Black Girl Selling Water," *New York Times,* June 25, 2018.

116. Bob D'Angelo, "Black Man Riding with White Grandmother Handcuffed After False Robbery Report," Fox 13 Memphis, Sept. 7, 2018.

117. "District Attorney Won't Charge 911 Caller in Kendrec McDade Killing," *Los Angeles Times,* Oct. 23, 2012.

118. "Pasadena Police Shooting of Kendrec McDade Was Justified, D.A. Says," *Los Angeles Times,* Dec. 17, 2012; Richard Winton, "Man Whose False Report Led to Police Shooting Won't Be Charged," *Los Angeles Times,* Oct. 25, 2012.

119. "911 Caller Proclaims Innocence Despite Pleading Guilty to False Report That Led to Teen's Death by Police," CBS Los Angeles, June 17, 2013.

120. Adrienne Hurst, "Black, Autistic, and Killed by the Police," *Chicago Reader,* Dec. 17, 2015.

121. Jason Tashea, "Looking Suspicious: Websites and Apps for Sharing Crime and Safety Data Have Become Outlets for Racial Profiling," *ABA Journal,* Aug. 1, 2016.

122. Ibid.; Jessi Hempel, "For Nextdoor, Eliminating Racism Is No Quick Fix," *Wired,* Feb. 16, 2017; Phil Simon, "How Nextdoor Addressed Racial Profiling on Its Platform," *Harvard Business Review,* May 11, 2018.

123. Rani Molla, "Activists Are Pressuring Lawmakers to Stop Amazon Ring's Police Surveillance Partnerships," *Vox,* Oct. 8, 2019; Jason Kelley and Matthew Guariglia, "Amazon Ring Must End Its Dangerous Partnerships with Police," Electronic Frontier Foundation, June 10, 2020; John Herrman, "Who's Watching Your Porch?," *New York Times,* Jan. 19, 2020.

124. Erin Baldassari, "Bay Transit's Suspicious Activity Reporting App Causes Racial Profiling, Privacy Concerns," *Government Technology,* Aug. 16, 2016.

125. "Georgetown Shops, Police Use App to Discuss 'Suspicious' Shoppers," NBC4 Washington, Oct. 15, 2015.

126. Terrance McCoy, "The Secret Surveillance of 'Suspicious' Blacks in One of the Nation's Poshest Neighborhoods," *Washington Post,* Oct. 13, 2015.

127. Jim Shay, "State Unveils New App to Report Suspicious Activity," *Connecticut Post,* Nov. 6, 2018.

128. Whitney Way, "Florida Launches Suspicious Activity Reporting App for Students," Florida Department of Education, Oct. 8, 2018.

129. Sebastian Larsson, "A First Line of Defence? Vigilant Surveillance, Participatory Policing, and the Reporting of 'Suspicious' Activity," *Surveillance and Society* 15 (2016): 94–107.

130. Karma Allen, "'I Felt Humiliated': 9-Year-Old Boy in 'Cornerstone Caroline' Video Speaks Out," *Good Morning America,* Oct. 19, 2018.

131. Farberov, "'Permit Patty' DID Call the Cops."

132. Charnee Perez, "Lost Key or Bike Thief: What Would You Do?," ABC News, May 4, 2010.

### 9. POLICING AS TRAUMA

1. Tauhid Chappell and Tom Jackman, "In the Murky World of D.C. Marijuana Law, 'Pop-Up' Markets Thrive," *Washington Post,* March 26, 2018.

2. *APA Dictionary of Psychology,* s.v. "trauma." See also Development Services Group, "Behind the Term: Trauma," National Registry of Evidence-Based Programs and Practices, 2016.

3. Thema Bryant-Davis et al., "The Trauma Lens of Police Violence Against Racial and Ethnic Minorities," *Journal of Social Issues* 73 (Dec. 2017): 852–71; Sirry Alang et al., "Police Brutality and Black Health: Setting the Agenda for Public Health Scholars," *American Journal of Public Health* 107 (May 2017): 633.

4. "Number of People Shot to Death by the Police in the United States by Race 2017–2020," *Washington Post,* Aug. 2020; www .statista.com.

5. "Rate of Fatal Police Shootings in the United States from 2015 to 2020, by Ethnicity," *Washington Post,* Aug. 2020.

6. D. Brian Burghart, Fatal Encounters, fatalencounters.org. Journalist-collected data on police shootings, from Fatal Encounters and *The Washington Post,* has proved more accurate than FBI-collected data. After a *Washington Post* investigation revealed the FBI was dramatically undercounting the number of fatal police shootings nationwide, the FBI instituted a new program to collect use-of-force data beginning in 2019. However, participation is volun-

tary, and only 40 percent of police departments nationwide have submitted data. Mark Berman et al., "Protests Spread over Police Shootings. Police Promised Reforms. Every Year, They Still Shoot and Kill Nearly 1,000 People," *Washington Post,* June 8, 2020.

7. Monica Anderson and Jingjing Jiang, "Teens, Social Media, and Technology 2018," Pew Research Center, May 31, 2018.

8. Brendesha M. Tynes et al., "Race-Related Traumatic Events Online and Mental Health Among Adolescents of Color," *Journal of Adolescent Health* 65 (Sept. 2019): 373.

9. Ibid., 372.

10. Ibid., 371–73.

11. Ibid.

12. Raja Staggers-Hakim, "The Nation's Unprotected Children and the Ghost of Mike Brown, or the Impact of National Police Killings on the Health and Social Development of African American Boys," *Journal of Human Behavior in the Social Environment* 26 (Feb. 2016): 390–99.

13. Ibid., 394–96.

14. Ibid., 395.

15. Maria Trent, Danielle G. Dooley, and Jacqueline Dougé, "The Impact of Racism on Child and Adolescent Health, Policy Statement of American Academy of Pediatrics," *Pediatrics* 144 (Aug. 2019): 4.

16. Dylan B. Jackson et al., "Police Stops Among At-Risk Youth: Repercussions for Mental Health," *Journal of Adolescent Health* 65 (Nov. 2019): 627 (citing Rod K. Brunson and Kashea Pegram, "'Kids Do Not So Much Make Trouble, They Are Trouble': Police-Youth Relations," *Future of Children* 28 (Spring 2018): 83–102); Juan José Medina Ariza, "Police-Initiated Contacts: Young People, Ethnicity, and the 'Usual Suspects,'" *Policing and Society* 24 (Spring 2014): 208–23.

17. Craig B. Futterman, Chadyn Hunt, and Jamie Kalven, "Youth/ Police Encounters on Chicago's South Side: Acknowledge the Realities," University of Chicago Legal Forum, March 23, 2016; Rod K. Brunson, "Police Don't Like Black People: African-American Young Men's Accumulated Police Experiences," *Criminology and Public Policy* 6, no. 1 (Feb. 2007): 84; Ariza, "Police-Initiated Contacts"; Nikki Jones, "'The Regular Routine': Proactive Policing and Adolescent Development Among Young Poor Black Men," *New Directions in Child and Adolescent Development*

2014 (Spring 2014): 33–54; Claudio Vera Sanchez and Erica B. Sanchez, "Sacrificed on the Altar of Public Safety: The Policing of Latina and African American Youth," *Journal of Contemporary Criminal Justice* 27 (July 2011): 322–41; Rod K. Brunson and Ronald Weitzer, "Police Relations with Black and White Youths in Different Urban Neighborhoods," *Urban Affairs Review* 44 (2009): 858–85.

18. Christopher Dunn and Michelle Shames, *Stop-and-Frisk in the de Blasio Era,* New York Civil Liberties Union, March 2019.

19. Juan Del Toro et al., "The Criminogenic and Psychological Effects of Police Stops on Adolescent Black and Latino Boys," *Proceedings of the National Academy of Sciences of the United States of America* 116, no. 7 (2019): 8261–68; Jones, " 'Regular Routine' "; Sanchez and Sanchez, "Sacrificed on the Altar of Public Safety"; Lee Ann Slocum and Stephanie Ann Wilely, " 'Experience of the Expected': Race and Ethnicity Differences in the Effects of Police Contact on Youth," *Criminology* 56, no. 2 (May 2018): 402–32.

20. Dunn and Shames, *Stop-and-Frisk in the de Blasio Era* (noting that between 2014 and 2017, the NYPD used force on more than 21,000 Black and Latino people and more than 2,200 White people); Kimberly Barsamian Kahn and Phillip Atiba Goff, "Protecting Whiteness: White Phenotypic Racial Stereotypicality Reduces Police Use of Force," *Social Psychological and Personality Science* 7 (Feb. 2016): 403–11. See also Jon Swaine et al., "Young Black Men Killed by US Police at Highest Rate in Year of 1,134 Deaths," *Guardian,* Dec. 31, 2015.

21. Center for Promise, *Barriers to Wellness: Voices and Views from Young People in Five Cities* (Washington, D.C.: America's Promise Alliance, 2016).

22. Amanda Geller et al., "Aggressive Policing and the Mental Health of Young Urban Men," *American Journal of Public Health* 104, no. 12 (Dec. 2014): 2321–27 (summarizing results of telephone survey of 1,261 mostly Black and Latino young men aged eighteen to twenty-four about police encounters in New York City between September 2012 and March 2013); Abigail A. Sewell et al., "Living Under Surveillance: Gender, Psychological Distress, and Stop-Question-and-Frisk Policing in New York City," *Social Science and Medicine* 159 (June 2016): 1–13.

23. Geller et al., "Aggressive Policing and the Mental Health of Young Urban Men."

24. Jackson et al., "Police Stops Among At-Risk Youth," 627–32.

25. Del Toro et al., "Criminogenic and Psychological Effects."

26. Ibid., 8263.

27. Dylan B. Jackson et al., "Police Stops and Sleep Behaviors Among At-Risk Youth," *Journal of the National Sleep Foundation* 6, no. 4 (2020): 1–7.

28. Bryant-Davis et al., "Trauma Lens of Police Violence," 854.

29. Sewell et al., "Living Under Surveillance"; Abigail Sewell and Kevin Jefferson, "Collateral Damage: The Health Effects of Invasive Police Encounters in New York City," *Journal of Urban Health: Bulletin of the New York Academy of Medicine* 93 (Jan. 2016): 542–67; Alang et al., "Police Brutality and Black Health," 664.

30. Jackson et al., "Police Stops Among At-Risk Youth," 628.

31. Brunson and Pegram, "'Kids Do Not So Much Make Trouble, They Are Trouble.'"

32. Bryant-Davis et al., "Trauma Lens of Police Violence," 854.

33. Jackson et al., "Police Stops Among At-Risk Youth," 629.

34. Advancement Project and the Alliance for Educational Justice, *We Came to Learn: A Call to Action for Police-Free Schools* (Washington, D.C.: Advancement Project, 2019), 55 (citing Niya Kenny's testimony in front of the UN Working Group on People of African Descent, Jackson, Miss., 2016).

35. *Ring the Alarm: The Crisis of Black Youth Suicide in America: A Report to Congress from the Congressional Black Caucus Emergency Taskforce on Black Youth Suicide and Mental Health* (Washington, D.C.: Congressional Black Caucus, 2019), 16. See also Staggers-Hakim, "Nation's Unprotected Children and the Ghost of Mike Brown."

36. Laura M. White et al., "Behavioral Health Service Utilization Among Detained Adolescents: A Meta-analysis of Prevalence and Potential Moderators," *Journal of Adolescent Health* 64 (June 2019): 701.

37. Jacqueline M. Swank and Joseph C. Gagnon, "Mental Health Services in Juvenile Correctional Facilities: A National Survey of Clinical Staff," *Journal of Child and Family Studies* 25 (June 2016): 2862–72.

38. Jackson et al., "Police Stops Among At-Risk Youth," 629.

39. Data from the Police-Public Contact Survey "is the only national data we are aware of that enables any intersectional analysis of

civilian experiences with police, and the Bureau of Justice Statistics (BJS) does not attempt this analysis in its report on the survey's results . . . [P]olice stops and arrests during these stops are relatively infrequent events, and . . . our findings are based on survey data from over 90,000 respondents, not the total U.S. population." Prison Policy Initiative, "Policing Women: Race and Gender Disparities in Police Stops, Searches, and Use of Force," May 14, 2019, prisonpolicy.org. Women are about twenty times less likely to be killed by police. Latina and Asian/Pacific Islander women are less likely than White women to be killed by police, but Black women and American Indian/Alaska Native women face a higher risk. Frank Edwards, Hedwig Lee, and Michael Esposito, "Risk of Being Killed by Police Use of Force in the United States by Age, Race-Ethnicity, and Sex," *Proceedings of the National Academy of Sciences,* Aug. 5, 2019, 16793–98.

40. Edwards, Lee, and Esposito, "Risk of Being Killed by Police" (Black women are about 1.4 times more likely to be killed by police than are White women).
41. Prison Policy Initiative, "Policing Women." The policing of women, especially women of color, has received much less attention than the policing of men, and state and federal governments have been particularly inadequate at tracking this data. Nonetheless, some nonprofit entities have attempted to track the intersectionality of race and gender in police stops, frisks, and use of force.
42. Andrea Ritchie, *Invisible No More: Police Violence Against Black Women and Women of Color* (Boston: Beacon Press, 2017), 43–58.
43. Jeff Todd, "Woman Describes Kids Getting Handcuffed by Aurora Police in Video That Went Viral: "I'm Livid." 4 CBS Denver, August 4, 2020; Madeline Holcombe, "The Black Children Who Had Guns Drawn on Them in a Stolen Vehicle Mix-up Are Traumatized, the Mother Says," CNN, August 6, 2020; Vanessa Romo, "No Charges for Colorado Officers Who Held Black Children at Gunpoint," NPR.org, January 8, 2021.
44. Justin Murphy and Victoria E. Freile, "A 9-Year-Old Was Pepper-Sprayed by Police. Here's What Should Have Happened Instead," *USA TODAY,* February 2, 2021.
45. Janelle Griffith, "'You Did It to Yourself,' Officer Tells 9-Year-Old Girl Pepper-Sprayed by Police in Newly Released Video," *NBC*

*News,* February 12, 2021; Laura Ly and Eric Levenson, "Rochester Police Officers Handcuff and Pepper-Spray a 9-Year-Old Girl After Call of 'Family Trouble,'" CNN.com, February 2, 2021.

46. African American Policy Forum, "Black Women and Girls Killed by Police: The Incomplete Stories of #SayHerName," *Portside,* June 20, 2020.
47. Rose Hackman, "'She Was Only a Baby': Last Charge Dropped in Police Raid That Killed Sleeping Detroit Child," *Guardian,* Jan. 31, 2015.
48. Alang et al., "Police Brutality and Black Health," 662.
49. Steve Large, "Family Asks for Apology from Police After Officers Put 'Spit Bag' on 12-Year-Old Boy Under Arrest," CBS Sacramento, May 21, 2019.
50. Christina Davidson and Patrick Madden, "In DC, Wiggling While Handcuffed Counts as Assaulting an Officer," *Reveal News,* May 2015.
51. Peter Hermann and Clarence Williams, "Police Say Youths, Including 10-Year-Old, Used Pellet Gun to Rob Boy of His Phone," *Washington Post,* April 1, 2019.
52. Lorenzo Hall, "'It Destroyed Him the Whole Night': Mom Speaks After 10-Year-Old Son Detained by DC Police," WUSA9, April 1, 2019.
53. Peter Hermann, "10-Year-Old Boy Handcuffed in Robbery Case Is 'Totally Innocent,' Authorities Say," *Washington Post,* April 5, 2019.
54. Evan Lambert, "DC Police Investigating After Video Shows Officer Handcuffing 9-Year-Old Boy," Fox 5 DC, April 24, 2019.
55. Theresa Vargas, "'It Hurt': A 9-Year-Old Boy Was Handcuffed. But How Many Other D.C. Youth Have Also Been?," *Washington Post,* April 27, 2019.
56. Michael Laris, "'Horseplay' by Boys at Metro Station Descends into Accusations of Assault and Excessive Force and 13-Year-Old in Cuffs," *Washington Post,* Feb. 9, 2020.
57. Brunson, "Police Don't Like Black People," 84.
58. Trent, Dooley, and Dougé, "Impact of Racism on Child and Adolescent Health," 4.
59. Devin English et al., "Daily Multidimensional Racial Discrimination Among Black U.S. American Adolescents," *Journal of Applied Developmental Psychology* 66 (Jan. 2020): 1–12.

Notes · 419

60. Ibid., 3; Trent, Dooley, and Dougé, "Impact of Racism on Child and Adolescent Health," 4.
61. Federal Bureau of Investigation, "Victims," *Uniform Crime Report Hate Crime Statistics, 2017* (2018).
62. English et al., "Daily Multidimensional Racial Discrimination," 7.
63. Ibid.
64. Ibid., 6–7.
65. Brunson, "Police Don't Like Black People," 81; Rod K. Brunson and Jody Miller, "Gender, Race, and Urban Policing: The Experience of African American Youths," *Gender and Society* 20, no. 4 (Aug. 2006): 534.
66. Trent, Dooley, and Dougé, "Impact of Racism on Child and Adolescent Health."
67. Tynes, "Race-Related Traumatic Events Online," 372.
68. English et al., "Daily Multidimensional Racial Discrimination" (citing Devin English et al., "Adding to the Education Debt: Depressive Symptoms Mediate the Association Between Racial Discrimination and Academic Performance in African American Adolescents," *Journal of School Psychology* 57 (2016): 29–40); Trent, Dooley, and Dougé, "Impact of Racism on Child and Adolescent Health," 4.
69. Bryant-Davis et al., "Trauma Lens of Police Violence," 854.
70. Ibid.
71. Donovan X. Ramsey, "White America's Silence on Police Brutality Is Consent," *Gawker Justice,* April 10, 2015.
72. Alang et al., "Police Brutality and Black Health."
73. Bryant-Davis et al., "Trauma Lens of Police Violence," 858.
74. Aprile D. Benner et al., "Racial/Ethnic Discrimination and Well-Being During Adolescence: A Meta-analytic Review," *American Psychologist* 73, no. 7 (Oct. 2018): 855–83; Trent, Dooley, and Dougé, "Impact of Racism on Child and Adolescent Health."
75. English et al., "Daily Multidimensional Racial Discrimination," 2.
76. Ibid. (citing Adriana J. Umaña-Taylor et al., "Ethnic and Racial Identity During Adolescence and into Young Adulthood: An Integrated Conceptualization," *Child Development* 85 (2014): 21–39).
77. English et al., "Daily Multidimensional Racial Discrimination";

Naomi Priest et al., "A Systematic Review of Studies Examining the Relationship Between Reported Racism and Health and Wellbeing for Children and Young People," *Social Science and Medicine* 95 (Oct. 2013): 115–27; Benner et al., "Racial/Ethnic Discrimination."

78. Bryant-Davis et al., "Trauma Lens of Police Violence," 854; Kim Gilhuly et al., *Reducing Youth Arrests Keeps Kids Healthy and Successful: A Health Analysis of Youth Arrest in Michigan* (Oakland: Human Impact Partners, 2017), 64; English et al., "Daily Multidimensional Racial Discrimination" (citing English et al., "Adding to the Education Debt").

79. English et al., "Daily Multidimensional Racial Discrimination."

80. Trent, Dooley, and Dougé, "Impact of Racism on Child and Adolescent Health," 2, 4.

81. Abigail A. Sewell, "The Illness Association of Police Violence: Differential Relationships by Ethnoracial Composition," *Sociological Forum* 32, no. S1 (Dec. 2017): 975–97; Sewell and Jefferson, "Collateral Damage."

82. English et al., "Daily Multidimensional Racial Discrimination" (citing Gene Brody et al., "Discrimination, Racial Identity, and Cytokine Levels Among African-American Adolescents," *Journal of Adolescent Health* 56, no. 5 (2015): 496–501).

83. Alang et al., "Police Brutality and Black Health," 663; Trent, Dooley, and Dougé, "Impact of Racism on Child and Adolescent Health."

84. Kristen Nunez and Timothy J. Legg, Ph.D., CRNP, "Fight, Flight, Freeze: What This Response Means," *Healthline*, Feb. 21, 2020; Kasia Kozlowskia et al., "Fear and the Defense Cascade: Clinical Implications and Management," *Harvard Review of Psychology* 23, no. 4 (2015).

85. Alang et al., "Police Brutality and Black Health," 663–64; Trent, Dooley, and Dougé, "Impact of Racism on Child and Adolescent Health"; Brody et al., "Discrimination, Racial Identity, and Cytokine Levels Among African-American Adolescents"; Sewell and Jefferson, "Collateral Damage."

86. *2020 KIDS COUNT Data Book: State Trends in Child Well-Being* (Baltimore: Annie E. Casey Foundation, 2020); Zara Abrams, "Sounding the Alarm on Black Youth Suicide," American Psychological Association, Jan. 28, 2020; Burghart, Fatal Encounters.

87. Congressional Black Caucus, *Ring the Alarm,* 16–17.

88. Ibid.
89. English et al., "Daily Multidimensional Racial Discrimination."
90. Gilhuly et al., *Reducing Youth Arrests*, 64.
91. Congressional Black Caucus, *Ring the Alarm*, 16.
92. Laurence Steinberg, *Age of Opportunity: Lessons from the New Science of Adolescence* (Boston: Houghton Mifflin Harcourt, 2014), 23.
93. Ibid., 9, 22.
94. Ibid., 25.
95. Ibid., 42–43.
96. Ibid., 30.
97. Ibid., 37–39.
98. Ibid., 42–43.
99. Congressional Black Caucus, *Ring the Alarm* (noting that the rate of Black youth committing suicide rose from 2.55 per 100,000 in 2007 to 4.82 per 100,000 in 2017; suicide attempts by Black adolescent boys and girls rose by 73 percent between 1991 and 2017; and injuries caused by attempted suicide among Black teens rose by 122 percent in that same time frame).
100. Ibid., 15.
101. Jason Jones et al., "Parent-Adolescent Agreement About Adolescents' Suicidal Thoughts," *Pediatrics* 143, no. 2 (Feb. 2019): 5.
102. "His Holiness the Dalai Lama Meets Vietnamese Group for the Second Time," Dalailama.com, Sept. 26, 2012.
103. Dunn and Shames, *Stop-and-Frisk in the de Blasio Era*, 4, 9.
104. New York Civil Liberties Union, *Stop-and-Frisk 2011, NYCLU Briefing*, May 9, 2012, 4 (noting that in 2011 as compared to 2003 (the earliest year a gun recovery figure is available), the NYPD conducted 524,873 more stops but recovered only 176 more guns, amounting to an additional recovery rate of three one-hundredths of a percent).
105. Dunn and Shames, *Stop-and-Frisk in the de Blasio Era*.
106. Sean Blackmon, letter to the editor, "The D.C. Police Chief Is Wrong. Stop and Frisk Is Racist," *Washington Post*, March 4, 2019; Occupation Free DC, "MPD Police Chief Newsham Lies About Stop-and-Frisk," YouTube, Feb. 8, 2019.
107. Blackmon, "D.C. Police Chief Is Wrong"; Patrick Madden, "Collateral Damage: Caught Between Gun Violence and Aggressive Policing," WAMU, Sept. 19, 2018 (Acknowledging that there are important caveats for this data, WAMU noted that its sample

includes only cases in which gun and ammunition possession were the sole charges. A handful of cases in the analysis might have been dismissed as part of a plea deal in a separate case, or due to court rulings on D.C. handgun laws. WAMU analyzed nearly 500 affidavits out of 1,713 total cases that were filed between 2010 and 2015 found in D.C. Superior Court records. Police affidavits explain why the individual was stopped and how police allegedly found the gun.).

108. The D.C. Council passed a criminal justice reform bill in 2016 requiring D.C. MPD to collect data, but MPD did not do so until the ACLU of D.C. sued the city in May 2018. Six months after the suit, a judge ordered the police department to start collecting and releasing the data. Matt Cohen, "Civil Rights and Activist Groups Sue Bowser over Stop-and-Frisk Data Collection," *Washington City Paper,* May 8, 2018; Kenyan McDuffie, "The NEAR Act," kenyanmcduffieward5.com; D.C. Law 21-125, Neighborhood Engagement Achieves Results Amendment Act of 2016.

109. Martin Austermuhle, "D.C. Police Release Long-Delayed Stop-and-Frisk Data, Showing Racial Disparities in Stops," WAMU, Sept. 10, 2019; Eric Flack, "'They Can't Hide It Anymore': Police Report Shows Racial Disparities in Stop and Frisk," WUSA9, Sept. 10, 2019.

110. Eric Flack and Jordan Fischer, "DC Police Underreported Stop and Frisk Numbers for Years. What Is the City Going to Do About It?," WUSA9, Sept. 13, 2019.

111. Brianne K. Nadeau, "End Stop and Frisk in D.C.," *Washington Post,* Feb. 15, 2019.

112. Metropolitan Police Department, *Stop Data Report: July 22–December 31, 2019* (Washington, D.C.: Metropolitan Police Department, 2019).

113. Occupation Free DC, "MPD Police Chief Newsham Lies About Stop-and-Frisk."

114. Jeffrey Fagan and Tracey L. Meares, "Punishment, Deterrence, and Social Control: The Paradox of Punishment in Minority Communities," *Ohio State Journal of Criminal Law* 6 (2008): 176–77, 180 (discussing the failure of punitive legal sanctions like incarceration to reduce crime, especially in poor communities of color).

115. Del Toro et al., "Criminogenic and Psychological Effects."

116. English et al., "Daily Multidimensional Racial Discrimination"

(citing Gerrard Gibbons et al., "Perceived Discrimination and Substance Use in African American Parents and Their Children: A Panel Study," *Journal of Personality and Social Psychology* 86 (2004): 517–29); Steinberg, *Age of Opportunity,* 1, 11–14.

117. Del Toro et al., "Criminogenic and Psychological Effects"; Stephanie A. Wiley and Finn-Aage Esbensen, "The Effect of Police Contact: Does Official Intervention Result in Deviance Amplification?," *Crime and Delinquency* 62, no. 3 (July 2013): 283–307; David S. Kirk and Andrew V. Papachristos, "Cultural Mechanisms and the Persistence of Neighborhood Violence," *American Journal of Sociology* 116 (2011): 1198–200.

118. Del Toro et al., "Criminogenic and Psychological Effects," 8263 (assessing delinquency at six, twelve, and eighteen months).

119. Congressional Black Caucus, *Ring the Alarm,* 16–17 (noting that assessment tools often lack culture-specific expressions of depression symptoms, leading to under- or misdiagnosis of youth in need of treatment).

120. See Madden, "Collateral Damage."

## 10. THE DEHUMANIZATION OF BLACK YOUTH: WHEN THE CHILDREN AREN'T CHILDREN ANYMORE

1. Lindsey Bever, "It Took 10 Minutes to Convict 14-Year-Old George Stinney Jr. It Took 70 Years After His Execution to Exonerate Him," *Washington Post,* Dec. 18, 2014; John J. O'Connor, "Review/Television; Reopening the Wounds of an Old Murder Case," *New York Times,* Sept. 30, 1991; Campbell Robertson, "South Carolina Judge Vacates Conviction of George Stinney in 1944 Execution," *New York Times,* Dec. 17, 2014; Lauren Barbato, "The Youngest American Executed Wasn't Guilty," *Bustle,* Dec. 17, 2014; Mark R. Jones, *South Carolina Killers: Crimes of Passion* (Charleston, S.C.: History Press, 2007).

2. Bever, "It Took 10 Minutes to Convict."

3. Ibid.

4. Ibid.

5. Robertson, "South Carolina Judge Vacates Conviction."

6. Arthur S. Miller and Jeffrey H. Bowman, "'Slow Dance on the Killing Ground': The Willie Francis Case Revisited," *DePaul Law Review* 32, no. 1 (1982): 5.

7. Deborah W. Denno, "When Willie Francis Died: The 'Disturbing' Story Behind One of the Eighth Amendment's Most Enduring

Standards of Risk," in *Death Penalty Stories,* ed. John H. Blume and Jordan M. Steiker (St. Paul: Foundation Press, 2009), 23.

8. Ibid., 25.
9. Ibid., 8.
10. Ibid., 13.
11. Ibid., 18.
12. Ibid., 21.
13. Ibid., 24–25.
14. Ibid., 21.
15. Miller, " 'Slow Dance on the Killing Ground,' " 7.
16. Denno, "When Willie Francis Died," 21.
17. Ibid., 22–23.
18. The death sentence was mandatory for murder in Louisiana at the time. Miller, " 'Slow Dance on the Killing Ground,' " 8 (citing Louisiana Code Crim. Law & Proc. Ch. 1, Art. 740-30 (Dart 1932 and Supp. 1942)).
19. Denno, "When Willie Francis Died," 44.
20. Miller, " 'Slow Dance on the Killing Ground,' " 8–10.
21. *Louisiana ex rel. Francis v. Resweber,* 329 U.S. 459, 462 (1947); Miller, " 'Slow Dance on the Killing Ground,' " 12–13; Gilbert King, "Cruel and Unusual History," *New York Times,* April 23, 2008.
22. Amnesty International, *The Exclusion of Child Offenders from the Death Penalty Under General International Law* (London: Amnesty International, 2003); UN Commission on Human Rights, *Convention on the Rights of the Child,* March 1990; UN General Assembly, "International Covenant on Civil and Political Rights," *United Nations Treaty Series* 999 (1996): 171; Organization of African Unity, *African Charter on the Rights and Welfare of the Child,* July 1990; Inter-American Commission on Human Rights, *American Convention on Human Rights "Pact of San Jose, Costa Rica"* (1969).
23. Mary Robinson, "Statement by Mary Robinson Urging Clemency for US Child Offenders T. J. Jones and Toronto Patterson," Office of the UN High Commissioner for Human Rights, press release, Aug. 1, 2002.
24. Death Penalty Information Center, "Executions of Juveniles in the U.S. 1976–2005."
25. Death Penalty Information Center, "Executions of Juveniles Outside of the U.S."

26. *Domingues v. United States,* Case 12.285, Report No. 62/02, Inter-Am. C.H.R., Doc. 5 rev. 1 at 913 (2002); ACLU, "Stop Killing Kids: Why It's Time to End the Indecent Practice of the Juvenile Death Penalty."

27. *Roper v. Simmons,* 543 U.S. 551 (2005).

28. Timothy B. Tyson, *The Blood of Emmett Till* (New York: Simon & Schuster, 2017).

29. Jones, *South Carolina Killers,* 38–42.

30. Karen McVeigh, "George Stinney Was Executed at 14. Can His Family Now Clear His Name?," *Guardian,* March 22, 2014.

31. Jones, *South Carolina Killers,* 38–42.

32. Nikki Gaskins Campbell, "Goose Creek Woman, Others Hope George Stinney Murder Conviction Sticks," *Berkeley Observer,* March 1, 2014; McVeigh, "George Stinney Was Executed."

33. Julian W. Mack, "The Juvenile Court," *Harvard Law Review* 23, no. 2 (1909): 104, 107.

34. Geoff K. Ward, *The Black Child-Savers: Racial Democracy and Juvenile Justice* (Chicago: University of Chicago Press, 2012), 38–39, 86–87. See also Robin Walker Sterling, "Fundamental Unfairness: *In re Gault* and the Road Not Taken," *Maryland Law Review* 72, no. 3 (2013): 607–81; James Bell and Laura J. Ridolfi, *Adoration of the Question: Reflections on the Failure to Reduce Racial and Ethnic Disparities in the Juvenile Justice System,* W. Haywood Burns Institute, Dec. 2008.

35. Berry C. Feld, "The Transformation of the Juvenile Court—Part II: Social Structure, Race, and the 'Crack Down' on Youth Crime," *Minnesota Law Review* 84 (1999): 332–34; see Ward, *Black Child-Savers,* 73.

36. Ward, *Black Child-Savers,* 39, 52–53, 60, 86–87.

37. Ibid., 53–56. See Bell and Ridolfi, *Adoration of the Question,* 3.

38. Ward, *Black Child-Savers,* 56–58, 74.

39. See Tamar R. Birckhead, "The Racialization of Juvenile Justice and the Role of the Defense Attorney," *Boston College Law Review* 58 (2017): 379, 394–405; Feld, "Transformation of the Juvenile Court," 333–34. For the most comprehensive treatment of the racialized history of juvenile justice and child welfare in America, see generally Ward, *Black Child-Savers.*

40. See Feld, "Transformation of the Juvenile Court," 340.

41. See David S. Tanenhaus, "The First Juvenile Court and the Problem of Difference in the Early Twentieth Century," in *Our Chil-*

*dren, Their Children: Confronting Racial and Ethnic Differences in American Juvenile Justice,* ed. Darnell F. Hawkins and Kimberly Kempf-Leonard (Chicago: University of Chicago Press, 2005), 108–10. See also Kenneth B. Nunn, "The Child as Other: Race and Differential Treatment in the Juvenile Justice System," *DePaul Law Review* 51 (2001–2): 706 (discussing how society's perception of Black youth as "others" leads to disproportionate treatment by the juvenile justice system).

42. Feld, "Transformation of the Juvenile Court," 340, 345–46; Barry C. Feld, *Bad Kids: Race and the Transformation of the Juvenile Court* (New York: Oxford University Press, 2002) (discussing Johnson's 1967 crime commission); Birckhead, "Racialization of Juvenile Justice," 404 (discussing increasing recidivism rates).

43. Birckhead, "Racialization of Juvenile Justice," 404–5, 408.

44. Ibid., 408; Feld, *Bad Kids;* Barry C. Feld, "Race, Politics, and Juvenile Justice: The Warren Court and the Conservative 'Backlash,'" *Minnesota Law Review* 87 (2003): 1507.

45. Feld, "Race, Politics, and Juvenile Justice," 1518, 1523. See also Perry L. Moriearty, "Framing Justice: Media, Bias, and Legal Decisionmaking," *Maryland Law Review* 69, no. 4 (2010): 870–73 (surveying media treatment of Black youth and crime in the 1990s).

46. Feld, "Race, Politics, and Juvenile Justice," 1558–68.

47. Kristin N. Henning, "Eroding Confidentiality in Delinquency Proceedings: Should Schools and Public Housing Authorities Be Notified," *New York Law Review* 79 (2004): 520–611.

48. Congress even encouraged states to adopt transfer policies by making some federal grants contingent on state policies allowing for children fourteen or older to be tried as adults. See Malcolm C. Young and Jenni Gainsborough, *Prosecuting Juveniles in Adult Court: An Assessment of Trends and Consequences* (Washington, D.C.: Sentencing Project, 2000).

49. Office of Juvenile Justice and Delinquency Prevention, *Statistical Briefing Book: Juveniles in Adult Jails and Prisons, Jail Inmates Younger Than Age 18, 1993–2018* (Washington, D.C.: U.S. Department of Justice, 2020).

50. Jeree M. Thomas and Mel Wilson, *The Color of Youth Transfer: Policy and Practice Recommendations* (Washington, D.C.: Campaign for Youth Justice and the National Association of Social Workers, 2018) (citing Charles Puzzanchera, Melissa Sickmund,

and Anthony Sladky, *Youth Younger Than 18 Prosecuted in Criminal Court: National Estimate, 2015 Cases* (Pittsburgh: National Center for Juvenile Justice, 2018)).

51. Sarah Hockenberry and Charles Puzzanchera, *Juvenile Court Statistics 2018* (Pittsburgh: National Center for Juvenile Justice, 2020), 21.

52. Black youth were waived to adult court by juvenile court judges in 1,872 cases of a total of 3,624 cases waived in 2018. Melissa Sickmund, Anthony Sladky, and W. Kang, "Easy Access to Juvenile Court Statistics: 1985–2018," National Center for Juvenile Justice and the Office of Juvenile Justice and Delinquency Prevention, 2020.

53. Ibid.

54. Hockenberry and Puzzanchera, *Juvenile Court Statistics 2018,* 21; Sickmund, Sladky, and Kang, "Easy Access to Juvenile Court Statistics: 1985–2018."

55. Thomas and Wilson, *Color of Youth Transfer,* 5.

56. *Disproportionate Minority Contact/Racial Ethnic Disparity Benchmark Report FY 2017–2018* (Florida: Department of Juvenile Justice, 2020).

57. Thomas and Wilson, *Color of Youth Transfer,* 13 (citing Supreme Court of Missouri Office of the State Court Administrator, *Missouri Juvenile and Family Division Annual Report,* 2016).

58. Sarah Gonzalez, "Kids in Prison: Getting Tried as an Adult Depends on Skin Color," WNYC News, Oct. 10, 2016; Charles Puzzanchera, Anthony Sladky, and W. Kang, "Easy Access to Juvenile Populations: 1990–2019," National Center for Juvenile Justice and the Office of Juvenile Justice and Delinquency Prevention, 2020.

59. Thomas and Wilson, *Color of Youth Transfer,* 7.

60. Ryan Deto, "Stark Racial Disparities Exist for Teens Tried as Adults in Allegheny County. Can Anything Be Done to Change It?," *Pittsburgh City Paper,* Dec. 11, 2018.

61. *Miller v. Alabama,* 132 S. Ct. 2455 (2012) (finding mandatory life sentences cruel and unusual); *Graham v. Florida,* 130 S. Ct. 2011 (2010) (banning life without parole in non-homicide cases).

62. Josh Rovner, *Juvenile Life Without Parole: An Overview* (Washington, D.C.: Sentencing Project, April 13, 2021).

63. John R. Mills, Anna M. Dorn, and Amelia C. Hritz, "Juvenile Life Without Parole in Law and Practice: Chronicling the Rapid

Change Underway," *American University Law Review* 65, no. 3 (2016): 575.

64. John R. Mills, Anna M. Dorn, and Amelia C. Hritz, *No Hope: Reexamining Lifetime Sentences for Juvenile Offenders* (Oakland: Phillips Black Project, 2015).

65. Mills, Dorn, and Hritz, "Juvenile Life Without Parole in Law and Practice," 603.

66. Puzzanchera, Sladky, and Kang, "Easy Access to Juvenile Populations."

67. Ibid.; Mills, Dorn, and Hritz, "Juvenile Life Without Parole in Law and Practice," 603.

68. Mills, Dorn, and Hritz, "Juvenile Life Without Parole in Law and Practice," 604.

69. *Miller v. Alabama,* 132 S. Ct. 2455 (2012).

70. Robert J. Smith and Justin D. Levinson, "The Impact of Implicit Racial Bias on the Exercise of Prosecutorial Discretion," *Seattle University Law Review* 35 (2012): 806 (noting that prosecutors who believe Blacks are dangerous are more likely to charge Black suspects than Whites even when their prior criminal records are the same); Carlos Berdejo, "Criminalizing Race: Racial Disparities in Plea-Bargaining," *Boston College Law Review* 59 (April 2018): 1187–249 (noting that prosecutors are more likely to offer Blacks less favorable plea bargains); Justin D. Levinson, "Forgotten Racial Equality: Implicit Bias, Decision-Making, and Misremembering," 57 (2007): 347–50, 381 (finding mock jurors significantly more likely to recall a fictional defendant as being aggressive when he was Black than when he was White or Hawaiian and finding judges prone to "stereotype-consistent memory errors," causing them to remember facts through a racially biased filter); Justin D. Levinson, Huajian Cai, and Danielle Young, "Guilty by Implicit Racial Bias: The Guilty/Not Guilty Implicit Association Test," *Ohio State Journal of Criminal Law* 8 (Sept. 2010): 189–90 (finding evidence of bias that causes judges and jurors to associate Black defendants with guilt); Justin D. Levinson and Danielle Young, "Different Shades of Bias: Skin Tone, Implicit Racial Bias, and Judgments of Ambiguous Evidence," *West Virginia Law Review* 112 (Jan. 2010): 310 (explaining mock jurors primed with Black perpetrator were significantly more likely to find ambiguous evidence to be indicative of guilt than White perpetrator).

71. George S. Bridges and Sara Steen, "Racial Disparities in Official

Assessments of Juvenile Offenders: Attributional Stereotypes as Mediating Mechanisms," *American Sociological Review* 63 (Aug. 1998): 557–84.

72. Ibid., 561, 563.

73. Ibid., 563–64.

74. Sandra Graham and Brian S. Lowery, "Priming Unconscious Racial Stereotypes About Adolescent Offenders," *Law and Human Behavior* 28 (Oct. 2004): 487, 490, 495.

75. Ibid. (finding that probation officers who were primed to think about Blacks judged alleged offenders to be more mature, more violent, more culpable, and more likely to re-offend than those who had not been primed).

76. Phillip Atiba Goff et al., "The Essence of Innocence: Consequences of Dehumanizing Black Children," *Journal of Personality and Social Psychology* 106 (Feb. 2014): 526–45.

77. Aneeta Rattan et al., "Race and the Fragility of the Legal Distinction Between Juveniles and Adults," *PLoS ONE* 7 (May 2012): 1–5.

78. Karen M. Kolivoski and Jeffrey J. Shook, "Incarcerating Juveniles in Adult Prisons: Examining the Relationship Between Age and Prison Behavior in Transferred Juveniles," *Criminal Justice and Behavior* 43 (March 2016): 1242–59; Eileen M. Ahlin and Don Hummer, "Sexual Victimization of Juveniles Incarcerated in Jails and Prisons: An Exploratory Study of Prevalence and Risk Factors," *Victims and Offenders* 14, no. 7 (2019): 793–810.

79. Wendy Sawyer, "Youth Confinement: The Whole Pie 2019," Prison Policy Initiative, Dec. 19, 2019.

80. Bureau of Justice Assistance, "Impact of PREA on Department of Justice Grants for Fiscal Year 2019."

81. Jasmine Awad, "Is It Enough? The Implementation of PREA's Youthful Inmate Standard," Campaign for Youth Justice, Sept. 4, 2018.

82. Prison Rape Elimination Act of 2003; Department of Justice, National Standards to Prevent, Detect, and Respond to Prison Rape: Final Rule, 28 C.F.R. § 115.14.

83. Awad, "Is It Enough?"

84. Ibid., 16.

85. Sarah Willets, "Federal Court Says Durham Must Separate Juveniles and Adults in County Jail," *Indy Week,* April 25, 2019.

86. Complaint for Plaintiff at 15, *Graves v. Durham County,* No.

1:19-CV-316 (M.D.N.C. March 20, 2019). Federal law provides that a "youthful inmate shall not be placed in a housing unit in which the youthful inmate will have sight, sound, or physical contact with any adult inmate." Prison Rape Elimination Act, 28 C.F.R. § 115.14.

87. Complaint for Plaintiff, *Graves,* No. 1:19-CV-316, 15, www .southerncoalition.org.

88. Celia Harris et al., *Juvenile InJustice: Charging Youth as Adults Is Ineffective, Biased, and Harmful* (Oakland: Human Impact Partners, 2017), 21 (citing Mark Soler, "Health Issues for Adolescents in the Justice System," *Journal of Adolescent Health* 31 (Dec. 2002): 321–33).

89. "Investigation into Violence Toward Teenagers at Rikers Island," *New York Times,* August 4, 2014; U.S. Attorney Southern District of New York Preet Bharara to Mayor Bill de Blasio, Commissioner Joseph Ponte, and Zachary Carter, *Re: CRIPA Investigation of the New York City Department of Correction Jails on Rikers Island,* Letter, Aug. 4, 2014.

90. "Investigation into Violence Toward Teenagers at Rikers Island"; Carol Marbin Miller and Audra D. S. Burch, "Teen Was Arrested and Strapped in a 'Barbaric-Looking' Chair—Even Though It's Banned," *Miami Herald,* Oct. 10, 2017; Helen Wilbers, "Teen Charged for Deputy Jail Assault," *Fulton Sun,* Sept. 10, 2019.

91. "Investigation into Violence."

92. Rachel Marshall, *Removing Youth from Adult Jails: A 50-State Scan of Pretrial Detention Laws for Youth* (Washington, D.C.: Campaign for Youth Justice, 2019).

93. Richard A. Mendel, *No Place for Kids: The Case for Reducing Juvenile Incarceration* (Baltimore: Annie E. Casey Foundation, 2011); Jessica Lahey, "The Steep Costs of Keeping Juveniles in Adult Prisons," *Atlantic,* Jan. 8, 2016.

94. Ahlin, "Sexual Victimization of Juveniles," 803; Eileen Ahlin, "Moving Beyond Prison Rape: Assessing Sexual Victimization Among Youth in Custody," *Aggression and Violent Behavior* 47 (March 2019): 163.

95. Ahlin and Hummer, "Sexual Victimization of Juveniles," 803; National Institute of Corrections, *Sexual Violence in Women's Prisons and Jails: Results from Focus Group Interviews,* 3rd ed. (Washington, D.C.: U.S. Department of Justice, 2009); Brenda V.

Smith et al., *An End to Silence: Inmates' Handbook on Identifying and Addressing Sexual Abuse,* 3rd ed., Project on Addressing Prison Rape at American University Washington College of Law, Sept. 2014.

96. Ahlin and Hummer, "Sexual Victimization of Juveniles," 803; National Institute of Corrections, *Sexual Violence in Women's Prisons;* Smith et al., *End to Silence;* Ahlin, "Moving Beyond Prison Rape," 163.

97. Harris et al., *Juvenile InJustice* (citing Michael Massoglia, "Incarceration as Exposure: The Prison, Infectious Disease, and Other Stress-Related Illnesses," *Journal of Health and Social Behavior* 49, no. 1 (2008): 56–71).

98. Harris et al., *Juvenile InJustice* (citing Matthew C. Aalsma et al., "Mortality of Youth Offenders Along a Continuum of Justice System Involvement," *American Journal of Preventive Medicine* 50 (2016): 303–10).

99. Harris et al., *Juvenile InJustice,* 19 (citing Evelyn J. Patterson, "The Dose-Response of Time Served in Prison on Mortality: New York State, 1989–2003," *American Journal of Public Health* 103, no. 3 (March 2013): 523–28).

100. Harris et al., *Juvenile InJustice* (citing National Commission on Correctional Health Care, *The Health Status of Soon-to-Be-Released Inmates* (Chicago: National Commission on Correctional Health Care, 2002)).

101. Harris et al., *Juvenile InJustice,* 26.

102. Ibid., 23 (citing Hans Steiner, Ivan G. Garcia, and Zakee Matthews, "Posttraumatic Stress Disorder in Incarcerated Juvenile Delinquents," *Journal of the American Academy of Child and Adolescent Psychiatry* 36 (March 1997): 357–65).

103. Harris et al., *Juvenile InJustice,* 23 (citing Karen M. Abram et al., "Posttraumatic Stress Disorder and Trauma in Youth in Juvenile Detention," *Archives of General Psychiatry* 61 (April 2004): 403–10); Sue Burrell, "Trauma and the Environment of Care in Juvenile Institutions," National Child Traumatic Stress Network, Aug. 2013, www.njjn.org.

104. Harris et al., *Juvenile InJustice,* 23 (citing Jason J. Washburn et al., "Detained Youth Processed in Juvenile and Adult Court: Psychiatric Disorders and Mental Health Needs," *Juvenile Justice Bulletin,* Sept. 2015).

105. Simone S. Hicks, "Behind Prison Walls: The Failing Treatment Choice for Mentally Ill Minority Youth," *Hofstra Law Review* 39, no. 4 (2011): 979–1010.

106. Office of Juvenile Justice and Delinquency Prevention, *Intersection Between Mental Health and the Juvenile Justice System* (Washington, D.C.: U.S. Department of Justice, 2017).

107. "Deaths at North Carolina Jail due to Lack of Medical, Mental Health Care," *Prison Legal News,* Sept. 2017, 20.

108. Virginia Bridges and Dan Kane, "Mother of Teen Who Died in Durham County Jail to Receive $650,000 in Settlement," *News and Observer,* March 21, 2019.

109. Complaint for Plaintiff, *Graves,* No. 1:19-CV-316.

110. Laurence Steinberg, *Age of Opportunity: Lessons from the New Science of Adolescence* (Boston: Houghton Mifflin Harcourt, 2014), 88–89; Edward P. Mulvey et al., "Trajectories of Desistance and Continuity in Antisocial Behavior Following Court Adjudication Among Serious Adolescent Offenders," *Development and Psychopathology* 22, no. 2 (2010): 454; Laurence Steinberg, Elizabeth Cauffman, and Kathryn C. Monahan, "Psychosocial Maturity and Desistance from Crime in a Sample of Serious Juvenile Offenders," *Juvenile Justice Bulletin,* March 2015, 3–4.

111. Steinberg, *Age of Opportunity,* 31.

112. Ibid., 207.

113. Ibid., 61–62; Julia Dmitrieva et al., "Arrested Development: The Effects of Incarceration on the Development of Psychosocial Maturity," *Development and Psychopathology* 24, no. 3 (Aug. 2012): 1073–90.

114. Dmitrieva et al., "Arrested Development," 1086.

115. Laurence Steinberg et al., "Reentry of Young Offenders from the Justice System: A Developmental Perspective," *Youth Violence and Juvenile Justice* 2 (Jan. 2004): 21–38.

116. Kristen Weir, "Maximizing Children's Resilience," *Monitor on Psychology* 48, no. 8 (Sept. 2017): 40 (quoting Suniya Luthar, PhD, who says, "Resilience rests, fundamentally, on relationships"); He Len Chung et al., "The Transition to Adulthood for Adolescents in the Juvenile Justice System: A Developmental Perspective," in *On Your Own Without a Net: The Transition to Adulthood for Vulnerable Populations,* ed. D. Wayne Osgood et al. (Chicago: University of Chicago Press, 2005), 68, 74, 83.

117. Weir, "Maximizing Children's Resilience"; Chung et al., "Transition to Adulthood," 68, 74, 83.

118. Kevin McGill, "Teen's Suicide a Sign of Big Problems at New Orleans Jail," *Times-Picayune,* July 9, 2017; Matt Sledge, "Suicide by 15-Year-Old Orleans Parish Inmate Likely to Refuel Controversy, Debate," *Times-Picayune,* Oct. 18, 2019.

119. McGill, "Teen's Suicide."

120. Donna A. Ruch et al., "Characteristics and Precipitating Circumstances of Suicide Among Incarcerated Youth," *Journal of the American Academy of Child and Adolescent Psychiatry* 58, no. 5 (May 2019): 514–24; Karen M. Abram et al., "Suicidal Thoughts and Behaviors Among Detained Youth," U.S. Department of Justice, Office of Juvenile Justice and Delinquency Prevention, July 2014; Lindsay M. Hayes, *Juvenile Suicide in Confinement: A National Survey* (Washington, D.C.: U.S. Department of Justice, Office of Justice Programs, 2009); Doug Gray et al., "Utah Youth Suicide Study, Phase I: Government Agency Contact Before Death," *Journal of the American Academy of Child and Adolescent Psychiatry* 41, no. 4 (April 2002): 427–34.

121. Arya Neelum, *Getting to Zero: A 50-State Strategy to Remove Youth from Adult Jails* (Los Angeles: UCLA School of Law Criminal Justice Reform Clinic, 2018), 22–23.

122. Dara Lind, "Teenagers in Prison Have a Shockingly High Suicide Rate," *Vox,* June 17, 2015.

123. Lara Zarum, "'Time: The Kalief Browder Story' Will Make Your Blood Boil," *Flavorwire,* Feb. 28, 2017; Jennifer Gonnerman, "Before the Law," *New Yorker,* Sept. 29, 2014.

124. Gonnerman, "Before the Law."

125. Ibid.

126. Jennifer Gonnerman, "Kalief Browder, 1993–2015," *New Yorker,* June 7, 2015; Jennifer Gonnerman, "Kalief Browder Learned How to Commit Suicide on Rikers," *New Yorker,* June 2, 2016.

127. "Kalief's Mother on Her Torment," Marshall Project, Oct. 17, 2016.

128. "Violence Inside Rikers," *New Yorker* video, April 22, 2015; Jennifer Gonnerman, "Exclusive Video: Violence Inside Rikers," *New Yorker,* April 23, 2015; Gonnerman, "Before the Law."

129. Gonnerman, "Exclusive Video."

130. Gonnerman, "Before the Law."

131. Stuart Marques, "Riots, Rebellion, and the City's Second Attempt to 'Sink' Rikers Island," NYC *Department of Records & Information Services* (blog), April 19, 2019; American Civil Liberties Union and Human Rights Watch, *Growing Up Locked Down: Youth in Solitary Confinement in Jails and Prisons in the United States* (New York: Human Rights Watch, 2012), 132 (reporting that 48 percent of adolescents in New York City Department of Correction custody had diagnosed mental health problems).

132. Office of Public Affairs, "Department of Justice Takes Legal Action to Address Pattern and Practice of Excessive Force and Violence at Rikers Island Jails That Violates the Constitutional Rights of Young Male Inmates," U.S. Department of Justice, Dec. 18, 2014.

133. Jennifer Gonnerman, "Kalief Browder, 1993–2015," *The New Yorker*, June 7, 2015; Jennifer Gonnerman, "Kalief Browder Learned How to Commit Suicide on Rikers," *The New Yorker*, June 2, 2016.

134. Gonnerman, "Before the Law."

135. Andrew B. Clark, "Juvenile Solitary Confinement as a Form of Child Abuse," *Journal of the American Academy of Psychiatry and the Law* 45, no. 3 (Sept. 2017): 350–57.

136. American Civil Liberties Union, *Growing Up Locked Down*, 37–43.

137. United Nations General Assembly, *Torture and Other Cruel, Inhuman, or Degrading Punishment, Interim Report of the Special Rapporteur of the Human Rights Council on Torture and Other Cruel, Inhuman, or Degrading Treatment or Punishment, Juan E. Méndez*, A/66/268, Aug. 5, 2011, 21.

138. Laura Dimon, "How Solitary Confinement Hurts the Teenage Brain," *Atlantic*, June 30, 2014.

139. Center for Children's Law and Policy; Center for Juvenile Justice Reform at Georgetown University; Council of Juvenile Justice Administrators; Justice Policy Institute; Stop Solitary for Kids. American Civil Liberties Union, *No Child Left Alone: Campaign to Stop the Solitary Confinement of Youth in Adult Jails and Prisons* (Washington, D.C.: American Civil Liberties Union, 2013); Duvall Ricks and David Crosby, "Torture by Another Name: The Use of Solitary Confinement on Youth and Young Adults in New Jersey Prisons," Center for Youth Justice, June 26, 2018.

140. Natali J. Kraner et al., *51-Jurisdiction Survey of Juvenile Solitary*

*Confinement Rules in Juvenile Justice System* (Washington, D.C.: Lowenstein Center for the Public Interest, 2016).

141. Maddy Troilo, "Locking Up Youth with Adults: An Update," Prison Policy Initiative, Feb. 27, 2018; Jessica Feierman et al., *Unlocking Youth: Legal Strategies to End Solitary Confinement in Juvenile Facilities* (Philadelphia: Juvenile Law Center, 2017).

142. Feierman et al., *Unblocking Youth*.

143. Dimon, "How Solitary Confinement Hurts the Teenage Brain"; American Civil Liberties Union, *Growing Up Locked Down*, 24.

144. Dimon, "How Solitary Confinement Hurts the Teenage Brain."

145. American Civil Liberties Union, *Alone and Afraid: Children Held in Solitary Confinement and Isolation in Juvenile Detention and Correctional Facilities* (New York: ACLU, 2013), 4.

146. Ibid., 5.

147. Nationwide Children's Hospital, "Suicide Death Among Incarcerated Youth," Jan. 23, 2019 (referencing Ruch et al., "Characteristics and Precipitating Circumstances of Suicide Among Incarcerated Youth").

148. Gonnerman, "Kalief Browder, 1993–2015"; Gonnerman, "Kalief Browder Learned."

149. Gonnerman, "Before the Law."

150. Gonnerman, "Kalief Browder, 1993–2015"; Gonnerman, "Kalief Browder Learned."

151. Marshall Project, "Kalief's Mother."

152. Gonnerman, "Kalief Browder Learned."

153. Gonnerman, "Kalief Browder, 1993–2015"; Gonnerman, "Kalief Browder Learned."

154. Camille Augustin, "Once Rikers Island Took Kalief Browder's Life, His Siblings Knew Their Mother Was Next," *Vibe*, March 1, 2017.

155. Christopher Mathias, "Here's Kalief Browder's Heartbreaking Research Paper on Solitary Confinement," *HuffPost*, June 23, 2015; Taylor Lewis, "Kalief Browder Penned Essay on Solitary Confinement One Month Before Committing Suicide," *Essence*, June 24, 2015.

156. Ayesha Delany-Brumsy, "Kalief Browder's Tragic Story Is Shocking, but Not Unique," *Vera Think Justice Blog*, June 15, 2015.

157. Delany-Brumsy, "Kalief Browder's Tragic Story."

158. Chung et al., "Transition to Adulthood," 72; Ashley Nellis and

Richard Hooks Wayman, *Back on Track: Supporting Youth Reentry from Out-of-Home Placement to the Community* (Washington, D.C.: Youth Reentry Task Force of the Juvenile Justice and Delinquency Prevention Coalition, 2009), 22–24.

159. Nellis and Wayman, *Back on Track.*

160. Suzanne Meiners-Levy, "Challenging the Prosecution of Young 'Sex Offenders': How Developmental Psychology and the Lessons of *Roper* Should Inform Daily Practice," *Temple Law Review* 79 (2006).

161. Young and Gainsborough, *Prosecuting Juveniles in Adult Court,* 7.

162. Thuc Vy H. Nguyen, "Juvenile Justice: Searching for a Flexible Alternative to the Strict and Over-inclusive Transfer System for Serious Juvenile Offenders," *Southern California Law Review* 90 (Jan. 2017): 364.

163. Zarum, "'Time: The Kalief Browder Story.'"

## 11. THINGS FALL APART:
### BLACK FAMILIES IN AN ERA OF MASS INCARCERATION

1. "Kalief's Mother on Her Torment," Marshall Project, Oct. 17, 2016.

2. Christopher Mathias, "Mother of Kalief Browder, the Teen Cruelly Held at Rikers Island, Dies of a 'Broken Heart,'" *HuffPost,* Oct. 17, 2016.

3. Alysia Santo, "What Kalief Browder's Mother Thinks Should Happen to Rikers," Marshall Project, Feb. 17, 2016.

4. Deion Browder, "My Mom Died Trying to Preserve the Legacy of Her Son. Keeping Kids Out of Solitary Will Preserve Hers," *USA Today,* April 23, 2019.

5. Daniel Trotta, "Trayvon Martin: Before the World Heard the Cries," Reuters, April 3, 2012; Post Staff Report, "Trayvon Martin's Parents Recall Learning That Their Son Died," *New York Post,* March 24, 2012.

6. Trotta, "Trayvon Martin"; Chitra Ramaswamy, "Trayvon Martin's Parents Five Years On: 'Racism Is Alive and Well in America,'" *Guardian,* Feb. 13, 2017.

7. Ramaswamy, "Trayvon Martin's Parents Five Years On."

8. Post Staff Report, "Trayvon Martin's Parents Recall."

9. Trotta, "Trayvon Martin."

10. Everytown for Gun Safety, "Lucy McBath—We Can End Gun Violence," YouTube, Dec. 25, 2015.

11. Madison Feller, "Lucy McBath Lost Her Son to Gun Violence. Next Came Activism. Now She's Running for Congress," *Elle,* June 26, 2018.

12. Everytown for Gun Safety, "Lucy McBath—We Can End Gun Violence."

13. Chris Parenteau, "Ron Davis Speaks 3 Years After Son's Death," News4Jax, Nov. 23, 2015.

14. Nicquel Terry Ellis, "'You Don't Get Over Nothing Like This': Mother of Tamir Rice Says Moving On Has Been Painful," *USA Today,* June 23, 2020.

15. Leila Atassi, "'America Has No Dreams for Black and Brown People': Samaria Rice's Continuing Journey, 5 Years After Police Killed Her Son Tamir," Cleveland.com, Nov. 22, 2019.

16. Ellis, "'You Don't Get Over Nothing Like This.'"

17. Wesley Lowery, "As Investigation Enters Fifth Month, Tamir Rice's Mother Has Moved into a Homeless Shelter," *Washington Post,* May 4, 2015.

18. Ellis, "'You Don't Get Over Nothing Like This.'"

19. Samaria Rice, "My 12-Year-Old Son, Tamir Rice, Was Killed by Police. I'm Not Allowed to Be Normal," ABC News, July 13, 2020.

20. Ellis, "'You Don't Get Over Nothing Like This.'"

21. Rice, "My 12-Year-Old Son."

22. Ellis, "'You Don't Get Over Nothing Like This.'"

23. Jim Salter, "AP Interview: Michael Brown's Mom's Book Recalls Death, Life," *Daily Herald,* May 9, 2016; Lezley McSpadden, *Tell the Truth and Shame the Devil: The Life, Legacy, and Love of My Son Michael Brown* (New York: Regan Arts, 2016), 9–11.

24. Laura Collins, "Who Was the Real Michael Brown? The Kid from a Broken Home Who Beat the Odds to Get into College, the Rapper Who Sang About 'Feds' and Smoking Weed, or the Robbery Suspect Caught on Video Minutes Before Cop Shot Him Dead," *Daily Mail,* Aug. 22, 2014.

25. McSpadden, *Tell the Truth and Shame the Devil,* 9–11; Salter, "AP Interview: Michael Brown's Mom's Book."

26. DeNeen L. Brown and Mark Berman, "Michael Brown's Mother: 'We Just Got Rudeness and Disrespect' from the Police," *Washington Post,* Sept. 27, 2014.

27. McSpadden, *Tell the Truth and Shame the Devil,* 13; Salter, "AP Interview: Michael Brown's Mom's Book."

28. Jarvis DeBerry, "Michael Brown's Mother at Xavier: 'The Only Thing Told to Me Was to Be Quiet and Calm Down,'" *Times-Picayune*, Oct. 25, 2016.

29. McSpadden, *Tell the Truth and Shame the Devil*, 14; Brown and Berman, "Michael Brown's Mother."

30. Brown and Berman, "Michael Brown's Mother."

31. DeNeen L. Brown, "For the Family of Michael Brown, Grief, Sorrow, and Anger Play Out in the Public Eye," *Washington Post*, Dec. 1, 2014.

32. Brown and Berman, "Michael Brown's Mother."

33. Seth Sandronsky and Michelle Renee Matisons, "For Survivors of Police Violence, Healing Remains Elusive," *Fix*, May 9, 2018.

34. Helen Pow, "'We've Had Enough of the Senseless Killings': Michael Brown's Father Screams Out in Pain and Family Tell How He 'Prophesized His Own Death' as Thousands of Mourners Attend Funeral," *Daily Mail*, Aug. 25, 2014; Brown, "For the Family of Michael Brown."

35. *3½ Minutes, Ten Bullets*, directed by Marc Silver (New York: Candescent Films, 2015).

36. Brown and Berman, "Michael Brown's Mother."

37. Santo, "What Kalief Browder's Mother Thinks."

38. Ibid.

39. Eli Rosenberg, "'This Is One of My First Steps'; Michael Brown's Mother Plans to Run for Ferguson City Council," *Chicago Tribune*, Aug. 10, 2018.

40. *Rest in Power: The Trayvon Martin Story*, directed by Jenner Furst and Julia Willoughby Nason (Hollywood, Calif.: Paramount Network, 2018); Sybrina Fulton and Tracy Martin, *Rest in Power: The Enduring Life of Trayvon Martin* (New York: Spiegel & Grau, 2017); Ramaswamy, "Trayvon Martin's Parents Five Years On."

41. Ramaswamy, "Trayvon Martin's Parents Five Years On."

42. Liz Fields, "Parents of Jordan Davis and Trayvon Martin in Constant Touch," ABC News, Feb. 19, 2014.

43. Browder, "My Mom Died Trying to Preserve."

44. William Neuman, "New York City Wants to Move 16- and 17-Year-Olds from Rikers Jail to Bronx Center," *New York Times*, July 20, 2016; Browder, "My Mom Died Trying to Preserve."

45. Mathias, "Mother of Kalief Browder"; Neuman, "New York City"; Jillian Jorgensen, "City Needs 'Some Type of Bail Reform,'

de Blasio Says After Kalief Browder Suicide," *Observer,* June 8, 2015; Jan Ransom and Nikita Stewart, "7 Key Questions as New York Moves Teenagers out of Rikers," *New York Times,* Sept. 28, 2018.

46. Ramaswamy, "Trayvon Martin's Parents Five Years On."

47. "We Are Trayvon," Trayvon Martin Foundation, 2020.

48. Everytown for Gun Safety, "Lucy McBath—We Can End Gun Violence"; Gracie Bonds Staples, "Lucy McBath's Son Was Shot to Death Outside a Jacksonville Convenience Store After a Dispute over Loud Music," *Atlanta Journal-Constitution,* March 29, 2014.

49. Ta-Nehisi Coates, "To Raise, Love, and Lose a Black Child," *Atlantic,* Oct. 8, 2014; Allyson Chiu and Samantha Schmidt, "Lucy McBath: Moved to Run for Congress by Son's Fatal Shooting, She Just Won Her Primary," *Washington Post,* July 25, 2018.

50. Cheyenne Haslett, "Lucy McBath, Lost Son to Gun Violence Wins Democratic Nomination in Georgia: 'To Not Do Anything Is a Tragedy,'" ABC News, July 25, 2018.

51. Ron Davis, "Standing My Ground—a Father's Story," filmed May 29, 2019, Florida State College at Jacksonville, TED video.

52. Lilly Workneh, "Michael Brown's Parents Advocate for Human Rights to U.N. Committee Against Torture," *HuffPost,* Nov. 11, 2014.

53. Fox 2 News St. Louis, "Michael Brown's Mother on Coping with the Loss of Her Son, 5 Years After His Death," YouTube, Aug. 9, 2019, www.youtube.com.

54. P. R. Lockhart, "Michael Brown Was Shot by Ferguson Police. It Inspired His Mother to Run for Office," *Vox,* April 3, 2019.

55. Ellis, "'You Don't Get Over Nothing Like This.'"

56. Rice, "My 12-Year-Old Son."

57. *Time: The Kalief Browder Story,* directed by Jenner Furst (New York: Roc Nation, Weinstein Company, and Cinemart, 2017), Netflix.

58. National Center for Mental Health and Juvenile Justice, "Policy Statement on Indiscriminate Shackling of Juveniles in Court," April 2015 (While shackling's purported purpose is to maintain order in courtrooms, it can actually have the opposite effect by causing youth to become emotionally dysregulated due to fear or anger).

59. Ibid.; David Fassler, "Policy Statement on Mandatory Shackling

in Juvenile Court Settings," American Academy of Child and Adolescent Psychiatry, Feb. 2015.

60. National Juvenile Defender Center, *A Right to Liberty: Reforming Juvenile Money Bail* (Washington, D.C.: National Juvenile Defender Center, 2019).

61. Wendy Sawyer, "How Race Impacts Who Is Detained Pretrial," Prison Policy Initiative, Oct. 9, 2019.

62. Shawn Bushway and Jonah Gelbach, "Testing for Racial Discrimination in Bail Setting Using Nonparametric Estimation of a Parametric Model," SSRN, Aug. 20, 2011, papers.ssrn.com (The five counties studied were Harris, Tex.; Dallas, Tex.; Cook, Ill.; Los Angeles, Calif.; and Broward, Fla.).

63. Ellen Donnelly and John Macdonald, "The Downstream Effects of Bail and Pretrial Detention on Racial Disparities in Incarceration," *Journal of Criminal Law and Criminology* 108, no. 4 (2018): 775–814.

64. David Arnold, Will Dobbie, and Crystal S. Yang, "Racial Bias in Bail Decisions," *Quarterly Journal of Economics* 133, no. 4 (Nov. 2018).

65. Browder, "My Mom Died Trying to Preserve."

66. Santo, "What Kalief Browder's Mother Thinks."

67. Lauren MacDougall, "The Effect of Youth Incarceration on Siblings and the Family," *Shared Justice*, May 25, 2017.

68. Development Services Group, *Family Engagement in Juvenile Justice*, Literature Review of the Office of Juvenile Justice and Delinquency Prevention, Feb. 2018.

69. Sandra Villalobos Agudelo, *The Impact of Family Visitation on Incarcerated Youth's Behavior and School Performance: Findings from the Families as Partners Project*, Vera Institute of Justice, April 2013.

70. Justice for Families and DataCenter, *Families Unlocking Futures: Solutions to the Crisis in Juvenile Justice* (Oakland: Justice for Families, 2012).

71. Ibid., 24.

72. Development Services Group, *Family Engagement in Juvenile Justice*.

73. Dorothy E. Roberts, "Black Women and Child Welfare: Lessons for Modern Reform," *Florida State University Law Review* 32, no. 3 (2005) (noting that Black children in the early twentieth century were more likely to be labeled delinquent and incarcer-

ated than to be admitted to orphanages established for destitute White children).

74. Marlene Moretti and Maya Peled, "Adolescent-Parent Attachment: Bonds That Support Healthy Development," *Paediatrics and Child Health* 9, no. 8 (Oct. 2004): 551–55; Development Services Group, *Family Engagement in Juvenile Justice.*

75. Moretti and Peled, "Adolescent-Parent Attachment."

76. Laurence Steinberg, "We Know Some Things: Parent-Adolescent Relationships in Retrospect and Prospect," *Journal of Research on Adolescence* 11 (March 2001): 1–19.

77. Santo, "What Kalief Browder's Mother Thinks."

78. Jessica Feierman et al., *Debtors' Prison for Kids? The High Cost of Fines and Fees in the Juvenile Justice System* (Philadelphia: Juvenile Law Center, 2016).

79. NY CLS Family Ct. Act § 305.2 (2019).

80. Sarah Burns, *The Central Park Five: The Untold Story Behind One of New York's Most Infamous Crimes* (New York: First Vintage Books, 2012), 28–65.

81. Ibid., 28–29, 61, 62.

82. Ibid., 31, 37–38, 39, 40.

83. Ibid., 41–42.

84. Ibid., 42–43.

85. Douglas Starr, "This Psychologist Explains Why People Confess to Crimes They Didn't Commit," *Science,* June 13, 2019.

86. Burns, *Central Park Five,* 3–4.

87. Ibid., 46–47.

88. Ibid., 53.

89. Santo, "What Kalief Browder's Mother Thinks."

90. John Edgar Wideman, *Brothers and Keepers: A Memoir* (New York: Holt, Rinehart and Winston, 1984).

91. J. Mark Eddy and Julie Poehlman-Tynan, eds., *Handbook on Children with Incarcerated Parents: Research, Policy, and Practice* (New York: Springer International, 2019); Annie E. Casey Foundation, *Children of Incarcerated Parents, a Shared Sentence* (Baltimore: Annie E. Casey Foundation, 2016); Donald Braman, *Doing Time on the Outside: Incarceration and Family Life in Urban America* (Ann Arbor: University of Michigan Press, 2007).

92. Juleyka Lantigua-Williams, "When a Sibling Goes to Prison," *Atlantic,* Nov. 14, 2016.

93. Katie Heaton, "The Sibling Experience: Grief and Coping with

Sibling Incarceration," Sophia, St. Catherine University, May 2014.

94. Juleyka Lantigua-Williams, "Getting Therapy Instead of Serving Time," *Atlantic*, Nov. 18, 2016.

95. Heaton, "Sibling Experience."

96. Ibid., 4.

97. Ibid., 7.

98. Lantigua-Williams, "Getting Therapy Instead of Serving Time."

99. Ibid.

100. Juleyka Lantigua-Williams, "In Prison, but Still a Big Sister," *Atlantic*, Nov. 15, 2016.

101. Chris Bodenner, "The Trauma of Visiting a Sibling in Prison," *Atlantic*, Nov. 23, 2016.

102. Heaton, "Sibling Experience," 4.

103. Santo, "What Kalief Browder's Mother Thinks."

104. Brown, "For the Family of Michael Brown."

105. P. R. Lockhart, "New York's Justice System Failed Kalief Browder. Now the City Will Pay His Family $3.3 Million," *Vox*, Jan. 25, 2019; Byron Pitts, Jasmine Brown, and Lauren Effron, "Kalief Browder's Siblings Hope New Documentary 'Time: The Story of Kalief Browder' Prevents Their Brother's Case from Repeating," ABC News, March 8, 2017.

106. Cory Shaffer, "Tamir Rice's Sister Says Cleveland Police Lacked 'Decency' and 'Respect' in Detaining Her After Shooting," Cleveland.com, Feb. 9, 2015.

107. Cory Shaffer, "Extended Tamir Rice Shooting Video Shows Officers Restrained Sister," Cleveland.com, Jan. 8, 2015.

108. Richard A. Oppel Jr., "National Questions over Police Hit Home in Cleveland," *New York Times*, Dec. 8, 2014.

109. Cleveland.com, "Tamir Rice and His 14-Year-Old Sister Tajai Were Inseparable," YouTube, March 31, 2015.

110. RT Ruptly, "USA: 'He Was Only 12.' Tamir Rice's Sister Makes Emotional Plea," YouTube, Nov. 24, 2014.

111. Shaffer, "Tamir Rice's Sister Says."

112. CNN, "Brother: Remember Trayvon as a Happy Teen," CNN video, April 13, 2012.

113. Timothy Bella, "At City Hall with Trayvon Martin's Brother, a Rising Community Organizer," *Vice*, May 19, 2017.

114. Matthew Desmond, *Evicted: Poverty and Profit in the American City* (New York: Crown, 2016).

115. Terrence McCoy, "As the Nation's Capital Booms, Poor Tenants Face Eviction over as Little as $25," *Washington Post,* Aug. 8, 2016; D.C. Code Mun. Regs. tit. 14 § 6109 (2020).

116. 24 C.F.R. § 966.4(f)(12)(2017).

117. 42 U.S.C. § 13661(c) (2012); *Scarborough v. Winn Residential LLP/Atlantic Terrace Apartments,* 890 A.2d 249 (D.C. 2006); *Calloway v. District of Columbia Housing Authority,* 916 A.2d 888 (D.C. 2006).

118. Wendy J. Kaplan and David Rossman, "Called 'Out' at Home: The One Strike Eviction Policy and Juvenile Court," *Duke Forum for Law and Social Change* 3 (2011): 109, 116.

119. Matthew Desmond, *Evicted: Poverty and Profit in the American City* (New York: Crown, 2016).

120. *Ensuring Young People Are Not Criminalized for Poverty: Bail, Fees, Fines, Costs, and Restitution in Juvenile Court* (Washington, D.C.: National Juvenile Defender Center, 2018).

121. Feierman et al., *Debtors' Prison for Kids?*

122. Rena Coen et al., *Electronic Monitoring of Youth in the California Juvenile Justice System* (Berkeley, Calif.: Berkeley School of Law, Samuelson Law, Technology & Public Policy Clinic, 2017), 1–20.

123. Eli Hager, "Your Kid Goes to Jail, You Get the Bill," Marshall Project, March 2, 2017.

124. Feierman et al., *Debtors' Prison for Kids?*

125. Erik Eckholm, "Court Costs Entrap Nonwhite, Poor Juvenile Offenders," *New York Times,* Aug. 31, 2016.

## 12. #BLACKBOYJOY AND #BLACKGIRLMAGIC: ADOLESCENT RESILIENCE AND SYSTEMS REFORM

1. Matt Perez, "Trump Threatens to Deploy Troops to End Protests After Tear Gas, Flashbangs Shot at Peaceful Demonstrators Outside White House," *Forbes,* June 1, 2020; Michelle Boorstein and Rachel Weiner, "Historic D.C. Church Where Trump Stood with a Bible Becomes a Symbol for His Religious Foes," *Washington Post,* June 3, 2020.

2. Collette Chapman-Hilliard and Valerie Adams-Bass, "A Conceptual Framework for Utilizing Black History Knowledge as a Path to Psychological Liberation for Black Youth," *Journal of Black Psychology* 42 (2016): 479–507.

3. Gemma Aburn, Merryn Gott, and Karen Hoare, "What Is Resilience? An Integrative Review of the Empirical Literature," *Journal*

*of Advanced Nursing* 72, no. 5 (2016): 980–1000. See also Alexa Curtis, "Defining Adolescence," *Journal of Adolescent and Family Health* 7, no. 2 (2015): 1–39; David Murphy, Megan Barry, and Brigitte Vaughn, "Adolescent Health Highlight, Positive Mental Health: Resilience," *Child Trends,* Jan. 2013.

4. American Psychological Association Task Force on Resilience and Strength in Black Children and Adolescents, *Resilience in African American Children and Adolescents: A Vision for Optimal Development* (Washington, D.C.: American Psychological Association, 2008), 29.

5. *Ring the Alarm: The Crisis of Black Youth Suicide in America: A Report to Congress from the Congressional Black Caucus Emergency Taskforce on Black Youth Suicide and Mental Health* (Washington, D.C.: Congressional Black Caucus, 2019), 21.

6. Ibid., 23; Daniel B. Lee and Enrique W. Neblett, "Religious Development in African American Adolescents: Growth Patterns That Offer Protection," *Child Development* 90 (2019); Dong Ha Kim et al., "The Protective Effects of Religious Beliefs on Behavioral Health Factors Among Low Income African American Adolescents in Chicago," *Journal of Child and Family Studies* 27, no. 6 (2018): 355–64. See also Callie Burt et al., "Racial Discrimination, Racial Socialization, and Crime: Understanding Mechanisms of Resilience," *Social Problems* 64, no. 3 (2017): 414–38; Michael Cunningham et al., "Resilience and Coping: An Example in African American Adolescents," *Research in Human Development* 15, no. 3–4 (2018): 317–31; Antoinette Landor et al., "Colorizing Self-Esteem Among African American Young Women: Linking Skin Tone, Parental Support, and Sexual Health," *Journal of Child and Family Studies* 28, no. 6 (2019): 1886–98; Kristin Neff and Pittman McGehee, "Self-Compassion and Psychological Resilience Among Adolescents and Young Adults," *Self and Identity* 9, no. 3 (2010): 225–40.

7. Congressional Black Caucus, *Ring the Alarm,* 23; Joseph B. Richardson Jr., "Beyond the Playing Field: Coaches as Social Capital for Inner-City Adolescent African-American Males," *Journal of African American Studies* 16, no. 2 (2012): 171–94; Paul Caldarella et al., "Adolescent Sports Participation and Parent Perceptions of Resilience: A Comparative Study," *Physical Educator* 76, no. 4 (2019): 1026–45.

8. Jacqueline O. Moses et al., "Black and Proud: The Role of Ethnic-

Racial Identity in the Development of Future Expectations Among At-Risk Adolescents," *Cultural Diversity and Ethnic Minority Psychology* 26 (2020): 112–23; Sheretta T. Butler-Barnes et al., "Promoting Resilience Among African American Girls: Racial Identity as a Protective Factor," *Child Development* 89, no. 6 (2018): e552–e571; Robert Sellers et al., "Racial Identity Matters: The Relationship Between Racial Discrimination and Psychological Functioning in African American Adolescents," *Journal of Research on Adolescence* 16 (2006): 187–216.

9. Moses et al., "Black and Proud," 117–19; Angelique J. Trask-Tate, Michael Cunningham, and Samantha Francois, "The Role of Racial Socialization in Promoting the Academic Expectations of African American Adolescents: Realities in a Post-*Brown* Era," *Journal of Negro Education* 83, no. 3 (2014): 281–99; Butler-Barnes et al., "Promoting Resilience."

10. Burt et al., "Racial Discrimination, Racial Socialization, and Crime," 431.

11. See Sellers et al., "Racial Identity Matters"; Trask-Tate, Cunningham, and Francois, "Role of Racial Socialization"; Riana Elyse Anderson et al., "What's Race Got to Do with It? Racial Socialization's Contribution to Black Adolescent Coping," *Journal of Research on Adolescence* 29, no. 4 (2018): 822–31.

12. Cunningham et al., "Resilience and Coping"; Landor et al., "Colorizing Self-Esteem," 1887.

13. Landor et al., "Colorizing Self-Esteem," 1887.

14. Anderson et al., "What's Race Got to Do with It?," 823–25.

15. Sellers et al., "Racial Identity Matters," 188–89 (citing Margaret Beale Spencer et al., "A Phenomenological Variant of Ecological Systems Theory (PVEST): A Self-Organization Perspective in Context," *Development and Psychopathology* 9 (1997): 817–33).

16. Chapman-Hilliard and Adams-Bass, "Conceptual Framework," 493; Trask-Tate, Cunningham, and Francois, "Role of Racial Socialization," 295.

17. Chapman-Hilliard and Adams-Bass, "Conceptual Framework," 493, 496.

18. Burt et al., "Racial Discrimination, Racial Socialization, and Crime," 416; Lee and Neblett, "Religious Development."

19. Lee and Neblett, "Religious Development," 254.

20. Kim et al., "Protective Effects of Religious Beliefs," 360–61.

21. Laurence Steinberg, *Age of Opportunity: Lessons from the New*

*Science of Adolescence* (Boston: Houghton Mifflin Harcourt), 10, 17.

22. Lee and Neblett, "Religious Development," 255–56.

23. Velma McBride Murry, "Healthy African American Families in the 21st Century: Navigating Opportunities and Transcending Adversities," *Family Relations* 68, no. 3 (2019): 342–57; Jonitha Watkins Johnson, "'All I Do Is Win . . . No Matter What': Low-Income, African American Single Mothers and Their Collegiate Daughters' Unrelenting Academic Achievement," *Journal of Negro Education* 85, no. 2 (2016): 156–71.

24. Donte L. Bernard et al., "Making the 'C-ACE' for a Culturally-Informed Adverse Childhood Experiences Framework to Understand the Pervasive Mental Health Impact of Racism on Black Youth," *Journal of Child & Adolescent Trauma* (2020).

25. Omnibus Juvenile Justice, Victim's Rights, and Parental Participation Act of 2003, Bill 15-537 in the Council of the District of Columbia, Introduced by Chairman Linda W. Cropp at the Request of the Mayor.

26. Vivian Yee and Alan Blinder, "National School Walkout: Thousands Protest Against Gun Violence Across the U.S.," *New York Times,* March 14, 2018.

27. P. R. Lockhart, "The Gun Reform Debate Has Largely Ignored Race. Black Students Made Sure the School Walkouts Didn't," *Vox,* March 14, 2018; P. R. Lockhart, "Parkland Is Sparking a Difficult Conversation about Race, Trauma, and Public Support," *Vox*, Feb. 24, 2018.

28. Emily Shapiro, "National School Walkout: Everything to Know About the Upcoming Event to End Gun Violence," ABC News, April 18, 2018.

29. Christopher Rim, "How Student Activism Shaped the Black Lives Matter Movement," *Forbes,* June 4, 2020; Phil Helsel, "Students Walk Out in Day of Protest Against Trump Immigration Plans," NBC News, Nov. 16, 2016; Moriah Banlingit, "Hundreds of Virginia High School Students Walk Out in Support of Immigrants," *Washington Post,* Feb. 10, 2017; Doug Stanglin, Grace Hauck, and Janet Wilson, "'Our House Is on Fire': Global Climate Strike Draws Out Hundreds of Thousands of Protesters in New York, DC," *USA Today,* Sept. 20, 2019.

30. Shawn A. Ginwright, "Peace Out to Revolution! Activism Among African American Youth: An Argument for Radical Healing,"

*Young* 18 (2010): 93; Shawn Ginwright and Julio Cammarota, "New Terrain in Youth Development: The Promise of a Social Justice Approach," *Social Justice* 29, no. 4 (2002): 92; Ben Kirshner, "Introduction: Youth Activism as a Context for Learning and Development," *American Behavioral Scientist* 51, no. 3 (2007): 368.

31. Ginwright and Cammarota, "New Terrain in Youth Development," 92; Ginwright, "Peace Out to Revolution!," 82.
32. Constance A. Flanagan et al., "Youth Civic Development: Theorizing a Domain with Evidence from Different Cultural Contexts," *New Directions for Child and Adolescent Development* 134 (2011): 99; Ginwright, "Peace Out to Revolution!," 82.
33. Michael Nakkula and Eric Toshalis, *Understanding Youth: Adolescent Development for Educators* (Cambridge, Mass.: Harvard Education Press, 2006), 120–22, 125; Philtrina Farquharson, "M-DCPS Votes 8–1 to Teach Anti-racism," *Miami Times,* June 24, 2020.
34. Shawn A. Ginwright, "Black Youth Activism and the Role of Critical Social Capital in Black Community Organizations," *American Behavioral Scientist* 51 (2007): 403–18.
35. Sophia Barnes, "DC Council Votes to Remove School Security Contract from MPD," NBC Washington, July 8, 2020.
36. The School Safety Division is a unit within MPD tasked with providing security services to DCPS. See Code of the District of Columbia, Establishment of the Metropolitan Police Department School Safety Division; Functions of the School Safety Division, § 5–132.02; Metropolitan Police Department, *School Safety and Security in the District of Columbia: SY 2009–2010* (Washington, D.C.: Metropolitan Police, 2009).
37. Metropolitan Police Department, *School Safety and Security.*
38. Barnes, "DC Council Votes to Remove School Security Contract from MPD"; "Positive Youth Development," Youth.gov (defining positive youth development as an intentional, pro-social approach that engages youth within their communities, schools, organizations, peer groups, and families in a manner that is productive and constructive; recognizes, utilizes, and enhances young people's strengths; and promotes positive outcomes for young people by providing opportunities, fostering positive relationships, and furnishing the support needed to build on their leadership strengths).
39. Black Swan Academy, "About Black Swan Academy."

40. D.C. Office of the State Superintendent of Education, "District of Columbia Report: Student Population," DC School Report Card, dcschoolreportcard.org (indicating in 2019 School Report Card that out of 338 total arrests of students across the District, 312 were of Black students, 26 were of Latino students, and 104 were for students with disabilities).

41. @EmpowerEdDC, "Strong teacher voice today with @EmpowerEdDC teacher leaders showing up to @councilofdc budget hearing asking to #DefundMPD and invest in school based mental health, fund relief for child care, raising revenues for #JustRecoveryDC, SPED and ELL support and more!," Twitter, June 17, 2020.

42. Nathan Diller, "Two-Thirds of D.C. Voters Surveyed Support Removing Police from Schools, Using Funds for Student Programs," WAMU, June 17, 2020; Public Policy Polling, "Just Recovery DC Poll," June 15–16, 2020.

43. Council Member David Grosso, *Draft Report and Recommendation of the Committee on Education on the Fiscal Year 2021 Budget for Agencies Under Its Purview*, Washington, D.C., Committee on Education, June 24, 2020; David Grosso, "Councilmember Grosso Files Resolution to Disapprove School Security Contract Administered by MPD," David Grosso DC Council At-Large, June 19, 2020; David Grosso et al., *A Proposed Resolution in the Council of the District of Columbia: Security Assurance Management Inc. Disapproval Resolution 2020*, Council of the District of Columbia, June 19, 2020.

44. See David Grosso, "Grosso Proposes Budget That Maintains D.C.'s Growing Investments in Education," David Grosso Council Member At-Large, June 24, 2020.

45. Samantha Davis, "To: D.C. Mayor, City Council, Deputy Mayor of Education & State Board of Education, Tell D.C. Leaders: We Demand Police-Free Schools!," Organize For, 2020; Department of Youth Rehabilitation Services, "Credible Messenger Initiative," dyrs.dc.gov.

46. Perry Stein, "D.C. Schools Chancellor Defends Police in Schools amid Questioning by Lawmakers," *Washington Post*, June 11, 2020.

47. Evie Blad, "United Nations Panel Recommends Changes to U.S. School Discipline," *EdWeek*, Feb. 1, 2016.

48. Dignity in Schools, "Youth and Parents Across the Country Call

for #CounselorsNotCops #PoliceFreeSchools," Dignity in Schools, June 19, 2020 (noting thirteen cities with active campaigns to remove police include Oakland; San Francisco; Los Angeles; Denver; Washington, D.C.; Chicago; Montgomery County, Maryland; Minneapolis; New York; Raleigh; Portland; Pittsburgh; Madison, Wisconsin).

49. Lois Beckett, "Minneapolis Public School Board Votes to Terminate Its Contract with Police," *Guardian,* June 2, 2020.

50. Dahlia Bazzaz and Hannah Furfaro, "Police Presence at Seattle Public Schools Halted Indefinitely," *Seattle Times,* June 24, 2020.

51. Dahlia Bazzaz, "What We Know About the Effort to Remove Police Stationed in Seattle Schools," *Seattle Times,* June 10, 2020.

52. Zack Haber, "How to Help Black Organizing Project's Fight to Remove Police from OUSD," *Post News Group,* June 10, 2020.

53. Ashley McBride, "For 9 Years, the Black Organizing Project Has Been Campaigning to Remove Police from Oakland Schools. Will It Finally Happen?," *Berkleyside,* June 5, 2020.

54. Wilson Walker, "Oakland School Board Votes to Remove OUSD Police from School Campuses," 5KPIX CBS San Francisco Area, June 24, 2020; Darwin BondGraham, "How 2 Oakland Students Got 15,000 People to March Against Police Violence on Monday," *Berkleyside,* June 2, 2020.

55. Libby Nelson and Dara Lind, "The School to Prison Pipeline, Explained," Justice Policy Institute, Feb. 24, 2015; American Civil Liberties Union, "School-to-Prison Pipeline," ACLU, 2020; Jessica Gould et al., "Students at Mostly Black NYC Schools More Likely to Have Negative Feelings About School Police," *Gothamist,* June 19, 2020.

56. See Bazzaz, "What We Know"; Thomasi McDonald, "Durham Students Plan Protest to Remove Cops from Schools," *Indy Week,* June 11, 2020; Mark McPherson, "Students Rally to Remove Police from Milwaukee Public Schools," WDJT-Milwaukee, June 17, 2020.

57. Adam Rogan, "Leader of Racine Teachers Union Wants Police out of Unified School," *Journal Times,* June 11, 2020.

58. Sarah Jones, "Protests Are Galvanizing Demands to Take Cops out of Schools," *Intelligencer,* June 12, 2020; Dave Stieber, "We Protest Police in the Streets, So Why Do We Let Police in Our Schools?," *Chicago Reporter,* June 3, 2020.

59. Meagan Day, "Teachers' Unions Are Demanding Police-Free

Schools," *Jacobin,* June 16, 2020; "Los Angeles Unified Reviews Budget and School Police Practices," City News Service, June 15, 2020; Yi-Jin Yu, "School Resource Officers: What Are They and Are They Necessary?," *Today,* June 19, 2020.

60. Melissa Gomez, "L.A. School Board Cuts Its Police Force and Diverts Funds for Black Student Achievement," *Los Angeles Times,* Feb. 16, 2021.

61. Indigo Oliver, "Chicago Teachers Join the Nationwide Movement to Kick Cops out of Schools," *In These Times,* June 17, 2020.

62. Elizabeth Miller, "Under Pressure, Portland Will Eliminate School Resource Officer Program," Oregon Public Broadcasting, June 4, 2020.

63. Rogan, "Leader of Racine Teachers"; Farquharson, "M-DCPS Votes 8–1 to Teach Anti-racism" (noting that on June 16, 2020, the Miami-Dade County Public Schools board approved a proposal to add antiracism to its multicultural curriculum).

64. Dana Goldstein, "Do Police Officers Make Schools Safer or More Dangerous?," *New York Times,* June 12, 2020; Victoria Freile, "School Resource Officers Eliminated from City Schools After Approval of Budget Tuesday," *Democrat and Chronicle,* June 17, 2020.

65. See McBride, "For 9 Years, the Black Organizing Project"; Ida Mojadad, "School District Considers Changing Relationship with Police: Board Members Debate Dropping Financial Support for Resource Officers Program," *SF Examiner,* June 9, 2020; Heather Graf, "Prince George's School Board Will Consider Proposal to Remove Armed Officers from Schools," ABC7, June 8, 2020.

66. Advancement Project and Alliance for Educational Justice, *We Came to Learn: A Call to Action for Police Free Schools* (Washington, D.C.: Advancement Project, 2019); McBride, "For 9 Years, the Black Organizing Project"; Mojadad, "School District Considers"; Graf, "Prince George's School Board Will Consider."

67. Mojadad, "School District Considers."

68. Christy Lopez, "Defund the Police? Here Is What That Really Means," *Washington Post,* June 7, 2020.

69. Katherine Tyson McCrea et al., "Understanding Violence and Developing Resilience with African American Youth in High-Poverty, High-Crime Communities," *Children and Youth Services Review* 99 (2019): 296–307.

70. Amir Whitaker et al., *Cops and No Counselors* (New York: American Civil Liberties Union, 2019), 4, 6; Richard Cleveland and Christopher Sink, "Student Happiness, School Climate, and School Improvement Plans: Implications for School Counseling Practice," *Professional School Counselling* 21 (2018); Richard Lapan, Sara Whitcomb, and Nancy Aleman, "Connecticut Professional School Counselors: College and Career Counseling Services and Smaller Ratios Benefit Students," *Professional School Counseling* 16 (2018): 117–24.
71. Mental Health America, "Position Statement 41: Early Identification of Mental Health Issues in Young People," Mental Health America, Sept. 18, 2016.
72. Congressional Black Caucus, *Ring the Alarm,* 8. See also Mental Health America, "Position Statement 45: Discipline and Positive Behavior Support in Schools," Mental Health America, Dec. 3, 2016; Paul Gionfriddo, "Ending Racism Is a Mental Health Imperative," Mental Health America, June 12, 2020.
73. Mental Health America, "Position Statement 41: Early Identification."
74. Mental Health America, "Position Statement 45: Discipline and Positive Behavior." See also Center on Positive Behavioral Interventions and Supports, "Getting Started," pbis.org.
75. Edmund Nocera et al., "Impact of School-Wide Positive Behavior Supports on Student Behavior in the Middle Grades," *Research in Middle Level Education Online* 37, no. 8 (2014); U.S. Department of Education, *Guiding Principles: A Resource Guide for Improving School Climate and Discipline,* Jan. 2014; Robert Horner and George Sugai, "School-Wide PBIS: An Example of Applied Behavior Analysis Implemented at a Scale of Social Importance," *Behavioral Analysis in Practice* 8 (2015): 81.
76. Horner and Sugai, "School-Wide PBIS"; U.S. Department of Education, *Guiding Principles.* For peer intervention strategies, see also National Institute of Justice, "Program Profile: Peers Making Peace," CrimeSolutions, Oct. 22, 2013, crimesolutions.ojp.gov; National Institute of Justice, "Practice Profile: School-Based Conflict Resolution Education," CrimeSolutions, Sept. 28, 2015, crimesolutions.ojp.gov.
77. Horner and Sugai, "School-Wide PBIS"; U.S. Department of Education, *Guiding Principles.*

78. Horner and Sugai, "School-Wide PBIS," 83; Mental Health America, "Position Statement 45: Discipline and Positive Behavior."

79. Nocera, "Impact of School-Wide Positive Behavior Supports."

80. Joie Acosta et al., "Evaluation of a Whole-School Change Intervention: Findings from a Two-Year Cluster Randomized Trial of the Restorative Practices Intervention," *Journal of Youth and Adolescence* 48, no. 5 (2019): 879.

81. Trevor Faonius et al., *Restorative Justice in U.S. Schools: A Research Review,* WestEd Justice and Prevention Research Center, Feb. 2016.

82. Catherine H. Augustine et al., *Can Restorative Practices Improve School Climate and Curb Suspensions?* (Santa Monica, Calif.: Rand, 2018) (noting that in Pittsburgh Public Schools, there were fewer suspensions for elementary, Black, low-income, and female students.); Faonius et al., *Restorative Justice in U.S. Schools.*

83. Barbara McMorris et al., *Applying Restorative Practices to Minneapolis Public Schools Students Recommended for Possible Expulsion: A Pilot Program Evaluation of the Family and Youth Restorative Conference Program* (Minneapolis: University of Minnesota Prevention Research Center, Department of Pediatrics, 2013).

84. John Bridgeland et al., *The Missing Piece: A National Teacher Survey on How Social and Emotional Learning Can Empower Children and Transform Schools* (Chicago: Collaborative for Academic, Social, and Emotional Learning, 2013), 16.

85. Roy Lubit and Rina Lubit, "Why Educators Should Care About Social and Emotional Learning?," *New Directions for Teaching and Learning* 2019, no. 160 (2019): 19.

86. John Payton et al., *The Positive Impact of Social and Emotional Learning for Kindergarten to Eighth-Grade Students: Findings from Three Scientific Reviews* (Chicago: Collaborative for Academic, Social, and Emotional Learning, 2008), 16; Roger P. Weissberg and Mary Utne O'Brien, "What Works in School-Based Social and Emotional Learning Programs for Positive Youth Development," *Annals of the American Academy of Political and Social Science* 591 (2004): 95.

87. See Bridgeland et al., *Missing Piece,* 27; David Osher et al., "Avoid Simple Solutions and Quick Fixes: Lessons Learned from a Comprehensive Districtwide Approach to Improving Student Behavior

and School Safety," *Journal of Applied Research on Children* 5 (2014): 1, 11, 19.

88. See Lubit and Lubit, "Why Educators Should Care"; Joseph L. Mahoney et al., "An Update on Social and Emotional Learning Outcome Research," *Phi Delta Kappa* 100 (2019): 21; Joseph A. Durak et al., "The Impact of Enhancing Students' Social and Emotional Learning: A Meta-analysis of School Based Universal Interventions," *Journal of Child Development* 82 (2011): 406–7; Lauri Massari, "Teaching Emotional Intelligence," *Leadership* 8 (2011): 8–9.

89. Gabriella C. Gonzalez et al., *Social and Emotional Learning, School Climate, and School Safety: A Randomized Controlled Trial Evaluation of Tools for Life in Elementary and Middle Schools XI* (Santa Monica, Calif.: Rand, 2020); Beverly Kingston et al., "Building Schools' Readiness to Implement a Comprehensive Approach to School Safety," *Clinical Child and Family Psychological Review* 21 (2018): 435.

90. American Civil Liberties Union, *Students Not Suspects: The Need to Reform School Policing in Washington State* (Seattle: American Civil Liberties Union of Washington, 2017).

91. Washington State Office of Superintendent of Public Instruction, "School Resource Officer Program."

92. See Sadie Gurman, "Agreement Keeps Denver Police out of Most School Discipline Problems," *Denver Post,* Feb. 19, 2013.

93. Dignity in Schools Campaign, *A Resource Guide on Counselors Not Cops: Supplemental Materials for DSC Policy Recommendations on Ending the Regular Presence of Law Enforcement in Schools* (New York: Dignity in Schools, 2016); Statement of Interest of the United States in *S.R. v. Kenton County,* Case No. 2:15-CV-143 (E.D. Ky. Oct. 2, 2015); *Hereford v. United States,* Consent Order No. 5:63-cv-00109-MHH (N.D. Al. Apr. 24, 2015).

94. Leadership for Educational Equity, *Emerging Models for Police Presence in Schools* (training goals); Catherine Y. Kim and India I. Geronimo, *Policing in Schools: Developing a Governance Document for School Resource Officers in K–12 Schools* (New York: American Civil Liberties Union, 2009) (distinguishing discipline from crime); U.S. Department of Justice, Office of Community Oriented Policing Services, "Memorandum of Understanding

Fact Sheet," 2017 (specifically not for discipline); Federal Bureau of Investigation, *Violence Prevention in Schools: Enhancement Through Law Enforcement Partnerships* (Washington, D.C.: U.S. Department of Justice, 2017) (legal issues).

95. Revised Code of Washington, School-Based Threat Assessment Program § 28A.320.123 (2019).

96. See Gurman, "Agreement Keeps Denver Police."

97. "Police in Schools: Arresting Developments," *Economist,* Jan. 9, 2016.

98. Olga Rodriguez, "San Francisco Police Won't Respond to Noncriminal Calls," Associated Press, June 11, 2020.

99. Federal Bureau of Investigation, *Violence Prevention in Schools.*

100. John Rosiak, "Developing Safe Schools Partnerships with Law Enforcement," *Forum on Public Policy* 1 (2009): 19.

101. Leadership for Educational Equity, *Emerging Models;* Lisa H. Thurau and Lany W. Or, *Two Billion Dollars Later: States Begin to Regulate School Resource Officers in the Nation's Schools* (Cambridge, Mass.: Strategies for Youth, 2019).

102. Thurau and Or, *Two Billion Dollars Later.* See also N. Todak and M.D. White, "Expert Officer Perceptions of De-escalation in Policing," *Policing: An International Journal* 42, no. 5 (2019): 832–46; Deborah Thompson Eisenberg, "School Conflict De-Escalation: A Coordinated Approach for Educators and SROs," *Dispute Resolution Journal* 74, no. 2 (2019).

103. Juleyka Williams-Lantigua, "Policing the Teenage Brain," *Atlantic,* Aug. 25, 2016.

104. *Hereford v. U.S.;* Statement of Interest of the United States in *S.R. v. Kenton County;* Settlement Agreement between the United States of America and the City of Meridian, Mississippi, Civil Action No. 3:13-CV-978-HTW-LRA (S.D. Miss. Nov. 18, 2015); Jennifer Counts et al., "School Resource Officers in Public Schools: A National Review," *Education and Treatment of Children* 41 (2018): 409; Thurau and Or, *Two Billion Dollars Later;* U.S. Department of Education, "Guiding Principles: A Resource Guide for Improving School Climate and Discipline"; Johanna Wald and Lisa Thurau, *First, Do No Harm: How Educators and Police Can Work Together More Effectively to Preserve School Safety and Protect Vulnerable Students* (Cambridge, Mass.: Harvard Law School Institute for Race and Justice, 2010); National Juvenile Justice Network, "School Discipline & Security Person-

nel: A Tip Sheet for Advocates on Maximizing School Safety and Student Success," Oct. 2015.

105. Thurau and Or, *Two Billion Dollars Later.*

106. Revised Code of Washington, School Resource Officer Programs § 28A.320.124 (2019).

107. National Association of School Resource Officers, "About NASRO." See Benjamin Fisher, "School Resource Officers, Exclusionary Discipline, and the Role of Context" (PhD diss., Vanderbilt University, 2016) (on file with Office of Justice Programs' National Criminal Justice Reference Service).

108. Elizabeth Shaver and Janet Decker, "Handcuffing a Third Grader? Interactions Between School Resource Officers and Students with Disabilities," *Utah Law Review* 2 (2017): 235; Caroletta Shuler Ivey, "Teaching, Counseling, and Law Enforcement Functions in South Carolina High Schools: A Study on the Perception of Time Spent Among School Resource Officers," *International Journal of Criminal Justice Science* 7 (2012): 553; Benjamin W. Fisher and Deanna N. Devlin, "School Crime and the Patterns of Roles of School Resource Officers: Evidence from a National Longitudinal Study," *Crime and Delinquency* 66, no. 11 (2019): 1, 15, 17–18.

109. National Association of School Resource Officers, "NASRO Position Statement on Police Involvement in Student Discipline," Aug. 14, 2015.

110. See Theresa Ochoa et al., "Integration of the School Resource Officer as Liaison Between Law Enforcement and School Administration in the Discipline of Students," *Law Enforcement Executive Forum* 13 (2013): 131; Shaver and Decker, "Handcuffing a Third Grader?," 235; Fisher, "School Resource Officers, Exclusionary Discipline, and the Role of Context," 7.

111. See Alice Speri, "New York Schools Gang Unit Pushes the Criminalization of Children," *Intercept,* Feb. 13, 2020; Paul Holland, "Schooling *Miranda:* Policing Interrogation in the Twenty-First Century Schoolhouse," *Loyola Law Review* 52 (2006): 113.

112. Rowan Moore Gerety, "An Alternative to Police That Police Can Get Behind," *Atlantic,* December 28, 2020.

113. Civil Rights Division, *Investigation of the Ferguson Police Department* (Washington, D.C.: U.S. Department of Justice, 2015), 91–92, 90–91, 94–96; Civil Rights Division, *Investigation of the Baltimore City Police Department* (Washington, D.C.: U.S. Department of Justice, 2016), 85–87.

114. President's Task Force on 21st Century Policing, *Final Report of the President's Task Force on 21st Century Policing* (Washington, D.C.: Office of Community Oriented Policing Services, 2015).

115. Campaign Zero, "We Can End Police Violence in America."

116. Community Oriented Policing Services, *Community Policing Defined* (Washington, D.C.: U.S. Department of Justice, 2012, revised 2014).

117. Civil Rights Division, *Investigation of the Baltimore City Police Department*, 85–87, 160–66; Civil Rights Division, *Investigation of the Ferguson Police Department*, 90. See also Jack Glaser, *Suspect Race: Causes and Consequences of Racial Profiling* (Oxford: Oxford University Press, 2014), 207–11 (discussing research showing that community policing and similar approaches can help reduce racial bias and stereotypes and improve community relations); L. Song Richardson and Phillip Atiba Goff, "Interrogating Racial Violence," *Ohio State Journal of Criminal Law* 12 (2014): 143–47 (describing how fully implemented and inclusive community policing can help avoid racial stereotyping and violence).

118. Civil Rights Division, *Investigation of the Ferguson Police Department*, 90; Civil Rights Division, *Investigation of the Baltimore City Police Department*, 160–61.

119. Thomas C. O'Brien and Tom R. Tyler, "Rebuilding Trust Between Police & Communities Through Procedural Justice & Reconciliation," *Behavioral Science and Policy* 5 (2019): 35–50; Lorraine Mazerolle et al., "Shaping Citizen Perceptions of Police Legitimacy: A Randomized Field Trial of Procedural Justice," *Criminology* 51 (2013): 33–63; Daniela Gilbert et al., *Procedural Justice and Police Legitimacy: Using Training as a Foundation for Strengthening Community-Police Relationships*, California Partnership for Safe Communities, 2015; Chicago Police Department, Instructional Design and Quality Control Section of the Education and Training Division, *Procedural Justice and Police Legitimacy: Facilitator Guide* (New York: National Institute for Building Community Trust & Justice).

120. O'Brien and Tyler, "Rebuilding Trust Between Police & Communities"; President's Task Force on 21st Century Policing, *Final Report of the President's Task Force*.

121. O'Brien and Tyler, "Rebuilding Trust Between Police & Commu-

nities"; Mazerolle et al., "Shaping Citizen Perceptions of Police Legitimacy," 33–34; George Wood, Tom Tyler, and Andrew Papachristos, "Procedural Justice Training Reduces Police Use of Force and Complaints Against Officers," *Proceedings of the National Academy of Sciences of the United States of America* 117, no. 18 (May 2020).

122. International Association of Chiefs of Police, *Practices in Modern Policing: Police-Youth Engagement* (Alexandria, Va.: IACP, 2018); Jennifer L. Woolard, Samantha Harvell, and Sandra Graham, "Anticipatory Injustice Among Adolescents: Age and Racial/Ethnic Differences in Perceived Unfairness of the Justice System," *Behavioral Sciences and the Law* 26 (2008): 207, 209; Norman J. Finkel, "But It's Not Fair! Commonsense Notions of Unfairness," *Psychology, Public Policy, and Law* 6 (2000): 898, 903–4 (finding children and teens twice as concerned with procedural justice as college-age or older adults).

123. Mazerolle et al., "Shaping Citizen Perceptions of Police Legitimacy," 33–34; Erika K. Penner et al., "Procedural Justice Versus Risk Factors for Offending: Predicting Recidivism in Youth," *Law and Human Behavior* 38 (2014): 234.

124. See John Irwin and Daniel L. Real, "Unconscious Influences on Judicial Decision-Making: The Illusion of Objectivity," *McGeorge Law Review* 42 (2010): 8–9 (summarizing research on strategies to reduce implicit judicial bias); Jerry Kang, "Trojan Horses of Race," *Harvard Law Review* 118 (2005): 1529–30; Jeffrey J. Rachlinski et al., "Does Unconscious Racial Bias Affect Trial Judges?," *Notre Dame Law Review* 84 (2009): 1195, 1196–97, 1221 (indicating that judges are able to control implicit biases when they are aware of them and motivated to do so).

125. Marie Pryor, Kim Shayo Buchanan, and Phillip Atiba Goff, "Risky Situations: Sources of Racial Disparity in Police Behavior," *Annual Review of Social Science* 16 (2020): 343–60 (citing John F. Dovidio and Samuel L. Gaertner, "Aversive Racism and Selection Decisions: 1989 and 1999," *Psychological Science* 11(4) (2000): 315–19).

126. Patricia G. Devine et al., "Long-Term Reduction in Implicit Race Bias: A Prejudice Habit-Breaking Intervention," *Journal of Experimental Psychology* 48 (2012): 1267.

127. Nakkula and Toshalis, *Understanding Youth,* 120–22, 144 (urging adults who work with youth to consider the historical, cultural,

and developmental contexts that shape their identity and threats to that identity).

128. Darryn Mumphrey and Grace Denoon, "Youth-Police Dialogue Toolkit," prepared May 2019 for Innovations in Policing class (on file with author).

129. Ibid., 2.

130. Nakkula and Toshalis, *Understanding Youth*, 125.

131. Ibid., 127, 4.

132. Ibid., 148.

133. Justin Fenton, "Baltimore School Police Officer Pleads Guilty to Slapping Student," *Baltimore Sun*, Feb. 14, 2017.

134. Karma Allen, "Florida School's Resource Officer Arrested After Video Shows Him Slamming 15-Year-Old Girl to Ground, Police Say," ABC News, Nov. 5, 2019.

135. Yu, "School Resource Officers: What Are They and Are They Necessary?"

136. Mariel Padilla, "Orlando Officer Is Terminated After Arresting 6-Year-Olds," *New York Times*, Sept. 23, 2019.

137. Julia Reinstein, "A Police Officer Who Slammed an 11-Year-Old to the Ground Has Reportedly Been Fired," *BuzzFeed News*, Dec. 16, 2019.

138. Daniel Kreps, "Campaign Zero's '8 Can't Wait Project' Aims to Curtail Police Violence," *Rolling Stone*, June 4, 2020; Advancement Project, *We Came to Learn*; Lopez, "Defund the Police?"

139. Advancement Project, *We Came to Learn; Hereford v. United States;* McBride, "For 9 Years, the Black Organizing Project"; Settlement Agreement between the United States of America and the City of Meridian, Mississippi, Civil Action No. 3:13-CV-978-HTW-LRA (S.D. Miss. Nov. 18, 2015).

140. Ian Millhiser, "Why Police Can Violate Your Constitutional Rights and Suffer No Consequences in Court," *Vox*, June 3, 2020; Institute for Justice, "Frequently Asked Questions About Ending Qualified Immunity," July 27, 2020.

141. *Gray v. Bostic*, 458 F.3d 1295 (11th Cir. 2006).

142. James Wynn Jr., "As a Judge, I Have to Follow the Supreme Court. It Should Fix This Mistake," *Washington Post*, June 20, 2020.

143. Nina Totenberg, "Supreme Court Weighs Qualified Immunity for Police Accused of Misconduct," NPR, June 8, 2020.

144. Christina Prignano, "Ayanna Pressley, Justin Amash Introduce Bill

to End Prohibition on Lawsuits Against Police Officers," *Boston Globe,* June 4, 2020.

145. Christy E. Lopez, "George Floyd's Death Could Have Been Prevented," *Washington Post,* May 29, 2020.

146. Libor Jany, "Minneapolis Police Reveal Changes to Use-of-Force Policy," *Star Tribune,* Aug. 9, 2016.

147. Working Group on Police-Involved Deadly Force Encounters, *Recommendations and Action Steps,* Minnesota Department of Public Safety, Feb. 2020.

148. New Orleans Police Department, "EPIC Ethical Policing Is Courageous," epic.nola.gov.

149. Georgetown University Law Center Innovative Policing Program, "Active Bystandership for Law Enforcement (ABLE) Project," law.georgetown.edu.

150. Nicole Porter, "Racial Impact Statements," Sentencing Project, Sept. 30, 2019; Marc Mauer, "Racial Impact Statements: Changing Policies to Address Disparities," *Criminal Justice* 23, no. 4 (2009).

151. See Porter, "Racial Impact Statements."

152. Amanda Ripley, "How America Outlawed Adolescence," *Atlantic,* Nov. 2016.

153. See Madeline List, "In Settlement with Activists, Providence Police Gang Database Is Now a Narrower Dragnet," *Providence Journal,* March 11, 2020; Maxine Bernstein, "Portland Police Discovered Nearly 100 Reports Still Contain Gang Designations, Despite Pledge to Purge Them in 2017," *Oregonian,* March 6, 2020; Anita Chabria, Kevin Rector, and Cindy Chang, "California Bars Police from Using LAPD Records in Gang Database. Critics Want It Axed," *Los Angeles Times,* July 14, 2020.

154. Michael Scotto, "Activists Rally at City Hall to Get NYPD to Erase Gang Database," Spectrum News NY 1, Dec. 12, 2019 (stating, "The NYPD says it has cut the database nearly in half, to about 17,500 people. But leaders of the 'Erase the Database Campaign' say even by the NYPD's own criteria, people can be in the database for non-criminal activity. In effect, they said, it leads to the monitoring of some people based solely on who they know and where they live.").

155. Maxine Bernstein, "Portland Police to Halt, Purge All Gang Designations," *Oregonian/OregonLive,* Sept. 8, 2017, oregonlive.com.

156. National Institute of Justice, "How CrimeSolutions Works," CrimeSolutions, July 31, 2020.

157. Blueprints for Healthy Development, "Program Search."

158. Emily Ekins, "Poll: 70% of Americans Oppose Racial Profiling by the Police," *Reason*, Oct. 14, 2014.

159. Proactive Team, "Racial Profiling: Toolkit on State Anti-racial Profiling Legislation," (2013): 2, 7.

160. *Born Suspect: Stop-and-Frisk Abuses & the Continued Fight to End Racial Profiling in America*, NAACP, Sept. 2014.

161. Anti-profiling laws would ban profiling based on race, ethnicity, national origin, immigration or citizenship status, religion, gender, gender identity, gender expression, sexual orientation, housing status, occupation, and disability status. "Appendix II: Components of an Effective Racial Profiling Law," in ibid.; Southern Poverty Law Center, "10 Best Practices for Writing Policies Against Racial Profiling," Oct. 23, 2018.

162. ACLU Iowa, "Anti-racial Profiling Efforts Gaining Momentum," Feb. 2019; Ian Kullgren, "Kate Brown Signs Bill Aimed at Stopping Police Profiling," *Oregonian*, July 13, 2015; Jonathan Maus, "Oregon Governor Signs Anti-profiling Bill Aimed at Racially Motivated Traffic Stops," *BikePortland*, Aug. 18, 2017.

163. Ben Cardin, "Cardin Introduces Bill to Ban Religious, Racial, and Discriminatory Profiling by Law Enforcement," press release, Feb. 16, 2017.

164. Ben Cardin, "Cardin Legislation Finally Would Prohibit Racial and Religious Profiling by All Levels of Law Enforcement," cardin.senate.gov, March 4, 2021. At the time of writing, S. 597 is in the Senate Committee on the Judiciary.

165. Candice Norwood, "Democrats' Police Reform Bill Faces Opposition in the Senate—but That's Only the First Hurdle," *PBS News Hour*, March 5, 2021; George Floyd Justice in Policing Act of 2021, H.R. 1280, 117th Congress (2021).

166. P. R. Lockhart, "Oregon Senate Passes Bill Punishing Racist 911 Callers," *Vox*, June 5, 2019.

167. See Jesse Hamilton, "Senator Jesse Hamilton Announces 911 Anti-discrimination, Anti-harassment Legislation in Wake of Living While Black Incidents in Brooklyn and Across the Country," press release, Aug. 15, 2018, nysenate.gov; "New Bill Seeks to Add Consequences for 911 Abuse," News 12 Brooklyn, Oct. 18, 2018.

168. Parker originally introduced a bill with criminal sanctions, but the final bill passed is a civil rights bill. An Act to Amend the Civil Rights Law, in Relation to Reporting a Nonemergency Incident Involving a Member of a Protected Class, S8492, New York State Senate, 2019–20 Leg. Sess. (NY 2020); Ariama Long, "Hamilton, Richardson Quarrel over 911 Legislation," *Kings County Politics,* June 15, 2020.

169. Long, "Hamilton, Richardson Quarrel."

170. Assembly Member Rob Bonta District 18, "Bonta to Introduce Bill to Add Racially-Motivated 911 Calls to Hate Crime Statute & Provide a Civil Remedy for Victims of Such Discrimination," press release, June 17, 2020; An Act to Add Section 52.35 to the Civil Code, and to Amend Sections 14.83 and 422.7 of the Penal Code, Relating to Discriminatory Emergency Calls, A.B. 1550, California Leg., 2019–20 Reg. Sess. (CA 2020), leginfo.legislature.ca.gov.

171. Shani Saxon, "Bye, Karen: San Francisco Officials Move to Ban Racist 911 Calls," *Colorlines,* Oct. 23, 2020; Ivan Pereira, "San Francisco Passes Caren Act to Criminalize Phony 911 Calls Based on Race," *ABC News,* Oct. 27, 2020.

172. Maria Cramer, "San Francisco Takes Action on Racial Profiling in 911 Calls," *New York Times,* Oct. 21, 2020; Janie Har, "San Francisco Passes 'CAREN' Bill in Effort to Stop White People from Calling 911 on People of Color for No Good Reason," *Chicago Tribune,* Oct. 21, 2020; City and County of San Francisco, Ordinance 219-20 Amending the Police Code- Discriminatory Reports to Law Enforcement, passed Oct. 27, 2020.

173. Nate Belt, "Grand Rapids Police Fighting False, Racially Biased 911 Calls," ABC13 On Your Side, May 26, 2020.

174. Lauren Dake, "Bill to Stop Racially Motivated 911 Calls Passes Oregon Senate," Oregon Public Broadcasting, June 3, 2019.

175. Abigail Hauslohner et al., "Incidents of Calling Police on Black People Lead States to Consider New Laws," *Philadelphia Inquirer,* May 28, 2020.

176. Evan Simko-Bednarski, "A False 911 Call in New Jersey Could Lead to More Jail Time if There's Bias," CNN, Sept. 2, 2020.

177. Kristin Henning, "The Reasonable Black Child: Race, Adolescence, and the Fourth Amendment," *American University Law Review* 67 (2018).

178. Kristin Henning and Rebba Omer, "Vulnerable and Valued: Protecting Youth from the Perils of Custodial Interrogation," *Arizona*

*State Law Journal* 52, no. 3 (Dec. 2020); Committee of the Whole and Committee on Education Public Roundtable, *School Security in District of Columbia Public Schools,* Council of the District of Columbia Joint Public Roundtable, Oct. 21, 2020.

179. Michael D. Shear, "Obama Bans Solitary Confinement of Juveniles in Federal Prisons," *New York Times,* Jan. 25, 2016.

180. *A Youth Mandate for Presidential Candidates: Permanently Dismantle the School-to-Prison-and-Deportation Pipeline* (Brooklyn, N.Y.: Center for Popular Democracy, 2020); Ellen Marrus and Nadia Seeratan, "What's Race Got to Do with It? Just About Everything: Challenging Implicit Bias to Reduce Minority Youth Incarceration in America," *John Marshall Law Journal* 8 (2015): 448–54.

181. Juvenile Justice and Delinquency Prevention Act of 1974, Pub. L. No. 93-415, 88 Stat. 1109 (1974); Heidi M. Hsia et al., *Disproportionate Minority Confinement: 2002 Update* (Washington, D.C.: Department of Justice, 2004).

182. Marrus and Seeratan, "What's Race Got to Do with It?," 449–50.

183. Juvenile Justice Reform Act, H.R. 6964 (Dec. 2018); Tshaka Barrows and Laura Ridolfi, "Public Safety Harmed in Reality by Excessively Targeting Youth of Color," *Juvenile Justice Information Exchange,* July 12, 2018 (noting that the Office of Juvenile Justice and Delinquency Prevention "backpedaled on efforts to require basic and fundamental data collection" on racial and ethnic disparities); Office of Juvenile Justice and Delinquency Prevention, "OJJDP Holds Core Requirements Training for States," *OJJDP News @ a Glance,* 2018.

184. Coalition for Juvenile Justice, "JJDPA Reauthorization: Updated Protections to Ensure Equity for Youth," Sept. 23, 2019, juvjustice .org.

185. Kristin Henning, "Criminalizing Normal Adolescent Behavior in Communities of Color: The Role of Prosecutors in Juvenile Justice Reform," *Cornell Law Review* 98 (2013): 444–45; Angela J. Davis, *Arbitrary Justice: The Power of the American Prosecutor* (Oxford: Oxford University Press, 2009).

186. Fair and Just Prosecution, Brennan Center for Justice, and the Justice Collaborative, *21 Principles for the 21st Century Prosecutor* (Washington, D.C.: Fair and Just Prosecution, 2018): 9–10.

187. *Floyd et al. v. City of New York et al.,* 959 F. Supp. 2d 540 (2013).

188. Henning, "Reasonable Black Child."

189. Tim Cushing, "Judge Calls Out Portland Police for Bogus 'Contempt of Cop' Arrest/Beating," *Techdirt*, March 27, 2015.

190. See Justice Policy Institute, "Bail Fail: Why the U.S. Should End the Practice of Using Money for Bail," Sept. 2012; Jessica Brand and Jessica Pishko, "Bail Reform: Explained," *Appeal*, June 14, 2018; Pretrial Justice Institute, *What's Happening in Pretrial Justice Q3 2020*, Oct. 2020.

191. Tamar R. Birckhead, "The Racialization of Juvenile Justice and the Role of the Defense Attorney," *Boston College Law Review* 58 (2017): 417–18; Angèle Christin et al., "Courts and Predictive Algorithms," *Data and Civil Rights: A New Era of Policing and Justice* (2015): 1–2; Sonja B. Starr, "Evidence-Based Sentencing and the Scientific Rationalization of Discrimination," *Stanford Law Review* 66 (2014): 821–23 (discussing the equal protection concerns of evidence-based sentencing based on socioeconomic status and demographics); Eric Holder, "Attorney General, U.S. Department of Justice, Address at the National Association of Criminal Defense Lawyers 57th Annual Meeting and 13th State Criminal Justice Network Conference," Aug. 1, 2014, transcript available at www.justice.gov) (expressing concern that risk assessments inject bias into the court system). See also Bernard Harcourt, "Risk as a Proxy for Race: The Dangers of Risk Assessment," *Federal Sentencing Reporter* 27 (2015): 237–38.

192. Joy Marcelle and Dakin Andone, "2nd Teen in 'Slenderman' Stabbing Gets 40 Years in Mental Institution," CNN, Feb. 1, 2018.

193. See Elizabeth S. Scott and Laurence Steinberg, *Rethinking Juvenile Justice* (Cambridge, Mass.: Harvard University Press, 2008), 217–20.

194. MST Services, *Multisystemic Therapy (MST) Research at a Glance: Published MST Outcome, Implementation, and Benchmarking Studies*, Jan. 2020.

195. Scott and Steinberg, *Rethinking Juvenile Justice*, 217–20; Katarzyna Celinska et al., "An Outcome Evaluation of Functional Family Therapy for Court-Involved Youth," *Journal of Family Therapy* 41, no. 2 (April 2019): 251–76 (finding FFT effective in reducing recidivism in delinquent youth); Clio Belle Weisman and Paul Montgomery, "Functional Family Therapy (FFT) for Behavior Disordered Youth Aged 10–18: An Overview of Reviews," *Research on Social Work Practice* 29, no. 3 (Sept. 2018): 333–46 (reporting modest but positive effects on reducing recidivism and

substance abuse, but concluding there need to be better studies on FFT before there is conclusive certainty it is effective).

196. See National Institute of Justice, "Program Profile: Trauma Focused Cognitive Behavioral Therapy," CrimeSolutions, June 21, 2011.

197. Center for Disease Control and Prevention, "The Public Health Approach to Violence Prevention," Jan. 28, 2020.

198. Andrea Lyon, "Racial Bias and the Importance of Consciousness for Criminal Defense Attorneys," *Seattle University Law Review* 35 (2012); Theodore Eisenberg and Sheri Lynn Johnson, "Implicit Racial Attitudes of Death Penalty Lawyers," *DePaul Law Review* 53 (2004); Vanessa Edkins, "Defense Attorney Plea Recommendations and Client Race: Does Zealous Representation Apply Equally to All?," *Law and Human Behavior* 35 (2011): 415.

199. Kristin Henning, "Race, Paternalism, and the Right to Counsel," *American Criminal Law Review* 54 (2017): 649.

200. Henning, "Race, Paternalism, and the Right to Counsel," 649.

201. Murugi Thande, "More Than Just a Hashtag: #BlackGirlMagic Is a Movement That Originated in DC," WUSA 9, Feb. 7, 2018.

202. Ikran Dahir, "People Are Sharing Their Black Boy Joy and It Is the Best Thing Ever," *BuzzFeed News,* Sept. 5, 2016; Danielle Young, "Thanks to Chance the Rapper, #BlackBoyJoy Is a Thing," *Root,* Aug. 30, 2016.

203. Jasmine Washington, "LeBron James Speaks Out After Brutal Police Arrest of Florida Teen," *Ebony,* April 22, 2019.

204. Abigail Freeman, "Lil Baby's 'The Bigger Picture' Is the Most Streamed Protest Track After Death of George Floyd," *Forbes,* July 2, 2020.

205. Zoe Johnson and Vernon C. Coleman III, "Here Are the Poignant Hip-Hop Songs Addressing Police Brutality, Racial Inequality, and Social Justice Right Now," *XXL,* June 15, 2020, www.xxlmag.com.

206. *Two Sides,* directed by Viola Davis, Julius Tennon, and Lemuel Plummer, TV One, Jan. 2020.

# Index

abuse
  or harrassment by police, *see*
    police brutality
  in prison or jail, *see* prison or
    jail, abuse in
  physical, and/or neglect, 104–5,
    137, 148–49, 208, 229, 262
  sexual, *see* prison or jail, sexual
    abuse in; juvenile detention
    facility, sexual victimization in
  substance, *see* alcohol; drugs;
    substance abuse
ACLU (American Civil Liberties
  Union), 47, 57, 138, 152, 316
Active Bystandership for Law
  Enforcement Project (ABLE),
  329
activism, youth, 117–21, 299–302,
  306–8
Adams, Michael Paul, 70–71
addiction(s)/addicts, 17–19, 229,
  233
ADHD (attention deficit and
  hyperactivity disorder), 142,
  168, 171, 318
adolescence, x–xi, 3–24, 228,
  279

adults' responses to behavior in,
  110
brain in, 11–13, 31, 134, 145,
  228, 241, 254, 256, 262, 334
identity development in, 110, 111;
  *see also* identity development,
  Black
impulsivity and risk-taking in,
  11–14, 31, 91, 132, 153–54,
  212, 250, 256, 257, 279, 305,
  334
invention of, 8–10
length of, 90–91
puberty in, *see* puberty
sexual development in, 83–84
worldwide similarities in, 12
adulthood, 90–91
  emerging, 91
  pre–Industrial Revolution view
    of, 9
affluenza, 22–23
African Methodist Episcopal
  church shooting, 85
*Age of Opportunity* (Steinberg), 11
aggression replacement therapy, 340
aggressive or hypermasculine
  persona, 153

agriculture, 9
Al-Amin, Elijah, 70–71
alcohol, 13, 14, 23, 31
Allen, Barry, 175, 176
Allen, Levar, 88–89
Allen, Vidal, 38–40
Alliance for Educational Justice
    (AEJ), 142
Amash, Justin, 328
Amazon, 200
American Academy of Child and
    Adolescent Psychiatry, 261
American Civil Liberties Union
    (ACLU), 47, 57, 138, 152, 316
Anderson, Tanisha, 219
anxiety, 137
Arbery, Ahmaud, 269
Arnett, Jeffrey, 91
Arnold, DeAndre, 65, 66
arrests, 321, 337
    contempt of cop, see "contempt
        of cop" arrests
    disparities in, 15
    disorderly conduct, 136, 150–52,
        154, 155, 329, 331, 337
    obstruction of justice, 151, 154
    parents and, 274, 334
    racial disparities in, 217
    rates of, xvi
    resisting, 119, 150, 152, 154,
        155, 329
    school-based, viii, 6, 119, 122,
        132, 133, 135–39, 141, 144,
        145, 216, 309, 316–19, 337
    video footage of, 159
Asperger's syndrome, 168, 170
assault on a police officer (APO),
    150–52, 221
Atlantic, 289–90
attention deficit and hyperactivity
    disorder (ADHD), 142, 168,
    171, 318

Austin, Tex., 46
authority, respect for, 157
autism, 142, 168, 170, 171, 318
autonomy, 31

bail, 275–77, 339
Bail Project, 343
Bakari, Jahda, 42–43
Balogun, Rakem, 120–21
Balser, David, 95
Baltimore, Md., 45–46, 128, 134,
    135, 151
Barris, Kenya, 343
Baton Rouge, La., 162
Bautista, Roberto, 259, 265
Bay Area Rapid Transit (BART),
    201
Becton, Dajerria, xv, 42–43
Bellille, Someko, 81–82, 84
Benjamin Franklin High School,
    144
Beyoncé, 158, 342
bias
    implicit, 99, 171
    subconscious, 89–90
    see also racial stereotypes
Bieber, Justin, 52
Billboard, 68
Binnicker, Betty June, 236–37,
    242, 243
Birth of a Nation, The, 85
Bivens, Richard, 55
#BlackBoyJoy, 341–42
Black Codes, 47, 329
#BlackGirlMagic, 341
Black Identity Extremists (BIE),
    120
Black-ish, 343
Black Lives Matter, 114, 118, 120,
    159, 307, 309, 343
Black Lives Matter Plaza, 300
Black Organizing Project, 311

Black Panthers, 52–53
Black Power, 62, 127
Black Pride, 114
Black Swan Academy, 306, 309
Bland, Sandra, 209, 217, 219, 271, 343
Bonta, Rob, 333
*Born Suspect* report, 332
Boston Marathon bombing, 210
Bowser, Muriel, 310
Boyd, Rekia, 119, 219
"boys will be boys," 92, 93, 95, 97
Bracey, Taylor, 142
brain
  in adolescence, 11–13, 31, 134, 145, 228, 241, 254, 256, 262, 334
  prefrontal cortex in, 229
  stress and trauma and, 141, 228–29
Brooks, Brandon, 42
Browder, Deion, 267
Browder, Kalief, 250, 258–65, 266–67, 271, 272, 274, 276, 277, 279, 284, 290, 335, 337–39
Browder, Venida, 258–59, 263, 266–67, 271, 272, 274, 276, 277, 279, 284, 290
Brown, Antonio, 342–43
Brown, Kristie, 94
Brown, Michael, 119, 125, 143, 160, 184–87, 189, 269–71, 322, 340
Brown, Michael, Sr., 270–73
Brown, Raheim, 311
*Brown v. Board of Education*
  decision on school segregation, 126, 145, 196
Bryant, Ma'Khia, 219
Bumpurs, Eleanor, 219
burglary, 3–5, 7–8

Burney, Brian, 144
Burrus, Barbara, 119
Bush, George H. W., 69

Cabey, Darrell, 175–77
CAHOOTS (Crisis Assistance Helping Out on the Streets), 320
Campaign Zero, 321
Canty, Troy, 175, 176
Cardin, Ben, 332
Carey, Miriam, 219
Carrillo, Oscar, 199
Carter, Akil, 198
Casebolt, Eric, 42–43
Cash, Johnny, 71
Castile, Philando, 209, 342
Caution Against Racially Exploitative Non-Emergencies (CAREN) Act, 333
CDC (Centers for Disease Control and Prevention), 13, 83, 171
cell phones, *see* smartphones
Center for Gender Equity in Science and Technology, 33
Center on Juvenile and Criminal Justice, 46
Central Park Five, 86–88, 90, 280–84, 339, 343
Chance the Rapper, 341
Chapman, William L., 184
Charleston church shooting, 85
Chatman, Cedrick LaMont, 184, 187, 189, 242
Chauvin, Derek, 328
*Chicago Tribune*, 188–89
childhood
  child labor, 9, 10
  pre–Industrial Revolution view of, 9
  presumption of innocence in, 241
  *see also* adolescence

child pornography laws, 88–89
Children's Defense Fund, 95
Childs, Anthony, 56
child welfare institutions, 244
Chinese immigrants, 18
*Chokehold* (Butler), xvii
Circle of Mothers and Circle of
    Fathers, 272–73
*City Journal*, 88
civic engagement, 117–18
  activism, 117–21, 299–302, 306–8
civil rights movement, 118–19,
    151, 245
  school policing as backlash
    against, 127–28, 133
Clark, Stephon, 209
Clinton, Bill, 19, 44, 131
cliques, 72–73
clothing and appearance, 52, 114
  dreadlocks (locs), 61, 62, 64–66
  durags, 62, 65
  fade haircuts, 65–66
  gangs and, 53–55, 57, 79, 80
  hair, 51, 61–66
  headwraps, 62, 64–65
  hijabs, 64
  hoodies, 48–51, 342
  prison associations of, 51–52,
    55, 57
  "respectability" debate and,
    57–58
  sagging pants, 51–58, 100, 329,
    331
  school dress codes and, 53, 55,
    58–66, 79
  ski masks, 48–51, 336
  tattoos, 55, 78, 79
  zoot suits, 56–57
cocaine, 15, 18, 19
  crack, 18, 19, 69, 76, 130
code switching, 117
Coffey, William, 169, 170

cognitive behavioral therapy, 340
cognitive disabilities, 166–72, 189
collateral consequences, 100, 245
college, 9, 141, 145
Colon, Natividad, 281–82
Columbine High School massacre,
    125, 131, 133, 139, 145–46,
    307
Commission on Law Enforcement
    and Administration of Justice,
    128–29
community, 30–31, 303
  police engagement with, 321–23,
    325
computers, 33
Congress of Racial Equality, 127
Connecticut, 202
consent decrees, 5, 7
Constitution, U.S., 149, 150, 161,
    319, 328
"contempt of cop" arrests,
    147–72, 325, 337, 338
  adolescent impulsivity and,
    153–54
  of adolescents with cognitive
    disabilities, 166–72
  assault on a police officer (APO),
    150–52, 221
  civil suits from, 152
  cover charges in, 10–52, 154
  data and studies on, 150–54
  disorderly conduct, 150–52, 154,
    155, 329, 331, 337
  and hypermasculine persona in
    teenage boys, 153
  intentional resistance and, 157–60
  nervousness and, 163–66
  obstruction of justice, 151, 154
  and officers' misunderstanding of
    slang, 172
  resisting arrest, 150, 152, 154, 155
Cook, Mya and Deanna, 63, 64, 66

COPS (Community Oriented Policing Services), 130, 131, 144, 335
"Cops Shot the Kid" (Nas), 160
Correll, Joshua, 40
Coston, Liz, 47
Couch, Ethan, 21–24, 339
courts, adult
  children in, xvi, 243, 245–46
  public records of, 264
  racial disparities in sentencing in, 98–99
courts, juvenile, see juvenile courts
crack, 18, 19, 69, 76, 130
Crawford, John, 343
crime(s), 130, 245
  and "aging out" of criminal behavior, 256–57
  by adolescents vs. children or adults, 11–12
  arrests for, see arrests
  civil penalties (collateral consequences) for, 245
  curfew laws and, 44–47
  in New York City, 230
  peer pressure and, 12
  stereotypes about Blackness and, see racial stereotypes about Black criminality
  and treating children like adults, 256, 264
  violent, xvi, 23, 184
CrimeSolutions database, 331
criminal justice system, 341
  bail in, 275
  Black Americans' refusal to participate in, 159
  courts in, see courts, adult; juvenile courts
  defense attorneys in, 340–41
  implicit bias in, 99
  judges in, see judges

jurors in, 19, 71
prison in, see prison and jail
prosecutors in, 336–39
racial bias in, 248
rap lyrics used as evidence in, 71
sentencing in, see sentences, sentencing
see also juvenile legal system
#CrimingWhileWhite, 16
Crump, Benjamin, 191
CT Safe, 202
Cudell Recreation Center, 26
Cuffee, Grace, 281
culture, Black adolescent, 48–80
  hip-hop and rap, 50, 52, 53, 62, 67–72, 342
  "respectability" and, 57–58, 117
  see also clothing and appearance
Cuomo, Andrew, 333
curfew laws, 44–47
Cusseaux, Michelle, 219
Cyberbullying Research Center, 83

Dalai Lama, 230
D'Alesandro, Thomas, III, 128
Dateline NBC, 178
Davis, Jordan, 71, 174–75, 182, 190–94, 196, 268, 270, 272, 273
Davis, Lorenzo, 187
Davis, Ron, 268, 270–73
Davis, Viola, 343
death penalty and execution of children, xv, 86, 236–43, 261, 265
defense attorneys, 340–41
Defense Department, U.S., 124–25
dehumanization of Black youth, 236–65, 273, 342
  courts and, 243–50
  executions, xv, 86, 236–43, 261, 265

dehumanization of Black youth (*continued*)
  laws allowing harsh penalties, 245
  "perennial lost cause" narrative, 244
  by police, 220–21
  solitary confinement, 251, 258–63, 335
  youth in adult jails and prisons, 245–47, 250–58, 264, 265
Democratic National Convention, 273
Democrats, 26, 54
Dennis, Andrea, 71
depression, 137, 210, 225, 227, 229, 255, 262, 318, 340
detention centers, *see* juvenile detention facilities
DiIulio, John, Jr., 87–88, 130, 179
disabilities, students with, 138, 142–43, 146
disorderly conduct arrests, 136, 150–52, 154, 155, 329, 331, 337
Dixon, Marcus, 94–96, 98
*Doonesbury,* 177
Douglass, Frederick, 226
dreadlocks (locs), 61, 62, 64–66
drugs, 14–15, 31, 54, 125, 130, 233, 245, 305, 331
  cocaine, 15, 18, 19
  crack, 18, 19, 69, 76, 130
  fentanyl, 17, 18
  heroin, 17
  law enforcement and "war on drugs," 18–19
  marijuana, 13, 14, 18, 205, 318
  opioids, 17–19
  opium, 18
Du, Soon Ja, 175, 179
Dunn, Michael David, 71, 174–75, 182, 184, 190–94, 272

durags, 62, 65
"duty to retreat" laws, 181
DuVernay, Ava, 86, 284, 343

Edelman, Marian Wright, 95
education, 9, 145, 303
  college, 9, 141, 145
  *see also* school
Education Department, U.S., 132, 170
Edwards, Charmaine, 37
Edwards, Jordan, 37–41, 184, 242
Edwards, Kevon, 38, 39
Edwards, Odell, 37, 38, 40
Eisenhower, Dwight D., 127
End Racial and Religious Profiling Act (ERRPA), 332
Ethical Policing Is Courageous (EPIC), 329
Ettel, Alison, 198, 202
Everette, Maximus, 38, 39
Everette, Maxwell, 38, 39
Everytown for Gun Safety, 273
evictions from public housing, 245, 292–95
execution of children, xv, 86, 236–43, 261, 265

Fairstein, Linda, 283
families, 266–97
  bail and, 275–77, 339
  evictions and, 292–95
  functional family therapy and, 340
  GPS monitors and, 296
  juvenile court fees and, 295–97
  and lasting effects of child's incarceration, 290
  resilience and, 303–6
  siblings, 284–92
  stigma of incarcerated children in, 289

viewed as cause of delinquency, 278–79, 305–6
and visiting child in detention or jail, 277–78, 288–89
*see also* parents
fashion, *see* clothing and appearance
FBI, 69, 120–21, 137, 239
Fennell, Demoraea, 251, 252, 255–58
Fennell, Niecey, 250–53, 255–58, 262, 276, 277, 284, 337, 339
Fennidy, Faith, 63
fentanyl, 17, 18
Ferebee, Lewis D., 310
Fields, Ben, 34–36, 142
Fields, Reggie, 197, 202
fight-flight-freeze response, 226–27
financial hardship, *see* poverty and financial hardship
Flake, Floyd, 178
Flint, Mich., 126, 128–30, 133, 144
Floyd, George, xviii, 119, 120, 209, 269, 300, 311, 328
Fly Rich Double, 70
Ford, Christine Blasey, 92
Ford, Ezell, 343
Forman, James, Jr., xiii–xiv
FortifyFL, 202
Francis, Willie, 238–43, 265
fraternities, 3–5, 76
Frey, Shelly, 219
Fried, Carrie, 68
friends, 72–73
Fry, Kevin, 187, 189
Fulton, Sybrina, 267–68, 271–73
functional family therapy (FFT), 340

Gaines, Korryn, 219
gangs, 20–21, 39, 73–80, 233, 253, 331

Black, first formation of, 75
Black, violence in 1980s and 1990s, 75–76
clothing and, 53–55, 57, 79, 80
databases on, 77–80, 331
decline of youth involvement in, 77
definitions and uses of term, 74–77
history of, 74–75
police surveillance and, 80
schools and, 54, 77, 79–80
White, in nineteenth and early twentieth centuries, 75
white supremacist, 76–77
Garner, Eric, 16, 119, 160, 209, 343
gentrification, 212–13
George Floyd Justice in Policing Act, 332
Georgetown Business Improvement District, 201
Georgetown Law, xiv, 101, 329
George Washington University, Jewish fraternity party at, 3–5
Gertner, Nancy, 93
Geyser, Morgan, 339
"ghetto riots," 129
Ghetto Tracker, 200, 202
Gilliam, Brittney, 218
girls, Black
abuse and trauma suffered by, 104–5
arrested at school, 122, 132, 136, 138–39, 144
arrests of, common reasons for, 47, 104–5
hair of, 61–66
incarceration rates of White girls versus, 105
in juvenile detention facilities, 105
juvenile legal system and, 101, 104–5

girls, Black (*continued*)
police killings of, 219
police officers' objectification of,
101–4
police violence against, xv,
41–44, 217–19
puberty in, 103–4
school dress codes for, 58–61
school punishment and, 101
self-esteem in, 304
sexual stereotypes and Jezebel
myth about, 58–60, 84, 85,
100–105
transgender, 219
Giuliani, Rudolph, 178
Goetz, Bernhard, 175–79, 181, 192
Golden, Pearlie, 219
Goodfellas, 73–74, 77
*Good Morning America,* 82
Good Part of Town, 200
GPS monitors, 296
Graham, Ramarley, 184, 189
Graves, Julia, 251–52, 257–58
Gray, Freddie, 119, 322
Great Migration of Blacks into
northern cities, 75, 126, 151
Greene, Wendy, 66
Griffin, Mathew, 189, 199
Grosso, David, 310
Guardian Angels, 177
Gun-Free Schools Act, 130
guns, 6–7, 14, 54, 107, 112, 130,
245
safety laws for, 307
stop and frisk and, 161–63, 231
toy, 25–29
Gurule, Thai, 155–56, 338
*Guyland* (Kimmel), 91, 97

hair, 51, 61–66
dreadlocks (locs), 61, 62, 64–66
fade cuts, 65–66

Haley, Alex, xiii
Hall, G. Stanley, 10
Hall, Mya, 219
Hamilton, Jesse, 333
Harlins, Latasha, 175, 179
Harris, Cheryl, 194
Harris, Eric, 131
Harvey, Jeremiah, 81–83, 89–90,
202, 332–33
Haste, Richard, 189
hate crimes, 223
discriminatory 911 calls as,
333
Jewish fraternity party crashing
and, 3–5
headwraps, 62, 64–65
health problems, 226–27, 254
Henning, Dustin, 284–87, 292
Henning, Kyle, 285
Henry, Asheem, 73–74, 77
Henry, Jelani, 73–74, 77
heroin, 17
hijabs, 64
hip-hop and rap, 50, 52, 53, 62,
67–72, 342
hippies, 52, 55
Hispanic and Latinx youth, xiii,
xv, 14, 19, 29, 47, 212, 217,
233
in gang databases, 77, 78
and police in schools, 132, 136,
138
history, Black, 304–5
Hitler, Adolf, 131
Holmes, Justin, 20
homicide
justifiable, 183
in New York City, 230
U.S. murder rate, 184
hoodies, 48–51, 342
Hooks, Benjamin, 177–78
Horwitz, Sari, 151

housing, 303
  evictions from, 245, 292–95
human rights agreements,
    241–42
Hunter, Wilford, 237
Hurricane Katrina, 210
Hynek, Robert, 169, 170

Ice-T, 69
identity development, 110, 111
identity development, Black,
    106–21, 304
  parents' role in, 111, 113–17
  policing's role in, 106–10, 112
  and protests against racial
    injustice, 118–21
  racial socialization and, 113–17,
    304, 305
immigrants, 18, 244–45, 332
incarceration, see prison and
    jail
Indianapolis Public Schools, 125
Industrial Revolution, 8–10
Institute of Behavioral Science,
    331
Inter-American Commission on
    Human Rights, 241–42
interrogation, 280–82

Jackson, Alvin, 95
Jackson, Dequan, 296–97
Jackson, Dominic, 256
jail, see prison and jail
James, LeBron, 342
Jay-Z, 158, 272
Jefferson, Atatiana, 219
Jewish fraternity party, 3–5
Jim Crow, 126, 242, 329
jobs
  incarceration and, 264
  Industrial Revolution and, 9, 10
  unemployment, 212–13

Johnson, Andrew "Drew," 66
Johnson, Duanna, 219
Johnson, Lyndon B., 128
Johnston, Kathryn, 219
Jomoh, Fatayi, 32
Jones, Kenneth and Peri, 94
Jordan Davis Foundation, 273
Judge, Mark, 92, 93
judges, 338–39
  bail set by, 275–76, 339
  bias in, 5–6, 19, 339
Justice Department, U.S., 18, 143,
    150, 321, 322
  Office of Community Oriented
    Policing Services, 130, 131, 144
  Office of Law Enforcement
    Assistance, 129
  Rikers Island prison and, 260
Justice for Families, 278
justifiable homicide, 183
juvenile courts, xvi, 13, 15,
    336–37
  bail and, 275–77, 339
  drug cases in, 15
  establishment of, 243–44
  fines and fees required by,
    295–97
  judges in, see judges
  jurors in, 19
  racial disparities in, 246
  White youth offered alternatives
    to jail by, 19, 23, 339
juvenile detention facilities, xvi,
    8, 15
  children chained in, xiii
  girls in, 105
  sexual victimization in, 101, 105
Juvenile Justice and Delinquency
    Prevention Act (JJDPA), 335–36
juvenile legal system, 234, 264, 336
  Black girls and, 101, 104–5
  children shackled in, xiii, 274–75

juvenile legal system (*continued*)
  creation of, 10, 279
  defense attorneys in, 340–41
  and dropping out of school, 141
  minorities overrepresented in, 47
  prosecutors in, 336–39
  public access to records of, 306
  reformers in, 243–45
  regulating and incentivizing
    humane contact with youth in,
    334–36
  "state as parent" (*parens patriae*)
    philosophy in, 279
  treatment of Black vs. White
    youth in, 15–16
  White youth in, 15–16, 19, 23
  youth with cognitive and
    language deficits in, 170–71

Kaepernick, Colin, 158, 307, 342
Kager, India, 219
Kalief Browder Memorial
  Scholarship, 272
Karlin, Joyce, 179
Kavanaugh, Brett, 92–93
Kennedy, John F., 127
Kenny, Matthew, 189
Kenny, Niya, 34–36, 144, 216
Kimmel, Michael, 91, 97
Klebold, Dylan, 131
Klein, Teresa, 81–83, 89–90, 202
Krakora, Linda, 197, 202
Ku Klux Klan, 49, 125, 175, 176,
  194

Lamar, Kendrick, 342
Lantigua-Williams, Juleyka, 289
Latinx youth, *see* Hispanic and
  Latinx youth
Law Enforcement Assistance
  (LEA), 129
leadership skills, 118, 307

Leap, Braden, 68
learning disabilities, 166–72, 189
Lee, Mekhi, 197
leisure and recreation, 30, 31, 303
  *see also* play, adolescent
life expectancy, 226, 254
Lil Baby, 342–43
Lindley, Bryce, 32
LL Cool J, 50, 51
*Locking Up Our Own* (Forman),
  xiii–xiv
Loehmann, Timothy, 26–29, 39,
  160, 189
Loftin, Myles, 342
Lopez, Christy, 328
Los Angeles, Calif., 126, 312
Los Angeles Rams, 342
Los Angeles School Police
  Department, 124
Los Angeles Unified School
  District (LAUSD), 125
Lott, Leon, 33, 35, 36
Lyles, Charleena, 219
lynchings, 57, 58, 85, 90, 160,
  183–84, 194, 196, 240, 242,
  244
  of Emmett Till, xv, 82, 85, 87,
    175, 242, 270–72

Mafia, 77
Males, Mike, 46
marijuana, 13, 14, 18, 205, 318
Marjory Stoneman Douglas High
  School shooting in Parkland,
  132, 139, 202, 307
Marshall Project, 162
Martin, Jahvaris, 291–92
Martin, Tracy, 267–68, 270–73
Martin, Trayvon, xv, 50, 51, 58,
  174, 180–82, 190–91, 195–96,
  267–68, 271, 291–92, 340, 342
mass incarceration, xvii, 133, 194

mass shootings, 55
  Charleston church, 85
  *see also* school shootings
Mayfield, Emilio, 156
McBath, Lucy, 268, 273
McBride, Renisha, 174, 175, 195, 196
McCarthy, Garry, 120
McCray, Antron, 86–87, 282–83
McCray, Bobby, 282–83
McCray, Linda, 282–83
McCulloch, Bob, 186–87
McDade, Kendrec, 184, 189, 199
McDonald, Laquan, 184, 187–90
McGinty, Tim, 26, 28
McKenna, Natasha, 219
McKinney, Tex., 41, 43, 44, 136
McMillian, Tremaine, 32, 154, 156
McSpadden, Lezley, 269–71, 273
Mead, Margaret, 10
Meili, Trisha, 280
memorandum of understanding (MOU), involving police in schools, 134, 317, 319
Mental Health America, 313
mental health issues, 137–38, 163, 189, 229, 305, 318, 339
  depression, 137, 210, 225, 227, 229, 255, 262, 318, 340
  exposure to police killings and, 210
  in incarcerated youth, 216, 254–55, 258
  mobile crises units for, 320
  policing and, 213–17
  reluctance to seek treatment for, 227–29
  schools and, 137–38, 312–14, 319, 320, 335
  suicide and, *see* suicide
Metropolitan Police Department (MPD), 151, 201, 222, 230–33, 309–10

Mexican Americans, 128
Mexican migrants, 18
Michael O. D. Brown We Love Our Sons and Daughters Foundation, 273
Michigan Civil Rights Commission, 130
Michigan statehouse, storming of, 120
Mikva Challenge, 306
Minnesota Lynx, 342
Molotov cocktail incident, vii–xii, 6, 136–37, 298–99, 336
Moms Demand Action, 273
Moore, Kayla, 219
Moore, Rita, 312
Morris, Monique, 101
Mothers of the Movement, 273
Mott Institute for Police-School Liaison Officers, 126
Mullen, Carmen, 238
multisystemic therapy, 340
murder rate, U.S., 184
music, 67–68, 114
  country, 68–69
  hip-hop and rap, 67–72
  pop, 68, 69
Murphy, Shakara, 33–36, 136, 142, 326

NAACP, 57, 95, 177, 240
  *Born Suspect* report of, 332
Nas, 158, 160
national anthem protests, 158, 342
National Association of Black Journalists, 343
National Association of School Resource Officers (NASRO), 125, 319
National Gang Center, 76, 77

National Institute of Justice, 331
National Juvenile Defender
  Center, xiv
National Rifle Association, 177
National Women's Law Center,
  59, 61, 64
Neighborhood Watch, 174, 180,
  190, 196
New Jim Crow, The (Alexander),
  xvii
Newlen, Jeffrey, 189, 199
New York, N.Y., 74, 200
  crime in, 230
  gang database in, 77, 80, 331
  gang prevention unit in, 79–80
  Rikers Island prison in, see
    Rikers Island prison
New York City Board of
  Education, 130–31
New York Police Department,
  76–77, 127, 131
  stops and frisks by, 211–12,
    230–31, 338
New York Times, 296–97
Nextdoor.com, 200
Nielson, Erik, 71
9/11 attacks, 210
Nixon, Richard, 18
Nordstrom Rack, 197–98
N.W.A., 69, 342

Oakland, Calif., 134, 311
Obama, Barack, 57, 321, 335
obstruction of justice arrests, 151,
  154
Oklahoma City bombing, 210
Oliver, Roy, 37–41
Omnibus Crime Control and Safe
  Streets Act, 245
Operation GroupMe, 201–2
opioids, 17–19
opium, 18

Pantaleo, Daniel, 16
pants, sagging, 51–58, 100, 329,
  331
parens patriae, 279
parents, 9–10, 31–32, 58, 279
  adolescent sexual development
    and, 83–84
  arrests and, 274, 334
  Black identity development and,
    111, 113–17
  of Central Park Five, 280–84
  and child's interrogation by
    police, 280
  of victims of police killings,
    267–71, 273
  of victims of racist civilian
    violence, 269, 271–73
  see also families
Parker, Kathleen, 93
Parker, Kevin, 333
Parkland, Fla., Stoneman Douglas
  High School shooting in, 132,
  139, 202, 307
parties, 37–44
Pathways 2 Power, 306
peers, 72–73
  influence of, 12, 257
Persky, Aaron, 96–98
Pew Research Group, 32
Phillips, Stone, 178
phones, see smartphones
play, adolescent, 25–47
  benefits of, 29–32
  parties, 37–44
  toy guns and war games, 25–29
Plowden, Charles, 237
police, 114, 301–2
  accountability of, 321, 326–29
  Black girls objectified by, 101–5
  Black identity development and,
    106–10, 112
  calls to, 197–200, 202, 332–34

children attacked by dogs of, 162
civil liability and, 327, 328
community-oriented policing
  and, 321–23, 325
as constant presence, 211
"contempt of cop" arrests by, see
  "contempt of cop" arrests
and decriminalization of Black
  adolescence, 329–34
dehumanization by, 220–21
demeaning language used by,
  158
dialogues between youth and,
  325–26
distrust of, 116, 140, 159, 212
interrogation by, 280–82
judges and, 338
lack of training of, 153
legitimacy of, 159, 322
parents' advice to children about
  encounters with, 115
procedural justice and, 322–23
qualified immunity doctrine and,
  327, 328
racial stereotypes and, see
  racial stereotypes about Black
  criminality, and police
rappers and, 69
reform strategies for, 321
slang and colloquialisms
  misunderstood by, 172
stops and frisks by, 80, 107,
  157–58, 161–64, 211–12, 220,
  230–33, 321, 332, 334, 337,
  338
surveillance by, 74, 79–80, 140,
  160, 289, 332
time and location of encounters
  with, 215–16
vicious cycles created by
  interactions between Black
  youth and, 141, 159–60

violence against, 120
White Americans killed by,
  208–9
police brutality, 140, 158, 212,
  342, 343
against girls, xv, 41–44, 217–19
grievance procedures and, 159
peer intervention in, 328–29
posted on social media, 158, 159,
  209–10
in schools, 141–44, 146
use of force, 28, 101, 142, 156,
  212, 217, 321, 322, 326–27, 328
White versus Black perceptions
  of, 158
youth blamed for, 156
police in schools, 122–46, 335,
  336
accountability of, 143, 326–28
arrests by, viii, 6, 119, 122, 132,
  133, 135–39, 141, 144, 145,
  216, 309, 316–19, 337
beginnings of school-police
  partnerships, 125–30, 133, 144
civil rights backlash and, 127–28,
  133
Columbine and, 125, 131, 133,
  139, 145–46
COPS grants for, 130, 131, 144,
  335
criminalization of school
  discipline by, 133–40, 145
"disturbing schools" laws and,
  135–36, 316, 329–31
funding for, 130–32, 141, 335
grievance procedures and, 143
"law and order" reforms and, 129
learning environment and,
  139–41, 145
limiting of, 316–20
memoranda of understanding
  and, 134, 317, 319

police in schools (*continued*)
Metropolitan Police Department,
309–10
military-grade weapons of,
124–25
multiple functions and lack of
clarity about role of, 133–34,
143, 319–20
police-free schools movement,
307, 309–13, 316
private security guards and
neighborhood officers, 124
racial disparities of, 132, 140–41,
145–46
safety and, 139–45
school resource officers (SROs),
123–24, 126, 131, 136, 139,
141, 335
and students with disabilities,
138, 142–43, 146
and students with emotional and
psychological issues, 137–38
success measurements of, 141
symbolic role of, 139
training of, 134–35, 316–20
vicious cycle created by, 141
violent force used by, 141–44, 146
police killings of Black Americans,
xvii, 160, 184–85, 242
accountability for, 41, 184,
189–90, 225
Brown, Michael, 119, 125, 143,
160, 184–87, 189, 269–71,
322, 340
Chatman, Cedrick LaMont, 184,
187, 189, 242
Childs, Anthony, 56
civilian vigilante violence and,
184, 190
common components of, 184
defense of police actions in, 184
Edwards, Jordan, 37–41, 184, 242

Floyd, George, xviii, 119, 120,
209, 269, 300, 311, 328
Garner, Eric, 16, 119, 209, 343
girls and women, 219
Gray, Freddie, 119, 322
McDonald, Laquan, 184, 187–90
mental health problems in
victims of, 168–71, 189
number of, 208
parents of victims of, 267–71,
273
prevalence of, versus other
ethnicities, 40, 171, 184, 208
and prevalence of violent crime,
184
prosecutions for, 41
publicized, effects of, 160–61,
208–10, 225
racial stereotypes and, 29, 39, 40,
184, 188
Rice, Tamir, xv, 26–30, 39, 51,
58, 119, 160, 184, 189, 242,
268–69, 273, 290–91
in schools, 142
siblings of victims of, 290–92
Taylor, Breonna, 119, 219, 269,
343
transgender women, 219
unjustifiability of, 184
vilification of victims of, 184–89,
271
Watts, Stephon, 168–71, 199
*Policing the Black Man* (Davis), xvii
policing as trauma, 204–35
Black girls and, 217–19
health problems and, 226–27
humiliation and, 220–23
memories of prior police contact,
215
mental health and, 213–17
racism and, 223–26
stop and frisk and, 232, 233

survival strategies and, 211
and viral videos of police killings,
208–10
policing by proxy, 173–203
calling the police, 197–200, 202,
332–34
crime watch services and apps,
200–202
parents of victims of, 269, 271–73
and securing the White space,
192–97
"see something, say something"
culture and, 200
siblings of victims of, 290–92
Stand Your Ground laws and,
180–82
vigilante shootings, 174–81,
183–84, 190, 194, 196
vilification of victims of, 191–92
post-traumatic stress disorder
(PTSD), 210, 216–17, 255, 340
poverty and financial hardship,
292
bail and, 276, 277, 339
evictions and, 245, 292–95
juvenile court fees and, 295–97
Powell, Danelene, 169
PPCS (Police-Public Contact
Survey), 217
presidential election of 2016, 223
President's Commission on
Combating Drug Addiction
and the Opioid Crisis, 18
Pressley, Ayanna, 328
Prestia, Paul V., 264–65
prison and jail, 337–39
abuse of youth in, 101, 105, 251,
253–54, 258, 259–60, 263, 277
adolescent development slowed
by, 257
adult, youth in, 245–47, 250–58,
264, 265, 277

clothing fashions associated with,
51–52, 55, 57
family visits to, 277–78, 288–89
mass incarceration, xvii, 133,
194
mental health problems among
youth in, 216, 254–55, 258
post-traumatic stress disorder
from being in, 255
psychological trauma caused by,
254
and relationships with loved
ones, 257–58, 278
sentencing and, see sentences,
sentencing
sexual abuse in, 101, 105, 251,
254
siblings and, 284–90
solitary confinement in, 251,
258–63, 335
suicide and, 255–56, 258,
262–64, 266–67, 271
violence in, 253
White youth offered alternatives
to, 19, 23
Prison Policy Initiative, 217
Prison Rape Elimination Act
(PREA), 251
privacy, right to, 161
probation and probation officers,
8, 23, 248–49
procedural justice, 322–23
property crimes, xvi, 3–5, 7–8, 162
prosecutors, 336–39
Proud Boys, 76–77
Pryor, Richard, 160
PTSD (post-traumatic stress
disorder), 210, 216–17, 255,
340
puberty, 11, 83–84, 90
of Black girls, 103–4
brain and, 228

Public Defender Service for the
District of Columbia, xiii–xiv
public housing, 43, 264
eviction from, 245, 292–95
*Pushout* (Morris), 101

Quiñones, John, 202–3

racial impact statements, 330
racial profiling, 200, 201, 210,
225, 271, 332
racial segregation, 194
Jim Crow laws, 126, 242, 329
school desegregation, 125–27,
145, 196
racial socialization, 113–17, 304,
305
racial stereotypes, 16–17, 40, 90,
111–12, 114
about Black adolescent sexuality,
99–100
about Black girls' sexuality,
58–60, 84, 85, 100–105
gangs and, 76–78
rap music and, 71
racial stereotypes about Black
criminality, 28, 36, 54, 113,
199, 248
child's age and, 90
Goetz and, 175–79
reality show experiment and,
202–3
studies on, 90, 249
racial stereotypes about Black
criminality, and police, 15, 36,
47, 54, 112, 157–62, 212, 338
and adolescents with cognitive
disabilities, 166–72
bias reduction strategies and,
323–26
and fatal shootings by police, 29,
39, 40, 184, 188

nervousness perceived as guilt in,
163–66
and officers' use of demeaning
language, 158
and perceived age of Black youth,
29, 192, 324
"stereotype threat" fear and,
164–66, 215
studies on, 40, 249
racism, 112, 114–17, 158, 159,
202, 223–26, 228
academic achievement and,
224–25
in country music lyrics, 69
depression and, 225
policing as, 223–26
Ramseur, James, 175, 176
rap and hip-hop, 50, 52, 53, 62,
67–72, 342
*Rap on Trial* (Nielson and
Dennis), 71
Reagan, Ronald, 18
*Reason*, 332
recreation and leisure, 30, 31, 303
*see also* play, adolescent
rehabilitative interventions, 339–40
religion and spirituality, 303, 305
Republicans, 54, 273
resilience in Black adolescents,
promoting, 302–6
"respectability," 57–58, 117
*Rest in Power* (Fulton and
Martin), 271
restorative justice, 314–15
Reyes, Matias, 87
Rhodes, Tatyana, 42
Rice, Samaria, 29–30, 32,
268–69, 273, 291
Rice, Tajai, 290–91
Rice, Tamir, xv, 26–30, 39, 51,
58, 119, 160, 184, 189, 242,
268–69, 273, 290–91

Richardson, Kevin, 86–87, 281
Rikers Island prison, 74, 259–60,
    262–63, 271, 272, 277, 290,
    337–38
Ring, 200
riots, "ghetto," 129
risky behavior and impulsivity,
    11–14, 31, 91, 132, 153–54,
    212, 250, 256, 257, 279, 305,
    334
Rivera, Geraldo, 51
Robert N. Davoren Complex
    (RNDC), 259, 260
Robinson, Tony, 184, 189
Rogers, Eric, II, 197–98
Rolle, Delucca, 155, 342
Roof, Dylann, 85
Roots, xiii
Ross, Jason, 15–16
Rouer, Rhonda, 193

sagging pants, 51–58, 100, 329,
    331
Salaam, Sharonne, 283
Salaam, Yusef, 86–87, 283
Sandy Hook Elementary School
    shooting, 132, 307
Santana, Raymond, 86–87, 281–82
Santana, Raymond, Sr., 281–82
#SayHerName, 219
Scheindlin, Shira, 338
school(s), 123
    academic achievement in, and
        racism, 224–25
    attendance laws for, 9, 10
    Black girls punished in, 101
    civic participation and activism
        and, 118, 308
    counselors at, 123, 138
    credible messengers, 310
    curfew laws and, 45
    curricula at, 127, 304–5

discipline in, 313–16
dress codes in, 53, 55, 58–66, 79
dropping out of, 141
expulsion from, 80, 121, 245
gangs and, 54, 77, 79–80
high school graduation rates, 141
incarceration and inability to
    complete, 257, 264
mental health issues and, 137–38,
    312–14, 319, 320, 335
police in, see police in schools
"positive youth development
    philosophy" in, 309
racial desegregation in, 125–27,
    145, 196
rap and hip-hop banned in, 70
recreation and, 30
restorative justice practices in,
    314–15
safety in, 139–45, 313–16
social and emotional learning
    (SEL) in, 315
test scores in, 141
violence interrupters, 310
walkouts for gun safety at, 307
school shootings, ix, 55, 131, 132,
    145, 307
    Columbine, 125, 131, 133, 139,
        145–46, 307
    Sandy Hook, 132, 307
    Stoneman Douglas High School in
        Parkland, 132, 139, 202, 307
    toy guns and, 25
Scott, Walter, 209
Scottsboro Boys, 85
"see something, say something"
    culture, 200
segregation, see racial segregation
self-defense, 181, 184, 192, 271,
    272
    Stand Your Ground laws and,
        180–82, 273

self-determination, 31
sentences, sentencing, 337, 339
  for drug offenses, 18–19
  for indeterminate period of time,
    277–78
  life without parole, 247–48
  mandatory minimum, 245
  racial disparities in, 98–99,
    247–49
  threat of, as deterrent, 249–50
Sentencing Commission, 98
Sentencing Project, 330
sex offender registration, 88, 245,
  264
sex trafficking victims, 105
sexuality, 14, 81–105, 305
  Black adolescent, 85–90, 99–100,
    242
  Black "Brute" stereotype and,
    84, 85
  Black female, stereotypes and
    Jezebel myth about, 58–60, 84,
    85, 100–105
  "boys will be boys" and, 92, 93,
    95, 97
  child pornography laws and,
    88–89
  sexting and, 83, 88
  sexual development, 83–84; see
    also puberty
  White adolescent, 90–94
shackles, xiii, 274–75
Sharpton, Al, 177
siblings, 284–92
Simmons, Darius, 174
Simpson, David, 85–86
SketchFactor, 200, 202
ski masks, 48–51, 336
skinheads, 4, 55, 77
Skyline High School, 311
slavery, xiii, 62, 100, 162, 183,
  194, 242, 244, 275

Slick Rick, 160
smartphones, 32–37, 209
  crime watch apps for, 200–202
Smith, Yvette, 219
social and emotional learning
  (SEL), 315
social media, 30, 33, 300
  police surveillance of Black youth
    on, 74, 79–80
  police violence posted on,
    121, 158, 159, 160,
    209–10, 326
solitary confinement, 251,
  258–63, 335
Sotomayor, Sonia, 328
South Boston High School, 130
Southern Manifesto, 126–27
spirituality and religion, 303,
  305
Spooner, John Henry, 174
Spring Valley High School, 33–36,
  136, 144
Stand Your Ground laws, 180–82,
  273
Stanford University, 249
Stanley-Jones, Aiyana, 219
Staub, Ervin, 329
Steinberg, Laurence, 11
stereotypes, see racial stereotypes
stereotype threat, 163–66, 215
Sterling, Alton, 342
Stinney, Aime, 236, 237
Stinney, George, xv, 86, 236–38,
  240–43, 265
Stinney, George, Sr., 236, 237
Stinney, Johnny, 236
Stone, Grace, 42
Stoneman Douglas High School
  shooting in Parkland, 132,
  139, 202, 307
Stop Solitary for Kids, 272
Strategies for Youth, 318–19

stress, 137, 212
  brain and, 141
  *see also* trauma
Stuart, Diana, 156, 338
Student Nonviolent Coordinating
  Committee, 127
substance abuse, 229, 233, 305
suicide, 229
  incarceration and, 255–56, 258,
    262–64, 266–67, 271
superpredator myth, 87–88, 130,
  133, 247, 342
Supreme Court, U.S.
  *Brown v. Board of Education*
    decision on school segregation,
    126, 145, 196
  and execution of children, 240,
    242
  life sentences and, 248
  qualified immunity and, 328
  stop and frisk and, 164
surveillance
  by civilians, 200, 201
  by police, 80, 140, 160, 289, 332

Tamir Rice Afrocentric Cultural
  Center, 273
Tamir Rice Foundation, 273
Task Force on 21st Century
  Policing, 321
tattoos, 55, 78, 79
Taylor, Breonna, 119, 219, 269,
  343
Taylor, Dirone, 197–98
*Tell the Truth and Shame the Devil*
  (McSpadden), 270
Tennon, Julius, 343
Terrell, Cameron, 19–21, 24, 276,
  339
testosterone, 11
Thames, Mary Emma, 236–37, 242
Thomas, Andrew, 238, 239, 242

Thomas, Clarence, 328
Thomas, Jaquin, 258, 339
Thompson, CaShawn, 341
Thompson, James Hanover,
  85–86
Till, Emmett, xv, 82, 85, 87, 175,
  242, 270–72
Till-Mobley, Mamie, 270, 272
toy guns, 25–29
transgender women, 219
trauma, 208, 258, 303, 308, 313,
  318
  abuse, 104–5, 137, 208, 229
  brain and, 228–29
  cognitive behavioral therapy for,
    340
  policing as, *see* policing as
    trauma
  post-traumatic stress disorder,
    210, 216–17, 255, 340
  survival strategies and, 211
Trayvon Martin Foundation, 272
Troiano, James, 97–98
Trump, Donald, 18, 76, 87, 92,
  120, 159, 300, 307, 335–36
Turner, Brock, 94, 96–98
Turner, Dan, 97
Twitter, 15–16

Unabomber, 50
unemployment, 212–13
United Nations, 261, 273
University of California, Irvine,
  68, 249
University of Colorado Boulder,
  331
University of Illinois, 78
University of Kentucky, 59
University of Michigan, 13
University of Pennsylvania, 249
Urban Institute, 183
*USA Today,* 269

Van Dyke, Jason, 187–90
Vera Institute of Justice, 278
vigilantes
  Goetz, 175–79, 181, 192
  lynchings by, *see* lynchings
  shootings by, 174–81, 183–84,
    190, 194, 196
  *see also* policing by proxy
violence, xvi, 11
  in lyrics, 68–70, 72
  toy guns and, 26
violent crime, xvi, 23, 184
Violent Crime Control and Law
  Enforcement Act, 130

Wafer, Theodore, 175, 195
Walker, Brennan, 173–74, 192,
  195, 196
Walton, Shamann, 333
Washington, Chasity, 89
Washington, D.C., xiii–xiv, 13, 32,
  112, 128, 151–52, 159, 163,
  200, 205, 223, 292–93, 295
  city agencies in, 293, 294
  D.C. Public Schools, 309–10
  Metropolitan Police Department,
    151, 201, 222, 230–33,
    309–10
*Washington Post,* 93, 151, 171,
  270
Watts, Steven, 169, 199
Watts, Stephon, 168–71, 199
*Wattstax,* 160
weapons, 14, 130
  *see also* guns
Weekley, Joseph, 219
Weier, Anissa, 339
West, Kanye, 160
We the Protesters, 321
*What Would You Do?,* 202–3

*When They See Us,* 86, 284, 343
Whiteness, 194–95
  and securing the White space,
    192–97
Whites
  arrests of, 217
  police killings of, 208–9
  police stops and frisks of, 212,
    232
White supremacists, 69, 85
  Ku Klux Klan, 49, 125, 175, 176,
    194
White youth
  boys' sexual behavior, 90–94
  in gangs in nineteenth and early
    twentieth centuries, 75
  girls' incarceration rates, 105
  in juvenile legal system, 15–16,
    19, 23
  police killings of, 40
  police misconduct as viewed by,
    158
Wilson, Darren, 185–87, 189, 271,
  340
Wilson, Tarika, 219
Wise, Deloris, 283, 284
Wise, Korey, 86–87, 283–84, 337,
  339
Wolfgang, Marvin E., 178, 179
Woodland Hills High School, 144
Wright, Lisa, 174
Wu-Tang Clan, 50

Zeigler, Dana, 173–74, 192
Zeigler, Jeffrey, 173–74, 192
Zimmerman, George, 51, 174,
  180–82, 184, 190–91, 196,
  271–72, 291, 340
Zimmerman, Jonathan, 93
zoot suits, 56–57

## A Note About the Author

Kristin Henning has been representing children accused of crime in Washington, D.C., for more than twenty-five years and is a nationally recognized trainer and consultant on the intersection of race, adolescence, and policing. Henning now serves as the Blume Professor of Law and director of the Juvenile Justice Clinic and Initiative at Georgetown Law and previously served as the lead attorney of the Juvenile Unit at the D.C. Public Defender Service. Henning is the recipient of many awards, including the 2021 Leadership Prize from the Juvenile Law Center and the 2013 Robert E. Shepherd Jr. Award for Excellence in Juvenile Defense by the National Juvenile Defender Center. She has written numerous law review articles and other publications advocating for reform in the juvenile legal system.

## A Note on the Type

The text of this book was set in Sabon, a typeface designed by Jan Tschichold (1902–1974), the well-known German typographer. Based loosely on the original designs by Claude Garamond (ca. 1480–1561), Sabon is unique in that it was explicitly designed for hot-metal composition on both the Monotype and Linotype machines as well as for filmsetting. Designed in 1966 in Frankfurt, Sabon was named for the famous Lyons punch cutter Jacques Sabon, who is thought to have brought some of Garamond's matrices to Frankfurt.

*Typeset by Scribe, Philadelphia, Pennsylvania*

*Printed and bound by Berryville Graphics,
Berryville, Virginia*

*Designed by Betty Lew*